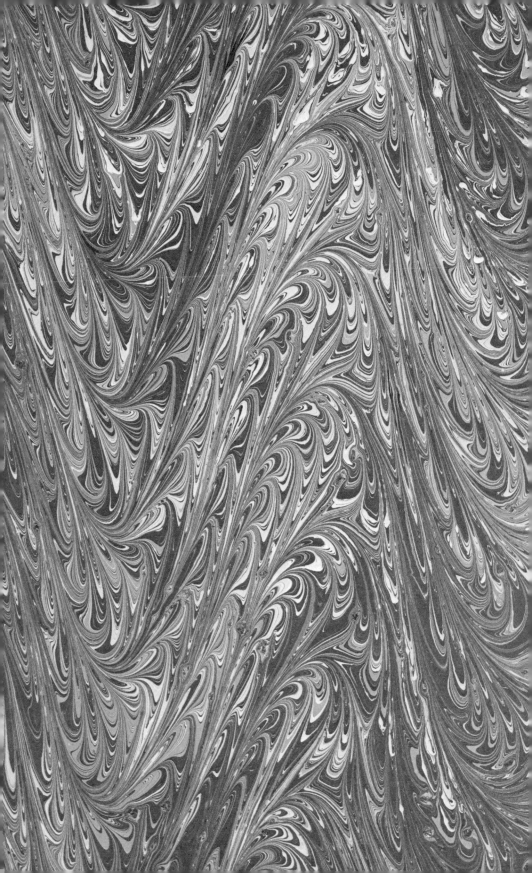

⚜ WILLIAM SHAKESPEARE
SELECTED PLAYS

WILLIAM SHAKESPEARE
SELECTED PLAYS

With the Illustrations of Henry Fuseli

THE FRANKLIN LIBRARY
Franklin Center, Pennsylvania

The pen-and-ink drawing "Fortuna hovering above the world" appearing in the front matter, and the engravings after Henry Fuseli's paintings for *A Midsummer Night's Dream* and *Macbeth* are reproduced by permission of the Trustees of the British Museum. The engravings after the artist's paintings for *Romeo and Juliet, Hamlet, Othello, King Lear,* and *The Tempest* are reproduced by permission of The Folger Shakespeare Library, Washington, D.C.

This edition of *Selected Plays* is based on *The Cambridge Shakespeare,* edited by William Aldis Wright, first published by Macmillan and Co., London and New York, 1863–66. The second edition under the editorship of Wright was published in 1891.

Special contents copyright © 1981 The Franklin Library. Printed in the United States of America.

✧   ✧   ✧   ✧   ✧   ✧   ✧   ✧   ✧   ✧   ✧

❧ ABOUT THE ILLUSTRATOR

"For a man with a soul the theatre in London is alone worth the journey." These words were written by Henry Fuseli (1741–1825), the Anglo-Swiss historical painter and author who was one of the most exotic, original, and sensual painters of the Romantic period. Born in Zurich to a family of painters, Fuseli grew up in an atmosphere of progressive and radical ideas. He himself possessed a remarkable aptitude for painting, but his father ignored his gift and decided to make a Zwinglian minister of him. Although he was ordained in 1761 and preached for a year or more, Fuseli regarded poetry as his true vocation and Milton and Shakespeare as his inspiration. He was one of the first translators of Shakespeare into German, attempting a version of *Macbeth* while still in his teens.

At the age of twenty-three Fuseli moved to London and plunged himself into the city's life. Theatre-going became and remained one of his great passions, and he came to know some of the great actors and actresses of his day. Fuseli worshipped Shakespeare as "the supreme master of passions and the ruler of our hearts," and memorized the plays so completely that he could recollect any passage to which one alluded. This intimate knowledge was remarked upon again and again by his colleagues. He continued to draw, but only as an avocation. Upon seeing some of Fuseli's sketches, Sir Joshua Reynolds encouraged him to abandon his literary projects altogether and devote himself to an artistic career. This he did, beginning in the spring of 1770. Although a late starter, he was never short of commissions from patrons and admirers.

In 1786, the noted engraver and publisher of prints John Boydell invited Fuseli, as well as other well-known artists, to participate in a monumental project: the creation of a Shakespeare Gallery. Boydell commissioned oil paintings of scenes from the plays, which would be exhibited in the Gallery in Pall Mall, London, and later engraved and published by subscription. Fuseli's contributions faithfully captured the conventions of the London stage: the exaggerated gestures of the declamatory style of acting, the minimal use of props, and the angle of view from the orchestra pit.

Although Henry Fuseli's art was long overshadowed by that of his friend William Blake, it has been acclaimed in recent years for its imagination and mysticism. Perhaps Fuseli foresaw the twentieth century's estimate of his work when he wrote, "Deserve, but expect not, to be praised by your contemporaries for any excellence; leave the dispensation of justice to posterity."

# CONTENTS

ROMEO AND JULIET

THE ACTORS

ESCALUS, *Prince of Verona*

PARIS, *a young nobleman, kinsman to the Prince*

MONTAGUE ⎱ *heads of two houses at*
CAPULET ⎰ *variance with one another*

COUSIN TO CAPULET

ROMEO, *son to Montague*

MERCUTIO, *kinsman to the Prince, and friend to Romeo*

BENVOLIO, *nephew to Montague, and friend to Romeo*

TYBALT, *nephew to Lady Capulet*

FRIAR LAURENCE ⎱ *Franciscans*
FRIAR JOHN ⎰

BALTHASAR, *servant to Romeo*

SAMPSON ⎱ *servants to Capulet*
GREGORY ⎰

PETER, *servant to Juliet's nurse*

ABRAHAM, *servant to Montague*

AN APOTHECARY

THREE MUSICIANS

PAGE *to Paris*

THREE WATCHMEN

FIRST CITIZEN *of Verona*

THREE SERVANTS *to Capulet*

LADY MONTAGUE, *wife to Montague*

LADY CAPULET, *wife to Capulet*

JULIET, *daughter to Capulet*

NURSE *to Juliet*

CHORUS

Non-Speaking: Citizens of Verona, Maskers, Torchbearers, Musicians, Page to Mercutio, Guards, Watchmen, and Attendants

SCENE: *Verona and Mantua*

ACT I

✿ PROLOGUE

Enter Chorus.

CHORUS   Two households, both alike in dignity,
    In fair Verona, where we lay our scene,
    From ancient grudge break to new mutiny,
    Where civil blood makes civil hands unclean.
    From forth the fatal loins of these two foes
    A pair of star-cross'd lovers take their life;
    Whose misadventured piteous overthrows
    Do with their death bury their parents' strife.
    The fearful passage of their death-mark'd love,
    And the continuance of their parents' rage,
    Which, but their children's end, nought could remove,
    Is now the two hours' traffic of our stage;
    The which if you with patient ears attend,
    What here shall miss, our toil shall strive to mend.   *Exeunt.*

✿ SCENE 1   *Verona. A public place.*

Enter Sampson and Gregory, of the House of Capulet, armed with swords and bucklers.

SAMPSON   Gregory, o' my word, we'll not carry coals.

GREGORY   No, for then we should be colliers.

SAMPSON   I mean, an we be in choler, we'll draw.

GREGORY   Ay, while you live, draw your neck out o' the collar.

5

SAMPSON I strike quickly, being moved.

GREGORY But thou art not quickly moved to strike.

SAMPSON A dog of the house of Montague moves me.

GREGORY To move is to stir; and to be valiant is to stand: therefore, if thou art moved, thou runn'st away.

SAMPSON A dog of that house shall move me to stand: I will take the wall of any man or maid of Montague's.

GREGORY That shows thee a weak slave; for the weakest goes to the wall.

SAMPSON True; and therefore women, being the weaker vessels, are ever thrust to the wall: therefore I will push Montague's men from the wall, and thrust his maids to the wall.

GREGORY The quarrel is between our masters and us their men.

SAMPSON 'Tis all one, I will show myself a tyrant: when I have fought with the men, I will be cruel with the maids and cut off their heads.

GREGORY The heads of the maids?

SAMPSON Ay, the heads of the maids, or their maidenheads; take it in what sense thou wilt.

GREGORY They must take it in sense that feel it.

SAMPSON Me they shall feel while I am able to stand: and 'tis known I am a pretty piece of flesh.

GREGORY 'Tis well thou art not fish; if thou hadst, thou hadst been poor John. Draw thy tool; here comes two of the house of the Montagues.

SAMPSON My naked weapon is out: quarrel, I will back thee.

GREGORY How! turn thy back and run?

SAMPSON Fear me not.

GREGORY No, marry: I fear thee!

SAMPSON Let us take the law of our sides; let them begin.

GREGORY I will frown as I pass by, and let them take it as they list.

SAMPSON Nay, as they dare. I will bite my thumb at them; which is a disgrace to them, if they bear it.

ACT I   Scene 1

Enter Abraham and Balthasar.

ABRAHAM   Do you bite your thumb at us, sir?

SAMPSON   I do bite my thumb, sir.

ABRAHAM   Do you bite your thumb at us, sir?

SAMPSON   [*Aside to Gregory.*] Is the law of our side, if I say ay?

GREGORY   No.

SAMPSON   No, sir, I do not bite my thumb at you, sir, but I bite my thumb, sir.

GREGORY   Do you quarrel, sir?

ABRAHAM   Quarrel, sir? no, sir.

SAMPSON   If you do, sir, I am for you: I serve as good a man as you.

ABRAHAM   No better.

SAMPSON   Well, sir.

GREGORY   Say "better": here comes one of my master's kinsmen.

SAMPSON   Yes, better, sir.

ABRAHAM   You lie.

SAMPSON   Draw, if you be men. Gregory, remember thy swashing blow.

They fight. Enter Benvolio.

BENVOLIO   Part, fools!
  Put up your swords; you know not what you do.

Beats down their swords. Enter Tybalt.

TYBALT   What, art thou drawn among these heartless hinds?
  Turn thee, Benvolio, look upon thy death.

BENVOLIO   I do but keep the peace: put up thy sword,
  Or manage it to part these men with me.

TYBALT   What, drawn, and talk of peace! I hate the word,
  As I hate hell, all Montagues, and thee:
  Have at thee, coward!

They fight. Enter several of both houses, who join the fray; then enter Citizens, with clubs.

7

FIRST CITIZEN   Clubs, bills, and partisans! strike! beat them down!
   Down with the Capulets! down with the Montagues!

Enter Capulet in his gown, and Lady Capulet.

CAPULET   What noise is this? Give me my longsword, ho!

LADY CAPULET   A crutch, a crutch! why call you for a sword?

CAPULET   My sword, I say! Old Montague is come,
   And flourishes his blade in spite of me.

Enter Montague and Lady Montague.

MONTAGUE   Thou villain Capulet. Hold me not, let me go.

LADY MONTAGUE   Thou shalt not stir a foot to seek a foe.

Enter Prince Escalus, with attendants.

PRINCE ESCALUS   Rebellious subjects, enemies to peace,
   Profaners of this neighbour-stained steel—
   Will they not hear?— What, ho! you men, you beasts,
   That quench the fire of your pernicious rage
   With purple fountains issuing from your veins,
   On pain of torture, from those bloody hands
   Throw your mistemper'd weapons to the ground,
   And hear the sentence of your moved Prince.
   Three civil brawls, bred of an airy word,
   By thee, old Capulet and Montague,
   Have thrice disturb'd the quiet of our streets,
   And made Verona's ancient citizens
   Cast by their grave beseeming ornaments
   To wield old partisans, in hands as old,
   Canker'd with peace, to part your canker'd hate:
   If ever you disturb our streets again,
   Your lives shall pay the forfeit of the peace.
   For this time, all the rest depart away:
   You, Capulet, shall go along with me:
   And, Montague, come you this afternoon,
   To know our further pleasure in this case,
   To old Free-town, our common judgement-place.
   Once more, on pain of death, all men depart.
                    Exeunt all but Montague, Lady Montague, and Benvolio.

MONTAGUE   Who set this ancient quarrel new abroach?
   Speak, nephew, were you by when it began?

8

BENVOLIO   Here were the servants of your adversary,
And yours, close fighting ere I did approach:
I drew to part them: in the instant came
The fiery Tybalt, with his sword prepared,
Which, as he breathed defiance to my ears,
He swung about his head and cut the winds,
Who nothing hurt withal hiss'd him in scorn:
While we were interchanging thrusts and blows,
Came more and more and fought on part and part,
Till the Prince came, who parted either part.

LADY MONTAGUE   O, where is Romeo? saw you him to-day?
Right glad I am he was not at this fray.

BENVOLIO   Madam, an hour before the worshipp'd sun
Peer'd forth the golden window of the east,
A troubled mind drave me to walk abroad;
Where, underneath the grove of sycamore
That westward rooteth from the city's side,
So early walking did I see your son:
Towards him I made, but he was ware of me
And stole into the covert of the wood:
I, measuring his affections by my own,
That most are busied when they're most alone,
Pursued my humour not pursuing his,
And gladly shunn'd who gladly fled from me.

MONTAGUE   Many a morning hath he there been seen,
With tears augmenting the fresh morning's dew,
Adding to clouds more clouds with his deep sighs;
But all so soon as the all-cheering sun
Should in the furthest east begin to draw
The shady curtains from Aurora's bed,
Away from light steals home my heavy son,
And private in his chamber pens himself,
Shuts up his windows, locks fair daylight out,
And makes himself an artificial night:
Black and portentous must this humour prove,
Unless good counsel may the cause remove.

BENVOLIO   My noble uncle, do you know the cause?

MONTAGUE   I neither know it nor can learn of him.

BENVOLIO   Have you importuned him by any means?

9

MONTAGUE   Both by myself and many other friends:
But he, his own affections' counsellor,
Is to himself—I will not say how true—
But to himself so secret and so close,
So far from sounding and discovery,
As is the bud bit with an envious worm,
Ere he can spread his sweet leaves to the air,
Or dedicate his beauty to the sun.
Could we but learn from whence his sorrows grow,
We would as willingly give cure as know.

Enter Romeo.

BENVOLIO   See, where he comes: so please you, step aside;
I'll know his grievance, or be much denied.

MONTAGUE   I would thou wert so happy by thy stay,
To hear true shrift. Come, madam, let's away.
                              Exeunt Montague and Lady Montague.

BENVOLIO   Good morrow, cousin.

ROMEO   Is the day so young?

BENVOLIO   But new struck nine.

ROMEO   Ay me! sad hours seem long.
Was that my father that went hence so fast?

BENVOLIO   It was. What sadness lengthens Romeo's hours?

ROMEO   Not having that, which, having, makes them short.

BENVOLIO   In love?

ROMEO   Out—

BENVOLIO   Of love?

ROMEO   Out of her favour, where I am in love.

BENVOLIO   Alas, that love, so gentle in his view,
Should be so tyrannous and rough in proof!

ROMEO   Alas, that love, whose view is muffled still,
Should, without eyes, see pathways to his will!
Where shall we dine? O me! What fray was here?
Yet tell me not, for I have heard it all.
Here's much to do with hate, but more with love.

Why, then, O brawling love! O loving hate!
O any thing, of nothing first create!
O heavy lightness! serious vanity!
Mis-shapen chaos of well-seeming forms!
Feather of lead, bright smoke, cold fire, sick health!
Still-waking sleep, that is not what it is!
This love feel I, that feel no love in this.
Dost thou not laugh?

BENVOLIO   No, coz, I rather weep.

ROMEO   Good heart, at what?

BENVOLIO   At thy good heart's oppression.

ROMEO   Why, such is love's transgression.
Griefs of mine own lie heavy in my breast,
Which thou wilt propagate, to have it prest
With more of thine: this love that thou hast shown
Doth add more grief to too much of mine own.
Love is a smoke raised with the fume of sighs;
Being purged, a fire sparkling in lovers' eyes;
Being vex'd, a sea nourish'd with lovers' tears:
What is it else? a madness most discreet,
A choking gall and a preserving sweet.
Farewell, my coz.

BENVOLIO   Soft! I will go along;
An if you leave me so, you do me wrong.

ROMEO   Tut, I have lost myself; I am not here;
This is not Romeo, he's some other where.

BENVOLIO   Tell me in sadness, who is that you love.

ROMEO   What, shall I groan and tell thee?

BENVOLIO   Groan! why, no;
But sadly tell me who.

ROMEO   Bid a sick man in sadness make his will:
Ah, word ill urged to one that is so ill!
In sadness, cousin, I do love a woman.

BENVOLIO   I aim'd so near, when I supposed you loved.

ROMEO   A right good mark-man! And she's fair I love.

11

BENVOLIO   A right fair mark, fair coz, is soonest hit.

ROMEO   Well, in that hit you miss: she'll not be hit
With Cupid's arrow; she hath Dian's wit;
And, in strong proof of chastity well arm'd,
From love's weak childish bow she lives unharm'd.
She will not stay the siege of loving terms,
Nor bide the encounter of assailing eyes,
Nor ope her lap to saint-seducing gold:
O, she is rich in beauty, only poor
That, when she dies, with beauty dies her store.

BENVOLIO   Then she hath sworn that she will still live chaste?

ROMEO   She hath, and in that sparing makes huge waste,
For beauty starved with her severity
Cuts beauty off from all posterity.
She is too fair, too wise, wisely too fair,
To merit bliss by making me despair:
She hath forsworn to love, and in that vow
Do I live dead that live to tell it now.

BENVOLIO   Be ruled by me, forget to think of her.

ROMEO   O, teach me how I should forget to think.

BENVOLIO   By giving liberty unto thine eyes;
Examine other beauties.

ROMEO   'Tis the way
To call hers exquisite, in question more:
These happy masks that kiss fair ladies' brows
Being black put us in mind they hide the fair;
He that is strucken blind cannot forget
The precious treasure of his eyesight lost:
Show me a mistress that is passing fair,
What doth her beauty serve, but as a note
Where I may read who pass'd that passing fair?
Farewell: thou canst not teach me to forget.

BENVOLIO   I'll pay that doctrine, or else die in debt.   *Exeunt.*

SCENE 2   *A street.*

Enter Capulet, Paris, and Servant.

CAPULET   But Montague is bound as well as I,
 In penalty alike; and 'tis not hard, I think,
 For men so old as we to keep the peace.

PARIS   Of honourable reckoning are you both;
 And pity 'tis you lived at odds so long.
 But now, my lord, what say you to my suit?

CAPULET   But saying o'er what I have said before:
 My child is yet a stranger in the world;
 She hath not seen the change of fourteen years;
 Let two more summers wither in their pride,
 Ere we may think her ripe to be a bride.

PARIS   Younger than she are happy mothers made.

CAPULET   And too soon marr'd are those so early made.
 The earth hath swallow'd all my hopes but she,
 She is the hopeful lady of my earth:
 But woo her, gentle Paris, get her heart,
 My will to her consent is but a part;
 An she agree, within her scope of choice
 Lies my consent and fair according voice.
 This night I hold an old accustom'd feast,
 Whereto I have invited many a guest,
 Such as I love; and you, among the store,
 One more, most welcome, makes my number more,
 At my poor house look to behold this night
 Earth-treading stars that make dark heaven light:
 Such comfort as do lusty young men feel
 When well-apparell'd April on the heel
 Of limping winter treads, even such delight
 Among fresh female buds shall you this night
 Inherit at my house; hear all, all see,
 And like her most whose merit most shall be:
 Which on more view, of many mine being one
 May stand in number, though in reckoning none.
 Come, go with me.

To Servant, giving a paper.

                        Go, sirrah, trudge about

Through fair Verona; find those persons out
Whose names are written there, and to them say,
My house and welcome on their pleasure stay.

Exeunt Capulet and Paris.

SERVANT   Find them out whose names are written here! It is written, that the shoemaker should meddle with his yard, and the tailor with his last, the fisher with his pencil, and the painter with his nets; but I am sent to find those persons whose names are here writ, and can never find what names the writing person hath here writ. I must to the learned. In good time!

Enter Benvolio and Romeo.

BENVOLIO   Tut, man, one fire burns out another's burning,
One pain is lessen'd by another's anguish;
Turn giddy, and be holp by backward turning;
One desperate grief cures with another's languish:
Take thou some new infection to thy eye,
And the rank poison of the old will die.

ROMEO   Your plaintain-leaf is excellent for that.

BENVOLIO   For what, I pray thee?

ROMEO   For your broken shin.

BENVOLIO   Why, Romeo, art thou mad?

ROMEO   Not mad, but bound more than a madman is;
Shut up in prison, kept without my food,
Whipp'd and tormented and—God-den, good fellow.

SERVANT   God gi' god-den. I pray, sir, can you read?

ROMEO   Ay, mine own fortune in my misery.

SERVANT   Perhaps you have learned it without book: but, I pray, can you read anything you see?

ROMEO   Ay, if I know the letters and the language.

SERVANT   Ye say honestly: rest you merry!

ROMEO   Stay, fellow; I can read. [*Reads.*]

"Signior Martino and his wife and daughters; County Anselme and his beauteous sisters; the lady widow of Vitruvio; Signior Placentio and his lovely nieces; Mercutio and his brother Valentine; mine uncle

14

Capulet, his wife, and daughters; my fair niece Rosaline; Livia; Signior
Valentio and his cousin Tybalt; Lucio and the lively Helena.''

A fair assembly: whither should they come?

SERVANT   Up.

ROMEO   Whither?

SERVANT   To supper; to our house.

ROMEO   Whose house?

SERVANT   My master's.

ROMEO   Indeed, I should have ask'd you that before.

SERVANT   Now I'll tell you without asking: my master is the great rich
Capulet; and if you be not of the house of Montagues, I pray, come and
crush a cup of wine. Rest you merry!   *Exit.*

BENVOLIO   At this same ancient feast of Capulet's
Sups the fair Rosaline whom thou so lovest,
With all the admired beauties of Verona:
Go thither; and, with unattainted eye,
Compare her face with some that I shall show,
And I will make thee think thy swan a crow.

ROMEO   When the devout religion of mine eye
Maintains such falsehood, then turn tears to fires;
And these, who often drown'd could never die,
Transparent heretics, be burnt for liars!
One fairer than my love! the all-seeing sun
Ne'er saw her match since first the world begun.

BENVOLIO   Tut, you saw her fair, none else being by,
Herself poised with herself in either eye:
But in that crystal scales let there be weigh'd
Your lady's love against some other maid
That I will show you shining at this feast,
And she shall scant show well that now shows best.

ROMEO   I'll go along, no such sight to be shown,
But to rejoice in splendour of mine own.   *Exeunt.*

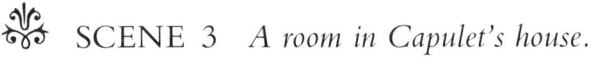 SCENE 3 *A room in Capulet's house.*

Enter Lady Capulet and Nurse.

LADY CAPULET Nurse, where's my daughter? call her forth to me.

NURSE Now, by my maidenhead at twelve year old,
I bade her come. What, lamb! what, lady-bird!
God forbid! Where's this girl? What, Juliet!

Enter Juliet.

JULIET How now? who calls?

NURSE   Your mother.

JULIET Madam, I am here. What is your will?

LADY CAPULET This is the matter:—Nurse, give leave awhile,
We must talk in secret:—nurse, come back again;
I have remember'd me, thou's hear our counsel.
Thou know'st my daughter's of a pretty age.

NURSE Faith, I can tell her age unto an hour.

LADY CAPULET She's not fourteen.

NURSE   I'll lay fourteen of my teeth—
And yet, to my teen be it spoken, I have but four—
She is not fourteen. How long is it now
To Lammas-tide?

LADY CAPULET   A fortnight and odd days.

NURSE Even or odd, of all days in the year,
Come Lammas-eve at night shall she be fourteen.
Susan and she—God rest all Christian souls!—
Were of an age: well, Susan is with God;
She was too good for me: but, as I said,
On Lammas-eve at night shall she be fourteen;
That shall she, marry; I remember it well.
'Tis since the earthquake now eleven years:
And she was wean'd—I never shall forget it—
Of all the days of the year, upon that day:
For I had then laid wormwood to my dug,
Sitting in the sun under the dove-house wall;
My lord and you were then at Mantua—

16

Nay, I do bear a brain—but, as I said,
When it did taste the wormwood on the nipple
Of my dug and felt it bitter, pretty fool,
To see it tetchy and fall out with the dug!
"Shake" quoth the dove-house: 'twas no need, I trow,
To bid me trudge:
And since that time it is eleven years;
For then she could stand alone; nay, by the rood,
She could have run and waddled all about;
For even the day before, she broke her brow:
And then my husband—God be with his soul!
A' was a merry man—took up the child:
"Yea," quoth he, "dost thou fall upon thy face?
Thou wilt fall backward when thou hast more wit;
Wilt thou not, Jule?" and, by my holidame,
The pretty wretch left crying and said, "Ay."
To see, now, how a jest shall come about!
I warrant, an I should live a thousand years,
I never should forget it: "Wilt thou not, Jule?" quoth he;
And, pretty fool, it stinted and said, "Ay."

LADY CAPULET   Enough of this; I pray thee, hold thy peace.

NURSE   Yes, madam: yet I cannot choose but laugh,
To think it should leave crying and say, "Ay,"
And yet, I warrant, it had upon its brow
A bump as big as a young cockerel's stone;
A parlous knock; and it cried bitterly:
"Yea," quoth my husband, "fall'st upon thy face?
Thou wilt fall backward when thou comest to age;
Wilt thou not, Jule?" it stinted and said, "Ay."

JULIET   And stint thou too, I pray thee, nurse, say I.

NURSE   Peace, I have done. God mark thee to his grace!
Thou wast the prettiest babe that e'er I nursed:
An I might live to see thee married once,
I have my wish.

LADY CAPULET   Marry, that "marry" is the very theme
I came to talk of. Tell me, daughter Juliet,
How stands your disposition to be married?

JULIET   It is an honour that I dream not of.

17

NURSE   An honour! were not I thine only nurse,
 I would say thou hadst suck'd wisdom from thy teat.

LADY CAPULET   Well, think of marriage now; younger than you,
 Here in Verona, ladies of esteem,
 Are made already mothers: by my count,
 I was your mother much upon these years
 That you are now a maid. Thus then in brief:
 The valiant Paris seeks you for his love.

NURSE   A man, young lady! lady, such a man
 As all the world—why, he's a man of wax.

LADY CAPULET   Verona's summer hath not such a flower.

NURSE   Nay, he's a flower; in faith, a very flower.

LADY CAPULET   What say you? can you love the gentleman?
 This night you shall behold him at our feast;
 Read o'er the volume of young Paris' face
 And find delight writ there with beauty's pen;
 Examine every married lineament
 And see how one another lends content,
 And what obscured in this fair volume lies
 Find written in the margent of his eyes.
 This precious book of love, this unbound lover,
 To beautify him, only lacks a cover:
 The fish lives in the sea, and 'tis much pride
 For fair without the fair within to hide:
 That book in many's eyes doth share the glory,
 That in gold clasps locks in the golden story;
 So shall you share all that he doth possess,
 By having him, making yourself no less.

NURSE   No less! nay, bigger; women grow by men.

LADY CAPULET   Speak briefly, can you like of Paris' love?

JULIET   I'll look to like, if looking liking move:
 But no more deep will I endart mine eye
 Than your consent gives strength to make it fly.

Enter a Servant.

SERVANT   Madam, the guests are come, supper served up, you called, my
 young lady asked for, the nurse cursed in the pantry, and everything in
 extremity. I must hence to wait; I beseech you, follow straight.

LADY CAPULET   We follow thee.   *Exit Servant.*
                              Juliet, the County stays.

NURSE   Go, girl, seek happy nights to happy days.   *Exeunt.*

❀ SCENE 4   *A street before Capulet's house.*

Enter Romeo, Mercutio, Benvolio, with five or six maskers, torchbearers, and others.

ROMEO   What, shall this speech be spoke for our excuse?
    Or shall we on without apology?

BENVOLIO   The date is out of such prolixity:
    We'll have not Cupid hoodwink'd with a scarf,
    Bearing a Tartar's painted bow of lath,
    Scaring the ladies like a crow-keeper;
    Nor no without-book prologue, faintly spoke
    After the prompter, for our entrance:
    But let them measure us by what they will;
    We'll measure them a measure and be gone.

ROMEO   Give me a torch: I am not for this ambling;
    Being but heavy, I will bear the light.

MERCUTIO   Nay, gentle Romeo, we must have you dance.

ROMEO   Not I, believe me: you have dancing shoes
    With nimble soles: I have a soul of lead
    So stakes me to the ground I cannot move.

MERCUTIO   You are a lover; borrow Cupid's wings,
    And soar with them above a common bound.

ROMEO   I am too sore enpiercèd with his shaft
    To soar with his light feathers, and so bound
    I cannot bound a pitch above dull woe:
    Under love's heavy burden do I sink.

MERCUTIO   And, to sink in it, should you burden love;
    Too great oppression for a tender thing.

ROMEO   Is love a tender thing? it is too rough,
    Too rude, too boisterous, and it pricks like thorn.

MERCUTIO   If love be rough with you, be rough with love;
    Prick love for pricking, and you beat love down.

19

Give me a case to put my visage in!
A visor for a visor! what care I
What curious eye doth quote deformities?
Here are the beetle brows shall blush for me.

BENVOLIO   Come, knock and enter; and no sooner in,
But every man betake him to his legs.

ROMEO   A torch for me: let wantons light of heart
Tickle the senseless rushes with their heels,
For I am proverb'd with a grandsire phrase;
I'll be a candle-holder, and look on.
The game was ne'er so fair, and I am done.

MERCUTIO   Tut, dun's the mouse, the constable's own word:
If thou art Dun, we'll draw thee from the mire
Of this sir-reverence love, wherein thou stick'st
Up to the ears. Come, we burn daylight, ho!

ROMEO   Nay, that's not so.

MERCUTIO   I mean, sir, in delay
We waste our lights in vain, like lamps by day.
Take our good meaning, for our judgement sits
Five times in that ere once in our five wits.

ROMEO   And we mean well in going to this mask;
But 'tis no wit to go.

MERCUTIO   Why, may one ask?

ROMEO   I dream'd a dream to-night.

MERCUTIO   And so did I.

ROMEO   Well, what was yours?

MERCUTIO   That dreamers often lie.

ROMEO   In bed asleep, while they do dream things true.

MERCUTIO   O, then, I see Queen Mab hath been with you.
She is the fairies' midwife, and she comes
In shape no bigger than an agate-stone
On the fore-finger of an alderman,
Drawn with a team of little atomies
Athwart men's noses as they lie asleep;
Her waggon-spokes made of long spinners' legs,

The cover of the wings of grasshoppers,
The traces of the smallest spider's web,
The collars of the moonshine's watery beams,
Her whip of cricket's bone, the lash of film,
Her waggoner a small grey-coated gnat,
Not half so big as a round little worm
Prick'd from the lazy finger of a maid;
Her chariot is an empty hazel-nut
Made by the joiner squirrel or old grub,
Time out o' mind the fairies' coachmakers.
And in this state she gallops night by night
Through lovers' brains, and then they dream of love;
O'er courtiers' knees, that dream on court'sies straight,
O'er lawyers' fingers, who straight dream on fees,
O'er ladies' lips, who straight on kisses dream,
Which oft the angry Mab with blisters plagues,
Because their breaths with sweetmeats tainted are:
Sometime she gallops o'er a courtier's nose,
And then dreams he of smelling out a suit;
And sometime comes she with a tithe-pig's tail
Tickling a parson's nose as a' lies asleep,
Then dreams he of another benefice:
Sometime she driveth o'er a soldier's neck,
And then dreams he of cutting foreign throats,
Of breaches, ambuscadoes, Spanish blades,
Of healths five-fathom deep; and then anon
Drums in his ear, at which he starts and wakes,
And being thus frighted swears a prayer or two
And sleeps again. This is that very Mab
That plats the manes of horses in the night,
And bakes the elf-locks in foul sluttish hairs,
Which once untangled much misfortune bodes:
This is the hag, when maids lie on their backs,
That presses them and learns them first to bear,
Making them women of good carriage:
This is she —

ROMEO   Peace, peace, Mercutio, peace!
    Thou talk'st of nothing.

MERCUTIO   True, I talk of dreams,
    Which are the children of an idle brain,
    Begot of nothing but vain fantasy,

21

Which is as thin of substance as the air
And more inconstant than the wind, who woos
Even now the frozen bosom of the north,
And, being anger'd, puffs away from thence,
Turning his face to the dew-dropping south.

BENVOLIO   This wind, you talk of, blows us from ourselves;
Supper is done, and we shall come too late.

ROMEO   I fear, too early: for my mind misgives
Some consequence yet hanging in the stars
Shall bitterly begin his fearful date
With this night's revels and expire the term
Of a despised life closed in my breast
By some vile forfeit of untimely death.
But He, that hath the steerage of my course,
Direct my sail! On, lusty gentlemen.

BENVOLIO   Strike, drum.   *Exeunt.*

❧ SCENE 5   *A hall in Capulet's house.*

Musicians waiting. Enter Servants, with napkins.

FIRST SERVANT   Where's Potpan, that he helps not to take away? He shift
a trencher? he scrape a trencher!

SECOND SERVANT   When good manners shall lie all in one or two men's
hands and they unwashed too, 'tis a foul thing.

FIRST SERVANT   Away with the joint-stools, remove the court-cupboard,
look to the plate. Good thou, save me a piece of marchpane; and, as
thou lovest me, let the porter let in Susan Grindstone and Nell. Antony, and Potpan!

SECOND SERVANT   Ay, boy, ready.

FIRST SERVANT   You are looked for and called for, asked for and sought
for, in the greater chamber.

SECOND SERVANT   We cannot be here and there too. Cheerly, boys; be
brisk awhile, and the longer liver take all.

*Enter Capulet, with Juliet, and others of his house, meeting the guests and
maskers.*

22

CAPULET Welcome, gentlemen! ladies that have their toes
   Unplagued with corns will have a bout with you.
   Ah ha, my mistresses! which of you all
   Will now deny to dance? she that makes dainty,
   She, I'll swear, hath corns; am I come near ye now?
   Welcome, gentlemen! I have seen the day
   That I have worn a visor and could tell
   A whispering tale in a fair lady's ear,
   Such as would please: 'tis gone, 'tis gone, 'tis gone:
   You are welcome, gentlemen! Come, musicians, play.
   A hall, a hall! give room! and foot it, girls.

Music plays, and they dance.

   More light, you knaves; and turn the tables up,
   And quench the fire, the room is grown too hot.
   Ah, sirrah, this unlook'd-for sport comes well.
   Nay, sit, nay, sit, good cousin Capulet;
   For you and I are past our dancing days:
   How long is't now since last yourself and I
   Were in a mask?

COUSIN TO CAPULET By'r lady, thirty years.

CAPULET What, man! 'tis not so much, 'tis not so much:
   'Tis since the nuptial of Lucentio,
   Come Pentecost as quickly as it will,
   Some five and twenty years; and then we mask'd.

COUSIN TO CAPULET 'Tis more, 'tis more: his son is elder, sir;
   His son is thirty.

CAPULET   Will you tell me that?
   His son was but a ward two years ago.

ROMEO [*To a Servant.*] What lady is that, which doth enrich the hand
   Of yonder knight?

SERVANT I know not, sir.

ROMEO O, she doth teach the torches to burn bright!
   It seems she hangs upon the cheek of night
   Like a rich jewel in an Ethiope's ear;
   Beauty too rich for use, for earth too dear!
   So shows a snowy dove trooping with crows,

23

As yonder lady o'er her fellows shows.
The measure done, I'll watch her place of stand,
And, touching hers, make blessed my rude hand.
Did my heart love till now? forswear it, sight!
For I ne'er saw true beauty till this night.

TYBALT   This, by his voice, should be a Montague.
Fetch me my rapier, boy. What dares the slave
Come hither, cover'd with an antic face,
To fleet and scorn at our solemnity?
Now, by the stock and honour of my kin,
To strike him dead I hold it not a sin.

CAPULET   Why, how now, kinsman? wherefore storm you so?

TYBALT   Uncle, this is a Montague, our foe,
A villain that is hither come in spite,
To scorn at our solemnity this night.

CAPULET   Young Romeo is it?

TYBALT   'Tis he, that villain Romeo.

CAPULET   Content thee, gentle coz, let him alone;
He bears him like a portly gentleman;
And, to say truth, Verona brags of him
To be a virtuous and well-govern'd youth:
I would not for the wealth of all the town
Here in my house do him disparagement:
Therefore be patient, take no note of him:
It is my will, the which if thou respect,
Show a fair presence and put off these frowns,
An ill-beseeming semblance for a feast.

TYBALT   It fits, when such a villain is a guest:
I'll not endure him.

CAPULET   He shall be endured:
What, goodman boy! I say, he shall: go to;
Am I the master here, or you? go to.
You'll not endure him! God shall mend my soul!
You'll make a mutiny among my guests!
You will set cock-a-hoop! you'll be the man!

TYBALT   Why, uncle, 'tis a shame.

CAPULET   Go to, go to;
  You are a saucy boy: is't so, indeed?
  This trick may chance to scathe you, I know what:
  You must contrary me! marry, 'tis time.
  Well said, my hearts! You are a princox; go:
  Be quiet, or— More light, more light!— For shame!
  I'll make you quiet— What, cheerly, my hearts!

TYBALT   Patience perforce with wilful choler meeting
  Makes my flesh tremble in their different greeting.
  I will withdraw: but this intrusion shall
  Now seeming sweet convert to bitter gall.   *Exit.*

ROMEO   [*To Juliet.*] If I profane with my unworthiest hand
  This holy shrine, the gentle fine is this:
  My lips, two blushing pilgrims, ready stand
  To smooth that rough touch with a tender kiss.

JULIET   Good pilgrim, you do wrong your hand too much,
  Which mannerly devotion shows in this;
  For saints have hands that pilgrims' hands do touch,
  And palm to palm is holy palmers' kiss.

ROMEO   Have not saints lips, and holy palmers too?

JULIET   Ay, pilgrim, lips that they must use in prayer.

ROMEO   O, then, dear saint, let lips do what hands do;
  They pray, grant thou, lest faith turn to despair.

JULIET   Saints do not move, though grant for prayers' sake.

ROMEO   Then move not, while my prayer's effect I take.
  Thus from my lips, by yours, my sin is purged.

Kisses her.

JULIET   Then have my lips the sin that they have took.

ROMEO   Sin from my lips? O trespass sweetly urged!
  Give me my sin again.

Kisses her.

JULIET   You kiss by the book.

NURSE   Madam, your mother craves a word with you.

25

ROMEO   What is her mother?

NURSE   Marry, bachelor,
   Her mother is the lady of the house,
   And a good lady, and a wise and virtuous:
   I nursed her daughter, that you talk'd withal;
   I tell you, he that can lay hold of her
   Shall have the chinks.

ROMEO   Is she a Capulet?
   O dear account! my life is my foe's debt.

BENVOLIO   Away, be gone; the sport is at the best.

ROMEO   Ay, so I fear; the more is my unrest.

CAPULET   Nay, gentlemen, prepare not to be gone;
   We have a trifling foolish banquet towards.
   Is it e'en so? why, then, I thank you all;
   I thank you, honest gentlemen; good night.
   More torches here! Come on then, let's to bed.
   Ah, sirrah, by my fay, it waxes late:
   I'll to my rest.   *Exeunt all but Juliet and Nurse.*

JULIET   Come hither, nurse. What is yond gentleman?

NURSE   The son and heir of old Tiberio.

JULIET   What's he that now is going out of door?

NURSE   Marry, that, I think, be young Petruchio.

JULIET   What's he that follows there, that would not dance?

NURSE   I know not.

JULIET   Go, ask his name: if he be married,
   My grave is like to be my wedding bed.

NURSE   His name is Romeo, and a Montague;
   The only son of your great enemy.

JULIET   My only love sprung from my only hate!
   Too early seen unknown, and known too late!
   Prodigious birth of love it is to me
   That I must love a loathed enemy.

26

NURSE   What's this? what's this?

JULIET   A rhyme I learn'd even now
 Of one I danced withal.

One calls within: "Juliet."

NURSE   Anon, anon!
 Come, let's away; the strangers all are gone.   *Exeunt.*

ACT II

 PROLOGUE

Enter Chorus.

CHORUS Now old desire doth in his death-bed lie,
    And young affection gapes to be his heir;
    That fair for which love groan'd for and would die,
    With tender Juliet match'd, is now not fair.
    Now Romeo is beloved and loves again,
    Alike bewitched by the charm of looks,
    But to his foe supposed he must complain,
    And she steal love's sweet bait from fearful hooks.
    Being held a foe, he may not have access
    To breathe such vows as lovers use to swear;
    And she as much in love, her means much less
    To meet her new-beloved anywhere:
    But passion lends them power, time means, to meet,
    Tempering extremities with extreme sweet.   *Exeunt.*

SCENE 1   *A lane by the wall of Capulet's orchard.*

Enter Romeo.

ROMEO Can I go forward when my heart is here?
    Turn back, dull earth, and find thy centre out.

He climbs the wall, and leaps down within it. Enter Benvolio and Mercutio.

BENVOLIO Romeo! my cousin Romeo!

MERCUTIO   He is wise;
    And, on my life, hath stol'n him home to bed.

28

BENVOLIO   He ran this way, and leap'd this orchard wall:
Call, good Mercutio.

MERCUTIO   Nay, I'll conjure too.
Romeo! humours! madman! passion! lover!
Appear thou in the likeness of a sigh:
Speak but one rhyme, and I am satisfied;
Cry but "Ay me!" pronounce but "love" and "dove";
Speak to my gossip Venus one fair word,
One nick-name for her purblind son and heir,
Young Adam Cupid, he that shot so trim,
When King Cophetua loved the beggar-maid!
He heareth not, he stirreth not, he moveth not;
The ape is dead, and I must conjure him.
I conjure thee by Rosaline's bright eyes,
By her high forehead and her scarlet lip,
By her fine foot, straight leg, and quivering thigh
And the demesnes that there adjacent lie,
That in thy likeness thou appear to us!

BENVOLIO   An if he hear thee, thou wilt anger him.

MERCUTIO   This cannot anger him: 'twould anger him
To raise a spirit in his mistress' circle
Of some strange nature, letting it there stand
Till she had laid it and conjured it down;
That were some spite: my invocation
Is fair and honest, and in his mistress' name
I conjure only but to raise up him.

BENVOLIO   Come, he hath hid himself among these trees.
To be consorted with the humorous night:
Blind is his love and best befits the dark.

MERCUTIO   If love be blind, love cannot hit the mark.
Now will he sit under a medlar tree,
And wish his mistress were that kind of fruit
As maids call medlars, when they laugh alone.
O, Romeo, that she were, O, that she were
An open et cetera, thou a poperin pear!
Romeo, good night: I'll to my truckle-bed;
This field-bed is too cold for me to sleep:
Come, shall we go?

BENVOLIO   Go, then; for 'tis in vain
To seek him here that means not to be found.   *Exeunt.*

❧ SCENE 2 *Capulet's orchard.*

Enter Romeo.

ROMEO   He jests at scars that never felt a wound.

Juliet appears above at a window.

But, soft! what light through yonder window breaks?
It is the east, and Juliet is the sun.
Arise, fair sun, and kill the envious moon,
Who is already sick and pale with grief,
That thou her maid art far more fair than she:
Be not her maid, since she is envious;
Her vestal livery is but sick and green
And none but fools do wear it; cast it off.
It is my lady, O, it is my love!
O, that she knew she were!
She speaks, yet she says nothing: what of that?
Her eye discourses; I will answer it.
I am too bold, 'tis not to me she speaks:
Two of the fairest stars in all the heaven,
Having some business, do entreat her eyes
To twinkle in their spheres till they return.
What if her eyes were there, they in her head?
The brightness of her cheek would shame those stars,
As daylight doth a lamp; her eyes in heaven
Would through the airy region stream so bright
That birds would sing and think it were not night.
See, how she leans her cheek upon her hand!
O, that I were a glove upon that hand,
That I might touch that cheek!

JULIET   Ay me!

ROMEO   She speaks!
O, speak again, bright angel! for thou art
As glorious to this night, being o'er my head,
As is a winged messenger of heaven
Unto the white-upturned wondering eyes
Of mortals that fall back to gaze on him

30

When he bestrides the lazy-pacing clouds
And sails upon the bosom of the air.

JULIET   O Romeo, Romeo! wherefore art thou Romeo?
Deny thy father and refuse thy name;
Or, if thou wilt not, be but sworn my love,
And I'll no longer be a Capulet.

ROMEO   [*Aside.*] Shall I hear more, or shall I speak at this?

JULIET   'Tis but thy name that is my enemy;
Thou art thyself, though not a Montague.
What's Montague? it is nor hand, nor foot,
Nor arm, nor face, nor any other part
Belonging to a man. O, be some other name!
What's in a name? that which we call a rose
By any other name would smell as sweet;
So Romeo would, were he not Romeo call'd,
Retain that dear perfection which he owes
Without that title. Romeo, doff thy name,
And for that name which is no part of thee
Take all myself.

ROMEO   I take thee at thy word:
Call me but love, and I'll be new baptized;
Henceforth I never will be Romeo.

JULIET   What man art thou that thus bescreen'd in night
So stumblest on my counsel?

ROMEO   By a name
I know not how to tell thee who I am:
My name, dear saint, is hateful to myself,
Because it is an enemy to thee;
Had I it written, I would tear the word.

JULIET   My ears have not yet drunk a hundred words
Of that tongue's utterance, yet I know the sound:
Art thou not Romeo and a Montague?

ROMEO   Neither, fair saint, if either thee dislike.

JULIET   How camest thou hither, tell me, and wherefore?
The orchard walls are high and hard to climb,
And the place death, considering who thou art,
If any of my kinsmen find thee here.

31

ROMEO   With love's light wings did I o'er-perch these walls;
For stony limits cannot hold love out,
And what love can do that dares love attempt;
Therefore thy kinsmen are no stop to me.

JULIET   If they do see thee, they will murder thee.

ROMEO   Alack, there lies more peril in thine eye
Than twenty of their swords: look thou but sweet,
And I am proof against their enmity.

JULIET   I would not for the world they saw thee here.

ROMEO   I have night's cloak to hide me from their sight;
And but thou love me, let them find me here:
My life were better ended by their hate,
Than death prorogued, wanting of thy love.

JULIET   By whose direction found'st thou out this place?

ROMEO   By love, who first did prompt me to inquire;
He lent me counsel and I lent him eyes.
I am no pilot; yet, wert thou as far
As that vast shore wash'd with the farthest sea,
I would adventure for such merchandise.

JULIET   Thou know'st the mask of night is on my face.
Else would a maiden blush bepaint my cheek
For that which thou hast heard me speak to-night.
Fain would I dwell on form, fain, fain deny
What I have spoke: but farewell compliment!
Dost thou love me? I know thou wilt say "Ay,"
And I will take thy word: yet, if thou swear'st,
Thou mayst prove false; at lovers' perjuries,
They say, Jove laughs. O gentle Romeo,
If thou dost love, pronounce it faithfully:
Or if thou think'st I am too quickly won,
I'll frown and be perverse and say thee nay,
So thou wilt woo; but else, not for the world.
In truth, fair Montague, I am too fond,
And therefore thou mayst think my 'haviour light:
But trust me, gentleman, I'll prove more true
Than those that have more cunning to be strange.
I should have been more strange, I must confess,
But that thou overheard'st, ere I was ware,

My true love's passion: therefore pardon me,
And not impute this yielding to light love,
Which the dark night hath so discovered.

ROMEO   Lady, by yonder blessed moon I swear
That tips with silver all these fruit-tree tops—

JULIET   O, swear not by the moon, the inconstant moon,
That monthly changes in her circled orb,
Lest that thy love prove likewise variable.

ROMEO   What shall I swear by?

JULIET   Do not swear at all;
Or, if thou wilt, swear by thy gracious self,
Which is the god of my idolatry,
And I'll believe thee.

ROMEO   If my heart's dear love—

JULIET   Well, do not swear: although I joy in thee,
I have no joy of this contract to-night:
It is too rash, too unadvised, too sudden;
Too like the lightning, which doth cease to be
Ere one can say "It lightens." Sweet, good night!
This bud of love, by summer's ripening breath,
May prove a beauteous flower when next we meet.
Good night, good night! as sweet repose and rest
Come to thy heart as that within my breast!

ROMEO   O, wilt thou leave me so unsatisfied?

JULIET   What satisfaction canst thou have to-night?

ROMEO   The exchange of thy love's faithful vow for mine.

JULIET   I gave thee mine before thou didst request it:
And yet I would it were to give again.

ROMEO   Wouldst thou withdraw it? for what purpose, love?

JULIET   But to be frank, and give it thee again.
And yet I wish but for the thing I have:
My bounty is as boundless as the sea,
My love as deep; the more I give to thee,
The more I have, for both are infinite.

Nurse calls within.

33

I hear some noise within; dear love, adieu!
Anon, good nurse! Sweet Montague, be true.
Stay but a little, I will come again.   *Exit, above.*

ROMEO   O blessed, blessed night! I am afeard,
  Being in night, all this is but a dream,
  Too flattering-sweet to be substantial.

Re-enter Juliet, above.

JULIET   Three words, dear Romeo, and good night indeed.
  If that thy bent of love be honourable,
  Thy purpose marriage, send me word to-morrow,
  By one that I'll procure to come to thee,
  Where and what time thou wilt perform the rite;
  And all my fortunes at thy foot I'll lay
  And follow thee my lord throughout the world.

NURSE   [*Within.*] Madam!

JULIET   I come, anon. But if thou mean'st not well,
  I do beseech thee—

NURSE   [*Within.*] Madam!

JULIET   By and by, I come:—
  To cease thy suit, and leave me to my grief:
  To-morrow will I send.

ROMEO   So thrive my soul—

JULIET   A thousand times good night!   *Exit, above.*

ROMEO   A thousand times the worse, to want thy light.
  Love goes toward love, as schoolboys from their books,
  But love from love, toward school with heavy looks.   *Retiring.*

Re-enter Juliet, above.

JULIET   Hist! Romeo, hist! O, for a falconer's voice,
  To lure this tassel-gentle back again!
  Bondage is hoarse, and may not speak aloud;
  Else would I tear the cave where Echo lies,
  And make her airy tongue more hoarse than mine,
  With repetition of my Romeo's name.

ROMEO   It is my soul that calls upon my name:
  How silver-sweet sound lovers' tongues by night,
  Like softest music to attending ears!

34

JULIET   Romeo!

ROMEO   My dear?

JULIET   At what o'clock to-morrow
　Shall I send to thee?

ROMEO   At the hour of nine.

JULIET   I will not fail: 'tis twenty years till then.
　I have forgot why I did call thee back.

ROMEO   Let me stand here till thou remember it.

JULIET   I shall forget, to have thee still stand there,
　Remembering how I love thy company.

ROMEO   And I'll still stay, to have thee still forget,
　Forgetting any other home but this.

JULIET   'Tis almost morning; I would have thee gone:
　And yet no further than a wanton's bird;
　Who lets it hop a little from her hand,
　Like a poor prisoner in his twisted gyves,
　And with a silk thread plucks it back again,
　So loving-jealous of his liberty.

ROMEO   I would I were thy bird.

JULIET   Sweet, so would I:
　Yet I should kill thee with much cherishing.
　Good night, good night! parting is such sweet sorrow,
　That I shall say good night till it be morrow.   *Exit, above.*

ROMEO   Sleep dwell upon thine eyes, peace in thy breast!
　Would I were sleep and peace, so sweet to rest!
　Hence will I to my ghostly father's cell,
　His help to crave, and my dear hap to tell.   *Exit.*

SCENE 3   *Friar Laurence' cell.*

Enter Friar Laurence, with a basket.

FRIAR LAURENCE   The grey-eyed morn smiles on the frowning night,
　Chequering the eastern clouds with streaks of light,
　And flecked darkness like a drunkard reels
　From forth day's path and Titan's fiery wheels:

Now, ere the sun advance his burning eye,
The day to cheer and night's dank dew to dry,
I must up-fill this osier cage of ours
With baleful weeds and precious-juiced flowers.
The earth that's nature's mother is her tomb;
What is her burying grave that is her womb,
And from her womb children of divers kind
We sucking on her natural bosom find,
Many for many virtues excellent,
None but for some, and yet all different.
O, mickle is the powerful grace that lies
In herbs, plants, stones, and their true qualities:
For nought so vile that on the earth doth live
But to the earth some special good doth give,
Nor aught so good but strain'd from that fair use
Revolts from true birth, stumbling on abuse:
Virtue itself turns vice, being misapplied;
And vice sometimes by action dignified.
Within the infant rind of this small flower
Poison hath residence and medicine power:
For this, being smelt, with that part cheers each part;
Being tasted, slays all senses with the heart.
Two such opposed kings encamp them still
In man as well as herbs, grace and rude will;
And where the worser is predominant,
Full soon the canker death eats up that plant.

Enter Romeo.

ROMEO   Good morrow, father.

FRIAR LAURENCE   *Benedicite!*
What early tongue so sweet saluteth me?
Young son, it argues a distemper'd head
So soon to bid good morrow to thy bed:
Care keeps his watch in every old man's eye,
And where care lodges, sleep will never lie;
But where unbruised youth with unstuff'd brain
Doth couch his limbs, there golden sleep doth reign:
Therefore thy earliness doth me assure
Thou art up-roused by some distemperature;
Or if not so, then here I hit it right,
Our Romeo hath not been in bed to-night.

ROMEO   That last is true; the sweeter rest was mine.

FRIAR LAURENCE   God pardon sin! wast thou with Rosaline?

ROMEO   With Rosaline, my ghostly father? no;
I have forgot that name, and that name's woe.

FRIAR LAURENCE   That's my good son: but where hast thou been, then?

ROMEO   I'll tell thee, ere thou ask it me again.
I have been feasting with mine enemy,
Where on a sudden one hath wounded me,
That's by me wounded: both our remedies
Within thy help and holy physic lies:
I bear no hatred, blessed man, for, lo,
My intercession likewise steads my foe.

FRIAR LAURENCE   Be plain, good son, and homely in thy drift;
Riddling confession finds but riddling shrift.

ROMEO   Then plainly know my heart's dear love is set
On the fair daughter of rich Capulet:
As mine on hers so hers is set on mine;
And all combined, save what thou must combine
By holy marriage: when and where and how
We met, we woo'd, and made exchange of vow,
I'll tell thee as we pass; but this I pray,
That thou consent to marry us to-day.

FRIAR LAURENCE   Holy Saint Francis, what a change is here!
Is Rosaline, whom thou didst love so dear,
So soon forsaken? young men's love then lies
Not truly in their hearts, but in their eyes.
Jesu Maria, what a deal of brine
Hath wash'd thy sallow cheeks for Rosaline!
How much salt water thrown away in waste,
To season love, that of it doth not taste!
The sun not yet thy sighs from heaven clears,
Thy old groans ring yet in my ancient ears;
Lo, here upon thy cheek the stain doth sit
Of an old tear that is not wash'd off yet:
If e'er thou wast thyself and those woes thine,
Thou and these woes were all for Rosaline:
And art thou changed? pronounce this sentence then:
Women may fall, when there's no strength in men.

37

ROMEO   Thou chid'st me oft for loving Rosaline.

FRIAR LAURENCE   For doting, not for loving, pupil mine.

ROMEO   And bad'st me bury love.

FRIAR LAURENCE   Not in a grave,
　　To lay one in, another out to have.

ROMEO   I pray thee, chide not: she whom I love now
　　Doth grace for grace and love for love allow;
　　The other did not so.

FRIAR LAURENCE   O, she knew well
　　Thy love did read by rote and could not spell.
　　But come, young waverer, come, go with me,
　　In one respect I'll thy assistant be;
　　For this alliance may so happy prove,
　　To turn your households' rancour to pure love.

ROMEO   O, let us hence; I stand on sudden haste.

FRIAR LAURENCE   Wisely and slow; they stumble that run fast.   *Exeunt.*

✿ SCENE 4   *A street.*

Enter Benvolio and Mercutio.

MERCUTIO   Where the devil should this Romeo be? Came he not home
to-night?

BENVOLIO   Not to his father's; I spoke with his man.

MERCUTIO   Ah, that same pale hard-hearted wench, that Rosaline,
Torments him so, that he will sure run mad.

BENVOLIO   Tybalt, the kinsman of old Capulet,
Hath sent a letter to his father's house.

MERCUTIO   A challenge, on my life.

BENVOLIO   Romeo will answer it.

MERCUTIO   Any man that can write may answer a letter.

BENVOLIO   Nay, he will answer the letter's master, how he dares, being
dared.

MERCUTIO   Alas, poor Romeo! he is already dead; stabbed with a white

wench's black eye; shot through the ear with a love-song; the very pin of his heart cleft with the blind bow-boy's butt-shaft: and is he a man to encounter Tybalt?

BENVOLIO   Why, what is Tybalt?

MERCUTIO   More than prince of cats, I can tell you. O, he is the coura-geous captain of compliments. He fights as you sing prick-song, keeps time, distance, and proportion; rests me his minim rest, one, two, and the third in your bosom: the very butcher of a silk button, a duellist, a duellist; a gentleman of the very first house, of the first and second cause: ah, the immortal *passado!* the *punto reverso!* the *hai!*

BENVOLIO   The what?

MERCUTIO   The pox of such antic, lisping, affecting fantasticoes; these new tuners of accents! "By Jesu, a very good blade! a very tall man! a very good whore!" Why, is not this a lamentable thing, grandsire, that we should be thus afflicted with these strange flies, these fashion-mon-gers, these *perdona-mi's,* who stand so much on the new form, that they cannot sit at ease on the old bench? O, their bones, their bones!

Enter Romeo.

BENVOLIO   Here comes Romeo, here comes Romeo.

MERCUTIO   Without his roe, like a dried herring: O flesh, flesh, how art thou fishified! Now is he for the numbers that Petrarch flowed in: Laura to his lady was but a kitchen-wench; marry, she had a better love to be-rhyme her; Dido a dowdy; Cleopatra a gipsy; Helen and Hero hildings and harlots; Thisbe a grey eye or so, but not to the purpose. Signior Romeo, *bon jour!* there's a French salutation to your French slop. You gave us the counterfeit fairly last night.

ROMEO   Good morrow to you both. What counterfeit did I give you?

MERCUTIO   The slip, sir, the slip; can you not conceive?

ROMEO   Pardon, good Mercutio, my business was great; and in such a case as mine a man may strain courtesy.

MERCUTIO   That's as much as to say, such a case as yours constrains a man to bow in the hams.

ROMEO   Meaning, to court'sy.

MERCUTIO   Thou hast most kindly hit it.

ROMEO   A most courteous exposition.

39

MERCUTIO   Nay, I am the very pink of courtesy.

ROMEO   Pink for flower.

MERCUTIO   Right.

ROMEO   Why, then is my pump well flowered.

MERCUTIO   Well said: follow me this jest now till thou hast worn out thy pump, that when the single sole of it is worn, the jest may remain after the wearing sole singular.

ROMEO   O single-soled jest, solely singular for the singleness!

MERCUTIO   Come between us, good Benvolio; my wits faint.

ROMEO   Switch and spurs, switch and spurs; or I'll cry a match.

MERCUTIO   Nay, if thy wits run the wild-goose chase, I have done, for thou hast more of the wild-goose in one of thy wits than, I am sure, I have in my whole five: was I with you there for the goose?

ROMEO   Thou wast never with me for any thing when thou wast not there for the goose.

MERCUTIO   I will bite thee by the ear for that jest.

ROMEO   Nay, good goose, bite not.

MERCUTIO   Thy wit is a very bitter sweeting; it is a most sharp sauce.

ROMEO   And is it not well served in to a sweet goose?

MERCUTIO   O, here's a wit of cheveril, that stretches from an inch narrow to an ell broad!

ROMEO   I stretch it out for that word "broad"; which added to the goose, proves thee far and wide a broad goose.

MERCUTIO   Why, is not this better now than groaning for love? now art thou sociable, now art thou Romeo; now art thou what thou art, by art as well as by nature: for this drivelling love is like a great natural, that runs lolling up and down to hide his bauble in a hole.

BENVOLIO   Stop there, stop there.

MERCUTIO   Thou desirest me to stop in my tale against the hair.

BENVOLIO   Thou wouldst else have made thy tale large.

MERCUTIO   O, thou art deceived; I would have made it short: for I was

come to the whole depth of my tale; and meant, indeed, to occupy the argument no longer.

ROMEO   Here's goodly gear!

Enter Nurse and Peter.

MERCUTIO   A sail, a sail!

BENVOLIO   Two, two; a shirt and a smock.

NURSE   Peter!

PETER   Anon!

NURSE   My fan, Peter.

MERCUTIO   Good Peter, to hide her face; for her fan's the fairer face.

NURSE   God ye good morrow, gentlemen.

MERCUTIO   God ye good den, fair gentlewoman.

NURSE   Is it good den?

MERCUTIO   'Tis no less, I tell you, for the bawdy hand of the dial is now upon the prick of noon.

NURSE   Out upon you! what a man are you!

ROMEO   One, gentlewoman, that God hath made for himself to mar.

NURSE   By my troth, it is well said; "for himself to mar," quoth a'? Gentlemen, can any of you tell me where I may find the young Romeo?

ROMEO   I can tell you; but young Romeo will be older when you have found him than he was when you sought him: I am the youngest of that name, for fault of a worse.

NURSE   You say well.

MERCUTIO   Yea, is the worst well? very well took, i' faith; wisely, wisely.

NURSE   If you be he, sir, I desire some confidence with you.

BENVOLIO   She will indite him to some supper.

MERCUTIO   A bawd, a bawd, a bawd! So ho!

ROMEO   What hast thou found?

41

MERCUTIO   No hare, sir; unless a hare, sir, in a lenten pie, that is some-thing stale and hoar ere it be spent. [*Sings.*]

> "An old hare hoar,
>   And an old hare hoar,
> Is very good meat in Lent:
>   But a hare that is hoar
>   Is too much for a score,
> When it hoars ere it be spent."

Romeo, will you come to your father's? we'll to dinner, thither.

ROMEO   I will follow you.

MERCUTIO   Farewell, ancient lady; farewell, [*Sings.*] "Lady, lady, lady."
Exeunt Mercutio and Benvolio.

NURSE   Marry, farewell I pray you, sir, what saucy merchant was this, that was so full of his ropery?

ROMEO   A gentleman, nurse, that loves to hear himself talk, and will speak more in a minute than he will stand to in a month.

NURSE   An a' speak any thing against me, I'll take him down, an a' were lustier than he is, and twenty such Jacks; and if I cannot, I'll find those that shall. Scurvy knave! I am none of his flirt-gills; I am none of his skains-mates. And thou must stand by too, and suffer every knave to use me at his pleasure?

PETER   I saw no man use you at his pleasure: if I had, my weapon should quickly have been out, I warrant you: I dare draw as soon as another man, if I see occasion in a good quarrel, and the law on my side.

NURSE   Now, afore God, I am so vexed, that every part about me quiv-ers. Scurvy knave! Pray you, sir, a word: and as I told you, my young lady bade me inquire you out; what she bade me say, I will keep to myself: but first let me tell ye, if ye should lead her into a fool's para-dise, as they say, it were a very gross kind of behaviour, as they say: for the gentlewoman is young; and, therefore, if you should deal double with her, truly it were an ill thing to be offered to any gentlewoman, and very weak dealing.

ROMEO   Nurse, commend me to thy lady and mistress. I protest unto thee—

NURSE   Good heart, and, i' faith, I will tell her as much: Lord, Lord, she will be a joyful woman.

ROMEO   What wilt thou tell her, nurse? thou dost not mark me.

NURSE   I will tell her, sir, that you do protest; which, as I take it, is a
gentlemanlike offer.

ROMEO   Bid her devise
Some means to come to shrift this afternoon;
And there she shall at Friar Laurence' cell
Be shrived and married. Here is for thy pains.

NURSE   No, truly, sir; not a penny.

ROMEO   Go to; I say you shall.

NURSE   This afternoon, sir? well, she shall be there.

ROMEO   And stay, good nurse, behind the abbey wall:
Within this hour my man shall be with thee,
And bring thee cords made like a tackled stair;
Which to the high top-gallant of my joy
Must be my convoy in the secret night.
Farewell; be trusty, and I'll quit thy pains:
Farewell; commend me to thy mistress.

NURSE   Now God in heaven bless thee! Hark you, sir.

ROMEO   What say'st thou, my dear nurse?

NURSE   Is your man secret? Did you ne'er hear say,
"Two may keep counsel, putting one away"?

ROMEO   I warrant thee, my man's as true as steel.

NURSE   Well, sir; my mistress is the sweetest lady—Lord, Lord! when
'twas a little prating thing:—O, there is a nobleman in town, one Paris,
that would fain lay knife aboard, but she, good soul, had as lief see a
toad, a very toad, as see him. I anger her sometimes and tell her that
Paris is the properer man; but, I'll warrant you, when I say so, she
looks as pale as any clout in the versal world. Doth not rosemary and
Romeo begin both with a letter?

ROMEO   Ay, nurse; what of that? both with an R.

NURSE   Ah, mocker! that's the dog's name; R is for the— No; I know it
begins with some other letter:—and she hath the prettiest sententious
of it, of you and rosemary, that it would do you good to hear it.

ROMEO   Commend me to thy lady.

NURSE   Ay, a thousand times.   *Exit Romeo.*
   Peter!

PETER   Anon!

NURSE   Peter, take my fan, and go before, and apace.   *Exeunt.*

❀ SCENE 5   *Capulet's orchard.*

Enter Juliet.

JULIET   The clock struck nine when I did send the nurse;
   In half an hour she promised to return.
   Perchance she cannot meet him: that's not so.
   O, she is lame! love's heralds should be thoughts,
   Which ten times faster glide than the sun's beams,
   Driving back shadows over louring hills:
   Therefore do nimble-pinion'd doves draw love,
   And therefore hath the wind-swift Cupid wings.
   Now is the sun upon the highmost hill
   Of this day's journey, and from nine till twelve
   Is three long hours, yet she is not come.
   Had she affections and warm youthful blood,
   She would be as swift in motion as a ball;
   My words would bandy her to my sweet love,
   And his to me:
   But old folks, many feign as they were dead;
   Unwieldy, slow, heavy, and pale as lead.
   O God, she comes!

Enter Nurse and Peter.

                     O honey nurse, what news?
   Hast thou met with him? Send thy man away.

NURSE   Peter, stay at the gate.   *Exit Peter.*

JULIET   Now, good sweet nurse—O Lord, why look'st thou sad?
   Though news be sad, yet tell them merrily;
   If good, thou shamest the music of sweet news
   By playing it to me with so sour a face.

NURSE   I am a-weary, give me leave awhile:
   Fie, how my bones ache! what a jaunt have I had!

JULIET   I would thou hadst my bones, and I thy news.
Nay, come, I pray thee, speak; good, good nurse, speak.

NURSE   Jesu, what haste? can you not stay awhile?
Do you not see that I am out of breath?

JULIET   How art thou out of breath, when thou hast breath
To say to me that thou art out of breath?
The excuse that thou dost make in this delay
Is longer than the tale thou dost excuse.
Is thy news good, or bad? answer to that;
Say either, and I'll stay the circumstance:
Let me be satisfied, is't good or bad?

NURSE   Well, you have made a simple choice; you know not how to
choose a man: Romeo! no, not he; though his face be better than any
man's, yet his leg excels all men's; and for a hand, and a foot, and a
body, though they be not to be talked on, yet they are past compare: he
is not the flower of courtesy, but, I'll warrant him, as gentle as a lamb.
Go thy ways, wench; serve God. What, have you dined at home?

JULIET   No, no: but all this did I know before.
What says he of our marriage? what of that?

NURSE   Lord, how my head aches! what a head have I!
It beats as it would fall in twenty pieces.
My back o' t' other side—O, my back, my back!
Beshrew your heart for sending me about
To catch my death with jaunting up and down!

JULIET   I' faith, I am sorry that thou are not well.
Sweet, sweet, sweet nurse, tell me, what says my love?

NURSE   Your love says, like an honest gentleman, and a courteous, and a
kind, and a handsome, and, I warrant, a virtuous— Where is your
mother?

JULIET   Where is my mother! why, she is within;
Where should she be? How oddly thou repliest!
"Your love says, like an honest gentleman,
'Where is your mother?'"

NURSE   O God's lady dear!
Are you so hot? marry, come up, I trow;
Is this the poultice for my aching bones?
Henceforward do your messages yourself.

45

JULIET Here's such a coil! come, what says Romeo?

NURSE Have you got leave to go to shrift to-day?

JULIET I have.

NURSE Then hie you hence to Friar Laurence' cell;
There stays a husband to make you a wife:
Now comes the wanton blood up in your cheeks,
They'll be in scarlet straight at any news.
Hie you to church; I must another way,
To fetch a ladder, by the which your love
Must climb a bird's nest soon when it is dark:
I am the drudge and toil in your delight,
But you shall bear the burden soon at night.
Go; I'll to dinner; hie you to the cell.

JULIET Hie to high fortune! Honest nurse, farewell.   *Exeunt.*

🎟 SCENE 6 *Friar Laurence' cell.*

Enter Friar Laurence and Romeo.

FRIAR LAURENCE So smile the heavens upon this holy act,
That after hours with sorrow chide us not!

ROMEO Amen, amen! but come what sorrow can,
It cannot countervail the exchange of joy
That one short minute gives me in her sight:
Do thou but close our hands with holy words,
Then love-devouring death do what he dare;
It is enough I may call her mine.

FRIAR LAURENCE These violent delights have violent ends
And in their triumph die, like fire and powder,
Which as they kiss consume: the sweetest honey
Is loathsome in his own deliciousness
And in the taste confounds the appetite:
Therefore love moderately; long love doth so;
Too swift arrives as tardy as too slow.

Enter Juliet.

Here comes the lady: O, so light a foot
Will ne'er wear out the everlasting flint:
A lover may bestride the gossamer

That idles in the wanton summer air,
And yet not fall; so light is vanity.

JULIET   Good even to my ghostly confessor.

FRIAR LAURENCE   Romeo shall thank thee, daughter, for us both.

JULIET   As much to him, else is his thanks too much.

ROMEO   Ah, Juliet, if the measure of thy joy
Be heap'd like mine and that thy skill be more
To blazon it, then sweeten with thy breath
This neighbour air, and let rich music's tongue
Unfold the imagined happiness that both
Receive in either by this dear encounter.

JULIET   Conceit, more rich in matter than in words,
Brags of his substance, not of ornament:
They are but beggars that can count their worth;
But my true love is grown to such excess
I cannot sum up sum of half my wealth.

FRIAR LAURENCE   Come, come with me, and we will make short work;
For, by your leaves, you shall not stay alone
Till holy church incorporate two in one.   *Exeunt.*

ACT III

SCENE 1 *Verona. A public place.*

Enter Mercutio, Benvolio, Page, and Servants.

BENVOLIO I pray thee, good Mercutio, let's retire:
The day is hot, the Capulets abroad,
And, if we meet, we shall not scape a brawl;
For now, these hot days, is the mad blood stirring.

MERCUTIO Thou art like one of those fellows that when he enters the
confines of a tavern claps me his sword upon the table and says, "God
send me no need of thee!" and by the operation of the second cup
draws it on the drawer, when indeed there is no need.

BENVOLIO Am I like such a fellow?

MERCUTIO Come, come, thou art as hot a Jack in thy mood as any in
Italy, and as soon moved to be moody, and as soon moody to be
moved.

BENVOLIO And what to?

MERCUTIO Nay, an there were two such, we should have none shortly,
for one would kill the other. Thou! why, thou wilt quarrel with a man
that hath a hair more, or a hair less, in his beard than thou hast: thou
wilt quarrel with a man for cracking nuts, having no other reason but
because thou hast hazel eyes: what eye but such an eye would spy out
such a quarrel? Thy head is as full of quarrels as an egg is full of meat,
and yet thy head hath been beaten as addle as an egg for quarrelling:
thou hast quarrelled with a man for coughing in the street, because he
hath wakened thy dog that hath lain asleep in the sun: didst thou not
fall out with a tailor for wearing his new doublet before Easter? with

48

another, for tying his new shoes with old riband? and yet thou wilt tutor me from quarrelling!

BENVOLIO   An I were so apt to quarrel as thou art, any man should buy the fee-simple of my life for an hour and a quarter.

MERCUTIO   The fee-simple—O simple!

BENVOLIO   By my head, here come the Capulets.

MERCUTIO   By my heel, I care not.

Enter Tybalt and others.

TYBALT   Follow me close, for I will speak to them.
Gentlemen, good den: a word with one of you.

MERCUTIO   And but one word with one of us? couple it with something; make it a word and a blow.

TYBALT   You shall find me apt enough to that, sir, an you will give me occasion.

MERCUTIO   Could you not take some occasion without giving?

TYBALT   Mercutio, thou consort'st with Romeo—

MERCUTIO   Consort! what, dost thou make us minstrels? an thou make minstrels of us, look to hear nothing but discords: here's my fiddle-stick; here's that shall make you dance. 'Zounds, consort!

BENVOLIO   We talk here in the public haunt of men:
Either withdraw unto some private place,
And reason coldly of your grievances,
Or else depart; here all eyes gaze on us.

MERCUTIO   Men's eyes were made to look, and let them gaze;
I will not budge for no man's pleasure, I.

Enter Romeo.

TYBALT   Well, peace be with you, sir: here comes my man.

MERCUTIO   But I'll be hang'd, sir, if he wear your livery:
Marry, go before to field, he'll be your follower;
Your worship in that sense may call him "man."

TYBALT   Romeo, the hate I bear thee can afford
No better term than this: thou art a villain.

ROMEO   Tybalt, the reason that I have to love thee

49

Doth much excuse the appertaining rage
To such a greeting: villain am I none;
Therefore farewell; I see thou know'st me not.

TYBALT Boy, this shall not excuse the injuries
That thou hast done me; therefore turn and draw.

ROMEO I do protest I never injured thee,
But love thee better than thou canst devise,
Till thou shalt know the reason of my love:
And so, good Capulet—which name I tender
As dearly as my own—be satisfied.

MERCUTIO O calm, dishonourable, vile submission!
Alla stoccata carries it away.

Draws.

Tybalt, you rat-catcher, will you walk?

TYBALT What wouldst thou have with me?

MERCUTIO Good king of cats, nothing but one of your nine lives; that I
mean to make bold withal, and, as you shall use me hereafter, dry-beat
the rest of the eight. Will you pluck your sword out of his pilcher by
the ears? make haste, lest mine be about your ears ere it be out.

TYBALT I am for you.

Draws.

ROMEO Gentle Mercutio, put thy rapier up.

MERCUTIO Come, sir, your *passado*.

They fight.

ROMEO Draw, Benvolio; beat down their weapons.
Gentlemen, for shame, forbear this outrage!
Tybalt, Mercutio, the Prince expressly hath
Forbidden bandying in Verona streets:
Hold, Tybalt! good Mercutio!

Tybalt under Romeo's arm stabs Mercutio, and flies with his followers.

MERCUTIO   I am hurt.
A plague o' both your houses! I am sped.
Is he gone, and hath nothing?

BENVOLIO   What, art thou hurt?

MERCUTIO   Ay, ay, a scratch, a scratch; marry, 'tis enough.
Where is my page? Go, villain, fetch a surgeon.   *Exit Page.*

ROMEO   Courage, man; the hurt cannot be much.

MERCUTIO   No, 'tis not so deep as a well, nor so wide as a church-door;
but 'tis enough, 'twill serve: ask for me to-morrow, and you shall find
me a grave man. I am peppered, I warrant, for this world. A plague o'
both your houses! 'Zounds, a dog, a rat, a mouse, a cat, to scratch a
man to death! a braggart, a rogue, a villain, that fights by the book of
arithmetic! Why the devil came you between us? I was hurt under your
arm.

ROMEO   I thought all for the best.

MERCUTIO   Help me into some house, Benvolio,
Or I shall faint. A plague o' both your houses!
They have made worms' meat of me: I have it,
And soundly too: your houses!   *Exeunt Mercutio and Benvolio.*

ROMEO   This gentleman, the Prince's near ally,
My very friend, hath got his mortal hurt
In my behalf; my reputation stain'd
With Tybalt's slander—Tybalt, that an hour
Hath been my kinsman! O sweet Juliet,
Thy beauty hath made me effeminate
And in my temper soften'd valour's steel!

Re-enter Benvolio.

BENVOLIO   O Romeo, Romeo, brave Mercutio's dead!
That gallant spirit hath aspired the clouds,
Which too untimely here did scorn the earth.

ROMEO   This day's black fate on more days doth depend;
This but begins the woe others must end.

BENVOLIO   Here comes the furious Tybalt back again.

ROMEO   Alive, in triumph! and Mercutio slain!
Away to heaven, respective lenity,
And fire-eyed fury be my conduct now!

Re-enter Tybalt.

Now, Tybalt, take the "villain" back again
That late thou gavest me; for Mercutio's soul
Is but a little way above our heads,

Staying for thine to keep him company:
Either thou, or I, or both, must go with him.

TYBALT Thou, wretched boy, that didst consort him here,
Shalt with him hence.

ROMEO   This shall determine that.

They fight; Tybalt falls.

BENVOLIO Romeo away, be gone!
The citizens are up, and Tybalt slain.
Stand not amazed: the Prince will doom thee death,
If thou art taken: hence, be gone, away!

ROMEO O, I am fortune's fool!

BENVOLIO   Why dost thou stay?   *Exit Romeo.*

Enter Citizens, &c.

FIRST CITIZEN Which way ran he that kill'd Mercutio?
Tybalt, that murderer, which way ran he?

BENVOLIO There lies that Tybalt.

FIRST CITIZEN   Up, sir, go with me;
I charge thee in the Prince's name, obey.

Enter Prince Escalus, attended; Montague, Capulet, their Wives, and others.

PRINCE ESCALUS Where are the vile beginners of this fray?

BENVOLIO O noble Prince, I can discover all
The unlucky manage of this fatal brawl:
There lies the man, slain by young Romeo,
That slew thy kinsman, brave Mercutio.

LADY CAPULET Tybalt, my cousin! O my brother's child!
O Prince! O cousin! husband! O, the blood is spilt
Of my dear kinsman! Prince, as thou art true,
For blood of ours, shed blood of Montague.
O cousin, cousin!

PRINCE ESCALUS Benvolio, who began this bloody fray?

BENVOLIO Tybalt, here slain, whom Romeo's hand did slay;
Romeo that spoke him fair, bade him bethink
How nice the quarrel was, and urged withal
Your high displeasure: all this uttered

With gentle breath, calm look, knees humbly bow'd,
Could not take truce with the unruly spleen
Of Tybalt deaf to peace, but that he tilts
With piercing steel at bold Mercutio's breast,
Who, all as hot, turns deadly point to point,
And, with a martial scorn, with one hand beats
Cold death aside, and with the other sends
It back to Tybalt, whose dexterity
Retorts it: Romeo he cried aloud,
"Hold friends! friends, part!" and, swifter than his tongue,
His agile arm beats down their fatal points,
And 'twixt them rushes; underneath whose arm
An envious thrust from Tybalt hit the life
Of stout Mercutio, and then Tybalt fled;
But by and by comes back to Romeo,
Who had but newly entertain'd revenge,
And to't they go like lightning, for, ere I
Could draw to part them, was stout Tybalt slain,
And, as he fell, did Romeo turn and fly.
This is the truth, or let Benvolio die.

LADY CAPULET   He is a kinsman to the Montague;
   Affection makes him false; he speaks not true:
   Some twenty of them fought in this black strife,
   And all those twenty could but kill one life.
   I beg for justice, which thou, Prince, must give;
   Romeo slew Tybalt, Romeo must not live.

PRINCE ESCALUS   Romeo slew him, he slew Mercutio;
   Who now the price of his dear blood doth owe?

MONTAGUE   Not Romeo, Prince, he was Mercutio's friend;
   His fault concludes but what the law should end,
   The life of Tybalt.

PRINCE ESCALUS   And for that offence
   Immediately we do exile him hence:
   I have an interest in your hate's proceeding,
   My blood for your rude brawls doth lie a-bleeding;
   But I'll amerce you with so strong a fine
   That you shall all repent the loss of mine:
   I will be deaf to pleading and excuses;
   Nor tears nor prayers shall purchase out abuses:
   Therefore use none: let Romeo hence in haste,

Else, when he's found, that hour is his last.
Bear hence this body and attend our will:
Mercy but murders, pardoning those that kill.   *Exeunt.*

SCENE 2 *Capulet's orchard.*

Enter Juliet.

JULIET   Gallop apace, you fiery-footed steeds,
  Towards Phoebus' lodging: such a waggoner
  As Phaethon would whip you to the west,
  And bring in cloudy night immediately.
  Spread thy close curtain, love-performing night,
  That runaways' eyes may wink, and Romeo
  Leap to these arms, untalk'd of and unseen.
  Lovers can see to do their amorous rites
  By their own beauties; or, if love be blind,
  It best agrees with night. Come, civil night,
  Thou sober-suited matron, all in black,
  And learn me how to lose a winning match,
  Play'd for a pair of stainless maidenhoods:
  Hood my unmann'd blood, bating in my cheeks,
  With thy black mantle; till strange love, grown bold,
  Think true love acted simple modesty.
  Come, night; come, Romeo; come, thou day in night;
  For thou wilt lie upon the wings of night
  Whiter than new snow on a raven's back.
  Come, gentle night, come, loving, black-brow'd night,
  Give me my Romeo; and, when he shall die,
  Take him and cut him out in little stars,
  And he will make the face of heaven so fine
  That all the world will be in love with night
  And pay no worship to the garish sun.
  O, I have bought the mansion of a love,
  But not possess'd it, and, though I am sold,
  Not yet enjoy'd: so tedious is this day
  As is the night before some festival
  To an impatient child that hath new robes
  And may not wear them. O, here comes my nurse,
  And she brings news; and every tongue that speaks
  But Romeo's name speaks heavenly eloquence.

Enter Nurse, with cords.

54

Now, nurse, what news? What hast thou there? the cords
That Romeo bid thee fetch?

NURSE   Ay, ay, the cords.

Throws them down.

JULIET   Ay me! what news! why dost thou wring thy hands?

NURSE   Ah, well-a-day! he's dead, he's dead!
  We are undone, lady, we are undone!
  Alack the day! he's gone, he's kill'd, he's dead!

JULIET   Can heaven be so envious?

NURSE   Romeo can,
  Though heaven cannot: O Romeo, Romeo!
  Who ever would have thought it? Romeo!

JULIET   What devil art thou, that dost torment me thus?
  This torture should be roar'd in dismal hell.
  Hath Romeo slain himself? say thou but ay,
  And that bare vowel I shall poison more
  Than the death-darting eye of cockatrice:
  I am not I, if there be such an ay,
  Or those eyes shut, that make thee answer ay.
  If he be slain, say ay; or if not, no:
  Brief sounds determine of my weal or woe.

NURSE   I saw the wound, I saw it with mine eyes—
  God save the mark!—here on his manly breast:
  A piteous corse, a bloody piteous corse;
  Pale, pale as ashes, all bedaub'd in blood,
  All in gore-blood; I swounded at the sight.

JULIET   O, break, my heart! poor bankrupt, break at once!
  To prison, eyes, ne'er look on liberty!
  Vile earth, to earth resign; end motion here;
  And thou and Romeo press one heavy bier!

NURSE   O Tybalt, Tybalt, the best friend I had!
  O courteous Tybalt! honest gentleman!
  That ever I should live to see thee dead!

JULIET   What storm is this that blows so contrary?
  Is Romeo slaughter'd, and is Tybalt dead?
  My dear-loved cousin, and my dearer lord?

55

Then, dreadful trumpet, sound the general doom!
For who is living, if those two are gone?

NURSE   Tybalt is gone, and Romeo banished;
Romeo that kill'd him, he is banished.

JULIET   O God! did Romeo's hand shed Tybalt's blood?

NURSE   It did, it did; alas the day, it did!

JULIET   O serpent heart, hid with a flowering face!
Did ever dragon keep so fair a cave?
Beautiful tyrant! fiend angelical!
Dove-feather'd raven! wolvish-ravening lamb!
Despised substance of divinest show!
Just opposite to what thou justly seem'st,
A damned saint, an honourable villain!
O nature, what hadst thou to do in hell,
When thou didst bower the spirit of a fiend
In mortal paradise of such sweet flesh?
Was ever book containing such vile matter
So fairly bound? O, that deceit should dwell
In such a gorgeous palace!

NURSE   There's no trust,
No faith, no honesty in men; all perjured,
All forsworn, all naught, all dissemblers.
Ah, where's my man? give me some aqua vitae:
These griefs, these woes, these sorrows make me old.
Shame come to Romeo!

JULIET   Blister'd be thy tongue
For such a wish! he was not born to shame:
Upon his brow shame is ashamed to sit;
For 'tis a throne where honour may be crown'd
Sole monarch of the universal earth.
O, what a beast was I to chide at him!

NURSE   Will you speak well of him that kill'd your cousin?

JULIET   Shall I speak ill of him that is my husband?
Ah, poor my lord, what tongue shall smooth thy name,
When I, thy three-hours wife, have mangled it?
But, wherefore, villain, didst thou kill my cousin?
That villain cousin would have kill'd my husband:
Back, foolish tears, back to your native spring;
Your tributary drops belong to woe,

Which you, mistaking, offer up to joy.
My husband lives, that Tybalt would have slain;
And Tybalt's dead, that would have slain my husband:
All this is comfort; wherefore weep I then?
Some word there was, worser than Tybalt's death,
That murder'd me: I would forget it fain;
But, O, it presses to my memory,
Like damned guilty deeds to sinners' minds:
"Tybalt is dead, and Romeo—banished";
That "banished," that one word "banished,"
Hath slain ten thousand Tybalts.   Tybalt's death
Was woe enough, if it had ended there:
Or, if sour woe delights in fellowship
And needly will be rank'd with other griefs,
Why follow'd not, when she said "Tybalt's dead,"
Thy father, or thy mother, nay, or both,
Which modern lamentation might have moved?
But with a rearward following Tybalt's death,
"Romeo is banished," to speak that word,
Is father, mother, Tybalt, Romeo, Juliet,
All slain, all dead. "Romeo is banished!"
There is no end, no limit, measure, bound,
In that word's death; no words can that woe sound.
Where is my father and my mother, nurse?

NURSE   Weeping and wailing over Tybalt's corse:
   Will you go to them? I will bring you thither.

JULIET   Wash they his wounds with tears: mine shall be spent,
   When theirs are dry, for Romeo's banishment.
   Take up those cords: poor ropes, you are beguiled,
   Both you and I; for Romeo is exiled:
   He made you for a highway to my bed;
   But I, a maid, die maiden-widowed.
   Come, cords, come, nurse; I'll to my wedding-bed;
   And death, not Romeo, take my maidenhead!

NURSE   Hie to your chamber: I'll find Romeo
   To comfort you: I wot well where he is.
   Hark ye, your Romeo will be here at night:
   I'll to him; he is hid at Laurence' cell.

JULIET   O, find him! give this ring to my true knight,
   And bid him come to take his last farewell.   *Exeunt.*

 SCENE 3 *Friar Laurence' cell.*

Enter Friar Laurence.

FRIAR LAURENCE   Romeo, come forth; come forth, thou fearful man:
  Affliction is enamour'd of thy parts,
  And thou art wedded to calamity.

Enter Romeo.

ROMEO   Father, what news? what is the Prince's doom?
  What sorrow craves acquaintance at my hand,
  That I yet know not?

FRIAR LAURENCE   Too familiar
  Is my dear son with such sour company:
  I bring thee tidings of the Prince's doom.

ROMEO   What less than dooms-day is the Prince's doom?

FRIAR LAURENCE   A gentler judgement vanish'd from his lips,
  Not body's death, but body's banishment.

ROMEO   Ha, banishment! be merciful, say "death";
  For exile hath more terror in his look,
  Much more than death: do not say "banishment."

FRIAR LAURENCE   Hence from Verona art thou banished:
  Be patient, for the world is broad and wide.

ROMEO   There is no world without Verona walls,
  But purgatory, torture, hell itself.
  Hence-banished is banish'd from the world,
  And world's exile is death: then "banished"
  Is death mis-term'd: calling death "banishment,"
  Thou cutt'st my head off with a golden axe,
  And smilest upon the stroke that murders me.

FRIAR LAURENCE   O deadly sin! O rude unthankfulness!
  Thy fault our law calls death; but the kind prince,
  Taking thy part, hath rush'd aside the law,
  And turn'd that black word "death" to "banishment":
  This is dear mercy, and thou seest it not.

ROMEO   'Tis torture, and not mercy: heaven is here,
  Where Juliet lives; and every cat and dog

58

And little mouse, every unworthy thing,
Live here in heaven and may look on her;
But Romeo may not: more validity,
More honourable state, more courtship lives
In carrion-flies than Romeo: they may seize
On the white wonder of dear Juliet's hand
And steal immortal blessing from her lips,
Who, even in pure and vestal modesty,
Still blush, as thinking their own kisses sin;
But Romeo may not; he is banished:
Flies may do this, but I from this must fly:
They are free men, but I am banished:
And say'st thou yet that exile is not death?
Hadst thou no poison mix'd, no sharp-ground knife,
No sudden mean of death, though ne'er so mean,
But "banished" to kill me?—"banished"?
O friar, the damned use that word in hell;
Howlings attend it: how hast thou the heart,
Being a divine, a ghostly confessor,
A sin-absolver, and my friend profess'd,
To mangle me with that word "banished"?

FRIAR LAURENCE   Thou fond madman, hear me but speak a word.

ROMEO   O, thou wilt speak again of banishment.

FRIAR LAURENCE   I'll give thee armour to keep off that word;
Adversity's sweet milk, philosophy,
To comfort thee, though thou art banished.

ROMEO   Yet "banished"? Hang up philosophy!
Unless philosophy can make a Juliet,
Displant a town, reverse a prince's doom,
It helps not, it prevails not: talk no more.

FRIAR LAURENCE   O, then I see that madmen have no ears.

ROMEO   How should they, when that wise men have no eyes?

FRIAR LAURENCE   Let me dispute with thee of thy estate.

ROMEO   Thou canst not speak of that thou dost not feel:
Wert thou as young as I, Juliet thy love,
An hour but married, Tybalt murdered,
Doting like me and like me banished,

Then mightst thou speak, then mightst thou tear thy hair,
And fall upon the ground, as I do now,
Taking the measure of an unmade grave.

Knocking within.

FRIAR LAURENCE   Arise; one knocks; good Romeo, hide thyself.

ROMEO   Not I; unless the breath of heart-sick groans,
  Mist-like, infold me from the search of eyes.

Knocking.

FRIAR LAURENCE   Hark, how they knock! Who's there? Romeo, arise;
  Thou wilt be taken. Stay awhile! Stand up;

Knocking.

  Run to my study. By and by! God's will,
  What simpleness is this! I come, I come!

Knocking.

  Who knocks so hard? whence come you? what's your will?

NURSE   [*Within.*] Let me come in, and you shall know my errand;
  I come from Lady Juliet.

FRIAR LAURENCE   Welcome, then.

Enter Nurse.

NURSE   O holy friar, O, tell me, holy friar,
  Where is my lady's lord, where's Romeo?

FRIAR LAURENCE   There on the ground, with his own tears made drunk.

NURSE   O, he is even in my mistress' case,
  Just in her case! O woeful sympathy!
  Piteous predicament! Even so lies she,
  Blubbering and weeping, weeping and blubbering.
  Stand up, stand up, stand, an you be a man:
  For Juliet's sake, for her sake, rise and stand;
  Why should you fall into so deep an O?

ROMEO   Nurse!

NURSE   Ah sir! ah sir! Well, death's the end of all.

ROMEO   Spakest thou of Juliet? how is it with her?
  Doth she not think me an old murderer,

Now I have stain'd the childhood of our joy
With blood removed but little from her own?
Where is she? and how doth she? and what says
My conceal'd lady to our cancell'd love?

NURSE   O, she says nothing, sir, but weeps and weeps;
And now falls on her bed, and then starts up,
And Tybalt calls; and then on Romeo cries,
And then down falls again.

ROMEO   As if that name,
Shot from the deadly level of a gun,
Did murder her; as that name's cursed hand
Murder'd her kinsman. O, tell me, friar, tell me,
In what vile part of this anatomy
Doth my name lodge? tell me, that I may sack
The hateful mansion.

Drawing his sword.

FRIAR LAURENCE   Hold thy desperate hand:
Art thou a man? thy form cries out thou art:
Thy tears are womanish; thy wild acts denote
The unreasonable fury of a beast:
Unseemly woman in a seeming man!
Or ill-beseeming beast in seeming both!
Thou hast amazed me: by my holy order,
I thought thy disposition better temper'd.
Hast thou slain Tybalt? wilt thou slay thyself?
And slay thy lady too that lives in thee,
By doing damned hate upon thyself?
Why rail'st thou on thy birth, the heaven, and earth?
Since birth, and heaven, and earth, all three do meet
In thee at once; which thou at once wouldst lose.
Fie, fie, thou shamest thy shape, thy love, thy wit;
Which, like a usurer, abound'st in all,
And usest none in that true use indeed
Which should bedeck thy shape, thy love, thy wit:
Thy noble shape is but a form of wax,
Digressing from the valour of a man;
Thy dear love sworn but hollow perjury,
Killing that love which thou hast vow'd to cherish;
Thy wit, that ornament to shape and love,
Mis-shapen in the conduct of them both,

61

Like powder in a skilless soldier's flask,
Is set a-fire by thine own ignorance,
And thou dismember'd with thine own defence.
What, rouse thee, man! thy Juliet is alive,
For whose dear sake thou wast but lately dead;
There art thou happy: Tybalt would kill thee,
But thou slew'st Tybalt; there art thou happy too:
The law that threaten'd death becomes thy friend
And turns it to exile; there art thou happy:
A pack of blessings lights upon thy back;
Happiness courts thee in her best array;
But, like a misbehaved and sullen wench,
Thou pout'st upon thy fortune and thy love:
Take heed, take heed, for such die miserable.
Go, get thee to thy love, as was decreed,
Ascend her chamber, hence and comfort her;
But look thou stay not till the watch be set,
For then thou canst not pass to Mantua;
Where thou shalt live, till we can find a time
To blaze your marriage, reconcile your friends,
Beg pardon of the Prince, and call thee back
With twenty hundred thousand times more joy
Than thou went'st forth in lamentation.
Go before, nurse: commend me to thy lady;
And bid her hasten all the house to bed,
Which heavy sorrow makes them apt unto:
Romeo is coming.

NURSE   O Lord, I could have stay'd here all the night
To hear good counsel: O, what learning is!
My lord, I'll tell my lady you will come.

ROMEO   Do so, and bid my sweet prepare to chide.

NURSE   Here, sir, a ring she bid me give you, sir:
Hie you, make haste, for it grows very late.   *Exit.*

ROMEO   How well my comfort is revived by this!

FRIAR LAURENCE   Go hence; good night; and here stands all your state:
Either be gone before the watch be set,
Or by the break of day disguised from hence:
Sojourn in Mantua; I'll find out your man,
And he shall signify from time to time

Every good hap to you that chances here:
Give me thy hand; 'tis late: farewell; good night.

ROMEO   But that a joy past joy calls out on me,
It were a grief, so brief to part with thee:
Farewell.   *Exeunt.*

🎋 SCENE 4   *A room in Capulet's house.*

Enter Capulet, Lady Capulet, and Paris.

CAPULET   Things have fall'n out, sir, so unluckily,
That we have had no time to move our daughter:
Look you, she loved her kinsman Tybalt dearly,
And so did I. Well, we were born to die.
'Tis very late, she'll not come down to-night:
I promise you, but for your company,
I would have been a-bed an hour ago.

PARIS   These times of woe afford no time to woo.
Madam, good night: commend me to your daughter.

LADY CAPULET   I will, and know her mind early to-morrow;
To-night she is mew'd up to her heaviness.

CAPULET   Sir Paris, I will make a desperate tender
Of my child's love: I think she will be ruled
In all respects by me; nay, more, I doubt it not.
Wife, go you to her ere you go to bed;
Acquaint her here of my son Paris' love;
And bid her, mark you me, on Wednesday next—
But, soft! what day is this?

PARIS   Monday, my lord.

CAPULET   Monday! ha, ha! Well, Wednesday is too soon,
O' Thursday let it be: o' Thursday, tell her,
She shall be married to this noble earl.
Will you be ready? do you like this haste?
We'll keep no great ado—a friend or two;
For, hark you, Tybalt being slain so late,
It may be thought we held him carelessly,
Being our kinsman, if we revel much:
Therefore we'll have some half a dozen friends,
And there an end. But what say you to Thursday?

PARIS My lord, I would that Thursday were to-morrow.

CAPULET Well, get you gone: o' Thursday be it, then.
Go you to Juliet ere you go to bed,
Prepare her, wife, against this wedding-day.
Farewell, my lord. Light to my chamber, ho!
Afore me! it is so very very late,
That we may call it early by and by.
Good night.   *Exeunt.*

❀ SCENE 5 *Capulet's orchard.*

Enter Romeo and Juliet above, at the window.

JULIET Wilt thou be gone? it is not yet near day:
It was the nightingale, and not the lark,
That pierced the fearful hollow of thine ear;
Nightly she sings on yon pomegranate-tree:
Believe me, love, it was the nightingale.

ROMEO It was the lark, the herald of the morn,
No nightingale: look, love, what envious streaks
Do lace the severing clouds in yonder east:
Night's candles are burnt out, and jocund day
Stands tiptoe on the misty mountain tops.
I must be gone and live, or stay and die.

JULIET Yon light is not day-light, I know it, I:
It is some meteor that the sun exhales,
To be to thee this night a torch-bearer,
And light thee on thy way to Mantua:
Therefore stay yet; thou need'st not to be gone.

ROMEO Let me be ta'en, let me be put to death;
I am content, so thou wilt have it so.
I'll say yon grey is not the morning's eye,
'Tis but the pale reflex of Cynthia's brow;
Nor that is not the lark, whose notes do beat
The vaulty heaven so high above our heads:
I have more care to stay than will to go:
Come, death, and welcome! Juliet wills it so.
How is't, my soul? let's talk; it is not day.

JULIET It is, it is: hie hence, be gone, away!

It is the lark that sings so out of tune,
Straining harsh discords and unpleasing sharps.
Some say the lark makes sweet division;
This doth not so, for she divideth us:
Some say the lark and loathed toad change eyes;
O, now I would they had changed voices too!
Since arm from arm that voice doth us affray,
Hunting thee hence with hunt's-up to the day.
O, now be gone; more light and light it grows.

ROMEO   More light and light; more dark and dark our woes!

Enter Nurse, to the chamber.

NURSE   Madam!

JULIET   Nurse?

NURSE   Your lady mother is coming to your chamber:
The day is broke; be wary, look about.   *Exit.*

JULIET   Then, window, let day in, and let life out.

ROMEO   Farewell, farewell! one kiss, and I'll descend.

He goeth down.

JULIET   Art thou gone so? love, lord, ay, husband, friend!
I must hear from thee every day in the hour,
For in a minute there are many days:
O, by this count I shall be much in years
Ere I again behold my Romeo!

ROMEO   Farewell!
I will omit no opportunity
That may convey my greetings, love, to thee.

JULIET   O, think'st thou we shall ever meet again?

ROMEO   I doubt it not; and all these woes shall serve
For sweet discourses in our time to come.

JULIET   O God, I have an ill-divining soul!
Methinks I see thee, now thou art below,
As one dead in the bottom of a tomb:
Either my eyesight fails, or thou look'st pale.

ROMEO   And trust me, love, in my eye so do you:
Dry sorrow drinks our blood. Adieu, adieu!   *Exit.*

JULIET   O Fortune, Fortune! all men call thee fickle:
If thou art fickle, what dost thou with him
That is renown'd for faith? Be fickle, Fortune;
For then, I hope, thou wilt not keep him long,
But send him back.

LADY CAPULET   [*Within.*] Ho, daughter! are you up?

JULIET   Who is't that calls? is it my lady mother?
Is she not down so late, or up so early?
What unaccustom'd cause procures her hither?

Enter Lady Capulet.

LADY CAPULET   Why, how now, Juliet?

JULIET   Madam, I am not well.

LADY CAPULET   Evermore weeping for your cousin's death?
What, wilt thou wash him from his grave with tears?
An if thou couldst, thou couldst not make him live;
Therefore, have done: some grief shows much of love;
But much of grief shows still some want of wit.

JULIET   Yet let me weep for such a feeling loss.

LADY CAPULET   So shall you feel the loss, but not the friend
Which you weep for.

JULIET   Feeling so the loss,
I cannot choose but ever weep the friend.

LADY CAPULET   Well, girl, thou weep'st not so much for his death,
As that the villain lives which slaughter'd him.

JULIET   What villain, madam?

LADY CAPULET   That same villain, Romeo.

JULIET   [*Aside.*] Villain and he be many miles asunder.
God pardon him! I do, with all my heart;
And yet no man like he doth grieve my heart.

LADY CAPULET   That is, because the traitor murderer lives.

JULIET   Ay, madam, from the reach of these my hands:
Would none but I might venge my cousin's death!

LADY CAPULET   We will have vengeance for it, fear thou not:
Then weep no more. I'll send to one in Mantua,

Where that same banish'd runagate doth live,
Shall give him such an unaccustom'd dram,
That he shall soon keep Tybalt company:
And then, I hope, thou wilt be satisfied.

JULIET   Indeed, I never shall be satisfied
With Romeo, till I behold him — dead —
Is my poor heart so for a kinsman vex'd:
Madam, if you could find out but a man
To bear a poison, I would temper it;
That Romeo should, upon receipt thereof,
Soon sleep in quiet. O, how my heart abhors
To hear him named, and cannot come to him,
To wreak the love I bore my cousin
Upon his body that hath slaughter'd him!

LADY CAPULET   Find thou the means, and I'll find such a man.
But now I'll tell thee joyful tidings, girl.

JULIET   And joy comes well in such a needy time:
What are they, I beseech your ladyship?

LADY CAPULET   Well, well, thou hast a careful father, child;
One who, to put thee from thy heaviness,
Hath sorted out a sudden day of joy,
That thou expect'st not nor I look'd not for.

JULIET   Madam, in happy time, what day is that?

LADY CAPULET   Marry, my child, early next Thursday morn,
The gallant, young and noble gentleman,
The County Paris, at Saint Peter's Church,
Shall happily make thee there a joyful bride.

JULIET   Now, by Saint Peter's Church and Peter too,
He shall not make me there a joyful bride.
I wonder at this haste; that I must wed
Ere he, that should be husband, comes to woo.
I pray you, tell my lord and father, madam,
I will not marry yet; and, when I do, I swear,
It shall be Romeo, whom you know I hate,
Rather than Paris. These are news indeed!

LADY CAPULET   Here comes your father; tell him so yourself,
And see how he will take it at your hands.

Enter Capulet and Nurse.

67

CAPULET   When the sun sets, the air doth drizzle dew;
But for the sunset of my brother's son
It rains downright.
How now? a conduit, girl? what, still in tears?
Evermore showering? In one little body
Thou counterfeit'st a bark, a sea, a wind;
For still thy eyes, which I may call the sea,
Do ebb and flow with tears; the bark thy body is,
Sailing in this salt flood; the winds, thy sighs;
Who, raging with thy tears, and they with them,
Without a sudden calm, will overset
Thy tempest-tossed body. How now, wife?
Have you deliver'd to her our decree?

LADY CAPULET   Ay, sir; but she will none, she gives you thanks.
I would the fool were married to her grave!

CAPULET   Soft! take me with you, take me with you, wife.
How? will she none? doth she not give us thanks?
Is she not proud? doth she not count her blest,
Unworthy as she is, that we have wrought
So worthy a gentleman to be her bridegroom?

JULIET   Not proud you have; but thankful that you have:
Proud can I never be of what I hate;
But thankful even for hate that is meant love.

CAPULET   How now, how now, chop-logic! What is this?
"Proud," and "I thank you," and "I thank you not";
And yet "not proud": mistress minion, you,
Thank me no thankings, nor proud me no prouds,
But fettle your fine joints 'gainst Thursday next,
To go with Paris to Saint Peter's Church,
Or I will drag thee on a hurdle thither.
Out, you green-sickness carrion! out, you baggage!
You tallow-face!

LADY CAPULET   Fie, fie! what, are you mad?

JULIET   Good father, I beseech you on my knees,
Hear me with patience but to speak a word.

CAPULET   Hang thee, young baggage! disobedient wretch!
I tell thee what: get thee to church o' Thursday,
Or never after look me in the face:

Speak not, reply not, do not answer me;
My fingers itch. Wife, we scarce thought us blest
That God had lent us but this only child;
But now I see this one is one too much,
And that we have a curse in having her:
Out on her, hilding!

NURSE   God in heaven bless her!
  You are to blame, my lord, to rate her so.

CAPULET   And why, my Lady Wisdom? hold your tongue,
  Good prudence; smatter with your gossips, go.

NURSE   I speak no treason.

CAPULET   O, God ye god-den.

NURSE   May not one speak?

CAPULET   Peace, you mumbling fool!
  Utter your gravity o'er a gossip's bowl;
  For here we need it not.

LADY CAPULET   You are too hot.

CAPULET   God's bread! it makes me mad:
  Day, night, hour, tide, time, work, play,
  Alone, in company, still my care hath been
  To have her match'd: and having now provided
  A gentleman of noble parentage,
  Of fair demesnes, youthful, and nobly train'd,
  Stuff'd, as they say, with honourable parts,
  Proportion'd as one's thought would wish a man;
  And then to have a wretched puling fool,
  A whining mammet, in her fortune's tender,
  To answer, "I'll not wed; I cannot love,
  I am too young; I pray you, pardon me."
  But, an you will not wed, I'll pardon you:
  Graze where you will, you shall not house with me:
  Look to't, think on't, I do not use to jest.
  Thursday is near; lay hand on heart, advise:
  An you be mine, I'll give you to my friend;
  An you be not, hang, beg, starve, die in the streets,
  For, by my soul, I'll ne'er acknowledge thee,
  Nor what is mine shall never do thee good:
  Trust to't, bethink you; I'll not be forsworn.   *Exit.*

JULIET   Is there no pity sitting in the clouds,
That sees into the bottom of my grief?
O, sweet my mother, cast me not away!
Delay this marriage for a month, a week;
Or, if you do not, make the bridal bed
In that dim monument where Tybalt lies.

LADY CAPULET   Talk not to me, for I'll not speak a word:
Do as thou wilt, for I have done with thee.   *Exit.*

JULIET   O God!—O nurse, how shall this be prevented?
My husband is on earth, my faith in heaven;
How shall that faith return again to earth,
Unless that husband send it me from heaven
By leaving earth? comfort me, counsel me.
Alack, alack, that heaven should practise stratagems
Upon so soft a subject as myself!
What say'st thou? hast thou not a word of joy?
Some comfort, nurse.

NURSE   Faith, here it is.
Romeo is banish'd; and all the world to nothing
That he dares ne'er come back to challenge you;
Or, if he do, it needs must be by stealth.
Then, since the case so stands as now it doth,
I think it best you married with the County.
O, he's a lovely gentleman!
Romeo's a dishclout to him: an eagle, madam,
Hath not so green, so quick, so fair an eye
As Paris hath. Beshrew my very heart,
I think you are happy in this second match,
For it excels your first: or if it did not,
Your first is dead; or 'twere as good he were
As living here and you no use of him.

JULIET   Speakest thou from thy heart?

NURSE   And from my soul too;
Or else beshrew them both.

JULIET   Amen!

NURSE   What?

JULIET   Well, thou hast comforted me marvellous much.
Go in; and tell my lady I am gone,

Having displeased my father, to Laurence' cell,
To make confession and to be absolved.

NURSE   Marry, I will; and this is wisely done.   *Exit.*

JULIET   Ancient damnation! O most wicked fiend!
Is it more sin to wish me thus forsworn,
Or to dispraise my lord with that same tongue
Which she hath praised him with above compare
So many thousand times? Go, counsellor;
Thou and my bosom henceforth shall be twain.
I'll to the friar, to know his remedy:
If all else fail, myself have power to die.   *Exit.*

ACT IV

❧ SCENE 1   *Friar Laurence' cell.*

Enter Friar Laurence and Paris.

FRIAR LAURENCE   On Thursday, sir? the time is very short.

PARIS   My father Capulet will have it so;
And I am nothing slow to slack his haste.

FRIAR LAURENCE   You say you do not know the lady's mind:
Uneven is the course, I like it not.

PARIS   Immoderately she weeps for Tybalt's death,
And therefore have I little talk'd of love;
For Venus smiles not in a house of tears.
Now, sir, her father counts it dangerous
That she doth give her sorrow so much sway,
And in his wisdom hastes our marriage,
To stop the inundation of her tears;
Which, too much minded by herself alone,
May be put from her by society:
Now do you know the reason of this haste.

FRIAR LAURENCE   [*Aside.*] I would I knew not why it should be slow'd.
Look, sir, here comes the lady towards my cell.

Enter Juliet.

PARIS   Happily met, my lady and my wife!

JULIET   That may be, sir, when I may be a wife.

PARIS   That may be must be, love, on Thursday next.

JULIET   What must be shall be.

FRIAR LAURENCE   That's a certain text.

PARIS   Come you to make confession to this father?

JULIET   To answer that, I should confess to you.

PARIS   Do not deny to him that you love me.

JULIET   I will confess to you that I love him.

PARIS   So will ye, I am sure, that you love me.

JULIET   If I do so, it will be of more price,
   Being spoke behind your back, than to your face.

PARIS   Poor soul, thy face is much abused with tears.

JULIET   The tears have got small victory by that;
   For it was bad enough before their spite.

PARIS   Thou wrong'st it, more than tears, with that report.

JULIET   That is no slander, sir, which is a truth;
   And what I spake, I spake it to my face.

PARIS   Thy face is mine, and thou hast slander'd it.

JULIET   It may be so, for it is not mine own.
   Are you at leisure, holy father, now;
   Or shall I come to you at evening mass?

FRIAR LAURENCE   My leisure serves me, pensive daughter, now.
   My lord, we must entreat the time alone.

PARIS   God shield I should disturb devotion!
   Juliet, on Thursday early will I rouse ye:
   Till then, adieu; and keep this holy kiss.   *Exit.*

JULIET   O, shut the door! and when thou hast done so,
   Come weep with me; past hope, past cure, past help!

FRIAR LAURENCE   Ah, Juliet. I already know thy grief;
   It strains me past the compass of my wits:
   I hear thou must, and nothing may prorogue it,
   On Thursday next be married to this County.

JULIET   Tell me not, friar, that thou hear'st of this,
   Unless thou tell me how I may prevent it:
   If, in thy wisdom, thou canst give no help,

73

Do thou but call my resolution wise,
And with this knife I'll help it presently.
God join'd my heart and Romeo's, thou our hands;
And ere this hand, by thee to Romeo seal'd,
Shall be the label to another deed,
Or my true heart with treacherous revolt
Turn to another, this shall slay them both:
Therefore, out of thy long-experienced time,
Give me some present counsel, or, behold,
'Twixt my extremes and me this bloody knife
Shall play the umpire, arbitrating that
Which the commission of thy years and art
Could to no issue of true honour bring.
Be not so long to speak; I long to die,
If what thou speak'st speak not of remedy.

FRIAR LAURENCE   Hold, daughter: I do spy a kind of hope,
Which craves as desperate an execution
As that is desperate which we would prevent.
If, rather than to marry County Paris,
Thou hast the strength of will to slay thyself,
Then it is likely thou wilt undertake
A thing like death to chide away this shame,
That copest with death himself to scape from it,
And, if thou darest, I'll give thee remedy.

JULIET   O, bid me leap, rather than marry Paris,
From off the battlements of yonder tower;
Or walk in thievish ways; or bid me lurk
Where serpents are; chain me with roaring bears;
Or shut me nightly in a charnel-house,
O'er-cover'd quite with dead men's rattling bones,
With reeky shanks and yellow chapless skulls;
Or bid me go into a new-made grave
And hide me with a dead man in his shroud;
Things that, to hear them told, have made me tremble;
And I will do it without fear or doubt,
To live an unstain'd wife to my sweet love.

FRIAR LAURENCE   Hold, then; go home, be merry, give consent
To marry Paris: Wednesday is to-morrow:
To-morrow night look that thou lie alone;
Let not thy nurse lie with thee in thy chamber:

Take thou this vial, being then in bed,
And this distilled liquor drink thou off;
When presently through all thy veins shall run
A cold and drowsy humour, for no pulse
Shall keep his native progress, but surcease:
No warmth, no breath, shall testify thou livest;
The roses in thy lips and cheeks shall fade
To paly ashes, thy eyes' windows fall,
Like death, when he shuts up the day of life;
Each part, deprived of supple government,
Shall, stiff and stark and cold, appear like death:
And in this borrow'd likeness of shrunk death
Thou shalt continue two and forty hours,
And then awake as from a pleasant sleep.
Now, when the bridegroom in the morning comes
To rouse thee from thy bed, there art thou dead:
Then, as the manner of our country is,
In thy best robes uncover'd on the bier
Thou shalt be borne to that same ancient vault
Where all the kindred of the Capulets lie.
In the meantime, against thou shalt awake,
Shall Romeo by my letters know our drift,
And hither shall he come: and he and I
Will watch thy waking, and that very night
Shall Romeo bear thee hence to Mantua.
And this shall free thee from this present shame;
If no inconstant toy, nor womanish fear,
Abate thy valour in the acting it.

JULIET   Give me, give me! O, tell not me of fear!

FRIAR LAURENCE   Hold; get you gone, be strong and prosperous
In this resolve: I'll send a friar with speed
To Mantua, with my letters to thy lord.

JULIET   Love give me strength! and strength shall help afford.
Farewell, dear father!   *Exeunt.*

 SCENE 2 *A hall in Capulet's house.*

Enter Capulet, Lady Capulet, Nurse, and two Servants.

CAPULET So many guests invite as here are writ.   *Exit First Servant.*
Sirrah, go hire me twenty cunning cooks.

SECOND SERVANT You shall have none ill, sir; for I'll try if they can lick
their fingers.

CAPULET How canst thou try them so?

SECOND SERVANT Marry, sir, 'tis an ill cook that cannot lick his own fingers: therefore he that cannot lick his fingers goes not with me.

CAPULET Go, be gone.   *Exit Second Servant.*
We shall be much unfurnish'd for this time.
What, is my daughter gone to Friar Laurence?

NURSE Ay, forsooth.

CAPULET Well, he may chance to do some good on her:
A peevish self-will'd harlotry it is.

NURSE See where she comes from shrift with merry look.

Enter Juliet.

CAPULET How now, my headstrong? where have you been gadding?

JULIET Where I have learn'd me to repent the sin
Of disobedient opposition
To you and your behests, and am enjoin'd
By holy Laurence to fall prostrate here,
And beg your pardon: pardon, I beseech you!
Henceforward I am ever ruled by you.

CAPULET Send for the County; go tell him of this:
I'll have this knot knit up to-morrow morning.

JULIET I met the youthful lord at Laurence' cell;
And gave him what becomed love I might,
Not stepping o'er the bounds of modesty.

CAPULET Why, I am glad on't; this is well: stand up:
This is as't should be. Let me see the County;
Ay, marry, go, I say, and fetch him hither.
Now, afore God! this reverend holy friar,
All our whole city is much bound to him.

JULIET   Nurse, will go with me into my closet,
    To help me sort such needful ornaments
    As you think fit to furnish me to-morrow?

LADY CAPULET   No, not till Thursday; there is time enough.

CAPULET   Go nurse, go with her: we'll to church to-morrow.

Exeunt Juliet and Nurse.

LADY CAPULET   We shall be short in our provision:
    'Tis now near night.

CAPULET   Tush, I will stir about,
    And all things shall be well, I warrant thee, wife:
    Go thou to Juliet, help to deck up her;
    I'll not to bed to-night; let me alone;
    I'll play the housewife for this once. What, ho!
    They are all forth. Well, I will walk myself
    To County Paris, to prepare him up
    Against to-morrow: my heart is wondrous light,
    Since this same wayward girl is so reclaim'd.   *Exeunt.*

❀ SCENE 3 *Juliet's chamber.*

Enter Juliet and Nurse.

JULIET   Ay, those attires are best: but, gentle nurse,
    I pray thee, leave me to myself to-night;
    For I have need of many orisons
    To move the heavens to smile upon my state,
    Which, well thou know'st, is cross and full of sin.

Enter Lady Capulet.

LADY CAPULET   What, are you busy, ho? need you my help?

JULIET   No, madam; we have cull'd such necessaries
    As are behoveful for our state to-morrow:
    So please you, let me now be left alone,
    And let the nurse this night sit up with you;
    For, I am sure, you have your hands full all,
    In this so sudden business.

LADY CAPULET   Good night:
    Get thee to bed, and rest; for thou hast need.

Exeunt Lady Capulet and Nurse.

77

JULIET Farewell! God knows when we shall meet again.
I have a faint cold fear thrills through my veins,
That almost freezes up the heat of life:
I'll call them back again to comfort me:
Nurse! What should she do here?
My dismal scene I needs must act alone.
Come, vial.
What if this mixture do not work at all?
Shall I be married then to-morrow morning?
No, no: this shall forbid it: lie thou there.

Laying down her dagger.

What if it be a poison, which the friar
Subtly hath minister'd to have me dead,
Lest in this marriage he should be dishonour'd,
Because he married me before to Romeo?
I fear it is: and yet, methinks, it should not,
For he hath still been tried a holy man.
How if, when I am laid into the tomb,
I wake before the time that Romeo
Come to redeem me? there's a fearful point!
Shall I not, then, be stifled in the vault,
To whose foul mouth no healthsome air breathes in,
And there die strangled ere my Romeo comes?
Or, if I live, is it not very like,
The horrible conceit of death and night,
Together with the terror of the place —
As in a vault, an ancient receptacle,
Where, for these many hundred years, the bones
Of all my buried ancestors are pack'd:
Where bloody Tybalt, yet but green in earth,
Lies festering in his shroud; where, as they say,
At some hours in the night spirits resort —
Alack, alack, is it not like that I,
So early waking, what with loathsome smells,
And shrieks like mandrakes' torn out of the earth,
That living mortals, hearing them, run mad:
O, if I wake, shall I not be distraught,
Environed with all these hideous fears?
And madly play with my forefathers' joints?
And pluck the mangled Tybalt from his shroud?
And, in this rage, with some great kinsman's bone,

As with a club, dash out my desperate brains?
O, look! methinks I see my cousin's ghost
Seeking out Romeo, that did spit his body
Upon a rapier's point: stay, Tybalt, stay!
Romeo, I come! this do I drink to thee.

She falls upon her bed, within the curtains.

SCENE 4   *A hall in Capulet's house.*

Enter Lady Capulet and Nurse.

LADY CAPULET   Hold, take these keys, and fetch more spices, nurse.

NURSE   They call for dates and quinces in the pastry.

Enter Capulet.

CAPULET   Come, stir, stir, stir! the second cock hath crow'd,
The curfew-bell hath rung, 'tis three o'clock:
Look to the baked meats, good Angelica:
Spare not for cost.

NURSE   Go, you cot-quean, go,
Get you to bed; faith, you'll be sick to-morrow
For this night's watching.

CAPULET   No, not a whit: what! I have watch'd ere now
All night for lesser cause, and ne'er been sick.

LADY CAPULET   Ay, you have been a mouse-hunt in your time;
But I will watch you from such watching now.

Exeunt Lady Capulet and Nurse.

CAPULET   A jealous-hood, a jealous-hood!

Enter three or four Servants, with spits, logs, and baskets.

Now, fellow, what's there?

FIRST SERVANT   Things for the cook, sir; but I know not what.

CAPULET   Make haste, make haste.   *Exit First Servant*
                    Sirrah, fetch drier logs:
Call Peter, he will show thee where they are.

SECOND SERVANT   I have a head, sir, that will find out logs,
And never trouble Peter for the matter.   *Exit.*

79

CAPULET   Mass, and well said; a merry whoreson, ha!
   Thou shalt be logger-head. Good faith, 'tis day:
   The County will be here with music straight,
   For so he said he would: I hear him near.

Music within.

   Nurse! Wife! What, ho! What, nurse, I say!

Re-enter Nurse.

   Go waken Juliet, go and trim her up;
   I'll go and chat with Paris: hie, make haste,
   Make haste; the bridegroom he is come already:
   Make haste, I say.   *Exeunt.*

SCENE 5 *Juliet's chamber.*

Enter Nurse.

NURSE   Mistress! what, mistress! Juliet! fast, I warrant her, she—
   Why, lamb! why, lady! fie, you slug-a-bed!
   Why, love, I say! madam! sweet-heart! why, bride!
   What, not a word! you take your pennyworths now;
   Sleep for a week; for the next night, I warrant,
   The County Paris hath set up his rest,
   That you shall rest but little. God forgive me,
   Marry, and amen, how sound is she asleep!
   I must needs wake her. Madam, madam, madam!
   Ay, let the County take you in your bed;
   He'll fright you up, i' faith. Will it not be?

Undraws the curtains.

   What, dress'd! and in your clothes! and down again!
   I must needs wake you: Lady! lady! lady!
   Alas, alas! Help, help! my lady's dead!
   O, well-a-day, that ever I was born!
   Some aqua vitae, ho! My lord! my lady!

Enter Lady Capulet.

LADY CAPULET   What noise is here?

NURSE   O lamentable day!

LADY CAPULET   What is the matter?

NURSE   Look, look! O heavy day!

LADY CAPULET   O me, O me! My child, my only life,
   Revive, look up, or I will die with thee!
   Help, help! Call help.

Enter Capulet.

CAPULET   For shame, bring Juliet forth; her lord is come.

NURSE   She's dead, deceased, she's dead; alack the day!

LADY CAPULET   Alack the day, she's dead, she's dead, she's dead!

CAPULET   Ha! let me see her: out, alas! she's cold;
   Her blood is settled, and her joints are stiff;
   Life and these lips have long been separated:
   Death lies on her like an untimely frost
   Upon the sweetest flower of all the field.

NURSE   O lamentable day!

LADY CAPULET   O woeful time!

CAPULET   Death, that hath ta'en her hence to make me wail,
   Ties up my tongue and will not let me speak.

Enter Friar Laurence and Paris, with Musicians.

FRIAR LAURENCE   Come, is the bride ready to go to church?

CAPULET   Ready to go, but never to return.
   O son! the night before thy wedding-day
   Hath Death lain with thy wife. There she lies,
   Flower as she was, deflowered by him.
   Death is my son-in-law, Death is my heir;
   My daughter he hath wedded: I will die,
   And leave him all; life, living, all is Death's.

PARIS   Have I thought long to see this morning's face,
   And doth it give me such a sight as this?

LADY CAPULET   Accursed, unhappy, wretched, hateful day!
   Most miserable hour that e'er time saw
   In lasting labour of his pilgrimage!
   But one, poor one, one poor and loving child,
   But one thing to rejoice and solace in,
   And cruel death hath catch'd it from my sight!

81

NURSE O woe! O woeful, woeful, woeful day!
Most lamentable day, most woeful day,
That ever, ever, I did yet behold!
O day! O day! O day! O hateful day!
Never was seen so black a day as this:
O woeful day, O woeful day!

PARIS Beguiled, divorced, wronged, spited, slain
Most detestable death, by thee beguiled,
By cruel cruel thee quite overthrown!
O love! O life! not life, but love in death!

CAPULET Despised, distressed, hated, martyr'd, kill'd!
Uncomfortable time, why camest thou now
To murder, murder our solemnity?
O child! O child! my soul, and not my child!
Dead art thou! Alack! my child is dead:
And with my child my joys are buried.

FRIAR LAURENCE Peace, ho, for shame! confusion's cure lives not
In these confusions. Heaven and yourself
Had part in this fair maid; now heaven hath all,
And all the better is it for the maid:
Your part in her you could not keep from death,
But heaven keeps his part in eternal life.
The most you sought was her promotion;
For 'twas your heaven she should be advanced:
And weep ye now, seeing she is advanced
Above the clouds, as high as heaven itself?
O, in this love, you love your child so ill
That you run mad, seeing that she is well:
She's not well married that lives married long;
But she's best married that dies married young.
Dry up your tears, and stick your rosemary
On this fair corse; and, as the custom is,
In all her best array bear her to church:
For though fond nature bids us all lament,
Yet nature's tears are reason's merriment.

CAPULET All things that we ordained festival,
Turn from their office to black funeral;
Our instruments to melancholy bells,
Our wedding cheer to a sad burial feast,

Our solemn hymns to sullen dirges change,
Our bridal flowers serve for a buried corse,
And all things change them to the contrary.

FRIAR LAURENCE   Sir, go you in; and, madam, go with him;
And go, Sir Paris; every one prepare
To follow this fair corse unto her grave:
The heavens do lour upon you for some ill;
Move them no more by crossing their high will.

Exeunt Capulet, Lady Capulet, Paris, and Friar.

FIRST MUSICIAN   Faith, we may put up our pipes and be gone.

NURSE   Honest good fellows, ah, put up, put up;
For, well you know, this is a pitiful case.   *Exit.*

FIRST MUSICIAN   Ay, by my troth, the case may be amended.

Enter Peter.

PETER   Musicians, O, musicians, "Heart's ease," "Heart's ease": O, an you will have me live, play "Heart's ease."

FIRST MUSICIAN   Why "Heart's ease"?

PETER   O, musicians, because my heart itself plays "My heart is full of woe": O, play me some merry dump, to comfort me.

FIRST MUSICIAN   Not a dump we; 'tis no time to play now.

PETER   You will not, then?

FIRST MUSICIAN   No.

PETER   I will then give it you soundly.

FIRST MUSICIAN   What will you give us?

PETER   No money, on my faith, but the gleek; I will give you the minstrel.

FIRST MUSICIAN   Then will I give you the serving-creature.

PETER   Then will I lay the serving-creature's dagger on your pate. I will carry no crotchets: I'll *re* you, I'll *fa* you; do you note me?

FIRST MUSICIAN   An you *re* us and *fa* us, you note us.

SECOND MUSICIAN   Pray you, put up your dagger, and put out your wit.

PETER   Then have at you with my wit! I will dry-beat you with an iron wit, and put up my iron dagger. Answer me like men:

> "When griping grief the heart doth wound,
> And doleful dumps the mind oppress,
> Then music with her silver sound"—

Why "silver sound"? why "music with her silver sound"? What say you, Simon Catling?

FIRST MUSICIAN   Marry, sir, because silver hath a sweet sound.

PETER   Pretty! What say you, Hugh Rebeck?

SECOND MUSICIAN   I say "silver sound," because musicians sound for silver.

PETER   Pretty too! What say you, James Soundpost?

THIRD MUSICIAN   Faith, I know not what to say.

PETER   O, I cry you mercy; you are the singer: I will say for you. It is "music with her silver sound," because musicians have no gold for sounding:

> "Then music with her silver sound
> With speedy help doth lend redress."   *Exit.*

FIRST MUSICIAN   What a pestilent knave is this same!

SECOND MUSICIAN   Hang him, Jack! Come, we'll in here; tarry for the mourners, and stay dinner.   *Exeunt.*

84

ACT V

Enter Romeo.

ROMEO   If I may trust the flattering truth of sleep,
  My dreams presage some joyful news at hand:
  My bosom's lord sits lightly in his throne;
  And all this day an unaccustom'd spirit
  Lifts me above the ground with cheerful thoughts.
  I dreamt my lady came and found me dead—
  Strange dream, that gives a dead man leave to think!—
  And breathed such life with kisses in my lips,
  That I revived, and was an emperor.
  Ah me! how sweet is love itself possess'd,
  When but love's shadows are so rich in joy!

Enter Balthasar, booted.

  News from Verona! How now, Balthasar?
  Dost thou not bring me letters from the friar?
  How doth my lady? Is my father well?
  How fares my Juliet? that I ask again;
  For nothing can be ill, if she be well.

BALTHASAR   Then she is well, and nothing can be ill:
  Her body sleeps in Capel's monument,
  And her immortal part with angels lives.
  I saw her laid low in her kindred's vault,
  And presently took post to tell it you:
  O, pardon me for bringing these ill news,
  Since you did leave it for my office, sir.

85

ROMEO Is it even so? then I defy you, stars!
  Thou know'st my lodging: get me ink and paper,
  And hire post-horses; I will hence to-night.

BALTHASAR I do beseech you, sir, have patience:
  Your looks are pale and wild, and do import
  Some misadventure.

ROMEO   Tush, thou art deceived:
  Leave me, and do the thing I bid thee do.
  Hast thou no letters to me from the friar?

BALTHASAR No, my good lord.

ROMEO   No matter: get thee gone,
  And hire those horses; I'll be with thee straight.   *Exit Balthasar.*
  Well, Juliet, I will lie with thee to-night.
  Let's see for means: O mischief, thou art swift
  To enter in the thoughts of desperate men!
  I do remember an apothecary—
  And hereabouts he dwells—which late I noted
  In tatter'd weeds, with overwhelming brows,
  Culling of simples; meagre were his looks,
  Sharp misery had worn him to the bones:
  And in his needy shop a tortoise hung,
  An alligator stuff'd, and other skins
  Of ill-shaped fishes; and about his shelves
  A beggarly account of empty boxes,
  Green earthen pots, bladders and musty seeds,
  Remnants of packthread and old cakes of roses,
  Were thinly scatter'd, to make up a show.
  Noting this penury, to myself I said,
  "An if a man did need a poison now,
  Whose sale is present death in Mantua,
  Here lives a caitiff wretch would sell it him."
  O, this same thought did but forerun my need;
  And this same needy man must sell it me.
  As I remember, this should be the house.
  Being holiday, the beggar's shop is shut.
  What, ho! apothecary!

Enter Apothecary.

APOTHECARY   Who calls so loud?

ROMEO Come hither, man. I see that thou art poor:

Hold, there is forty ducats: let me have
A dram of poison, such soon-speeding gear
As will disperse itself through all the veins
That the life-weary taker may fall dead
And that the trunk may be discharged of breath
As violently as hasty powder fired
Doth hurry from the fatal cannon's womb.

APOTHECARY   Such mortal drugs I have; but Mantua's law
Is death to any he that utters them.

ROMEO   Art thou so bare and full of wretchedness,
And fear'st to die? famine is in thy cheeks,
Need and oppression starveth in thine eyes,
Contempt and beggary hangs upon thy back;
The world is not thy friend nor the world's law;
The world affords no law to make thee rich;
Then be not poor, but break it, and take this.

APOTHECARY   My poverty, but not my will, consents.

ROMEO   I pay thy poverty, and not thy will.

APOTHECARY   Put this in any liquid thing you will,
And drink it off; and, if you had the strength
Of twenty men, it would dispatch you straight.

ROMEO   There is thy gold, worse poison to men's souls,
Doing more murders in this loathsome world
Than these poor compounds that thou mayst not sell.
I sell thee poison; thou hast sold me none.
Farewell: buy food, and get thyself in flesh.
Come, cordial and not poison, go with me
To Juliet's grave; for there must I use thee.   *Exeunt.*

✿ SCENE 2   *Verona. Friar Laurence' cell.*

Enter Friar John.

FRIAR JOHN   Holy Franciscan friar! brother, ho!

Enter Friar Laurence.

FRIAR LAURENCE   This same should be the voice of Friar John.
Welcome from Mantua: what says Romeo?
Or, if his mind be writ, give me his letter.

FRIAR JOHN   Going to find a bare-foot brother out,
One of our order, to associate me,
Here in this city visiting the sick,
And finding him, the searchers of the town,
Suspecting that we both were in a house
Where the infectious pestilence did reign,
Seal'd up the doors, and would not let us forth;
So that my speed to Mantua there was stay'd.

FRIAR LAURENCE   Who bare my letter, then, to Romeo?

FRIAR JOHN   I could not send it—here it is again—
Nor get a messenger to bring it thee,
So fearful were they of infection.

FRIAR LAURENCE   Unhappy fortune! by my brotherhood,
The letter was not nice but full of charge
Of dear import, and the neglecting it
May do much danger. Friar John, go hence;
Get me an iron crow, and bring it straight
Unto my cell.

FRIAR JOHN   Brother, I'll go and bring it thee.   *Exit.*

FRIAR LAURENCE   Now must I to the monument alone;
Within this three hours will fair Juliet wake:
She will beshrew me much that Romeo
Hath had no notice of these accidents;
But I will write again to Mantua,
And keep her at my cell till Romeo come;
Poor living corse, closed in a dead man's tomb!   *Exit.*

❀ SCENE 3   *A churchyard. In it a tomb belonging to the Capulets.*

Enter Paris, and his Page, bearing flowers and a torch.

PARIS   Give me thy torch, boy: hence, and stand aloof:
Yet put it out, for I would not be seen.
Under yond yew-trees lay thee all along,
Holding thine ear close to the hollow ground;
So shall no foot upon the churchyard tread,
Being loose, unfirm, with digging up of graves,
But thou shalt hear it: whistle then to me,

As signal that thou hear'st something approach.
Give me those flowers. Do as I bid thee, go.

PAGE   [*Aside.*] I am almost afraid to stand alone
Here in the churchyard; yet I will adventure.   *Retires.*

PARIS   Sweet flower, with flowers thy bridal bed I strew —
O woe! thy canopy is dust and stones —
Which with sweet water nightly I will dew,
Or, wanting that, with tears distill'd by moans:
The obsequies that I for thee will keep
Nightly shall be to strew thy grave and weep.

The Page whistles.

The boy gives warning something doth approach.
What cursed foot wanders this way to-night,
To cross my obsequies and true love's rite?
What, with a torch! muffle me, night, awhile.   *Retires.*

Enter Romeo and Balthasar, with a torch, mattock,&c.

ROMEO   Give me that mattock and the wrenching iron.
Hold, take this letter; early in the morning
See thou deliver it to my lord and father.
Give me the light: upon thy life, I charge thee,
Whate'er thou hear'st or seest, stand all aloof,
And do not interrupt me in my course.
Why I descend into this bed of death,
Is partly to behold my lady's face;
But chiefly to take thence from her dead finger
A precious ring, a ring that I must use
In dear employment: therefore hence, be gone:
But if thou, jealous, dost return to pry
In what I further shall intend to do,
By heaven, I will tear thee joint by joint
And strew this hungry churchyard with thy limbs:
The time and my intents are savage-wild,
More fierce and more inexorable far
Than empty tigers or the roaring sea.

BALTHASAR   I will be gone, sir, and not trouble you.

ROMEO   So shalt thou show me friendship. Take thou that:
Live, and be prosperous: and farewell, good fellow.

89

BALTHASAR   [*Aside.*] For all this same, I'll hide me hereabout:
  His looks I fear, and his intents I doubt.   *Retires.*

ROMEO   Thou detestable maw, thou womb of death,
  Gorged with the dearest morsel of the earth,
  Thus I enforce thy rotten jaws to open,
  And, in despite, I'll cram thee with more food!

Opens the tomb.

PARIS   This is that banish'd haughty Montague,
  That murder'd my love's cousin, with which grief,
  It is supposed, the fair creature died;
  And here is come to do some villainous shame
  To the dead bodies: I will apprehend him.

Comes forward.

  Stop thy unhallow'd toil, vile Montague!
  Can vengeance be pursued further than death?
  Condemned villain, I do apprehend thee:
  Obey, and go with me; for thou must die.

ROMEO   I must indeed; and therefore came I hither.
  Good gentle youth, tempt not a desperate man;
  Fly hence, and leave me: think upon these gone;
  Let them affright thee. I beseech thee, youth,
  Put not another sin upon my head,
  By urging me to fury: O, be gone!
  By heaven, I love thee better than myself;
  For I come hither arm'd against myself:
  Stay not, be gone; live, and hereafter say,
  A madman's mercy bade thee run away.

PARIS   I do defy thy conjurations,
  And apprehend thee for a felon here.

ROMEO   Wilt thou provoke me? then have at thee, boy!

They fight.

PAGE   O Lord, they fight! I will go call the watch.   *Exit.*

PARIS   O, I am slain! [*Falls.*] If thou be merciful,
  Open the tomb, lay me with Juliet.   *Dies.*

ROMEO   In faith, I will. Let me peruse this face.
  Mercutio's kinsman, noble County Paris!

What said my man, when my betossed soul
Did not attend him as we rode? I think
He told me Paris should have married Juliet:
Said he not so? or did I dream it so?
Or am I mad, hearing him talk of Juliet,
To think it was so? O, give me thy hand,
One writ with me in sour misfortune's book!
I'll bury thee in a triumphant grave;
A grave? O, no! a lantern, slaughter'd youth,
For here lies Juliet, and her beauty makes
This vault a feasting presence full of light.
Death, lie thou there, by a dead man interr'd.

Laying Paris in the tomb.

How oft when men are at the point of death
Have they been merry! which their keepers call
A lightning before death: O, how may I
Call this a lightning? O my love! my wife!
Death, that hath suck'd the honey of thy breath,
Hath had no power yet upon thy beauty:
Thou art not conquer'd; beauty's ensign yet
Is crimson in thy lips and in thy cheeks,
And death's pale flag is not advanced there.
Tybalt, liest thou there in thy bloody sheet?
O, what more favour can I do to thee,
Than with that hand that cut thy youth in twain
To sunder his that was thine enemy?
Forgive me, cousin! Ah, dear Juliet,
Why art thou yet so fair? shall I believe
That unsubstantial death is amorous,
And that the lean abhorred monster keeps
Thee here in dark to be his paramour?
For fear of that, I still will stay with thee;
And never from this palace of dim night
Depart again: here, here will I remain
With worms that are thy chamber-maids; O, here
Will I set up my everlasting rest,
And shake the yoke of inauspicious stars
From this world-wearied flesh. Eyes, look your last!
Arms, take your last embrace! and, lips, O you
The doors of breath, seal with a righteous kiss
A dateless bargain to engrossing death!

Come, bitter conduct, come, unsavoury guide!
Thou desperate pilot, now at once run on
The dashing rocks thy sea-sick weary bark!
Here's to my love! [*Drinks.*] O true apothecary!
Thy drugs are quick. Thus with a kiss I die.   *Dies.*

Enter, at the other end of the churchyard, Friar Laurence, with a lantern, crow, and spade.

FRIAR LAURENCE   Saint Francis be my speed! how oft to-night
Have my old feet stumbled at graves! Who's there?

BALTHASAR   Here's one, a friend, and one that knows you well.

FRIAR LAURENCE   Bliss be upon you! Tell me, good my friend,
What torch is yond, that vainly lends his light
To grubs and eyeless skulls? as I discern,
It burneth in the Capels' monument.

BALTHASAR   It doth so, holy sir; and there's my master,
One that you love.

FRIAR LAURENCE   Who is it?

BALTHASAR   Romeo.

FRIAR LAURENCE   How long hath he been there?

BALTHASAR   Full half an hour.

FRIAR LAURENCE   Go with me to the vault.

BALTHASAR   I dare not, sir:
My master knows not but I am gone hence;
And fearfully did menace me with death,
If I did stay to look on his intents.

FRIAR LAURENCE   Stay, then; I'll go alone. Fear comes upon me:
O, much I fear some ill unlucky thing.

BALTHASAR   As I did sleep under this yew-tree here,
I dreamt my master and another fought,
And that my master slew him.

FRIAR LAURENCE   Romeo!

Advances.

Alack, alack, what blood is this, which stains
The stony entrance of this sepulchre?

What mean these masterless and gory swords
To lie discolour'd by this place of peace?

Enters the tomb.

Romeo! O, pale! Who else? what, Paris too?
And steep'd in blood? Ah, what an unkind hour
Is guilty of this lamentable chance!
The lady stirs.

Juliet wakes.

JULIET   O comfortable friar! where is my lord?
I do remember well where I should be,
And there I am. Where is my Romeo?

Noise within.

FRIAR LAURENCE   I hear some noise. Lady, come from that nest
Of death, contagion, and unnatural sleep:
A greater power than we can contradict
Hath thwarted our intents. Come, come away.
Thy husband in thy bosom there lies dead;
And Paris too. Come, I'll dispose of thee
Among a sisterhood of holy nuns:
Stay not to question, for the watch is coming;
Come, go, good Juliet [*Noise again.*], I dare no longer stay.

JULIET   Go, get thee hence, for I will not away.   *Exit Friar Laurence.*
What's here? a cup, closed in my true love's hand?
Poison, I see, hath been his timeless end:
O churl! drunk all, and left no friendly drop
To help me after? I will kiss thy lips;
Haply some poison yet doth hang on them,
To make me die with a restorative.

Kisses him.

Thy lips are warm.

FIRST WATCHMAN   [*Within.*] Lead, boy: which way?

JULIET   Yea, noise? then I'll be brief. O happy dagger!

Snatching Romeo's dagger.

This is thy sheath [*Stabs herself.*]; there rust, and let me die.
                                    Falls on Romeo's body, and dies.

Enter First Watchman, with the Page of Paris.

PAGE This is the place; there, where the torch doth burn.

FIRST WATCHMAN The ground is bloody; search about the churchyard:
Go, some of you, whoe'er you find attach.
Pitiful sight! here lies the County slain;
And Juliet bleeding, warm, and newly dead,
Who here hath lain these two days buried.
Go, tell the Prince: run to the Capulets:
Raise up the Montagues: some others search:
We see the ground whereon these woes do lie;
But the true ground of all these piteous woes
We cannot without circumstance descry.

Re-enter some of the Watch, with Balthasar.

SECOND WATCHMAN Here's Romeo's man; we found him in the churchyard.

FIRST WATCHMAN Hold him in safety, till the Prince come hither.

Re-enter others of the Watch, with Friar Laurence.

THIRD WATCHMAN Here is a friar, that trembles, sighs, and weeps:
We took this mattock and this spade from him,
As he was coming from this churchyard side.

FIRST WATCHMAN A great suspicion: stay the friar too.

Enter Prince Escalus and attendants.

PRINCE ESCALUS What misadventure is so early up,
That calls our person from our morning's rest?

Enter Capulet, Lady Capulet, and others.

CAPULET What should it be, that they so shriek abroad?

LADY CAPULET The people in the street cry "Romeo,"
Some "Juliet," and some "Paris"; and all run,
With open outcry, toward our monument.

PRINCE ESCALUS What fear is this which startles in our ears?

FIRST WATCHMAN Sovereign, here lies the County Paris slain;
And Romeo dead; and Juliet, dead before,
Warm and new kill'd.

PRINCE ESCALUS Search, seek, and know how this foul murder comes.

94

FIRST WATCHMAN   Here is a friar, and slaughter'd Romeo's man;
   With instruments upon them, fit to open
   These dead men's tombs.

CAPULET   O heavens! O wife, look how our daughter bleeds!
   This dagger hath mista'en—for, lo, his house
   Is empty on the back of Montague—
   And it mis-sheathed in my daughter's bosom!

LADY CAPULET   O me! this sight of death is as a bell,
   That warns my old age to a sepulchre.

Enter Montague and others.

PRINCE ESCALUS   Come, Montague; for thou art early up,
   To see thy son and heir more early down.

MONTAGUE   Alas, my liege, my wife is dead to-night;
   Grief of my son's exile hath stopp'd her breath:
   What further woe conspires against mine age?

PRINCE ESCALUS   Look, and thou shalt see.

MONTAGUE   O thou untaught! what manners is in this,
   To press before thy father to a grave?

PRINCE ESCALUS   Seal up the mouth of outrage for a while,
   Till we can clear these ambiguities,
   And know their spring, their head, their true descent;
   And then will I be general of your woes
   And lead you even to death: meantime forbear,
   And let mischance be slave to patience.
   Bring forth the parties of suspicion.

FRIAR LAURENCE   I am the greatest, able to do least,
   Yet most suspected, as the time and place
   Doth make against me, of this direful murder;
   And here I stand, both to impeach and purge
   Myself condemned and myself excused.

PRINCE ESCALUS   Then say at once what thou dost know in this.

FRIAR LAURENCE   I will be brief, for my short date of breath
   Is not so long as is a tedious tale.
   Romeo, there dead, was husband to that Juliet;
   And she, there dead, that Romeo's faithful wife:
   I married them; and their stol'n marriage-day

Was Tybalt's dooms-day, whose untimely death
Banish'd the new-made bridegroom from this city,
For whom, and not for Tybalt, Juliet pined.
You, to remove that siege of grief from her,
Betroth'd and would have married her perforce
To County Paris: then comes she to me,
And, with wild looks, bid me devise some mean
To rid her from this second marriage,
Or in my cell there would she kill herself.
Then gave I her, so tutor'd by my art,
A sleeping potion; which so took effect
As I intended, for it wrought on her
The form of death: meantime I writ to Romeo,
That he should hither come as this dire night,
To help to take her from her borrow'd grave,
Being the time the potion's force should cease.
But he which bore my letter, Friar John,
Was stay'd by accident, and yesternight
Return'd my letter back. Then all alone
At the prefixed hour of her waking,
Came I to take her from her kindred's vault;
Meaning to keep her closely at my cell,
Till I conveniently could send to Romeo:
But when I came, some minute ere the time
Of her awaking, here untimely lay
The noble Paris and true Romeo dead.
She wakes; and I entreated her come forth,
And bear this work of heaven with patience:
But then a noise did scare me from the tomb;
And she, too desperate, would not go with me,
But, as it seems, did violence on herself.
All this I know; and to the marriage
Her nurse is privy; and, if aught in this
Miscarried by my fault, let my old life
Be sacrificed, some hour before his time,
Unto the rigour of severest law.

PRINCE ESCALUS   We still have known thee for a holy man.
  Where's Romeo's man? what can he say in this?

BALTHASAR   I brought my master news of Juliet's death;
  And then in post he came from Mantua
  To this same place, to this same monument.

This letter he early bid me give his father,
And threaten'd me with death, going in the vault,
If I departed not and left him there.

PRINCE ESCALUS   Give me the letter; I will look on it.
Where is the County's page, that raised the watch?
Sirrah, what made your master in this place?

PAGE   He came with flowers to strew his lady's grave;
And bid me stand aloof, and so I did:
Anon comes one with light to ope the tomb;
And by and by my master drew on him;
And then I ran away to call the watch.

PRINCE ESCALUS   This letter doth make good the friar's words,
Their course of love, the tidings of her death:
And here he writes that he did buy a poison
Of a poor 'pothecary, and therewithal
Came to this vault to die, and lie with Juliet.
Where be these enemies? Capulet! Montague!
See, what a scourge is laid upon your hate,
That heaven finds means to kill your joys with love.
And I for winking at your discords too
Have lost a brace of kinsmen: all are punish'd.

CAPULET   O brother Montague, give me thy hand:
This is my daughter's jointure, for no more
Can I demand.

MONTAGUE   But I can give thee more:
For I will raise her statue in pure gold;
That while Verona by that name is known,
There shall no figure at such rate be set
As that of true and faithful Juliet.

CAPULET   As rich shall Romeo's by his lady's lie;
Poor sacrifices of our enmity!

PRINCE ESCALUS   A glooming peace this morning with it brings;
The sun, for sorrow, will not show his head:
Go hence, to have more talk of these sad things;
Some shall be pardon'd, and some punished:
For never was a story of more woe
Than this of Juliet and her Romeo.   *Exeunt.*

A MIDSUMMER NIGHT'S DREAM

THE ACTORS

THESEUS, *Duke of Athens*

EGEUS, *father to Hermia*

LYSANDER
DEMETRIUS } *in love with Hermia*

PHILOSTRATE, *master of the revels to Theseus*

QUINCE, *a carpenter*

SNUG, *a joiner*

BOTTOM, *a weaver*

FLUTE, *a bellows-mender*

SNOUT, *a tinker*

STARVELING, *a tailor*

HIPPOLYTA, *Queen of the Amazons, betrothed to Theseus*

HERMIA, *daughter to Egeus, in love with Lysander*

HELENA, *in love with Demetrius*

OBERON, *King of the Fairies*

TITANIA, *Queen of the Fairies*

PUCK, *or Robin Goodfellow*

PEASEBLOSSOM
COBWEB
MOTH
MUSTARDSEED } *Fairies*

Non-Speaking: Attendants on Theseus and Hippolyta; Fairies attending their King and Queen

SCENE: *Athens, and a wood near it*

ACT I

SCENE 1   *Athens. The palace of Theseus.*

Enter Theseus, Hippolyta, Philostrate, and Attendants.

THESEUS   Now, fair Hippolyta, our nuptial hour
Draws on apace; four happy days bring in
Another moon: but, O, methinks, how slow
This old moon wanes! she lingers my desires,
Like to a step-dame or a dowager
Long withering out a young man's revenue.

HIPPOLYTA   Four days will quickly steep themselves in night;
Four nights will quickly dream away the time;
And then the moon, like to a silver bow
New-bent in heaven, shall behold the night
Of our solemnities.

THESEUS   Go, Philostrate,
Stir up the Athenian youth to merriments;
Awake the pert and nimble spirit of mirth:
Turn melancholy forth to funerals;
The pale companion is not for our pomp.   *Exit Philostrate.*
Hippolyta, I woo'd thee with my sword,
And won thy love, doing thee injuries;
But I will wed thee in another key,
With pomp, with triumph, and with revelling.

Enter Egeus, Hermia, Lysander, and Demetrius.

EGEUS   Happy be Theseus, our renowned Duke!

THESEUS   Thanks, good Egeus: what's the news with thee?

103

EGEUS   Full of vexation come I, with complaint
  Against my child, my daughter Hermia.
  Stand forth, Demetrius. My noble lord,
  This man hath my consent to marry her.
  Stand forth, Lysander: and, my gracious Duke,
  This man hath bewitch'd the bosom of my child:
  Thou, thou, Lysander, thou hast given her rhymes
  And interchanged love-tokens with my child:
  Thou hast by moonlight at her window sung
  With feigning voice verses of feigning love,
  And stolen the impression of her fantasy
  With bracelets of thy hair, rings, gawds, conceits,
  Knacks, trifles, nosegays, sweetmeats, messengers
  Of strong prevailment in unharden'd youth:
  With cunning hast thou filch'd my daughter's heart,
  Turn'd her obedience, which is due to me,
  To stubborn harshness: and, my gracious Duke,
  Be it so she will not here before your Grace
  Consent to marry with Demetrius,
  I beg the ancient privilege of Athens,
  As she is mine, I may dispose of her:
  Which shall be either to this gentleman
  Or to her death, according to our law
  Immediately provided in that case.

THESEUS   What say you, Hermia? be advised, fair maid:
  To you your father should be as a god;
  One that composed your beauties, yea, and one
  To whom you are but as a form in wax
  By him imprinted and within his power
  To leave the figure or disfigure it.
  Demetrius is a worthy gentleman.

HERMIA   So is Lysander.

THESEUS   In himself he is;
  But in this kind, wanting your father's voice,
  The other must be held the worthier.

HERMIA   I would my father look'd but with my eyes.

THESEUS   Rather your eyes must with his judgement look.

HERMIA   I do entreat your Grace to pardon me.
  I know not by what power I am made bold,

Nor how it may concern my modesty,
In such a presence here to plead my thoughts;
But I beseech your Grace that I may know
The worst that may befall me in this case,
If I refuse to wed Demetrius.

THESEUS   Either to die the death or to abjure
For ever the society of men.
Therefore, fair Hermia, question your desires;
Know of your youth, examine well your blood,
Whether, if you yield not to your father's choice,
You can endure the livery of a nun,
For aye to be in shady cloister mew'd,
To live a barren sister all your life,
Chanting faint hymns to the cold fruitless moon.
Thrice-blessed they that master so their blood
To undergo such maiden pilgrimage;
But earthlier happy is the rose distill'd
Than that which withering on the virgin thorn
Grows, lives, and dies in single blessedness.

HERMIA   So will I grow, so live, so die, my lord,
Ere I will yield my virgin patent up
Unto his lordship, whose unwished yoke
My soul consents not to give sovereignty.

THESEUS   Take time to pause; and, by the next new moon—
The sealing-day betwixt my love and me,
For everlasting bond of fellowship—
Upon that day either prepare to die
For disobedience to your father's will,
Or else to wed Demetrius, as he would;
Or on Diana's altar to protest
For aye austerity and single life.

DEMETRIUS   Relent, sweet Hermia: and, Lysander, yield
Thy crazed title to my certain right.

LYSANDER   You have her father's love, Demetrius;
Let me have Hermia's: do you marry him.

EGEUS   Scornful Lysander! true, he hath my love,
And what is mine my love shall render him.
And she is mine, and all my right of her
I do estate unto Demetrius.

105

LYSANDER   I am, my lord, as well derived as he,
As well possess'd; my love is more than his;
My fortunes every way as fairly rank'd,
If not with vantage, as Demetrius';
And, which is more than all these boasts can be,
I am beloved of beauteous Hermia:
Why should not I then prosecute my right?
Demetrius, I'll avouch it to his head,
Made love to Nedar's daughter, Helena,
And won her soul; and she, sweet lady, dotes,
Devoutly dotes, dotes in idolatry,
Upon this spotted and inconstant man.

THESEUS   I must confess that I have heard so much,
And with Demetrius thought to have spoke thereof;
But, being over-full of self-affairs,
My mind did lose it. But, Demetrius, come;
And come, Egeus; you shall go with me,
I have some private schooling for you both.
For you, fair Hermia, look you arm yourself
To fit your fancies to your father's will;
Or else the law of Athens yields you up —
Which by no means we may extenuate —
To death, or to a vow of single life.
Come, my Hippolyta: what cheer, my love?
Demetrius and Egeus, go along:
I must employ you in some business
Against our nuptial and confer with you
Of something nearly that concerns yourselves.

EGEUS   With duty and desire we follow you.

Exeunt all but Lysander and Hermia.

LYSANDER   How now, my love! why is your cheek so pale?
How chance the roses there do fade so fast?

HERMIA   Belike for want of rain, which I could well
Beteem them from the tempest of my eyes.

LYSANDER   Ay me! for aught that I could ever read,
Could ever hear by tale or history,
The course of true love never did run smooth;
But, either it was different in blood —

HERMIA   O cross! too high to be enthrall'd to low.

106

LYSANDER   Or else misgraffed in respect of years —

HERMIA   O spite! too old to be engaged to young.

LYSANDER   Or else it stood upon the choice of friends —

HERMIA   O hell! to choose love by another's eyes.

LYSANDER   Or, if there were a sympathy in choice,
War, death, or sickness did lay siege to it,
Making it momentany as a sound,
Swift as a shadow, short as any dream;
Brief as the lightning in the collied night,
That, in a spleen, unfolds both heaven and earth,
And ere a man hath power to say "Behold!"
The jaws of darkness do devour it up:
So quick bright things come to confusion.

HERMIA   If then true lovers have been ever cross'd,
It stands as an edict in destiny:
Then let us teach our trial patience,
Because it is a customary cross,
As due to love as thoughts and dreams and sighs,
Wishes and tears, poor Fancy's followers.

LYSANDER   A good persuasion: therefore, hear me, Hermia.
I have a widow aunt, a dowager
Of great revenue, and she hath no child:
From Athens is her house remote seven leagues;
And she respects me as her only son.
There, gentle Hermia, may I marry thee;
And to that place the sharp Athenian law
Cannot pursue us. If thou lovest me then,
Steal forth thy father's house to-morrow night;
And in the wood, a league without the town,
Where I did meet thee once with Helena
To do observance to a morn of May,
There will I stay for thee.

HERMIA   My good Lysander!
I swear to thee, by Cupid's strongest bow,
By his best arrow with the golden head,
By the simplicity of Venus' doves,
By that which knitteth souls and prospers loves,
And by that fire which burn'd the Carthage queen,

107

When the false Troyan under sail was seen,
By all the vows that ever men have broke,
In number more than ever women spoke,
In that same place thou hast appointed me,
To-morrow truly will I meet with thee.

LYSANDER Keep promise, love. Look, here comes Helena.

Enter Helena.

HERMIA God speed fair Helena! whither away?

HELENA Call you me fair? that fair again unsay.
  Demetrius loves your fair: O happy fair!
  Your eyes are lode-stars; and your tongue's sweet air
  More tuneable than lark to shepherd's ear,
  When wheat is green, when hawthorn buds appear.
  Sickness is catching: O, were favour so,
  Yours would I catch, fair Hermia, ere I go;
  My ear should catch your voice, my eye your eye,
  My tongue should catch your tongue's sweet melody.
  Were the world mine, Demetrius being bated,
  The rest I'd give to be to you translated.
  O, teach me how you look, and with what art
  You sway the motion of Demetrius' heart.

HERMIA I frown upon him, yet he loves me still.

HELENA O that your frowns would teach my smiles such skill!

HERMIA I give him curses, yet he gives me love.

HELENA O that my prayers could such affection move!

HERMIA The more I hate, the more he follows me.

HELENA The more I love, the more he hateth me.

HERMIA His folly, Helena, is no fault of mine.

HELENA None, but your beauty: would that fault were mine!

HERMIA Take comfort: he no more shall see my face;
  Lysander and myself will fly this place.
  Before the time I did Lysander see,
  Seem'd Athens as a paradise to me:
  O, then, what graces in my love do dwell,
  That he hath turn'd a heaven unto a hell!

LYSANDER   Helen, to you our minds we will unfold:
   To-morrow night, when Phoebe doth behold
   Her silver visage in the watery glass,
   Decking with liquid pearl the bladed grass,
   A time that lovers' flights doth still conceal,
   Through Athens' gates have we devised to steal.

HERMIA   And in the wood, where often you and I
   Upon faint primrose-beds were wont to lie,
   Emptying our bosoms of their counsel sweet,
   There my Lysander and myself shall meet;
   And thence from Athens turn away our eyes,
   To seek new friends and stranger companies.
   Farewell, sweet playfellow: pray thou for us;
   And good luck grant thee thy Demetrius!
   Keep word, Lysander: we must starve our sight
   From lovers' food till morrow deep midnight.

LYSANDER   I will, my Hermia.   *Exit Hermia.*
                 Helena, adieu:
   As you on him, Demetrius dote on you!   *Exit.*

HELENA   How happy some o'er other some can be!
   Through Athens I am thought as fair as she.
   But what of that? Demetrius thinks not so;
   He will not know what all but he do know:
   And as he errs, doting on Hermia's eyes,
   So I, admiring of his qualities:
   Things base and vile, holding no quantity,
   Love can transpose to form and dignity:
   Love looks not with the eyes, but with the mind;
   And therefore is wing'd Cupid painted blind:
   Nor hath Love's mind of any judgement taste;
   Wings and no eyes figure unheedy haste:
   And therefore is Love said to be a child,
   Because in choice he is so oft beguiled.
   As waggish boys in game themselves forswear,
   So the boy Love is perjured every where:
   For ere Demetrius look'd on Hermia's eyne,
   He hail'd down oaths that he was only mine;
   And when this hail some heat from Hermia felt,
   So he dissolved, and showers of oaths did melt.
   I will go tell him of fair Hermia's flight:

Then to the wood will he to-morrow night
Pursue her; and for this intelligence
If I have thanks, it is a dear expense:
But herein mean I to enrich my pain,
To have his sight thither and back again.   *Exit.*

✤ SCENE 2 *Athens. Quince's house.*

Enter Quince, Snug, Bottom, Flute, Snout, and Starveling.

QUINCE   Is all our company here?

BOTTOM   You were best to call them generally, man by man, according to the scrip.

QUINCE   Here is the scroll of every man's name, which is thought fit, through all Athens, to play in our interlude before the Duke and the Duchess, on his wedding-day at night.

BOTTOM   First, good Peter Quince, say what the play treats on, then read the names of the actors, and so grow to a point.

QUINCE   Marry, our play is *The most lamentable comedy, and most cruel death of Pyramus and Thisby.*

BOTTOM   A very good piece of work, I assure you, and a merry. Now, good Peter Quince, call forth your actors by the scroll. Masters, spread yourselves.

QUINCE   Answer as I call you. Nick Bottom, the weaver.

BOTTOM   Ready. Name what part I am for, and proceed.

QUINCE   You, Nick Bottom, are set down for Pyramus.

BOTTOM   What is Pyramus? a lover, or a tyrant?

QUINCE   A lover, that kills himself most gallant for love.

BOTTOM   That will ask some tears in the true performing of it: if I do it, let the audience look to their eyes; I will move storms, I will condole in some measure. To the rest: yet my chief humour is for a tyrant: I could play Ercles rarely, or a part to tear a cat in, to make all split.

> "The raging rocks
> And shivering shocks
> Shall break the locks
> Of prison gates;

110

> And Phibbus' car
> Shall shine from far
> And make and mar
> The foolish Fates."

This was lofty! Now name the rest of the players. This is Ercles' vein, a tyrant's vein; a lover is more condoling.

QUINCE Francis Flute, the bellows-mender.

FLUTE Here, Peter Quince.

QUINCE Flute, you must take Thisby on you.

FLUTE What is Thisby? a wandering knight?

QUINCE It is the lady that Pyramus must love.

FLUTE Nay, faith, let not me play a woman; I have a beard coming.

QUINCE That's all one: you shall play it in a mask, and you may speak as small as you will.

BOTTOM An I may hide my face, let me play Thisby too, I'll speak in a monstrous little voice, "Thisne, Thisne"; "Ah Pyramus, my lover dear! thy Thisby dear, and lady dear!"

QUINCE No, no; you must play Pyramus: and Flute, you Thisby.

BOTTOM Well, proceed.

QUINCE Robin Starveling, the tailor.

STARVELING Here, Peter Quince.

QUINCE Robin Starveling, you must play Thisby's mother. Tom Snout, the tinker.

SNOUT Here, Peter Quince.

QUINCE You, Pyramus' father: myself, Thisby's father. Snug, the joiner; you, the lion's part: and, I hope, here is a play fitted.

SNUG Have you the lion's part written? pray you, if it be, give it me, for I am slow of study.

QUINCE You may do it extempore, for it is nothing but roaring.

BOTTOM Let me play the lion too: I will roar, that I will do any man's heart good to hear me; I will roar, that I will make the Duke say, "Let him roar again, let him roar again."

111

QUINCE An you should do it too terribly, you would fright the Duchess and the ladies, that they would shriek; and that were enough to hang us all.

ALL That would hang us, every mother's son.

BOTTOM I grant you, friends, if that you should fright the ladies out of their wits, they would have no more discretion but to hang us: but I will aggravate my voice so that I will roar you as gently as any sucking dove; I will roar you an 'twere any nightingale.

QUINCE You can play no part but Pyramus; for Pyramus is a sweet-faced man; a proper man, as one shall see in a summer's day; a most lovely gentleman-like man: therefore you must needs play Pyramus.

BOTTOM Well, I will undertake it. What beard were I best to play it in?

QUINCE Why, what you will.

BOTTOM I will discharge it in either your straw-colour beard, your orange-tawny beard, your purple-in-grain beard, or your French-crown-colour beard, your perfect yellow.

QUINCE Some of your French crowns have no hair at all, and then you will play barefaced. But, masters, here are your parts: and I am to entreat you, request you and desire you, to con them by to-morrow night; and meet me in the palace wood, a mile without the town, by moonlight; there will we rehearse, for if we meet in the city, we shall be dogged with company, and our devices known. In the meantime I will draw a bill of properties, such as our play wants. I pray you, fail me not.

BOTTOM We will meet; and there we may rehearse most obscenely and courageously. Take pains; be perfect: adieu.

QUINCE At the Duke's oak we meet.

BOTTOM Enough; hold or cut bow-strings.   *Exeunt.*

ACT II

Enter, from opposite sides, a Fairy, and Puck.

PUCK   How now, spirit! whither wander you?

FAIRY   Over hill, over dale,
                    Thorough bush, thorough brier,
                    Over park, over pale,
                    Thorough flood, thorough fire,
                    I do wander every where,
                    Swifter than the moon's sphere;
                    And I serve the fairy Queen,
                    To dew her orbs upon the green.
                    The cowslips tall her pensioners be:
                    In their gold coats spots you see;
                    Those be rubies, fairy favours,
                    In those freckles live their savours:
                    I must go seek some dewdrops here
                    And hang a pearl in every cowslip's ear.
                    Farewell, thou lob of spirits; I'll be gone:
                    Our Queen and all her elves come here anon.

PUCK   The King doth keep his revels here to-night:
        Take heed the Queen come not within his sight;
        For Oberon is passing fell and wrath,
        Because that she as her attendant hath
        A lovely boy, stolen from an Indian king;
        She never had so sweet a changeling;
        And jealous Oberon would have the child

113

Knight of his train, to trace the forests wild;
But she perforce withholds the loved boy,
Crowns him with flowers and makes him all her joy:
And now they never meet in grove or green,
By fountain clear, or spangled starlight sheen,
But they do square, that all their elves for fear
Creep into acorn-cups and hide them there.

FAIRY   Either I mistake your shape and making quite,
  Or else you are that shrewd and knavish sprite
  Call'd Robin Goodfellow: are not you he
  That frights the maidens of the villagery;
  Skim milk, and sometimes labour in the quern
  And bootless make the breathless housewife churn;
  And sometime make the drink to bear no barm;
  Mislead night-wanderers, laughing at their harm?
  Those that Hobgoblin call you and sweet Puck,
  You do their work, and they shall have good luck:
  Are not you he?

PUCK   Thou speak'st aright;
  I am that merry wanderer of the night.
  I jest to Oberon and make him smile
  When I a fat and bean-fed horse beguile,
  Neighing in likeness of a filly foal:
  And sometime lurk I in a gossip's bowl,
  In very likeness of a roasted crab,
  And when she drinks, against her lips I bob
  And on her wither'd dewlap pour the ale.
  The wisest aunt, telling the saddest tale,
  Sometime for three-foot stool mistaketh me;
  Then slip I from her bum, down topples she,
  And "tailor" cries, and falls into a cough;
  And then the whole quire hold their hips and laugh,
  And waxen in their mirth and neeze and swear
  A merrier hour was never wasted there.
  But, room, fairy! here comes Oberon.

FAIRY   And here my mistress. Would that he were gone!

Enter, from one side, Oberon, with his train; from the other, Titania, with hers.

OBERON   Ill met by moonlight, proud Titania.

TITANIA   What, jealous Oberon! Fairies, skip hence:
I have forsworn his bed and company.

OBERON   Tarry, rash wanton: am not I thy lord?

TITANIA   Then I must be thy lady: but I know
When thou hast stolen away from fairy land,
And in the shape of Corin sat all day,
Playing on pipes of corn and versing love
To amorous Phillida. Why art thou here,
Come from the farthest steppe of India?
But that, forsooth, the bouncing Amazon,
Your buskin'd mistress and your warrior love,
To Theseus must be wedded, and you come
To give their bed joy and prosperity.

OBERON   How canst thou thus for shame, Titania,
Glance at my credit with Hippolyta,
Knowing I know thy love to Theseus?
Didst thou not lead him through the glimmering night
From Perigenia, whom he ravished?
And make him with fair Aegle break his faith,
With Ariadne and Antiopa?

TITANIA   These are the forgeries of jealousy:
And never, since the middle summer's spring,
Met we on hill, in dale, forest or mead,
By paved fountain or by rushy brook,
Or in the beached margent of the sea,
To dance our ringlets to the whistling wind,
But with thy brawls thou hast disturb'd our sport.
Therefore the winds, piping to us in vain,
As in revenge, have suck'd up from the sea
Contagious fogs; which falling in the land
Have every pelting river made so proud
That they have overborne their continents:
The ox hath therefore stretch'd his yoke in vain,
The ploughman lost his sweat, and the green corn
Hath rotted ere his youth attain'd a beard;
The fold stands empty in the drowned field,
And crows are fatted with the murrion flock;
The nine men's morris is fill'd up with mud,
And the quaint mazes in the wanton green

115

For lack of tread are undistinguishable:
The human mortals want their winter here;
No night is now with hymn or carol blest:
Therefore the moon, the governess of floods,
Pale in her anger, washes all the air,
That rheumatic diseases do abound:
And thorough this distemperature we see
The seasons alter: hoary-headed frosts
Fall in the fresh lap of the crimson rose,
And on old Hiems' thin and icy crown
An odorous chaplet of sweet summer buds
Is, as in mockery, set: the spring, the summer,
The childing autumn, angry winter, change
Their wonted liveries, and the mazed world,
By their increase, now knows not which is which:
And this same progeny of evils comes
From our debate, from our dissension;
We are their parents and original.

OBERON   Do you amend it then; it lies in you:
Why should Titania cross her Oberon?
I do but beg a little changeling boy
To be my henchman.

TITANIA   Set your heart at rest:
The fairy land buys not the child of me.
His mother was a votaress of my order:
And, in the spiced Indian air, by night,
Full often hath she gossip'd by my side,
And sat with me on Neptune's yellow sands,
Marking the embarked traders on the flood,
When we have laugh'd to see the sails conceive
And grow big-bellied with the wanton wind;
Which she, with pretty and with swimming gait
Following—her womb then rich with my young squire—
Would imitate, and sail upon the land,
To fetch me trifles, and return again,
As from a voyage, rich with merchandise.
But she, being mortal, of that boy did die;
And for her sake do I rear up her boy,
And for her sake I will not part with him.

OBERON   How long within this wood intend you stay?

TITANIA   Perchance till after Theseus' wedding-day.
    If you will patiently dance in our round
    And see our moonlight revels, go with us;
    If not, shun me, and I will spare your haunts.

OBERON   Give me that boy, and I will go with thee.

TITANIA   Not for thy fairy kingdom. Fairies, away!
    We shall chide downright, if I longer stay.

Exit Titania with her train.

OBERON   Well, go thy way: thou shalt not from this grove
    Till I torment thee for this injury.
    My gentle Puck, come hither. Thou rememb'rest
    Since once I sat upon a promontory,
    And heard a mermaid on a dolphin's back
    Uttering such dulcet and harmonious breath
    That the rude sea grew civil at her song
    And certain stars shot madly from their spheres,
    To hear the sea-maid's music.

PUCK   I remember.

OBERON   That very time I saw, but thou couldst not,
    Flying between the cold moon and the earth,
    Cupid all arm'd: a certain aim he took
    At a fair vestal throned by the west,
    And loosed his love-shaft smartly from his bow,
    As it should pierce a hundred thousand hearts;
    But I might see young Cupid's fiery shaft
    Quench'd in the chaste beams of the watery moon,
    And the imperial votaress passed on,
    In maiden meditation, fancy-free.
    Yet mark'd I where the bolt of Cupid fell:
    It fell upon a little western flower,
    Before milk-white, now purple with love's wound,
    And maidens call it love-in-idleness.
    Fetch me that flower; the herb I shew'd thee once:
    The juice of it on sleeping eye-lids laid
    Will make or man or woman madly dote
    Upon the next live creature that it sees.
    Fetch me this herb; and be thou here again
    Ere the leviathan can swim a league.

PUCK   I'll put a girdle round about the earth
  In forty minutes.   *Exit.*

OBERON   Having once this juice,
  I'll watch Titania when she is asleep,
  And drop the liquor of it in her eyes.
  The next thing then she waking looks upon,
  Be it on lion, bear, or wolf, or bull,
  On meddling monkey, or on busy ape,
  She shall pursue it with the soul of love:
  And ere I take this charm from off her sight,
  As I can take it with another herb,
  I'll make her render up her page to me.
  But who comes here? I am invisible;
  And I will overhear their conference.

Enter Demetrius, Helena following him.

DEMETRIUS   I love thee not, therefore pursue me not.
  Where is Lysander and fair Hermia?
  The one I'll slay, the other slayeth me.
  Thou told'st me they were stolen unto this wood;
  And here am I, and wood within this wood,
  Because I cannot meet my Hermia.
  Hence, get thee gone, and follow me no more.

HELENA   You draw me, you hard-hearted adamant;
  But yet you draw not iron, for my heart
  Is true as steel: leave you your power to draw,
  And I shall have no power to follow you.

DEMETRIUS   Do I entice you? do I speak you fair?
  Or, rather, do I not in plainest truth
  Tell you, I do not, nor I cannot love you?

HELENA   And even for that do I love you the more.
  I am your spaniel; and, Demetrius,
  The more you beat me, I will fawn on you:
  Use me but as your spaniel, spurn me, strike me,
  Neglect me, lose me; only give me leave,
  Unworthy as I am, to follow you.
  What worser place can I beg in your love —
  And yet a place of high respect with me —
  Than to be used as you use your dog?

118

DEMETRIUS   Tempt not too much the hatred of my spirit,
For I am sick when I do look on thee.

HELENA   And I am sick when I look not on you.

DEMETRIUS   You do impeach your modesty too much,
To leave the city and commit yourself
Into the hands of one that loves you not;
To trust the opportunity of night
And the ill counsel of a desert place
With the rich worth of your virginity.

HELENA   Your virtue is my privilege: for that
It is not night when I do see your face,
Therefore I think I am not in the night;
Nor doth this wood lack worlds of company,
For you in my respect are all the world:
Then how can it be said I am alone,
When all the world is here to look on me?

DEMETRIUS   I'll run from thee and hide me in the brakes,
And leave thee to the mercy of wild beasts.

HELENA   The wildest hath not such a heart as you.
Run when you will, the story shall be changed:
Apollo flies, and Daphne holds the chase;
The dove pursues the griffin; the mild hind
Makes speed to catch the tiger; bootless speed,
When cowardice pursues and valour flies.

DEMETRIUS   I will not stay thy questions; let me go:
Or, if thou follow me, do not believe
But I shall do thee mischief in the wood.

HELENA   Ay, in the temple, in the town, the field,
You do me mischief. Fie, Demetrius!
Your wrongs do set a scandal on my sex:
We cannot fight for love, as men may do;
We should be woo'd and were not made to woo.   *Exit Demetrius.*
I'll follow thee and make a heaven of hell,
To die upon the hand I love so well.   *Exit.*

OBERON   Fare thee well, nymph: ere he do leave this grove,
Thou shalt fly him and he shall seek thy love.

119

Re-enter Puck.

Hast thou the flower there? Welcome, wanderer.

PUCK   Ay, there it is.

OBERON   I pray thee, give it me.
  I know a bank where the wild thyme blows,
  Where oxlips and the nodding violet grows,
  Quite over-canopied with luscious woodbine,
  With sweet musk-roses and with eglantine:
  There sleeps Titania sometime of the night,
  Lull'd in these flowers with dances and delight;
  And there the snake throws her enamell'd skin,
  Weed wide enough to wrap a fairy in:
  And with the juice of this I'll streak her eyes,
  And make her full of hateful fantasies.
  Take thou some of it, and seek through this grove:
  A sweet Athenian lady is in love
  With a disdainful youth: anoint his eyes;
  But do it when the next thing he espies
  May be the lady; thou shalt know the man
  By the Athenian garments he hath on.
  Effect it with some care that he may prove
  More fond on her than she upon her love:
  And look thou meet me ere the first cock crow.

PUCK   Fear not, my lord, your servant shall do so.   *Exeunt.*

❧ SCENE 2   *Another part of the wood.*

Enter Titania, with her train.

TITANIA   Come, now a roundel and a fairy song;
  Then, for the third part of a minute, hence;
  Some to kill cankers in the musk-rose buds,
  Some war with rere-mice for their leathern wings,
  To make my small elves coats, and some keep back
  The clamorous owl that nightly hoots and wonders
  At our quaint spirits. Sing me now asleep;
  Then to your offices and let me rest.

The Fairies sing.

FIRST FAIRY   You spotted snakes with double tongue,

120

Thorny hedgehogs, be not seen;
Newts and blind-worms, do no wrong,
Come not near our fairy queen.

CHORUS   Philomel, with melody
Sing in our sweet lullaby;
Lulla, lulla, lullaby, lulla, lulla, lullaby:
Never harm,
Nor spell nor charm,
Come our lovely lady nigh;
So, good night, with lullaby.

FIRST FAIRY   Weaving spiders, come not here;
Hence, you long-legg'd spinners, hence!
Beetles black, approach not near;
Worm nor snail, do no offence.

CHORUS   Philomel, with melody, &c.

SECOND FAIRY   Hence, away! now all is well:
One aloof stand sentinel.   *Exeunt Fairies.*

Titania sleeps. Enter Oberon, and squeezes the flower on Titania's eyelids.

OBERON   What thou seest when thou dost wake,
Do it for thy true-love take,
Love and languish for his sake:
Be it ounce, or cat, or bear,
Pard, or boar with bristled hair,
In thy eye that shall appear
When thou wakest, it is thy dear:
Wake when some vile thing is near.   *Exit.*

Enter Lysander and Hermia.

LYSANDER   Fair love, you faint with wandering in the wood;
   And to speak troth, I have forgot our way:
   We'll rest us, Hermia, if you think it good,
   And tarry for the comfort of the day.

HERMIA   Be it so, Lysander: find you out a bed;
   For I upon this bank will rest my head.

LYSANDER   One turf shall serve as pillow for us both;
   One heart, one bed, two bosoms, and one troth.

HERMIA   Nay, good Lysander; for my sake, my dear,
   Lie further off yet, do not lie so near.

121

LYSANDER   O, take the sense, sweet, of my innocence!
Love takes the meaning in love's conference.
I mean that my heart unto yours is knit
So that but one heart we can make of it;
Two bosoms interchained with an oath;
So then two bosoms and a single troth.
Then by your side no bed-room me deny;
For lying so, Hermia, I do not lie.

HERMIA   Lysander riddles very prettily:
Now much beshrew my manners and my pride,
If Hermia meant to say Lysander lied.
But, gentle friend, for love and courtesy
Lie further off; in human modesty,
Such separation as may well be said
Becomes a virtuous bachelor and a maid,
So far be distant; and, good night, sweet friend:
Thy love ne'er alter till thy sweet life end!

LYSANDER   Amen, amen, to that fair prayer, say I;
And then end life when I end loyalty!
Here is my bed: sleep give thee all his rest!

HERMIA   With half that wish the wisher's eyes be press'd!

They sleep. Enter Puck.

PUCK   Through the forest have I gone,
                But Athenian found I none,
                On whose eyes I might approve
                This flower's force in stirring love.
                Night and silence. Who is here?
                Weeds of Athens he doth wear:
                This is he, my master said,
                Despised the Athenian maid;
                And here the maiden, sleeping sound,
                On the dank and dirty ground.
                Pretty soul! she durst not lie
                Near this lack-love, this kill-courtesy.
                Churl, upon thy eyes I throw
                All the power this charm doth owe.
                When thou wakest, let love forbid
                Sleep his seat on thy eyelid:
                So awake when I am gone;
                For I must now to Oberon.   *Exit.*

Enter Demetrius and Helena, running.

HELENA   Stay, though thou kill me, sweet Demetrius.

DEMETRIUS   I charge thee, hence, and do not haunt me thus.

HELENA   O, wilt thou darkling leave me? do not so.

DEMETRIUS   Stay, on thy peril: I alone will go.   *Exit.*

HELENA   O, I am out of breath in this fond chase!
  The more my prayer, the lesser is my grace.
  Happy is Hermia, wheresoe'er she lies;
  For she hath blessed and attractive eyes.
  How came her eyes so bright? Not with salt tears:
  If so, my eyes are oftener wash'd than hers.
  No, no, I am as ugly as a bear;
  For beasts that meet me run away for fear:
  Therefore no marvel though Demetrius
  Do, as a monster, fly my presence thus.
  What wicked and dissembling glass of mine
  Made me compare with Hermia's sphery eyne?
  But who is here? Lysander! on the ground!
  Dead? or asleep? I see no blood, no wound.
  Lysander, if you live, good sir, awake.

LYSANDER   [*Awaking.*] And run through fire I will for thy sweet sake.
  Transparent Helena! Nature shows art,
  That through thy bosom makes me see thy heart.
  Where is Demetrius? O, how fit a word
  Is that vile name to perish on my sword!

HELENA   Do not say so, Lysander; say not so.
  What though he love your Hermia? Lord, what though?
  Yet Hermia still loves you: then be content.

LYSANDER   Content with Hermia! No; I do repent
  The tedious minutes I with her have spent.
  Not Hermia but Helena I love:
  Who will not change a raven for a dove?
  The will of man is by his reason sway'd;
  And reason says you are the worthier maid.
  Things growing are not ripe until their season:
  So I, being young, till now ripe not to reason;
  And touching now the point of human skill,
  Reason becomes the marshal to my will

123

And leads me to your eyes, where I o'erlook
Love's stories written in love's richest book.

HELENA   Wherefore was I to this keen mockery born?
When at your hands did I deserve this scorn?
Is't not enough, is't not enough, young man,
That I did never, no, nor never can,
Deserve a sweet look from Demetrius' eye,
But you must flout my insufficiency?
Good troth, you do me wrong, good sooth, you do,
In such disdainful manner me to woo.
But fare you well: perforce I must confess
I thought you lord of more true gentleness.
O, that a lady, of one man refused,
Should of another therefore be abused!   *Exit.*

LYSANDER   She sees not Hermia. Hermia, sleep thou there:
And never mayst thou come Lysander near!
For as a surfeit of the sweetest things
The deepest loathing to the stomach brings,
Or as the heresies that men do leave
Are hated most of those they did deceive,
So thou, my surfeit and my heresy,
Of all be hated, but the most of me!
And, all my powers, address your love and might
To honour Helen and to be her knight!   *Exit.*

HERMIA   [*Awaking.*] Help me, Lysander, help me! do thy best
To pluck this crawling serpent from my breast!
Ay me, for pity! what a dream was here!
Lysander, look how I do quake with fear:
Methought a serpent eat my heart away,
And you sat smiling at his cruel prey.
Lysander! what, removed? Lysander! lord!
What, out of hearing? gone? no sound, no word?
Alack, where are you? speak, an if you hear;
Speak, of all loves! I swoon almost with fear.
No? then I well perceive you are not nigh:
Either death or you I'll find immediately.   *Exit.*

ACT III

The wood. Titania lying asleep.

Enter Quince, Snug, Bottom, Flute, Snout, and Starveling.

BOTTOM   Are we all met?

QUINCE   Pat, pat; and here's a marvellous convenient place for our re-
hearsal. This green plot shall be our stage, this hawthorn-brake our tir-
ing-house; and we will do it in action as we will do it before the Duke.

BOTTOM   Peter Quince—

QUINCE   What sayest thou, bully Bottom?

BOTTOM   There are things in this comedy of Pyramus and Thisby that
will never please. First, Pyramus must draw a sword to kill himself,
which the ladies cannot abide. How answer you that?

SNOUT   By'r lakin, a parlous fear.

STARVELING   I believe we must leave the killing out, when all is done.

BOTTOM   Not a whit: I have a device to make all well. Write me a prologue; and let the prologue seem to say, we will do no harm with our
swords and that Pyramus is not killed indeed; and, for the more better
assurance, tell them that I Pyramus am not Pyramus, but Bottom the
weaver: this will put them out of fear.

QUINCE   Well, we will have such a prologue; and it shall be written in
eight and six.

BOTTOM   No, make it two more; let it be written in eight and eight.

SNOUT   Will not the ladies be afeard of the lion?

125

STARVELING   I fear it, I promise you.

BOTTOM   Masters, you ought to consider with yourselves: to bring in—God shield us!—a lion among ladies, is a most dreadful thing; for there is not a more fearful wild-fowl than your lion living; and we ought to look to't.

SNOUT   Therefore another prologue must tell he is not a lion.

BOTTOM   Nay, you must name his name, and half his face must be seen through the lion's neck; and he himself must speak through, saying thus, or to the same defect, "Ladies," or "Fair ladies, I would wish you," or "I would request you," or "I would entreat you, not to fear, not to tremble: my life for yours. If you think I come hither as a lion, it were a pity of my life: no, I am no such thing; I am a man as other men are"; and there indeed let him name his name, and tell them plainly he is Snug the joiner.

QUINCE   Well, it shall be so. But there is two hard things; that is, to bring the moonlight into a chamber; for, you know, Pyramus and Thisby meet by moonlight.

SNOUT   Doth the moon shine that night we play our play?

BOTTOM   A calendar, a calendar! look in the almanac; find out moonshine, find out moonshine.

QUINCE   Yes, it doth shine that night.

BOTTOM   Why, then may you leave a casement of the great chamber window, where we play, open, and the moon may shine in at the casement.

QUINCE   Ay; or else one must come in with a bush of thorns and a lanthorn, and say he comes to disfigure, or to present, the person of Moonshine. Then, there is another thing: we must have a wall in the great chamber; for Pyramus and Thisby, says the story, did talk through the chink of a wall.

SNOUT   You can never bring in a wall. What say you, Bottom?

BOTTOM   Some man or other must present Wall: and let him have some plaster, or some loam, or some rough-cast about him, to signify wall; and let him hold his fingers thus, and through that cranny shall Pyramus and Thisby whisper.

QUINCE   If that may be, then all is well. Come, sit down, every mother's

son, and rehearse your parts. Pyramus, you begin: when you have spoken your speech, enter into that brake: and so every one according to
his cue.

Enter Puck behind.

PUCK   What hempen home-spuns have we swaggering here,
So near the cradle of the fairy queen?
What, a play toward! I'll be an auditor;
An actor too perhaps, if I see cause.

QUINCE   Speak, Pyramus. Thisby, stand forth.

BOTTOM   "Thisby, the flowers of odious savours sweet—"

QUINCE   Odours, odours.

BOTTOM   "—odours savours sweet:
So hath thy breath, my dearest Thisby dear.
But hark, a voice! stay thou but here awhile,
And by and by I will to thee appear."   *Exit.*

PUCK   A stranger Pyramus than e'er played here.   *Exit.*

FLUTE   Must I speak now?

QUINCE   Ay, marry, must you; for you must understand he goes but to
see a noise that he heard, and is to come again.

FLUTE   "Most radiant Pyramus, most lily-white of hue,
Of colour like the red rose on triumphant brier,
Most brisky juvenal and eke most lovely Jew,
As true as truest horse, that yet would never tire,
I'll meet thee, Pyramus, at Ninny's tomb."

QUINCE   "Ninus' tomb," man: why, you must not speak that yet; that
you answer to Pyramus: you speak all your part at once, cues and all.
Pyramus enter: your cue is past; it is, "never tire."

FLUTE   O—"As true as truest horse, that yet would never tire."

Re-enter Puck, and Bottom with an ass's head.

BOTTOM   "If I were fair, Thisby, I were only thine."

QUINCE   O monstrous! O strange! we are haunted.
Pray, masters! fly, masters! Help!
                        Exeunt Quince, Snug, Flute, Snout, and Starveling.

127

PUCK   I'll follow you, I'll lead you about a round,
  Through bog, through bush, through brake, through brier:
  Sometime a horse I'll be, sometime a hound,
  A hog, a headless bear, sometime a fire;
  And neigh, and bark, and grunt, and roar, and burn,
  Like horse, hound, hog, bear, fire, at every turn.   *Exit.*

BOTTOM   Why do they run away? this is a knavery of them to make me
  afeard.

Re-enter Snout.

SNOUT   O Bottom, thou art changed! what do I see on thee?

BOTTOM   What do you see? you see an ass-head of your own, do you?
                                                                Exit Snout.

Re-enter Quince.

QUINCE   Bless thee, Bottom! bless thee! thou art translated.   *Exit.*

BOTTOM   I see their knavery: this is to make an ass of me; to fright me, if
  they could. But I will not stir from this place, do what they can: I will
  walk up and down here, and I will sing, that they shall hear I am not
  afraid. [*Sings.*]

> "The ousel cock so black of hue,
>   With orange-tawny bill,
> The throstle with his note so true,
>   The wren with little quill—"

TITANIA   [*Awaking.*] What angel wakes me from my flowery bed?

BOTTOM   [*Sings.*]
> "The finch, the sparrow and the lark,
>   The plain-song cuckoo gray,
> Whose note full many a man doth mark,
>   And dares not answer nay."

For, indeed, who would set his wit to so foolish a bird? who would
give a bird the lie, though he cry "cuckoo" never so?

TITANIA   I pray thee, gentle mortal, sing again:
  Mine ear is much enamour'd of thy note;
  So is mine eye enthralled to thy shape;
  And thy fair virtue's force perforce doth move me
  On the first view to say, to swear, I love thee.

BOTTOM   Methinks, mistress, you should have little reason for that: and yet, to say the truth, reason and love keep little company together now-a-days; the more the pity that some honest neighbours will not make them friends. Nay, I can gleek upon occasion.

TITANIA   Thou art as wise as thou art beautiful.

BOTTOM   Not so, neither: but if I had wit enough to get out of this wood, I have enough to serve mine own turn.

TITANIA   Out of this wood do not desire to go:
Thou shalt remain here, whether thou wilt or no.
I am a spirit of no common rate:
The summer still doth tend upon my state;
And I do love thee: therefore, go with me;
I'll give thee fairies to attend on thee,
And they shall fetch thee jewels from the deep,
And sing while thou on pressed flowers dost sleep:
And I will purge thy mortal grossness so
That thou shalt like an airy spirit go.
Peaseblossom! Cobweb! Moth! and Mustardseed!

Enter Peaseblossom, Cobweb, Moth, and Mustardseed.

PEASEBLOSSOM   Ready.

COBWEB   And I.

MOTH   And I.

MUSTARDSEED   And I.

ALL   Where shall we go?

TITANIA   Be kind and courteous to this gentleman;
Hop in his walks and gambol in his eyes;
Feed him with apricocks and dewberries,
With purple grapes, green figs, and mulberries;
The honey-bags steal from the humble-bees,
And for night-tapers crop their waxen thighs
And light them at the fiery glow-worm's eyes,
To have my love to bed and to arise;
And pluck the wings from painted butterflies
To fan the moonbeams from his sleeping eyes:
Nod to him, elves, and do him courtesies.

PEASEBLOSSOM   Hail, mortal!

129

COBWEB   Hail!

MOTH   Hail!

MUSTARDSEED   Hail!

BOTTOM   I cry your worships mercy, heartily: I beseech your worship's name.

COBWEB   Cobweb.

BOTTOM   I shall desire you of more acquaintance, good Master Cobweb: if I cut my finger, I shall make bold with you. Your name, honest gentleman?

PEASEBLOSSOM   Peaseblossom.

BOTTOM   I pray you, commend me to Mistress Squash, your mother, and to Master Peascod, your father. Good Master Peaseblossom, I shall desire you of more acquaintance too. Your name, I beseech you, sir?

MUSTARDSEED   Mustardseed.

BOTTOM   Good Master Mustardseed, I know your patience well: that same cowardly, giant-like ox-beef hath devoured many a gentleman of your house: I promise you your kindred hath made my eyes water ere now. I desire you of more acquaintance, good Master Mustardseed.

TITANIA   Come, wait upon him; lead him to my bower.
  The moon methinks looks with a watery eye;
  And when she weeps, weeps every little flower,
  Lamenting some enforced chastity.
  Tie up my love's tongue, bring him silently.   *Exeunt.*

✿ SCENE 2   *Another part of the wood.*

Enter Oberon.

OBERON   I wonder if Titania be awaked;
  Then, what it was that next came in her eye,
  Which she must dote on in extremity.
  Here comes my messenger.

Enter Puck.

                    How now, mad spirit!
  What night-rule now about this haunted grove?

130

PUCK   My mistress with a monster is in love.
  Near to her close and consecrated bower,
  While she was in her dull and sleeping hour,
  A crew of patches, rude mechanicals,
  That work for bread upon Athenian stalls,
  Were met together to rehearse a play
  Intended for great Theseus' nuptial-day.
  The shallowest thick-skin of that barren sort,
  Who Pyramus presented, in their sport
  Forsook his scene and enter'd in a brake:
  When I did him at this advantage take,
  An ass's nole I fixed on his head:
  Anon his Thisby must be answered,
  And forth my mimic comes. When they him spy,
  As wild geese that the creeping fowler eye,
  Or russet-pated choughs, many in sort,
  Rising and cawing at the gun's report,
  Sever themselves and madly sweep the sky,
  So, at his sight, away his fellows fly;
  And, at our stamp, here o'er and o'er one falls;
  He murder cries and help from Athens calls.
  Their sense thus weak, lost with their fears thus strong,
  Made senseless things begin to do them wrong;
  For briers and thorns at their apparel snatch;
  Some sleeves, some hats, from yielders all things catch.
  I led them on in this distracted fear,
  And left sweet Pyramus translated there:
  When in that moment, so it came to pass,
  Titania waked and straightway loved an ass.

OBERON   This falls out better than I could devise.
  But hast thou yet latch'd the Athenian's eyes
  With the love-juice, as I did bid thee do?

PUCK   I took him sleeping—that is finish'd too—
  And the Athenian woman by his side;
  That, when he waked, of force she must be eyed.

Enter Hermia and Demetrius.

OBERON   Stand close: this is the same Athenian.

PUCK   This is the woman, but not this the man.

131

DEMETRIUS O, why rebuke you him that loves you so?
  Lay breath so bitter on your bitter foe.

HERMIA Now I but chide; but I should use thee worse.
  For thou, I fear, hast given me cause to curse.
  If thou hast slain Lysander in his sleep,
  Being o'er shoes in blood, plunge in the deep,
  And kill me too.
  The sun was not so true unto the day
  As he to me: would he have stolen away
  From sleeping Hermia? I'll believe as soon
  This whole earth may be bored and that the moon
  May through the centre creep and so displease
  Her brother's noontide with the Antipodes.
  It cannot be but thou hast murder'd him;
  So should a murderer look, so dead, so grim.

DEMETRIUS So should the murder'd look, and so should I,
  Pierced through the heart with your stern cruelty:
  Yet you, the murderer, look as bright, as clear,
  As yonder Venus in her glimmering sphere.

HERMIA What's this to my Lysander? where is he?
  Ah, good Demetrius, wilt thou give him me?

DEMETRIUS I had rather give his carcass to my hounds.

HERMIA Out, dog! out, cur! thou drivest me past the bounds
  Of maiden's patience. Hast thou slain him, then?
  Henceforth be never number'd among men!
  O, once tell true, tell true, even for my sake!
  Durst thou have look'd upon him being awake,
  And hast thou kill'd him sleeping? O brave touch!
  Could not a worm, an adder, do so much?
  An adder did it; for with doubler tongue
  Than thine, thou serpent, never adder stung.

DEMETRIUS You spend your passion on a misprised mood:
  I am not guilty of Lysander's blood;
  Nor is he dead, for aught that I can tell.

HERMIA I pray thee, tell me then that he is well.

DEMETRIUS An if I could, what should I get therefore?

HERMIA A privilege never to see me more.

And from thy hated presence part I so:
See me no more, whether he be dead or no.   *Exit.*

DEMETRIUS   There is no following her in this fierce vein:
Here therefore for a while I will remain.
So sorrow's heaviness doth heavier grow
For debt that bankrupt sleep doth sorrow owe;
Which now in some slight measure it will pay,
If for his tender here I make some stay.

Lies down and sleeps.

OBERON   What hast thou done? thou hast mistaken quite
And laid the love-juice on some true-love's sight:
Of thy misprision must perforce ensue
Some true love turn'd and not a false turn'd true.

PUCK   Then fate o'er-rules, that, one man holding troth,
A million fail, confounding oath on oath.

OBERON   About the wood go swifter than the wind,
And Helena of Athens look thou find:
All fancy-sick she is and pale of cheer,
With sighs of love, that costs the fresh blood dear:
By some illusion see thou bring her here:
I'll charm his eyes against she do appear.

PUCK   I go, I go; look how I go,
Swifter than arrow from the Tartar's bow.   *Exit.*

OBERON   Flower of this purple dye,
                      Hit with Cupid's archery,
                      Sink in apple of his eye.
                      When his love he doth espy,
                      Let her shine as gloriously
                      As the Venus of the sky.
                      When thou wakest, if she be by,
                      Beg of her for remedy.

Re-enter Puck.

PUCK   Captain of our fairy band,
                      Helena is here at hand;
                      And the youth, mistook by me,
                      Pleading for a lover's fee.
                      Shall we their fond pageant see?
                      Lord, what fools these mortals be!

OBERON   Stand aside: the noise they make
                      Will cause Demetrius to awake.

PUCK   Then will two at once woo one;
                      That must needs be sport alone;
                      And those things do best please me
                      That befall preposterously.

Enter Lysander and Helena.

LYSANDER Why should you think that I should woo in scorn?
Scorn and derision never come in tears:
Look, when I vow, I weep; and vows so born,
In their nativity all truth appears.
How can these things in me seem scorn to you,
Bearing the badge of faith, to prove them true?

HELENA You do advance your cunning more and more.
When truth kills truth, O devilish-holy fray!
These vows are Hermia's: will you give her o'er?
Weigh oath with oath, and you will nothing weigh:
Your vows to her and me, put in two scales,
Will even weigh, and both as light as tales.

LYSANDER I had no judgement when to her I swore.

HELENA Nor none, in my mind, now you give her o'er.

LYSANDER Demetrius loves her, and he loves not you.

DEMETRIUS [*Awaking.*] O Helen, goddess, nymph, perfect, divine!
To what, my love, shall I compare thine eyne?
Crystal is muddy. O, how ripe in show
Thy lips, those kissing cherries, tempting grow!
That pure congealed white, high Taurus' snow,
Fann'd with the eastern wind, turns to a crow
When thou hold'st up thy hand: O, let me kiss
This princess of pure white, this seal of bliss!

HELENA O spite! O hell! I see you all are bent
To set against me for your merriment:
If you were civil and knew courtesy,
You would not do me thus much injury.
Can you not hate me, as I know you do,
But you must join in souls to mock me too?
If you were men, as men you are in show,

134

You would not use a gentle lady so;
To vow, and swear, and superpraise my parts,
When I am sure you hate me with your hearts.
You both are rivals, and love Hermia;
And now both rivals, to mock Helena:
A trim exploit, a manly enterprise,
To conjure tears up in a poor maid's eyes
With your derision! none of noble sort
Would so offend a virgin and extort
A poor soul's patience, all to make you sport.

LYSANDER   You are unkind, Demetrius; be not so;
For you love Hermia; this you know I know:
And here, with all good will, with all my heart,
In Hermia's love I yield you up my part;
And yours of Helena to me bequeath,
Whom I do love and will do till my death.

HELENA   Never did mockers waste more idle breath.

DEMETRIUS   Lysander, keep thy Hermia; I will none:
If e'er I loved her, all that love is gone.
My heart to her but as guest-wise sojourn'd,
And now to Helen is it home return'd,
There to remain.

LYSANDER   Helen, it is not so.

DEMETRIUS   Disparage not the faith thou dost not know,
Lest, to thy peril, thou aby it dear.
Look, where thy love comes; yonder is thy dear.

Re-enter Hermia.

HERMIA   Dark night, that from the eye his function takes,
The ear more quick of apprehension makes;
Wherein it doth impair the seeing sense,
It pays the hearing double recompense.
Thou art not by mine eye, Lysander, found;
Mine ear, I thank it, brought me to thy sound.
But why unkindly didst thou leave me so?

LYSANDER   Why should he stay, whom love doth press to go?

HERMIA   What love could press Lysander from my side?

LYSANDER   Lysander's love, that would not let him bide,

    Fair Helena, who more engilds the night
    Than all yon fiery oes and eyes of light.
    Why seek'st thou me? could not this make thee know,
    The hate I bear thee made me leave thee so?

HERMIA   You speak not as you think: it cannot be.

HELENA   Lo, she is one of this confederacy!
  Now I perceive they have conjoin'd all three
  To fashion this false sport, in spite of me.
  Injurious Hermia! most ungrateful maid!
  Have you conspired, have you with these contrived
  To bait me with this foul derision?
  Is all the counsel that we two have shared,
  The sisters' vows, the hours that we have spent,
  When we have chid the hasty-footed time
  For parting us—O, is it all forgot?
  All school-days' friendship, childhood innocence?
  We, Hermia, like two artificial gods,
  Have with our needles created both one flower,
  Both on one sampler, sitting on one cushion,
  Both warbling of one song, both in one key,
  As if our hands, our sides, voices and minds,
  Had been incorporate. So we grew together,
  Like to a double cherry, seeming parted,
  But yet an union in partition;
  Two lovely berries moulded on one stem;
  So, with two seeming bodies, but one heart;
  Two of the first, like coats in heraldry,
  Due but to one and crowned with one crest.
  And will you rend our ancient love asunder,
  To join with men in scorning your poor friend?
  It is not friendly, 'tis not maidenly:
  Our sex, as well as I, may chide you for it,
  Though I alone do feel the injury.

HERMIA   I am amazed at your passionate words.
  I scorn you not: it seems that you scorn me.

HELENA   Have you not set Lysander, as in scorn,
  To follow me and praise my eyes and face?
  And made your other love, Demetrius,
  Who even but now did spurn me with his foot,
  To call me goddess, nymph, divine and rare,

136

Precious, celestial? Wherefore speaks he this
To her he hates? and wherefore doth Lysander
Deny your love, so rich within his soul,
And tender me, forsooth, affection,
But by your setting on, by your consent?
What though I be not so in grace as you,
So hung upon with love, so fortunate,
But miserable most, to love unloved?
This you should pity rather than despise.

HERMIA   I understand not what you mean by this.

HELENA   Ay, do, persever, counterfeit sad looks,
Make mouths upon me when I turn my back;
Wink each at other; hold the sweet jest up:
This sport, well carried, shall be chronicled.
If you have any pity, grace, or manners,
You would not make me such an argument.
But fare ye well: 'tis partly my own fault;
Which death or absence soon shall remedy.

LYSANDER   Stay, gentle Helena; hear my excuse:
My love, my life, my soul, fair Helena!

HELENA   O excellent!

HERMIA   Sweet, do not scorn her so.

DEMETRIUS   If she cannot entreat, I can compel.

LYSANDER   Thou canst compel no more than she entreat:
Thy threats have no more strength than her weak prayers.
Helen, I love thee, by my life, I do:
I swear by that which I will lose for thee,
To prove him false that says I love thee not.

DEMETRIUS   I say I love thee more than he can do.

LYSANDER   If thou say so, withdraw, and prove it too.

DEMETRIUS   Quick, come!

HERMIA   Lysander, whereto tends all this?

LYSANDER   Away, you Ethiope!

DEMETRIUS   No, no; he'll but
Seem to break loose; take on as you would follow,
But yet come not: you are a tame man, go!

LYSANDER   Hang off, thou cat, thou burr! vile thing, let loose,
Or I will shake thee from me like a serpent!

HERMIA   Why are you grown so rude? what change is this?
Sweet love —

LYSANDER   Thy love! out, tawny Tartar, out!
Out, loathed medicine! hated potion, hence!

HERMIA   Do you not jest?

HELENA   Yes, sooth; and so do you.

LYSANDER   Demetrius, I will keep my word with thee.

DEMETRIUS   I would I had your bond, for I perceive
A weak bond holds you: I'll not trust your word.

LYSANDER   What, should I hurt her, strike her, kill her dead?
Although I hate her, I'll not harm her so.

HERMIA   What, can you do me greater harm than hate?
Hate me! wherefore? O me! what news, my love!
Am not I Hermia? are not you Lysander?
I am as fair now as I was erewhile.
Since night you loved me; yet since night you left me:
Why, then you left me — O, the gods forbid! —
In earnest, shall I say?

LYSANDER   Ay, by my life;
And never did desire to see thee more.
Therefore be out of hope, of question, of doubt;
Be certain, nothing truer; 'tis no jest
That I do hate thee and love Helena.

HERMIA   O me! you juggler! you canker-blossom!
You thief of love! what, have you come by night
And stolen my love's heart from him?

HELENA   Fine, i'faith!
Have you no modesty, no maiden shame,
No touch of bashfulness? What, will you tear
Impatient answers from my gentle tongue?
Fie, fie! you counterfeit, you puppet, you!

HERMIA   "Puppet"? why so? ay, that way goes the game.
Now I perceive that she hath made compare
Between our statures; she hath urged her height;

And with her personage, her tall personage,
Her height, forsooth, she hath prevail'd with him.
And are you grown so high in his esteem,
Because I am so dwarfish and so low?
How low am I, thou painted maypole? speak;
How low am I? I am not yet so low
But that my nails can reach unto thine eyes.

HELENA   I pray you, though you mock me, gentlemen,
Let her not hurt me: I was never curst;
I have no gift at all in shrewishness;
I am a right maid for my cowardice:
Let her not strike me. You perhaps may think,
Because she is something lower than myself,
That I can match her.

HERMIA   "Lower"! hark, again.

HELENA   Good Hermia, do not be so bitter with me.
I evermore did love you, Hermia,
Did ever keep your counsels, never wrong'd you;
Save that, in love unto Demetrius,
I told him of your stealth unto this wood.
He follow'd you; for love I follow'd him;
But he hath chid me hence and threaten'd me
To strike me, spurn me, nay, to kill me too:
And now, so you will let me quiet go,
To Athens will I bear my folly back
And follow you no further: let me go:
You see how simple and how fond I am.

HERMIA   Why, get you gone: who is't that hinders you?

HELENA   A foolish heart, that I leave here behind.

HERMIA   What, with Lysander?

HELENA   With Demetrius.

LYSANDER   Be not afraid; she shall not harm thee, Helena.

DEMETRIUS   No, sir, she shall not, though you take her part.

HELENA   O, when she's angry, she is keen and shrewd!
She was a vixen when she went to school;
And though she be but little, she is fierce.

139

HERMIA "Little" again! nothing but "low" and "little"!
Why will you suffer her to flout me thus?
Let me come to her.

LYSANDER   Get you gone, you dwarf;
You minimus, of hindering knot-grass made;
You bead, you acorn.

DEMETRIUS   You are too officious
In her behalf that scorns your services.
Let her alone: speak not of Helena;
Take not her part; for, if thou dost intend
Never so little show of love to her,
Thou shalt aby it.

LYSANDER   Now she holds me not;
Now follow, if thou darest, to try whose right,
Of thine or mine, is most in Helena.

DEMETRIUS Follow! nay, I'll go with thee, cheek by jole.
                    Exeunt Lysander and Demetrius.

HERMIA You, mistress, all this coil is 'long of you:
Nay, go not back.

HELENA   I will not trust you, I,
Nor longer stay in your curst company.
Your hands than mine are quicker for a fray,
My legs are longer though, to run away.   *Exit.*

HERMIA I am amazed, and know not what to say.   *Exit.*

OBERON This is thy negligence: still thou mistakest,
Or else committ'st thy knaveries wilfully.

PUCK Believe me, king of shadows, I mistook.
Did not you tell me I should know the man
By the Athenian garments he had on?
And so far blameless proves my enterprise,
That I have 'nointed an Athenian's eyes;
And so far am I glad it so did sort
As this their jangling I esteem a sport.

OBERON Thou see'st these lovers seek a place to fight:
Hie therefore, Robin, overcast the night;
The starry welkin cover thou anon
With drooping fog as black as Acheron,

And lead these testy rivals so astray
As one come not within another's way.
Like to Lysander sometime frame thy tongue,
Then stir Demetrius up with bitter wrong;
And sometime rail thou like Demetrius;
And from each other look thou lead them thus,
Till o'er their brows death-counterfeiting sleep
With leaden legs and batty wings doth creep:
Then crush this herb into Lysander's eye;
Whose liquor hath this virtuous property,
To take from thence all error with his might,
And make his eyeballs roll with wonted sight.
When they next wake, all this derision
Shall seem a dream and fruitless vision,
And back to Athens shall the lovers wend,
With league whose date till death shall never end.
Whiles I in this affair do thee employ,
I'll to my queen and beg her Indian boy;
And then I will her charmed eye release
From monster's view, and all things shall be peace.

PUCK   My fairy lord, this must be done with haste,
For night's swift dragons cut the clouds full fast,
And yonder shines Aurora's harbinger;
At whose approach, ghosts, wandering here and there,
Troop home to churchyards: damned spirits all,
That in crossways and floods have burial,
Already to their wormy beds are gone;
For fear lest day should look their shames upon,
They wilfully themselves exile from light
And must for aye consort with black-brow'd night.

OBERON   But we are spirits of another sort:
I with the morning's love have oft made sport,
And, like a forester, the groves may tread,
Even till the eastern gate, all fiery-red,
Opening on Neptune with fair blessed beams,
Turns into yellow gold his salt green streams.
But, notwithstanding, haste; make no delay:
We may effect this business yet ere day.   *Exit.*

PUCK   Up and down, up and down,
                    I will lead them up and down:

141

I am fear'd in field and town:
Goblin, lead them up and down.
Here comes one.

Re-enter Lysander.

LYSANDER   Where art thou, proud Demetrius? speak thou now.

PUCK   Here, villain; drawn and ready. Where art thou?

LYSANDER   I will be with thee straight.

PUCK   Follow me, then,
   To plainer ground.   *Exit Lysander, as following the voice.*

Re-enter Demetrius.

DEMETRIUS   Lysander! speak again:
   Thou runaway, thou coward, art thou fled?
   Speak! In some bush? Where dost thou hide thy head?

PUCK   Thou coward, art thou bragging to the stars,
   Telling the bushes that thou look'st for wars,
   And wilt not come? Come, recreant; come, thou child;
   I'll whip thee with a rod: he is defiled
   That draws a sword on thee.

DEMETRIUS   Yea, art thou there?

PUCK   Follow my voice: we'll try no manhood here.   *Exeunt.*

Re-enter Lysander.

LYSANDER   He goes before me and still dares me on:
   When I come where he calls, then he is gone.
   The villain is much lighter-heel'd than I:
   I follow'd fast, but faster he did fly;
   That fallen am I in dark uneven way,
   And here will rest me. [*Lies down.*] Come, thou gentle day!
   For if but once thou show me thy grey light,
   I'll find Demetrius and revenge this spite.

Sleeps. Re-enter Puck and Demetrius.

PUCK   Ho, ho, ho! Coward, why comest thou not?

DEMETRIUS   Abide, me, if thou darest; for well I wot
   Thou runn'st before me, shifting every place,

And darest not stand, nor look me in the face.
Where art thou now?

PUCK   Come hither: I am here.

DEMETRIUS   Nay, then, thou mock'st me. Thou shalt buy this dear,
If ever I thy face by daylight see:
Now, go thy way. Faintness constraineth me
To measure out my length on this cold bed.
By day's approach look to be visited.

Lies down and sleeps. Re-enter Helena.

HELENA   O weary night, O long and tedious night,
Abate thy hours! Shine comforts from the east,
That I may back to Athens by daylight,
From these that my poor company detest:
And sleep, that sometimes shuts up sorrow's eye,
Steal me awhile from mine own company.

Lies down and sleeps.

PUCK   Yet but three? Come one more;
Two of both kinds makes up four.
Here she comes, curst and sad:
Cupid is a knavish lad,
Thus to make poor females mad.

Re-enter Hermia.

HERMIA   Never so weary, never so in woe,
Bedabbled with the dew and torn with briers,
I can no further crawl, no further go;
My legs can keep no pace with my desires.
Here will I rest me till the break of day.
Heavens shield Lysander, if they mean a fray!

Lies down and sleeps.

PUCK   On the ground
Sleep sound:
I'll apply
To your eye,
Gentle lover, remedy.

Squeezing the juice on Lysander's eyes.

143

When thou wakest,
Thou takest
True delight
In the sight
Of thy former lady's eye:
And the country proverb known,
That every man should take his own,
In your waking shall be shown:
    Jack shall have Jill;
    Nought shall go ill;
The man shall have his mare again, and all shall be well.   *Exit.*

ACT IV

❧ SCENE 1 *The same. Lysander, Demetrius, Helena, and Hermia lying asleep.*

Enter Titania and Bottom; Peaseblossom, Cobweb, Moth, Mustardseed, and other Fairies attending; Oberon behind unseen.

TITANIA   Come, sit thee down upon this flowery bed,
While I thy amiable cheeks do coy,
And stick musk-roses in thy sleek smooth head,
And kiss thy fair large ears, my gentle joy.

BOTTOM   Where's Peaseblossom?

PEASEBLOSSOM   Ready.

BOTTOM   Scratch my head, Peaseblossom. Where's Mounsieur Cobweb?

COBWEB   Ready.

BOTTOM   Mounsieur Cobweb, good mounsieur, get you your weapons in your hand, and kill me a red-hipped humble-bee on the top of a thistle; and, good mounsieur, bring me the honey-bag. Do not fret yourself too much in the action, mounsieur; and, good mounsieur, have a care the honey-bag break not; I would be loath to have you overflown with a honey-bag, signior. Where's Mounsieur Mustardseed?

MUSTARDSEED   Ready.

BOTTOM   Give me your neaf, Mounsieur Mustardseed. Pray you, leave your courtesy, good mounsieur.

MUSTARDSEED   What's your will?

BOTTOM   Nothing, good mounsieur, but to help Cavalery Cobweb to

145

scratch. I must to the barber's, mounsieur; for methinks I am marvellous hairy about the face; and I am such a tender ass, if my hair do but
tickle me, I must scratch.

TITANIA What, wilt thou hear some music, my sweet love?

BOTTOM I have a reasonable good ear in music.
Let's have the tongs and the bones.

TITANIA Or say, sweet love, what thou desirest to eat.

BOTTOM Truly, a peck of provender: I could munch your good dry oats.
Methinks I have a great desire to a bottle of hay: good hay, sweet hay,
hath no fellow.

TITANIA I have a venturous fairy that shall seek
The squirrel's hoard, and fetch thee new nuts.

BOTTOM I had rather have a handful or two of dried peas. But, I pray
you, let none of your people stir me: I have an exposition of sleep come
upon me.

TITANIA Sleep thou, and I will wind thee in my arms.
Fairies, be gone, and be all ways away.   *Exeunt Fairies.*
So doth the woodbine the sweet honeysuckle
Gently entwist; the female ivy so
Enrings the barky fingers of the elm.
O, how I love thee! how I dote on thee!

They sleep. Enter Puck.

OBERON [*Advancing.*] Welcome, good Robin.
See'st thou this sweet sight?
Her dotage now I do begin to pity:
For, meeting her of late behind the wood,
Seeking sweet favours for this hateful fool,
I did upbraid her and fall out with her;
For she his hairy temples then had rounded
With coronet of fresh and fragrant flowers;
And that same dew, which sometime on the buds
Was wont to swell like round and orient pearls,
Stood now within the pretty flowerets' eyes
Like tears that did their own disgrace bewail.
When I had at my pleasure taunted her
And she in mild terms begg'd my patience,
I then did ask her of her changeling child;

146

Which straight she gave me, and her fairy sent
To bear him to my bower in fairy land.
And now I have the boy, I will undo
This hateful imperfection of her eyes:
And, gentle Puck, take this transformed scalp
From off the head of this Athenian swain;
That, he awaking when the other do,
May all to Athens back again repair
And think no more of this night's accidents
But as the fierce vexation of a dream.
But first I will release the fairy queen.

Touching her eyes.

               Be as thou wast wont to be;
               See as thou wast wont to see:
               Dian's bud o'er Cupid's flower
               Hath such force and blessed power.
Now, my Titania; wake you, my sweet queen.

TITANIA   My Oberon! what visions have I seen!
Methought I was enamour'd of an ass.

OBERON   There lies your love.

TITANIA   How came these things to pass?
O, how mine eyes do loathe his visage now!

OBERON   Silence awhile. Robin, take off this head.
Titania, music call; and strike more dead
Than common sleep of all these five the sense.

TITANIA   Music, ho! music, such as charmeth sleep!

Music, still.

PUCK   Now, when thou wakest, with thine own fool's eyes peep.

OBERON   Sound, music! Come, my queen, take hands with me,
And rock the ground whereon these sleepers be.
Now thou and I are new in amity
And will to-morrow midnight solemnly
Dance in Duke Theseus' house triumphantly
And bless it to all fair prosperity:
There shall the pairs of faithful lovers be
Wedded, with Theseus, all in jollity.

147

PUCK   Fairy king, attend, and mark:
I do hear the morning lark.

OBERON   Then, my queen, in silence sad
Trip we after night's shade:
We the globe can compass soon,
Swifter than the wandering moon.

TITANIA   Come, my lord, and in our flight
Tell me how it came this night
That I sleeping here was found
With these mortals on the ground.   *Exeunt.*

Horns winded within. Enter Theseus, Hippolyta, Egeus, and train.

THESEUS   Go, one of you, find out the forester;
For now our observation is perform'd;
And since we have the vaward of the day,
My love shall hear the music of my hounds.
Uncouple in the western valley; let them go:
Dispatch, I say, and find the forester.   *Exit an Attendant.*
We will, fair queen, up to the mountain's top
And mark the musical confusion
Of hounds and echo in conjunction.

HIPPOLYTA   I was with Hercules and Cadmus once,
When in a wood of Crete they bay'd the bear
With hounds of Sparta: never did I hear
Such gallant chiding; for, besides the groves,
The skies, the fountains, every region near
Seem'd all one mutual cry: I never heard
So musical a discord, such sweet thunder.

THESEUS   My hounds are bred out of the Spartan kind,
So flew'd, so sanded, and their heads are hung
With ears that sweep away the morning dew;
Crook-knee'd, and dew-lapp'd like Thessalian bulls;
Slow in pursuit, but match'd in mouth like bells,
Each under each. A cry more tuneable
Was never holla'd to, nor cheer'd with horn,
In Crete, in Sparta, nor in Thessaly:
Judge when you hear. But, soft! what nymphs are these?

EGEUS   My lord, this is my daughter here asleep;
And this, Lysander; this Demetrius is;

148

ACT IV   Scene 1

This Helena, old Nedar's Helena:
I wonder of their being here together.

THESEUS   No doubt they rose up early to observe
The rite of May, and, hearing our intent,
Came here in grace of our solemnity.
But speak, Egeus; is not this the day
That Hermia should give answer of her choice?

EGEUS   It is, my lord.

THESEUS   Go, bid the huntsmen wake them with their horns.

Horns and shout within. Lysander, Demetrius, Helena, and Hermia wake and start up.

Good morrow, friends. Saint Valentine is past:
Begin these wood-birds but to couple now?

LYSANDER   Pardon, my lord.

THESEUS   I pray you all, stand up.
I know you two are rival enemies:
How comes this gentle concord in the world,
That hatred is so far from jealousy
To sleep by hate and fear no enmity?

LYSANDER   My lord, I shall reply amazedly,
Half sleep, half waking: but as yet, I swear,
I cannot truly say how I came here;
But, as I think—for truly would I speak,
And now I do bethink me, so it is—
I came with Hermia hither: our intent
Was to be gone from Athens, where we might,
Without the peril of the Athenian law—

EGEUS   Enough, enough, my lord; you have enough:
I beg the law, the law, upon his head.
They would have stolen away; they would, Demetrius,
Thereby to have defeated you and me,
You of your wife and me of my consent,
Of my consent that she should be your wife.

DEMETRIUS   My lord, fair Helen told me of their stealth,
Of this their purpose hither to this wood;
And I in fury hither follow'd them,
Fair Helena in fancy following me.

149

But, my good lord, I wot not by what power—
But by some power it is—my love to Hermia,
Melted as the snow, seems to me now
As the remembrance of an idle gawd
Which in my childhood I did dote upon;
And all the faith, the virtue of my heart,
The object and the pleasure of mine eye,
Is only Helena. To her, my lord,
Was I betroth'd ere I saw Hermia:
But like in sickness did I loathe this food;
But, as in health, come to my natural taste,
Now I do wish it, love it, long for it,
And will for evermore be true to it.

THESEUS Fair lovers, you are fortunately met:
Of this discourse we more will hear anon.
Egeus, I will overbear your will;
For in the temple, by and by, with us
These couples shall eternally be knit:
And, for the morning now is something worn,
Our purposed hunting shall be set aside.
Away with us to Athens; three and three,
We'll hold a feast in great solemnity.
Come, Hippolyta.   *Exeunt Theseus, Hippolyta, Egeus, and train.*

DEMETRIUS These things seem small and undistinguishable,
Like far-off mountains turned into clouds.

HERMIA Methinks I see these things with parted eye,
When every thing seems double.

HELENA   So methinks:
And I have found Demetrius like a jewel,
Mine own, and not mine own.

DEMETRIUS   Are you sure
That we are awake? It seems to me
That yet we sleep, we dream. Do not you think
The Duke was here, and bid us follow him?

HERMIA Yea; and my father.

HELENA   And Hippolyta.

LYSANDER And he did bid us follow to the temple.

DEMETRIUS   Why, then, we are awake: let's follow him;
And by the way let us recount our dreams.   *Exeunt.*

BOTTOM   [*Awaking.*] When my cue comes, call me, and I will answer:
my next is, "Most fair Pyramus." Heigh-ho! Peter Quince! Flute, the
bellows-mender! Snout, the tinker! Starveling! God's my life, stolen
hence, and left me asleep! I have had a most rare vision. I have had a
dream, past the wit of man to say what dream it was: man is but an ass,
if he go about to expound this dream. Methought I was—there is no
man can tell what. Methought I was—and methought I had—but
man is but a patched fool, if he will offer to say what methought I had.
The eye of man hath not heard, the ear of man hath not seen, man's
hand is not able to taste, his tongue to conceive, nor his heart to report,
what my dream was. I will get Peter Quince to write a ballad of this
dream: it shall be called "Bottom's Dream," because it hath no bottom; and I will sing it in the latter end of a play, before the Duke:
peradventure, to make it the more gracious, I shall sing it at her death.
                                                              Exit.

✣ SCENE 2   *Athens. Quince's house.*

Enter Quince, Flute, Snout, and Starveling.

QUINCE   Have you sent to Bottom's house? is he come home yet?

STARVELING   He cannot be heard of. Out of doubt he is transported.

FLUTE   If he come not, then the play is marred: it goes not forward, doth
it?

QUINCE   It is not possible: you have not a man in all Athens able to discharge Pyramus but he.

FLUTE   No, he hath simply the best wit of any handicraft man in Athens.

QUINCE   Yea, and the best person too; and he is a very paramour for a
sweet voice.

FLUTE   You must say "paragon": a paramour is, God bless us, a thing of
naught.

Enter Snug.

SNUG   Masters, the Duke is coming from the temple, and there is two or
three lords and ladies more married: if our sport had gone forward, we
had all been made men.

151

FLUTE O sweet bully Bottom! Thus hath he lost sixpence a day during his life; he could not have 'scaped sixpence a day: an the Duke had not given him sixpence a day for playing Pyramus, I'll be hanged; he would have deserved it: sixpence a day in Pyramus, or nothing.

Enter Bottom.

BOTTOM Where are these lads? where are these hearts?

QUINCE Bottom! O most courageous day! O most happy hour!

BOTTOM Masters, I am to discourse wonders: but ask me not what: for if I tell you, I am no true Athenian. I will tell you everything, right as it fell out.

QUINCE Let us hear, sweet Bottom.

BOTTOM Not a word of me. All that I will tell you is, that the Duke hath dined. Get your apparel together, good strings to your beards, new ribbons to your pumps; meet presently at the palace; every man look o'er his part; for the short and the long is, our play is preferred. In any case, let Thisby have clean linen; and let not him that plays the lion pare his nails, for they shall hang out for the lion's claws. And, most dear actors, eat no onions nor garlic, for we are to utter sweet breath; and I do not doubt but to hear them say, it is a sweet comedy. No more words: away! go, away!   *Exeunt.*

ACT V

✿ SCENE 1 *Athens. The palace of Theseus.*

Enter Theseus, Hippolyta, Philostrate, Lords, and Attendants.

HIPPOLYTA 'Tis strange, my Theseus, that these lovers speak of.

THESEUS More strange than true: I never may believe
These antique fables, nor these fairy toys.
Lovers and madmen have such seething brains,
Such shaping fantasies, that apprehend
More than cool reason ever comprehends.
The lunatic, the lover, and the poet
Are of imagination all compact:
One sees more devils than vast hell can hold,
That is, the madman: the lover, all as frantic,
Sees Helen's beauty in a brow of Egypt:
The poet's eye, in a fine frenzy rolling,
Doth glance from heaven to earth, from earth to heaven;
And as imagination bodies forth
The forms of things unknown, the poet's pen
Turns them to shapes and gives to airy nothing
A local habitation and a name.
Such tricks hath strong imagination,
That, if it would but apprehend some joy,
It comprehends some bringer of that joy;
Or in the night, imagining some fear,
How easy is a bush supposed a bear!

HIPPOLYTA But all the story of the night told over,
And all their minds transfigured so together,

153

More witnesseth than fancy's images
And grows to something of great constancy;
But, howsoever, strange and admirable.

THESEUS   Here come the lovers, full of joy and mirth.

Enter Lysander, Demetrius, Hermia, and Helena.

Joy, gentle friends! joy and fresh days of love
Accompany your hearts!

LYSANDER   More than to us
Wait in your royal walks, your board, your bed!

THESEUS   Come now; what masques, what dances shall we have,
To wear away this long age of three hours
Between our after-supper and bed-time?
Where is our usual manager of mirth?
What revels are in hand? Is there no play,
To ease the anguish of a torturing hour?
Call Philostrate.

PHILOSTRATE   Here, mighty Theseus.

THESEUS   Say, what abridgement have you for this evening?
What masque? what music? How shall we beguile
The lazy time, if not with some delight?

PHILOSTRATE   There is a brief how many sports are ripe:
Make choice of which your highness will see first.

Giving a paper.

THESEUS   [*Reads.*]
"The battle with the Centaurs, to be sung
By an Athenian eunuch to the harp."

We'll none of that: that have I told my love,
In glory of my kinsman Hercules.

"The riot of the tipsy Bacchanals,
Tearing the Thracian singer in their rage."

That is an old device; and it was play'd
When I from Thebes came last a conqueror.

"The thrice three Muses mourning for the death
Of learning, late deceased in beggary."

154

That is some satire, keen and critical,
Not sorting with a nuptial ceremony.

"A tedious brief scene of young Pyramus
And his love Thisby; very tragical mirth."

Merry and tragical! tedious and brief!
That is, hot ice and wondrous strange snow.
How shall we find the concord of this discord?

PHILOSTRATE   A play there is, my lord, some ten words long,
Which is as brief as I have known a play;
But by ten words, my lord, it is too long,
Which makes it tedious; for in all the play
There is not one word apt, one player fitted:
And tragical, my noble lord, it is;
For Pyramus therein doth kill himself.
Which, when I saw rehearsed, I must confess,
Made mine eyes water; but more merry tears
The passion of loud laughter never shed.

THESEUS   What are they that do play it?

PHILOSTRATE   Hard-handed men that work in Athens here,
Which never labour'd in their minds till now,
And now have toil'd their unbreathed memories
With this same play, against your nuptial.

THESEUS   And we will hear it.

PHILOSTRATE   No, my noble lord;
It is not for you: I have heard it over,
And it is nothing, nothing in the world;
Unless you can find sport in their intents,
Extremely stretch'd and conn'd with cruel pain,
To do you service.

THESEUS   I will hear that play;
For never anything can be amiss,
When simpleness and duty tender it.
Go, bring them in: and take your places ladies.   *Exit Philostrate.*

HIPPOLYTA   I love not to see wretchedness o'ercharged
And duty in his service perishing.

THESEUS   Why, gentle sweet, you shall see no such thing.

155

HIPPOLYTA   He says they can do nothing in this kind.

THESEUS   The kinder we, to give them thanks for nothing.
  Our sport shall be to take what they mistake:
  And what poor duty cannot do, noble respect
  Takes it in might, not merit.
  Where I have come, great clerks have purposed
  To greet me with premeditated welcomes;
  Where I have seen them shiver and look pale,
  Make periods in the midst of sentences,
  Throttle their practised accent in their fears
  And in conclusion dumbly have broke off,
  Not paying me a welcome. Trust me, sweet,
  Out of this silence yet I pick'd a welcome;
  And in the modesty of fearful duty
  I read as much as from the rattling tongue
  Of saucy and audacious eloquence.
  Love, therefore, and tongue-tied simplicity
  In least speak most, to my capacity.

Re-enter Philostrate.

PHILOSTRATE   So please your Grace, the Prologue is address'd.

THESEUS   Let him approach.

Flourish of trumpets. Enter Quince for the Prologue.

PROLOGUE   If we offend, it is with our good will.
  That you should think, we come not to offend,
  But with good will. To show our simple skill,
  That is the true beginning of our end.
  Consider then we come but in despite.
  We do not come as minding to content you,
  Our true intent is. All for your delight
  We are not here. That you should here repent you,
  The actors are at hand and by their show
  You shall know all that you are like to know.

THESEUS   This fellow doth not stand upon points.

LYSANDER   He hath rid his prologue like a rough colt; he knows not the
  stop. A good moral, my lord: it is not enough to speak, but to speak
  true.

HIPPOLYTA   Indeed he hath played on his prologue like a child on a re-corder; a sound, but not in government.

THESEUS   His speech was like a tangled chain; nothing impaired, but all disordered. Who is next?

Enter Pyramus and Thisbe, Wall, Moonshine, and Lion.

PROLOGUE   Gentles, perchance you wonder at this show;
But wonder on, till truth make all things plain.
This man is Pyramus, if you would know;
This beauteous lady Thisby is certain.
This man, with lime and rough-cast, doth present
Wall, that vile Wall which did these lovers sunder;
And through Wall's chink, poor souls, they are content
To whisper. At the which let no man wonder.
This man, with lanthorn, dog, and bush of thorn,
Presenteth Moonshine; for, if you will know,
By moonshine did these lovers think no scorn
To meet at Ninus' tomb, there, there to woo.
This grisly beast, which Lion hight by name,
The trusty Thisby, coming first by night,
Did scare away, or rather did affright;
And, as she fled, her mantle she did fall,
Which Lion vile with bloody mouth did stain.
Anon comes Pyramus, sweet youth and tall,
And finds his trusty Thisby's mantle slain:
Whereat, with blade, with bloody blameful blade,
He bravely broach'd his boiling bloody breast;
And Thisby, tarrying in mulberry shade,
His dagger drew, and died. For all the rest,
Let Lion, Moonshine, Wall, and lovers twain
At large discourse, while here they do remain.
                    Exeunt Prologue, Pyramus, Thisbe, Lion, and Moonshine.

THESEUS   I wonder if the lion be to speak.

DEMETRIUS   No wonder, my lord: one lion may, when many asses do.

WALL   In this same interlude it doth befall
That I, one Snout by name, present a wall;
And such a wall, as I would have you think,
That had in it a crannied hole or chink,
Through which the lovers, Pyramus and Thisby,

Did whisper often very secretly.
This loam, this rough-cast, and this stone doth show
That I am that same wall; the truth is so:
And this the cranny is, right and sinister,
Through which the fearful lovers are to whisper.

THESEUS Would you desire lime and hair to speak better?

DEMETRIUS It is the wittiest partition that ever I heard discourse, my
lord.

Re-enter Pyramus.

THESEUS Pyramus draws near the wall: silence!

PYRAMUS O grim-look'd night! O night with hue so black!
O night, which ever art when day is not!
O night, O night! alack, alack, alack,
I fear my Thisby's promise is forgot!
And thou, O wall, O sweet, O lovely wall,
That stand'st between her father's ground and mine!
Thou wall, O wall, O sweet and lovely wall,
Show me thy chink, to blink through with mine eyne!

Wall holds up his fingers.

Thanks, courteous wall: Jove shield thee well for this!
But what see I? No Thisby do I see.
O wicked wall, through whom I see no bliss!
Curs'd be thy stones for thus deceiving me!

THESEUS The wall, methinks, being sensible, should curse again.

PYRAMUS No, in truth, sir, he should not. "Deceiving me" is Thisby's
cue: she is to enter now, and I am to spy her through the wall. You
shall see, it will fall pat as I told you. Yonder she comes.

Re-enter Thisbe.

THISBE O wall, full often hast thou heard my moans,
For parting my fair Pyramus and me!
My cherry lips have often kiss'd thy stones,
Thy stones with lime and hair knit up in thee.

PYRAMUS I see a voice: now will I to the chink,
To spy an I can hear my Thisby's face.
Thisby!

158

THISBE   My love thou art, my love I think.

PYRAMUS   Think what thou wilt, I am thy lover's grace;
And, like Limander, am I trusty still.

THISBE   And I like Helen, till the Fates me kill.

PYRAMUS   Not Shafalus to Procrus was so true.

THISBE   As Shafalus to Procrus, I to you.

PYRAMUS   O, kiss me through the hole of this vile wall!

THISBE   I kiss the wall's hole, not your lips at all.

PYRAMUS   Wilt thou at Ninny's tomb meet me straightway?

THISBE   'Tide life, 'tide death, I come without delay.

Exeunt Pyramus and Thisbe.

WALL   Thus have I, Wall, my part discharged so;
And, being done, thus Wall away doth go.   *Exit.*

THESEUS   Now is the mural down between the two neighbours.

DEMETRIUS   No remedy, my lord, when walls are so wilful to hear without warning.

HIPPOLYTA   This is the silliest stuff that ever I heard.

THESEUS   The best in this kind are but shadows; and the worst are no worse, if imagination amend them.

HIPPOLYTA   It must be your imagination then, and not theirs.

THESEUS   If we imagine no worse of them than they of themselves, they may pass for excellent men. Here come two noble beasts in, a man and a lion.

Re-enter Lion and Moonshine.

LION   You, ladies, you, whose gentle hearts do fear
The smallest monstrous mouse that creeps on floor,
May now perchance both quake and tremble here,
When lion rough in wildest rage doth roar.
Then know that I, one Snug the joiner, am
A lion fell, nor else no lion's dam;
For, if I should as lion come in strife
Into this place, 'twere pity on my life.

THESEUS   A very gentle beast, and of a good conscience.

159

DEMETRIUS   The very best at a beast, my lord, that e'er I saw.

LYSANDER   This lion is a very fox for his valour.

THESEUS   True; and a goose for his discretion.

DEMETRIUS   Not so, my lord; for his valour cannot carry his discretion; and the fox carries the goose.

THESEUS   His discretion, I am sure, cannot carry his valour; for the goose carries not the fox. It is well: leave it to his discretion, and let us listen to the moon.

MOONSHINE   This lanthorn doth the horned moon present—

DEMETRIUS   He should have worn the horns on his head.

THESEUS   He is no crescent, and his horns are invisible within the circumference.

MOONSHINE   This lanthorn doth the horned moon present;
Myself the man i' the moon do seem to be.

THESEUS   This is the greatest error of all the rest: the man should be put into the lanthorn. How is it else the man i' the moon?

DEMETRIUS   He dares not come there for the candle; for, you see, it is already in snuff.

HIPPOLYTA   I am aweary of this moon: would he would change!

THESEUS   It appears, by his small light of discretion, that he is in the wane; but yet, in courtesy, in all reason, we must stay the time.

LYSANDER   Proceed, Moon.

MOONSHINE   All that I have to say, is, to tell you that the lanthorn is the moon; I, the man in the moon; this thorn-bush, my thorn-bush; and this dog, my dog.

DEMETRIUS   Why, all these should be in the lanthorn; for all these are in the moon. But, silence! here comes Thisbe.

Re-enter Thisbe.

THISBE   This is old Ninny's tomb. Where is my love?

LION   [*Roaring.*] Oh—   *Thisbe runs off.*

DEMETRIUS   Well roared, Lion.

THESEUS   Well run, Thisbe.

HIPPOLYTA   Well shone, Moon. Truly, the moon shines with a good
grace.   *The Lion shakes Thisbe's mantle, and exit.*

THESEUS   Well moused, Lion.

LYSANDER   And so the lion vanished.

DEMETRIUS   And then came Pyramus.

Re-enter Pyramus.

PYRAMUS   Sweet Moon, I thank thee for thy sunny beams;
I thank thee, Moon, for shining now so bright;
For, by thy gracious, golden, glittering gleams,
I trust to take of truest Thisby sight.
                    But stay, O spite!
                    But mark, poor knight,
            What dreadful dole is here!
                    Eyes, do you see?
                    How can it be?
            O dainty duck! O dear!
                    Thy mantle good,
                    What, stain'd with blood!
            Approach, ye Furies fell!
                    O Fates, come, come,
                    Cut thread and thrum;
            Quail, crush, conclude, and quell!

THESEUS   This passion, and the death of a dear friend, would go near to
make a man look sad.

HIPPOLYTA   Beshrew my heart, but I pity the man.

PYRAMUS   O wherefore, Nature, didst thou lions frame?
Since lion vile hath here deflower'd my dear:
Which is—no, no—which was the fairest dame
That lived, that loved, that liked, that look'd with cheer.
                    Come, tears, confound;
                    Out, sword, and wound
            The pap of Pyramus;
                    Ay, that left pap,
                    Where heart doth hop:

Stabs himself.

                    Thus die I, thus, thus, thus.
                    Now am I dead,

> Now am I fled;
> My soul is in the sky:
> Tongue, lose thy light;
> Moon take thy flight: *Exit Moonshine.*
> Now die, die, die, die, die.   *Dies.*

DEMETRIUS   No die, but an ace, for him; for he is but one.

LYSANDER   Less than an ace, man; for he is dead; he is nothing.

THESEUS   With the help of a surgeon he might yet recover, and prove an ass.

HIPPOLYTA   How chance Moonshine is gone before
Thisbe comes back and finds her lover?

THESEUS   She will find him by starlight. Here she comes; and her passion ends the play.

Re-enter Thisbe.

HIPPOLYTA   Methinks she should not use a long one for such a Pyramus: I hope she will be brief.

DEMETRIUS   A mote will turn the balance, which Pyramus, which Thisbe, is the better; he for a man, God warrant us; she for a woman, God bless us.

LYSANDER   She hath spied him already with those sweet eyes.

DEMETRIUS   And thus she moans, *videlicet* —

THISBE
> Asleep, my love?
> What, dead, my dove?
> O Pyramus, arise!
> Speak, speak. Quite dumb?
> Dead, dead? A tomb
> Must cover thy sweet eyes.
> These lily lips,
> This cherry nose,
> These yellow cowslip cheeks,
> Are gone, are gone:
> Lovers, make moan:
> His eyes were green as leeks.
> O Sisters Three,
> Come, come to me,
> With hands as pale as milk;

> Lay them in gore,
> Since you have shore
> With shears his thread of silk.
> Tongue, not a word:
> Come, trusty sword;
> Come, blade, my breast imbrue:

Stabs herself.

> And, farewell, friends;
> Thus Thisby ends:
> Adieu, adieu, adieu.   *Dies.*

THESEUS Moonshine and Lion are left to bury the dead.

DEMETRIUS Ay, and Wall too.

BOTTOM [*Starting up.*] No, I assure you; the wall is down that parted their fathers. Will it please you to see the epilogue, or to hear a Bergomask dance between two of our company?

THESEUS No epilogue, I pray you; for your play needs no excuse. Never excuse; for when the players are all dead, there need none to be blamed. Marry, if he that writ it had played Pyramus and hanged himself in Thisbe's garter, it would have been a fine tragedy: and so it is, truly; and very notably discharged. But, come, your Bergomask: let your epilogue alone.

A dance.

> The iron tongue of midnight hath told twelve:
> Lovers, to bed; 'tis almost fairy time.
> I fear we shall out-sleep the coming morn
> As much as we this night have overwatch'd.
> This palpable-gross play hath well beguiled
> The heavy gait of night. Sweet friends, to bed.
> A fortnight hold we this solemnity,
> In nightly revels and new jollity.   *Exeunt.*

Enter Puck.

PUCK Now the hungry lion roars,
> And the wolf behowls the moon;
> Whilst the heavy ploughman snores,
> All with weary task fordone.
> Now the wasted brands do glow,
> Whilst the screech-owl, screeching loud,

Puts the wretch that lies in woe
In remembrance of a shroud.
Now it is the time of night
That the graves all gaping wide,
Every one lets forth his sprite,
In the church-way paths to glide:
And we fairies, that do run
By the triple Hecate's team,
From the presence of the sun,
Following darkness like a dream,
Now are frolic: not a mouse
Shall disturb this hallow'd house:
I am sent with broom before,
To sweep the dust behind the door.

Enter Oberon and Titania with their train.

OBERON   Through the house give glimmering light,
By the dead and drowsy fire:
Every elf and fairy sprite
Hop as light as bird from brier;
And this ditty, after me,
Sing, and dance it trippingly.

TITANIA   First, rehearse your song by rote,
To each word a warbling note:
Hand in hand, with fairy grace,
Will we sing, and bless this place.

Song and dance.

OBERON   Now, until the break of day,
Through this house each fairy stray.
To the best bride-bed will we,
Which by us shall blessed be;
And the issue there create
Ever shall be fortunate.
So shall all the couples three
Ever true in loving be;
And the blots of Nature's hand
Shall not in their issue stand;
Never mole, hare lip, nor scar,
Nor mark prodigious, such as are
Despised in nativity,

164

Shall upon their children be.
With this field-dew consecrate,
Every fairy take his gait;
And each several chamber bless,
Through this palace, with sweet peace;
And the owner of it blest
Ever shall in safety rest.
Trip away; make no stay;
Meet me all by break of day.   *Exeunt Oberon, Titania, and train.*

PUCK   If we shadows have offended,
Think but this, and all is mended,
That you have but slumber'd here
While these visions did appear.
And this weak and idle theme,
No more yielding but a dream,
Gentles, do not reprehend:
If you pardon, we will mend:
And, as I am an honest Puck,
If we have unearned luck
Now to 'scape the serpent's tongue,
We will make amends ere long;
Else the Puck a liar call:
So, good night unto you all.
Give me your hands, if we be friends,
And Robin shall restore amends.   *Exit.*

HAMLET,
PRINCE OF DENMARK

THE ACTORS

CLAUDIUS, *King of Denmark*

HAMLET, *son to the late, and nephew to the present, King*

POLONIUS, *Lord Chamberlain*

HORATIO, *friend to Hamlet*

LAERTES, *son to Polonius*

VOLTIMAND
CORNELIUS
ROSENCRANTZ
GUILDENSTERN } *courtiers*
OSRIC
A GENTLEMAN

A PRIEST

MARCELLUS } *officers*
BERNARDO

FRANCISCO, *a soldier*

REYNALDO, *servant to Polonius*

FIVE PLAYERS

TWO CLOWNS, *gravediggers*

FORTINBRAS, *Prince of Norway*

A CAPTAIN

AN ENGLISH AMBASSADOR

A LORD

A SAILOR

TWO MESSENGERS

A SERVANT *to Horatio*

DANES

GHOST *of Hamlet's father*

GERTRUDE, *Queen of Denmark, and mother to Hamlet*

OPHELIA, *daughter to Polonius*

Non-Speaking: Lords, Ladies, Officers, Soldiers, Priests, Ambassadors, Sailors, and other Attendants

SCENE: *Denmark*

ACT I

❦ SCENE 1 *Elsinore. A platform before the castle.*

Francisco at his post. Enter to him Bernardo.

BERNARDO Who's there?

FRANCISCO Nay, answer me: stand, and unfold yourself.

BERNARDO Long live the King!

FRANCISCO Bernardo?

BERNARDO He.

FRANCISCO You come most carefully upon your hour.

BERNARDO 'Tis now struck twelve; get thee to bed, Francisco.

FRANCISCO For this relief much thanks: 'tis bitter cold,
  And I am sick at heart.

BERNARDO Have you had quiet guard?

FRANCISCO   Not a mouse stirring.

BERNARDO Well, good night.
  If you do meet Horatio and Marcellus,
  The rivals of my watch, bid them make haste.

FRANCISCO I think I hear them. Stand, ho! Who's there?

Enter Horatio and Marcellus.

HORATIO Friends to this ground.

MARCELLUS   And liegemen to the Dane.

171

FRANCISCO   Give you good night.

MARCELLUS   O, farewell, honest soldier:
   Who hath relieved you?

FRANCISCO   Bernardo has my place.
   Give you good night.   *Exit.*

MARCELLUS   Holla! Bernardo!

BERNARDO   Say,
   What, is Horatio there?

HORATIO   A piece of him.

BERNARDO   Welcome, Horatio: welcome, good Marcellus.

MARCELLUS   What, has this thing appear'd again to-night?

BERNARDO   I have seen nothing.

MARCELLUS   Horatio says 'tis but our fantasy,
   And will not let belief take hold of him
   Touching this dreaded sight, twice seen of us:
   Therefore I have entreated him along
   With us to watch the minutes of this night,
   That if again this apparition come,
   He may approve our eyes and speak to it.

HORATIO   Tush, tush, 'twill not appear.

BERNARDO   Sit down awhile;
   And let us once again assail your ears,
   That are so fortified against our story,
   What we have two nights seen.

HORATIO   Well, sit we down,
   And let us hear Bernardo speak of this.

BERNARDO   Last night of all,
   When yond same star that's westward from the pole
   Had made his course to illume that part of heaven
   Where now it burns, Marcellus and myself,
   The bell then beating one—

Enter Ghost.

MARCELLUS   Peace, break thee off; look, where it comes again!

BERNARDO   In the same figure, like the King that's dead.

172

MARCELLUS   Thou art a scholar; speak to it, Horatio.

BERNARDO   Looks it not like the King? mark it, Horatio.

HORATIO   Most like: it harrows me with fear and wonder.

BERNARDO   It would be spoke to.

MARCELLUS   Question it, Horatio.

HORATIO   What art thou that usurp'st this time of night,
　Together with that fair and warlike form
　In which the majesty of buried Denmark
　Did sometimes march? by heaven I charge thee, speak!

MARCELLUS   It is offended.

BERNARDO   See, it stalks away!

HORATIO   Stay! speak, speak! I charge thee, speak!　　　*Exit Ghost.*

MARCELLUS   'Tis gone, and will not answer.

BERNARDO   How now, Horatio! you tremble and look pale:
　Is not this something more than fantasy?
　What think you on't?

HORATIO   Before my God, I might not this believe
　Without the sensible and true avouch
　Of mine own eyes.

MARCELLUS   Is it not like the King?

HORATIO   As thou art to thyself:
　Such was the very armour he had on
　When he the ambitious Norway combated;
　So frown'd he once, when, in an angry parle,
　He smote the sledded Polacks on the ice.
　'Tis strange.

MARCELLUS   Thus twice before, and jump at this dead hour,
　With martial stalk hath he gone by our watch.

HORATIO   In what particular thought to work I know not;
　But in the gross and scope of my opinion,
　This bodes some strange eruption to our state.

MARCELLUS   Good now, sit down, and tell me, he that knows,
　Why this same strict and most observant watch
　So nightly toils the subject of the land,

And why such daily cast of brazen cannon,
And foreign mart for implements of war;
Why such impress of shipwrights, whose sore task
Does not divide the Sunday from the week;
What might be toward, that this sweaty haste
Doth make the night joint-labourer with the day:
Who is't that can inform me?

HORATIO   That can I;
At least, the whisper goes so. Our last king,
Whose image even but now appear'd to us,
Was, as you know, by Fortinbras of Norway,
Thereto prick'd on by a most emulate pride,
Dared to the combat; in which our valiant Hamlet —
For so this side of our known world esteem'd him —
Did slay this Fortinbras; who, by a seal'd compact,
Well ratified by law and heraldry,
Did forfeit, with his life, all those his lands
Which he stood seized of, to the conqueror:
Against the which, a moiety competent
Was gaged by our king; which had return'd
To the inheritance of Fortinbras,
Had he been vanquisher; as, by the same covenant,
And carriage of the article design'd,
His fell to Hamlet. Now, sir, young Fortinbras,
Of unimproved mettle hot and full,
Hath in the skirts of Norway here and there
Shark'd up a list of lawless resolutes,
For food and diet, to some enterprise
That hath a stomach in't; which is no other —
As it doth well appear unto our state —
But to recover of us, by strong hand
And terms compulsatory, those foresaid lands
So by his father lost: and this, I take it,
Is the main motive of our preparations,
The source of this our watch and the chief head
Of this post-haste and romage in the land.

BERNARDO   I think it be no other but e'en so:
Well may it sort that this portentous figure
Comes armed through our watch; so like the King
That was and is the question of these wars.

174

HORATIO   A mote it is to trouble the mind's eye.
  In the most high and palmy state of Rome,
  A little ere the mightiest Julius fell,
  The graves stood tenantless and the sheeted dead
  Did squeak and gibber in the Roman streets.
  As stars with trains of fire and dews of blood,
  Disasters in the sun; and the moist star
  Upon whose influence Neptune's empire stands
  Was sick almost to doomsday with eclipse.
  And even the like precurse of fierce events,
  As harbingers preceding still the fates
  And prologue to the omen coming on,
  Have heaven and earth together demonstrated
  Unto our climatures and countrymen.
  But soft, behold! lo, where it comes again!

Re-enter Ghost.

  I'll cross it, though it blast me. Stay, illusion!
  If thou hast any sound, or use of voice,
  Speak to me:
  If there be any good thing to be done,
  That may to thee do ease and grace to me,
  Speak to me:
  If thou art privy to thy country's fate,
  Which, happily, foreknowing may avoid,
  O, speak!
  Or if thou hast uphoarded in thy life
  Extorted treasure in the womb of earth,
  For which, they say, you spirits oft walk in death,
  Speak of it: [*Cock crows.*] stay, and speak! Stop it, Marcellus.

MARCELLUS   Shall I strike at it with my partisan?

HORATIO   Do, if it will not stand.

BERNARDO   'Tis here!

HORATIO   'Tis here!

MARCELLUS   'Tis gone!   *Exit Ghost.*
  We do it wrong, being so majestical,
  To offer it the show of violence;
  For it is, as the air, invulnerable,
  And our vain blows malicious mockery.

175

BERNARDO It was about to speak, when the cock crew.

HORATIO And then it started like a guilty thing
Upon a fearful summons. I have heard,
The cock, that is the trumpet to the morn,
Doth with his lofty and shrill-sounding throat
Awake the god of day; and, at his warning,
Whether in sea or fire, in earth or air,
The extravagant and erring spirit hies
To his confine: and of the truth herein
This present object made probation.

MARCELLUS It faded on the crowing of the cock.
Some say that ever 'gainst that season comes
Wherein our Saviour's birth is celebrated,
The bird of dawning singeth all night long:
And then, they say, no spirit dare stir abroad;
The nights are wholesome; then no planets strike,
No fairy takes, nor witch hath power to charm,
So hallow'd and so gracious is the time.

HORATIO So have I heard and do in part believe it.
But, look, the morn, in russet mantle clad,
Walks o'er the dew of yon high eastward hill:
Break we our watch up; and by my advice,
Let us impart what we have seen to-night
Unto young Hamlet; for, upon my life,
This spirit, dumb to us, will speak to him.
Do you consent we shall acquaint him with it,
As needful in our loves, fitting our duty?

MARCELLUS Let's do't, I pray; and I this morning know
Where we shall find him most conveniently.   *Exeunt.*

SCENE 2 *A room of state in the castle.*

*Enter the King, Queen, Hamlet, Polonius, Laertes, Voltimand, Cornelius,
Lords, and Attendants.*

KING Though yet of Hamlet our dear brother's death
The memory be green, and that it us befitted
To bear our hearts in grief and our whole kingdom
To be contracted in one brow of woe,
Yet so far hath discretion fought with nature

176

That we with wisest sorrow think on him,
Together with remembrance of ourselves.
Therefore our sometime sister, now our queen,
The imperial jointress to this warlike state,
Have we, as 'twere with a defeated joy—
With an auspicious and a dropping eye,
With mirth in funeral and with dirge in marriage,
In equal scale weighing delight and dole—
Taken to wife: nor have we herein barr'd
Your better wisdoms, which have freely gone
With this affair along. For all, our thanks.
Now follows, that you know, young Fortinbras,
Holding a weak supposal of our worth,
Or thinking by our late dear brother's death
Our state to be disjoint and out of frame,
Colleagued with the dream of his advantage,
He hath not fail'd to pester us with message,
Importing the surrender of those lands
Lost by his father, with all bonds of law,
To our most valiant brother. So much for him.
Now for ourself and for this time of meeting:
Thus much the business is: we have here writ
To Norway, uncle of young Fortinbras—
Who, impotent and bed-rid, scarcely hears
Of this his nephew's purpose—to suppress
His further gait herein; in that the levies,
The lists, and full proportions are all made
Out of his subject: and we here dispatch
You, good Cornelius, and you, Voltimand,
For bearers of this greeting to old Norway;
Giving to you no further personal power
To business with the king, more than the scope
Of these delated articles allow.
Farewell, and let your haste commend your duty.

CORNELIUS AND VOLTIMAND   In that and all things will we show our
    duty.

KING   We doubt it nothing: heartily farewell.
                                        Exeunt Voltimand and Cornelius.
And now, Laertes, what's the news with you?
You told us of some suit; what is't, Laertes?
You cannot speak of reason to the Dane,

And lose your voice: what wouldst thou beg, Laertes,
That shall not be my offer, not thy asking?
The head is not more native to the heart,
The hand more instrumental to the mouth,
Than is the throne of Denmark to thy father.
What wouldst thou have, Laertes?

LAERTES   My dread lord,
  Your leave and favour to return to France;
  From whence though willingly I came to Denmark,
  To show my duty in your coronation,
  Yet now, I must confess, that duty done,
  My thoughts and wishes bend again toward France
  And bow them to your gracious leave and pardon.

KING   Have you your father's leave? What says Polonius?

POLONIUS   He hath, my lord, wrung from me my slow leave
  By laboursome petition, and at last
  Upon his will I seal'd my hard consent:
  I do beseech you, give him leave to go.

KING   Take thy fair hour, Laertes; time be thine,
  And thy best graces spend it at thy will!
  But now, my cousin Hamlet, and my son—

HAMLET   [*Aside.*] A little more than kin, and less than kind.

KING   How is it that the clouds still hang on you?

HAMLET   Not so, my lord; I am too much i' the sun.

QUEEN   Good Hamlet, cast thy nighted colour off,
  And let thine eye look like a friend on Denmark.
  Do not for ever with thy vailed lids
  Seek for thy noble father in the dust.
  Thou know'st 'tis common; all that lives must die,
  Passing through nature to eternity.

HAMLET   Ay, madam, it is common.

QUEEN   If it be,
  Why seems it so particular with thee?

HAMLET   Seems, madam! nay, it is; I know not "seems."
  'Tis not alone my inky cloak, good mother,
  Nor customary suits of solemn black,

178

Nor windy suspiration of forced breath,
No, nor the fruitful river in the eye,
Nor the dejected 'haviour of the visage,
Together with all forms, moods, shapes of grief,
That can denote me truly: these indeed seem,
For they are actions that a man might play:
But I have that within which passeth show;
These but the trappings and the suits of woe.

KING   'Tis sweet and commendable in your nature, Hamlet,
To give these mourning duties to your father:
But, you must know, your father lost a father;
That father lost, lost his, and the survivor bound
In filial obligation for some term
To do obsequious sorrow: but to persever
In obstinate condolement is a course
Of impious stubbornness; 'tis unmanly grief;
It shows a will most incorrect to heaven,
A heart unfortified, a mind impatient,
An understanding simple and unschool'd:
For what we know must be and is as common
As any the most vulgar thing to sense,
Why should we in our peevish opposition
Take it to heart? Fie! 'tis a fault to heaven,
A fault against the dead, a fault to nature,
To reason most absurd; whose common theme
Is death of fathers, and who still hath cried,
From the first corse till he that died to-day,
"This must be so." We pray you, throw to earth
This unprevailing woe, and think of us
As of a father: for let the world take note,
You are the most immediate to our throne;
And with no less nobility of love
Than that which dearest father bears his son,
Do I impart toward you. For your intent
In going back to school in Wittenberg,
It is most retrograde to our desire:
And we beseech you, bend you to remain
Here, in the cheer and comfort of our eye,
Our chiefest courtier, cousin, and our son.

QUEEN   Let not thy mother lose her prayers, Hamlet:
I pray thee, stay with us; go not to Wittenberg.

179

HAMLET   I shall in all my best obey you, madam.

KING   Why, 'tis a loving and a fair reply:
  Be as ourself in Denmark. Madam, come;
  This gentle and unforced accord of Hamlet
  Sits smiling to my heart: in grace whereof,
  No jocund health that Denmark drinks to-day,
  But the great cannon to the clouds shall tell,
  And the King's rouse the heavens shall bruit again,
  Re-speaking earthly thunder. Come away.   *Exeunt all but Hamlet.*

HAMLET   O, that this too too solid flesh would melt,
  Thaw, and resolve itself into a dew!
  Or that the Everlasting had not fix'd
  His canon 'gainst self-slaughter! O God! God!
  How weary, stale, flat, and unprofitable,
  Seem to me all the uses of this world!
  Fie on't! ah fie! 'tis an unweeded garden,
  That grows to seed; things rank and gross in nature
  Possess it merely. That it should come to this!
  But two months dead: nay, not so much, not two:
  So excellent a king; that was, to this,
  Hyperion to a satyr; so loving to my mother
  That he might not beteem the winds of heaven
  Visit her face too roughly. Heaven and earth!
  Must I remember? why, she would hang on him,
  As if increase of appetite had grown
  By what it fed on: and yet, within a month—
  Let me not think on't— Frailty, thy name is woman!
  A little month, or ere those shoes were old
  With which she follow'd my poor father's body,
  Like Niobe, all tears: why she, even she—
  O God! a beast, that wants discourse of reason,
  Would have mourn'd longer—married with my uncle,
  My father's brother, but no more like my father
  Than I to Hercules: within a month:
  Ere yet the salt of most unrighteous tears
  Had left the flushing in her galled eyes,
  She married. O, most wicked speed, to post
  With such dexterity to incestuous sheets!
  It is not nor it cannot come to good:
  But break, my heart; for I must hold my tongue.

180

Enter Horatio, Marcellus, and Bernardo.

HORATIO   Hail to your lordship!

HAMLET   I am glad to see you well:
  Horatio—or I do forget myself.

HORATIO   The same, my lord, and your poor servant ever.

HAMLET   Sir, my good friend; I'll change that name with you:
  And what make you from Wittenberg, Horatio?
  Marcellus?

MARCELLUS   My good lord—

HAMLET   I am very glad to see you. [*To Bernardo.*] Good even, sir.
  But what, in faith, make you from Wittenberg?

HORATIO   A truant disposition, good my lord.

HAMLET   I would not hear your enemy say so,
  Nor shall you do mine ear that violence,
  To make it truster of your own report
  Against yourself: I know you are no truant.
  But what is your affair in Elsinore?
  We'll teach you to drink deep ere you depart.

HORATIO   My lord, I came to see your father's funeral.

HAMLET   I pray thee, do not mock me, fellow-student;
  I think it was to see my mother's wedding.

HORATIO   Indeed, my lord, it follow'd hard upon.

HAMLET   Thrift, thrift, Horatio! the funeral baked meats
  Did coldly furnish forth the marriage tables.
  Would I had met my dearest foe in heaven
  Or ever I had seen that day, Horatio!
  My father!—methinks I see my father.

HORATIO   Where, my lord?

HAMLET   In my mind's eye, Horatio.

HORATIO   I saw him once; he was a goodly king.

HAMLET   He was a man, take him for all in all,
  I shall not look upon his like again.

HORATIO   My lord, I think I saw him yesternight.

181

HAMLET   Saw? who?

HORATIO   My lord, the King your father.

HAMLET   The King my father?

HORATIO   Season your admiration for a while
With an attent ear, till I may deliver,
Upon the witness of these gentlemen,
This marvel to you.

HAMLET   For God's love, let me hear.

HORATIO   Two nights together had these gentlemen,
Marcellus and Bernardo, on their watch,
In the dead vast and middle of the night,
Been thus encounter'd. A figure like your father,
Armed at point exactly, cap-a-pie,
Appears before them, and with solemn march
Goes slow and stately by them: thrice he walk'd
By their oppress'd and fear-surprised eyes,
Within his truncheon's length; whilst they, distill'd
Almost to jelly with the act of fear,
Stand dumb and speak not to him. This to me
In dreadful secrecy impart they did;
And I with them the third night kept the watch:
Where, as they had deliver'd, both in time,
Form of the thing, each word made true and good,
The apparition comes: I knew your father;
These hands are not more like.

HAMLET   But where was this?

MARCELLUS   My lord, upon the platform where we watch'd.

HAMLET   Did you not speak to it?

HORATIO   My lord, I did;
But answer made it none: yet once methought
It lifted up it head and did address
Itself to motion, like as it would speak;
But even then the morning cock crew loud,
And at the sound it shrunk in haste away,
And vanish'd from our sight.

HAMLET   'Tis very strange.

HORATIO As I do live, my honour'd lord, 'tis true;
And we did think it writ down in our duty
To let you know of it.

HAMLET Indeed, indeed, sirs, but this troubles me.
Hold you the watch to-night?

MARCELLUS AND BERNARDO We do, my lord.

HAMLET Arm'd, say you?

MARCELLUS AND BERNARDO Arm'd, my lord.

HAMLET From top to toe?

MARCELLUS AND BERNARDO My lord, from head to foot.

HAMLET Then saw you not his face?

HORATIO O, yes, my lord; he wore his beaver up.

HAMLET What, look'd he frowningly?

HORATIO A countenance more in sorrow than in anger.

HAMLET Pale or red?

HORATIO Nay, very pale.

HAMLET And fix'd his eyes upon you?

HORATIO Most constantly.

HAMLET I would I had been there.

HORATIO It would have much amazed you.

HAMLET Very like, very like. Stay'd it long?

HORATIO While one with moderate haste might tell a hundred.

MARCELLUS AND BERNARDO Longer, longer.

HORATIO Not when I saw't.

HAMLET His beard was grizzled, no?

HORATIO It was, as I have seen it in his life,
A sable silver'd.

HAMLET I will watch to-night;
Perchance 'twill walk again.

HORATIO I warrant it will.

183

HAMLET If it assume my noble father's person,
I'll speak to it, though hell itself should gape
And bid me hold my peace. I pray you all,
If you have hitherto conceal'd this sight,
Let it be tenable in your silence still;
And whatsoever else shall hap to-night,
Give it an understanding, but no tongue:
I will requite your loves. So, fare you well:
Upon the platform, 'twixt eleven and twelve,
I'll visit you.

ALL Our duty to your honour.

HAMLET Your loves, as mine to you: farewell. *Exeunt all but Hamlet.*
My father's spirit in arms! all is not well;
I doubt some foul play. Would the night were come!
Till then sit still, my soul. Foul deeds will rise,
Though all the earth o'erwhelm them, to men's eyes. *Exit.*

❧ SCENE 3 *A room in Polonius' house.*

Enter Laertes and Ophelia.

LAERTES My necessaries are embark'd: farewell:
And, sister, as the winds give benefit
And convoy is assistant, do not sleep,
But let me hear from you.

OPHELIA Do you doubt that?

LAERTES For Hamlet and the trifling of his favour,
Hold it a fashion and a toy in blood,
A violet in the youth of primy nature,
Forward, not permanent, sweet, not lasting,
The perfume and suppliance of a minute;
No more.

OPHELIA No more but so?

LAERTES Think it no more:
For nature, crescent, does not grow alone

184

In thews and bulk, but, as this temple waxes,
The inward service of the mind and soul
Grows wide withal. Perhaps he loves you now,
And now no soil nor cautel doth besmirch
The virtue of his will: but you must fear,
His greatness weigh'd, his will is not his own;
For he himself is subject to his birth.
He may not, as unvalued persons do,
Carve for himself; for on his choice depends
The safety and health of this whole state;
And therefore must his choice be circumscribed
Unto the voice and yielding of that body
Whereof he is the head. Then if he says he loves you,
It fits your wisdom so far to believe it
As he in his particular act and place
May give his saying deed; which is no further
Than the main voice of Denmark goes withal.
Then weigh what loss your honour may sustain,
If with too credent ear you list his songs,
Or lose your heart, or your chaste treasure open
To his unmaster'd importunity.
Fear it, Ophelia, fear it, my dear sister,
And keep you in the rear of your affection,
Out of the shot and danger of desire.
The chariest maid is prodigal enough,
If she unmask her beauty to the moon:
Virtue itself 'scapes not calumnious strokes:
The canker galls the infants of the spring,
Too oft before their buttons be disclosed,
And in the morn and liquid dew of youth
Contagious blastments are most imminent.
Be wary then; best safety lies in fear:
Youth to itself rebels, though none else near.

OPHELIA   I shall the effect of this good lesson keep,
As watchman to my heart. But, good my brother,
Do not, as some ungracious pastors do,
Show me the steep and thorny way to heaven;
Whiles, like a puff'd and reckless libertine,
Himself the primrose path of dalliance treads,
And recks not his own rede.

185

LAERTES   O, fear me not.
  I stay too long: but here my father comes.

Enter Polonius.

  A double blessing is a double grace;
  Occasion smiles upon a second leave.

POLONIUS   Yet here, Laertes! aboard, aboard, for shame!
  The wind sits in the shoulder of your sail,
  And you are stay'd for. There; my blessing with thee!
  And these few precepts in thy memory
  See thou character. Give thy thoughts no tongue,
  Nor any unproportion'd thought his act.
  Be thou familiar, but by no means vulgar.
  Those friends thou hast, and their adoption tried,
  Grapple them to thy soul with hoops of steel;
  But do not dull thy palm with entertainment
  Of each new-hatch'd, unfledged comrade. Beware
  Of entrance to a quarrel, but being in,
  Bear't that the opposed may beware of thee.
  Give every man thy ear, but few thy voice;
  Take each man's censure, but reserve thy judgement.
  Costly thy habit as thy purse can buy,
  But not express'd in fancy; rich, not gaudy;
  For the apparel oft proclaims the man,
  And they in France of the best rank and station
  Are of a most select and generous chief in that.
  Neither a borrower nor a lender be;
  For loan oft loses both itself and friend,
  And borrowing dulls the edge of husbandry.
  This above all: to thine own self be true,
  And it must follow, as the night the day,
  Thou canst not then be false to any man.
  Farewell: my blessing season this in thee!

LAERTES   Most humbly do I take my leave, my lord.

POLONIUS   The time invites you; go; your servants tend.

LAERTES   Farewell, Ophelia; and remember well
  What I have said to you.

OPHELIA   'Tis in my memory lock'd,
  And you yourself shall keep the key of it.

LAERTES   Farewell.   *Exit.*

POLONIUS   What is't, Ophelia, he hath said to you?

OPHELIA   So please you, something touching the Lord Hamlet.

POLONIUS   Marry, well bethought:
  'Tis told me, he hath very oft of late
  Given private time to you; and you yourself
  Have of your audience been most free and bounteous:
  If it be so, as so 'tis put on me,
  And that in way of caution, I must tell you,
  You do not understand yourself so clearly
  As it behoves my daughter and your honour.
  What is between you? give me up the truth.

OPHELIA   He hath, my lord, of late made many tenders
  Of his affection to me.

POLONIUS   Affection! pooh! you speak like a green girl,
  Unsifted in such perilous circumstance.
  Do you believe his tenders, as you call them?

OPHELIA   I do not know, my lord, what I should think.

POLONIUS   Marry, I'll teach you: think yourself a baby;
  That you have ta'en these tenders for true pay,
  Which are not sterling. Tender yourself more dearly;
  Or—not to crack the wind of the poor phrase,
  Running it thus—you'll tender me a fool.

OPHELIA   My lord, he hath importuned me with love
  In honourable fashion.

POLONIUS   Ay, fashion you may call it; go to, go to.

OPHELIA   And hath given countenance to his speech, my lord,
  With almost all the holy vows of heaven.

POLONIUS   Ay, springes to catch woodcocks. I do know,
  When the blood burns, how prodigal the soul
  Lends the tongue vows: these blazes, daughter,
  Giving more light than heat, extinct in both,
  Even in their promise, as it is a-making,

187

You must not take for fire. From this time
Be somewhat scanter of your maiden presence;
Set your entreatments at a higher rate
Than a command to parley. For Lord Hamlet,
Believe so much in him, that he is young,
And with a larger tether may he walk
Than may be given you: in few, Ophelia,
Do not believe his vows; for they are brokers,
Not of that dye which their investments show,
But mere implorators of unholy suits,
Breathing like sanctified and pious bawds,
The better to beguile. This is for all:
I would not, in plain terms, from this time forth,
Have you so slander any moment leisure,
As to give words or talk with the Lord Hamlet.
Look to't, I charge you: come your ways.

OPHELIA   I shall obey, my lord.   *Exeunt.*

✿ SCENE 4   *The platform.*

Enter Hamlet, Horatio, and Marcellus.

HAMLET   The air bites shrewdly; it is very cold.

HORATIO   It is a nipping and an eager air.

HAMLET   What hour now?

HORATIO   I think it lacks of twelve.

MARCELLUS   No, it is struck.

HORATIO   Indeed? I heard it not: then it draws near the season
Wherein the spirit held his wont to walk.

A flourish of trumpets, and ordnance shot off, within.

What does this mean, my lord?

HAMLET   The King doth wake to-night and takes his rouse,
Keeps wassail, and the swaggering up-spring reels;
And, as he drains his draughts of Rhenish down,
The kettle-drum and trumpet thus bray out
The triumph of his pledge.

HORATIO   Is it a custom?

HAMLET   Ay, marry, is't:
   But to my mind, though I am native here
   And to the manner born, it is a custom
   More honour'd in the breach than the observance.
   This heavy-headed revel east and west
   Makes us traduced and tax'd of other nations:
   They clepe us drunkards, and with swinish phrase
   Soil our addition; and indeed it takes
   From our achievements, though perform'd at height,
   The pith and marrow of our attribute.
   So, oft it chances in particular men,
   That for some vicious mole of nature in them,
   As, in their birth—wherein they are not guilty,
   Since nature cannot choose his origin—
   By the o'ergrowth of some complexion,
   Oft breaking down the pales and forts of reason,
   Or by some habit that too much o'er-leavens
   The form of plausive manners, that these men,
   Carrying, I say, the stamp of one defect,
   Being nature's livery, or fortune's star—
   Their virtues else—be they as pure as grace,
   As infinite as man may undergo—
   Shall in the general censure take corruption
   From that particular fault: the dram of eale
   Doth all the noble substance of a doubt
   To his own scandal.

HORATIO   Look, my lords, it comes!

Enter Ghost.

HAMLET   Angels and ministers of grace defend us!
   Be thou a spirit of health or goblin damn'd,
   Bring with thee airs from heaven or blasts from hell,
   Be thy intents wicked or charitable,
   Thou comest in such a questionable shape
   That I will speak to thee. I'll call thee Hamlet,
   King, father, royal Dane: O, answer me!
   Let me not burst in ignorance; but tell
   Why thy canonized bones, hearsed in death,
   Have burst their cerements; why the sepulchre,
   Wherein we saw thee quietly inurn'd,
   Hath oped his ponderous and marble jaws,

189

To cast thee up again. What may this mean,
That thou, dead corse, again in complete steel
Revisit'st thus the glimpses of the moon,
Making night hideous; and we fools of nature
So horridly to shake our disposition
With thoughts beyond the reaches of our souls?
Say, why is this? wherefore? what should we do?

Ghost beckons Hamlet.

HORATIO   It beckons you to go away with it,
As if it some impartment did desire
To you alone.

MARCELLUS   Look, with what courteous action
It waves you to a more removed ground:
But do not go with it.

HORATIO   No, by no means.

HAMLET   It will not speak; then I will follow it.

HORATIO   Do not, my lord.

HAMLET   Why, what should be the fear?
I do not set my life at a pin's fee;
And for my soul, what can it do to that,
Being a thing immortal as itself?
It waves me forth again: I'll follow it.

HORATIO   What if it tempt you toward the flood, my lord,
Or to the dreadful summit of the cliff
That beetles o'er his base into the sea,
And there assume some other horrible form,
Which might deprive your sovereignty of reason
And draw you into madness? think of it.
The very place puts toys of desperation,
Without more motive, into every brain
That looks so many fathoms to the sea
And hears it roar beneath.

HAMLET   It waves me still.
Go on; I'll follow thee.

MARCELLUS   You shall not go, my lord.

HAMLET   Hold off your hands.

HORATIO   Be ruled; you shall not go.

HAMLET   My fate cries out,
   And makes each petty artery in this body
   As hardy as the Nemean lion's nerve.
   Still am I call'd. Unhand me, gentlemen.
   By heaven, I'll make a ghost of him that lets me!
   I say, away! Go on; I'll follow thee.   *Exeunt Ghost and Hamlet.*

HORATIO   He waxes desperate with imagination.

MARCELLUS   Let's follow; 'tis not fit thus to obey him.

HORATIO   Have after. To what issue will this come?

MARCELLUS   Something is rotten in the state of Denmark.

HORATIO   Heaven will direct it.

MARCELLUS   Nay, let's follow him.   *Exeunt.*

✤ SCENE 5   *Another part of the platform.*

Enter Ghost and Hamlet.

HAMLET   Where wilt thou lead me? speak; I'll go no further.

GHOST   Mark me.

HAMLET   I will.

GHOST   My hour is almost come,
   When I to sulphurous and tormenting flames
   Must render up myself.

HAMLET   Alas, poor ghost!

GHOST   Pity me not, but lend thy serious hearing
   To what I shall unfold.

HAMLET   Speak; I am bound to hear.

GHOST   So art thou to revenge, when thou shalt hear.

HAMLET   What?

GHOST   I am thy father's spirit,
   Doom'd for a certain term to walk the night,
   And for the day confined to fast in fires,
   Till the foul crimes done in my days of nature

191

Are burnt and purged away. But that I am forbid
To tell the secrets of my prison-house,
I could a tale unfold whose lightest word
Would harrow up thy soul, freeze thy young blood,
Make thy two eyes, like stars, start from their spheres,
Thy knotted and combined locks to part
And each particular hair to stand an end,
Like quills upon the fretful porpentine.
But this eternal blazon must not be
To ears of flesh and blood. List, list, O, list!
If thou didst ever thy dear father love —

HAMLET   O God!

GHOST   Revenge his foul and most unnatural murder.

HAMLET   Murder!

GHOST   Murder most foul, as in the best it is;
But this most foul, strange, and unnatural.

HAMLET   Haste me to know't, that I, with wings as swift
As meditation or the thoughts of love,
May sweep to my revenge.

GHOST   I find thee apt;
And duller shouldst thou be than the fat weed
That roots itself in ease on Lethe wharf,
Wouldst thou not stir in this. Now, Hamlet, hear:
'Tis given out that, sleeping in my orchard,
A serpent stung me; so the whole ear of Denmark
Is by a forged process of my death
Rankly abused: but know, thou noble youth,
The serpent that did sting thy father's life
Now wears his crown.

HAMLET   O my prophetic soul!
My uncle!

GHOST   Ay, that incestuous, that adulterate beast,
With witchcraft of his wit, with traitorous gifts —
O wicked wit and gifts, that have the power
So to seduce! — won to his shameful lust
The will of my most seeming-virtuous queen:
O Hamlet, what a falling-off was there!

192

From me, whose love was of that dignity
That it went hand in hand even with the vow
I made to her in marriage, and to decline
Upon a wretch whose natural gifts were poor
To those of mine!
But virtue, as it never will be moved,
Though lewdness court it in a shape of heaven,
So lust, though to a radiant angel link'd,
Will sate itself in a celestial bed,
And prey on garbage.
But, soft! methinks I scent the morning air;
Brief let me be. Sleeping within my orchard,
My custom always of the afternoon,
Upon my secure hour thy uncle stole,
With juice of cursed hebenon in a vial,
And in the porches of my ears did pour
The leperous distilment; whose effect
Holds such an enmity with blood of man
That swift as quicksilver it courses through
The natural gates and alleys of the body,
And with a sudden vigour it doth posset
And curd, like eager droppings into milk,
The thin and wholesome blood. So did it mine;
And a most instant tetter bark'd about,
Most lazar-like, with vile and loathsome crust,
All my smooth body.
Thus was I, sleeping, by a brother's hand
Of life, of crown, of queen, at once dispatch'd:
Cut off even in the blossoms of my sin,
Unhousel'd, disappointed, unaneled,
No reckoning made, but sent to my account
With all my imperfections on my head.
O, horrible! O, horrible! most horrible!
If thou hast nature in thee, bear it not;
Let not the royal bed of Denmark be
A couch for luxury and damned incest.
But, howsoever thou pursuest this act,
Taint not thy mind, nor let thy soul contrive
Against thy mother aught: leave her to heaven
And to those thorns that in her bosom lodge,
To prick and sting her. Fare thee well at once!

The glow-worm shows the matin to be near,
And 'gins to pale his uneffectual fire:
Adieu, adieu! Hamlet, remember me.   *Exit.*

HAMLET   O all you host of heaven! O earth! what else?
And shall I couple hell? O, fie! Hold, hold, my heart;
And you, my sinews, grow not instant old,
But bear me stiffly up. Remember thee!
Ay, thou poor ghost, while memory holds a seat
In this distracted globe. Remember thee!
Yea, from the table of my memory
I'll wipe away all trivial fond records,
All saws of books, all forms, all pressures past,
That youth and observation copied there;
And thy commandment all alone shall live
Within the book and volume of my brain,
Unmix'd with baser matter. Yes, by heaven!
O most pernicious woman!
O villain, villain, smiling, damned villain!
My tables—meet it is I set it down,
That one may smile, and smile, and be a villain;
At least I'm sure it may be so in Denmark:

Writing.

So, uncle, there you are. Now to my word;
It is "Adieu, adieu! remember me."
I have sworn't.

MARCELLUS AND HORATIO   [*Within.*] My lord, my lord—

MARCELLUS   [*Within.*] Lord Hamlet—

HORATIO   [*Within.*] Heaven secure him!

HAMLET   So be it!

HORATIO   [*Within.*] Hillo, ho, ho, my lord!

HAMLET   Hillo, ho, ho, boy! come, bird, come.

Enter Horatio and Marcellus.

MARCELLUS   How is't, my noble lord?

HORATIO   What news, my lord?

HAMLET   O, wonderful!

194

HORATIO   Good my lord, tell it.

HAMLET   No; you'll reveal it.

HORATIO   Not I, my lord, by heaven.

MARCELLUS   Nor I, my lord.

HAMLET   How say you, then; would heart of man once think it?
  But you'll be secret?

HORATIO AND MARCELLUS   Ay, by heaven, my lord.

HAMLET   There's ne'er a villain dwelling in all Denmark
  But he's an arrant knave.

HORATIO   There needs no ghost, my lord, come from the grave
  To tell us this.

HAMLET   Why, right; you are i' the right;
  And so, without more circumstance at all,
  I hold it fit that we shake hands and part:
  You, as your business and desire shall point you;
  For every man has business and desire,
  Such as it is; and for mine own poor part,
  Look you, I'll go pray.

HORATIO   These are but wild and whirling words, my lord.

HAMLET   I'm sorry they offend you, heartily;
  Yes, 'faith, heartily.

HORATIO   There's no offence, my lord.

HAMLET   Yes, by Saint Patrick, but there is, Horatio,
  And much offence too. Touching this vision here,
  It is an honest ghost, that let me tell you,
  For your desire to know what is between us,
  O'ermaster't as you may. And now, good friends,
  As you are friends, scholars, and soldiers,
  Give me one poor request.

HORATIO   What is't, my lord? we will.

HAMLET   Never make known what you have seen to-night.

HORATIO AND MARCELLUS   My Lord, we will not.

HAMLET   Nay, but swear't.

195

HORATIO   In faith,
  My lord, not I.

MARCELLUS   Nor I, my lord, in faith.

HAMLET   Upon my sword.

MARCELLUS   We have sworn, my lord, already.

HAMLET   Indeed, upon my sword, indeed.

GHOST   [*Beneath.*] Swear.

HAMLET   Ah, ha, boy! say'st thou so? art thou there, truepenny?
  Come on—you hear this fellow in the cellarage—
  Consent to swear.

HORATIO   Propose the oath, my lord.

HAMLET   Never to speak of this that you have seen,
  Swear by my sword.

GHOST   [*Beneath.*] Swear.

HAMLET   *Hic et ubique?* then we'll shift our ground.
  Come higher, gentlemen,
  And lay your hands again upon my sword:
  Never to speak of this that you have heard,
  Swear by my sword.

GHOST   [*Beneath.*] Swear.

HAMLET   Well said, old mole! canst work i' the earth so fast?
  A worthy pioner! Once more remove, good friends.

HORATIO   O day and night, but this is wondrous strange!

HAMLET   And therefore as a stranger give it welcome.
  There are more things in heaven and earth, Horatio,
  Than are dreamt of in your philosophy.
  But come;
  Here, as before, never, so help you mercy,
  How strange or odd soe'er I bear myself,
  As I perchance hereafter shall think meet
  To put an antic disposition on,
  That you, at such times seeing me, never shall,
  With arms encumber'd thus, or this headshake,
  Or by pronouncing of some doubtful phrase,
  As "Well, well, we know," or "We could, an if we would,"

196

Or "If we list to speak," or "There be, an if they might,"
Or such ambiguous giving out, to note
That you know aught of me: this not to do,
So grace and mercy at your most need help you,
Swear.

GHOST [*Beneath.*] Swear.

They swear.

HAMLET Rest, rest, perturbed spirit! So, gentlemen,
With all my love I do commend me to you:
And what so poor a man as Hamlet is
May do, to express his love and friending to you,
God willing, shall not lack. Let us go in together;
And still your fingers on your lips, I pray.
The time is out of joint: O cursed spite,
That ever I was born to set it right!
Nay, come, let's go together.   *Exeunt.*

ACT II

SCENE 1   *A room in Polonius' house.*

Enter Polonius and Reynaldo.

POLONIUS   Give him this money and these notes, Reynaldo.

REYNALDO   I will, my lord.

POLONIUS   You shall do marvellous wisely, good Reynaldo,
Before you visit him, to make inquire
Of his behaviour.

REYNALDO   My lord, I did intend it.

POLONIUS   Marry, well said; very well said. Look you, sir,
Inquire me first what Danskers are in Paris;
And how, and who, what means, and where they keep,
What company, at what expense; and finding
By this encompassment and drift of question
That they do know my son, come you more nearer
Than your particular demands will touch it.
Take you, as 'twere, some distant knowledge of him;
As thus, "I know his father and his friends,
And in part him": do you mark this, Reynaldo?

REYNALDO   Ay, very well, my lord.

POLONIUS   "And in part him; but" you may say "not well:
But, if't be he I mean, he's very wild;
Addicted so and so": and there put on him
What forgeries you please; marry, none so rank
As may dishonour him; take heed of that;

198

But, sir, such wanton, wild, and usual slips
As are companions noted and most known
To youth and liberty.

REYNALDO   As gaming, my lord.

POLONIUS   Ay, or drinking, fencing, swearing, quarrelling,
  Drabbing: you may go so far.

REYNALDO   My lord, that would dishonour him.

POLONIUS   'Faith, no; as you may season it in the charge.
  You must not put another scandal on him,
  That he is open to incontinency;
  That's not my meaning. But breathe his faults so quaintly
  That they may seem the taints of liberty,
  The flash and outbreak of a fiery mind,
  A savageness in unreclaimed blood,
  Of general assault.

REYNALDO   But, my good lord—

POLONIUS   Wherefore should you do this?

REYNALDO   Ay, my lord,
  I would know that.

POLONIUS   Marry, sir, here's my drift;
  And, I believe, it is a fetch of wit.
  You laying these slight sullies on my son,
  As 'twere a thing a little soil'd i' the working,
  Mark you,
  Your party in converse, him you would sound,
  Having ever seen in the prenominate crimes
  The youth you breathe of guilty, be assured
  He closes with you in this consequence;
  "Good sir," or so, or "friend," or "gentleman,"
  According to the phrase or the addition
  Of man and country.

REYNALDO   Very good, my lord.

POLONIUS   And then, sir, does he this—he does—what was I about to
  say? By the mass, I was about to say something. Where did I leave?

REYNALDO   At "closes in the consequence," at "friend or so," and "gentleman."

199

POLONIUS   At "closes in the consequence," ay, marry;
　　He closes thus: "I know the gentleman;
　　I saw him yesterday, or t'other day,
　　Or then, or then; with such, or such; and, as you say,
　　There was a' gaming; there o'ertook in's rouse;
　　There falling out at tennis": or perchance,
　　"I saw him enter such a house of sale,"
　　Videlicet, a brothel, or so forth.
　　See you now;
　　Your bait of falsehood takes this carp of truth:
　　And thus do we of wisdom and of reach,
　　With windlasses and with assays of bias,
　　By indirections find directions out.
　　So by my former lecture and advice,
　　Shall you my son. You have me, have you not?

REYNALDO   My lord, I have.

POLONIUS   God be wi' you; fare you well.

REYNALDO   Good my lord!

POLONIUS   Observe his inclination in yourself.

REYNALDO   I shall, my lord.

POLONIUS   And let him ply his music.

REYNALDO   Well, my lord.

POLONIUS   Farewell!   *Exit Reynaldo.*

Enter Ophelia.

　　　　　　　　How now, Ophelia! what's the matter?

OPHELIA   O, my lord, my lord, I have been so affrighted!

POLONIUS   With what, i' the name of God?

OPHELIA   My lord, as I was sewing in my closet,
　　Lord Hamlet, with his doublet all unbraced;
　　No hat upon his head; his stockings foul'd,
　　Ungarter'd, and down-gyved to his ankle;
　　Pale as his shirt; his knees knocking each other;
　　And with a look so piteous in purport
　　As if he had been loosed out of hell
　　To speak of horrors—he comes before me.

200

POLONIUS   Mad for thy love?

OPHELIA   My lord, I do not know;
  But truly, I do fear it.

POLONIUS   What said he?

OPHELIA   He took me by the wrist and held me hard;
  Then goes he to the length of all his arm;
  And, with his other hand thus o'er his brow,
  He falls to such perusal of my face
  As he would draw it. Long stay'd he so;
  At last, a little shaking of mine arm
  And thrice his head thus waving up and down,
  He raised a sigh so piteous and profound
  As it did seem to shatter all his bulk
  And end his being. That done, he lets me go;
  And, with his head over his shoulder turn'd,
  He seem'd to find his way without his eyes;
  For out o'doors he went without their helps,
  And, to the last, bended their light on me.

POLONIUS   Come, go with me: I will go seek the King.
  This is the very ecstasy of love,
  Whose violent property fordoes itself
  And leads the will to desperate undertakings
  As oft as any passion under heaven
  That does afflict our natures. I am sorry.
  What, have you given him any hard words of late?

OPHELIA   No, my good lord, but, as you did command,
  I did repel his letters and denied
  His access to me.

POLONIUS   That hath made him mad.
  I am sorry that with better heed and judgement
  I had not quoted him. I fear'd he did but trifle,
  And meant to wreck thee; but, beshrew my jealousy!
  By heaven, it is as proper to our age
  To cast beyond ourselves in our opinions
  As it is common for the younger sort
  To lack discretion. Come, go we to the King:
  This must be known; which, being kept close, might move
  More grief to hide than hate to utter love.   *Exeunt.*

201

❧ SCENE 2   *A room in the castle.*

Enter King, Queen, Rosencrantz, Guildenstern, and Attendants.

KING   Welcome, dear Rosencrantz and Guildenstern!
  Moreover that we much did long to see you,
  The need we have to use you did provoke
  Our hasty sending. Something have you heard
  Of Hamlet's transformation; so call it,
  Sith nor the exterior nor the inward man
  Resembles that it was. What it should be,
  More than his father's death, that thus hath put him
  So much from the understanding of himself,
  I cannot dream of. I entreat you both
  That, being of so young days brought up with him,
  And sith so neighbour'd to his youth and humour,
  That you vouchsafe your rest here in our court
  Some little time; so by your companies
  To draw him on to pleasures, and to gather,
  So much as from occasion you may glean,
  Whether aught, to us unknown, afflicts him thus,
  That, open'd, lies within our remedy.

QUEEN   Good gentlemen, he hath much talk'd of you;
  And sure I am two men there are not living
  To whom he more adheres. If it will please you
  To show us so much gentry and good will
  As to expend your time with us awhile,
  For the supply and profit of our hope,
  Your visitation shall receive such thanks
  As fits a king's remembrance.

ROSENCRANTZ   Both your Majesties
  Might, by the sovereign power you have of us,
  Put your dread pleasures more into command
  Than to entreaty.

GUILDENSTERN   But we both obey,
  And here give up ourselves, in the full bent
  To lay our service freely at your feet,
  To be commanded.

KING   Thanks, Rosencrantz and gentle Guildenstern.

QUEEN   Thanks, Guildenstern and gentle Rosencrantz:

And I beseech you instantly to visit
My too much changed son. Go, some of you,
And bring these gentlemen where Hamlet is.

GUILDENSTERN   Heavens make our presence and our practices
Pleasant and helpful to him!

QUEEN   Ay, amen!
                    Exeunt Rosencrantz, Guildenstern, and some Attendants.

Enter Polonius.

POLONIUS   The ambassadors from Norway, my good lord,
Are joyfully return'd.

KING   Thou still hast been the father of good news.

POLONIUS   Have I, my lord? I assure my good liege,
I hold my duty, as I hold my soul,
Both to my God and to my gracious king:
And I do think, or else this brain of mine
Hunts not the trail of policy so sure
As it hath used to do, that I have found
The very cause of Hamlet's lunacy.

KING   O, speak of that; that do I long to hear.

POLONIUS   Give first admittance to the ambassadors;
My news shall be the fruit to that great feast.

KING   Thyself do grace to them, and bring them in.   *Exit Polonius.*
He tells me, my dear Gertrude, he hath found
The head and source of all your son's distemper.

QUEEN   I doubt it is no other but the main;
His father's death, and our o'erhasty marriage.

KING   Well, we shall sift him.

Re-enter Polonius, with Voltimand and Cornelius.

                                Welcome, my good friends!
Say, Voltimand, what from our brother Norway?

VOLTIMAND   Most fair return of greetings and desires.
Upon our first, he sent out to suppress
His nephew's levies; which to him appear'd
To be a preparation 'gainst the Polack;
But, better look'd into, he truly found

It was against your Highness: whereat grieved,
That so to his sickness, age, and impotence
Was falsely borne in hand, sends out arrests
On Fortinbras; which he, in brief, obeys;
Receives rebuke from Norway, and in fine
Makes vow before his uncle never more
To give the assay of arms against your Majesty.
Whereon old Norway, overcome with joy,
Gives him three thousand crowns in annual fee,
And his commission to employ those soldiers,
So levied as before, against the Polack:
With an entreaty, herein further shown,

Giving a paper.

That it might please you to give quiet pass
Through your dominions for this enterprise,
On such regards of safety and allowance
As therein are set down.

KING   It likes us well;
And at our more consider'd time we'll read,
Answer, and think upon this business.
Meantime we thank you for your well-took labour.
Go to your rest; at night we'll feast together.
Most welcome home!   *Exeunt Voltimand and Cornelius.*

POLONIUS   This business is well ended.
My liege, and madam, to expostulate
What majesty should be, what duty is,
Why day is day, night night, and time is time,
Were nothing but to waste night, day, and time.
Therefore, since brevity is the soul of wit,
And tediousness the limbs and outward flourishes,
I will be brief: your noble son is mad.
Mad call I it; for, to define true madness,
What is't but to be nothing else but mad?
But let that go.

QUEEN   More matter, with less art.

POLONIUS   Madam, I swear I use no art at all.
That he is mad, 'tis true: 'tis true 'tis pity;
And pity 'tis 'tis true. A foolish figure;
But farewell it, for I will use no art.

204

Mad let us grant him, then; and now remains
That we find out the cause of this effect,
Or rather say, the cause of this defect,
For this effect defective comes by cause.
Thus it remains and the remainder thus.
Perpend.
I have a daughter—have while she is mine—
Who, in her duty and obedience, mark,
Hath given me this. Now gather, and surmise. [*Reads.*]

"To the celestial and my soul's idol, the most beautified Ophelia"—

That's an ill phrase, a vile phrase; "beautified" is a vile phrase: but you
shall hear. Thus: [*Reads.*]

"In her excellent white bosom, these, &c."

QUEEN   Came this from Hamlet to her?

POLONIUS   Good madam, stay awhile; I will be faithful. [*Reads.*]

> "Doubt thou the stars are fire;
>   Doubt that the sun doth move;
>   Doubt truth to be a liar;
>   But never doubt I love.

"O dear Ophelia, I am ill at these numbers; I have not art to reckon
my groans: but that I love thee best, O most best, believe it, Adieu.

"Thine evermore, most dear lady, whilst this machine is to him,
Hamlet."

This, in obedience, hath my daughter shown me,
And more above, hath his solicitings,
As they fell out by time, by means, and place,
All given to mine ear.

KING   But how hath she
Received his love?

POLONIUS   What do you think of me?

KING   As of a man faithful and honourable.

POLONIUS   I would fain prove so. But what might you think,
When I had seen this hot love on the wing—
As I perceived it, I must tell you that,
Before my daughter told me—what might you,
Or my dear Majesty your queen here, think,

205

If I had play'd the desk or table-book,
Or given my heart a winking, mute and dumb,
Or look'd upon this love with idle sight;
What might you think? No, I went round to work,
And my young mistress thus I did bespeak:
"Lord Hamlet is a prince, out of thy star;
This must not be": and then I prescripts gave her,
That she should lock herself from his resort,
Admit no messengers, receive no tokens.
Which done, she took the fruits of my advice;
And he, repulsed—a short tale to make—
Fell into a sadness, then into a fast,
Thence to a watch, thence into a weakness,
Thence to a lightness, and, by this declension,
Into the madness wherein now he raves,
And all we mourn for.

KING   Do you think 'tis this?

QUEEN   It may be, very likely.

POLONIUS   Hath there been such a time—I'd fain know that—
    That I have positively said " 'Tis so,"
    When it proved otherwise?

KING   Not that I know.

POLONIUS   [*Pointing to his head and shoulder.*] Take this from this, if this be
    otherwise:
    If circumstances lead me, I will find
    Where truth is hid, though it were hid indeed
    Within the centre.

KING   How may we try it further?

POLONIUS   You know, sometimes he walks four hours together
    Here in the lobby.

QUEEN   So he does indeed.

POLONIUS   At such a time I'll loose my daughter to him:
    Be you and I behind an arras then;
    Mark the encounter. If he love her not
    And be not from his reason fall'n thereon,
    Let me be no assistant for a state,
    But keep a farm and carters.

206

ACT II   Scene 2

KING   We will try it.

QUEEN   But, look, where sadly the poor wretch comes reading.

POLONIUS   Away, I do beseech you, both away:
I'll board him presently.   *Exeunt King, Queen, and Attendants.*

Enter Hamlet, reading.

O, give me leave,
How does my good Lord Hamlet?

HAMLET   Well, God-a-mercy.

POLONIUS   Do you know me, my lord?

HAMLET   Excellent well; you are a fishmonger.

POLONIUS   Not I, my lord.

HAMLET   Then I would you were so honest a man.

POLONIUS   Honest, my lord!

HAMLET   Ay, sir; to be honest, as this world goes, is to be one man picked out of ten thousand.

POLONIUS   That's very true, my lord.

HAMLET   For if the sun breed maggots in a dead dog, being a god kissing carrion— Have you a daughter?

POLONIUS   I have, my lord.

HAMLET   Let her not walk i' the sun. Conception is a blessing, but not as your daughter may conceive. Friend, look to't.

POLONIUS   [*Aside.*] How say you by that? Still harping on my daughter: yet he knew me not at first; he said I was a fishmonger: he is far gone, far gone, and truly in my youth I suffered much extremity for love; very near this. I'll speak to him again. What do you read, my lord?

HAMLET   Words, words, words.

POLONIUS   What is the matter, my lord?

HAMLET   Between who?

POLONIUS   I mean, the matter that you read, my lord.

HAMLET   Slanders, sir: for the satirical rogue says here that old men have grey beards, that their faces are wrinkled, their eyes purging thick

207

amber and plum-tree gum and that they have a plentiful lack of wit, together with most weak hams; all which, sir, though I most power-fully and potently believe, yet I hold it not honesty to have it thus set down, for yourself, sir, should be old as I am, if like a crab you could go backward.

POLONIUS [*Aside.*] Though this be madness, yet there is method in't. Will you walk out of the air, my lord?

HAMLET Into my grave.

POLONIUS Indeed, that is out o' the air. [*Aside.*] How pregnant some-times his replies are! a happiness that often madness hits on, which rea-son and sanity could not so prosperously be delivered of. I will leave him, and suddenly contrive the means of meeting between him and my daughter.—My honourable lord, I will most humbly take my leave of you.

HAMLET You cannot, sir, take from me any thing that I will more will-ingly part withal: except my life, except my life, except my life.

POLONIUS Fare you well, my lord.

HAMLET These tedious old fools!

Enter Rosencrantz and Guildenstern.

POLONIUS You go to seek the Lord Hamlet; there he is.

ROSENCRANTZ [*To Polonius.*] God save you, sir!   *Exit Polonius.*

GUILDENSTERN My honoured lord!

ROSENCRANTZ My most dear lord!

HAMLET My excellent good friends! How dost thou, Guildenstern? Ah, Rosencrantz! Good lads, how do ye both?

ROSENCRANTZ As the indifferent children of the earth.

GUILDENSTERN Happy, in that we are not over-happy;
On fortune's cap we are not the very button.

HAMLET Nor the soles of her shoe?

ROSENCRANTZ Neither, my lord.

HAMLET Then you live about her waist, or in the middle of her favours?

GUILDENSTERN 'Faith, her privates we.

208

HAMLET   In the secret parts of fortune? O, most true; she is a strumpet. What's the news?

ROSENCRANTZ   None, my lord, but that the world's grown honest.

HAMLET   Then is doomsday near. But your news is not true. Let me question more in particular. What have you, my good friends, deserved at the hands of fortune, that she sends you to prison hither?

GUILDENSTERN   Prison, my lord!

HAMLET   Denmark's a prison.

ROSENCRANTZ   Then is the world one.

HAMLET   A goodly one; in which there are many confines, wards, and dungeons, Denmark being one o' the worst.

ROSENCRANTZ   We think not so, my lord.

HAMLET   Why, then, 'tis none to you; for there is nothing either good or bad, but thinking makes it so. To me it is a prison.

ROSENCRANTZ   Why then, your ambition makes it one; 'tis too narrow for your mind.

HAMLET   O God, I could be bounded in a nutshell and count myself a king of infinite space, were it not that I have bad dreams.

GUILDENSTERN   Which dreams indeed are ambition, for the very substance of the ambitious is merely the shadow of a dream.

HAMLET   A dream itself is but a shadow.

ROSENCRANTZ   Truly, and I hold ambition of so airy and light a quality that it is but a shadow's shadow.

HAMLET   Then are our beggars bodies, and our monarchs and outstretched heroes the beggars' shadows. Shall we to the court? for, by my fay, I cannot reason.

ROSENCRANTZ AND GUILDENSTERN   We'll wait upon you.

HAMLET   No such matter. I will not sort you with the rest of my servants, for, to speak to you like an honest man, I am most dreadfully attended. But, in the beaten way of friendship, what make you at Elsinore?

ROSENCRANTZ   To visit you, my lord; no other occasion.

HAMLET   Beggar that I am, I am even poor in thanks; but I thank you:

209

and sure, dear friends, my thanks are too dear a halfpenny. Were you not sent for? Is it your own inclining? Is it a free visitation? Come, deal justly with me. Come, come; nay, speak.

GUILDENSTERN   What should we say, my lord?

HAMLET   Why, any thing, but to the purpose. You were sent for; and there is a kind of confession in your looks which your modesties have not craft enough to colour. I know the good King and Queen have sent for you.

ROSENCRANTZ   To what end, my lord?

HAMLET   That you must teach me. But let me conjure you, by the rights of our fellowship, by the consonancy of our youth, by the obligation of our ever-preserved love, and by what more dear a better proposer could charge you withal, be even and direct with me, whether you were sent for, or no?

ROSENCRANTZ   [Aside to Guildenstern.] What say you?

HAMLET   [Aside.] Nay, then, I have an eye of you. —If you love me, hold not off.

GUILDENSTERN   My lord, we were sent for.

HAMLET   I will tell you why; so shall my anticipation prevent your discovery, and your secrecy to the King and Queen moult no feather. I have of late —but wherefore I know not—lost all my mirth, forgone all custom of exercises; and indeed it goes so heavily with my disposition that this goodly frame, the earth, seems to me a sterile promontory, this most excellent canopy, the air, look you, this brave o'erhanging firmament, this majestical roof fretted with golden fire, why, it appears no other thing to me than a foul and pestilent congregation of vapours. What a piece of work is a man! how noble in reason! how infinite in faculty! in form and moving how express and admirable! in action how like an angel! in apprehension how like a god! the beauty of the world! the paragon of animals! And yet, to me, what is this quintessence of dust? man delights not me: no, nor woman neither, though by your smiling you seem to say so.

ROSENCRANTZ   My lord, there was no such stuff in my thoughts.

HAMLET   Why did you laugh then, when I said "man delights not me"?

ROSENCRANTZ   To think, my lord, if you delight not in man, what lenten

entertainment the players shall receive from you. We coted them on the way; and hither are they coming, to offer you service.

HAMLET   He that plays the king shall be welcome; his Majesty shall have tribute of me; the adventurous knight shall use his foil and target; the lover shall not sigh *gratis;* the humorous man shall end his part in peace; the clown shall make those laugh whose lungs are tickle o' the sere; and the lady shall say her mind freely, or the blank verse shall halt for't. What players are they?

ROSENCRANTZ   Even those you were wont to take delight in, the tragedians of the city.

HAMLET   How chances it they travel? their residence, both in reputation and profit, was better both ways.

ROSENCRANTZ   I think their inhibition comes by the means of the late innovation.

HAMLET   Do they hold the same estimation they did when I was in the city? are they so followed?

ROSENCRANTZ   No, indeed, are they not.

HAMLET   How comes it? do they grow rusty?

ROSENCRANTZ   Nay, their endeavour keeps in the wonted pace; but there is, sir, an aery of children, little eyases, that cry out on the top of question, and are most tyrannically clapped for't. These are now the fashion, and so berattle the common stages—so they call them—that many wearing rapiers are afraid of goose-quills and dare scarce come thither.

HAMLET   What, are they children? who maintains 'em? how are they escoted? Will they pursue the quality no longer than they can sing? will they not say afterwards, if they should grow themselves to common players—as it is most like, if their means are no better—their writers do them wrong, to make them exclaim against their own succession?

ROSENCRANTZ   'Faith, there has been much to-do on both sides; and the nation holds it no sin to tarre them to controversy. There was, for a while, no money bid for argument, unless the poet and the player went to cuffs in the question.

HAMLET   Is't possible?

GUILDENSTERN   O, there has been much throwing about of brains.

211

HAMLET   Do the boys carry it away?

ROSENCRANTZ   Ay, that they do, my lord; Hercules and his load too.

HAMLET   It is not very strange; for mine uncle is King of Denmark, and those that would make mows at him while my father lived, give twenty, forty, fifty, an hundred ducats a-piece for his picture in little. 'Sblood, there is something in this more than natural, if philosophy could find it out.

Flourish of trumpets, within.

GUILDENSTERN   There are the players.

HAMLET   Gentlemen, you are welcome to Elsinore. Your hands, come then. The appurtenance of welcome is fashion and ceremony. Let me comply with you in this garb, lest my extent to the players, which, I tell you, must show fairly outward, should more appear like entertainment than yours. You are welcome; but my uncle-father and aunt-mother are deceived.

GUILDENSTERN   In what, my dear lord?

HAMLET   I am but mad north-north-west. When the wind is southerly I know a hawk from a handsaw.

Re-enter Polonius.

POLONIUS   Well be with you, gentlemen!

HAMLET   Hark you, Guildenstern; and you too: at each ear a hearer: that great baby you see there is not yet out of his swaddling-clouts.

ROSENCRANTZ   Happily he's the second time come to them; for they say an old man is twice a child.

HAMLET   I will prophesy he comes to tell me of the players; mark it. [*Aloud.*] You say right, sir: o' Monday morning; 'twas so indeed.

POLONIUS   My lord, I have news to tell you.

HAMLET   My lord, I have news to tell you. When Roscius was an actor in Rome —

POLONIUS   The actors are come hither, my lord.

HAMLET   Buz, buz!

POLONIUS   Upon mine honour —

HAMLET   Then came each actor on his ass —

POLONIUS   The best actors in the world, either for tragedy, comedy, history, pastoral, pastoral-comical, historical-pastoral, tragical-historical, tragical-comical-historical-pastoral, scene individable, or poem unlimited; Seneca cannot be too heavy, nor Plautus too light. For the law of writ and the liberty, these are the only men.

HAMLET   O Jephthah, judge of Israel, what a treasure hadst thou!

POLONIUS   What a treasure had he, my lord?

HAMLET   Why,

> "One fair daughter, and no more,
>   The which he loved passing well."

POLONIUS   [*Aside.*] Still on my daughter.

HAMLET   Am I not i' the right, old Jephthah?

POLONIUS   If you call me Jephthah, my lord, I have a daughter that I love passing well.

HAMLET   Nay, that follows not.

POLONIUS   What follows, then, my lord?

HAMLET   Why,

> "As by lot, God wot,"

and then, you know,

> "It came to pass, as most like it was"

The first row of the pious chanson will show you more; for look, where my abridgement comes.

Enter four or five Players.

You are welcome, masters; welcome, all. I am glad to see thee well. Welcome, good friends. O, my old friend! thy face is valanced since I saw thee last; comest thou to beard me in Denmark? What, my young lady and mistress! By'r lady, your ladyship is nearer to heaven than when I saw you last, by the altitude of a chopine. Pray God, your voice, like a piece of uncurrent gold, be not cracked within the ring. Masters, you are all welcome. We'll e'en to't like French falconers, fly at anything we see: we'll have a speech straight. Come, give us a taste of your quality; come, a passionate speech.

FIRST PLAYER   What speech, my lord?

213

HAMLET I heard thee speak me a speech once, but it was never acted; or, if it was, not above once; for the play, I remember, pleased not the million; 'twas caviare to the general; but it was—as I received it, and others, whose judgements in such matters cried in the top of mine—an excellent play, well digested in the scenes, set down with as much modesty as cunning. I remember, one said there were no sallets in the lines to make the matter savoury, nor no matter in the phrase that might indict the author of affectation; but called it an honest method, as wholesome as sweet, and by very much more handsome than fine. One speech in it I chiefly loved: 'twas Aeneas' tale to Dido; and thereabout of it especially, where he speaks of Priam's slaughter. If it live in your memory, begin at this line: let me see, let me see—

"The rugged Pyrrhus, like the Hyrcanian beast—"

It is not so. It begins with Pyrrhus:

"The rugged Pyrrhus, he whose sable arms,
Black as his purpose, did the night resemble
When he lay couched in the ominous horse,
Hath now this dread and black complexion smear'd
With heraldry more dismal; head to foot
Now is he total gules; horridly trick'd
With blood of fathers, mothers, daughters, sons,
Baked and impasted with the parching streets,
That lend a tyrannous and damned light
To their lord's murder: roasted in wrath and fire,
And thus o'er-sized with coagulate gore,
With eyes like carbuncles, the hellish Pyrrhus
Old grandsire Priam seeks."

So, proceed you.

POLONIUS 'Fore God, my lord, well spoken, with good accent and good discretion.

FIRST PLAYER "Anon he finds him
Striking too short at Greeks; his antique sword,
Rebellious to his arm, lies where it falls,
Repugnant to command. Unequal match'd,
Pyrrhus at Priam drives; in rage strikes wide;
But with the whiff and wind of his fell sword
The unnerved father falls. Then senseless Ilium,
Seeming to feel this blow, with flaming top
Stoops to his base, and with a hideous crash

214

Takes prisoner Pyrrhus' ear; for, lo! his sword,
Which was declining on the milky head
Of reverend Priam, seem'd i' the air to stick.
So, as a painted tyrant, Pyrrhus stood,
And like a neutral to his will and matter,
Did nothing.
But, as we often see, against some storm,
A silence in the heavens, the rack stand still,
The bold winds speechless, and the orb below
As hush as death, anon the dreadful thunder
Doth rend the region, so, after Pyrrhus' pause,
Aroused vengeance sets him new a-work;
And never did the Cyclops' hammers fall
On Mars' armour forged for proof eterne
With less remorse than Pyrrhus' bleeding sword
Now falls on Priam.
Out, out, thou strumpet, Fortune! All you gods,
In general synod, take away her power;
Break all the spokes and fellies from her wheel,
And bowl the round nave down the hill of heaven,
As low as to the fiends!"

POLONIUS   This is too long.

HAMLET   It shall to the barber's, with your beard. Prithee, say on; he's
for a jig or a tale of bawdry, or he sleeps. Say on; come to Hecuba.

FIRST PLAYER   "But who, O, who had seen the mobled queen—"

HAMLET   "The mobled queen"?

POLONIUS   That's good; "mobled queen" is good.

FIRST PLAYER   "Run barefoot up and down, threatening the flames
With bisson rheum; a clout upon that head
Where late the diadem stood, and for a robe,
About her lank and all o'er-teemed loins,
A blanket, in the alarm of fear caught up;
Who this had seen, with tongue in venom steep'd,
'Gainst Fortune's state would treason have pronounced:
But if the gods themselves did see her then
When she saw Pyrrhus make malicious sport
In mincing with his sword her husband's limbs,
The instant burst of clamour that she made,

215

Unless things mortal move them not at all,
Would have made milch the burning eyes of heaven,
And passion in the gods."

POLONIUS   Look, whether he has not turned his colour and has tears in's eyes. Pray you, no more.

HAMLET   'Tis well; I'll have thee speak out the rest soon. Good my lord, will you see the players well bestowed? Do you hear, let them be well used; for they are the abstract and brief chronicles of the time; after your death you were better have a bad epitaph than their ill report while you live.

POLONIUS   My lord, I will use them according to their desert.

HAMLET   God's bodykins, man, much better. Use every man after his desert, and who should 'scape whipping? Use them after your own honour and dignity; the less they deserve, the more merit is in your bounty. Take them in.

POLONIUS   Come, sirs.

HAMLET   Follow him, friends: we'll hear a play to-morrow.
                    Exit Polonius with all the Players but the First.
Dost thou hear me, old friend; can you play "The Murder of Gonzago"?

FIRST PLAYER   Ay, my lord.

HAMLET   We'll ha't to-morrow night. You could, for a need, study a speech of some dozen or sixteen lines, which I would set down and insert in't, could you not?

FIRST PLAYER   Ay, my lord.

HAMLET   Very well. Follow that lord; and look you mock him not.
                              Exit First Player.
My good friends, I'll leave you till night: you are welcome to Elsinore.

ROSENCRANTZ   Good my lord!

HAMLET   Ay, so, God be wi' ye;   *Exeunt Rosencrantz and Guildenstern.*
                    Now I am alone.
O, what a rogue and peasant slave am I!
Is it not monstrous that this player here,
But in a fiction, in a dream of passion,
Could force his soul so to his own conceit
That from her working all his visage wann'd,

216

Tears in his eyes, distraction in's aspect,
A broken voice, and his whole function suiting
With forms to his conceit? and all for nothing!
For Hecuba!
What's Hecuba to him, or he to Hecuba,
That he should weep for her? What would he do,
Had he the motive and the cue for passion
That I have? He would drown the stage with tears
And cleave the general ear with horrid speech,
Make mad the guilty and appal the free,
Confound the ignorant, and amaze indeed
The very faculties of eyes and ears.
Yet I,
A dull and muddy-mettled rascal, peak,
Like John-a-dreams, unpregnant of my cause,
And can say nothing; no, not for a king,
Upon whose property and most dear life
A damn'd defeat was made. Am I a coward?
Who calls me villain? breaks my pate across?
Plucks off my beard, and blows it in my face?
Tweaks me by the nose? gives me the lie i' the throat,
As deep as to the lungs? who does me this?
Ha!
'Swounds, I should take it: for it cannot be
But I am pigeon-liver'd and lack gall
To make oppression bitter, or ere this
I should have fatted all the region kites
With this slave's offal. Bloody, bawdy villain!
Remorseless, treacherous, lecherous, kindless villain!
O, vengeance!
Why, what an ass am I! This is most brave,
That I, the son of a dear father murder'd,
Prompted to my revenge by heaven and hell,
Must, like a whore, unpack my heart with words,
And fall a-cursing, like a very drab,
A scullion!
Fie upon't! foh! About, my brain! I have heard
That guilty creatures sitting at a play
Have by the very cunning of the scene
Been struck so to the soul that presently
They have proclaim'd their malefactions;
For murder, though it have no tongue, will speak

With most miraculous organ. I'll have these players
Play something like the murder of my father
Before mine uncle. I'll observe his looks;
I'll tent him to the quick. If he but blench,
I know my course. The spirit that I have seen
May be the devil; and the devil hath power
To assume a pleasing shape; yea, and perhaps
Out of my weakness and my melancholy,
As he is very potent with such spirits,
Abuses me to damn me. I'll have grounds
More relative than this. The play's the thing
Wherein I'll catch the conscience of the King.   *Exit.*

ACT III

✿ SCENE 1 *A room in the castle.*

Enter King, Queen, Polonius, Ophelia, Rosencrantz, and Guildenstern.

KING   And can you, by no drift of circumstance,
   Get from him why he puts on this confusion,
   Grating so harshly all his days of quiet
   With turbulent and dangerous lunacy?

ROSENCRANTZ   He does confess he feels himself distracted;
   But from what cause he will by no means speak.

GUILDENSTERN   Nor do we find him forward to be sounded,
   But, with a crafty madness, keeps aloof,
   When we would bring him on to some confession
   Of his true state.

QUEEN   Did he receive you well?

ROSENCRANTZ   Most like a gentleman.

GUILDENSTERN   But with much forcing of his disposition.

ROSENCRANTZ   Niggard of question; but, of our demands,
   Most free in his reply.

QUEEN   Did you assay him
   To any pastime?

ROSENCRANTZ   Madam, it so fell out, that certain players
   We o'er-raught on the way; of these we told him,
   And there did seem in him a kind of joy
   To hear of it. They are about the court,

219

And, as I think, they have already order
This night to play before him.

POLONIUS   'Tis most true.
And he beseech'd me to entreat your Majesties
To hear and see the matter.

KING   With all my heart; and it doth much content me
To hear him so inclined.
Good gentlemen, give him a further edge,
And drive his purpose on to these delights.

ROSENCRANTZ   We shall, my lord.   *Exeunt Rosencrantz and Guildenstern.*

KING   Sweet Gertrude, leave us too;
For we have closely sent for Hamlet hither,
That he, as 'twere by accident, may here
Affront Ophelia.
Her father and myself, lawful espials,
Will so bestow ourselves that, seeing, unseen,
We may of their encounter frankly judge,
And gather by him, as he is behaved,
If't be the affliction of his love or no
That thus he suffers for.

QUEEN   I shall obey you.
And for your part, Ophelia, I do wish
That your good beauties be the happy cause
Of Hamlet's wildness: so shall I hope your virtues
Will bring him to his wonted way again,
To both your honours.

OPHELIA   Madam, I wish it may.   *Exit Queen.*

POLONIUS   Ophelia, walk you here. Gracious, so please you,
We will bestow ourselves. [*To Ophelia.*] Read on this book;
That show of such an exercise may colour
Your loneliness. We are oft to blame in this—
'Tis too much proved—that with devotion's visage
And pious action we do sugar o'er
The devil himself.

KING   [*Aside.*] O, 'tis too true!
How smart a lash that speech doth give my conscience!
The harlot's cheek, beautied with plastering art,
Is not more ugly to the thing that helps it

220

Than is my deed to my most painted word:
O heavy burthen!

POLONIUS   I hear him coming: let's withdraw, my lord.

Exeunt King and Polonius.

Enter Hamlet.

HAMLET   To be, or not to be: that is the question.
Whether 'tis nobler in the mind to suffer
The slings and arrows of outrageous fortune,
Or to take arms against a sea of troubles,
And by opposing end them? To die; to sleep;
No more; and by a sleep to say we end
The heart-ache and the thousand natural shocks
That flesh is heir to, 'tis a consummation
Devoutly to be wish'd. To die, to sleep;
To sleep? perchance to dream. Ay, there's the rub;
For in that sleep of death what dreams may come
When we have shuffled off this mortal coil,
Must give us pause. There's the respect
That makes calamity of so long life;
For who would bear the whips and scorns of time,
The oppressor's wrong, the proud man's contumely,
The pangs of despised love, the law's delay,
The insolence of office and the spurns
That patient merit of the unworthy takes,
When he himself might his quietus make
With a bare bodkin? who would fardels bear,
To grunt and sweat under a weary life,
But that the dread of something after death,
The undiscover'd country from whose bourn
No traveller returns, puzzles the will
And makes us rather bear those ills we have
Than fly to others that we know not of?
Thus conscience does make cowards of us all;
And thus the native hue of resolution
Is sicklied o'er with the pale cast of thought,
And enterprises of great pitch and moment
With this regard their currents turn awry,
And lose the name of action.—Soft you now!
The fair Ophelia! Nymph, in thy orisons
Be all my sins remember'd.

221

OPHELIA   Good my lord,
  How does your honour for this many a day?

HAMLET   I humbly thank you; well, well, well.

OPHELIA   My lord, I have remembrances of yours,
  That I have longed long to re-deliver;
  I pray you, now receive them.

HAMLET   No, not I;
  I never gave you aught.

OPHELIA   My honour'd lord, you know right well you did;
  And, with them, words of so sweet breath composed
  As made the things more rich. Their perfume lost,
  Take these again; for to the noble mind
  Rich gifts wax poor when givers prove unkind.
  There, my lord.

HAMLET   Ha, ha! are you honest?

OPHELIA   My lord?

HAMLET   Are you fair?

OPHELIA   What means your lordship?

HAMLET   That if you be honest and fair, your honesty should admit no
  discourse to your beauty.

OPHELIA   Could beauty, my lord, have better commerce than with honesty?

HAMLET   Ay, truly; for the power of beauty will sooner transform honesty from what it is to a bawd than the force of honesty can translate
  beauty into his likeness. This was sometime a paradox, but now the
  time gives it proof. I did love you once.

OPHELIA   Indeed, my lord, you made me believe so.

HAMLET   You should not have believed me; for virtue cannot so inocu-
  late our old stock but we shall relish of it. I loved you not.

OPHELIA   I was the more deceived.

HAMLET   Get thee to a nunnery; why wouldst thou be a breeder of sinners? I am myself indifferent honest; but yet I could accuse me of such
  things that it were better my mother had not borne me. I am very
  proud, revengeful, ambitious, with more offences at my beck than I

have thoughts to put them in, imagination to give them shape, or time to act them in. What should such fellows as I do crawling between earth and heaven? We are arrant knaves, all; believe none of us. Go thy ways to a nunnery. Where's your father?

OPHELIA   At home, my lord.

HAMLET   Let the doors be shut upon him, that he may play the fool nowhere but in's own house. Farewell.

OPHELIA   O, help him, you sweet heavens!

HAMLET   If thou dost marry, I'll give thee this plague for thy dowry: be thou as chaste as ice, as pure as snow, thou shalt not escape calumny. Get thee to a nunnery, go. Farewell. Or, if thou wilt needs marry, marry a fool; for wise men know well enough what monsters you make of them. To a nunnery, go, and quickly too. Farewell.

OPHELIA   O heavenly powers, restore him!

HAMLET   I have heard of your paintings too, well enough; God has given you one face, and you make yourselves another. You jig, you amble, and you lisp, and nick-name God's creatures, and make your wantonness your ignorance. Go to, I'll no more on't; it hath made me mad. I say, we will have no more marriages. Those that are married already, all but one, shall live; the rest shall keep as they are. To a nunnery, go.
Exit.

OPHELIA   O, what a noble mind is here o'erthrown!
    The courtier's, soldier's, scholar's, eye, tongue, sword,
    The expectancy and rose of the fair state,
    The glass of fashion and the mould of form,
    The observed of all observers, quite, quite down!
    And I, of ladies most deject and wretched,
    That suck'd the honey of his music vows,
    Now see that noble and most sovereign reason,
    Like sweet bells jangled, out of tune and harsh;
    That unmatch'd form and feature of blown youth
    Blasted with ecstasy: O, woe is me,
    To have seen what I have seen, see what I see!

Re-enter King and Polonius.

KING   Love! his affections do not that way tend;
    Nor what he spake, though it lack'd form a little,
    Was not like madness. There's something in his soul,

223

O'er which his melancholy sits on brood;
And I do doubt the hatch and the disclose
Will be some danger; which for to prevent,
I have in quick determination
Thus set it down: he shall with speed to England,
For the demand of our neglected tribute.
Haply the seas and countries different
With variable objects shall expel
This something-settled matter in his heart,
Whereon his brains still beating puts him thus
From fashion of himself. What think you on't?

POLONIUS   It shall do well: but yet do I believe
The origin and commencement of his grief
Sprung from neglected love. How now, Ophelia!
You need not tell us what Lord Hamlet said;
We heard it all. My lord, do as you please;
But, if you hold it fit, after the play
Let his queen mother all alone entreat him
To show his grief: let her be round with him;
And I'll be placed, so please you, in the ear
Of all their conference. If she find him not,
To England send him, or confine him where
Your wisdom best shall think.

KING   It shall be so.
Madness in great ones must not unwatch'd go.   *Exeunt.*

 SCENE 2   *A hall in the castle.*

Enter Hamlet and Players.

HAMLET   Speak the speech, I pray you, as I pronounced it to you, trippingly on the tongue: but if you mouth it, as many of your players do,
I had as lief the town-crier spoke my lines. Nor do not saw the air too
much with your hand, thus, but use all gently; for in the very torrent,
tempest, and, as I may say, the whirlwind of passion, you must acquire
and beget a temperance that may give it smoothness. O, it offends me
to the soul to hear a robustious periwig-pated fellow tear a passion to
tatters, to very rags, to split the ears of the groundlings, who for the
most part are capable of nothing but inexplicable dumb-shows and
noise. I would have such a fellow whipped for o'erdoing Termagant. It
out-herods Herod. Pray you, avoid it.

FIRST PLAYER   I warrant your honour.

HAMLET   Be not too tame neither, but let your own discretion be your tutor. Suit the action to the word, the word to the action; with this special observance, that you o'erstep not the modesty of nature; for anything so overdone is from the purpose of playing, whose end, both at the first and now, was and is, to hold, as 'twere, the mirror up to nature; to show virtue her own feature, scorn her own image, and the very age and body of the time his form and pressure. Now this over-done, or come tardy off, though it make the unskilful laugh, cannot but make the judicious grieve; the censure of the which one must in your allowance o'erweigh a whole theatre of others. O, there be play-ers that I have seen play, and heard others praise, and that highly, not to speak it profanely, that, neither having the accent of Christians nor the gait of Christian, pagan, nor man, have so strutted and bellowed that I have thought some of nature's journeymen had made men and not made them well, they imitated humanity so abominably.

FIRST PLAYER   I hope we have reformed that indifferently with us, sir.

HAMLET   O, reform it altogether. And let those that play your clowns speak no more than is set down for them; for there be of them that will themselves laugh, to set on some quantity of barren spectators to laugh too; though, in the mean time, some necessary question of the play be then to be considered: that's villainous, and shows a most pitiful ambi-tion in the fool that uses it. Go, make you ready.   *Exeunt Players.*

Enter Polonius, Rosencrantz, and Guildenstern.

How now, my lord! will the King hear this piece of work?

POLONIUS   And the Queen too, and that presently.

HAMLET   Bid the players make haste.   *Exit Polonius.*
     Will you two help to hasten them?

ROSENCRANTZ AND GUILDENSTERN   We will, my lord.
                         Exeunt Rosencrantz and Guildenstern.

HAMLET   What ho! Horatio!

Enter Horatio.

HORATIO   Here, sweet lord, at your service.

HAMLET   Horatio, thou art e'en as just a man
     As e'er my conversation coped withal.

225

HORATIO   O, my dear lord—

HAMLET   Nay, do not think I flatter;
For what advancement may I hope from thee
That no revenue hast but thy good spirits,
To feed and clothe thee? Why should the poor be flatter'd?
No, let the candied tongue lick absurd pomp,
And crook the pregnant hinges of the knee
Where thrift may follow fawning. Dost thou hear?
Since my dear soul was mistress of her choice
And could of men distinguish, her election
Hath seal'd thee for herself; for thou hast been
As one, in suffering all, that suffers nothing,
A man that fortune's buffets and rewards
Hast ta'en with equal thanks; and blest are those
Whose blood and judgement are so well commingled,
That they are not a pipe for fortune's finger
To sound what stop she please. Give me that man
That is not passion's slave, and I will wear him
In my heart's core, ay, in my heart of heart,
As I do thee. Something too much of this.
There is a play to-night before the King.
One scene of it comes near the circumstance
Which I have told thee of my father's death:
I prithee, when thou seest that act afoot,
Even with the very comment of thy soul
Observe mine uncle. If his occulted guilt
Do not itself unkennel in one speech,
It is a damned ghost that we have seen,
And my imaginations are as foul
As Vulcan's stithy. Give him heedful note;
For I mine eyes will rivet to his face,
And after we will both our judgements join
In censure of his seeming.

HORATIO   Well, my lord.
If he steal aught the whilst this play is playing,
And 'scape detecting, I will pay the theft.

HAMLET   They are coming to the play; I must be idle.
Get you a place.

*Danish march. A flourish. Enter King, Queen, Polonius, Ophelia, Rosen-
crantz, Guildenstern, and others.*

226

KING   How fares our cousin Hamlet?

HAMLET   Excellent, i' faith; of the chameleon's dish. I eat the air, promise-crammed. You cannot feed capons so.

KING   I have nothing with this answer, Hamlet; these words are not mine.

HAMLET   No, nor mine now. [*To Polonius.*] My lord, you played once i' the university, you say?

POLONIUS   That did I, my lord; and was accounted a good actor.

HAMLET   What did you enact?

POLONIUS   I did enact Julius Caesar. I was killed i' the Capitol; Brutus killed me.

HAMLET   It was a brute part of him to kill so capital a calf there. Be the players ready?

ROSENCRANTZ   Ay, my lord; they stay upon your patience.

QUEEN   Come hither, my dear Hamlet, sit by me.

HAMLET   No, good mother, here's metal more attractive.

POLONIUS   [*To the King.*] O, ho! do you mark that?

HAMLET   Lady, shall I lie in your lap?

Lying down at Ophelia's feet.

OPHELIA   No, my lord.

HAMLET   I mean, my head upon your lap?

OPHELIA   Ay, my lord.

HAMLET   Do you think I meant country matters?

OPHELIA   I think nothing, my lord.

HAMLET   That's a fair thought to lie between maids' legs.

OPHELIA   What is, my lord?

HAMLET   Nothing.

OPHELIA   You are merry, my lord.

HAMLET   Who, I?

OPHELIA   Ay, my lord.

227

HAMLET   O God, your only jig-maker. What should a man do but be
   merry? for, look you, how cheerfully my mother looks, and my father
   died within these two hours.

OPHELIA   Nay, 'tis twice two months, my lord.

HAMLET   So long? Nay then, let the devil wear black, for I'll have a suit
   of sables. O heavens! die two months ago, and not forgotten yet? Then
   there's hope a great man's memory may outlive his life half a year; but,
   by'r lady, he must build churches, then; or else shall he suffer not
   thinking on, with the hobby-horse, whose epitaph is "For, O, for, O,
   the hobby-horse is forgot."

*Hautboys play. The dumb-show enters. Enter a King and a Queen very lov-
ingly; the Queen embracing him, and he her. She kneels and makes show of
protestation unto him. He takes her up, and declines his head upon her neck; lays
him down upon a bank of flowers. She, seeing him asleep, leaves him. Anon
comes in a fellow, takes off his crown, kisses it, and pours poison in the King's
ears, and exit. The Queen returns; finds the King dead, and makes passionate
action. The Poisoner, with some two or three Mutes, comes in again, seeming to
lament with her. The dead body is carried away. The Poisoner woos the Queen
with gifts; she seems loath and unwilling awhile, but in the end accepts his love.
Exeunt.*

OPHELIA   What means this, my lord?

HAMLET   Marry, this is miching mallecho; it means mischief.

OPHELIA   Belike this show imports the argument of the play.

Enter Prologue.

HAMLET   We shall know by this fellow. The players cannot keep counsel;
   they'll tell all.

OPHELIA   Will he tell us what this show meant?

HAMLET   Ay, or any show that you'll show him. Be not you ashamed to
   show, he'll not shame to tell you what it means.

OPHELIA   You are naught, you are naught: I'll mark the play.

PROLOGUE   For us, and for our tragedy,
                    Here stooping to your clemency,
                    We beg your hearing patiently.   *Exit.*

HAMLET   Is this a prologue, or the posy of a ring?

OPHELIA   'Tis brief, my lord.

228

HAMLET   As woman's love.

Enter two Players as King and Queen.

PLAYER KING   Full thirty times hath Phoebus' cart gone round
 Neptune's salt wash and Tellus' orbed ground,
 And thirty dozen moons with borrow'd sheen
 About the world have times twelve thirties been,
 Since love our hearts and Hymen did our hands
 Unite commutual in most sacred bands.

PLAYER QUEEN   So many journeys may the sun and moon
 Make us again count o'er ere love be done!
 But, woe is me, you are so sick of late,
 So far from cheer and from your former state,
 That I distrust you. Yet, though I distrust,
 Discomfort you, my lord, it nothing must;
 For women's fear and love holds quantity,
 In neither aught, or in extremity.
 Now, what my love is, proof hath made you know;
 And as my love is sized, my fear is so.
 Where love is great, the littlest doubts are fear;
 Where little fears grow great, great love grows there.

PLAYER KING   'Faith, I must leave thee, love, and shortly too;
 My operant powers their functions leave to do;
 And thou shalt live in this fair world behind,
 Honour'd, beloved; and haply one as kind
 For husband shalt thou —

PLAYER QUEEN   O, confound the rest!
 Such love must needs be treason in my breast.
 In second husband let me be accurst!
 None wed the second but who kill'd the first.

HAMLET   [*Aside.*] Wormwood, wormwood.

PLAYER QUEEN   The instances that second marriage move
 Are base respects of thrift, but none of love:
 A second time I kill my husband dead,
 When second husband kisses me in bed.

PLAYER KING   I do believe you think what now you speak;
 But what we do determine oft we break.
 Purpose is but the slave to memory,
 Of violent birth, but poor validity:

229

Which now, like fruit unripe, sticks on the tree;
But fall, unshaken, when they mellow be.
Most necessary 'tis that we forget
To pay ourselves what to ourselves is debt:
What to ourselves in passion we propose,
The passion ending, doth the purpose lose.
The violence of either grief or joy
Their own enactures with themselves destroy.
Where joy most revels, grief doth most lament;
Grief joys, joy grieves, on slender accident.
This world is not for aye, nor 'tis not strange
That even our loves should with our fortunes change;
For 'tis a question left us yet to prove,
Whether love lead fortune, or else fortune love.
The great man down, you mark his favourite flies;
The poor advanced makes friends of enemies.
And hitherto doth love on fortune tend;
For who not needs shall never lack a friend,
And who in want a hollow friend doth try,
Directly seasons him his enemy.
But, orderly to end where I begun,
Our wills and fates do so contrary run
That our devices still are overthrown;
Our thoughts are ours, their ends none of our own.
So think thou wilt no second husband wed;
But die thy thoughts when thy first lord is dead.

PLAYER QUEEN   Nor earth to me give food, nor heaven light!
Sport and repose lock from me day and night!
To desperation turn my trust and hope!
An anchor's cheer in prison be my scope!
Each opposite that blanks the face of joy
Meet what I would have well and it destroy!
Both here and hence pursue me lasting strife,
If, once a widow, ever I be wife!

HAMLET   If she should break it now!

PLAYER KING   'Tis deeply sworn. Sweet, leave me here awhile;
My spirits grow dull, and fain I would beguile
The tedious day with sleep.

Sleeps.

230

PLAYER QUEEN   Sleep rock thy brain;
  And never come mischance between us twain!   *Exit.*

HAMLET   Madam, how like you this play?

QUEEN   The lady doth protest too much, methinks.

HAMLET   O, but she'll keep her word.

KING   Have you heard the argument? Is there no offence in't?

HAMLET   No, no, they do but jest, poison in jest; no offence i' the world.

KING   What do you call the play?

HAMLET   "The Mouse-trap." Marry, how? Tropically. This play is the
  image of a murder done in Vienna. Gonzago is the duke's name; his
  wife, Baptista. You shall see anon; 'tis a knavish piece of work, but
  what o' that? Your Majesty and we that have free souls, it touches us
  not. Let the galled jade wince, our withers are unwrung.

Enter Lucianus.

  This is one Lucianus, nephew to the king.

OPHELIA   You are as good as a chorus, my lord.

HAMLET   I could interpret between you and your love, if I could see the
  puppets dallying.

OPHELIA   You are keen, my lord, you are keen.

HAMLET   It would cost you a groaning to take off my edge.

OPHELIA   Still better, and worse.

HAMLET   So you must take your husbands. Begin, murderer; pox, leave
  thy damnable faces, and begin. Come, "the croaking raven doth bellow for revenge."

LUCIANUS   Thoughts black, hands apt, drugs fit, and time agreeing;
  Confederate season, else no creature seeing;
  Thou mixture rank, of midnight weeds collected,
  With Hecate's ban thrice blasted, thrice infected,
  Thy natural magic and dire property,
  On wholesome life usurp immediately.

Pours the poison into the sleeper's ears.

HAMLET   He poisons him i' the garden for's estate. His name's Gonzago;

231

the story is extant, and writ in choice Italian. You shall see anon how the murderer gets the love of Gonzago's wife.

OPHELIA   The King rises.

HAMLET   What, frighted with false fire!

QUEEN   How fares my lord?

POLONIUS   Give o'er the play.

KING   Give me some light. Away!

ALL   Lights, lights, lights!   *Exeunt all but Hamlet and Horatio.*

HAMLET   Why, let the stricken deer go weep,
                    The hart ungalled play;
              For some must watch, while some must sleep;
                    So runs the world away.
Would not this, sir, and a forest of feathers—if the rest of my fortunes turn Turk with me—with two Provincial roses on my razed shoes, get me a fellowship in a cry of players, sir?

HORATIO   Half a share.

HAMLET   A whole one, I.
                    For thou dost know, O Damon dear,
                        This realm dismantled was
                    Of Jove himself; and now reigns here
                        A very, very—pajock.

HORATIO   You might have rhymed.

HAMLET   O good Horatio, I'll take the ghost's word for a thousand pound. Didst perceive?

HORATIO   Very well, my lord.

HAMLET   Upon the talk of the poisoning?

HORATIO   I did very well note him.

HAMLET   Ah, ha! Come, some music! come, the recorders!
For if the king like not the comedy,
Why then, belike, he likes it not, perdy.
Come, some music!

Re-enter Rosencrantz and Guildenstern.

GUILDENSTERN   Good my lord, vouchsafe me a word with you.

232

HAMLET   Sir, a whole history.

GUILDENSTERN   The King, sir—

HAMLET   Ay, sir, what of him?

GUILDENSTERN   Is in his retirement marvellous distempered.

HAMLET   With drink, sir?

GUILDENSTERN   No, my lord, rather with choler.

HAMLET   Your wisdom should show itself more richer to signify this to his doctor; for, for me to put him to his purgation would perhaps plunge him into far more choler.

GUILDENSTERN   Good my lord, put your discourse into some frame and start not so wildly from my affair.

HAMLET   I am tame, sir; pronounce.

GUILDENSTERN   The Queen, your mother, in most great affliction of spirit, hath sent me to you.

HAMLET   You are welcome.

GUILDENSTERN   Nay, good my lord, this courtesy is not of the right breed. If it shall please you to make me a wholesome answer, I will do your mother's commandment; if not, your pardon and my return shall be the end of my business.

HAMLET   Sir, I cannot.

GUILDENSTERN   What, my lord?

HAMLET   Make you a wholesome answer; my wit's diseased. But, sir, such answer as I can make, you shall command; or, rather, as you say, my mother. Therefore no more, but to the matter. My mother, you say—

ROSENCRANTZ   Then thus she says; your behaviour hath struck her into amazement and admiration.

HAMLET   O wonderful son, that can so astonish a mother! But is there no sequel at the heels of this mother's admiration? Impart.

ROSENCRANTZ   She desires to speak with you in her closet, ere you go to bed.

HAMLET   We shall obey, were she ten times our mother. Have you any further trade with us?

ROSENCRANTZ My lord, you once did love me.

HAMLET So I do still, by these pickers and stealers.

ROSENCRANTZ Good my lord, what is your cause of distemper? You do, surely, bar the door upon your own liberty, if you deny your griefs to your friend.

HAMLET Sir, I lack advancement.

ROSENCRANTZ How can that be, when you have the voice of the King himself for your succession in Denmark?

HAMLET Ay, sir, but, "While the grass grows"—the proverb is something musty.

Re-enter Players with recorders.

O, the recorders! let me see one. To withdraw with you—why do you go about to recover the wind of me, as if you would drive me into a toil?

GUILDENSTERN O, my lord, if my duty be too bold, my love is too unmannerly.

HAMLET I do not well understand that. Will you play upon this pipe?

GUILDENSTERN My lord, I cannot.

HAMLET I pray you.

GUILDENSTERN Believe me, I cannot.

HAMLET I do beseech you.

GUILDENSTERN I know no touch of it, my lord.

HAMLET 'Tis as easy as lying. Govern these ventages with your fingers and thumb, give it breath with your mouth, and it will discourse most eloquent music. Look you, these are the stops.

GUILDENSTERN But these cannot I command to any utterance of harmony; I have not the skill.

HAMLET Why, look you now, how unworthy a thing you make of me! You would play upon me; you would seem to know my stops; you would pluck out the heart of my mystery; you would sound me from my lowest note to the top of my compass; and there is much music, excellent voice, in this little organ, yet cannot you make it speak. 'Sblood, do you think I am easier to be played on than a pipe? Call me

234

what instrument you will, though you can fret me, yet you cannot play upon me.

Enter Polonius.

God bless you, sir!

POLONIUS   My lord, the Queen would speak with you, and presently.

HAMLET   Do you see yonder cloud that's almost in shape of a camel?

POLONIUS   By the mass, and 'tis like a camel, indeed.

HAMLET   Methinks it is like a weasel.

POLONIUS   It is backed like a weasel.

HAMLET   Or like a whale?

POLONIUS   Very like a whale.

HAMLET   Then I will come to my mother by and by. They fool me to the top of my bent. I will come by and by.

POLONIUS   I will say so.

HAMLET   By and by is easily said.   *Exit Polonius.*
Leave me, friends.   *Exeunt all but Hamlet.*
'Tis now the very witching time of night,
When churchyards yawn and hell itself breathes out
Contagion to this world. Now could I drink hot blood,
And do such bitter business as the day
Would quake to look on. Soft! now to my mother.
O heart, lose not thy nature; let not ever
The soul of Nero enter this firm bosom.
Let me be cruel, not unnatural.
I will speak daggers to her, but use none;
My tongue and soul in this be hypocrites;
How in my words soever she be shent,
To give them seals never, my soul, consent!   *Exit.*

❧ SCENE 3   *A room in the castle.*

Enter King, Rosencrantz, and Guildenstern.

KING   I like him not, nor stands it safe with us
To let his madness range. Therefore prepare you;
I your commission will forthwith dispatch,

And he to England shall along with you:
The terms of our estate may not endure
Hazard so near us as doth hourly grow
Out of his lunacies.

GUILDENSTERN   We will ourselves provide.
Most holy and religious fear it is
To keep those many many bodies safe
That live and feed upon your Majesty.

ROSENCRANTZ   The single and peculiar life is bound,
With all the strength and armour of the mind,
To keep itself from noyance; but much more
That spirit upon whose weal depend and rest
The lives of many. The cease of majesty
Dies not alone; but, like a gulf, doth draw
What's near it with it. It is a massy wheel,
Fix'd on the summit of the highest mount,
To whose huge spokes ten thousand lesser things
Are mortised and adjoin'd; which, when it falls,
Each small annexment, petty consequence,
Attends the boisterous ruin. Never alone
Did the King sigh, but with a general groan.

KING   Arm you, I pray you, to this speedy voyage;
For we will fetters put upon this fear,
Which now goes too free-footed.

ROSENCRANTZ AND GUILDENSTERN   We will haste us.
                                   Exeunt Rosencrantz and Guildenstern.

Enter Polonius.

POLONIUS   My lord, he's going to his mother's closet:
Behind the arras I'll convey myself,
To hear the process; I'll warrant she'll tax him home:
And, as you said, and wisely was it said,
'Tis meet that some more audience than a mother,
Since nature makes them partial, should o'erhear
The speech, of vantage. Fare you well, my liege.
I'll call upon you ere you go to bed,
And tell you what I know.

KING   Thanks, dear my lord.   *Exit Polonius.*
O, my offence is rank, it smells to heaven;

236

It hath the primal eldest curse upon't,
A brother's murder. Pray can I not,
Though inclination be as sharp as will.
My stronger guilt defeats my strong intent;
And, like a man to double business bound,
I stand in pause where I shall first begin,
And both neglect. What if this cursed hand
Were thicker than itself with brother's blood,
Is there not rain enough in the sweet heavens
To wash it white as snow? Whereto serves mercy
But to confront the visage of offence?
And what's in prayer but this two-fold force,
To be forestalled ere we come to fall,
Or pardon'd being down? Then I'll look up;
My fault is past. But, O, what form of prayer
Can serve my turn? "Forgive me my foul murder"?
That cannot be; since I am still possess'd
Of those effects for which I did the murder,
My crown, mine own ambition, and my queen.
May one be pardon'd and retain the offence?
In the corrupted currents of this world
Offence's gilded hand may shove by justice,
And oft 'tis seen the wicked prize itself
Buys out the law: but 'tis not so above;
There is no shuffling, there the action lies
In his true nature; and we ourselves compell'd,
Even to the teeth and forehead of our faults,
To give in evidence. What then? what rests?
Try what repentance can. What can it not?
Yet what can it when one can not repent?
O wretched state! O bosom black as death!
O limed soul, that, struggling to be free,
Art more engaged! Help, angels! Make assay!
Bow, stubborn knees; and, heart with strings of steel,
Be soft as sinews of the new-born babe!
All may be well.   *Retires and kneels.*

Enter Hamlet.

HAMLET   Now might I do it pat, now he is praying;
And now I'll do't. And so he goes to heaven;
And so am I revenged. That would be scann'd.
A villain kills my father; and for that,

237

I, his sole son, do this same villain send
To heaven.
O, this is hire and salary, not revenge.
He took my father grossly, full of bread;
With all his crimes broad blown, as flush as May;
And how his audit stands who knows save heaven?
But in our circumstance and course of thought,
'Tis heavy with him. And am I then revenged,
To take him in the purging of his soul,
When he is fit and season'd for his passage?
No!
Up, sword; and know thou a more horrid hent.
When he is drunk asleep, or in his rage,
Or in the incestuous pleasure of his bed;
At gaming, swearing, or about some act
That has no relish of salvation in't;
Then trip him, that his heels may kick at heaven,
And that his soul may be as damn'd and black
As hell, whereto it goes. My mother stays.
This physic but prolongs thy sickly days.   *Exit.*

KING   [*Rising.*] My words fly up, my thoughts remain below.
    Words without thoughts never to heaven go.   *Exit.*

❀ SCENE 4   *The Queen's closet.*

Enter Queen and Polonius.

POLONIUS   He will come straight. Look you lay home to him.
    Tell him his pranks have been too broad to bear with,
    And that your Grace hath screen'd and stood between
    Much heat and him. I'll sconce me even here.
    Pray you, be round with him.

HAMLET   [*Within.*] Mother, mother, mother!

QUEEN   I'll warrant you,
    Fear me not. Withdraw, I hear him coming.

Polonius hides behind the arras. Enter Hamlet.

HAMLET   Now, mother, what's the matter?

QUEEN   Hamlet, thou hast thy father much offended.

HAMLET   Mother, you have my father much offended.

QUEEN   Come, come, you answer with an idle tongue.

HAMLET   Go, go, you question with a wicked tongue.

QUEEN   Why, how now, Hamlet!

HAMLET   What's the matter now?

QUEEN   Have you forgot me?

HAMLET   No, by the rood, not so:
   You are the Queen, your husband's brother's wife;
   And—would it were not so!—you are my mother.

QUEEN   Nay, then, I'll set those to you that can speak.

HAMLET   Come, come, and sit you down; you shall not budge;
   You go not till I set you up a glass
   Where you may see the inmost part of you.

QUEEN   What wilt thou do? thou wilt not murder me?
   Help, help, ho!

POLONIUS   [Behind.] What, ho! help, help, help!

HAMLET   [Drawing.] How now! a rat? Dead, for a ducat, dead!

Makes a pass through the arras.

POLONIUS   [Behind.] O, I am slain!   *Falls and dies.*

QUEEN   O me, what hast thou done?

HAMLET   Nay, I know not: Is it the King?

QUEEN   O, what a rash and bloody deed is this!

HAMLET   A bloody deed! almost as bad, good mother,
   As kill a king, and marry with his brother.

QUEEN   As kill a king!

HAMLET   Ay, lady, 'twas my word.

Lifts up the arras and discovers Polonius.

   Thou wretched, rash, intruding fool, farewell!
   I took thee for thy better. Take thy fortune;
   Thou find'st to be too busy is some danger.
   Leave wringing of your hands. Peace! sit you down,

And let me wring your heart; for so I shall,
If it be made of penetrable stuff,
If damned custom have not brass'd it so
That it be proof and bulwark against sense.

QUEEN What have I done, that thou darest wag thy tongue
In noise so rude against me?

HAMLET   Such an act
That blurs the grace and blush of modesty,
Calls virtue hypocrite, takes off the rose
From the fair forehead of an innocent love
And sets a blister there, makes marriage-vows
As false as dicers' oaths; O, such a deed
As from the body of contraction plucks
The very soul, and sweet religion makes
A rhapsody of words. Heaven's face doth glow;
Yea, this solidity and compound mass,
With tristful visage, as against the doom,
Is thought-sick at the act.

QUEEN   Ay me, what act,
That roars so loud, and thunders in the index?

HAMLET Look here, upon this picture, and on this,
The counterfeit presentment of two brothers.
See, what a grace was seated on this brow;
Hyperion's curls; the front of Jove himself;
An eye like Mars, to threaten and command;
A station like the herald Mercury
New-lighted on a heaven-kissing hill;
A combination and a form indeed,
Where every god did seem to set his seal,
To give the world assurance of a man.
This was your husband. Look you now, what follows:
Here is your husband; like a mildew'd ear,
Blasting his wholesome brother. Have you eyes?
Could you on this fair mountain leave to feed,
And batten on this moor? Ha! have you eyes?
You cannot call it love; for at your age
The hey-day in the blood is tame, it's humble,
And waits upon the judgement; and what judgement
Would step from this to this? Sense, sure, you have,
Else could you not have motion; but sure, that sense

240

Is apoplex'd; for madness would not err,
Nor sense to ecstasy was ne'er so thrall'd
But it reserved some quantity of choice,
To serve in such a difference. What devil was't
That thus hath cozen'd you at hoodman-blind?
Eyes without feeling, feeling without sight,
Ears without hands or eyes, smelling sans all,
Or but a sickly part of one true sense
Could not so mope.
O shame! where is thy blush? Rebellious hell,
If thou canst mutine in a matron's bones,
To flaming youth let virtue be as wax,
And melt in her own fire. Proclaim no shame
When the compulsive ardour gives the charge,
Since frost itself as actively doth burn
And reason panders will.

QUEEN   O Hamlet, speak no more.
  Thou turn'st mine eyes into my very soul;
  And there I see such black and grained spots
  As will not leave their tinct.

HAMLET   Nay, but to live
  In the rank sweat of an enseamed bed,
  Stew'd in corruption, honeying and making love
  Over the nasty sty—

QUEEN   O, speak to me no more;
  These words, like daggers, enter in mine ears;
  No more, sweet Hamlet!

HAMLET   A murderer and a villain;
  A slave that is not twentieth part the tithe
  Of your precedent lord; a vice of kings;
  A cutpurse of the empire and the rule,
  That from a shelf the precious diadem stole,
  And put it in his pocket!

QUEEN   No more!

HAMLET   A king of shreds and patches—

Enter Ghost.

  Save me, and hover o'er me with your wings,
  You heavenly guards! What would your gracious figure?

241

QUEEN Alas, he's mad!

HAMLET Do you not come your tardy son to chide,
That, lapsed in time and passion, lets go by
The important acting of your dread command?
O, say!

GHOST Do not forget! This visitation
Is but to whet thy almost blunted purpose.
But, look, amazement on thy mother sits.
O, step between her and her fighting soul.
Conceit in weakest bodies strongest works.
Speak to her, Hamlet.

HAMLET   How is it with you, lady?

QUEEN Alas, how is't with you,
That you do bend your eye on vacancy
And with the incorporal air do hold discourse?
Forth at your eyes your spirits wildly peep;
And, as the sleeping soldiers in the alarm,
Your bedded hair, like life in excrements,
Start up, and stand an end. O gentle son,
Upon the heat and flame of thy distemper
Sprinkle cool patience. Whereon do you look?

HAMLET On him, on him! Look you, how pale he glares!
His form and cause conjoin'd, preaching to stones,
Would make them capable. Do not look upon me;
Lest with this piteous action you convert
My stern effects; then what I have to do
Will want true colour, tears perchance for blood.

QUEEN To whom do you speak this?

HAMLET   Do you see nothing there?

QUEEN Nothing at all; yet all that is I see.

HAMLET Nor did you nothing hear?

QUEEN   No, nothing but ourselves.

HAMLET Why, look you there! look, how it steals away!
My father, in his habit as he lived!
Look, where he goes, even now, out at the portal!   *Exit Ghost.*

242

QUEEN   This is the very coinage of your brain.
This bodiless creation ecstasy
Is very cunning in.

HAMLET   Ecstasy!
My pulse, as yours, doth temperately keep time,
And makes as healthful music. It is not madness
That I have utter'd. Bring me to the test,
And I the matter will re-word; which madness
Would gambol from. Mother, for love of grace,
Lay not that flattering unction to your soul,
That not your trespass, but my madness speaks.
It will but skin and film the ulcerous place,
Whiles rank corruption, mining all within,
Infects unseen. Confess yourself to heaven;
Repent what's past; avoid what is to come;
And do not spread the compost on the weeds,
To make them ranker. Forgive me this my virtue;
For in the fatness of these pursy times
Virtue itself of vice must pardon beg,
Yea, curb and woo for leave to do him good.

QUEEN   O Hamlet, thou hast cleft my heart in twain.

HAMLET   O, throw away the worser part of it,
And live the purer with the other half.
Good night; but go not to mine uncle's bed.
Assume a virtue, if you have it not.
That monster, custom, who all sense doth eat,
Of habits devil, is angel yet in this,
That to the use of actions fair and good
He likewise gives a frock or livery,
That aptly is put on. Refrain to-night,
And that shall lend a kind of easiness
To the next abstinence; the next more easy;
For use almost can change the stamp of nature,
And either master the devil, or throw him out
With wondrous potency. Once more, good night;
And when you are desirous to be bless'd,
I'll blessing beg of you. For this same lord,

Pointing to Polonius.

I do repent; but heaven hath pleased it so,
To punish me with this and this with me,
That I must be their scourge and minister.
I will bestow him, and will answer well
The death I gave him. So, again, good night.
I must be cruel, only to be kind.
Thus bad begins and worse remains behind.
One word more, good lady.

QUEEN   What shall I do?

HAMLET   Not this, by no means, that I bid you do:
Let the bloat king tempt you again to bed;
Pinch wanton on your cheek; call you his mouse;
And let him, for a pair of reechy kisses,
Or paddling in your neck with his damn'd fingers,
Make you to ravel all this matter out,
That I essentially am not in madness,
But mad in craft. 'Twere good you let him know;
For who, that's but a queen, fair, sober, wise,
Would from a paddock, from a bat, a gib,
Such dear concernings hide? who would do so?
No, in despite of sense and secrecy,
Unpeg the basket on the house's top,
Let the birds fly, and, like the famous ape,
To try conclusions, in the basket creep,
And break your own neck down.

QUEEN   Be thou assured, if words be made of breath,
And breath of life, I have no life to breathe
What thou hast said to me.

HAMLET   I must to England; you know that?

QUEEN   Alack,
I had forgot. 'Tis so concluded on.

HAMLET   There's letters seal'd, and my two school-fellows,
Whom I will trust as I will adders fang'd,
They bear the mandate; they must sweep my way,
And marshal me to knavery. Let it work;
For 'tis the sport to have the enginer
Hoist with his own petar; and 't shall go hard
But I will delve one yard below their mines,
And blow them at the moon. O, 'tis most sweet,

244

When in one line two crafts directly meet.
This man shall set me packing.
I'll lug the guts into the neighbour room.
Mother, good night. Indeed this counsellor
Is now most still, most secret, and most grave,
Who was in life a foolish prating knave.
Come, sir, to draw toward an end with you.
Good night, mother.   *Exeunt severally; Hamlet dragging in Polonius.*

ACT IV

SCENE 1 *A room in the castle.*

Enter King, Queen, Rosencrantz, and Guildenstern.

KING   There's matter in these sighs; these profound heaves
You must translate; 'tis fit we understand them.
Where is your son?

QUEEN   Bestow this place on us a little while.
Exeunt Rosencrantz and Guildenstern.
Ah, mine own lord, what have I seen to-night!

KING   What, Gertrude? How does Hamlet?

QUEEN   Mad as the sea and wind, when both contend
Which is the mightier. In his lawless fit,
Behind the arras hearing something stir,
Whips out his rapier, cries, "A rat, a rat!"
And, in this brainish apprehension, kills
The unseen good old man.

KING   O heavy deed!
It had been so with us, had we been there.
His liberty is full of threats to all;
To you yourself, to us, to every one.
Alas, how shall this bloody deed be answer'd?
It will be laid to us, whose providence
Should have kept short, restrain'd, and out of haunt,
This mad young man. But so much was our love,
We would not understand what was most fit;
But, like the owner of a foul disease,

246

To keep it from divulging, let it feed
Even on the pith of life. Where is he gone?

QUEEN   To draw apart the body he hath kill'd,
O'er whom his very madness, like some ore
Among a mineral of metals base,
Shows itself pure; he weeps for what is done.

KING   O Gertrude, come away!
The sun no sooner shall the mountains touch,
But we will ship him hence, and this vile deed
We must, with all our majesty and skill,
Both countenance and excuse. Ho, Guildenstern!

Re-enter Rosencrantz and Guildenstern.

Friends both, go join you with some further aid.
Hamlet in madness hath Polonius slain,
And from his mother's closet hath he dragg'd him.
Go seek him out; speak fair, and bring the body
Into the chapel. I pray you, haste in this.
                    Exeunt Rosencrantz and Guildenstern.
Come, Gertrude, we'll call up our wisest friends;
And let them know, both what we mean to do,
And what's untimely done; so, haply, slander,
Whose whisper o'er the world's diameter,
As level as the cannon to his blank,
Transports his poison'd shot, may miss our name,
And hit the woundless air. O, come away!
My soul is full of discord and dismay.   *Exeunt.*

SCENE 2   *Another room in the castle.*

Enter Hamlet.

HAMLET   Safely stowed.

ROSENCRANTZ AND GUILDENSTERN   [*Within.*] Hamlet! Lord Hamlet!

HAMLET   But soft, what noise? who calls on Hamlet? O, here they come.

Enter Rosencrantz and Guildenstern.

ROSENCRANTZ   What have you done, my lord, with the dead body?

HAMLET   Compounded it with dust, whereto 'tis kin.

ROSENCRANTZ   Tell us where 'tis, that we may take it thence
And bear it to the chapel.

HAMLET   Do not believe it.

ROSENCRANTZ   Believe what?

HAMLET   That I can keep your counsel and not mine own. Besides, to be
demanded of a sponge, what replication should be made by the son of
a king?

ROSENCRANTZ   Take you me for a sponge, my lord?

HAMLET   Ay, sir, that soaks up the King's countenance, his rewards, his
authorities. But such officers do the King best service in the end. He
keeps them, like an ape, in the corner of his jaw; first mouthed, to be
last swallowed. When he needs what you have gleaned, it is but
squeezing you, and, sponge, you shall be dry again.

ROSENCRANTZ   I understand you not, my lord.

HAMLET   I am glad of it. A knavish speech sleeps in a foolish ear.

ROSENCRANTZ   My lord, you must tell us where the body is, and go with
us to the King.

HAMLET   The body is with the King, but the King is not with the body.
The King is a thing—

GUILDENSTERN   A thing, my lord!

HAMLET   Of nothing. Bring me to him. Hide fox, and all after.

Exeunt.

SCENE 3   *Another room in the castle.*

Enter King, attended.

KING   I have sent to seek him, and to find the body.
How dangerous is it that this man goes loose!
Yet must not we put the strong law on him.
He's loved of the distracted multitude,
Who like not in their judgement, but their eyes:
And where 'tis so, the offender's scourge is weigh'd,
But never the offence. To bear all smooth and even,
This sudden sending him away must seem

Deliberate pause. Diseases desperate grown
By desperate appliance are relieved,
Or not at all.

Enter Rosencrantz.

     How now! what hath befall'n?

ROSENCRANTZ Where the dead body is bestow'd, my lord,
We cannot get from him.

KING   But where is he?

ROSENCRANTZ Without, my lord; guarded, to know your pleasure.

KING Bring him before us.

ROSENCRANTZ Ho, Guildenstern! bring in my lord.

Enter Hamlet and Guildenstern.

KING Now, Hamlet, where's Polonius?

HAMLET At supper.

KING At supper! where?

HAMLET Not where he eats, but where he is eaten. A certain convoca-
tion of politic worms are e'en at him. Your worm is your only emperor for diet. We fat all creatures else to fat us, and we fat ourselves for
maggots. Your fat king and your lean beggar is but variable service,
two dishes, but to one table; that's the end.

KING Alas, alas!

HAMLET A man may fish with the worm that hath eat of a king, and eat
of the fish that hath fed of that worm.

KING What dost thou mean by this?

HAMLET Nothing but to show you how a king may go a progress
through the guts of a beggar.

KING Where is Polonius?

HAMLET In heaven; send thither to see. If your messenger find him not
there, seek him i' the other place yourself. But indeed, if you find him
not within this month, you shall nose him as you go up the stairs into
the lobby.

249

KING [*To some Attendants.*] Go seek him there.

HAMLET He will stay till you come. *Exeunt Attendants.*

KING Hamlet, this deed, for thine especial safety—
Which we do tender, as we dearly grieve
For that which thou hast done—must send thee hence
With fiery quickness. Therefore prepare thyself;
The bark is ready, and the wind at help,
The associates tend, and everything is bent
For England.

HAMLET For England!

KING Ay, Hamlet.

HAMLET Good.

KING So is it, if thou knew'st our purposes.

HAMLET I see a cherub that sees them. But, come; for England! Farewell,
dear mother.

KING Thy loving father, Hamlet.

HAMLET My mother. Father and mother is man and wife; man and wife
is one flesh; and so, my mother. Come, for England! *Exit.*

KING Follow him at foot; tempt him with speed aboard;
Delay it not; I'll have him hence to-night.
Away! for every thing is seal'd and done
That else leans on the affair. Pray you, make haste.
  Exeunt Rosencrantz and Guildenstern.
And, England, if my love thou hold'st at aught—
As my great power thereof may give thee sense,
Since yet thy cicatrice looks raw and red
After the Danish sword, and thy free awe
Pays homage to us—thou mayst not coldly set
Our sovereign process; which imports at full,
By letters congruing to that effect,
The present death of Hamlet. Do it, England;
For like the hectic in my blood he rages,
And thou must cure me. Till I know 'tis done,
Howe'er my haps, my joys were ne'er begun. *Exit.*

SCENE 4   *A plain in Denmark.*

Enter Fortinbras, a Captain, and Soldiers, marching.

FORTINBRAS   Go, captain, from me greet the Danish king:
Tell him that, by his license, Fortinbras
Craves the conveyance of a promised march
Over his kingdom. You know the rendezvous.
If that his Majesty would aught with us,
We shall express our duty in his eye;
And let him know so.

CAPTAIN   I will do't, my lord.

FORTINBRAS   Go softly on.   *Exeunt Fortinbras and Soldiers.*

Enter Hamlet, Rosencrantz, Guildenstern, and others.

HAMLET   Good sir, whose powers are these?

CAPTAIN   They are of Norway, sir.

HAMLET   How purposed, sir, I pray you?

CAPTAIN   Against some part of Poland.

HAMLET   Who commands them, sir?

CAPTAIN   The nephew to old Norway, Fortinbras.

HAMLET   Goes it against the main of Poland, sir,
Or for some frontier?

CAPTAIN   Truly to speak, and with no addition,
We go to gain a little patch of ground
That hath in it no profit but the name.
To pay five ducats, five, I would not farm it;
Nor will it yield to Norway or the Pole
A ranker rate, should it be sold in fee.

HAMLET   Why, then the Polack never will defend it.

CAPTAIN   Yes, it is already garrison'd.

HAMLET   Two thousand souls and twenty thousand ducats
Will not debate the question of this straw.
This is the imposthume of much wealth and peace,

251

That inward breaks, and shows no cause without
Why the man dies. I humbly thank you, sir.

CAPTAIN   God be wi' you, sir.   *Exit.*

ROSENCRANTZ   Will't please you go, my lord?

HAMLET   I'll be with you straight. Go a little before.
                                        Exeunt all except Hamlet.

How all occasions do inform against me,
And spur my dull revenge! What is a man,
If his chief good and market of his time
Be but to sleep and feed? a beast, no more.
Sure, he that made us with such large discourse,
Looking before and after, gave us not
That capability and god-like reason
To fust in us unused. Now, whether it be
Bestial oblivion, or some craven scruple
Of thinking too precisely on the event,
A thought which, quarter'd, hath but one part wisdom
And ever three parts coward, I do not know
Why yet I live to say "This thing's to do";
Sith I have cause and will and strength and means
To do't. Examples gross as earth exhort me;
Witness this army of such mass and charge
Led by a delicate and tender prince,
Whose spirit with divine ambition puff'd
Makes mouths at the invisible event,
Exposing what is mortal and unsure
To all that fortune, death, and danger dare,
Even for an egg-shell. Rightly to be great
Is not to stir without great argument,
But greatly to find quarrel in a straw
When honour's at the stake. How stand I then,
That have a father kill'd, a mother stain'd,
Excitements of my reason and my blood,
And let me sleep? while, to my shame, I see
The imminent death of twenty thousand men,
That, for a fantasy and trick of fame,
Go to their graves like beds, fight for a plot
Whereon the numbers cannot try the cause,
Which is not tomb enough and continent

To hide the slain? O, from this time forth,
My thoughts be bloody, or be nothing worth!   *Exit.*

❦ SCENE 5   *Elsinore. A room in the castle.*

Enter Queen, Horatio, and a Gentleman.

QUEEN   I will not speak with her.

GENTLEMAN   She is importunate, indeed distract.
   Her mood will needs be pitied.

QUEEN   What would she have?

GENTLEMAN   She speaks much of her father; says she hears
   There's tricks i' the world; and hems, and beats her heart;
   Spurns enviously at straws; speaks things in doubt,
   That carry but half sense. Her speech is nothing,
   Yet the unshaped use of it doth move
   The hearers to collection; they aim at it,
   And botch the words up fit to their own thoughts;
   Which, as her winks, and nods, and gestures yield them,
   Indeed would make one think there might be thought,
   Though nothing sure, yet much unhappily.

HORATIO   'Twere good she were spoken with; for she may strew
   Dangerous conjectures in ill-breeding minds.

QUEEN   Let her come in.   *Exit Horatio.*
   To my sick soul, as sin's true nature is,
   Each toy seems prologue to some great amiss;
   So full of artless jealousy is guilt,
   It spills itself in fearing to be spilt.

Re-enter Horatio, with Ophelia.

OPHELIA   Where is the beauteous majesty of Denmark?

QUEEN   How now, Ophelia!

OPHELIA   [*Sings.*]
                  "How should I your true love know
                     From another one?
                  By his cockle hat and staff,
                     And his sandal shoon."

253

QUEEN   Alas, sweet lady, what imports this song?

OPHELIA   Say you? nay, pray you, mark. [*Sings.*]

> "He is dead and gone, lady,
>   He is dead and gone;
> At his head a grass-green turf,
>   At his heels a stone."

QUEEN   Nay, but, Ophelia—

OPHELIA   Pray you, mark. [*Sings.*]

> "White his shroud as the mountain snow—"

Enter King.

QUEEN   Alas, look here, my lord.

OPHELIA   [*Sings.*]

> "Larded with sweet flowers;
> Which bewept to the grave did go
>   With true-love showers."

KING   How do you, pretty lady?

OPHELIA   Well, God 'ild you! They say the owl was a baker's daughter. Lord, we know what we are, but know not what we may be. God be at your table!

KING   Conceit upon her father.

OPHELIA   Pray you, let's have no words of this; but when they ask you what it means, say you this: [*Sings.*]

> "To-morrow is Saint Valentine's day,
>   All in the morning betime,
> And I a maid at your window,
>   To be your Valentine.
>
> Then up he rose, and donn'd his clothes,
>   And dupp'd the chamber-door;
> Let in the maid, that out a maid
>   Never departed more."

KING   Pretty Ophelia!

OPHELIA   Indeed, la, without an oath, I'll make an end on't: [*Sings.*]

> "By Gis and by Saint Charity,
>   Alack, and fie for shame!
> Young men will do't, if they come to't;
>   By cock, they are to blame.
> Quoth she, before you tumbled me,
>   You promised me to wed."

He answers:

> "So would I ha' done, by yonder sun,
>   An thou hadst not come to my bed."

KING   How long hath she been thus?

OPHELIA   I hope all will be well. We must be patient; but I cannot choose but weep, to think they should lay him i' the cold ground. My brother shall know of it; and so I thank you for your good counsel. Come, my coach! Good night, ladies; good night, sweet ladies; good night, good night.   *Exit.*

KING   Follow her close; give her good watch, I pray you.

Exit Horatio.

O, this is the poison of deep grief; it springs
All from her father's death. O Gertrude, Gertrude,
When sorrows come, they come not single spies,
But in battalions. First, her father slain;
Next, your son gone; and he most violent author
Of his own just remove; the people muddied,
Thick and unwholesome in their thoughts and whispers,
For good Polonius' death; and we have done but greenly,
In hugger-mugger to inter him; poor Ophelia
Divided from herself and her fair judgement,
Without the which we are pictures, or mere beasts;
Last, and as much containing as all these,
Her brother is in secret come from France;
Feeds on his wonder, keeps himself in clouds,
And wants not buzzers to infect his ear
With pestilent speeches of his father's death;
Wherein necessity, of matter beggar'd,
Will nothing stick our person to arraign
In ear and ear. O my dear Gertrude, this,
Like to a murdering-piece, in many places
Gives me superfluous death.

A noise within.

QUEEN   Alack, what noise is this?

Enter another Gentleman.

KING   Where are my Switzers? Let them guard the door.
   What is the matter?

GENTLEMAN   Save yourself, my lord:
   The ocean, overpeering of his list,
   Eats not the flats with more impetuous haste
   Than young Laertes, in a riotous head,
   O'erbears your officers. The rabble call him lord;
   And, as the world were now but to begin,
   Antiquity forgot, custom not known,
   The ratifiers and props of every word,
   They cry, "Choose we: Laertes shall be king!"
   Caps, hands, and tongues, applaud it to the clouds:
   "Laertes shall be king, Laertes king!"

QUEEN   How cheerfully on the false trail they cry!
   O, this is counter, you false Danish dogs!

KING   The doors are broke.

Noise within. Enter Laertes, armed; Danes following.

LAERTES   Where is this king? Sirs, stand you all without.

DANES   No, let's come in.

LAERTES   I pray you, give me leave.

DANES   We will, we will.   *They retire without the door.*

LAERTES   I thank you; keep the door. O thou vile king,
   Give me my father!

QUEEN   Calmly, good Laertes.

LAERTES   That drop of blood that's calm proclaims me bastard,
   Cries cuckold to my father, brands the harlot
   Even here, between the chaste unsmirched brow
   Of my true mother.

KING   What is the cause, Laertes,
   That thy rebellion looks so giant-like?
   Let him go, Gertrude; do not fear our person:
   There's such divinity doth hedge a king,
   That treason can but peep to what it would,

256

Acts little of his will. Tell me, Laertes,
Why thou art thus incensed. Let him go, Gertrude.
Speak, man.

LAERTES   Where is my father?

KING   Dead.

QUEEN   But not by him.

KING   Let him demand his fill.

LAERTES   How came he dead? I'll not be juggled with.
To hell, allegiance! vows, to the blackest devil!
Conscience and grace, to the profoundest pit!
I dare damnation. To this point I stand,
That both the worlds I give to negligence,
Let come what comes; only I'll be revenged
Most throughly for my father.

KING   Who shall stay you?

LAERTES   My will, not all the world:
And for my means, I'll husband them so well,
They shall go far with little.

KING   Good Laertes,
If you desire to know the certainty
Of your dear father's death, is't writ in your revenge,
That, swoopstake, you will draw both friend and foe,
Winner and loser?

LAERTES   None but his enemies.

KING   Will you know them then?

LAERTES   To his good friends thus wide I'll ope my arms;
And like the kind life-rendering pelican,
Repast them with my blood.

KING   Why, now you speak
Like a good child and a true gentleman.
That I am guiltless of your father's death,
And am most sensibly in grief for it,
It shall as level to your judgement pierce
As day does to your eye.

DANES   [*Within.*] Let her come in.

257

HAMLET, PRINCE OF DENMARK

LAERTES   How now! what noise is that?

Re-enter Ophelia.

O heat, dry up my brains! tears seven times salt,
Burn out the sense and virtue of mine eye!
By heaven, thy madness shall be paid with weight,
Till our scale turn the beam. O rose of May!
Dear maid, kind sister, sweet Ophelia!
O heavens! is't possible, a young maid's wits
Should be as mortal as an old man's life?
Nature is fine in love, and where 'tis fine,
It sends some precious instance of itself
After the thing it loves.

OPHELIA   [*Sings.*]
        "They bore him barefaced on the bier;
        Hey non nonny, nonny, hey nonny;
        And in his grave rain'd many a tear—"

Fare you well, my dove!

LAERTES   Hadst thou thy wits, and didst persuade revenge,
It could not move thus.

OPHELIA   [*Sings.*]
        "You must sing a-down a-down,
        An you call him a-down-a."

O, how the wheel becomes it! It is the false steward, that stole his master's daughter.

LAERTES   This nothing's more than matter.

OPHELIA   There's rosemary, that's for remembrance; pray, love, remember; and there is pansies, that's for thoughts.

LAERTES   A document in madness, thoughts and remembrance fitted.

OPHELIA   There's fennel for you, and columbines; there's rue for you, and here's some for me; we may call it herb-grace o' Sundays. O, you must wear your rue with a difference. There's a daisy. I would give you some violets, but they withered all when my father died. They say he made a good end—[*Sings.*]

        "For bonny sweet Robin is all my joy."

258

LAERTES   Thought and affliction, passion, hell itself,
She turns to favour and to prettiness.

OPHELIA   [*Sings.*]
                    "And will he not come again?
                    And will he not come again?
                        No, no, he is dead;
                        Go to thy death-bed;
                    He never will come again.

                    His beard was as white as snow,
                    All flaxen was his poll.
                        He is gone, he is gone,
                        And we cast away moan.
                    God ha' mercy on his soul!"

And of all Christian souls, I pray God. God be wi' ye.   *Exit.*

LAERTES   Do you see this, O God?

KING   Laertes, I must commune with your grief,
Or you deny me right. Go but apart,
Make choice of whom your wisest friends you will,
And they shall hear and judge 'twixt you and me.
If by direct or by collateral hand
They find us touch'd, we will our kingdom give,
Our crown, our life, and all that we call ours,
To you in satisfaction; but if not,
Be you content to lend your patience to us,
And we shall jointly labour with your soul
To give it due content.

LAERTES   Let this be so;
His means of death, his obscure funeral—
No trophy, sword, nor hatchment o'er his bones,
No noble rite nor formal ostentation—
Cry to be heard, as 'twere from heaven to earth,
That I must call't in question.

KING   So you shall;
And where the offence is let the great axe fall.
I pray you, go with me.   *Exeunt.*

259

SCENE 6 *Another room in the castle.*

Enter Horatio and a Servant.

HORATIO   What are they that would speak with me?

SERVANT   Sailors, sir. They say they have letters for you.

HORATIO   Let them come in.   *Exit Servant.*
I do not know from what part of the world
I should be greeted, if not from Lord Hamlet.

Enter Sailors.

FIRST SAILOR   God bless you, sir.

HORATIO   Let Him bless thee too.

FIRST SAILOR   He shall, sir, an't please Him. There's a letter for you, sir. It comes from the ambassador that was bound for England; if your name be Horatio, as I am let to know it is.

HORATIO   [*Reads.*]
"Horatio, when thou shalt have overlooked this, give these fellows some means to the King; they have letters for him. Ere we were two days old at sea, a pirate of very warlike appointment gave us chase. Finding ourselves too slow of sail, we put on a compelled valour, and in the grapple I boarded them. On the instant they got clear of our ship; so I alone became their prisoner. They have dealt with me like thieves of mercy, but they knew what they did; I am to do a good turn for them. Let the King have the letters I have sent; and repair thou to me with as much speed as thou wouldst fly death. I have words to speak in thine ear will make thee dumb; yet are they much too light for the bore of the matter. These good fellows will bring thee where I am. Rosencrantz and Guildenstern hold their course for England; of them I have much to tell thee. Farewell.
He that thou knowest thine, Hamlet"

Come, I will make you way for these your letters;
And do't the speedier, that you may direct me
To him from whom you brought them.   *Exeunt.*

 SCENE 7   *Another room in the castle.*

Enter King and Laertes.

KING   Now must your conscience my acquittance seal,
And you must put me in your heart for friend,
Sith you have heard, and with a knowing ear,
That he which hath your noble father slain
Pursued my life.

LAERTES   It well appears: but tell me
Why you proceeded not against these feats,
So crimeful and so capital in nature,
As by your safety, wisdom, all things else,
You mainly were stirr'd up.

KING   O, for two special reasons;
Which may to you, perhaps, seem much unsinew'd,
But yet to me they are strong. The Queen his mother
Lives almost by his looks; and for myself—
My virtue or my plague, be it either which—
She's so conjunctive to my life and soul,
That, as the star moves not but in his sphere,
I could not but by her. The other motive,
Why to a public count I might not go,
Is the great love the general gender bear him;
Who, dipping all his faults in their affection,
Would, like the spring that turneth wood to stone,
Convert his gyves to graces; so that my arrows,
Too slightly timber'd for so loud a wind,
Would have reverted to my bow again,
And not where I had aim'd them.

LAERTES   And so have I a noble father lost;
A sister driven into desperate terms,
Whose worth, if praises may go back again,
Stood challenger on mount of all the age
For her perfections. But my revenge will come.

KING   Break not your sleeps for that. You must not think
That we are made of stuff so flat and dull
That we can let our beard be shook with danger
And think it pastime. You shortly shall hear more.

261

I loved your father, and we love ourself;
And that, I hope, will teach you to imagine—

Enter a Messenger.

How now! what news?

MESSENGER   Letters, my lord, from Hamlet.
This to your Majesty; this to the Queen.

KING   From Hamlet! who brought them?

MESSENGER   Sailors, my lord, they say; I saw them not:
They were given me by Claudio; he received them
Of him that brought them.

KING   Laertes, you shall hear them.
Leave us.   *Exit Messenger.*

[*Reads.*]
"High and mighty, You shall know I am set naked on your kingdom.
To-morrow shall I beg leave to see your kingly eyes, when I shall, first
asking your pardon thereunto, recount the occasion of my sudden and
more strange return.
                                                    Hamlet"

What should this mean? Are all the rest come back?
Or is it some abuse, and no such thing?

LAERTES   Know you the hand?

KING   'Tis Hamlet's character. "Naked!"
And in a postscript here, he says "alone."
Can you advise me?

LAERTES   I'm lost in it, my lord. But let him come;
It warms the very sickness in my heart,
That I shall live and tell him to his teeth,
"Thus didest thou."

KING   If it be so, Laertes—
As how should it be so? how otherwise?—
Will you be ruled by me?

LAERTES   Ay, my lord;
So you will not o'errule me to a peace.

KING   To thine own peace. If he be now return'd,
As checking at his voyage, and that he means

No more to undertake it, I will work him
To an exploit, now ripe in my device,
Under the which he shall not choose but fall;
And for his death no wind of blame shall breathe,
But even his mother shall uncharge the practice
And call it accident.

LAERTES   My lord, I will be ruled;
  The rather, if you could devise it so
  That I might be the organ.

KING   It falls right.
  You have been talk'd of since your travel much,
  And that in Hamlet's hearing, for a quality
  Wherein, they say, you shine: your sum of parts
  Did not together pluck such envy from him
  As did that one, and that, in my regard,
  Of the unworthiest siege.

LAERTES   What part is that, my lord?

KING   A very riband in the cap of youth,
  Yet needful too; for youth no less becomes
  The light and careless livery that it wears
  Than settled age his sables and his weeds,
  Importing health and graveness. Two months since,
  Here was a gentleman of Normandy;
  I've seen myself, and served against, the French,
  And they can well on horseback: but this gallant
  Had witchcraft in't; he grew unto his seat;
  And to such wondrous doing brought his horse,
  As had he been incorpsed and demi-natured
  With the brave beast. So far he topp'd my thought,
  That I, in forgery of shapes and tricks,
  Come short of what he did.

LAERTES   A Norman was't?

KING   A Norman.

LAERTES   Upon my life, Lamond.

KING   The very same.

LAERTES   I know him well. He is the brooch indeed
  And gem of all the nation.

KING   He made confession of you,
    And gave you such a masterly report
    For art and exercise in your defence
    And for your rapier most especial,
    That he cried out, 'twould be a sight indeed,
    If one could match you. The scrimers of their nation,
    He swore, had neither motion, guard, nor eye,
    If you opposed them. Sir, this report of his
    Did Hamlet so envenom with his envy
    That he could nothing do but wish and beg
    Your sudden coming o'er, to play with him.
    Now, out of this—

LAERTES   What out of this, my lord?

KING   Laertes, was your father dear to you?
    Or are you like the painting of a sorrow,
    A face without a heart?

LAERTES   Why ask you this?

KING   Not that I think you did not love your father;
    But that I know love is begun by time;
    And that I see, in passages of proof,
    Time qualifies the spark and fire of it.
    There lives within the very flame of love
    A kind of wick or snuff that will abate it;
    And nothing is at a like goodness still;
    For goodness, growing to a plurisy,
    Dies in his own too much. That we would do,
    We should do when we would; for this "would" changes
    And hath abatements and delays as many
    As there are tongues, are hands, are accidents;
    And then this "should" is like a spendthrift sigh,
    That hurts by easing. But, to the quick o' the ulcer—
    Hamlet comes back. What would you undertake,
    To show yourself your father's son in deed
    More than in words?

LAERTES   To cut his throat i' the church.

KING   No place, indeed, should murder sanctuarize;
    Revenge should have no bounds. But, good Laertes,
    Will you do this, keep close within your chamber.
    Hamlet return'd shall know you are come home.

We'll put on those shall praise your excellence
And set a double varnish on the fame
The Frenchman gave you, bring you in fine together
And wager on your heads. He, being remiss,
Most generous and free from all contriving,
Will not peruse the foils; so that, with ease,
Or with a little shuffling, you may choose
A sword unbated, and in a pass of practice
Requite him for your father.

LAERTES   I will do't;
And, for that purpose, I'll anoint my sword.
I bought an unction of a mountebank,
So mortal that, but dip a knife in it,
Where it draws blood no cataplasm so rare,
Collected from all simples that have virtue
Under the moon, can save the thing from death
That is but scratch'd withal. I'll touch my point
With this contagion, that, if I gall him slightly,
It may be death.

KING   Let's further think of this;
Weigh what convenience both of time and means
May fit us to our shape: if this should fail,
And that our drift look through our bad performance,
'Twere better not assay'd: therefore this project
Should have a back or second, that might hold,
If this should blast in proof. Soft! let me see:
We'll make a solemn wager on your cunnings.
I ha't:
When in your motion you are hot and dry—
As make your bouts more violent to that end—
And that he calls for drink, I'll have prepared him
A chalice for the nonce, whereon but sipping,
If he by chance escape your venom'd stuck,
Our purpose may hold there.

Enter Queen.

                        How now, sweet queen!

QUEEN One woe doth tread upon another's heel,
  So fast they follow. Your sister's drown'd, Laertes.

LAERTES Drown'd! O, where?

QUEEN   There is a willow grows aslant a brook,
That shows his hoar leaves in the glassy stream;
There with fantastic garlands did she come
Of crow-flowers, nettles, daisies, and long purples
That liberal shepherds give a grosser name,
But our cold maids do dead men's fingers call them;
There, on the pendent boughs her coronet weeds
Clambering to hang, an envious sliver broke;
When down her weedy trophies and herself
Fell in the weeping brook. Her clothes spread wide;
And, mermaid-like, awhile they bore her up;
Which time she chanted snatches of old tunes;
As one incapable of her own distress,
Or like a creature native and indued
Unto that element. But long it could not be
Till that her garments, heavy with their drink,
Pull'd the poor wretch from her melodious lay
To muddy death.

LAERTES   Alas, then, she is drown'd?

QUEEN   Drown'd, drown'd.

LAERTES   Too much of water hast thou, poor Ophelia,
And therefore I forbid my tears. But yet
It is our trick; Nature her custom holds,
Let shame say what it will; when these are gone,
The woman will be out. Adieu, my lord:
I have a speech of fire, that fain would blaze,
But that this folly douts it.   *Exit.*

KING   Let's follow, Gertrude.
How much I had to do to calm his rage!
Now fear I this will give it start again;
Therefore let's follow.   *Exeunt.*

ACT V

❀ SCENE 1 *A churchyard.*

Enter Two Clowns, with spades, &c.

FIRST CLOWN   Is she to be buried in Christian burial that wilfully seeks her own salvation?

SECOND CLOWN   I tell thee she is; and therefore make her grave straight. The crowner hath sat on her, and finds it Christian burial.

FIRST CLOWN   How can that be, unless she drowned herself in her own defence?

SECOND CLOWN   Why, 'tis found so.

FIRST CLOWN   It must be *se offendendo;* it cannot be else. For here lies the point: if I drown myself wittingly, it argues an act, and an act hath three branches; it is, to act, to do, and to perform: argal, she drowned herself wittingly.

SECOND CLOWN   Nay, but hear you, goodman delver —

FIRST CLOWN   Give me leave. Here lies the water; good. Here stands the man; good. If the man go to this water, and drown himself, it is, will he, nill he, he goes — mark you that. But if the water come to him and drown him, he drowns not himself; argal, he that is not guilty of his own death shortens not his own life.

SECOND CLOWN   But is this law?

FIRST CLOWN   Ay, marry, is't; crowner's quest law.

SECOND CLOWN   Will you ha' the truth on't? If this had not been a gentlewoman, she should have been buried out o' Christian burial.

267

FIRST CLOWN   Why, there thou say'st; and the more pity that great folk should have countenance in this world to drown or hang themselves, more than their even Christian. Come, my spade. There is no ancient gentlemen but gardeners, ditchers, and grave-makers; they hold up Adam's profession.

SECOND CLOWN   Was he a gentleman?

FIRST CLOWN   A' was the first that ever bore arms.

SECOND CLOWN   Why, he had none.

FIRST CLOWN   What, art a heathen? How dost thou understand the Scripture? The Scripture says "Adam digged"; could he dig without arms? I'll put another question to thee. If thou answerest me not to the purpose, confess thyself—

SECOND CLOWN   Go to.

FIRST CLOWN   What is he that builds stronger than either the mason, the shipwright, or the carpenter?

SECOND CLOWN   The gallows-maker; for that frame outlives a thousand tenants.

FIRST CLOWN   I like thy wit well, in good faith. The gallows does well; but how does it well? it does well to those that do ill. Now thou dost ill to say the gallows is built stronger than the church; argal, the gallows may do well to thee. To't again, come.

SECOND CLOWN   "Who builds stronger than a mason, a shipwright, or a carpenter?"

FIRST CLOWN   Ay, tell me that, and unyoke.

SECOND CLOWN   Marry, now I can tell.

FIRST CLOWN   To't.

SECOND CLOWN   Mass, I cannot tell.

Enter Hamlet and Horatio, at a distance.

FIRST CLOWN   Cudgel thy brains no more about it, for your dull ass will not mend his pace with beating; and, when you are asked this question next, say "a grave-maker": the houses that he makes last till doomsday. Go, get thee to Yaughan: fetch me a stoup of liquor.

Exit Second Clown.

He digs, and sings.

"In youth, when I did love, did love,
   Methought it was very sweet,
To contract, O, the time, for, ah, my behove,
   O, methought, there was nothing meet."

HAMLET Has this fellow no feeling of his business, that he sings at grave-making?

HORATIO Custom hath made it in him a property of easiness.

HAMLET 'Tis e'en so. The hand of little employment hath the daintier sense.

FIRST CLOWN [*Sings.*]
"But age, with his stealing steps,
   Hath claw'd me in his clutch,
And hath shipped me intil the land,
   As if I had never been such."

Throws up a skull.

HAMLET That skull had a tongue in it, and could sing once. How the knave jowls it to the ground, as if it were Cain's jaw-bone, that did the first murder! It might be the pate of a politician, which this ass now o'er-reaches; one that would circumvent God, might it not?

HORATIO It might, my lord.

HAMLET Or of a courtier; which could say "Good morrow, sweet lord! How dost thou, good lord?" This might be my Lord Such-a-one, that praised my Lord Such-a-one's horse, when he meant to beg it; might it not?

HORATIO Ay, my lord.

HAMLET Why, e'en so; and now my Lady Worm's; chapless, and knocked about the mazzard with a sexton's spade. Here's fine revolution, an we had the trick to see't. Did these bones cost no more the breeding, but to play at loggats with 'em? mine ache to think on't.

FIRST CLOWN [*Sings.*]
"A pick-axe, and a spade, a spade,
   For and a shrouding sheet;
O, a pit of clay for to be made
   For such a guest is meet."

Throws up another skull.

269

HAMLET   There's another. Why may not that be the skull of a lawyer? Where be his quiddities now, his quillets, his cases, his tenures, and his tricks? Why does he suffer this rude knave now to knock him about the sconce with a dirty shovel, and will not tell him of his action of battery? Hum! This fellow might be in's time a great buyer of land, with his statutes, his recognizances, his fines, his double vouchers, his recoveries. Is this the fine of his fines, and the recovery of his recoveries, to have his fine pate full of fine dirt? Will his vouchers vouch him no more of his purchases, and double ones too, than the length and breadth of a pair of indentures? The very conveyances of his lands will hardly lie in this box; and must the inheritor himself have no more, ha?

HORATIO   Not a jot more, my lord.

HAMLET   Is not parchment made of sheep-skins?

HORATIO   Ay, my lord, and of calf-skins too.

HAMLET   They are sheep and calves which seek out assurance in that. I will speak to this fellow. Whose grave's this, sirrah?

FIRST CLOWN   Mine, sir. [Sings.]

> "O, a pit of clay for to be made
> For such a guest is meet."

HAMLET   I think it be thine, indeed; for thou liest in't.

FIRST CLOWN   You lie out on't, sir, and therefore it is not yours. For my part, I do not lie in't, and yet it is mine.

HAMLET   Thou dost lie in't, to be in't and say it is thine. 'Tis for the dead, not for the quick; therefore thou liest.

FIRST CLOWN   'Tis a quick lie, sir; 'twill away again, from me to you.

HAMLET   What man dost thou dig it for?

FIRST CLOWN   For no man, sir.

HAMLET   What woman, then?

FIRST CLOWN   For none, neither.

HAMLET   Who is to be buried in't?

FIRST CLOWN   One that was a woman, sir; but, rest her soul, she's dead.

HAMLET   How absolute the knave is! we must speak by the card, or equivocation will undo us. By the Lord, Horatio, these three years I

have taken note of it; the age is grown so picked that the toe of the peasant comes so near the heel of the courtier, he galls his kibe. How long hast thou been a grave-maker?

FIRST CLOWN   Of all the days i' the year, I came to't that day that our last King Hamlet overcame Fortinbras.

HAMLET   How long is that since?

FIRST CLOWN   Cannot you tell that? every fool can tell that. It was the very day that young Hamlet was born; he that is mad, and sent into England.

HAMLET   Ay, marry, why was he sent into England?

FIRST CLOWN   Why, because he was mad. He shall recover his wits there; or, if he do not, it's no great matter there.

HAMLET   Why?

FIRST CLOWN   'Twill not be seen in him there; there the men are as mad as he.

HAMLET   How came he mad?

FIRST CLOWN   Very strangely, they say.

HAMLET   How strangely?

FIRST CLOWN   Faith, e'en with losing his wits.

HAMLET   Upon what ground?

FIRST CLOWN   Why, here in Denmark. I have been sexton here, man and boy, thirty years.

HAMLET   How long will a man lie i' the earth ere he rot?

FIRST CLOWN   I' faith, if he be not rotten before he die—as we have many pocky corses now-a-days, that will scarce hold the laying in— he will last you some eight year or nine year. A tanner will last you nine year.

HAMLET   Why he more than another?

FIRST CLOWN   Why, sir, his hide is so tanned with his trade, that he will keep out water a great while; and your water is a sore decayer of your whoreson dead body. Here's a skull now; this skull has lain in the earth three and twenty years.

HAMLET   Whose was it?

271

FIRST CLOWN   A whoreson mad fellow's it was. Whose do you think it was?

HAMLET   Nay, I know not.

FIRST CLOWN   A pestilence on him for a mad rogue! a' poured a flagon of Rhenish on my head once. This same skull, sir, was Yorick's skull, the King's jester.

HAMLET   This?

FIRST CLOWN   E'en that.

HAMLET   Let me see. [*Takes the skull.*] Alas, poor Yorick! I knew him, Horatio; a fellow of infinite jest, of most excellent fancy. He hath borne me on his back a thousand times; and now, how abhorred in my imagination it is! my gorge rises at it. Here hung those lips that I have kissed I know not how oft. Where be your gibes now? your gambols? your songs? your flashes of merriment, that were wont to set the table on a roar? Not one now, to mock your own grinning? quite chap-fallen? Now get you to my lady's chamber, and tell her, let her paint an inch thick, to this favour she must come; make her laugh at that. Prithee, Horatio, tell me one thing.

HORATIO   What's that, my lord?

HAMLET   Dost thou think Alexander looked o' this fashion i' the earth?

HORATIO   E'en so.

HAMLET   And smelt so? pah!

Puts down the skull.

HORATIO   E'en so, my lord.

HAMLET   To what base uses we may return, Horatio! Why may not imagination trace the noble dust of Alexander, till he find it stopping a bung-hole?

HORATIO   'Twere to consider too curiously, to consider so.

HAMLET   No, faith, not a jot; but to follow him thither with modesty enough, and likelihood to lead it; as thus: Alexander died, Alexander was buried, Alexander returneth into dust; the dust is earth; of earth we make loam; and why of that loam, whereto he was converted, might they not stop a beer-barrel?

272

Imperious Caesar, dead and turn'd to clay,
Might stop a hole to keep the wind away.
O, that that earth, which kept the world in awe,
Should patch a wall to expel the winter's flaw!
But soft, but soft! aside: here comes the King,

Enter Priests, &c. in procession; the corpse of Ophelia, Laertes and mourners following; King, Queen, their trains, &c.

The Queen, the courtiers. Who is this they follow?
And with such maimed rites? This doth betoken
The corse they follow did with desperate hand
Fordo its own life. 'Twas of some estate.
Couch we awhile, and mark.   *Retiring with Horatio.*

LAERTES What ceremony else?

HAMLET   That is Laertes,
A very noble youth; mark.

LAERTES What ceremony else?

FIRST PRIEST Her obsequies have been as far enlarged
As we have warranty. Her death was doubtful;
And, but that great command o'ersways the order,
She should in ground unsanctified have lodged
Till the last trumpet; for charitable prayers,
Shards, flints, and pebbles should be thrown on her:
Yet here she is allow'd her virgin crants,
Her maiden strewments, and the bringing home
Of bell and burial.

LAERTES Must there no more be done?

FIRST PRIEST   No more be done.
We should profane the service of the dead
To sing a requiem and such rest to her
As to peace-parted souls.

LAERTES   Lay her i' the earth,
And from her fair and unpolluted flesh
May violets spring! I tell thee, churlish priest,
A ministering angel shall my sister be,
When thou liest howling.

HAMLET   What, the fair Ophelia!

QUEEN   Sweets to the sweet; farewell!

Scattering flowers.

> I hoped thou shouldst have been my Hamlet's wife;
> I thought thy bride-bed to have deck'd, sweet maid,
> And not have strew'd thy grave.

LAERTES   O, treble woe
> Fall ten times treble on that cursed head,
> Whose wicked deed thy most ingenious sense
> Deprived thee of! Hold off the earth awhile,
> Till I have caught her once more in mine arms.

Leaps into the grave.

> Now pile your dust upon the quick and dead,
> Till of this flat a mountain you have made,
> To o'ertop old Pelion, or the skyish head
> Of blue Olympus.

HAMLET   [*Advancing.*] What is he whose grief
> Bears such an emphasis? whose phrase of sorrow
> Conjures the wandering stars, and makes them stand
> Like wonder-wounded hearers? This is I,
> Hamlet the Dane.

Leaps into the grave.

LAERTES   The devil take thy soul!

Grappling with him.

HAMLET   Thou pray'st not well.
> I prithee, take thy fingers from my throat;
> For, though I am not splenitive and rash,
> Yet have I something in me dangerous,
> Which let thy wiseness fear: hold off thy hand.

KING   Pluck them asunder.

QUEEN   Hamlet, Hamlet!

ALL   Gentlemen—

HORATIO   Good my lord, be quiet.

The Attendants part them, and they come out of the grave.

HAMLET   Why, I will fight with him upon this theme
  Until my eyelids will no longer wag.

QUEEN   O my son, what theme?

HAMLET   I loved Ophelia. Forty thousand brothers
  Could not, with all their quantity of love,
  Make up my sum. What wilt thou do for her?

KING   O, he is mad, Laertes.

QUEEN   For love of God, forbear him.

HAMLET   'Swounds, show me what thou'lt do.
  Woo't weep? woo't fight? woo't fast? woo't tear thyself?
  Woo't drink up eisel? eat a crocodile?
  I'll do't. Dost thou come here to whine?
  To outface me with leaping in her grave?
  Be buried quick with her, and so will I;
  And, if thou prate of mountains, let them throw
  Millions of acres on us, till our ground,
  Singeing his pate against the burning zone,
  Make Ossa like a wart! Nay, an thou'lt mouth,
  I'll rant as well as thou.

QUEEN   This is mere madness,
  And thus awhile the fit will work on him;
  Anon, as patient as the female dove,
  When that her golden couplets are disclosed,
  His silence will sit drooping.

HAMLET   Hear you, sir;
  What is the reason that you use me thus?
  I loved you ever. But it is no matter;
  Let Hercules himself do what he may,
  The cat will mew and dog will have his day.   *Exit.*

KING   I pray you, good Horatio, wait upon him.   *Exit Horatio.*
  [*To Laertes.*] Strengthen your patience in our last night's speech;
  We'll put the matter to the present push.
  Good Gertrude, set some watch over your son.
  This grave shall have a living monument.
  An hour of quiet shortly shall we see;
  Till then, in patience our proceeding be.   *Exeunt.*

✤ SCENE 2 *A hall in the castle.*

Enter Hamlet and Horatio.

HAMLET So much for this, sir; now shall you see the other;
You do remember all the circumstance?

HORATIO Remember it, my lord!

HAMLET Sir, in my heart there was a kind of fighting,
That would not let me sleep. Methought I lay
Worse than the mutines in the bilboes. Rashly,
And praised be rashness for it, let us know,
Our indiscretion sometimes serves us well,
When our deep plots do pall; and that should teach us
There's a divinity that shapes our ends,
Rough-hew them how we will—

HORATIO   That is most certain.

HAMLET Up from my cabin,
My sea-gown scarf'd about me, in the dark
Groped I to find out them; had my desire,
Finger'd their packet, and in fine withdrew
To mine own room again; making so bold,
My fears forgetting manners, to unseal
Their grand commission; where I found, Horatio—
O royal knavery!—an exact command,
Larded with many several sorts of reasons
Importing Denmark's health and England's too,
With, ho! such bugs and goblins in my life,
That, on the supervise, no leisure bated,
No, not to stay the grinding of the axe,
My head should be struck off.

HORATIO   Is't possible?

HAMLET Here's the commission; read it at more leisure.
But wilt thou hear me how I did proceed?

HORATIO I beseech you.

HAMLET Being thus be-netted round with villainies—
Ere I could make a prologue to my brains,
They had begun the play—I sat me down,
Devised a new commission, wrote it fair.

276

I once did hold it, as our statists do,
A baseness to write fair and labour'd much
How to forget that learning, but, sir, now
It did me yeoman's service. Wilt thou know
The effect of what I wrote?

HORATIO   Ay, good my lord.

HAMLET   An earnest conjuration from the King,
As England was his faithful tributary,
As love between them like the palm might flourish,
As peace should still her wheaten garland wear
And stand a comma 'tween their amities,
And many such-like as's of great charge,
That, on the view and knowing of these contents,
Without debatement further, more or less,
He should the bearers put to sudden death,
Not shriving-time allow'd.

HORATIO   How was this seal'd?

HAMLET   Why, even in that was heaven ordinant.
I had my father's signet in my purse,
Which was the model of that Danish seal;
Folded the writ up in form of the other,
Subscribed it, gave't the impression, placed it safely,
The changeling never known. Now, the next day
Was our sea-fight; and what to this was sequent
Thou know'st already.

HORATIO   So Guildenstern and Rosencrantz go to't.

HAMLET   Why, man, they did make love to this employment;
They are not near my conscience; their defeat
Does by their own insinuation grow.
'Tis dangerous when the baser nature comes
Between the pass and fell incensed points
Of mighty opposites.

HORATIO   Why, what a king is this!

HAMLET   Does it not, think'st thee, stand me now upon—
He that hath kill'd my king and whored my mother,
Popp'd in between the election and my hopes,
Thrown out his angle for my proper life,
And with such cozenage—is't not perfect conscience,

277

To quit him with this arm? and is't not to be damn'd,
To let this canker of our nature come
In further evil?

HORATIO   It must be shortly known to him from England
What is the issue of the business there.

HAMLET   It will be short; the interim is mine,
And a man's life's no more than to say "One."
But I am very sorry, good Horatio,
That to Laertes I forgot myself;
For, by the image of my cause, I see
The portraiture of his. I'll court his favours.
But, sure, the bravery of his grief did put me
Into a towering passion.

HORATIO   Peace! who comes here?

Enter Osric.

OSRIC   Your lordship is right welcome back to Denmark.

HAMLET   I humbly thank you, sir. Dost know this water-fly?

HORATIO   No, my good lord.

HAMLET   Thy state is the more gracious; for 'tis a vice to know him. He hath much land, and fertile; let a beast be lord of beasts, and his crib shall stand at the King's mess. 'Tis a chough; but, as I say, spacious in the possession of dirt.

OSRIC   Sweet lord, if your lordship were at leisure, I should impart a thing to you from his Majesty.

HAMLET   I will receive it, sir, with all diligence of spirit. Put your bonnet to his right use; 'tis for the head.

OSRIC   I thank your lordship, it is very hot.

HAMLET   No, believe me, 'tis very cold; the wind is northerly.

OSRIC   It is indifferent cold, my lord, indeed.

HAMLET   But yet methinks it is very sultry and hot for my complexion.

OSRIC   Exceedingly, my lord; it is very sultry—as 'twere—I cannot tell how. But, my lord, his Majesty bade me signify to you that he has laid a great wager on your head. Sir, this is the matter—

HAMLET   I beseech you, remember—

Hamlet moves him to put on his hat.

OSRIC   Nay, good my lord; for mine ease, in good faith. Sir, here is newly come to court Laertes; believe me, an absolute gentleman, full of most excellent differences, of very soft society and great showing; indeed, to speak feelingly of him, he is the card or calendar of gentry, for you shall find in him the continent of what part a gentleman would see.

HAMLET   Sir, his definement suffers no perdition in you; though, I know, to divide him inventorially would dizzy the arithmetic of memory, and yet but yaw neither, in respect of his quick sail. But, in the verity of extolment, I take him to be a soul of great article; and his infusion of such dearth and rareness, as, to make true diction of him, his semblable is his mirror; and who else would trace him, his umbrage, nothing more.

OSRIC   Your lordship speaks most infallibly of him.

HAMLET   The concernancy, sir? why do we wrap the gentleman in our more rawer breath?

OSRIC   Sir?

HORATIO   Is't not possible to understand in another tongue? You will do't, sir, really.

HAMLET   What imports the nomination of this gentleman?

OSRIC   Of Laertes?

HORATIO   His purse is empty already; all's golden words are spent.

HAMLET   Of him, sir.

OSRIC   I know you are not ignorant—

HAMLET   I would you did, sir; yet, in faith, if you did, it would not much approve me. Well, sir?

OSRIC   You are not ignorant of what excellence Laertes is—

HAMLET   I dare not confess that, lest I should compare with him in excellence; but, to know a man well, were to know himself.

OSRIC   I mean, sir, for his weapon; but in the imputation laid on him by them, in his meed he's unfellowed.

279

HAMLET   What's his weapon?

OSRIC   Rapier and dagger.

HAMLET   That's two of his weapons; but, well.

OSRIC   The King, sir, hath wagered with him six Barbary horses, against the which he has imponed, as I take it, six French rapiers and poniards, with their assigns, as girdle, hangers, and so. Three of the carriages, in faith, are very dear to fancy, very responsive to the hilts, most delicate carriages, and of very liberal conceit.

HAMLET   What call you the carriages?

HORATIO   I knew you must be edified by the margent ere you had done.

OSRIC   The carriages, sir, are the hangers.

HAMLET   The phrase would be more germane to the matter, if we could carry cannon by our sides; I would it might be hangers till then. But, on: six Barbary horses against six French swords, their assigns, and three liberal-conceited carriages; that's the French bet against the Danish. Why is this "imponed," as you call it?

OSRIC   The King, sir, hath laid, that in a dozen passes between yourself and him, he shall not exceed you three hits. He hath laid on twelve for nine; and it would come to immediate trial, if your lordship would vouchsafe the answer.

HAMLET   How if I answer "no"?

OSRIC   I mean, my lord, the opposition of your person in trial.

HAMLET   Sir, I will walk here in the hall; if it please his Majesty, 'tis the breathing time of day with me; let the foils be brought, the gentleman willing, and the King hold his purpose, I will win for him an I can; if not, I will gain nothing but my shame and the odd hits.

OSRIC   Shall I re-deliver you e'en so?

HAMLET   To this effect, sir; after what flourish your nature will.

OSRIC   I commend my duty to your lordship.

HAMLET   Yours, yours.   *Exit Osric.*
He does well to commend it himself; there are no tongues else for's turn.

HORATIO   This lapwing runs away with the shell on his head.

HAMLET   He did comply with his dug, before he sucked it. Thus has he
—and many more of the same breed that I know the drossy age dotes
on—only got the tune of the time and outward habit of encounter; a
kind of yesty collection, which carries them through and through the
most fond and winnowed opinions; and do but blow them to their
trial, the bubbles are out.

Enter a Lord.

LORD   My Lord, his Majesty commended him to you by young Osric,
who brings back to him, that you attend him in the hall. He sends to
know if your pleasure hold to play with Laertes, or that you will take
longer time.

HAMLET   I am constant to my purposes; they follow the King's pleasure.
If his fitness speaks, mine is ready; now or whensoever, provided I be
so able as now.

LORD   The King and Queen and all are coming down.

HAMLET   In happy time.

LORD   The Queen desires you to use some gentle entertainment to
Laertes before you fall to play.

HAMLET   She well instructs me.   *Exit Lord.*

HORATIO   You will lose this wager, my lord.

HAMLET   I do not think so; since he went into France, I have been in con-
tinual practice; I shall win at the odds. But thou wouldst not think how
ill all's here about my heart. But it is no matter.

HORATIO   Nay, good my lord—

HAMLET   It is but foolery; but it is such a kind of gain-giving, as would
perhaps trouble a woman.

HORATIO   If your mind dislike anything, obey it. I will forestall their repair hither, and say you are not fit.

HAMLET   Not a whit, we defy augury. There's a special providence in the
fall of a sparrow. If it be now, 'tis not to come; if it be not to come, it
will be now; if it be not now, yet it will come; the readiness is all. Since
no man has aught of what he leaves, what is't to leave betimes? Let be.

*Enter King, Queen, Laertes, Osric, Lords, and Attendants with foils and gaunt-
lets; a table and flagons of wine on it.*

281

KING Come, Hamlet, come, and take this hand from me.

The King puts Laertes' hand into Hamlet's.

HAMLET Give me your pardon, sir. I've done you wrong;
But pardon't, as you are a gentleman.
This presence knows,
And you must needs have heard, how I am punish'd
With sore distraction. What I have done,
That might your nature, honour, and exception
Roughly awake, I here proclaim was madness.
Was't Hamlet wrong'd Laertes? Never Hamlet:
If Hamlet from himself be ta'en away,
And when he's not himself does wrong Laertes,
Then Hamlet does it not, Hamlet denies it.
Who does it, then? His madness. If't be so,
Hamlet is of the faction that is wrong'd;
His madness is poor Hamlet's enemy.
Sir, in this audience,
Let my disclaiming from a purposed evil
Free me so far in your most generous thoughts,
That I have shot mine arrow o'er the house,
And hurt my brother.

LAERTES   I am satisfied in nature,
Whose motive, in this case, should stir me most
To my revenge; but in my terms of honour
I stand aloof, and will no reconcilement,
Till by some elder masters, of known honour,
I have a voice and precedent of peace,
To keep my name ungored. But till that time,
I do receive your offer'd love like love,
And will not wrong it.

HAMLET   I embrace it freely;
And will this brother's wager frankly play.
Give us the foils. Come on.

LAERTES   Come, one for me.

HAMLET I'll be your foil, Laertes; in mine ignorance
Your skill shall, like a star i' the darkest night,
Stick fiery off indeed.

LAERTES   You mock me, sir.

HAMLET   No, by this hand.

KING   Give them the foils, young Osric. Cousin Hamlet,
  You know the wager?

HAMLET   Very well, my lord;
  Your Grace hath laid the odds o' the weaker side.

KING   I do not fear it; I have seen you both;
  But since he is better'd, we have therefore odds.

LAERTES   This is too heavy, let me see another.

HAMLET   This likes me well. These foils have all a length?

They prepare to play.

OSRIC   Ay, my good lord.

KING   Set me the stoups of wine upon that table.
  If Hamlet give the first or second hit,
  Or quit in answer of the third exchange,
  Let all the battlements their ordnance fire;
  The King shall drink to Hamlet's better breath;
  And in the cup an union shall he throw,
  Richer than that which four successive kings
  In Denmark's crown have worn. Give me the cups;
  And let the kettle to the trumpet speak,
  The trumpet to the cannoneer without,
  The cannons to the heavens, the heavens to earth,
  "Now the King drinks to Hamlet." Come, begin;
  And you, the judges, bear a wary eye.

HAMLET   Come on, sir.

LAERTES   Come, my lord.

They play.

HAMLET   One.

LAERTES   No.

HAMLET   Judgement.

OSRIC   A hit, a very palpable hit.

LAERTES   Well; again.

283

KING   Stay; give me drink. Hamlet, this pearl is thine;
  Here's to thy health.

Trumpets sound, and cannon shot off within.

                              Give him the cup.
HAMLET   I'll play this bout first; set it by awhile.
  Come. [*They play.*] Another hit; what say you?

LAERTES   A touch, a touch, I do confess.

KING   Our son shall win.

QUEEN   He's fat, and scant of breath.
  Here, Hamlet, take my napkin, rub thy brows.
  The Queen carouses to thy fortune, Hamlet.

HAMLET   Good madam!

KING   Gertrude, do not drink.

QUEEN   I will, my lord; I pray you, pardon me.

KING   [*Aside.*] It is the poison'd cup; it is too late.

HAMLET   I dare not drink yet, madam; by and by.

QUEEN   Come, let me wipe thy face.

LAERTES   My lord, I'll hit him now.

KING   I do not think't.

LAERTES   [*Aside.*] And yet 'tis almost 'gainst my conscience.

HAMLET   Come, for the third, Laertes; you but dally.
  I pray you, pass with your best violence;
  I am afeard you make a wanton of me.

LAERTES   Say you so? come on.

They play.

OSRIC   Nothing, neither way.

LAERTES   Have at you now!

Laertes wounds Hamlet; then, in scuffling, they change rapiers, and Hamlet wounds Laertes.

KING   Part them; they are incensed.

HAMLET   Nay, come, again.

The Queen falls.

OSRIC   Look to the Queen there, ho!

HORATIO   They bleed on both sides. How is it, my lord?

OSRIC   How is't, Laertes?

LAERTES   Why, as a woodcock to mine own springe, Osric;
   I am justly kill'd with mine own treachery.

HAMLET   How does the Queen?

KING   She swounds to see them bleed.

QUEEN   No, no, the drink, the drink—O my dear Hamlet—
   The drink, the drink! I am poison'd.   *Dies.*

HAMLET   O villainy! Ho! let the door be lock'd;
   Treachery! Seek it out.

LAERTES   It is here, Hamlet. Hamlet, thou art slain.
   No medicine in the world can do thee good;
   In thee there is not half an hour of life;
   The treacherous instrument is in thy hand,
   Unbated and envenom'd. The foul practice
   Hath turn'd itself on me; lo, here I lie,
   Never to rise again. Thy mother's poison'd.
   I can no more. The King, the King's to blame.

HAMLET   The point envenom'd too!
   Then, venom, to thy work.

Stabs the King.

ALL   Treason! treason!

KING   O, yet defend me, friends; I am but hurt.

HAMLET   Here, thou incestuous, murderous, damned Dane,
   Drink off this potion. Is thy union here?
   Follow my mother.   *King dies.*

LAERTES   He is justly served;
   It is a poison temper'd by himself.
   Exchange forgiveness with me, noble Hamlet.
   Mine and my father's death come not upon thee,
   Nor thine on me!   *Dies.*

285

HAMLET   Heaven make thee free of it! I follow thee.
  I am dead, Horatio. Wretched Queen, adieu!
  You that look pale and tremble at this chance,
  That are but mutes or audiences to this act,
  Had I but time—as this fell sergeant, Death,
  Is strict in his arrest—O, I could tell you—
  But let it be. Horatio, I am dead;
  Thou livest; report me and my cause aright
  To the unsatisfied.

HORATIO   Never believe it.
  I am more an antique Roman than a Dane;
  Here's yet some liquor left.

HAMLET   As thou'rt a man,
  Give me the cup. Let go! By heaven, I'll have't.
  O good Horatio, what a wounded name,
  Things standing thus unknown, shall live behind me!
  If thou didst ever hold me in thy heart,
  Absent thee from felicity awhile,
  And in this harsh world draw thy breath in pain,
  To tell my story.

March afar off, and shot within.

                    What warlike noise is this?

OSRIC   Young Fortinbras, with conquest come from Poland,
  To the ambassadors of England gives
  This warlike volley.

HAMLET   O, I die, Horatio;
  The potent poison quite o'er-crows my spirit.
  I cannot live to hear the news from England,
  But I do prophesy the election lights
  On Fortinbras; he has my dying voice.
  So tell him, with the occurrents, more and less,
  Which have solicited. The rest is silence.   *Dies.*

HORATIO   Now cracks a noble heart. Good night, sweet prince;
  And flights of angels sing thee to thy rest!

March within.

  Why does the drum come hither?

Enter Fortinbras, the English Ambassadors, and others.

FORTINBRAS   Where is this sight?

HORATIO   What is it ye would see?
   If aught of woe or wonder, cease your search.

FORTINBRAS   This quarry cries on havoc. O proud Death,
   What feast is toward in thine eternal cell,
   That thou so many princes at a shot
   So bloodily hast struck?

FIRST AMBASSADOR   The sight is dismal;
   And our affairs from England come too late.
   The ears are senseless that should give us hearing,
   To tell him his commandment is fulfill'd,
   That Rosencrantz and Guildenstern are dead.
   Where should we have our thanks?

HORATIO   Not from his mouth,
   Had it the ability of life to thank you.
   He never gave commandment for their death.
   But since, so jump upon this bloody question,
   You from the Polack wars, and you from England,
   Are here arrived, give order that these bodies
   High on a stage be placed to the view;
   And let me speak to the yet unknowing world
   How these things came about. So shall you hear
   Of carnal, bloody, and unnatural acts,
   Of accidental judgements, casual slaughters,
   Of deaths put on by cunning and forced cause,
   And, in this upshot, purposes mistook
   Fall'n on the inventors' heads: all this can I
   Truly deliver.

FORTINBRAS   Let us haste to hear it,
   And call the noblest to the audience.
   For me, with sorrow I embrace my fortune.
   I have some rights of memory in this kingdom,
   Which now to claim my vantage doth invite me.

HORATIO   Of that I shall have also cause to speak,
   And from his mouth whose voice will draw on more.
   But let this same be presently perform'd,

287

Even while men's minds are wild; lest more mischance,
On plots and errors, happen.

FORTINBRAS   Let four captains
  Bear Hamlet, like a soldier, to the stage;
  For he was likely, had he been put on,
  To have proved most royally; and, for his passage,
  The soldiers' music and the rites of war
  Speak loudly for him.
  Take up the bodies. Such a sight as this
  Becomes the field, but here shows much amiss.
  Go, bid the soldiers shoot.
    A dead march. Exeunt, bearing off the dead bodies; after which a peal of
                                                                    ordnance is shot off.

OTHELLO,
THE MOOR OF VENICE

THE ACTORS

DUKE OF VENICE

BRABANTIO, *a senator*

TWO SENATORS

GRATIANO, *brother to Brabantio*

LODOVICO, *kinsman to Brabantio*

OTHELLO, *a noble Moor in the service of the Venetian state*

CASSIO, *his lieutenant*

IAGO, *his ancient*

RODERIGO, *a Venetian gentleman*

MONTANO, *Othello's predecessor in the government of Cyprus*

CLOWN, *servant to Othello*

TWO GENTLEMEN *of Venice*

FOUR GENTLEMEN *of Cyprus*

AN OFFICER

A HERALD

A MESSENGER

A SAILOR

A MUSICIAN

DESDEMONA, *daughter to Brabantio and wife to Othello*

EMILIA, *wife to Iago*

BIANCA, *mistress to Cassio*

Non-Speaking: Officers, Gentlemen, Musicians, and Attendants

SCENE: *Venice, and a sea-port in Cyprus*

ACT I

SCENE 1 *Venice. A street.*

Enter Roderigo and Iago.

RODERIGO Tush! never tell me; I take it much unkindly
That thou, Iago, who hast had my purse
As if the strings were thine, shouldst know of this.

IAGO 'Sblood, but you will not hear me.
If ever I did dream of such a matter,
Abhor me.

RODERIGO Thou told'st me thou didst hold him in thy hate.

IAGO Despise me, if I do not. Three great ones of the city,
In personal suit to make me his lieutenant,
Off-capp'd to him; and, by the faith of man,
I know my price, I am worth no worse a place.
But he, as loving his own pride and purposes,
Evades them, with a bombast circumstance
Horribly stuff'd with epithets of war,
And, in conclusion,
Nonsuits my mediators; for, "Certes," says he,
"I have already chose my officer."
And what was he?
Forsooth, a great arithmetician,
One Michael Cassio, a Florentine,
A fellow almost damn'd in a fair wife;
That never set a squadron in the field,
Nor the division of a battle knows
More than a spinster; unless the bookish theoric,

293

Wherein the toged consuls can propose
As masterly as he. Mere prattle, without practice,
Is all his soldiership. But he, sir, had the election;
And I, of whom his eyes had seen the proof
At Rhodes, at Cyprus and on other grounds
Christian and heathen, must be be-lee'd and calm'd
By debitor and creditor; this counter-caster,
He, in good time, must his lieutenant be,
And I—God bless the mark!—his Moorship's ancient.

RODERIGO   By heaven, I rather would have been his hangman.

IAGO   Why, there's no remedy; 'tis the curse of service.
Preferment goes by letter and affection,
And not by old gradation, where each second
Stood heir to the first. Now, sir, be judge yourself
Whether I in any just term am affined
To love the Moor.

RODERIGO   I would not follow him then.

IAGO   O, sir, content you;
I follow him to serve my turn upon him.
We cannot all be masters, nor all masters
Cannot be truly follow'd. You shall mark
Many a duteous and knee-crooking knave
That, doting on his own obsequious bondage,
Wears out his time, much like his master's ass,
For nought but provender, and when he's old, cashier'd.
Whip me such honest knaves. Others there are
Who, trimm'd in forms and visages of duty,
Keep yet their hearts attending on themselves,
And, throwing but shows of service on their lords,
Do well thrive by them, and when they have lined their coats,
Do themselves homage. These fellows have some soul;
And such a one do I profess myself. For, sir,
It is as sure as you are Roderigo,
Were I the Moor, I would not be Iago.
In following him, I follow but myself;
Heaven is my judge, not I for love and duty,
But seeming so, for my peculiar end;
For when my outward action doth demonstrate
The native act and figure of my heart
In compliment extern, 'tis not long after

294

But I will wear my heart upon my sleeve
For daws to peck at. I am not what I am.

RODERIGO   What a full fortune does the thick-lips owe,
  If he can carry't thus!

IAGO   Call up her father,
  Rouse him. Make after him, poison his delight,
  Proclaim him in the streets. Incense her kinsmen,
  And, though he in a fertile climate dwell,
  Plague him with flies. Though that his joy be joy,
  Yet throw such changes of vexation on't,
  As it may lose some colour.

RODERIGO   Here is her father's house; I'll call aloud.

IAGO   Do, with like timorous accent and dire yell
  As when, by night and negligence, the fire
  Is spied in populous cities.

RODERIGO   What, ho, Brabantio! Signior Brabantio, ho!

IAGO   Awake! what, ho, Brabantio! thieves! thieves! thieves!
  Look to your house, your daughter, and your bags!
  Thieves! Thieves!

Brabantio appears above, at a window.

BRABANTIO   What is the reason of this terrible summons?
  What is the matter there?

RODERIGO   Signior, is all your family within?

IAGO   Are your doors lock'd?

BRABANTIO   Why, wherefore ask you this?

IAGO   'Zounds, sir, you're robb'd; for shame, put on your gown;
  Your heart is burst, you have lost half your soul;
  Even now, now, very now, an old black ram
  Is tupping your white ewe. Arise, arise;
  Awake the snorting citizens with the bell,
  Or else the devil will make a grandsire of you.
  Arise, I say.

BRABANTIO   What, have you lost your wits?

RODERIGO   Most reverend signior, do you know my voice?

BRABANTIO   Not I. What are you?

RODERIGO   My name is Roderigo.

BRABANTIO   The worser welcome.
 I have charged thee not to haunt about my doors.
 In honest plainness thou hast heard me say
 My daughter is not for thee; and now, in madness,
 Being full of supper and distempering draughts,
 Upon malicious bravery, dost thou come
 To start my quiet.

RODERIGO   Sir, sir, sir —

BRABANTIO   But thou must needs be sure
 My spirit and my place have in them power
 To make this bitter to thee.

RODERIGO   Patience, good sir.

BRABANTIO   What tell'st thou me of robbing? this is Venice;
 My house is not a grange.

RODERIGO   Most grave Brabantio,
 In simple and pure soul I come to you.

IAGO   'Zounds, sir, you are one of those that will not serve God, if the
 devil bid you. Because we come to do you service and you think we
 are ruffians, you'll have your daughter covered with a Barbary horse;
 you'll have your nephews neigh to you; you'll have coursers for cousins and gennets for germans.

BRABANTIO   What profane wretch art thou?

IAGO   I am one, sir, that comes to tell you your daughter and the Moor
 are now making the beast with two backs.

BRABANTIO   Thou art a villain.

IAGO   You are — a senator.

BRABANTIO   This thou shalt answer; I know thee, Roderigo.

RODERIGO   Sir, I will answer anything. But, I beseech you,
 If't be your pleasure and most wise consent,
 As partly I find it is, that your fair daughter,
 At this odd-even and dull watch o' the night,
 Transported, with no worse nor better guard
 But with a knave of common hire, a gondolier,

296

To the gross clasps of a lascivious Moor—
If this be known to you and your allowance,
We then have done you bold and saucy wrongs;
But if you know not this, my manners tell me
We have your wrong rebuke. Do not believe
That, from the sense of all civility,
I thus would play and trifle with your reverence.
Your daughter, if you have not given her leave,
I say again, hath made a gross revolt;
Tying her duty, beauty, wit, and fortunes
In an extravagant and wheeling stranger
Of here and everywhere. Straight satisfy yourself.
If she be in her chamber or your house,
Let loose on me the justice of the state
For thus deluding you.

BRABANTIO   Strike on the tinder, ho!
  Give me a taper! call up all my people!
  This accident is not unlike my dream;
  Belief of it oppresses me already.
  Light, I say! light!   *Exit above.*

IAGO   Farewell; for I must leave you.
  It seems not meet, nor wholesome to my place,
  To be produced—as, if I stay, I shall—
  Against the Moor; for, I do know, the state,
  However this may gall him with some check,
  Cannot with safety cast him, for he's embark'd
  With such loud reason to the Cyprus wars,
  Which even now stand in act, that, for their souls,
  Another of his fathom they have none
  To lead their business; in which regard,
  Though I do hate him as I do hell-pains,
  Yet, for necessity of present life,
  I must show out a flag and sign of love,
  Which is indeed but sign. That you shall surely find him,
  Lead to the Sagittary the raised search;
  And there will I be with him. So, farewell.   *Exit.*

Enter, below, Brabantio, and Servants with torches.

BRABANTIO It is too true an evil; gone she is;
  And what's to come of my despised time
  Is nought but bitterness. Now, Roderigo,

Where didst thou see her? O unhappy girl!
With the Moor, say'st thou? Who would be a father!
How didst thou know 'twas she? O, she deceives me
Past thought! What said she to you? Get more tapers.
Raise all my kindred. Are they married, think you?

RODERIGO   Truly, I think they are.

BRABANTIO   O heaven! How got she out? O treason of the blood!
Fathers, from hence trust not your daughters' minds
By what you see them act. Is there not charms
By which the property of youth and maidhood
May be abused? Have you not read, Roderigo,
Of some such thing?

RODERIGO   Yes, sir, I have indeed.

BRABANTIO   Call up my brother. O, would you had had her!
Some one way, some another. Do you know
Where we may apprehend her and the Moor?

RODERIGO   I think I can discover him, if you please
To get good guard and go along with me.

BRABANTIO   Pray you, lead on. At every house I'll call;
I may command at most. Get weapons, ho!
And raise some special officers of night.
On, good Roderigo; I'll deserve your pains.   *Exeunt.*

❦ SCENE 2   *Another street.*

Enter Othello, Iago, and Attendants with torches.

IAGO   Though in the trade of war I have slain men,
Yet do I hold it very stuff o' the conscience
To do no contrived murder. I lack iniquity
Sometimes to do me service. Nine or ten times
I had thought to have yerk'd him here under the ribs.

OTHELLO   'Tis better as it is.

IAGO   Nay, but he prated,
And spoke such scurvy and provoking terms
Against your honour,
That, with the little godliness I have,
I did full hard forbear him. But, I pray you, sir,

298

Are you fast married? Be assured of this,
That the magnifico is much beloved,
And hath in his effect a voice potential
As double as the Duke's. He will divorce you;
Or put upon you what restraint and grievance
The law, with all his might to enforce it on,
Will give him cable.

OTHELLO   Let him do his spite;
My services which I have done the signiory
Shall out-tongue his complaints. 'Tis yet to know —
Which, when I know that boasting is an honour,
I shall promulgate — I fetch my life and being
From men of royal siege, and my demerits
May speak unbonneted to as proud a fortune
As this that I have reach'd; for know, Iago,
But that I love the gentle Desdemona,
I would not my unhoused free condition
Put into circumscription and confine
For the sea's worth. But, look! what lights come yond?

IAGO   Those are the raised father and his friends.
You were best go in.

OTHELLO   Not I; I must be found.
My parts, my title, and my perfect soul
Shall manifest me rightly. Is it they?

IAGO   By Janus, I think no.

Enter Cassio, and certain Officers with torches.

OTHELLO   The servants of the Duke, and my lieutenant.
The goodness of the night upon you, friends!
What is the news?

CASSIO   The Duke does greet you, general,
And he requires your haste-post-haste appearance,
Even on the instant.

OTHELLO   What is the matter, think you?

CASSIO   Something from Cyprus, as I may divine;
It is a business of some heat. The galleys
Have sent a dozen sequent messengers
This very night at one another's heels,

And many of the consuls, raised and met,
Are at the Duke's already. You have been hotly call'd for;
When, being not at your lodging to be found,
The senate hath sent about three several quests
To search you out.

OTHELLO 'Tis well I am found by you.
I will but spend a word here in the house,
And go with you. *Exit.*

CASSIO Ancient, what makes he here?

IAGO 'Faith, he to-night hath boarded a land carack.
If it prove lawful prize, he's made for ever.

CASSIO I do not understand.

IAGO He's married.

CASSIO To who?

Re-enter Othello.

IAGO Marry, to— Come, captain, will you go?

OTHELLO Have with you.

CASSIO Here comes another troop to seek for you.

IAGO It is Brabantio. General, be advised;
He comes to bad intent.

Enter Brabantio, Roderigo, and Officers with torches and weapons.

OTHELLO Holla! stand there!

RODERIGO Signior, it is the Moor.

BRABANTIO Down with him, thief!

They draw on both sides.

IAGO You, Roderigo! come, sir, I am for you.

OTHELLO Keep up your bright swords, for the dew will rust them.
Good signior, you shall more command with years
Than with your weapons.

BRABANTIO O thou foul thief, where hast thou stow'd my daughter?
Damn'd as thou art, thou hast enchanted her;

300

For I'll refer me to all things of sense,
If she in chains of magic were not bound,
Whether a maid so tender, fair, and happy,
So opposite to marriage that she shunn'd
The wealthy curled darlings of our nation,
Would ever have, to incur a general mock,
Run from her guardage to the sooty bosom
Of such a thing as thou—to fear, not to delight.
Judge me the world, if 'tis not gross in sense
That thou hast practised on her with foul charms,
Abused her delicate youth with drugs or minerals
That weaken motion. I'll have't disputed on;
'Tis probable and palpable to thinking.
I therefore apprehend and do attach thee
For an abuser of the world, a practiser
Of arts inhibited and out of warrant.
Lay hold upon him. If he do resist,
Subdue him at his peril.

OTHELLO   Hold your hands,
Both you of my inclining, and the rest.
Were it my cue to fight, I should have known it
Without a prompter. Where will you that I go
To answer this your charge?

BRABANTIO   To prison, till fit time
Of law and course of direct session
Call thee to answer.

OTHELLO   What if I do obey?
How may the Duke be therewith satisfied,
Whose messengers are here about my side,
Upon some present business of the state
To bring me to him?

FIRST OFFICER   'Tis true, most worthy signior;
The Duke's in council, and your noble self,
I am sure, is sent for.

BRABANTIO   How! the Duke in council!
In this time of the night! Bring him away.
Mine's not an idle cause. The Duke himself,
Or any of my brothers of the state,

301

Cannot but feel this wrong as 'twere their own;
For if such actions may have passage free,
Bond-slaves and pagans shall our statesmen be.   *Exeunt.*

❦ SCENE 3 *A council-chamber.*

The Duke and Senators sitting at a table; Officers attending.

DUKE   There is no composition in these news
That gives them credit.

FIRST SENATOR   Indeed, they are disproportion'd;
My letters say a hundred and seven galleys.

DUKE   And mine, a hundred and forty.

SECOND SENATOR   And mine, two hundred.
But though they jump not on a just account—
As in these cases, where the aim reports,
'Tis oft with difference—yet do they all confirm
A Turkish fleet, and bearing up to Cyprus.

DUKE   Nay, it is possible enough to judgement.
I do not so secure me in the error,
But the main article I do approve
In fearful sense.

SAILOR   [*Within.*] What, ho! what, ho! what, ho!

FIRST OFFICER   A messenger from the galleys.

Enter a Sailor.

DUKE   Now, what's the business?

SAILOR   The Turkish preparation makes for Rhodes;
So was I bid report here to the state
By Signior Angelo.

DUKE   How say you by this change?

FIRST SENATOR   This cannot be,
By no assay of reason; 'tis a pageant,
To keep us in false gaze. When we consider
The importancy of Cyprus to the Turk,
And let ourselves again but understand,
That as it more concerns the Turk than Rhodes,

So may he with more facile question bear it,
For that it stands not in such warlike brace,
But altogether lacks the abilities
That Rhodes is dress'd in. If we make thought of this,
We must not think the Turk is so unskilful
To leave that latest which concerns him first,
Neglecting an attempt of ease and gain
To wake and wage a danger profitless.

DUKE   Nay, in all confidence, he's not for Rhodes.

FIRST OFFICER   Here is more news.

Enter a Messenger.

MESSENGER   The Ottomites, reverend and gracious,
Steering with due course towards the isle of Rhodes,
Have there injointed them with an after fleet.

FIRST SENATOR   Ay, so I thought. How many, as you guess?

MESSENGER   Of thirty sail; and now they do re-stem
Their backward course, bearing with frank appearance
Their purposes toward Cyprus. Signior Montano,
Your trusty and most valiant servitor,
With his free duty recommends you thus,
And prays you to believe him.

DUKE   'Tis certain, then, for Cyprus.
Marcus Luccicos, is not he in town?

FIRST SENATOR   He's now in Florence.

DUKE   Write from us to him; post-post-haste dispatch.

FIRST SENATOR   Here comes Brabantio and the valiant Moor.

Enter Brabantio, Othello, Iago, Roderigo, and Officers.

DUKE   Valiant Othello, we must straight employ you
Against the general enemy Ottoman.
[*To Brabantio.*] I did not see you; welcome, gentle signior;
We lack'd your counsel and your help to-night.

BRABANTIO   So did I yours. Good your Grace, pardon me;
Neither my place nor aught I heard of business
Hath raised me from my bed, nor doth the general care
Take hold on me, for my particular grief

303

Is of so flood-gate and o'erbearing nature
That it engluts and swallows other sorrows
And it is still itself.

DUKE   Why, what's the matter?

BRABANTIO My daughter! O, my daughter!

ALL   Dead?

BRABANTIO   Ay, to me;
  She is abused, stol'n from me, and corrupted
  By spells and medicines bought of mountebanks;
  For nature so preposterously to err,
  Being not deficient, blind, or lame of sense,
  Sans witchcraft could not.

DUKE Whoe'er he be that in this foul proceeding
  Hath thus beguiled your daughter of herself
  And you of her, the bloody book of law
  You shall yourself read in the bitter letter
  After your own sense, yea, though our proper son
  Stood in your action.

BRABANTIO   Humbly I thank your Grace.
  Here is the man, this Moor, whom now, it seems,
  Your special mandate for the state affairs
  Hath hither brought.

ALL   We are very sorry for't.

DUKE [To Othello.] What, in your own part, can you say to this?

BRABANTIO Nothing, but this is so.

OTHELLO Most potent, grave, and reverend signiors,
  My very noble and approved good masters,
  That I have ta'en away this old man's daughter,
  It is most true; true, I have married her:
  The very head and front of my offending
  Hath this extent, no more. Rude am I in my speech,
  And little bless'd with the soft phrase of peace.
  For since these arms of mine had seven years' pith,
  Till now some nine moons wasted, they have used
  Their dearest action in the tented field,
  And little of this great world can I speak
  More than pertains to feats of broil and battle,

304

And therefore little shall I grace my cause
In speaking for myself. Yet, by your gracious patience,
I will a round unvarnish'd tale deliver
Of my whole course of love; what drugs, what charms,
What conjuration, and what mighty magic,
For such proceeding I am charged withal,
I won his daughter.

BRABANTIO   A maiden never bold;
    Of spirit so still and quiet that her motion
    Blush'd at herself; and she, in spite of nature,
    Of years, of country, credit, everything,
    To fall in love with what she fear'd to look on!
    It is a judgement maim'd and most imperfect
    That will confess perfection so could err
    Against all rules of nature, and must be driven
    To find out practices of cunning hell,
    Why this should be. I therefore vouch again
    That with some mixtures powerful o'er the blood,
    Or with some dram conjured to this effect,
    He wrought upon her.

DUKE   To vouch this is no proof,
    Without more wider and more overt test
    Than these thin habits and poor likelihoods
    Of modern seeming do prefer against him.

FIRST SENATOR   But, Othello, speak.
    Did you by indirect and forced courses
    Subdue and poison this young maid's affections?
    Or came it by request and such fair question
    As soul to soul affordeth?

OTHELLO   I do beseech you,
    Send for the lady to the Sagittary,
    And let her speak of me before her father.
    If you do find me foul in her report,
    The trust, the office I do hold of you,
    Not only take away, but let your sentence
    Even fall upon my life.

DUKE   Fetch Desdemona hither.

OTHELLO   Ancient, conduct them; you best know the place.
                                    Exeunt Iago and Attendants.

305

And, till she come, as truly as to heaven
I do confess the vices of my blood,
So justly to your grave ears I'll present
How I did thrive in this fair lady's love,
And she in mine.

DUKE Say it, Othello.

OTHELLO Her father loved me; oft invited me;
Still question'd me the story of my life,
From year to year, the battles, sieges, fortunes,
That I have pass'd.
I ran it through, even from my boyish days,
To the very moment that he bade me tell it;
Wherein I spake of most disastrous chances,
Of moving accidents by flood and field,
Of hair-breadth scapes i' the imminent deadly breach,
Of being taken by the insolent foe
And sold to slavery, of my redemption thence
And portance in my travels' history;
Wherein of antres vast and deserts idle,
Rough quarries, rocks, and hills whose heads touch heaven,
It was my hint to speak—such was the process—
And of the Cannibals that each other eat,
The Anthropophagi and men whose heads
Do grow beneath their shoulders. This to hear
Would Desdemona seriously incline;
But still the house-affairs would draw her thence,
Which ever as she could with haste dispatch,
She'd come again, and with a greedy ear
Devour up my discourse; which I observing,
Took once a pliant hour, and found good means
To draw from her a prayer of earnest heart
That I would all my pilgrimage dilate,
Whereof by parcels she had something heard,
But not intentively. I did consent,
And often did beguile her of her tears
When I did speak of some distressful stroke
That my youth suffer'd. My story being done,
She gave me for my pains a world of sighs.
She swore, in faith, 'twas strange, 'twas passing strange,
'Twas pitiful, 'twas wondrous pitiful.

She wish'd she had not heard it, yet she wish'd
That heaven had made her such a man. She thank'd me,
And bade me, if I had a friend that loved her,
I should but teach him how to tell my story,
And that would woo her. Upon this hint I spake:
She loved me for the dangers I had pass'd,
And I loved her that she did pity them.
This only is the witchcraft I have used.
Here comes the lady; let her witness it.

Enter Desdemona, Iago, and Attendants.

DUKE   I think this tale would win my daughter too.
  Good Brabantio,
  Take up this mangled matter at the best;
  Men do their broken weapons rather use
  Than their bare hands.

BRABANTIO   I pray you, hear her speak.
  If she confess that she was half the wooer,
  Destruction on my head, if my bad blame
  Light on the man! Come hither, gentle mistress.
  Do you perceive in all this noble company
  Where most you owe obedience?

DESDEMONA   My noble father,
  I do perceive here a divided duty:
  To you I am bound for life and education;
  My life and education both do learn me
  How to respect you; you are the lord of duty;
  I am hitherto your daughter. But here's my husband,
  And so much duty as my mother show'd
  To you, preferring you before her father,
  So much I challenge that I may profess
  Due to the Moor my lord.

BRABANTIO   God be wi' you! I have done.
  Please it your Grace, on to the state-affairs.
  I had rather to adopt a child than get it.
  Come hither, Moor.
  I here do give thee that with all my heart
  Which, but thou hast already, with all my heart
  I would keep from thee. For your sake, jewel,

307

I am glad at soul I have no other child;
For thy escape would teach me tyranny,
To hang clogs on them. I have done, my lord.

DUKE Let me speak like yourself, and lay a sentence,
  Which, as a grise or step, may help these lovers
  Into your favour.
  When remedies are past, the griefs are ended
  By seeing the worst, which late on hopes depended.
  To mourn a mischief that is past and gone
  Is the next way to draw new mischief on.
  What cannot be preserved when fortune takes,
  Patience her injury a mockery makes.
  The robb'd that smiles steals something from the thief;
  He robs himself that spends a bootless grief.

BRABANTIO So let the Turk of Cyprus us beguile;
  We lose it not, so long as we can smile.
  He bears the sentence well that nothing bears
  But the free comfort which from thence he hears,
  But he bears both the sentence and the sorrow
  That, to pay grief, must of poor patience borrow.
  These sentences, to sugar, or to gall,
  Being strong on both sides, are equivocal.
  But words are words; I never yet did hear
  That the bruised heart was pierced through the ear.
  I humbly beseech you, proceed to the affairs of state.

DUKE The Turk with a most mighty preparation makes for Cyprus.
  Othello, the fortitude of the place is best known to you; and though
  we have there a substitute of most allowed sufficiency, yet opinion, a
  sovereign mistress of effects, throws a more safer voice on you. You
  must therefore be content to slubber the gloss of your new fortunes
  with this more stubborn and boisterous expedition.

OTHELLO The tyrant custom, most grave senators,
  Hath made the flinty and steel couch of war
  My thrice-driven bed of down. I do agnize
  A natural and prompt alacrity
  I find in hardness, and do undertake
  These present wars against the Ottomites.
  Most humbly therefore bending to your state,
  I crave fit disposition for my wife,
  Due reference of place and exhibition,

With such accommodation and besort
As levels with her breeding.

DUKE   If you please,
    Be't at her father's.

BRABANTIO   I'll not have it so.

OTHELLO   Nor I.

DESDEMONA   Nor I; I would not there reside,
    To put my father in impatient thoughts
    By being in his eye. Most gracious Duke,
    To my unfolding lend your prosperous ear;
    And let me find a charter in your voice,
    To assist my simpleness.

DUKE   What would you, Desdemona?

DESDEMONA   That I did love the Moor to live with him,
    My downright violence and storm of fortunes
    May trumpet to the world. My heart's subdued
    Even to the very quality of my lord.
    I saw Othello's visage in his mind,
    And to his honours and his valiant parts
    Did I my soul and fortunes consecrate.
    So that, dear lords, if I be left behind,
    A moth of peace, and he go to the war,
    The rites for which I love him are bereft me,
    And I a heavy interim shall support
    By his dear absence. Let me go with him.

OTHELLO   Let her have your voices.
    Vouch with me, heaven, I therefore beg it not,
    To please the palate of my appetite,
    Nor to comply with heat—the young affects
    In me defunct—and proper satisfaction,
    But to be free and bounteous to her mind;
    And heaven defend your good souls, that you think
    I will your serious and great business scant
    For she is with me. No, when light-wing'd toys
    Of feather'd Cupid seel with wanton dullness
    My speculative and officed instruments,
    That my disports corrupt and taint my business,
    Let housewives make a skillet of my helm,

309

And all indign and base adversities
Make head against my estimation!

DUKE   Be it as you shall privately determine,
Either for her stay or going. The affair cries haste,
And speed must answer it.

FIRST SENATOR   You must away to-night.

OTHELLO   With all my heart.

DUKE   At nine i' the morning here we'll meet again.
Othello, leave some officer behind,
And he shall our commission bring to you,
With such things else of quality and respect
As doth import you.

OTHELLO   So please your Grace, my ancient;
A man he is of honesty and trust.
To his conveyance I assign my wife,
With what else needful your good Grace shall think
To be sent after me.

DUKE   Let it be so.
Good night to every one. [*To Brabantio.*] And, noble signior,
If virtue no delighted beauty lack,
Your son-in-law is far more fair than black.

FIRST SENATOR   Adieu, brave Moor; use Desdemona well.

BRABANTIO   Look to her, Moor, if thou hast eyes to see;
She has deceived her father, and may thee.
                    Exeunt Duke, Senators, Officers, &c.

OTHELLO   My life upon her faith! Honest Iago,
My Desdemona must I leave to thee.
I prithee, let thy wife attend on her;
And bring them after in the best advantage.
Come, Desdemona; I have but an hour
Of love, of worldly matters and direction,
To spend with thee. We must obey the time.
                    Exeunt Othello and Desdemona.

RODERIGO   Iago —

IAGO   What say'st thou, noble heart?

RODERIGO   What will I do, thinkest thou?

310

IAGO   Why, go to bed and sleep.

RODERIGO   I will incontinently drown myself.

IAGO   If thou dost, I shall never love thee after. Why, thou silly gentleman!

RODERIGO   It is silliness to live when to live is torment; and then have we
a prescription to die when death is our physician.

IAGO   O villainous! I have looked upon the world for four times seven
years; and since I could distinguish betwixt a benefit and an injury, I
never found a man that knew how to love himself. Ere I would say I
would drown myself for the love of a guinea-hen, I would change my
humanity with a baboon.

RODERIGO   What should I do? I confess it is my shame to be so fond; but
it is not in my virtue to amend it.

IAGO   Virtue! a fig! 'tis in ourselves that we are thus or thus. Our bodies
are our gardens, to the which our wills are gardeners; so that if we will
plant nettles, or sow lettuce, set hyssop and weed up thyme, supply it
with one gender of herbs, or distract it with many, either to have it
sterile with idleness or manured with industry, why, the power and
corrigible authority of this lies in our wills. If the balance of our lives
had not one scale of reason to poise another of sensuality, the blood
and baseness of our natures would conduct us to most preposterous
conclusions; but we have reason to cool our raging motions, our carnal
stings, our unbitted lusts, whereof I take this that you call love to be a
sect or scion.

RODERIGO   It cannot be.

IAGO   It is merely a lust of the blood and a permission of the will. Come,
be a man. Drown thyself! drown cats and blind puppies. I have professed me thy friend and I confess me knit to thy deserving with cables
of perdurable toughness; I could never better stead thee than now. Put
money in thy purse; follow thou the wars; defeat thy favour with an
usurped beard; I say, put money in thy purse. It cannot be that Desdemona should long continue her love to the Moor—put money in thy
purse—nor he his to her. It was a violent commencement, and thou
shalt see an answerable sequestration—put but money in thy purse.
These Moors are changeable in their wills—fill thy purse with money
—the food that to him now is as luscious as locusts, shall be to him
shortly as bitter as coloquintida. She must change for youth; when she
is sated with his body, she will find the error of her choice; she must

311

have change, she must; therefore put money in thy purse. If thou wilt needs damn thyself, do it a more delicate way than drowning. Make all the money thou canst. If sanctimony and a frail vow betwixt an erring barbarian and a supersubtle Venetian be not too hard for my wits and all the tribe of hell, thou shalt enjoy her; therefore make money. A pox of drowning thyself! it is clean out of the way. Seek thou rather to be hanged in compassing thy joy than to be drowned and go without her.

RODERIGO   Wilt thou be fast to my hopes, if I depend on the issue?

IAGO   Thou art sure of me. Go, make money. I have told thee often, and I re-tell thee again and again, I hate the Moor; my cause is hearted; thine hath no less reason. Let us be conjunctive in our revenge against him. If thou canst cuckold him, thou dost thyself a pleasure, me a sport. There are many events in the womb of time which will be delivered. Traverse! go, provide thy money. We will have more of this to-morrow. Adieu.

RODERIGO   Where shall we meet i' the morning?

IAGO   At my lodging.

RODERIGO   I'll be with thee betimes.

IAGO   Go to, farewell. Do you hear, Roderigo?

RODERIGO   What say you?

IAGO   No more of drowning, do you hear?

RODERIGO   I am changed. I'll go sell all my land.   *Exit.*

IAGO   Thus do I ever make my fool my purse;
   For I mine own gain'd knowledge should profane,
   If I would time expend with such a snipe,
   But for my sport and profit. I hate the Moor;
   And it is thought abroad that 'twixt my sheets
   He has done my office. I know not if't be true;
   But I, for mere suspicion in that kind,
   Will do as if for surety. He holds me well;
   The better shall my purpose work on him.
   Cassio's a proper man; let me see now;
   To get his place and to plume up my will
   In double knavery— How, how?— Let's see—
   After some time, to abuse Othello's ear
   That he is too familiar with his wife.
   He hath a person and a smooth dispose

To be suspected, framed to make women false.
The Moor is of a free and open nature
That thinks men honest that but seem to be so,
And will as tenderly be led by the nose
As asses are.
I have't. It is engender'd. Hell and night
Must bring this monstrous birth to the world's light.   *Exit.*

ACT II

SCENE 1   *A sea-port in Cyprus. An open place near the quay.*

Enter Montano and Two Gentlemen.

MONTANO   What from the cape can you discern at sea?

FIRST GENTLEMAN   Nothing at all; it is a high-wrought flood.
I cannot, 'twixt the heaven and the main,
Descry a sail.

MONTANO   Methinks the wind hath spoke aloud at land;
A fuller blast ne'er shook our battlements.
If it hath ruffian'd so upon the sea,
What ribs of oak, when mountains melt on them,
Can hold the mortise? What shall we hear of this?

SECOND GENTLEMAN   A segregation of the Turkish fleet.
For do but stand upon the foaming shore,
The chidden billow seems to pelt the clouds;
The wind-shaked surge, with high and monstrous mane,
Seems to cast water on the burning bear,
And quench the guards of the ever-fixed pole.
I never did like molestation view
On the enchafed flood.

MONTANO   If that the Turkish fleet
Be not enshelter'd and embay'd, they are drown'd;
It is impossible they bear it out.

Enter a Third Gentleman.

314

THIRD GENTLEMAN   News, lads! our wars are done.
The desperate tempest hath so bang'd the Turks
That their designment halts. A noble ship of Venice
Hath seen a grievous wreck and sufferance
On most part of their fleet.

MONTANO   How! is this true?

THIRD GENTLEMAN   The ship is here put in.
A Veronesa, Michael Cassio,
Lieutenant to the warlike Moor Othello,
Is come on shore; the Moor himself at sea,
And is in full commission here for Cyprus.

MONTANO   I am glad on't; 'tis a worthy governor.

THIRD GENTLEMAN   But this same Cassio, though he speak of comfort
Touching the Turkish loss, yet he looks sadly,
And prays the Moor be safe, for they were parted
With foul and violent tempest.

MONTANO   Pray heavens he be;
For I have served him, and the man commands
Like a full soldier. Let's to the seaside, ho!
As well to see the vessel that's come in
As to throw out our eyes for brave Othello,
Even till we make the main and the aerial blue
An indistinct regard.

THIRD GENTLEMAN   Come, let's do so;
For every minute is expectancy
Of more arrivance.

Enter Cassio.

CASSIO   Thanks, you the valiant of this warlike isle,
That so approve the Moor! O, let the heavens
Give him defence against the elements,
For I have lost him on a dangerous sea.

MONTANO   Is he well shipp'd?

CASSIO   His bark is stoutly timber'd, and his pilot
Of very expert and approved allowance;
Therefore my hopes, not surfeited to death,
Stand in bold cure.

315

A cry within, "A sail, a sail, a sail!" Enter a Fourth Gentleman.

CASSIO   What noise?

FOURTH GENTLEMAN   The town is empty; on the brow o' the sea
Stand ranks of people, and they cry, "A sail!"

CASSIO   My hopes do shape him for the governor.

Guns heard.

SECOND GENTLEMAN   They do discharge their shot of courtesy.
Our friends at least.

CASSIO   I pray you, sir, go forth,
And give us truth who 'tis that is arrived.

SECOND GENTLEMAN   I shall.   *Exit.*

MONTANO   But, good lieutenant, is your general wived?

CASSIO   Most fortunately. He hath achieved a maid
That paragons description and wild fame;
One that excels the quirks of blazoning pens,
And in the essential vesture of creation
Does tire the ingener.

Re-enter Second Gentleman.

                         How now! who has put in?

SECOND GENTLEMAN   'Tis one Iago, ancient to the general.

CASSIO   He has had most favourable and happy speed.
Tempests themselves, high seas and howling winds,
The gutter'd rocks and congregated sands —
Traitors ensteep'd to clog the guiltless keel —
As having sense of beauty, do omit
Their mortal natures, letting go safely by
The divine Desdemona.

MONTANO   What is she?

CASSIO   She that I spake of, our great captain's captain,
Left in the conduct of the bold Iago,
Whose footing here anticipates our thoughts
A se'nnight's speed. Great Jove, Othello guard,
And swell his sail with thine own powerful breath,
That he may bless this bay with his tall ship,

316

Make love's quick pants in Desdemona's arms,
Give renew'd fire to our extinced spirits,
And bring all Cyprus comfort!

Enter Desdemona, Emilia, Iago, Roderigo, and Attendants.

                        O, behold,
The riches of the ship is come on shore!
Ye men of Cyprus, let her have your knees.
Hail to thee, lady! and the grace of heaven,
Before, behind thee, and on every hand,
Enwheel thee round!

DESDEMONA   I thank you, valiant Cassio.
What tidings can you tell me of my lord?

CASSIO   He is not yet arrived; nor know I aught
But that he's well and will be shortly here.

DESDEMONA   O, but I fear—how lost you company?

CASSIO   The great contention of the sea and skies
Parted our fellowship— But, hark! a sail.

Within, "A sail, a sail!" Guns heard.

SECOND GENTLEMAN   They give their greeting to the citadel.
This likewise is a friend.

CASSIO   See for the news.   *Exit Gentleman.*
Good ancient, you are welcome. [*To Emilia.*] Welcome, mistress.
Let it not gall your patience, good Iago,
That I extend my manners; 'tis my breeding
That gives me this bold show of courtesy.

Kissing her.

IAGO   Sir, would she give you so much of her lips
As of her tongue she oft bestows on me,
You'd have enough.

DESDEMONA   Alas, she has no speech.

IAGO   In faith, too much;
I find it still, when I have list to sleep.
Marry, before your ladyship, I grant,
She puts her tongue a little in her heart,
And chides with thinking.

317

EMILIA You have little cause to say so.

IAGO Come on, come on; you are pictures out of doors,
  Bells in your parlours, wild-cats in your kitchens,
  Saints in your injuries, devils being offended,
  Players in your housewifery, and housewives in your beds.

DESDEMONA O, fie upon thee, slanderer!

IAGO Nay, it is true, or else I am a Turk;
  You rise to play and go to bed to work.

EMILIA You shall not write my praise.

IAGO   No, let me not.

DESDEMONA What wouldst thou write of me, if thou shouldst praise
  me?

IAGO O gentle lady, do not put me to't;
  For I am nothing, if not critical.

DESDEMONA Come on, assay. There's one gone to the harbour?

IAGO Ay, madam.

DESDEMONA I am not merry; but I do beguile
  The thing I am by seeming otherwise.
  Come, how wouldst thou praise me?

IAGO I am about it; but indeed my invention
  Comes from my pate as birdlime does from frize;
  It plucks out brains and all. But my Muse labours,
  And thus she is deliver'd.
  If she be fair and wise, fairness and wit,
  The one's for use, the other useth it.

DESDEMONA Well praised! How if she be black and witty?

IAGO If she be black, and thereto have a wit,
  She'll find a white that shall her blackness fit.

DESDEMONA Worse and worse.

EMILIA How if fair and foolish?

IAGO She never yet was foolish that was fair;
  For even her folly help'd her to an heir.

318

DESDEMONA   These are old fond paradoxes to make fools laugh i' the ale-
house. What miserable praise hast thou for her that's foul and foolish?

IAGO   There's none so foul and foolish thereunto,
But does foul pranks which fair and wise ones do.

DESDEMONA   O heavy ignorance! thou praisest the worst best. But what
praise couldst thou bestow on a deserving woman indeed, one that, in
the authority of her merit, did justly put on the vouch of very malice
itself?

IAGO   She that was ever fair and never proud,
Had tongue at will and yet was never loud,
Never lack'd gold and yet went never gay,
Fled from her wish and yet said, "Now I may";
She that being anger'd, her revenge being nigh,
Bade her wrong stay and her displeasure fly,
She that in wisdom never was so frail
To change the cod's head for the salmon's tail,
She that could think and ne'er disclose her mind,
See suitors following and not look behind,
She was a wight, if ever such wight were—

DESDEMONA   To do what?

IAGO   To suckle fools and chronicle small beer.

DESDEMONA   O most lame and impotent conclusion! Do not learn of
him, Emilia, though he be thy husband. How say you, Cassio? is he
not a most profane and liberal counsellor?

CASSIO   He speaks home, madam. You may relish him more in the soldier than in the scholar.

IAGO   [Aside.] He takes her by the palm; ay, well said, whisper. With as
little a web as this will I ensnare as great a fly as Cassio. Ay, smile upon
her, do; I will gyve thee in thine own courtship. You say true; 'tis so,
indeed. If such tricks as these strip you out of your lieutenantry, it had
been better you had not kissed your three fingers so oft, which now
again you are most apt to play the sir in. Very good; well kissed! an
excellent courtesy! 'tis so, indeed. Yet again your fingers to your lips?
would they were clyster-pipes for your sake! [Trumpet within.] The
Moor! I know his trumpet.

CASSIO   'Tis truly so.

319

DESDEMONA   Let's meet him and receive him.

CASSIO   Lo, where he comes!

Enter Othello and Attendants.

OTHELLO   O my fair warrior!

DESDEMONA   My dear Othello!

OTHELLO   It gives me wonder great as my content
To see you here before me. O my soul's joy!
If after every tempest come such calms,
May the winds blow till they have waken'd death!
And let the labouring bark climb hills of seas
Olympus-high and duck again as low
As hell's from heaven! If it were now to die,
'Twere now to be most happy; for, I fear,
My soul hath her content so absolute
That not another comfort like to this
Succeeds in unknown fate.

DESDEMONA   The heavens forbid
But that our loves and comforts should increase,
Even as our days do grow!

OTHELLO   Amen to that, sweet powers!
I cannot speak enough of this content;
It stops me here; it is too much of joy.
And this, and this, the greatest discords be

Kissing her.

That e'er our hearts shall make!

IAGO   [*Aside.*] O, you are well tuned now!
But I'll set down the pegs that make this music,
As honest as I am.

OTHELLO   Come, let us to the castle.
News, friends; our wars are done, the Turks are drown'd.
How does my old acquaintance of this isle?
Honey, you shall be well desired in Cyprus;
I have found great love amongst them. O my sweet,
I prattle out of fashion, and I dote
In mine own comforts. I prithee, good Iago,
Go to the bay and disembark my coffers.

320

Bring thou the master to the citadel;
He is a good one, and his worthiness
Does challenge much respect. Come, Desdemona,
Once more, well met at Cyprus.

Exeunt Othello, Desdemona, and Attendants.

IAGO   Do thou meet me presently at the harbour. Come hither. If thou be'st valiant—as, they say, base men being in love have then a nobility in their natures more than is native to them—list me. The lieutenant to-night watches on the court of guard. First, I must tell thee this— Desdemona is directly in love with him.

RODERIGO   With him! why, 'tis not possible.

IAGO   Lay thy finger thus, and let thy soul be instructed. Mark me with what violence she first loved the Moor, but for bragging and telling her fantastical lies; and will she love him still for prating? let not thy discreet heart think it. Her eye must be fed; and what delight shall she have to look on the devil? When the blood is made dull with the act of sport, there should be, again to inflame it and to give satiety a fresh appetite, loveliness in favour, sympathy in years, manners, and beauties; all which the Moor is defective in. Now, for want of these required conveniences, her delicate tenderness will find itself abused, begin to heave the gorge, disrelish and abhor the Moor; very nature will instruct her in it and compel her to some second choice. Now, sir, this granted—as it is a most pregnant and unforced position—who stands so eminent in the degree of this fortune as Cassio does? a knave very voluble; no further conscionable than in putting on the mere form of civil and humane seeming, for the better compassing of his salt and most hidden loose affection? Why, none; why, none; a slipper and subtle knave, a finder of occasions, that has an eye can stamp and counterfeit advantages, though true advantage never present itself; a devilish knave. Besides, the knave is handsome, young, and hath all those requisites in him that folly and green minds look after; a pestilent complete knave; and the woman hath found him already.

RODERIGO   I cannot believe that in her; she's full of most blessed condition.

IAGO   Blessed fig's-end! the wine she drinks is made of grapes. If she had been blessed, she would never have loved the Moor. Blessed pudding! Didst thou not see her paddle with the palm of his hand? didst not mark that?

RODERIGO   Yes, that I did; but that was but courtesy.

321

IAGO Lechery, by this hand; an index and obscure prologue to the history of lust and foul thoughts. They met so near with their lips that their breaths embraced together. Villainous thoughts, Roderigo! when these mutualities so marshal the way, hard at hand comes the master and main exercise, the incorporate conclusion. Pish! But, sir, be you ruled by me; I have brought you from Venice. Watch you to-night; for the command, I'll lay't upon you. Cassio knows you not. I'll not be far from you. Do you find some occasion to anger Cassio, either by speaking too loud, or tainting his discipline; or from what other course you please, which the time shall more favourably minister.

RODERIGO Well.

IAGO Sir, he is rash and very sudden in choler, and haply may strike at you. Provoke him, that he may; for even out of that will I cause these of Cyprus to mutiny; whose qualification shall come into no true taste again but by the displanting of Cassio. So shall you have a shorter journey to your desires by the means I shall then have to prefer them; and the impediment most profitably removed, without the which there were no expectation of our prosperity.

RODERIGO I will do this, if I can bring it to any opportunity.

IAGO I warrant thee. Meet me by and by at the citadel. I must fetch his necessaries ashore. Farewell.

RODERIGO Adieu.   *Exit.*

IAGO That Cassio loves her, I do well believe it;
That she loves him, 'tis apt and of great credit.
The Moor, howbeit that I endure him not,
Is of a constant, loving, noble nature,
And I dare think he'll prove to Desdemona
A most dear husband. Now, I do love her too;
Not out of absolute lust, though peradventure
I stand accountant for as great a sin,
But partly led to diet my revenge,
For that I do suspect the lusty Moor
Hath leap'd into my seat; the thought whereof
Doth, like a poisonous mineral, gnaw my inwards;
And nothing can or shall content my soul
Till I am even'd with him, wife for wife,
Or failing so, yet that I put the Moor
At least into a jealousy so strong
That judgement cannot cure. Which thing to do,

322

If this poor trash of Venice, whom I trace
For his quick hunting, stand the putting on,
I'll have our Michael Cassio on the hip,
Abuse him to the Moor in the rank garb—
For I fear Cassio with my night-cap too—
Make the Moor thank me, love me, and reward me,
For making him egregiously an ass
And practising upon his peace and quiet
Even to madness. 'Tis here, but yet confused;
Knavery's plain face is never seen till used.   *Exit.*

SCENE 2   *A street.*

Enter a Herald with a proclamation; people following.

HERALD   It is Othello's pleasure, our noble and valiant general, that, upon certain tidings now arrived, importing the mere perdition of the Turkish fleet, every man put himself into triumph; some to dance, some to make bonfires, each man to what sport and revels his addiction leads him; for, besides these beneficial news, it is the celebration of his nuptial. So much was his pleasure should be proclaimed. All offices are open, and there is full liberty of feasting from this present hour of five till the bell have told eleven. Heaven bless the isle of Cyprus and our noble general Othello!   *Exeunt.*

SCENE 3   *A hall in the castle.*

Enter Othello, Desdemona, Cassio, and Attendants.

OTHELLO   Good Michael, look you to the guard to-night.
Let's teach ourselves that honourable stop,
Not to outsport discretion.

CASSIO   Iago hath direction what to do;
But, notwithstanding, with my personal eye
Will I look to't.

OTHELLO   Iago is most honest.
Michael, good night. To-morrow with your earliest
Let me have speech with you. [*To Desdemona.*] Come, my dear love,
The purchase made, the fruits are to ensue;
That profit's yet to come 'tween me and you.
Good night.   *Exeunt Othello, Desdemona, and Attendants.*

323

Enter Iago.

CASSIO   Welcome, Iago; we must to the watch.

IAGO   Not this hour, lieutenant; 'tis not yet ten o'clock. Our general cast us thus early for the love of his Desdemona; who let us not therefore blame. He hath not yet made wanton the night with her; and she is sport for Jove.

CASSIO   She's a most exquisite lady.

IAGO   And, I'll warrant her, full of game.

CASSIO   Indeed, she's a most fresh and delicate creature.

IAGO   What an eye she has! methinks it sounds a parley of provocation.

CASSIO   An inviting eye; and yet methinks right modest.

IAGO   And when she speaks, is it not an alarum to love?

CASSIO   She is indeed perfection.

IAGO   Well, happiness to their sheets! Come, lieutenant, I have a stoup of wine; and here without are a brace of Cyprus gallants that would fain have a measure to the health of black Othello.

CASSIO   Not to-night, good Iago. I have very poor and unhappy brains for drinking. I could well wish courtesy would invent some other custom of entertainment.

IAGO   O, they are our friends; but one cup; I'll drink for you.

CASSIO   I have drunk but one cup to-night, and that was craftily qualified too, and, behold, what innovation it makes here. I am unfortunate in the infirmity, and dare not task my weakness with any more.

IAGO   What, man! 'tis a night of revels. The gallants desire it.

CASSIO   Where are they?

IAGO   Here at the door; I pray you, call them in.

CASSIO   I'll do't; but it dislikes me.   *Exit.*

IAGO   If I can fasten but one cup upon him,
With that which he hath drunk to-night already,
He'll be as full of quarrel and offence
As my young mistress' dog. Now, my sick fool Roderigo,
Whom love hath turn'd almost the wrong side out,
To Desdemona hath to-night caroused

Potations pottle-deep; and he's to watch.
Three lads of Cyprus, noble swelling spirits,
That hold their honours in a wary distance,
The very elements of this warlike isle,
Have I to-night fluster'd with flowing cups,
And they watch too. Now, 'mongst this flock of drunkards,
Am I to put our Cassio in some action
That may offend the isle. But here they come.
If consequence do but approve my dream,
My boat sails freely, both with wind and stream.

Re-enter Cassio; with him Montano and Gentlemen; Servants following with wine.

CASSIO   'Fore God, they have given me a rouse already.

MONTANO   Good faith, a little one; not past a pint, as I am a soldier.

IAGO   Some wine, ho! [*Sings.*]

> "And let me the canakin clink, clink;
>   And let me the canakin clink.
>   A soldier's a man;
>   A life's but a span;
>   Why, then, let a soldier drink."

Some wine, boys!

CASSIO   'Fore God, an excellent song.

IAGO   I learned it in England, where, indeed, they are most potent in potting; your Dane, your German, and your swag-bellied Hollander—Drink, ho!—are nothing to your English.

CASSIO   Is your Englishman so expert in his drinking?

IAGO   Why, he drinks you, with facility, your Dane dead drunk; he sweats not to overthrow your Almain; he gives your Hollander a vomit, ere the next pottle can be filled.

CASSIO   To the health of our general!

MONTANO   I am for it, lieutenant; and I'll do you justice.

IAGO   O sweet England! [*Sings.*]

> "King Stephen was a worthy peer,
>   His breeches cost him but a crown;

325

> He held them sixpence all too dear,
>> With that he call'd the tailor lown.

> "He was a wight of high renown,
>> And thou art but of low degree.
> 'Tis pride that pulls the country down;
>> Then take thine auld cloak about thee."

Some wine, ho!

CASSIO Why, this is a more exquisite song than the other.

IAGO Will you hear't again?

CASSIO No; for I hold him to be unworthy of his place that does those things. Well, God's above all; and there be souls must be saved, and there be souls must not be saved.

IAGO It's true, good lieutenant.

CASSIO For mine own part—no offence to the general, nor any man of quality—I hope to be saved.

IAGO And so do I too, lieutenant.

CASSIO Ay, but, by your leave, not before me; the lieutenant is to be saved before the ancient. Let's have no more of this; let's to our affairs. Forgive us our sins! Gentlemen, let's look to our business. Do not think, gentlemen, I am drunk. This is my ancient; this is my right hand, and this is my left. I am not drunk now; I can stand well enough, and speak well enough.

ALL Excellent well.

CASSIO Why, very well then; you must not think then that I am drunk.

Exit.

MONTANO To the platform, masters; come, let's set the watch.

IAGO You see this fellow that is gone before;
He is a soldier fit to stand by Caesar
And give direction; and do but see his vice.
'Tis to his virtue a just equinox,
The one as long as the other; 'tis pity of him.
I fear the trust Othello puts him in,
On some odd time of his infirmity,
Will shake this island.

MONTANO   But is he often thus?

IAGO   'Tis evermore the prologue to his sleep.
  He'll watch the horologe a double set,
  If drink rock not his cradle.

MONTANO   It were well
  The general were put in mind of it.
  Perhaps he sees it not; or his good nature
  Prizes the virtue that appears in Cassio,
  And looks not on his evils. Is not this true?

Enter Roderigo.

IAGO   [*Aside to him.*] How now, Roderigo!
  I pray you, after the lieutenant; go.   *Exit Roderigo.*

MONTANO   And 'tis great pity that the noble Moor
  Should hazard such a place as his own second
  With one of an ingraft infirmity.
  It were an honest action to say
  So to the Moor.

IAGO   Not I, for this fair island.
  I do love Cassio well; and would do much
  To cure him of this evil— But, hark! What noise?

A cry within, "Help! help!" Re-enter Cassio, driving in Roderigo.

CASSIO   You rogue! you rascal!

MONTANO   What's the matter, lieutenant?

CASSIO   A knave teach me my duty! I'll beat the knave into a twiggen
  bottle.

RODERIGO   Beat me!

CASSIO   Dost thou prate, rogue?

Striking Roderigo.

MONTANO   Nay, good lieutenant; I pray you, sir, hold your hand.

Staying him.

CASSIO   Let me go, sir, or I'll knock you o'er the mazzard.

MONTANO   Come, come, you're drunk.

327

CASSIO Drunk!

They fight.

IAGO [*Aside to Roderigo.*] Away, I say; go out, and cry a mutiny.

Exit Roderigo.

Nay, good lieutenant—alas, gentlemen—
Help, ho!—Lieutenant—sir—Montano—sir—
Help, masters! Here's a goodly watch indeed!

Bell rings.

Who's that which rings the bell?—Diablo, ho!
The town will rise. God's will, lieutenant, hold!
You will be shamed for ever.

Re-enter Othello and Attendants.

OTHELLO   What is the matter here?

MONTANO 'Zounds, I bleed still; I am hurt to the death.

Faints.

OTHELLO Hold, for your lives!

IAGO Hold, ho! Lieutenant—sir—Montano—gentlemen—
Have you forgot all sense of place and duty?
Hold! the general speaks to you; hold, hold, for shame!

OTHELLO Why, how now, ho! from whence ariseth this?
Are we turn'd Turks, and to ourselves do that
Which heaven hath forbid the Ottomites?
For Christian shame, put by this barbarous brawl.
He that stirs next to carve for his own rage
Holds his soul light; he dies upon his motion.
Silence that dreadful bell; it frights the isle
From her propriety. What is the matter, masters?
Honest Iago, that look'st dead with grieving,
Speak, who began this? on thy love, I charge thee.

IAGO I do not know. Friends all but now, even now,
In quarter, and in terms like bride and groom
Devesting them for bed; and then, but now—
As if some planet had unwitted men—
Swords out, and tilting one at other's breast,

328

In opposition bloody. I cannot speak
Any beginning to this peevish odds;
And would in action glorious I had lost
Those legs that brought me to a part of it!

OTHELLO   How comes it, Michael, you are thus forgot?

CASSIO   I pray you, pardon me; I cannot speak.

OTHELLO   Worthy Montano, you were wont be civil;
The gravity and stillness of your youth
The world hath noted, and your name is great
In mouths of wisest censure. What's the matter,
That you unlace your reputation thus
And spend your rich opinion for the name
Of a night-brawler? give me answer to it.

MONTANO   Worthy Othello, I am hurt to danger.
Your officer, Iago, can inform you—
While I spare speech, which something now offends me—
Of all that I do know; nor know I aught
By me that's said or done amiss this night;
Unless self-charity be sometimes a vice,
And to defend ourselves it be a sin
When violence assails us.

OTHELLO   Now, by heaven,
My blood begins my safer guides to rule;
And passion, having my best judgement collied,
Assays to lead the way. If I once stir,
Or do but lift this arm, the best of you
Shall sink in my rebuke. Give me to know
How this foul rout began, who set it on;
And he that is approved in this offence,
Though he had twinn'd with me, both at a birth,
Shall lose me. What! in a town of war,
Yet wild, the people's hearts brimful of fear,
To manage private and domestic quarrel,
In night, and on the court and guard of safety!
'Tis monstrous. Iago, who began't?

MONTANO   If partially affined, or leagued in office,
Thou dost deliver more or less than truth,
Thou art no soldier.

329

IAGO   Touch me not so near.
I had rather have this tongue cut from my mouth
Than it should do offence to Michael Cassio;
Yet, I persuade myself, to speak the truth
Shall nothing wrong him. Thus it is, general.
Montano and myself being in speech,
There comes a fellow crying out for help;
And Cassio following him with determined sword,
To execute upon him. Sir, this gentleman
Steps in to Cassio, and entreats his pause.
Myself the crying fellow did pursue,
Lest by his clamour—as it so fell out—
The town might fall in fright. He, swift of foot,
Outran my purpose; and I return'd the rather
For that I heard the clink and fall of swords,
And Cassio high in oath; which till to-night
I ne'er might say before. When I came back—
For this was brief—I found them close together,
At blow and thrust; even as again they were
When you yourself did part them.
More of this matter cannot I report.
But men are men; the best sometimes forget.
Though Cassio did some little wrong to him,
As men in rage strike those that wish them best,
Yet surely Cassio, I believe, received
From him that fled some strange indignity
Which patience could not pass.

OTHELLO   I know, Iago,
Thy honesty and love doth mince this matter,
Making it light to Cassio. Cassio, I love thee;
But never more be officer of mine.

Re-enter Desdemona, attended.

Look, if my gentle love be not raised up!
I'll make thee an example.

DESDEMONA   What's the matter?

OTHELLO   All's well now, sweeting; come away to bed.
[*To Montano.*] Sir, for your hurts, myself will be your surgeon.
Lead him off.   *Exit Montano, attended.*
Iago, look with care about the town,

330

And silence those whom this vile brawl distracted.
Come, Desdemona; 'tis the soldiers' life
To have their balmy slumbers waked with strife.

Exeunt all but Iago and Cassio.

IAGO   What, are you hurt, lieutenant?

CASSIO   Ay, past all surgery.

IAGO   Marry, heaven forbid!

CASSIO   Reputation, reputation, reputation! O, I have lost my reputation! I have lost the immortal part of myself, and what remains is bestial. My reputation, Iago, my reputation!

IAGO   As I am an honest man, I thought you had received some bodily wound; there is more sense in that than in reputation. Reputation is an idle and most false imposition; oft got without merit, and lost without deserving. You have lost no reputation at all, unless you repute yourself such a loser. What, man! there are ways to recover the general again. You are but now cast in his mood, a punishment more in policy than in malice; even so as one would beat his offenceless dog to affright an imperious lion. Sue to him again, and he's yours.

CASSIO   I will rather sue to be despised than to deceive so good a commander with so slight, so drunken, and so indiscreet an officer. Drunk? and speak parrot? and squabble? swagger? swear? and discourse fustian with one's own shadow? O thou invisible spirit of wine, if thou hast no name to be known by, let us call thee devil!

IAGO   What was he that you followed with your sword? What had he done to you?

CASSIO   I know not.

IAGO   Is't possible?

CASSIO   I remember a mass of things, but nothing distinctly; a quarrel, but nothing wherefore. O God, that men should put an enemy in their mouths to steal away their brains! that we should, with joy, pleasance, revel, and applause, transform ourselves into beasts!

IAGO   Why, but you are now well enough. How came you thus recovered?

CASSIO   It hath pleased the devil drunkenness to give place to the devil wrath. One unperfectness shows me another, to make me frankly despise myself.

331

IAGO   Come, you are too severe a moraler. As the time, the place, and the condition of this country stands, I could heartily wish this had not befallen; but, since it is as it is, mend it for your own good.

CASSIO   I will ask him for my place again; he shall tell me I am a drunkard! Had I as many mouths as Hydra, such an answer would stop them all. To be now a sensible man, by and by a fool, and presently a beast! O strange! Every inordinate cup is unblessed and the ingredient is a devil.

IAGO   Come, come, good wine is a good familiar creature, if it be well used; exclaim no more against it. And, good lieutenant, I think you think I love you.

CASSIO   I have well approved it, sir. I drunk!

IAGO   You or any man living may be drunk at a time, man. I'll tell you what you shall do. Our general's wife is now the general. I may say so in this respect, for that he hath devoted and given up himself to the contemplation, mark, and denotement of her parts and graces. Confess yourself freely to her; importune her help to put you in your place again. She is of so free, so kind, so apt, so blessed a disposition, she holds it a vice in her goodness not to do more than she is requested. This broken joint between you and her husband entreat her to splinter; and, my fortunes against any lay worth naming, this crack of your love shall grow stronger than it was before.

CASSIO   You advise me well.

IAGO   I protest, in the sincerity of love and honest kindness.

CASSIO   I think it freely; and betimes in the morning I will beseech the virtuous Desdemona to undertake for me. I am desperate of my fortunes if they check me here.

IAGO   You are in the right. Good night, lieutenant; I must to the watch.

CASSIO   Good night, honest Iago.   *Exit.*

IAGO   And what's he then that says I play the villain?
When this advice is free I give and honest,
Probal to thinking and indeed the course
To win the Moor again? For 'tis most easy
The inclining Desdemona to subdue
In any honest suit; she's framed as fruitful
As the free elements. And then for her

332

To win the Moor—were't to renounce his baptism,
All seals and symbols of redeemed sin,
His soul is so enfetter'd to her love,
That she may make, unmake, do what she list,
Even as her appetite shall play the god
With his weak function. How am I then a villain
To counsel Cassio to this parallel course,
Directly to his good? Divinity of hell!
When devils will the blackest sins put on,
They do suggest at first with heavenly shows,
As I do now; for whiles this honest fool
Plies Desdemona to repair his fortunes
And she for him pleads strongly to the Moor,
I'll pour this pestilence into his ear,
That she repeals him for her body's lust;
And by how much she strives to do him good,
She shall undo her credit with the Moor.
So will I turn her virtue into pitch,
And out of her own goodness make the net
That shall enmesh them all.

Re-enter Roderigo.

How now, Roderigo!

RODERIGO   I do follow here in the chase, not like a hound that hunts, but
   one that fills up the cry. My money is almost spent; I have been to-
   night exceedingly well cudgelled; and I think the issue will be, I shall
   have so much experience for my pains, and so, with no money at all
   and a little more wit, return again to Venice.

IAGO   How poor are they that have not patience!
   What wound did ever heal but by degrees?
   Thou know'st we work by wit, and not by witchcraft;
   And wit depends on dilatory time.
   Does't not go well? Cassio hath beaten thee,
   And thou, by that small hurt, hast cashier'd Cassio.
   Though other things grow fair against the sun,
   Yet fruits that blossom first will first be ripe.
   Content thyself awhile. By the mass, 'tis morning;
   Pleasure and action make the hours seem short.
   Retire thee; go where thou art billeted.

333

Away, I say; thou shalt know more hereafter.
Nay, get thee gone.   *Exit Roderigo.*
             Two things are to be done:
My wife must move for Cassio to her mistress;
I'll set her on;
Myself the while to draw the Moor apart,
And bring him jump when he may Cassio find
Soliciting his wife. Ay, that's the way;
Dull not device by coldness and delay.   *Exit.*

ACT III

SCENE 1 *Before the castle.*

Enter Cassio and some Musicians.

CASSIO Masters, play here; I will content your pains;
Something that's brief; and bid "Good morrow, general."

Music. Enter Clown.

CLOWN Why, masters, have your instruments been in Naples, that they speak i' the nose thus?

FIRST MUSICIAN How, sir, how!

CLOWN Are these, I pray you, wind-instruments?

FIRST MUSICIAN Ay, marry, are they, sir.

CLOWN O, thereby hangs a tail.

FIRST MUSICIAN Whereby hangs a tale, sir?

CLOWN Marry, sir, by many a wind-instrument that I know. But, masters, here's money for you; and the general so likes your music, that he desires you, for love's sake, to make no more noise with it.

FIRST MUSICIAN Well, sir, we will not.

CLOWN If you have any music that may not be heard, to't again; but, as they say, to hear music the general does not greatly care.

FIRST MUSICIAN We have none such, sir.

CLOWN Then put up your pipes in your bag, for I'll away. Go; vanish into air; away! *Exeunt Musicians.*

335

CASSIO Dost thou hear, my honest friend?

CLOWN No, I hear not your honest friend; I hear you.

CASSIO Prithee, keep up thy quillets. There's a poor piece of gold for
thee. If the gentlewoman that attends the general's wife be stirring, tell
her there's one Cassio entreats her a little favour of speech. Wilt thou
do this?

CLOWN She is stirring, sir. If she will stir hither, I shall seem to notify
unto her.

CASSIO Do, good my friend.   *Exit Clown.*

Enter Iago.

> In happy time, Iago.

IAGO You have not been a-bed, then?

CASSIO Why, no; the day had broke
Before we parted. I have made bold, Iago,
To send in to your wife. My suit to her
Is that she will to virtuous Desdemona
Procure me some access.

IAGO   I'll send her to you presently;
And I'll devise a mean to draw the Moor
Out of the way, that your converse and business
May be more free.

CASSIO I humbly thank you for't.   *Exit Iago.*
> I never knew
A Florentine more kind and honest.

Enter Emilia.

EMILIA Good morrow, good lieutenant. I am sorry
For your displeasure; but all will sure be well.
The general and his wife are talking of it;
And she speaks for you stoutly. The Moor replies
That he you hurt is of great fame in Cyprus
And great affinity and that in wholesome wisdom
He might not but refuse you, but he protests he loves you
And needs no other suitor but his likings
To take the safest occasion by the front
To bring you in again.

336

CASSIO   Yet, I beseech you,
If you think fit, or that it may be done,
Give me advantage of some brief discourse
With Desdemona alone.

EMILIA   Pray you, come in.
I will bestow you where you shall have time
To speak your bosom freely.

CASSIO   I am much bound to you.   *Exeunt.*

SCENE 2   *A room in the castle.*

Enter Othello, Iago, and Gentlemen.

OTHELLO   These letters give, Iago, to the pilot;
And by him do my duties to the senate.
That done, I will be walking on the works;
Repair there to me.

IAGO   Well, my good lord, I'll do't.

OTHELLO   This fortification, gentlemen, shall we see't?

GENTLEMEN   We'll wait upon your lordship.   *Exeunt.*

SCENE 3   *The garden of the castle.*

Enter Desdemona, Cassio, and Emilia.

DESDEMONA   Be thou assured, good Cassio, I will do
All my abilities in thy behalf.

EMILIA   Good madam, do. I warrant it grieves my husband,
As if the case were his.

DESDEMONA   O, that's an honest fellow. Do not doubt, Cassio,
But I will have my lord and you again
As friendly as you were.

CASSIO   Bounteous madam,
Whatever shall become of Michael Cassio,
He's never anything but your true servant.

DESDEMONA   I know't; I thank you. You do love my lord;
You have known him long; and be you well assured

He shall in strangeness stand no further off
Than in a politic distance.

CASSIO   Ay, but, lady,
  That policy may either last so long,
  Or feed upon such nice and waterish diet,
  Or breed itself so out of circumstance,
  That, I being absent and my place supplied,
  My general will forget my love and service.

DESDEMONA   Do not doubt that; before Emilia here
  I give thee warrant of thy place. Assure thee,
  If I do vow a friendship, I'll perform it
  To the last article. My lord shall never rest;
  I'll watch him tame and talk him out of patience;
  His bed shall seem a school, his board a shrift;
  I'll intermingle everything he does
  With Cassio's suit. Therefore be merry, Cassio;
  For thy solicitor shall rather die
  Than give thy cause away.

Enter Othello and Iago.

EMILIA   Madam, here comes my lord.

CASSIO   Madam, I'll take my leave.

DESDEMONA   Why, stay, and hear me speak.

CASSIO   Madam, not now; I am very ill at ease,
  Unfit for mine own purposes.

DESDEMONA   Well, do your discretion.   *Exit Cassio.*

IAGO   Ha! I like not that.

OTHELLO   What dost thou say?

IAGO   Nothing, my lord; or if—I know not what.

OTHELLO   Was not that Cassio parted from my wife?

IAGO   Cassio, my lord! No, sure, I cannot think it,
  That he would steal away so guilty-like,
  Seeing you coming.

OTHELLO   I do believe 'twas he.

338

DESDEMONA   How now, my lord!
  I have been talking with a suitor here,
  A man that languishes in your displeasure.

OTHELLO   Who is't you mean?

DESDEMONA   Why, your lieutenant, Cassio. Good my lord,
  If I have any grace or power to move you,
  His present reconciliation take;
  For if he be not one that truly loves you,
  That errs in ignorance and not in cunning,
  I have no judgement in an honest face.
  I prithee, call him back.

OTHELLO   Went he hence now?

DESDEMONA   Ay, sooth; so humbled
  That he hath left part of his grief with me,
  To suffer with him. Good love, call him back.

OTHELLO   Not now, sweet Desdemona; some other time.

DESDEMONA   But shall't be shortly?

OTHELLO   The sooner, sweet, for you.

DESDEMONA   Shall't be to-night at supper?

OTHELLO   No, not to-night.

DESDEMONA   To-morrow dinner, then?

OTHELLO   I shall not dine at home;
  I meet the captains at the citadel.

DESDEMONA   Why, then, to-morrow night; or Tuesday morn;
  On Tuesday noon, or night; on Wednesday morn.
  I prithee, name the time, but let it not
  Exceed three days. In faith, he's penitent;
  And yet his trespass, in our common reason—
  Save that, they say, the wars must make examples
  Out of their best—is not almost a fault
  To incur a private check. When shall he come?
  Tell me, Othello. I wonder in my soul
  What you would ask me that I should deny,
  Or stand so mammering on. What! Michael Cassio,
  That came a-wooing with you, and so many a time,

When I have spoke of you dispraisingly,
Hath ta'en your part; to have so much to do
To bring him in! Trust me, I could do much—

OTHELLO   Prithee, no more. Let him come when he will;
I will deny thee nothing.

DESDEMONA   Why, this is not a boon;
'Tis as I should entreat you wear your gloves,
Or feed on nourishing dishes, or keep you warm,
Or sue to you to do a peculiar profit
To your own person. Nay, when I have a suit
Wherein I mean to touch your love indeed,
It shall be full of poise and difficult weight
And fearful to be granted.

OTHELLO   I will deny thee nothing;
Whereon, I do beseech thee, grant me this,
To leave me but a little to myself.

DESDEMONA   Shall I deny you? no. Farewell, my lord.

OTHELLO   Farewell, my Desdemona. I'll come to thee straight.

DESDEMONA   Emilia, come. Be as your fancies teach you;
Whate'er you be, I am obedient.   *Exeunt Desdemona and Emilia.*

OTHELLO   Excellent wretch! Perdition catch my soul,
But I do love thee! and when I love thee not,
Chaos is come again.

IAGO   My noble lord—

OTHELLO   What dost thou say, Iago?

IAGO   Did Michael Cassio, when you woo'd my lady,
Know of your love?

OTHELLO   He did, from first to last. Why dost thou ask?

IAGO   But for a satisfaction of my thought;
No further harm.

OTHELLO   Why of thy thought, Iago?

IAGO   I did not think he had been acquainted with her.

OTHELLO   O, yes; and went between us very oft.

IAGO   Indeed!

OTHELLO   Indeed! ay, indeed. Discern'st thou aught in that?
Is he not honest?

IAGO   Honest, my lord!

OTHELLO   Honest! ay, honest.

IAGO   My lord, for aught I know.

OTHELLO   What dost thou think?

IAGO   Think, my lord!

OTHELLO   Think, my lord!
By heaven, he echoes me,
As if there were some monster in his thought
Too hideous to be shown. Thou dost mean something.
I heard thee say even now, thou likedst not that,
When Cassio left my wife. What didst not like?
And when I told thee he was of my counsel
In my whole course of wooing, thou criedst "Indeed!"
And didst contract and purse thy brow together,
As if thou then hadst shut up in thy brain
Some horrible conceit. If thou dost love me,
Show me thy thought.

IAGO   My lord, you know I love you.

OTHELLO   I think thou dost;
And, for I know thou'rt full of love and honesty,
And weigh'st thy words before thou givest them breath,
Therefore these stops of thine fright me the more;
For such things in a false disloyal knave
Are tricks of custom, but in a man that's just
They are close delations, working from the heart
That passion cannot rule.

IAGO   For Michael Cassio,
I dare be sworn I think that he is honest.

OTHELLO   I think so too.

IAGO   Men should be what they seem;
Or those that be not, would they might seem none!

OTHELLO   Certain, men should be what they seem.

IAGO   Why, then, I think Cassio's an honest man.

341

OTHELLO   Nay, yet there's more in this.
  I prithee, speak to me as to thy thinkings,
  As thou dost ruminate, and give thy worst of thoughts
  The worst of words.

IAGO   Good my lord, pardon me.
  Though I am bound to every act of duty,
  I am not bound to that all slaves are free to.
  Utter my thoughts? Why, say they are vile and false;
  As where's that palace whereinto foul things
  Sometimes intrude not? who has a breast so pure,
  But some uncleanly apprehensions
  Keep leets and law-days and in session sit
  With meditations lawful?

OTHELLO   Thou dost conspire against thy friend, Iago,
  If thou but think'st him wrong'd and makest his ear
  A stranger to thy thoughts.

IAGO   I do beseech you—
  Though I perchance am vicious in my guess,
  As, I confess, it is my nature's plague
  To spy into abuses, and oft my jealousy
  Shapes faults that are not—that your wisdom yet,
  From one that so imperfectly conceits,
  Would take no notice, nor build yourself a trouble
  Out of his scattering and unsure observance.
  It were not for your quiet nor your good,
  Nor for my manhood, honesty, or wisdom,
  To let you know my thoughts.

OTHELLO   What dost thou mean?

IAGO   Good name in man and woman, dear my lord,
  Is the immediate jewel of their souls.
  Who steals my purse steals trash; 'tis something, nothing;
  'Twas mine, 'tis his, and has been slave to thousands;
  But he that filches from me my good name
  Robs me of that which not enriches him
  And makes me poor indeed.

OTHELLO   By heaven, I'll know thy thoughts.

IAGO   You cannot, if my heart were in your hand;
  Nor shall not, whilst 'tis in my custody.

OTHELLO Ha!

IAGO   O, beware, my lord, of jealousy;
  It is the green-eyed monster which doth mock
  The meat it feeds on. The cuckold lives in bliss
  Who, certain of his fate, loves not his wronger;
  But, O, what damned minutes tells he o'er
  Who dotes, yet doubts, suspects, yet strongly loves!

OTHELLO O misery!

IAGO Poor and content is rich and rich enough,
  But riches fineless is as poor as winter
  To him that ever fears he shall be poor.
  Good heaven, the souls of all my tribe defend
  From jealousy!

OTHELLO   Why, why is this?
  Think'st thou I'd make a life of jealousy,
  To follow still the changes of the moon
  With fresh suspicions? No; to be once in doubt
  Is once to be resolved. Exchange me for a goat,
  When I shall turn the business of my soul
  To such exsufflicate and blown surmises,
  Matching thy inference. 'Tis not to make me jealous
  To say my wife is fair, feeds well, loves company,
  Is free of speech, sings, plays, and dances well;
  Where virtue is, these are more virtuous.
  Nor from mine own weak merits will I draw
  The smallest fear or doubt of her revolt;
  For she had eyes, and chose me. No, Iago;
  I'll see before I doubt; when I doubt, prove;
  And on the proof, there is no more but this—
  Away at once with love or jealousy!

IAGO I am glad of it; for now I shall have reason
  To show the love and duty that I bear you
  With franker spirit; therefore, as I am bound,
  Receive it from me. I speak not yet of proof.
  Look to your wife; observe her well with Cassio;
  Wear your eye thus, not jealous nor secure.
  I would not have your free and noble nature,
  Out of self-bounty, be abused; look to't.
  I know our country disposition well;

In Venice they do let heaven see the pranks
They dare not show their husbands; their best conscience
Is not to leave't undone, but keep't unknown.

OTHELLO   Dost thou say so?

IAGO   She did deceive her father, marrying you;
And when she seem'd to shake and fear your looks,
She loved them most.

OTHELLO   And so she did.

IAGO   Why, go to then;
She that, so young, could give out such a seeming,
To seel her father's eyes up close as oak—
He thought 'twas witchcraft—but I am much to blame;
I humbly do beseech you of your pardon
For too much loving you.

OTHELLO   I am bound to thee for ever.

IAGO   I see this hath a little dash'd your spirits.

OTHELLO   Not a jot, not a jot.

IAGO   I' faith, I fear it has.
I hope you will consider what is spoke
Comes from my love. But I do see you're moved.
I am to pray you not to strain my speech
To grosser issues nor to larger reach
Than to suspicion.

OTHELLO   I will not.

IAGO   Should you do so, my lord,
My speech should fall into such vile success
As my thoughts aim not at. Cassio's my worthy friend—
My lord, I see you're moved.

OTHELLO   No, not much moved.
I do not think but Desdemona's honest.

IAGO   Long live she so! and long live you to think so!

OTHELLO   And yet, how nature erring from itself—

IAGO   Ay, there's the point; as—to be bold with you—
Not to affect many proposed matches
Of her own clime, complexion, and degree,

Whereto we see in all things nature tends—
Foh! one may smell in such a will most rank,
Foul disproportion, thoughts unnatural.
But pardon me; I do not in position
Distinctly speak of her; though I may fear
Her will, recoiling to her better judgement,
May fall to match you with her country forms
And happily repent.

OTHELLO   Farewell, farewell.
  If more thou dost perceive, let me know more;
  Set on thy wife to observe. Leave me, Iago.

IAGO [*Going.*] My lord, I take my leave.

OTHELLO Why did I marry? This honest creature doubtless
  Sees and knows more, much more, than he unfolds.

IAGO [*Returning.*] My lord, I would I might entreat your honour
  To scan this thing no further; leave it to time.
  Though it be fit that Cassio have his place,
  For, sure, he fills it up with great ability,
  Yet, if you please to hold him off awhile,
  You shall by that perceive him and his means.
  Note, if your lady strain his entertainment
  With any strong or vehement importunity;
  Much will be seen in that. In the mean time,
  Let me be thought too busy in my fears—
  As worthy cause I have to fear I am—
  And hold her free, I do beseech your honour.

OTHELLO Fear not my government.

IAGO I once more take my leave.   *Exit.*

OTHELLO This fellow's of exceeding honesty,
  And knows all qualities, with a learned spirit,
  Of human dealings. If I do prove her haggard,
  Though that her jesses were my dear heart-strings,
  I'd whistle her off and let her down the wind,
  To prey at fortune. Haply, for I am black
  And have not those soft parts of conversation
  That chamberers have, or for I am declined
  Into the vale of years—yet that's not much—
  She's gone. I am abused; and my relief

Must be to loathe her. O curse of marriage,
That we can call these delicate creatures ours,
And not their appetites! I had rather be a toad,
And live upon the vapour of a dungeon,
Than keep a corner in the thing I love
For others' uses. Yet, 'tis the plague of great ones;
Prerogatived are they less than the base;
'Tis destiny unshunnable, like death.
Even then this forked plague is fated to us
When we do quicken. Desdemona comes;

Re-enter Desdemona and Emilia.

If she be false, O, then heaven mocks itself!
I'll not believe't.

DESDEMONA   How now, my dear Othello!
Your dinner, and the generous islanders
By you invited, do attend your presence.

OTHELLO   I am to blame.

DESDEMONA   Why do you speak so faintly?
Are you not well?

OTHELLO   I have a pain upon my forehead here.

DESDEMONA   'Faith, that's with watching; 'twill away again.
Let me but bind it hard, within this hour
It will be well.

OTHELLO   Your napkin is too little.

He puts the handkerchief from him; and it drops.

Let it alone. Come, I'll go in with you.

DESDEMONA   I am very sorry that you are not well.
                              Exeunt Othello and Desdemona.

EMILIA   I am glad I have found this napkin;
This was her first remembrance from the Moor.
My wayward husband hath a hundred times
Woo'd me to steal it; but she so loves the token,
For he conjured her she should ever keep it,
That she reserves it evermore about her
To kiss and talk to. I'll have the work ta'en out,
And give't Iago. What he will do with it

Heaven knows, not I;
I nothing but to please his fantasy.

Re-enter Iago.

IAGO   How now! what do you here alone?

EMILIA   Do not you chide; I have a thing for you.

IAGO   A thing for me? it is a common thing—

EMILIA   Ha!

IAGO   To have a foolish wife.

EMILIA   O, is that all? What will you give me now
For that same handkerchief?

IAGO   What handkerchief?

EMILIA   What handkerchief!
Why, that the Moor first gave to Desdemona;
That which so often you did bid me steal.

IAGO   Hast stol'n it from her?

EMILIA   No, 'faith; she let it drop by negligence,
And, to the advantage, I, being here, took't up.
Look, here it is.

IAGO   A good wench; give it me.

EMILIA   What will you do with't, that you have been so earnest
To have me filch it?

IAGO   [*Snatching it.*] Why, what's that to you?

EMILIA   If it be not for some purpose of import,
Give't me again. Poor lady, she'll run mad
When she shall lack it.

IAGO   Be not acknown on't; I have use for it.
Go, leave me.   *Exit Emilia.*
I will in Cassio's lodging lose this napkin,
And let him find it. Trifles light as air
Are to the jealous confirmations strong
As proofs of holy writ; this may do something.
The Moor already changes with my poison.
Dangerous conceits are, in their natures, poisons,
Which at the first are scarce found to distaste,

347

But with a little act upon the blood,
Burn like the mines of sulphur. I did say so.
Look, where he comes!

Re-enter Othello.

                        Not poppy, nor mandragora,
Nor all the drowsy syrups of the world,
Shall ever medicine thee to that sweet sleep
Which thou owedst yesterday.

OTHELLO   Ha! ha! false to me?

IAGO   Why, how now, general! no more of that.

OTHELLO   Avaunt! be gone! thou hast set me on the rack.
I swear 'tis better to be much abused
Than but to know't a little.

IAGO   How now, my lord!

OTHELLO   What sense had I of her stol'n hours of lust?
I saw't not, thought it not, it harm'd not me.
I slept the next night well, was free and merry;
I found not Cassio's kisses on her lips.
He that is robb'd, not wanting what is stol'n,
Let him not know't, and he's not robb'd at all.

IAGO   I am sorry to hear this.

OTHELLO   I had been happy, if the general camp,
Pioners and all, had tasted her sweet body,
So I had nothing known. O, now, for ever
Farewell the tranquil mind! farewell content!
Farewell the plumed troop, and the big wars,
That make ambition virtue! O, farewell!
Farewell the neighing steed, and the shrill trump,
The spirit-stirring drum, the ear-piercing fife,
The royal banner, and all quality,
Pride, pomp, and circumstance of glorious war!
And, O you mortal engines, whose rude throats
The immortal Jove's dread clamours counterfeit,
Farewell! Othello's occupation's gone!

IAGO   Is't possible, my lord?

OTHELLO   Villain, be sure thou prove my love a whore,

348

Be sure of it; give me the ocular proof;
Or, by the worth of man's eternal soul,
Thou hadst been better have been born a dog
Than answer my waked wrath!

IAGO   Is't come to this?

OTHELLO   Make me to see't; or, at the least, so prove it
That the probation bear no hinge nor loop
To hang a doubt on; or woe upon thy life!

IAGO   My noble lord—

OTHELLO   If thou dost slander her and torture me,
Never pray more; abandon all remorse;
On horror's head horrors accumulate;
Do deeds to make heaven weep, all earth amazed;
For nothing canst thou to damnation add
Greater than that.

IAGO   O grace! O heaven forgive me!
Are you a man? have you a soul or sense?
God be wi' you; take mine office. O wretched fool,
That livest to make thine honesty a vice!
O monstrous world! Take note, take note, O world,
To be direct and honest is not safe.
I thank you for this profit; and from hence
I'll love no friend, sith love breeds such offence.

OTHELLO   Nay, stay. Thou shouldst be honest.

IAGO   I should be wise, for honesty's a fool
And loses that it works for.

OTHELLO   By the world,
I think my wife be honest and think she is not;
I think that thou art just and think thou art not.
I'll have proof. Her name, that was as fresh
As Dian's visage, is now begrimed and black
As mine own face. If there be cords, or knives,
Poison, or fire, or suffocating streams,
I'll not endure it. Would I were satisfied!

IAGO   I see, sir, you are eaten up with passion.
I do repent me that I put it to you.
You would be satisfied?

OTHELLO   Would! nay, I will.

IAGO   And may; but, how? how satisfied, my lord?
  Would you, the supervisor, grossly gape on—
  Behold her topp'd?

OTHELLO   Death and damnation! O!

IAGO   It were a tedious difficulty, I think,
  To bring them to that prospect. Damn them then,
  If ever mortal eyes do see them bolster
  More than their own! What then? how then?
  What shall I say? Where's satisfaction?
  It is impossible you should see this,
  Were they as prime as goats, as hot as monkeys,
  As salt as wolves in pride, and fools as gross
  As ignorance made drunk. But yet, I say,
  If imputation and strong circumstances,
  Which lead directly to the door of truth,
  Will give you satisfaction, you may have't.

OTHELLO   Give me a living reason she's disloyal.

IAGO   I do not like the office;
  But, sith I am enter'd in this cause so far,
  Prick'd to't by foolish honesty and love,
  I will go on. I lay with Cassio lately;
  And, being troubled with a raging tooth,
  I could not sleep.
  There are a kind of men so loose of soul,
  That in their sleeps will mutter their affairs;
  One of this kind is Cassio.
  In sleep I heard him say, "Sweet Desdemona,
  Let us be wary, let us hide our loves";
  And then, sir, would he gripe and wring my hand,
  Cry, "O sweet creature!" and then kiss me hard,
  As if he pluck'd up kisses by the roots
  That grew upon my lips; then laid his leg
  Over my thigh, and sigh'd, and kiss'd; and then
  Cried, "Cursed fate that gave thee to the Moor!"

OTHELLO   O monstrous! monstrous!

IAGO   Nay, this was but his dream.

350

OTHELLO   But this denoted a foregone conclusion.
'Tis a shrewd doubt, though it be but a dream.

IAGO   And this may help to thicken other proofs
That do demonstrate thinly.

OTHELLO   I'll tear her all to pieces.

IAGO   Nay, but be wise; yet we see nothing done;
She may be honest yet. Tell me but this,
Have you not sometimes seen a handkerchief
Spotted with strawberries in your wife's hand?

OTHELLO   I gave her such a one; 'twas my first gift.

IAGO   I know not that; but such a handkerchief—
I am sure it was your wife's—did I to-day
See Cassio wipe his beard with.

OTHELLO   If it be that—

IAGO   If it be that, or any that was hers,
It speaks against her with the other proofs.

OTHELLO   O, that the slave had forty thousand lives!
One is too poor, too weak for my revenge.
Now do I see 'tis true. Look here, Iago;
All my fond love thus do I blow to heaven.
'Tis gone.
Arise, black vengeance, from thy hollow cell!
Yield up, O love, thy crown and hearted throne
To tyrannous hate! Swell, bosom, with thy fraught,
For 'tis of aspics' tongues!

IAGO   Yet be content.

OTHELLO   O, blood, blood, blood!

IAGO   Patience, I say; your mind perhaps may change.

OTHELLO   Never, Iago. Like to the Pontic sea,
Whose icy current and compulsive course
Ne'er feels retiring ebb, but keeps due on
To the Propontic and the Hellespont,
Even so my bloody thoughts, with violent pace,
Shall ne'er look back, ne'er ebb to humble love,
Till that a capable and wide revenge

351

Swallow them up. Now, by yond marble heaven,
[*Kneels.*] In the due reverence of a sacred vow
I here engage my words.

IAGO   Do not rise yet.
[*Kneels.*] Witness, you ever-burning lights above,
You elements that clip us round about,
Witness that here Iago doth give up
The execution of his wit, hands, heart,
To wrong'd Othello's service! Let him command,
And to obey shall be in me remorse,
What bloody business ever.

They rise.

OTHELLO   I greet thy love,
Not with vain thanks, but with acceptance bounteous,
And will upon the instant put thee to't.
Within these three days let me hear thee say
That Cassio's not alive.

IAGO   My friend is dead; 'tis done at your request.
But let her live.

OTHELLO   Damn her, lewd minx! O, damn her!
Come, go with me apart; I will withdraw,
To furnish me with some swift means of death
For the fair devil. Now art thou my lieutenant.

IAGO   I am your own for ever.   *Exeunt.*

SCENE 4   *Before the castle.*

Enter Desdemona, Emilia, and Clown.

DESDEMONA   Do you know, sirrah, where Lieutenant Cassio lies?

CLOWN   I dare not say he lies anywhere.

DESDEMONA   Why, man?

CLOWN   He's a soldier, and for one to say a soldier lies, is stabbing.

DESDEMONA   Go to. Where lodges he?

CLOWN   To tell you where he lodges, is to tell you where I lie.

DESDEMONA   Can anything be made of this?

CLOWN   I know not where he lodges, and for me to devise a lodging and say he lies here or he lies there, were to lie in mine own throat.

DESDEMONA   Can you inquire him out, and be edified by report?

CLOWN   I will catechize the world for him; that is, make questions, and by them answer.

DESDEMONA   Seek him, bid him come hither. Tell him I have moved my lord on his behalf, and hope all will be well.

CLOWN   To do this is within the compass of man's wit; and therefore I will attempt the doing it.   *Exit.*

DESDEMONA   Where should I lose that handkerchief, Emilia?

EMILIA   I know not, madam.

DESDEMONA   Believe me, I had rather have lost my purse
Full of crusadoes; and, but my noble Moor
Is true of mind and made of no such baseness
As jealous creatures are, it were enough
To put him to ill thinking.

EMILIA   Is he not jealous?

DESDEMONA   Who, he? I think the sun where he was born
Drew all such humours from him.

EMILIA   Look, where he comes.

DESDEMONA   I will not leave him now till Cassio
Be call'd to him.

Enter Othello

                        How is't with you, my lord?

OTHELLO   Well, my good lady. [*Aside.*] O, hardness to dissemble!—
How do you, Desdemona?

DESDEMONA   Well, my good lord.

OTHELLO   Give me your hand. This hand is moist, my lady.

DESDEMONA   It yet hath felt no age nor known no sorrow.

OTHELLO   This argues fruitfulness and liberal heart;
Hot, hot, and moist. This hand of yours requires
A sequester from liberty, fasting, and prayer,
Much castigation, exercise devout;

353

For here's a young and sweating devil here,
That commonly rebels. 'Tis a good hand,
A frank one.

DESDEMONA   You may, indeed, say so;
For 'twas that hand that gave away my heart.

OTHELLO   A liberal hand. The hearts of old gave hands;
But our new heraldry is hands, not hearts.

DESDEMONA   I cannot speak of this. Come now, your promise.

OTHELLO   What promise, chuck?

DESDEMONA   I have sent to bid Cassio come speak with you.

OTHELLO   I have a salt and sorry rheum offends me;
Lend me thy handkerchief.

DESDEMONA   Here, my lord.

OTHELLO   That which I gave you.

DESDEMONA   I have it not about me.

OTHELLO   Not?

DESDEMONA   No, indeed, my lord.

OTHELLO   That is a fault.
That handkerchief
Did an Egyptian to my mother give;
She was a charmer, and could almost read
The thoughts of people. She told her, while she kept it,
'Twould make her amiable and subdue my father
Entirely to her love, but if she lost it
Or made a gift of it, my father's eye
Should hold her loathed and his spirits should hunt
After new fancies. She, dying, gave it me;
And bid me, when my fate would have me wive,
To give it her. I did so; and take heed on't;
Make it a darling like your precious eye;
To lose't or give't away were such perdition
As nothing else could match.

DESDEMONA   Is't possible?

OTHELLO   'Tis true; there's magic in the web of it.
A sibyl, that had number'd in the world

354

The sun to course two hundred compasses,
In her prophetic fury sew'd the work;
The worms were hallow'd that did breed the silk;
And it was dyed in mummy which the skilful
Conserved of maidens' hearts.

DESDEMONA   Indeed! is't true?

OTHELLO   Most veritable; therefore look to't well.

DESDEMONA   Then would to God that I had never seen't!

OTHELLO   Ha! wherefore?

DESDEMONA   Why do you speak so startingly and rash?

OTHELLO   Is't lost? is't gone? speak, is it out o' the way?

DESDEMONA   Heaven bless us!

OTHELLO   Say you?

DESDEMONA   It is not lost; but what an if it were?

OTHELLO   How!

DESDEMONA   I say, it is not lost.

OTHELLO   Fetch't, let me see't.

DESDEMONA   Why, so I can, sir, but I will not now.
   This is a trick to put me from my suit.
   Pray you, let Cassio be received again.

OTHELLO   Fetch me the handkerchief. My mind misgives.

DESDEMONA   Come, come;
   You'll never meet a more sufficient man.

OTHELLO   The handkerchief!

DESDEMONA   I pray, talk me of Cassio.

OTHELLO   The handkerchief!

DESDEMONA   A man that all his time
   Hath founded his good fortunes on your love,
   Shared dangers with you—

OTHELLO   The handkerchief!

355

DESDEMONA   In sooth, you are to blame.

OTHELLO   Away!   *Exit.*

EMILIA   Is not this man jealous?

DESDEMONA   I ne'er saw this before.
  Sure, there's some wonder in this handkerchief.
  I am most unhappy in the loss of it.

EMILIA   'Tis not a year or two shows us a man.
  They are all but stomachs, and we all but food;
  They eat us hungerly, and when they are full,
  They belch us. Look you, Cassio and my husband!

Enter Cassio and Iago.

IAGO   There is no other way; 'tis she must do't.
  And, lo, the happiness! go, and importune her.

DESDEMONA   How now, good Cassio! what's the news with you?

CASSIO   Madam, my former suit. I do beseech you
  That by your virtuous means I may again
  Exist, and be a member of his love
  Whom I with all the office of my heart
  Entirely honour. I would not be delay'd.
  If my offence be of such mortal kind
  That nor my service past, nor present sorrows,
  Nor purposed merit in futurity,
  Can ransom me into his love again,
  But to know so must be my benefit;
  So shall I clothe me in a forced content,
  And shut myself up in some other course,
  To fortune's alms.

DESDEMONA   Alas, thrice-gentle Cassio!
  My advocation is not now in tune;
  My lord is not my lord; nor should I know him,
  Were he in favour as in humour alter'd.
  So help me every spirit sanctified,
  As I have spoken for you all my best
  And stood within the blank of his displeasure
  For my free speech! you must awhile be patient.

What I can do I will; and more I will
Than for myself I dare. Let that suffice you.

IAGO   Is my lord angry?

EMILIA   He went hence but now,
And certainly in strange unquietness.

IAGO   Can he be angry? I have seen the cannon,
When it hath blown his ranks into the air,
And, like the devil, from his very arm
Puff'd his own brother—and can he be angry?
Something of moment then. I will go meet him.
There's matter in't indeed, if he be angry.

DESDEMONA   I prithee, do so.   *Exit Iago.*
                              Something, sure, of state,
Either from Venice, or some unhatch'd practice
Made demonstrable here in Cyprus to him,
Hath puddled his clear spirit; and in such cases
Men's natures wrangle with inferior things,
Though great ones are their object. 'Tis even so;
For let our finger ache, and it indues
Our other healthful members even to that sense
Of pain. Nay, we must think men are not gods,
Nor of them look for such observances
As fit the bridal. Beshrew me much, Emilia,
I was, unhandsome warrior as I am,
Arraigning his unkindness with my soul;
But now I find I had suborn'd the witness,
And he's indicted falsely.

EMILIA   Pray heaven it be state-matters, as you think,
And no conception nor no jealous toy
Concerning you.

DESDEMONA   Alas the day! I never gave him cause.

EMILIA   But jealous souls will not be answer'd so;
They are not ever jealous for the cause,
But jealous for they are jealous. 'Tis a monster
Begot upon itself, born on itself.

DESDEMONA   Heaven keep that monster from Othello's mind!

357

EMILIA   Lady, amen.

DESDEMONA   I will go seek him. Cassio, walk here about.
  If I do find him fit, I'll move your suit
  And seek to effect it to my uttermost.

CASSIO   I humbly thank your ladyship.   *Exeunt Desdemona and Emilia.*

Enter Bianca.

BIANCA   Save you, friend Cassio!

CASSIO   What make you from home?
  How is it with you, my most fair Bianca?
  I' faith, sweet love, I was coming to your house.

BIANCA   And I was going to your lodging, Cassio.
  What, keep a week away? seven days and nights?
  Eight score eight hours? and lovers' absent hours,
  More tedious than the dial eight score times?
  O weary reckoning!

CASSIO   Pardon me, Bianca.
  I have this while with leaden thoughts been press'd;
  But I shall, in a more continuate time,
  Strike off this score of absence. Sweet Bianca,

Giving her Desdemona's handkerchief.

  Take me this work out.

BIANCA   O Cassio, whence came this?
  This is some token from a newer friend.
  To the felt absence now I feel a cause;
  Is't come to this? Well, well.

CASSIO   Go to, woman!
  Throw your vile guesses in the devil's teeth,
  From whence you have them. You are jealous now
  That this is from some mistress, some remembrance.
  No, by my faith, Bianca.

BIANCA   Why, whose is it?

CASSIO   I know not, sweet. I found it in my chamber.
  I like the work well. Ere it be demanded—
  As like enough it will—I'd have it copied.
  Take it, and do't; and leave me for this time.

ACT III   Scene 4

BIANCA   Leave you! wherefore?

CASSIO   I do attend here on the general;
And think it no addition, nor my wish,
To have him see me woman'd.

BIANCA   Why, I pray you?

CASSIO   Not that I love you not.

BIANCA   But that you do not love me.
I pray you, bring me on the way a little,
And say if I shall see you soon at night.

CASSIO   'Tis but a little way that I can bring you;
For I attend here; but I'll see you soon.

BIANCA   'Tis very good; I must be circumstanced.   *Exeunt.*

359

ACT IV

✿ SCENE 1 *Cyprus. Before the castle.*

Enter Othello and Iago.

IAGO Will you think so?

OTHELLO   Think so, Iago!

IAGO   What,
 To kiss in private?

OTHELLO   An unauthorized kiss.

IAGO Or to be naked with her friend in bed
 An hour or more, not meaning any harm?

OTHELLO Naked in bed, Iago, and not mean harm!
 It is hypocrisy against the devil.
 They that mean virtuously, and yet do so,
 The devil their virtue tempts, and they tempt heaven.

IAGO So they do nothing, 'tis a venial slip.
 But if I give my wife a handkerchief—

OTHELLO What then?

IAGO Why, then, 'tis hers, my lord; and, being hers,
 She may, I think, bestow't on any man.

OTHELLO She is protectress of her honour too.
 May she give that?

IAGO Her honour is an essence that's not seen;

They have it very oft that have it not.
But, for the handkerchief—

OTHELLO   By heaven, I would most gladly have forgot it.
Thou said'st—O, it comes o'er my memory,
As doth the raven o'er the infected house,
Boding to all—he had my handkerchief.

IAGO   Ay, what of that?

OTHELLO   That's not so good now.

IAGO   What,
If I had said I had seen him do you wrong?
Or heard him say—as knaves be such abroad,
Who having, by their own importunate suit,
Or voluntary dotage of some mistress,
Convinced or supplied them, cannot choose
But they must blab—

OTHELLO   Hath he said anything?

IAGO   He hath, my lord; but be you well assured,
No more than he'll unswear.

OTHELLO   What hath he said?

IAGO   'Faith, that he did—I know not what he did.

OTHELLO   What? what?

IAGO   Lie—

OTHELLO   With her?

IAGO   With her, on her; what you will.

OTHELLO   Lie with her! lie on her! We say lie on her, when they belie her.
Lie with her! that's fulsome. Handkerchief—confessions—handkerchief! To confess, and be hanged for his labour—first, to be hanged,
and then to confess. I tremble at it. Nature would not invest herself in
such shadowing passion without some instruction. It is not words that
shake me thus. Pish! Noses, ears, and lips. Is't possible? Confess—
handkerchief! O devil!

Falls in a trance.

IAGO   Work on,
My medicine, work! Thus credulous fools are caught;

361

And many worthy and chaste dames even thus,
All guiltless, meet reproach. What, ho! my lord!
My lord, I say! Othello!

Enter Cassio.

                    How now, Cassio!

CASSIO What's the matter?

IAGO My lord is fall'n into an epilepsy.
  This is his second fit; he had one yesterday.

CASSIO Rub him about the temples.

IAGO   No, forbear;
  The lethargy must have his quiet course;
  If not, he foams at mouth and by and by
  Breaks out to savage madness. Look, he stirs.
  Do you withdraw yourself a little while,
  He will recover straight. When he is gone,   *Exit Cassio.*
  I would on great occasion speak with you.
  How is it, general? have you not hurt your head?

OTHELLO Dost thou mock me?

IAGO   I mock you! no, by heaven.
  Would you would bear your fortune like a man!

OTHELLO A horned man's a monster and a beast.

IAGO There's many a beast then in a populous city,
  And many a civil monster.

OTHELLO Did he confess it?

IAGO   Good sir, be a man;
  Think every bearded fellow that's but yoked
  May draw with you. There's millions now alive
  That nightly lie in those unproper beds
  Which they dare swear peculiar; your case is better.
  O, 'tis the spite of hell, the fiend's arch-mock,
  To lip a wanton in a secure couch,
  And to suppose her chaste! No, let me know;
  And knowing what I am, I know what she shall be.

OTHELLO O, thou art wise; 'tis certain.

IAGO   Stand you awhile apart;

362

Confine yourself but in a patient list.
Whilst you were here o'erwhelmed with your grief—
A passion most unsuiting such a man—
Cassio came hither. I shifted him away,
And laid good 'scuse upon your ecstasy,
Bade him anon return and here speak with me;
The which he promised. Do but encave yourself,
And mark the fleers, the gibes, and notable scorns,
That dwell in every region of his face;
For I will make him tell the tale anew,
Where, how, how oft, how long ago, and when
He hath, and is again to cope your wife.
I say, but mark his gesture. Marry, patience;
Or I shall say you are all in all in spleen,
And nothing of a man.

OTHELLO   Dost thou hear, Iago?
  I will be found most cunning in my patience;
  But—dost thou hear?—most bloody.

IAGO   That's not amiss;
  But yet keep time in all. Will you withdraw?   *Othello retires.*
  Now will I question Cassio of Bianca,
  A housewife that by selling her desires
  Buys herself bread and clothes; it is a creature
  That dotes on Cassio; as 'tis the strumpet's plague
  To beguile many and be beguiled by one.
  He, when he hears of her, cannot refrain
  From the excess of laughter. Here he comes.

Re-enter Cassio.

  As he shall smile, Othello shall go mad;
  And his unbookish jealousy must construe
  Poor Cassio's smiles, gestures, and light behaviour,
  Quite in the wrong. How do you now, lieutenant?

CASSIO   The worser that you give me the addition
  Whose want even kills me.

IAGO   Ply Desdemona well, and you are sure on't.
  [*Speaking lower.*] Now, if this suit lay in Bianca's power,
  How quickly should you speed!

CASSIO   Alas, poor caitiff!

363

OTHELLO Look, how he laughs already!

IAGO I never knew woman love man so.

CASSIO Alas, poor rogue! I think, i' faith, she loves me.

OTHELLO Now he denies it faintly, and laughs it out.

IAGO Do you hear, Cassio?

OTHELLO   Now he importunes him
  To tell it o'er. Go to; well said, well said.

IAGO She gives it out that you shall marry her.
  Do you intend it?

CASSIO Ha, ha, ha!

OTHELLO Do you triumph, Roman? do you triumph?

CASSIO I marry her! what? a customer! Prithee, bear some charity to my
  wit; do not think it so unwholesome. Ha, ha, ha!

OTHELLO So, so, so, so; they laugh that win.

IAGO 'Faith, the cry goes that you shall marry her.

CASSIO Prithee, say true.

IAGO I am a very villain else.

OTHELLO Have you scored me? Well.

CASSIO This is the monkey's own giving out: she is persuaded I will
  marry her, out of her own love and flattery, not out of my promise.

OTHELLO Iago beckons me; now he begins the story.

CASSIO She was here even now; she haunts me in every place. I was the
  other day talking on the sea-bank with certain Venetians; and thither
  comes the bauble, and, by this hand, she falls me thus about my
  neck—

OTHELLO Crying, "O dear Cassio!" as it were; his gesture imports it.

CASSIO So hangs, and lolls, and weeps upon me; so hales, and pulls me.
  Ha, ha, ha!

OTHELLO Now he tells how she plucked him to my chamber. O, I see
  that nose of yours, but not that dog I shall throw it to.

CASSIO Well, I must leave her company.

IAGO   Before me! look, where she comes.

CASSIO   'Tis such another fitchew! marry, a perfumed one.

Enter Bianca.

What do you mean by this haunting of me?

BIANCA   Let the devil and his dam haunt you! What did you mean by
that same handkerchief you gave me even now? I was a fine fool to
take it. I must take out the work? A likely piece of work, that you
should find it in your chamber, and not know who left it there! This is
some minx's token, and I must take out the work? There; give it your
hobby-horse. Wheresoever you had it, I'll take out no work on't.

CASSIO   How now, my sweet Bianca! how now! how now!

OTHELLO   By heaven, that should be my handkerchief!

BIANCA   An you'll come to supper to-night, you may; an you will not,
come when you are next prepared for.   *Exit.*

IAGO   After her, after her.

CASSIO   'Faith, I must; she'll rail in the street else.

IAGO   Will you sup there?

CASSIO   'Faith, I intend so.

IAGO   Well, I may chance to see you; for I would very fain speak with
you.

CASSIO   Prithee, come; will you?

IAGO   Go to; say no more.   *Exit Cassio.*

OTHELLO   [*Advancing.*] How shall I murder him, Iago?

IAGO   Did you perceive how he laughed at his vice?

OTHELLO   O Iago!

IAGO   And did you see the handkerchief?

OTHELLO   Was that mine?

IAGO   Yours, by this hand; and to see how he prizes the foolish woman
your wife! she gave it him, and he hath given it his whore.

OTHELLO   I would have him nine years a-killing. A fine woman! a fair
woman! a sweet woman!

IAGO Nay, you must forget that.

OTHELLO Ay, let her rot, and perish, and be damned to-night; for she shall not live. No, my heart is turned to stone; I strike it, and it hurts my hand. O, the world hath not a sweeter creature! She might lie by an emperor's side and command him tasks.

IAGO Nay, that's not your way.

OTHELLO Hang her! I do but say what she is: so delicate with her needle; an admirable musician: O! she will sing the savageness out of a bear. Of so high and plenteous wit and invention—

IAGO She's the worse for all this.

OTHELLO O, a thousand thousand times. And then, of so gentle a condition!

IAGO Ay, too gentle.

OTHELLO Nay, that's certain; but yet the pity of it, Iago! O Iago, the pity of it, Iago!

IAGO If you are so fond over her iniquity, give her patent to offend; for, if it touch not you, it comes near nobody.

OTHELLO I will chop her into messes. Cuckold me!

IAGO O, 'tis foul in her.

OTHELLO With mine officer!

IAGO That's fouler.

OTHELLO Get me some poison, Iago; this night. I'll not expostulate with her, lest her body and beauty unprovide my mind again. This night, Iago.

IAGO Do it not with poison; strangle her in her bed, even the bed she hath contaminated.

OTHELLO Good, good; the justice of it pleases; very good.

IAGO And for Cassio, let me be his undertaker. You shall hear more by midnight.

OTHELLO Excellent good.

A trumpet within.

What trumpet is that same?

ACT IV   Scene 1

IAGO   Something from Venice, sure. 'Tis Lodovico
   Come from the Duke. And, see, your wife is with him.

Enter Lodovico, Desdemona, and Attendants.

LODOVICO   Save you, worthy general!

OTHELLO   With all my heart, sir.

LODOVICO   The Duke and Senators of Venice greet you.

Gives him a letter.

OTHELLO   I kiss the instrument of their pleasures.

Opens the letter, and reads.

DESDEMONA   And what's the news, good cousin Lodovico?

IAGO   I am very glad to see you, signior;
   Welcome to Cyprus.

LODOVICO   I thank you. How does Lieutenant Cassio?

IAGO   Lives, sir.

DESDEMONA   Cousin, there's fall'n between him and my lord
   An unkind breach; but you shall make all well.

OTHELLO   Are you sure of that?

DESDEMONA   My lord?

OTHELLO   [*Reads.*] "This fail you not to do, as you will—"

LODOVICO   He did not call; he's busy in the paper.
   Is there division 'twixt my lord and Cassio?

DESDEMONA   A most unhappy one. I would do much
   To atone them, for the love I bear to Cassio.

OTHELLO   Fire and brimstone!

DESDEMONA   My lord?

OTHELLO   Are you wise?

DESDEMONA   What, is he angry?

LODOVICO   May be the letter moved him;
   For, as I think, they do command him home,
   Deputing Cassio in his government.

367

DESDEMONA   Trust me, I am glad on't.

OTHELLO   Indeed!

DESDEMONA   My lord?

OTHELLO   I am glad to see you mad.

DESDEMONA   Why, sweet Othello—

OTHELLO   [*Striking her.*] Devil!

DESDEMONA   I have not deserved this.

LODOVICO   My lord, this would not be believed in Venice,
   Though I should swear I saw't. 'Tis very much.
   Make her amends; she weeps.

OTHELLO   O devil, devil!
   If that the earth could teem with woman's tears,
   Each drop she falls would prove a crocodile.
   Out of my sight!

DESDEMONA   I will not stay to offend you.

Going.

LODOVICO   Truly, an obedient lady.
   I do beseech your lordship, call her back.

OTHELLO   Mistress!

DESDEMONA   My lord?

OTHELLO   What would you with her, sir?

LODOVICO   Who, I, my lord?

OTHELLO   Ay; you did wish that I would make her turn.
   Sir, she can turn, and turn, and yet go on,
   And turn again; and she can weep, sir, weep;
   And she's obedient, as you say, obedient,
   Very obedient. Proceed you in your tears.
   Concerning this, sir—O well-painted passion!—
   I am commanded home. Get you away;
   I'll send for you anon. Sir, I obey the mandate,
   And will return to Venice. Hence, avaunt!   *Exit Desdemona.*
   Cassio shall have my place. And, sir, to-night,
   I do entreat that we may sup together.
   You are welcome, sir, to Cyprus. Goats and monkeys!   *Exit.*

LODOVICO   Is this the noble Moor whom our full senate
 Call all in all sufficient? Is this the nature
 Whom passion could not shake? whose solid virtue
 The shot of accident, nor dart of chance,
 Could neither graze nor pierce?

IAGO   He is much changed.

LODOVICO   Are his wits safe? Is he not light of brain?

IAGO   He's that he is; I may not breathe my censure
 What he might be. If what he might he is not,
 I would to heaven he were!

LODOVICO   What, strike his wife!

IAGO   'Faith, that was not so well; yet would I knew
 That stroke would prove the worst!

LODOVICO   Is it his use?
 Or did the letters work upon his blood
 And new-create this fault?

IAGO   Alas, alas!
 It is not honesty in me to speak
 What I have seen and known. You shall observe him,
 And his own courses will denote him so
 That I may save my speech. Do but go after,
 And mark how he continues.

LODOVICO   I am sorry that I am deceived in him.   *Exeunt.*

SCENE 2   *A room in the castle.*

Enter Othello and Emilia.

OTHELLO   You have seen nothing then?

EMILIA   Nor ever heard, nor ever did suspect.

OTHELLO   Yes, you have seen Cassio and she together.

EMILIA   But then I saw no harm, and then I heard
 Each syllable that breath made up between them.

OTHELLO   What, did they never whisper?

EMILIA   Never, my lord.

369

OTHELLO Nor send you out o' the way?

EMILIA Never.

OTHELLO To fetch her fan, her gloves, her mask, nor nothing?

EMILIA Never, my lord.

OTHELLO That's strange.

EMILIA I durst, my lord, to wager she is honest,
Lay down my soul at stake. If you think other,
Remove your thought; it doth abuse your bosom.
If any wretch have put this in your head,
Let heaven requite it with the serpent's curse!
For, if she be not honest, chaste, and true,
There's no man happy; the purest of their wives
Is foul as slander.

OTHELLO   Bid her come hither; go.   *Exit Emilia.*
She says enough; yet she's a simple bawd
That cannot say as much. This is a subtle whore,
A closet lock and key of villainous secrets;
And yet she'll kneel and pray; I have seen her do't.

Enter Desdemona with Emilia.

DESDEMONA My lord, what is your will?

OTHELLO   Pray, chuck, come hither.

DESDEMONA What is your pleasure?

OTHELLO   Let me see your eyes;
Look in my face.

DESDEMONA   What horrible fancy's this?

OTHELLO [*To Emilia.*] Some of your function, mistress;
Leave procreants alone and shut the door;
Cough, or cry "hem," if anybody come.
Your mystery, your mystery; nay, dispatch.   *Exit Emilia.*

DESDEMONA Upon my knees, what doth your speech import?
I understand a fury in your words,
But not the words.

OTHELLO Why, what art thou?

370

DESDEMONA   Your wife, my lord; your true
　　And loyal wife.

OTHELLO   Come, swear it, damn thyself;
　　Lest, being like one of heaven, the devils themselves
　　Should fear to seize thee; therefore be double damn'd.
　　Swear thou art honest.

DESDEMONA   Heaven doth truly know it.

OTHELLO   Heaven truly knows that thou art false as hell.

DESDEMONA   To whom, my lord? with whom? how am I false?

OTHELLO   O Desdemona! away! away! away!

DESDEMONA   Alas the heavy day! Why do you weep?
　　Am I the motive of these tears, my lord?
　　If haply you my father do suspect
　　An instrument of this your calling back,
　　Lay not your blame on me. If you have lost him,
　　Why, I have lost him too.

OTHELLO   Had it pleased heaven
　　To try me with affliction; had they rain'd
　　All kinds of sores and shames on my bare head,
　　Steep'd me in poverty to the very lips,
　　Given to captivity me and my utmost hopes,
　　I should have found in some place of my soul
　　A drop of patience; but, alas, to make me
　　A fixed figure for the time of scorn
　　To point his slow unmoving finger at!
　　Yet could I bear that too; well, very well;
　　But there, where I have garner'd up my heart,
　　Where either I must live, or bear no life;
　　The fountain from the which my current runs,
　　Or else dries up; to be discarded thence!
　　Or keep it as a cistern for foul toads
　　To knot and gender in! Turn thy complexion there,
　　Patience, thou young and rose-lipp'd cherubin—
　　Ay, there, look grim as hell!

DESDEMONA   I hope my noble lord esteems me honest.

OTHELLO   O, ay; as summer flies are in the shambles,
　　That quicken even with blowing. O thou weed,

Who art so lovely fair and smell'st so sweet
That the sense aches at thee, would thou hadst ne'er been born!

DESDEMONA   Alas, what ignorant sin have I committed?

OTHELLO   Was this fair paper, this most goodly book,
Made to write "whore" upon? What committed!
Committed! O thou public commoner!
I should make very forges of my cheeks,
That would to cinders burn up modesty,
Did I but speak thy deeds. What committed!
Heaven stops the nose at it and the moon winks,
The bawdy wind that kisses all it meets
Is hush'd within the hollow mine of earth,
And will not hear it. What committed!
Impudent strumpet!

DESDEMONA   By heaven, you do me wrong.

OTHELLO   Are not you a strumpet?

DESDEMONA   No, as I am a Christian.
If to preserve this vessel for my lord
From any other foul unlawful touch
Be not to be a strumpet, I am none.

OTHELLO   What, not a whore?

DESDEMONA   No, as I shall be saved.

OTHELLO   Is't possible?

DESDEMONA   O, heaven forgive us!

OTHELLO   I cry you mercy, then.
I took you for that cunning whore of Venice
That married with Othello. [*Raising his voice.*] You, mistress,
That have the office opposite to Saint Peter,
And keep the gate of hell!

Re-enter Emilia.

                            You, you, ay, you!
We have done our course; there's money for your pains.
I pray you, turn the key and keep our counsel.   *Exit.*

EMILIA   Alas, what does this gentleman conceive?
How do you, madam? how do you, my good lady?

372

DESDEMONA   'Faith, half asleep.

EMILIA   Good madam, what's the matter with my lord?

DESDEMONA   With who?

EMILIA   Why, with my lord, madam.

DESDEMONA   Who is thy lord?

EMILIA   He that is yours, sweet lady.

DESDEMONA   I have none. Do not talk to me, Emilia;
  I cannot weep; nor answer have I none,
  But what should go by water. Prithee, to-night
  Lay on my bed my wedding sheets, remember;
  And call thy husband hither.

EMILIA   Here's a change indeed!   *Exit.*

DESDEMONA   'Tis meet I should be used so, very meet.
  How have I been behaved, that he might stick
  The small'st opinion on my least misuse?

Re-enter Emilia with Iago.

IAGO   What is your pleasure, madam? How is't with you?

DESDEMONA   I cannot tell. Those that do teach young babes
  Do it with gentle means and easy tasks.
  He might have chid me so; for, in good faith,
  I am a child to chiding.

IAGO   What's the matter, lady?

EMILIA   Alas, Iago, my lord hath so bewhored her,
  Thrown such despite and heavy terms upon her,
  As true hearts cannot bear.

DESDEMONA   Am I that name, Iago?

IAGO   What name, fair lady?

DESDEMONA   Such as she says my lord did say I was.

EMILIA   He call'd her whore. A beggar in his drink
  Could not have laid such terms upon his callet.

IAGO   Why did he so?

DESDEMONA   I do not know; I am sure I am none such.

373

IAGO Do not weep, do not weep. Alas the day!

EMILIA Hath she forsook so many noble matches,
Her father and her country and her friends,
To be call'd whore? would it not make one weep?

DESDEMONA It is my wretched fortune.

IAGO   Beshrew him for't!
How comes this trick upon him?

DESDEMONA   Nay, heaven doth know.

EMILIA I will be hang'd, if some eternal villain,
Some busy and insinuating rogue,
Some cogging, cozening slave, to get some office,
Have not devised this slander; I'll be hang'd else.

IAGO Fie, there is no such man; it is impossible.

DESDEMONA If any such there be, heaven pardon him!

EMILIA A halter pardon him! and hell gnaw his bones!
Why should he call her whore? who keeps her company?
What place? what time? what form? what likelihood?
The Moor's abused by some most villainous knave,
Some base notorious knave, some scurvy fellow.
O heaven, that such companions thou'dst unfold,
And put in every honest hand a whip
To lash the rascals naked through the world
Even from the east to the west!

IAGO   Speak within door.

EMILIA O, fie upon them! Some such squire he was
That turn'd your wit the seamy side without,
And made you to suspect me with the Moor.

IAGO You are a fool; go to.

DESDEMONA   O good Iago,
What shall I do to win my lord again?
Good friend, go to him; for, by this light of heaven,
I know not how I lost him. Here I kneel.
If e'er my will did trespass 'gainst his love,
Either in discourse of thought or actual deed,
Or that mine eyes, mine ears, or any sense,
Delighted them in any other form;

374

Or that I do not yet, and ever did,
And ever will—though he do shake me off
To beggarly divorcement—love him dearly,
Comfort forswear me! Unkindness may do much;
And his unkindness may defeat my life,
But never taint my love. I cannot say "whore."
It doth abhor me now I speak the word;
To do the act that might the addition earn
Not the world's mass of vanity could make me.

IAGO   I pray you, be content; 'tis but his humour.
The business of the state does him offence,
And he does chide with you.

DESDEMONA   If 'twere no other—

IAGO   'Tis but so, I warrant.

Trumpets within.

Hark, how these instruments summon to supper!
The messengers of Venice stay the meat.
Go in, and weep not; all things shall be well.
                                   Exeunt Desdemona and Emilia.

Enter Roderigo.

How now, Roderigo!

RODERIGO   I do not find that thou dealest justly with me.

IAGO   What in the contrary?

RODERIGO   Every day thou daffest me with some device, Iago; and
rather, as it seems to me now, keepest from me all conveniency than
suppliest me with the least advantage of hope. I will indeed no longer
endure it, nor am I yet persuaded to put up in peace what already I
have foolishly suffered.

IAGO   Will you hear me, Roderigo?

RODERIGO   'Faith, I have heard too much, for your words and performances are no kin together.

IAGO   You charge me most unjustly.

RODERIGO   With nought but truth. I have wasted myself out of my
means. The jewels you have had from me to deliver to Desdemona
would half have corrupted a votarist. You have told me she hath re-

ceived them and returned me expectations and comforts of sudden respect and acquaintance, but I find none.

IAGO   Well; go to; very well.

RODERIGO   Very well! go to! I cannot go to, man; nor 'tis not very well.
Nay, I think it is scurvy, and begin to find myself fopped in it.

IAGO   Very well.

RODERIGO   I tell you 'tis not very well. I will make myself known to
Desdemona. If she will return me my jewels, I will give over my suit
and repent my unlawful solicitation; if not, assure yourself I will seek
satisfaction of you.

IAGO   You have said now.

RODERIGO   Ay, and said nothing but what I protest intendment of doing.

IAGO   Why, now I see there's mettle in thee, and even from this instant
do build on thee a better opinion than ever before. Give me thy hand,
Roderigo. Thou hast taken against me a most just exception; but yet, I
protest, I have dealt most directly in thy affair.

RODERIGO   It hath not appeared.

IAGO   I grant indeed it hath not appeared, and your suspicion is not
without wit and judgement. But, Roderigo, if thou hast that in thee
indeed, which I have greater reason to believe now than ever, I mean
purpose, courage, and valour, this night show it. If thou the next night
following enjoy not Desdemona, take me from this world with treachery and devise engines for my life.

RODERIGO   Well, what is it? is it within reach and compass?

IAGO   Sir, there is especial commission come from Venice to depute Cassio in Othello's place.

RODERIGO   Is that true? why, then Othello and Desdemona return again
to Venice.

IAGO   O, no; he goes into Mauritania and takes away with him the fair
Desdemona, unless his abode be lingered here by some accident;
wherein none can be so determinate as the removing of Cassio.

RODERIGO   How do you mean, removing of him?

IAGO   Why, by making him uncapable of Othello's place; knocking out
his brains.

RODERIGO   And that you would have me to do?

IAGO   Ay, if you dare do yourself a profit and a right. He sups to-night with a harlotry, and thither will I go to him; he knows not yet of his honourable fortune. If you will watch his going thence, which I will fashion to fall out between twelve and one, you may take him at your pleasure. I will be near to second your attempt, and he shall fall be-tween us. Come, stand not amazed at it, but go along with me; I will show you such a necessity in his death that you shall think yourself bound to put it on him. It is now high supper-time, and the night grows to waste. About it.

RODERIGO   I will hear further reason for this.

IAGO   And you shall be satisfied.   *Exeunt.*

SCENE 3   *Another room in the castle.*

Enter Othello, Lodovico, Desdemona, Emilia, and Attendants.

LODOVICO   I do beseech you, sir, trouble yourself no further.

OTHELLO   O, pardon me; 'twill do me good to walk.

LODOVICO   Madam, good night; I humbly thank your ladyship.

DESDEMONA   Your honour is most welcome.

OTHELLO   Will you walk, sir?
    O—Desdemona—

DESDEMONA   My lord?

OTHELLO   Get you to bed on the instant; I will be returned forthwith. Dismiss your attendant there. Look it be done.

DESDEMONA   I will, my lord.   *Exeunt Othello, Lodovico, and Attendants.*

EMILIA   How goes it now? he looks gentler than he did.

DESDEMONA   He says he will return incontinent.
    He hath commanded me to go to bed,
    And bade me to dismiss you.

EMILIA   Dismiss me!

DESDEMONA   It was his bidding; therefore, good Emilia,
    Give me my nightly wearing, and adieu.
    We must not now displease him.

377

EMILIA   I would you had never seen him!

DESDEMONA   So would not I. My love doth so approve him,
That even his stubbornness, his checks, his frowns—
Prithee, unpin me—have grace and favour in them.

EMILIA   I have laid those sheets you bade me on the bed.

DESDEMONA   All's one. Good faith, how foolish are our minds!
If I do die before thee, prithee, shroud me
In one of those same sheets.

EMILIA   Come, come, you talk.

DESDEMONA   My mother had a maid call'd Barbara;
She was in love, and he she loved proved mad
And did forsake her. She had a song of "Willow";
An old thing 'twas, but it express'd her fortune,
And she died singing it. That song to-night
Will not go from my mind; I have much to do,
But to go hang my head all at one side,
And sing it like poor Barbara. Prithee, dispatch.

EMILIA   Shall I go fetch your night-gown?

DESDEMONA   No, unpin me here.
This Lodovico is a proper man.

EMILIA   A very handsome man.

DESDEMONA   He speaks well.

EMILIA   I know a lady in Venice would have walked barefoot to Palestine
for a touch of his nether lip.

DESDEMONA   [Sings.]
"The poor soul sat sighing by a sycamore tree,
    Sing all a green willow;
Her hand on her bosom, her head on her knee,
    Sing willow, willow, willow.
The fresh streams ran by her, and murmur'd her moans;
    Sing willow, willow, willow;
Her salt tears fell from her, and soften'd the stones—"

Lay by these:—

[Sings.]
"Sing willow, willow, willow";

Prithee, hie thee; he'll come anon—

[*Sings.*]

> "Sing all a green willow must be my garland.
> Let nobody blame him; his scorn I approve—"

Nay, that's not next. Hark! who is't that knocks?

EMILIA   It's the wind.

DESDEMONA   [*Sings.*]

> "I call'd my love false love; but what said he then?
>   Sing willow, willow, willow.
> If I court moe women, you'll couch with moe men."

So, get thee gone; good night. Mine eyes do itch;
Doth that bode weeping?

EMILIA   'Tis neither here nor there.

DESDEMONA   I have heard it said so. O, these men, these men!
Dost thou in conscience think—tell me, Emilia—
That there be women do abuse their husbands
In such gross kind?

EMILIA   There be some such, no question.

DESDEMONA   Wouldst thou do such a deed for all the world?

EMILIA   Why, would not you?

DESDEMONA   No, by this heavenly light!

EMILIA   Nor I neither by this heavenly light;
I might do't as well i' the dark.

DESDEMONA   Wouldst thou do such a deed for all the world?

EMILIA   The world's a huge thing; it is a great price
For a small vice.

DESDEMONA   In troth, I think thou wouldst not.

EMILIA   In troth, I think I should; and undo't when I had done. Marry, I
would not do such a thing for a joint-ring, nor for measures of lawn,
nor for gowns, petticoats, nor caps, nor any petty exhibition; but, for
the whole world—why, who would not make her husband a cuckold
to make him a monarch? I should venture purgatory for't.

DESDEMONA   Beshrew me, if I would do such a wrong
For the whole world.

EMILIA   Why, the wrong is but a wrong i' the world; and having the
world for your labour, 'tis a wrong in your own world, and you might
quickly make it right.

DESDEMONA   I do not think there is any such woman.

EMILIA   Yes, a dozen; and as many to the vantage as would store the
world they played for.
But I do think it is their husbands' faults
If wives do fall. Say that they slack their duties,
And pour our treasures into foreign laps,
Or else break out in peevish jealousies,
Throwing restraint upon us; or say they strike us,
Or scant our former having in despite;
Why, we have galls, and though we have some grace,
Yet have we some revenge. Let husbands know
Their wives have sense like them; they see and smell
And have their palates both for sweet and sour,
As husbands have. What is it that they do
When they change us for others? Is it sport?
I think it is. And doth affection breed it?
I think it doth. Is't frailty that thus errs?
It is so too. And have not we affections,
Desires for sport, and frailty, as men have?
Then let them use us well; else let them know,
The ills we do, their ills instruct us so.

DESDEMONA   Good night, good night. Heaven me such uses send,
Not to pick bad from bad, but by bad mend!   *Exeunt.*

380

ACT V

SCENE 1 *Cyprus. A street.*

Enter Iago and Roderigo.

IAGO Here, stand behind this bulk; straight will he come.
   Wear thy good rapier bare, and put it home.
   Quick, quick; fear nothing; I'll be at thy elbow.
   It makes us, or it mars us; think on that,
   And fix most firm thy resolution.

RODERIGO Be near at hand; I may miscarry in't.

IAGO Here, at thy hand; be bold, and take thy stand.   *Retires.*

RODERIGO I have no great devotion to the deed;
   And yet he hath given me satisfying reasons.
   'Tis but a man gone. Forth, my sword; he dies.

IAGO I have rubb'd this young quat almost to the sense,
   And he grows angry. Now, whether he kill Cassio,
   Or Cassio him, or each do kill the other,
   Every way makes my gain. Live Roderigo,
   He calls me to a restitution large
   Of gold and jewels that I bobb'd from him,
   As gifts to Desdemona;
   It must not be. If Cassio do remain,
   He hath a daily beauty in his life
   That makes me ugly; and, besides, the Moor
   May unfold me to him; there stand I in much peril.
   No, he must die. But so; I hear him coming.

Enter Cassio.

RODERIGO   I know his gait, 'tis he. Villain, thou diest!

Makes a pass at Cassio.

CASSIO   That thrust had been mine enemy indeed,
   But that my coat is better than thou know'st.
   I will make proof of thine.

Draws, and wounds Roderigo.

RODERIGO   O, I am slain!

Iago, from behind, wounds Cassio in the leg, and exits.

CASSIO   I am maim'd for ever. Help, ho! murder! murder!

Falls. Enter Othello.

OTHELLO   The voice of Cassio. Iago keeps his word.

RODERIGO   O, villain that I am!

OTHELLO   It is even so.

CASSIO   O, help, ho! light! a surgeon!

OTHELLO   'Tis he. O brave Iago, honest and just,
   That hast such noble sense of thy friend's wrong!
   Thou teachest me. Minion, your dear lies dead,
   And your unblest fate hies; strumpet, I come.
   Forth of my heart those charms, thine eyes, are blotted;
   Thy bed, lust-stain'd, shall with lust's blood be spotted.   *Exit.*

Enter Lodovico and Gratiano.

CASSIO   What, ho! no watch? no passage? murder! murder!

GRATIANO   'Tis some mischance; the cry is very direful.

CASSIO   O, help!

LODOVICO   Hark!

RODERIGO   O wretched villain!

LODOVICO   Two or three groan. It is a heavy night,
   These may be counterfeits; let's think't unsafe
   To come in to the cry without more help.

RODERIGO   Nobody come? then shall I bleed to death.

LODOVICO   Hark!

382

ACT V   Scene 1

Re-enter Iago, with a light.

GRATIANO Here's one comes in his shirt, with light and weapons.

IAGO Who's there? whose noise is this that cries on murder?

LODOVICO We do not know.

IAGO   Did not you hear a cry?

CASSIO Here, here! for heaven's sake, help me!

IAGO   What's the matter?

GRATIANO This is Othello's ancient, as I take it.

LODOVICO The same indeed; a very valiant fellow.

IAGO What are you here that cry so grievously?

CASSIO Iago? O, I am spoil'd, undone by villains!
   Give me some help.

IAGO O me, lieutenant! what villains have done this?

CASSIO I think that one of them is hereabout,
   And cannot make away.

IAGO   O treacherous villains!
   [*To Lodovico and Gratiano.*] What are you there? come in, and give some
   help.

RODERIGO O, help me here!

CASSIO That's one of them.

IAGO   O murderous slave! O villain!

Stabs Roderigo.

RODERIGO O damn'd Iago! O inhuman dog!

IAGO Kill men i' the dark! Where be these bloody thieves?
   How silent is this town! Ho! murder! murder!
   What may you be? are you of good or evil?

LODOVICO As you shall prove us, praise us.

IAGO Signior Lodovico?

LODOVICO He, sir.

IAGO I cry you mercy. Here's Cassio hurt by villains.

383

GRATIANO Cassio!

IAGO How is't, brother!

CASSIO My leg is cut in two.

IAGO   Marry, heaven forbid!
  Light, gentlemen. I'll bind it with my shirt.

Enter Bianca.

BIANCA What is the matter, ho? who is't that cried?

IAGO Who is't that cried!

BIANCA O my dear Cassio! my sweet Cassio!
  O Cassio, Cassio, Cassio!

IAGO O notable strumpet! Cassio, may you suspect
  Who they should be that have thus mangled you?

CASSIO No.

GRATIANO I am sorry to find you thus. I have been to seek you.

IAGO Lend me a garter. So. O, for a chair,
  To bear him easily hence!

BIANCA Alas, he faints! O Cassio, Cassio, Cassio!

IAGO Gentlemen all, I do suspect this trash
  To be a party in this injury.
  Patience awhile, good Cassio. Come, come;
  Lend me a light. Know we this face or no?
  Alas, my friend and my dear countryman
  Roderigo! no. Yes, sure. O heaven! Roderigo.

GRATIANO What, of Venice?

IAGO Even he, sir. Did you know him?

GRATIANO   Know him! ay.

IAGO Signior Gratiano? I cry you gentle pardon;
  These bloody accidents must excuse my manners,
  That so neglected you.

GRATIANO   I am glad to see you.

IAGO How do you, Cassio? O, a chair, a chair!

GRATIANO Roderigo!

IAGO   He, he, 'tis he. [*A chair brought in.*] O, that's well said; the chair.
   Some good man bear him carefully from hence;
   I'll fetch the general's surgeon. [*To Bianca.*] For you, mistress,
   Save you your labour. He that lies slain here, Cassio,
   Was my dear friend. What malice was between you?

CASSIO   None in the world; nor do I know the man.

IAGO   [*To Bianca.*] What, look you pale? O, bear him out o' the air.
                              Cassio and Roderigo are borne off.
   Stay you, good gentlemen. Look you pale, mistress?
   Do you perceive the gastness of her eye?
   Nay, if you stare, we shall hear more anon.
   Behold her well; I pray you, look upon her;
   Do you see, gentlemen? nay, guiltiness will speak,
   Though tongues were out of use.

Enter Emilia.

EMILIA   'Las, what's the matter? what's the matter, husband?

IAGO   Cassio hath here been set on in the dark
   By Roderigo and fellows that are scaped.
   He's almost slain, and Roderigo dead.

EMILIA   Alas, good gentleman! alas, good Cassio!

IAGO   This is the fruit of whoring. Prithee, Emilia,
   Go know of Cassio where he supp'd to-night.
   [*To Bianca.*] What, do you shake at that?

BIANCA   He supp'd at my house; but I therefore shake not.

IAGO   O, did he so? I charge you, go with me.

EMILIA   Fie, fie upon thee, strumpet!

BIANCA   I am no strumpet; but of life as honest
   As you that thus abuse me.

EMILIA   As I! foh! fie upon thee!

IAGO   Kind gentlemen, let's go see poor Cassio dress'd.
   Come, mistress, you must tell's another tale.
   Emilia, run you to the citadel,
   And tell my lord and lady what hath happ'd.
   Will you go on? I pray. [*Aside.*] This is the night
   That either makes me or fordoes me quite.   *Exeunt.*

SCENE 2 *A bedchamber in the castle. Desdemona in bed asleep; a light burning.*

Enter Othello.

OTHELLO   It is the cause, it is the cause, my soul—
Let me not name it to you, you chaste stars!—
It is the cause. Yet I'll not shed her blood;
Nor scar that whiter skin of hers than snow,
And smooth as monumental alabaster.
Yet she must die, else she'll betray more men.
Put out the light, and then put out the light.
If I quench thee, thou flaming minister,
I can again thy former light restore,
Should I repent me; but once put out thy light,
Thou cunning'st pattern of excelling nature,
I know not where is that Promethean heat
That can thy light relume. When I have pluck'd the rose,
I cannot give it vital growth again,
It needs must wither. I'll smell it on the tree.

Kissing her.

Ah, balmy breath, that dost almost persuade
Justice to break her sword! One more, one more.
Be thus when thou art dead, and I will kill thee,
And love thee after. One more, and this the last;
So sweet was ne'er so fatal. I must weep,
But they are cruel tears. This sorrow's heavenly;
It strikes where it doth love. She wakes.

DESDEMONA   Who's there? Othello?

OTHELLO   Ay, Desdemona.

DESDEMONA   Will you come to bed, my lord?

OTHELLO   Have you pray'd to-night, Desdemona?

DESDEMONA   Ay, my lord.

OTHELLO   If you bethink yourself of any crime
Unreconciled as yet to heaven and grace,
Solicit for it straight.

DESDEMONA   Alas, my lord, what do you mean by that?

386

OTHELLO   Well, do it, and be brief; I will walk by.
  I would not kill thy unprepared spirit;
  No; heaven forfend! I would not kill thy soul.

DESDEMONA   Talk you of killing?

OTHELLO   Ay, I do.

DESDEMONA   Then heaven
  Have mercy on me!

OTHELLO   Amen, with all my heart!

DESDEMONA   If you say so, I hope you will not kill me.

OTHELLO   Hum!

DESDEMONA   And yet I fear you; for you are fatal then
  When your eyes roll so. Why I should fear I know not,
  Since guiltiness I know not; but yet I feel I fear.

OTHELLO   Think on thy sins.

DESDEMONA   They are loves I bear to you.

OTHELLO   Ay, and for that thou diest.

DESDEMONA   That death's unnatural that kills for loving.
  Alas, why gnaw you so your nether lip?
  Some bloody passion shakes your very frame.
  These are portents; but yet I hope, I hope,
  They do not point on me.

OTHELLO   Peace, and be still!

DESDEMONA   I will so. What's the matter?

OTHELLO   That handkerchief which I so loved and gave thee
  Thou gav'st to Cassio.

DESDEMONA   No, by my life and soul!
  Send for the man, and ask him.

OTHELLO   Sweet soul, take heed,
  Take heed of perjury; thou art on thy death-bed.

DESDEMONA   Ay, but not yet to die.

OTHELLO   Yes, presently;
  Therefore confess thee freely of thy sin;
  For to deny each article with oath

387

Cannot remove nor choke the strong conception
That I do groan withal. Thou art to die.

DESDEMONA   Then Lord have mercy on me!

OTHELLO   I say, amen.

DESDEMONA   And have you mercy too! I never did
Offend you in my life; never loved Cassio
But with such general warranty of heaven
As I might love; I never gave him token.

OTHELLO   By heaven, I saw my handkerchief in's hand.
O perjured woman! thou dost stone my heart,
And mak'st me call what I intend to do
A murder, which I thought a sacrifice.
I saw the handkerchief.

DESDEMONA   He found it then;
I never gave it him. Send for him hither;
Let him confess a truth.

OTHELLO   He hath confess'd.

DESDEMONA   What, my lord?

OTHELLO   That he hath used thee.

DESDEMONA   How? unlawfully?

OTHELLO   Ay.

DESDEMONA   He will not say so.

OTHELLO   No, his mouth is stopp'd;
Honest Iago hath ta'en order for't.

DESDEMONA   O! my fear interprets. What, is he dead?

OTHELLO   Had all his hairs been lives, my great revenge
Had stomach for them all.

DESDEMONA   Alas! he is betray'd and I undone.

OTHELLO   Out, strumpet! weep'st thou for him to my face?

DESDEMONA   O, banish me, my lord, but kill me not!

OTHELLO   Down, strumpet!

DESDEMONA   Kill me to-morrow; let me live to-night!

388

OTHELLO Nay, if you strive—

DESDEMONA But half an hour!

OTHELLO   Being done, there is no pause.

DESDEMONA But while I say one prayer!

OTHELLO   It is too late.

He stifles her.

EMILIA [*Within.*] My lord, my lord! what, ho! my lord, my lord!

OTHELLO What noise is this? Not dead? not yet quite dead?
  I that am cruel am yet merciful;
  I would not have thee linger in thy pain.
  So, so.

EMILIA [*Within.*] What, ho! my lord, my lord!

OTHELLO   Who's there?

EMILIA [*Within.*] O, good my lord, I would speak a word with you!

OTHELLO Yes, 'tis Emilia. By and by. She's dead.
  'Tis like she comes to speak of Cassio's death.
  The noise was here. Ha! no more moving?
  Still as the grave. Shall she come in? were't good?
  I think she stirs again. No. What's best to do?
  If she come in, she'll sure speak to my wife.
  My wife! my wife! what wife? I have no wife.
  O, insupportable! O heavy hour!
  Methinks it should be now a huge eclipse
  Of sun and moon, and that the affrighted globe
  Should yawn at alteration.

EMILIA [*Within.*]   I do beseech you
  That I may speak with you, O, good my lord!

OTHELLO I had forgot thee. O, come in, Emilia.
  Soft; by and by. Let me the curtains draw.
  Where art thou?

Unlocks the door. Enter Emilia.

              What's the matter with thee now?

EMILIA O, my good lord, yonder's foul murders done!

OTHELLO   What, now?

EMILIA   But now, my lord.

OTHELLO   It is the very error of the moon;
    She comes more nearer earth than she was wont,
    And makes men mad.

EMILIA   Cassio, my lord, hath kill'd a young Venetian
    Call'd Roderigo.

OTHELLO   Roderigo kill'd!
    And Cassio kill'd!

EMILIA   No, Cassio is not kill'd.

OTHELLO   Not Cassio kill'd! then murder's out of tune,
    And sweet revenge grows harsh.

DESDEMONA   O, falsely, falsely murder'd!

EMILIA   Alas, what cry is that?

OTHELLO   That! what?

EMILIA   Out, and alas! that was my lady's voice.
    Help! help, ho! help! O lady, speak again!
    Sweet Desdemona! O sweet mistress, speak!

DESDEMONA   A guiltless death I die.

EMILIA   O, who hath done this deed?

DESDEMONA   Nobody; I myself. Farewell.
    Commend me to my kind lord. O, farewell!   *Dies.*

OTHELLO   Why, how should she be murder'd?

EMILIA   Alas, who knows?

OTHELLO   You heard her say herself, it was not I.

EMILIA   She said so. I must needs report the truth.

OTHELLO   She's, like a liar, gone to burning hell.
    'Twas I that kill'd her.

EMILIA   O, the more angel she,
    And you the blacker devil!

OTHELLO   She turn'd to folly, and she was a whore.

390

EMILIA   Thou dost belie her, and thou art a devil.

OTHELLO   She was false as water.

EMILIA   Thou art rash as fire to say
  That she was false. O, she was heavenly true!

OTHELLO   Cassio did top her; ask thy husband else.
  O, I were damn'd beneath all depth in hell,
  But that I did proceed upon just grounds
  To this extremity. Thy husband knew it all.

EMILIA   My husband!

OTHELLO   Thy husband.

EMILIA   That she was false to wedlock?

OTHELLO   Ay, with Cassio. Nay, had she been true,
  If heaven would make me such another world
  Of one entire and perfect chrysolite,
  I'd not have sold her for it.

EMILIA   My husband!

OTHELLO   Ay, 'twas he that told me first.
  An honest man he is, and hates the slime
  That sticks on filthy deeds.

EMILIA   My husband!

OTHELLO   What needs this iteration, woman? I say thy husband.

EMILIA   O mistress, villainy hath made mocks with love!
  My husband say that she was false!

OTHELLO   He, woman;
  I say thy husband. Dost understand the word?
  My friend, thy husband, honest, honest Iago.

EMILIA   If he say so, may his pernicious soul
  Rot half a grain a day! he lies to the heart.
  She was too fond of her most filthy bargain.

OTHELLO   Ha!

EMILIA   Do thy worst.
  This deed of thine is no more worthy heaven
  Than thou wast worthy her.

OTHELLO   Peace, you were best.

EMILIA   Thou hast not half that power to do me harm
As I have to be hurt. O gull! O dolt!
As ignorant as dirt! thou hast done a deed—
I care not for thy sword; I'll make thee known,
Though I lost twenty lives. Help! help, ho! help!
The Moor hath kill'd my mistress! Murder! murder!

Enter Montano, Gratiano, Iago, and others.

MONTANO   What is the matter? How now, general!

EMILIA   O, are you come, Iago? you have done well,
That men must lay their murders on your neck.

GRATIANO   What is the matter?

EMILIA   Disprove this villain, if thou be'st a man.
He says thou told'st him that his wife was false.
I know thou didst not, thou'rt not such a villain.
Speak, for my heart is full.

IAGO   I told him what I thought, and told no more
Than what he found himself was apt and true.

EMILIA   But did you ever tell him she was false?

IAGO   I did.

EMILIA   You told a lie; an odious, damned lie;
Upon my soul, a lie, a wicked lie.
She false with Cassio! Did you say with Cassio?

IAGO   With Cassio, mistress. Go to, charm your tongue.

EMILIA   I will not charm my tongue; I am bound to speak.
My mistress here lies murder'd in her bed—

ALL   O heavens forfend!

EMILIA   And your reports have set the murder on.

OTHELLO   Nay, stare not, masters. It is true, indeed.

GRATIANO   'Tis a strange truth.

MONTANO   O monstrous act!

EMILIA   Villainy, villainy, villainy!
I think upon't, I think, I smell't. O villainy!

392

I thought so then. I'll kill myself for grief.
O villainy, villainy!

IAGO   What, are you mad? I charge you, get you home.

EMILIA   Good gentlemen, let me have leave to speak;
'Tis proper I obey him, but not now.
Perchance, Iago, I will ne'er go home.

OTHELLO   O! O! O!

He falls on the bed.

EMILIA   Nay, lay thee down and roar;
For thou hast kill'd the sweetest innocent
That e'er did lift up eye.

OTHELLO   [*Rising.*]   O, she was foul!
I scarce did know you, uncle. There lies your niece,
Whose breath, indeed, these hands have newly stopp'd.
I know this act shows horrible and grim.

GRATIANO   Poor Desdemona! I am glad thy father's dead.
Thy match was mortal to him, and pure grief
Shore his old thread in twain. Did he live now,
This sight would make him do a desperate turn,
Yea, curse his better angel from his side,
And fall to reprobation.

OTHELLO   'Tis pitiful; but yet Iago knows
That she with Cassio hath the act of shame
A thousand times committed; Cassio confess'd it.
And she did gratify his amorous works
With that recognizance and pledge of love
Which I first gave her; I saw it in his hand;
It was a handkerchief, an antique token
My father gave my mother.

EMILIA   O heaven! O heavenly powers!

IAGO   Come, hold your peace.

EMILIA   'Twill out, 'twill out! I peace!
No, I will speak as liberal as the north.
Let heaven and men and devils, let them all,
All, all, cry shame against me, yet I'll speak.

IAGO   Be wise, and get you home.

EMILIA   I will not.

Iago offers to stab Emilia.

GRATIANO   Fie!
  Your sword upon a woman?

EMILIA   O thou dull Moor! that handkerchief thou speak'st of
  I found by fortune and did give my husband;
  For often, with a solemn earnestness,
  More than indeed belong'd to such a trifle,
  He begg'd of me to steal it.

IAGO   Villainous whore!

EMILIA   She give it Cassio! No, alas! I found it,
  And I did give't my husband.

IAGO   Filth, thou liest!

EMILIA   By heaven, I do not, I do not, gentlemen.
  O murderous coxcomb! what should such a fool
  Do with so good a woman?

OTHELLO   Are there no stones in heaven
  But what serve for the thunder? Precious villain!

He runs at Iago. Iago, from behind, stabs Emilia, and exits.

GRATIANO   The woman falls; sure, he hath kill'd his wife.

EMILIA   Ay, ay. O, lay me by my mistress' side.

GRATIANO   He's gone, but his wife's kill'd.

MONTANO   'Tis a notorious villain. Take you this weapon,
  Which I have here recover'd from the Moor.
  Come, guard the door without; let him not pass,
  But kill him rather. I'll after that same villain,
  For 'tis a damned slave.   *Exeunt Montano and Gratiano.*

OTHELLO   I am not valiant neither,
  But every puny whipster gets my sword.
  But why should honour outlive honesty?
  Let it go all.

EMILIA   What did thy song bode, lady?
  Hark, canst thou hear me? I will play the swan,
  And die in music. [*Sings.*] "Willow, willow, willow."

394

Moor, she was chaste; she loved thee, cruel Moor;
So come my soul to bliss, as I speak true;
So speaking as I think, I die, I die.   *Dies.*

OTHELLO   I have another weapon in this chamber;
It is a sword of Spain, the ice-brook's temper.
O, here it is. Uncle, I must come forth.

GRATIANO   [*Within.*] If thou attempt it, it will cost thee dear.
Thou hast no weapon, and perforce must suffer.

OTHELLO   Look in upon me then and speak with me,
Or, naked as I am, I will assault thee.

Re-enter Gratiano.

GRATIANO   What is the matter?

OTHELLO   Behold, I have a weapon;
A better never did itself sustain
Upon a soldier's thigh. I have seen the day
That, with this little arm and this good sword,
I have made my way through more impediments
Than twenty times your stop. But, O vain boast!
Who can control his fate? 'tis not so now.
Be not afraid, though you do see me weapon'd;
Here is my journey's end, here is my butt,
And very sea-mark of my utmost sail.
Do you go back dismay'd? 'tis a lost fear;
Man but a rush against Othello's breast,
And he retires. Where should Othello go?
Now, how dost thou look now? O ill-starr'd wench!
Pale as thy smock! when we shall meet at compt,
This look of thine will hurl my soul from heaven,
And fiends will snatch at it. Cold, cold, my girl!
Even like thy chastity. O cursed slave!
Whip me, ye devils,
From the possession of this heavenly sight!
Blow me about in winds! roast me in sulphur!
Wash me in steep-down gulfs of liquid fire!
O Desdemona! Desdemona! dead!
O! O! O!

*Enter Lodovico, Montano, Cassio carried in a chair, and Officers with Iago,
prisoner.*

395

LODOVICO   Where is this rash and most unfortunate man?

OTHELLO   That's he that was Othello. Here I am.

LODOVICO   Where is that viper? bring the villain forth.

OTHELLO   I look down towards his feet; but that's a fable.
   If that thou be'st a devil, I cannot kill thee.

Wounds Iago.

LODOVICO   Wrench his sword from him.

IAGO   I bleed, sir; but not kill'd.

OTHELLO   I am not sorry neither. I'd have thee live;
   For, in my sense, 'tis happiness to die.

LODOVICO   O thou Othello, that wert once so good,
   Fall'n in the practice of a damned slave,
   What shall be said to thee?

OTHELLO   Why, anything;
   An honourable murderer, if you will;
   For nought I did in hate, but all in honour.

LODOVICO   This wretch hath part confess'd his villainy.
   Did you and he consent in Cassio's death?

OTHELLO   Ay.

CASSIO   Dear general, I never gave you cause.

OTHELLO   I do believe it, and I ask you pardon.
   Will you, I pray, demand that demi-devil
   Why he hath thus ensnared my soul and body?

IAGO   Demand me nothing. What you know, you know.
   From this time forth I never will speak word.

LODOVICO   What, not to pray?

GRATIANO   Torments will ope your lips.

OTHELLO   Well, thou dost best.

LODOVICO   Sir, you shall understand what hath befall'n,
   Which, as I think, you know not. Here is a letter
   Found in the pocket of the slain Roderigo;
   And here another. The one of them imports

The death of Cassio to be undertook
By Roderigo.

OTHELLO   O villain!

CASSIO   Most heathenish and most gross!

LODOVICO   Now here's another discontented paper,
Found in his pocket too; and this, it seems,
Roderigo meant to have sent this damned villain;
But that belike Iago in the interim
Came in and satisfied him.

OTHELLO   O the pernicious caitiff!
How came you, Cassio, by that handkerchief
That was my wife's?

CASSIO   I found it in my chamber;
And he himself confess'd but even now
That there he dropp'd it for a special purpose
Which wrought to his desire.

OTHELLO   O fool! fool! fool!

CASSIO   There is besides in Roderigo's letter,
How he upbraids Iago, that he made him
Brave me upon the watch; whereon it came
That I was cast. And even but now he spake,
After long seeming dead, Iago hurt him,
Iago set him on.

LODOVICO   You must forsake this room, and go with us;
Your power and your command is taken off,
And Cassio rules in Cyprus. For this slave,
If there be any cunning cruelty
That can torment him much and hold him long,
It shall be his. You shall close prisoner rest,
Till that the nature of your fault be known
To the Venetian state. Come, bring him away.

OTHELLO   Soft you; a word or two before you go.
I have done the state some service, and they know't.
No more of that. I pray you, in your letters,
When you shall these unlucky deeds relate,
Speak of me as I am; nothing extenuate,
Nor set down aught in malice. Then must you speak

Of one that loved not wisely but too well;
Of one not easily jealous, but being wrought,
Perplex'd in the extreme; of one whose hand,
Like the base Indian, threw a pearl away
Richer than all his tribe; of one whose subdued eyes,
Albeit unused to the melting mood,
Drop tears as fast as the Arabian trees
Their medicinable gum. Set you down this;
And say besides, that in Aleppo once,
Where a malignant and a turban'd Turk
Beat a Venetian and traduced the state,
I took by the throat the circumcised dog,
And smote him, thus.

Stabs himself.

LODOVICO   O bloody period!

GRATIANO   All that's spoke is marr'd.

OTHELLO   I kiss'd thee ere I kill'd thee. No way but this,
   Killing myself, to die upon a kiss.   *Falls on the bed and dies.*

CASSIO   This did I fear, but thought he had no weapon;
   For he was great of heart.

LODOVICO   [*To Iago.*]   O Spartan dog,
   More fell than anguish, hunger, or the sea!
   Look on the tragic loading of this bed;
   This is thy work. The object poisons sight;
   Let it be hid. Gratiano, keep the house,
   And seize upon the fortunes of the Moor,
   For they succeed on you. To you, lord governor,
   Remains the censure of this hellish villain;
   The time, the place, the torture. O, enforce it!
   Myself will straight aboard; and to the state
   This heavy act with heavy heart relate.   *Exeunt.*

KING LEAR

THE ACTORS

LEAR, *King of Britain*

KING OF FRANCE

DUKE OF BURGUNDY

DUKE OF CORNWALL

DUKE OF ALBANY

EARL OF KENT

EARL OF GLOUCESTER

EDGAR, *son to Gloucester*

EDMUND, *bastard son to Gloucester*

CURAN, *a courtier*

OLD MAN, *tenant to Gloucester*

A DOCTOR

FOOL

OSWALD, *steward to Goneril*

TWO CAPTAINS

A GENTLEMAN, *attendant on Cordelia*

A GENTLEMAN, *attendant on Lear*

A KNIGHT, *attendant on Lear*

A HERALD

THREE SERVANTS *to Cornwall*

TWO MESSENGERS

GONERIL
REGAN *} daughters to Lear*
CORDELIA

Non-Speaking: Knights of Lear's train,
Captains, Soldiers, and Attendants

SCENE: *Britain*

ACT I

✿ SCENE 1 *King Lear's palace.*

Enter Kent, Gloucester, and Edmund.

KENT I thought the King had more affected the Duke of Albany than Cornwall.

GLOUCESTER It did always seem so to us; but now, in the division of the kingdom, it appears not which of the Dukes he values most; for equalities are so weighed, that curiosity in neither can make choice of either's moiety.

KENT Is not this your son, my lord?

GLOUCESTER His breeding, sir, hath been at my charge. I have so often blushed to acknowledge him, that now I am brazed to it.

KENT I cannot conceive you.

GLOUCESTER Sir, this young fellow's mother could; whereupon she grew round-wombed, and had, indeed, sir, a son for her cradle ere she had a husband for her bed. Do you smell a fault?

KENT I cannot wish the fault undone, the issue of it being so proper.

GLOUCESTER But I have, sir, a son by order of law, some year elder than this, who yet is no dearer in my account. Though this knave came something saucily into the world before he was sent for, yet was his mother fair; there was good sport at his making, and the whoreson must be acknowledged. Do you know this noble gentleman, Edmund?

EDMUND No, my lord.

GLOUCESTER   My Lord of Kent. Remember him hereafter as my honourable friend.

EDMUND   My services to your lordship.

KENT   I must love you, and sue to know you better.

EDMUND   Sir, I shall study deserving.

GLOUCESTER   He hath been out nine years, and away he shall again. The
King is coming.

*Sennet. Enter King Lear, Cornwall, Albany, Goneril, Regan, Cordelia, and
Attendants.*

LEAR   Attend the lords of France and Burgundy, Gloucester.

GLOUCESTER   I shall, my liege.   *Exeunt Gloucester and Edmund.*

LEAR   Meantime we shall express our darker purpose.
    Give me the map there. Know that we have divided
    In three our kingdom; and 'tis our fast intent
    To shake all cares and business from our age;
    Conferring them on younger strengths, while we
    Unburthen'd crawl toward death. Our son of Cornwall,
    And you, our no less loving son of Albany,
    We have this hour a constant will to publish
    Our daughters' several dowers, that future strife
    May be prevented now. The Princes, France and Burgundy,
    Great rivals in our youngest daughter's love,
    Long in our court have made their amorous sojourn,
    And here are to be answer'd. Tell me, my daughters—
    Since now we will divest us, both of rule,
    Interest of territory, cares of state—
    Which of you shall we say doth love us most?
    That we our largest bounty may extend
    Where nature doth with merit challenge. Goneril,
    Our eldest-born, speak first.

GONERIL   Sir, I love you more than words can wield the matter;
    Dearer than eye-sight, space, and liberty;
    Beyond what can be valued, rich or rare;
    No less than life, with grace, health, beauty, honour;
    As much as child e'er loved, or father found;
    A love that makes breath poor, and speech unable;
    Beyond all manner of so much I love you.

404

CORDELIA   [*Aside.*] What shall Cordelia do? Love, and be silent.

LEAR   Of all these bounds, even from this line to this,
With shadowy forests and with champains rich'd,
With plenteous rivers and wide-skirted meads,
We make thee lady; to thine and Albany's issue
Be this perpetual. What says our second daughter,
Our dearest Regan, wife to Cornwall? Speak.

REGAN   Sir, I am made
Of the self-same metal that my sister is,
And prize me at her worth. In my true heart
I find she names my very deed of love;
Only she comes too short; that I profess
Myself an enemy to all other joys,
Which the most precious square of sense possesses;
And find I am alone felicitate
In your dear Highness' love.

CORDELIA   [*Aside.*]   Then poor Cordelia!
And yet not so; since, I am sure, my love's
More richer than my tongue.

LEAR   To thee and thine hereditary ever
Remain this ample third of our fair kingdom;
No less in space, validity, and pleasure,
Than that conferr'd on Goneril. Now, our joy,
Although the last, not least; to whose young love
The vines of France and milk of Burgundy
Strive to be interessed; what can you say to draw
A third more opulent than your sisters? Speak.

CORDELIA   Nothing, my lord.

LEAR   Nothing!

CORDELIA   Nothing.

LEAR   Nothing will come of nothing. Speak again.

CORDELIA   Unhappy that I am, I cannot heave
My heart into my mouth. I love your Majesty
According to my bond; nor more nor less.

LEAR   How, how, Cordelia! mend your speech a little,
Lest it may mar your fortunes.

405

CORDELIA   Good my lord,
  You have begot me, bred me, loved me. I
  Return those duties back as are right fit,
  Obey you, love you, and most honour you.
  Why have my sisters husbands, if they say
  They love you all? Haply, when I shall wed,
  That lord whose hand must take my plight shall carry
  Half my love with him, half my care and duty.
  Sure, I shall never marry like my sisters,
  To love my father all.

LEAR   But goes thy heart with this?

CORDELIA   Ay, good my lord.

LEAR   So young, and so untender?

CORDELIA   So young, my lord, and true.

LEAR   Let it be so; thy truth, then, be thy dower;
  For, by the sacred radiance of the sun,
  The mysteries of Hecate, and the night;
  By all the operation of the orbs
  From whom we do exist, and cease to be;
  Here I disclaim all my paternal care,
  Propinquity and property of blood,
  And as a stranger to my heart and me
  Hold thee, from this, for ever. The barbarous Scythian,
  Or he that makes his generation messes
  To gorge his appetite, shall to my bosom
  Be as well neighbour'd, pitied, and relieved,
  As thou my sometime daughter.

KENT   Good my liege—

LEAR   Peace, Kent!
  Come not between the dragon and his wrath.
  I loved her most, and thought to set my rest
  On her kind nursery. Hence, and avoid my sight!
  So be my grave my peace, as here I give
  Her father's heart from her! Call France; who stirs?
  Call Burgundy. Cornwall and Albany,
  With my two daughters' dowers digest this third.
  Let pride, which she calls plainness, marry her.
  I do invest you jointly with my power,

Pre-eminence, and all the large effects
That troop with majesty. Ourself, by monthly course,
With reservation of an hundred knights,
By you to be sustain'd, shall our abode
Make with you by due turns. Only we still retain
The name, and all the additions to a king;
The sway, revenue, execution of the rest,
Beloved sons, be yours; which to confirm,
This coronet part betwixt you.

Giving the crown.

KENT   Royal Lear,
  Whom I have ever honour'd as my king,
  Loved as my father, as my master follow'd,
  As my great patron thought on in my prayers—

LEAR   The bow is bent and drawn, make from the shaft.

KENT   Let it fall rather, though the fork invade
  The region of my heart: be Kent unmannerly,
  When Lear is mad. What wilt thou do, old man?
  Think'st thou that duty shall have dread to speak,
  When power to flattery bows? To plainness honour's bound
  When majesty stoops to folly. Reverse thy doom;
  And, in thy best consideration, check
  This hideous rashness. Answer my life my judgement,
  Thy youngest daughter does not love thee least;
  Nor are those empty-hearted whose low sound
  Reverbs no hollowness.

LEAR   Kent, on thy life, no more.

KENT   My life I never held but as a pawn
  To wage against thy enemies; nor fear to lose it,
  Thy safety being the motive.

LEAR   Out of my sight!

KENT   See better, Lear; and let me still remain
  The true blank of thine eye.

LEAR   Now, by Apollo—

KENT   Now, by Apollo, King,
  Thou swear'st thy gods in vain.

LEAR   O, vassal! miscreant!

Laying his hand on his sword.

ALBANY AND CORNWALL   Dear sir, forbear.

KENT   Do;
   Kill thy physician, and the fee bestow
   Upon thy foul disease. Revoke thy doom;
   Or, whilst I can vent clamour from my throat,
   I'll tell thee thou dost evil.

LEAR   Hear me, recreant!
   On thine allegiance, hear me!
   Since thou hast sought to make us break our vow,
   Which we durst never yet, and with strain'd pride
   To come between our sentence and our power,
   Which nor our nature nor our place can bear,
   Our potency made good, take thy reward.
   Five days we do allot thee, for provision
   To shield thee from diseases of the world;
   And on the sixth to turn thy hated back
   Upon our kingdom. If, on the tenth day following,
   Thy banish'd trunk be found in our dominions,
   The moment is thy death. Away! by Jupiter,
   This shall not be revoked.

KENT   Fare thee well, King! Sith thus thou wilt appear,
   Freedom lives hence, and banishment is here.
   [*To Cordelia.*] The gods to their dear shelter take thee, maid,
   That justly think'st, and hast most rightly said!
   [*To Regan and Goneril.*] And your large speeches may your deeds
   approve,
   That good effects may spring from words of love.
   Thus Kent, O Princes, bids you all adieu;
   He'll shape his old course in a country new.   *Exit.*

Flourish. Re-enter Gloucester, with France, Burgundy, and Attendants.

GLOUCESTER   Here's France and Burgundy, my noble lord.

LEAR   My Lord of Burgundy,
   We first address towards you, who with this king
   Hath rivall'd for our daughter: what, in the least,
   Will you require in present dower with her,
   Or cease your quest of love?

BURGUNDY   Most royal Majesty,
  I crave no more than what your Highness offer'd,
  Nor will you tender less.

LEAR   Right noble Burgundy,
  When she was dear to us, we did hold her so;
  But now her price is fall'n. Sir, there she stands:
  If aught within that little seeming substance,
  Or all of it, with our displeasure pieced,
  And nothing more, may fitly like your Grace,
  She's there, and she is yours.

BURGUNDY   I know no answer.

LEAR   Will you, with those infirmities she owes,
  Unfriended, new-adopted to our hate,
  Dower'd with our curse, and stranger'd with our oath,
  Take her, or leave her?

BURGUNDY   Pardon me, royal sir;
  Election makes not up on such conditions.

LEAR   Then leave her, sir; for, by the power that made me,
  I tell you all her wealth. [*To France.*] For you, great King,
  I would not from your love make such a stray,
  To match you where I hate; therefore beseech you
  To avert your liking a more worthier way
  Than on a wretch whom nature is ashamed
  Almost to acknowledge hers.

FRANCE   This is most strange,
  That she, that even but now was your best object,
  The argument of your praise, balm of your age,
  Most best, most dearest, should in this trice of time
  Commit a thing so monstrous, to dismantle
  So many folds of favour. Sure, her offence
  Must be of such unnatural degree,
  That monsters it, or your fore-vouch'd affection
  Fall'n into taint; which to believe of her,
  Must be a faith that reason without miracle
  Could never plant in me.

CORDELIA   I yet beseech your Majesty —
  If for I want that glib and oily art
  To speak and purpose not; since what I well intend,

409

I'll do't before I speak—that you make known
It is no vicious blot, murder, or foulness,
No unchaste action, or dishonour'd step,
That hath deprived me of your grace and favour;
But even for want of that for which I am richer,
A still-soliciting eye, and such a tongue
As I am glad I have not, though not to have it
Hath lost me in your liking.

LEAR   Better thou
  Hadst not been born than not to have pleased me better.

FRANCE Is it but this—a tardiness in nature
  Which often leaves the history unspoke
  That it intends to do? My Lord of Burgundy,
  What say you to the lady? Love's not love
  When it is mingled with regards that stand
  Aloof from the entire point. Will you have her?
  She is herself a dowry.

BURGUNDY   Royal King,
  Give but that portion which yourself proposed,
  And here I take Cordelia by the hand,
  Duchess of Burgundy.

LEAR Nothing. I have sworn; I am firm.

BURGUNDY I am sorry, then, you have so lost a father
  That you must lose a husband.

CORDELIA   Peace be with Burgundy!
  Since that respects of fortune are his love,
  I shall not be his wife.

FRANCE Fairest Cordelia, that art most rich, being poor;
  Most choice, forsaken; and most loved, despised!
  Thee and thy virtues here I seize upon,
  Be it lawful I take up what's cast away.
  Gods, gods! 'tis strange that from their cold'st neglect
  My love should kindle to inflamed respect.
  Thy dowerless daughter, King, thrown to my chance,
  Is queen of us, of ours, and our fair France.
  Not all the dukes of waterish Burgundy
  Can buy this unprized precious maid of me.

Bid them farewell, Cordelia, though unkind;
Thou losest here, a better where to find.

LEAR   Thou hast her, France. Let her be thine; for we
Have no such daughter, nor shall ever see
That face of hers again. Therefore be gone
Without our grace, our love, our benison.
Come, noble Burgundy.
Flourish. Exeunt all but France, Goneril, Regan, and Cordelia.

FRANCE   Bid farewell to your sisters.

CORDELIA   The jewels of our father, with wash'd eyes
Cordelia leaves you. I know you what you are;
And like a sister am most loath to call
Your faults as they are named. Use well our father;
To your professed bosoms I commit him.
But yet, alas, stood I within his grace,
I would prefer him to a better place.
So, farewell to you both.

REGAN   Prescribe not us our duties.

GONERIL   Let your study
Be to content your lord, who hath received you
At fortune's alms. You have obedience scanted,
And well are worth the want that you have wanted.

CORDELIA   Time shall unfold what plaited cunning hides;
Who cover faults, at last shame them derides.
Well may you prosper!

FRANCE   Come, my fair Cordelia.
Exeunt France and Cordelia.

GONERIL   Sister, it is not a little I have to say of what most nearly apper-
tains to us both. I think our father will hence to-night.

REGAN   That's most certain, and with you; next month with us.

GONERIL   You see how full of changes his age is; the observation we have
made of it hath not been little. He always loved our sister most; and
with what poor judgement he hath now cast her off appears too
grossly.

REGAN   'Tis the infirmity of his age. Yet he hath ever but slenderly
known himself.

411

GONERIL   The best and soundest of his time hath been but rash; then must we look to receive from his age, not alone the imperfections of long-engraffed condition, but therewithal the unruly waywardness that infirm and choleric years bring with them.

REGAN   Such unconstant starts are we like to have from him as this of Kent's banishment.

GONERIL   There is further compliment of leave-taking between France and him. Pray you, let's hit together. If our father carry authority with such dispositions as he bears, this last surrender of his will but offend us.

REGAN   We shall further think on't.

GONERIL   We must do something, and i' the heat.   *Exeunt.*

SCENE 2   *The Earl of Gloucester's castle.*

Enter Edmund, with a letter.

EDMUND   Thou, nature, art my goddess; to thy law
        My services are bound. Wherefore should I
        Stand in the plague of custom, and permit
        The curiosity of nations to deprive me,
        For that I am some twelve or fourteen moonshines
        Lag of a brother? Why bastard? wherefore base?
        When my dimensions are as well compact,
        My mind as generous, and my shape as true,
        As honest madam's issue? Why brand they us
        With base? with baseness? bastardy? base, base?
        Who, in the lusty stealth of nature, take
        More composition and fierce quality
        Than doth, within a dull, stale, tired bed,
        Go to the creating a whole tribe of fops,
        Got 'tween asleep and wake? Well, then,
        Legitimate Edgar, I must have your land.
        Our father's love is to the bastard Edmund
        As to the legitimate. Fine word, "legitimate!"
        Well, my legitimate, if this letter speed,
        And my invention thrive, Edmund the base
        Shall top the legitimate. I grow; I prosper.
        Now, gods, stand up for bastards!

Enter Gloucester.

GLOUCESTER   Kent banish'd thus! and France in choler parted!
And the King gone to-night! subscribed his power!
Confined to exhibition! All this done
Upon the gad! Edmund, how now! what news?

EDMUND   So please your lordship, none.

Putting up the letter.

GLOUCESTER   Why so earnestly seek you to put up that letter?

EDMUND   I know no news, my lord.

GLOUCESTER   What paper were you reading?

EDMUND   Nothing, my lord.

GLOUCESTER   No? What needed, then, that terrible dispatch of it into
your pocket? the quality of nothing hath not such need to hide itself.
Let's see. Come, if it be nothing, I shall not need spectacles.

EDMUND   I beseech you, sir, pardon me. It is a letter from my brother
that I have not all o'er-read; and for so much as I have perused, I find it
not fit for your o'er-looking.

GLOUCESTER   Give me the letter, sir.

EDMUND   I shall offend, either to detain or give it. The contents, as in
part I understand them, are to blame.

GLOUCESTER   Let's see, let's see.

EDMUND   I hope, for my brother's justification, he wrote this but as an
essay or taste of my virtue.

GLOUCESTER   [*Reads.*]
"This policy and reverence of age makes the world bitter to the best of
our times; keeps our fortunes from us till our oldness cannot relish
them. I begin to find an idle and fond bondage in the oppression of
aged tyranny; who sways, not as it hath power, but as it is suffered.
Come to me, that of this I may speak more. If our father would sleep
till I waked him, you should enjoy half his revenue for ever, and live
the beloved of your brother,

Edgar."

413

Hum, conspiracy! "Sleep till I waked him, you should enjoy half his revenue." My son Edgar! Had he a hand to write this? a heart and brain to breed it in? When came this to you? who brought it?

EDMUND   It was not brought me, my lord; there's the cunning of it; I found it thrown in at the casement of my closet.

GLOUCESTER   You know the character to be your brother's?

EDMUND   If the matter were good, my lord, I durst swear it were his; but, in respect of that, I would fain think it were not.

GLOUCESTER   It is his.

EDMUND   It is his hand, my lord; but I hope his heart is not in the contents.

GLOUCESTER   Hath he never heretofore sounded you in this business?

EDMUND   Never, my lord; but I have heard him oft maintain it to be fit that, sons at perfect age, and fathers declining, the father should be as ward to the son, and the son manage his revenue.

GLOUCESTER   O villain, villain! His very opinion in the letter! Abhorred villain! Unnatural, detested, brutish villain! worse than brutish! Go, sirrah, seek him; I'll apprehend him. Abominable villain! Where is he?

EDMUND   I do not well know, my lord. If it shall please you to suspend your indignation against my brother till you can derive from him better testimony of his intent, you shall run a certain course; where, if you violently proceed against him, mistaking his purpose, it would make a great gap in your own honour, and shake in pieces the heart of his obedience. I dare pawn down my life for him, that he hath writ this to feel my affection to your honour, and to no other pretence of danger.

GLOUCESTER   Think you so?

EDMUND   If your honour judge it meet, I will place you where you shall hear us confer of this, and by an auricular assurance have your satisfaction; and that without any further delay than this very evening.

GLOUCESTER   He cannot be such a monster—

EDMUND   Nor is not, sure.

GLOUCESTER   To his father, that so tenderly and entirely loves him. Heaven and earth! Edmund, seek him out; wind me into him, I pray

414

you. Frame the business after your own wisdom. I would unstate my-self, to be in a due resolution.

EDMUND   I will seek him, sir, presently; convey the business as I shall find means, and acquaint you withal.

GLOUCESTER   These late eclipses in the sun and moon portend no good to us. Though the wisdom of nature can reason it thus and thus, yet na-ture finds itself scourged by the sequent effects. Love cools, friendship falls off, brothers divide; in cities, mutinies; in countries, discord; in palaces, treason; and the bond cracked 'twixt son and father. This vil-lain of mine comes under the prediction; there's son against father. The King falls from bias of nature; there's father against child. We have seen the best of our time: machinations, hollowness, treachery, and all ruinous disorders, follow us disquietly to our graves. Find out this vil-lain, Edmund; it shall lose thee nothing; do it carefully. And the noble and true-hearted Kent banished! his offence, honesty! 'Tis strange.

Exit.

EDMUND   This is the excellent foppery of the world, that, when we are sick in fortune—often the surfeit of our own behaviour—we make guilty of our disasters the sun, the moon, and the stars, as if we were villains by necessity, fools by heavenly compulsion, knaves, thieves, and treachers, by spherical predominance, drunkards, liars, and adul-terers, by an enforced obedience of planetary influence, and all that we are evil in, by a divine thrusting on. An admirable evasion of whore-master man, to lay his goatish disposition to the charge of a star! My father compounded with my mother under the dragon's tail; and my nativity was under *Ursa major;* so that it follows, I am rough and lech-erous. Tut, I should have been that I am, had the maidenliest star in the firmament twinkled on my bastardizing. Edgar—

Enter Edgar.

And pat he comes like the catastrophe of the old comedy. My cue is villainous melancholy, with a sigh like Tom o' Bedlam. O, these eclipses do portend these divisions! *fa, sol, la, mi.*

EDGAR   How now, brother Edmund! what serious contemplation are you in?

EDMUND   I am thinking, brother, of a prediction I read this other day, what should follow these eclipses.

EDGAR   Do you busy yourself about that?

415

EDMUND   I promise you, the effects he writes of succeed unhappily; as of unnaturalness between the child and the parent; death, dearth, dissolutions of ancient amities; divisions in state, menaces and maledictions against king and nobles; needless diffidences, banishment of friends, dissipation of cohorts, nuptial breaches, and I know not what.

EDGAR   How long have you been a sectary astronomical?

EDMUND   Come, come; when saw you my father last?

EDGAR   Why, the night gone by.

EDMUND   Spake you with him?

EDGAR   Ay, two hours together.

EDMUND   Parted you in good terms? Found you no displeasure in him by word or countenance?

EDGAR   None at all.

EDMUND   Bethink yourself wherein you may have offended him; and at my entreaty forbear his presence till some little time hath qualified the heat of his displeasure, which at this instant so rageth in him, that with the mischief of your person it would scarcely allay.

EDGAR   Some villain hath done me wrong.

EDMUND   That's my fear. I pray you, have a continent forbearance till the speed of his rage goes slower; and, as I say, retire with me to my lodging, from whence I will fitly bring you to hear my lord speak. Pray ye, go; there's my key. If you do stir abroad, go armed.

EDGAR   Armed, brother!

EDMUND   Brother, I advise you to the best; go armed. I am no honest man if there be any good meaning towards you. I have told you what I have seen and heard; but faintly, nothing like the image and horror of it. Pray you, away.

EDGAR   Shall I hear from you anon?

EDMUND   I do serve you in this business.   *Exit Edgar.*
   A credulous father! and a brother noble,
   Whose nature is so far from doing harms
   That he suspects none; on whose foolish honesty
   My practices ride easy! I see the business.
   Let me, if not by birth, have lands by wit;
   All with me's meet that I can fashion fit.   *Exit.*

SCENE 3   *The Duke of Albany's palace.*

Enter Goneril, and Oswald, her steward.

GONERIL   Did my father strike my gentleman for chiding of his fool?

OSWALD   Yes, madam.

GONERIL   By day and night he wrongs me; every hour
He flashes into one gross crime or other,
That sets us all at odds. I'll not endure it.
His knights grow riotous, and himself upbraids us
On every trifle. When he returns from hunting,
I will not speak with him; say I am sick.
If you come slack of former services,
You shall do well; the fault of it I'll answer.

OSWALD   He's coming, madam; I hear him.

Horns within.

GONERIL   Put on what weary negligence you please,
You and your fellows; I'd have it come to question.
If he dislike it, let him to our sister,
Whose mind and mine, I know, in that are one,
Not to be over-ruled. Idle old man,
That still would manage those authorities
That he hath given away! Now, by my life,
Old fools are babes again; and must be used
With checks as flatteries—when they are seen abused.
Remember what I tell you.

OSWALD   Well, madam.

GONERIL   And let his knights have colder looks among you;
What grows of it, no matter; advise your fellows so.
I would breed from hence occasions, and I shall,
That I may speak. I'll write straight to my sister,
To hold my very course. Prepare for dinner.   *Exeunt.*

 SCENE 4   *A hall in the same.*

Enter Kent, disguised.

KENT   If but as well I other accents borrow,
That can my speech defuse, my good intent

417

May carry through itself to that full issue
For which I razed my likeness. Now, banish'd Kent,
If thou canst serve where thou dost stand condemn'd,
So may it come, thy master, whom thou lovest,
Shall find thee full of labours.

Horns within. Enter Lear, Knights, and Attendants.

LEAR   Let me not stay a jot for dinner; go get it ready.

Exit an Attendant.

How now! what art thou?

KENT   A man, sir.

LEAR   What dost thou profess? what wouldst thou with us?

KENT   I do profess to be no less than I seem; to serve him truly that will put me in trust; to love him that is honest; to converse with him that is wise, and says little; to fear judgement; to fight when I cannot choose; and to eat no fish.

LEAR   What art thou?

KENT   A very honest-hearted fellow, and as poor as the King.

LEAR   If thou be as poor for a subject as he is for a king, thou art poor enough. What wouldst thou?

KENT   Service.

LEAR   Who wouldst thou serve?

KENT   You.

LEAR   Dost thou know me, fellow?

KENT   No, sir; but you have that in your countenance which I would fain call master.

LEAR   What's that?

KENT   Authority.

LEAR   What services canst thou do?

KENT   I can keep honest counsel, ride, run, mar a curious tale in telling it, and deliver a plain message bluntly. That which ordinary men are fit for, I am qualified in; and the best of me is diligence.

LEAR   How old art thou?

418

KENT   Not so young, sir, to love a woman for singing, nor so old to dote on her for anything. I have years on my back forty eight.

LEAR   Follow me; thou shalt serve me. If I like thee no worse after dinner, I will not part from thee yet. Dinner, ho, dinner! Where's my knave? My fool? Go you, and call my fool hither.

Exit an Attendant.

Enter Oswald.

You, you, sirrah, where's my daughter?

OSWALD   So please you—   *Exit.*

LEAR   What says the fellow there? Call the clotpoll back.

Exit a Knight.

Where's my fool, ho? I think the world's asleep.

Re-enter Knight.

How now! where's that mongrel?

KNIGHT   He says, my lord, your daughter is not well.

LEAR   Why came not the slave back to me when I called him?

KNIGHT   Sir, he answered me in the roundest manner, he would not.

LEAR   He would not!

KNIGHT   My lord, I know not what the matter is; but, to my judgement, your Highness is not entertained with that ceremonious affection as you were wont; there's a great abatement of kindness appears as well in the general dependants as in the Duke himself also and your daughter.

LEAR   Ha! sayest thou so?

KNIGHT   I beseech you, pardon me, my lord, if I be mistaken; for my duty cannot be silent when I think your Highness wronged.

LEAR   Thou but rememberest me of mine own conception. I have perceived a most faint neglect of late, which I have rather blamed as mine own jealous curiosity than as a very pretence and purpose of unkindness. I will look further into't. But where's my fool? I have not seen him this two days.

KNIGHT   Since my young lady's going into France, sir, the fool hath much pined away.

419

LEAR   No more of that; I have noted it well. Go you, and tell my daughter I would speak with her.   *Exit an Attendant.*
                    Go you, call hither my fool.
                                            Exit an Attendant.

Re-enter Oswald.

O, you sir, you, come you hither, sir. Who am I, sir?

OSWALD   My lady's father.

LEAR   "My lady's father"! my lord's knave! You whoreson dog! you
slave! you cur!

OSWALD   I am none of these, my lord; I beseech your pardon.

LEAR   Do you bandy looks with me, you rascal?

Striking him.

OSWALD   I'll not be struck, my lord.

KENT   Nor tripped neither, you base foot-ball player.

Tripping up his heels.

LEAR   I thank thee, fellow; thou servest me, and I'll love thee.

KENT   Come, sir, arise, away! I'll teach you differences. Away, away! If
you will measure your lubber's length again, tarry. But away! go to;
have you wisdom? so.   *Pushes Oswald out.*

LEAR   Now, my friendly knave, I thank thee. There's earnest of thy service.

Giving Kent money. Enter Fool.

FOOL   Let me hire him too. Here's my coxcomb.

Offering Kent his cap.

LEAR   How now my pretty knave! how dost thou?

FOOL   Sirrah, you were best take my coxcomb.

KENT   Why, fool?

FOOL   Why, for taking one's part that's out of favour. Nay, an thou canst
not smile as the wind sits, thou'lt catch cold shortly. There, take my
coxcomb. Why, this fellow has banished two on's daughters, and did
the third a blessing against his will; if thou follow him, thou must
needs wear my coxcomb. How now, nuncle! Would I had two coxcombs and two daughters!

420

LEAR   Why, my boy?

FOOL   If I gave them all my living, I'd keep my coxcombs myself.
There's mine; beg another of thy daughters.

LEAR   Take heed, sirrah; the whip.

FOOL   Truth's a dog must to kennel; he must be whipped out, when
Lady the brach may stand by the fire and stink.

LEAR   A pestilent gall to me!

FOOL   Sirrah, I'll teach thee a speech.

LEAR   Do.

FOOL   Mark it, nuncle:

> "Have more than thou showest,
> Speak less than thou knowest,
> Lend less than thou owest,
> Ride more than thou goest,
> Learn more than thou trowest,
> Set less than thou throwest,
> Leave thy drink and thy whore,
> And keep in-a-door,
> And thou shalt have more
> Than two tens to a score."

KENT   This is nothing, fool.

FOOL   Then 'tis like the breath of an unfee'd lawyer; you gave me
nothing for't. Can you make no use of nothing, nuncle?

LEAR   Why, no, boy; nothing can be made out of nothing.

FOOL   [*To Kent.*] Prithee, tell him, so much the rent of his land comes to.
He will not believe a fool.

LEAR   A bitter fool!

FOOL   Dost thou know the difference, my boy, between a bitter fool and
a sweet fool?

LEAR   No, lad; teach me.

FOOL
> "That lord that counsell'd thee
> To give away thy land,
> Come place him here by me,
> Do thou for him stand.

> The sweet and bitter fool
>   Will presently appear;
>   The one in motley here,
>   The other found out there."

LEAR   Dost thou call me fool, boy?

FOOL   All thy other titles thou hast given away; that thou wast born with.

KENT   This is not altogether fool, my lord.

FOOL   No, faith, lords and great men will not let me; if I had a monopoly out, they would have part on't. And ladies too, they will not let me have all fool to myself; they'll be snatching. Give me an egg, nuncle, and I'll give thee two crowns.

LEAR   What two crowns shall they be?

FOOL   Why, after I have cut the egg i' the middle, and eat up the meat, the two crowns of the egg. When thou clovest thy crown i' the middle, and gavest away both parts, thou borest thy ass on thy back o'er the dirt. Thou hadst little wit in thy bald crown when thou gavest thy golden one away. If I speak like myself in this, let him be whipped that first finds it so. [*Sings.*]

> "Fools had ne'er less wit in a year;
>   For wise men are grown foppish,
> They know not how their wits to wear,
>   Their manners are so apish."

LEAR   When were you wont to be so full of songs, sirrah?

FOOL   I have used it, nuncle, ever since thou madest thy daughters thy mother; for when thou gavest them the rod, and put'st down thine own breeches, [*Sings.*]

> "Then they for sudden joy did weep,
>   And I for sorrow sung,
> That such a king should play bo-peep,
>   And go the fools among."

Prithee, nuncle, keep a schoolmaster that can teach thy fool to lie. I would fain learn to lie.

LEAR   An you lie, sirrah, we'll have you whipped.

FOOL   I marvel what kin thou and thy daughters are. They'll have me

whipped for speaking true, thou'lt have me whipped for lying; and sometimes I am whipped for holding my peace. I had rather be any kind o' thing than a fool; and yet I would not be thee, nuncle; thou hast pared thy wit o' both sides, and left nothing i' the middle. Here comes one o' the parings.

Enter Goneril.

LEAR   How now, daughter! what makes that frontlet on? Methinks you are too much of late i' the frown.

FOOL   Thou wast a pretty fellow when thou hadst no need to care for her frowning; now thou art an O without a figure. I am better than thou art now; I am a fool, thou art nothing. [*To Goneril.*] Yes, forsooth, I will hold my tongue; so your face bids me, though you say nothing. Mum, mum,

> "He that keeps nor crust nor crum,
>   Weary of all, shall want some."

[*Pointing to Lear.*] That's a shealed peascod.

GONERIL   Not only, sir, this your all-licensed fool,
But other of your insolent retinue
Do hourly carp and quarrel, breaking forth
In rank and not-to-be-endured riots. Sir,
I had thought, by making this well known unto you,
To have found a safe redress; but now grow fearful
By what yourself too late have spoke and done,
That you protect this course, and put it on
By your allowance; which if you should, the fault
Would not 'scape censure, nor the redresses sleep,
Which, in the tender of a wholesome weal,
Might in their working do you that offence,
Which else were shame, that then necessity
Will call discreet proceeding.

FOOL   For, you know, nuncle,

> "The hedge-sparrow fed the cuckoo so long,
>   That it's had it head bit off by it young."

So, out went the candle, and we were left darkling.

LEAR   Are you our daughter?

GONERIL   Come, sir.

I would you would make use of that good wisdom,
Whereof I know you are fraught; and put away
These dispositions, that of late transform you
From what you rightly are.

FOOL May not an ass know when the cart draws the horse? "Whoop,
Jug! I love thee."

LEAR Doth any here know me? This is not Lear.
Doth Lear walk thus? speak thus? Where are his eyes?
Either his notion weakens, his discernings
Are lethargied— Ha! waking? 'tis not so.
Who is it that can tell me who I am?

FOOL Lear's shadow.

LEAR I would learn that; for, by the marks of sovereignty, knowledge,
and reason, I should be false persuaded I had daughters.

FOOL Which they will make an obedient father.

LEAR Your name, fair gentlewoman?

GONERIL This admiration, sir, is much o' the savour
Of other your new pranks. I do beseech you
To understand my purposes aright.
As you are old and reverend, you should be wise.
Here do you keep a hundred knights and squires;
Men so disorder'd, so debosh'd and bold,
That this our court, infected with their manners,
Shows like a riotous inn. Epicurism and lust
Make it more like a tavern or a brothel
Than a graced palace. The shame itself doth speak
For instant remedy. Be then desired
By her, that else will take the thing she begs,
A little to disquantity your train;
And the remainder, that shall still depend
To be such men as may besort your age,
And know themselves and you.

LEAR   Darkness and devils!
Saddle my horses; call my train together.
Degenerate bastard! I'll not trouble thee;
Yet have I left a daughter.

GONERIL You strike my people; and your disorder'd rabble
  Make servants of their betters.

Enter Albany.

LEAR Woe, that too late repents—[*To Albany.*] O, sir, are you come?
  Is it your will? Speak, sir. Prepare my horses.
  Ingratitude, thou marble-hearted fiend,
  More hideous when thou show'st thee in a child
  Than the sea-monster!

ALBANY   Pray, sir, be patient.

LEAR [*To Goneril.*] Detested kite! thou liest.
  My train are men of choice and rarest parts,
  That all particulars of duty know,
  And in the most exact regard support
  The worships of their name. O most small fault,
  How ugly didst thou in Cordelia show!
  That, like an engine, wrench'd my frame of nature
  From the fix'd place; drew from my heart all love,
  And added to the gall. O Lear, Lear, Lear!
  Beat at this gate, that let thy folly in,

Striking his head.

  And thy dear judgement out! Go, go, my people.

ALBANY My lord, I am guiltless, as I am ignorant
  Of what hath moved you.

LEAR   It may be so, my lord.
  Hear, Nature, hear; dear goddess, hear!
  Suspend thy purpose, if thou didst intend
  To make this creature fruitful!
  Into her womb convey sterility!
  Dry up in her the organs of increase;
  And from her derogate body never spring
  A babe to honour her! If she must teem,
  Create her child of spleen; that it may live,
  And be a thwart disnatured torment to her!
  Let it stamp wrinkles in her brow of youth;
  With cadent tears fret channels in her cheeks;
  Turn all her mother's pains and benefits

425

To laughter and contempt; that she may feel
How sharper than a serpent's tooth it is
To have a thankless child! Away, away!   *Exit.*

ALBANY   Now, gods that we adore, whereof comes this?

GONERIL   Never afflict yourself to know the cause;
But let his disposition have that scope
That dotage gives it.

Re-enter Lear.

LEAR   What, fifty of my followers at a clap!
Within a fortnight!

ALBANY   What's the matter, sir?

LEAR   I'll tell thee. [*To Goneril.*] Life and death! I am ashamed.
That thou hast power to shake my manhood thus;
That these hot tears, which break from me perforce,
Should make thee worth them. Blasts and fogs upon thee!
The untented woundings of a father's curse
Pierce every sense about thee! Old fond eyes,
Beweep this cause again, I'll pluck ye out,
And cast you, with the waters that you lose,
To temper clay. Yea, is it come to this?
Let it be so: yet have I left a daughter,
Who, I am sure, is kind and comfortable.
When she shall hear this of thee, with her nails
She'll flay thy wolvish visage. Thou shalt find
That I'll resume the shape which thou dost think
I have cast off for ever. Thou shalt, I warrant thee.
                    Exeunt Lear, Kent, and Attendants.

GONERIL   Do you mark that, my lord?

ALBANY   I cannot be so partial, Goneril,
To the great love I bear you—

GONERIL   Pray you, content. What, Oswald, ho!
[*To the Fool.*] You, sir, more knave than fool, after your master.

FOOL   Nuncle Lear, nuncle Lear, tarry and take the fool with thee.

          "A fox, when one has caught her,
              And such a daughter,

426

> Should sure to the slaughter,
> If my cap would buy a halter.
> So the fool follows after."   *Exit.*

GONERIL   This man hath had good counsel; a hundred knights!
'Tis politic and safe to let him keep
At point a hundred knights; yes, that, on every dream,
Each buzz, each fancy, each complaint, dislike,
He may enguard his dotage with their powers,
And hold our lives in mercy. Oswald, I say!

ALBANY   Well, you may fear too far.

GONERIL   Safer than trust too far.
Let me still take away the harms I fear,
Not fear still to be taken. I know his heart.
What he hath utter'd I have writ my sister.
If she sustain him and his hundred knights,
When I have show'd the unfitness—

Re-enter Oswald.

                                    How now, Oswald!
What, have you writ that letter to my sister?

OSWALD   Yes, madam.

GONERIL   Take you some company, and away to horse.
Inform her full of my particular fear;
And thereto add such reasons of your own
As may compact it more. Get you gone;
And hasten your return.   *Exit Oswald.*
                        No, no, my lord,
This milky gentleness and course of yours
Though I condemn not, yet, under pardon,
You are much more attask'd for want of wisdom
Than praised for harmful mildness.

ALBANY   How far your eyes may pierce I cannot tell.
Striving to better, oft we mar what's well.

GONERIL   Nay, then—

ALBANY   Well, well; the event.   *Exeunt.*

427

 SCENE 5 *Court before the same.*

Enter Lear, Kent, and Fool.

LEAR Go you before to Gloucester with these letters. Acquaint my daughter no further with anything you know than comes from her demand out of the letter. If your diligence be not speedy, I shall be there afore you.

KENT I will not sleep, my lord, till I have delivered your letter. *Exit.*

FOOL If a man's brains were in's heels, were't not in danger of kibes?

LEAR Ay, boy.

FOOL Then, I prithee, be merry; thy wit shall ne'er go slip-shod.

LEAR Ha, ha, ha!

FOOL Shalt see thy other daughter will use thee kindly; for though she's as like this as a crab's like an apple, yet I can tell what I can tell.

LEAR Why, what canst thou tell, my boy?

FOOL She will taste as like this as a crab does to a crab. Thou canst tell why one's nose stands i' the middle on's face?

LEAR No.

FOOL Why, to keep one's eyes of either side's nose; that what a man cannot smell out, he may spy into.

LEAR I did her wrong—

FOOL Canst tell how an oyster makes his shell?

LEAR No.

FOOL Nor I neither; but I can tell why a snail has a house.

LEAR Why?

FOOL Why, to put his head in; not to give it away to his daughters, and leave his horns without a case.

LEAR I will forget my nature. So kind a father! Be my horses ready?

FOOL Thy asses are gone about 'em. The reason why the seven stars are no more than seven is a pretty reason.

LEAR Because they are not eight?

428

FOOL   Yes, indeed. Thou wouldst make a good fool.

LEAR   To take't again perforce! Monster ingratitude!

FOOL   If thou wert my fool, nuncle, I'd have thee beaten for being old before thy time.

LEAR   How's that?

FOOL   Thou shouldst not have been old till thou hadst been wise.

LEAR   O, let me not be mad, not mad, sweet heaven!
Keep me in temper. I would not be mad!

Enter Gentleman.

How now! are the horses ready?

GENTLEMAN   Ready, my lord.

LEAR   Come, boy.

FOOL   She that's a maid now, and laughs at my departure,
Shall not be a maid long, unless things be cut shorter.   *Exeunt.*

ACT II

❀ SCENE 1 *The Earl of Gloucester's castle.*

Enter Edmund, and Curan meets him.

EDMUND Save thee, Curan.

CURAN And you, sir. I have been with your father, and given him notice that the Duke of Cornwall and Regan his duchess will be here with him this night.

EDMUND How comes that?

CURAN Nay, I know not. You have heard of the news abroad; I mean the whispered ones, for they are yet but ear-kissing arguments?

EDMUND Not I. Pray you, what are they?

CURAN Have you heard of no likely wars toward, 'twixt the Dukes of Cornwall and Albany?

EDMUND Not a word.

CURAN You may do, then, in time. Fare you well, sir.   *Exit.*

EDMUND The Duke be here to-night? The better! best!
This weaves itself perforce into my business.
My father hath set guard to take my brother;
And I have one thing, of a queasy question,
Which I must act. Briefness and fortune, work!
Brother, a word; descend, Brother, I say!

Enter Edgar.

My father watches. O sir, fly this place;

430

Intelligence is given where you are hid;
You have now the good advantage of the night.
Have you not spoken 'gainst the Duke of Cornwall?
He's coming hither; now, i' the night, i' the haste,
And Regan with him. Have you nothing said
Upon his party 'gainst the Duke of Albany?
Advise yourself.

EDGAR   I am sure on't, not a word.

EDMUND   I hear my father coming. Pardon me;
In cunning I must draw my sword upon you:
Draw; seem to defend yourself; now quit you well.
Yield. Come before my father. Light, ho, here!
Fly, brother. Torches, torches! So, farewell.   *Exit Edgar.*
Some blood drawn on me would beget opinion

Wounds his arm.

Of my more fierce endeavour. I have seen drunkards
Do more than this in sport. Father, father!
Stop, stop! No help?

Enter Gloucester, and Servants with torches.

GLOUCESTER   Now, Edmund, where's the villain?

EDMUND   Here stood he in the dark, his sharp sword out,
Mumbling of wicked charms, conjuring the moon
To stand auspicious mistress—

GLOUCESTER   But where is he?

EDMUND   Look, sir, I bleed.

GLOUCESTER   Where is the villain, Edmund?

EDMUND   Fled this way, sir. When by no means he could—

GLOUCESTER   Pursue him, ho! Go after.   *Exeunt some Servants.*
                    By no means what?

EDMUND   Persuade me to the murder of your lordship;
But that I told him, the revenging gods
'Gainst parricides did all their thunders bend;
Spoke, with how manifold and strong a bond
The child was bound to the father; sir, in fine,
Seeing how loathly opposite I stood

431

To his unnatural purpose, in fell motion,
With his prepared sword, he charges home
My unprovided body, lanced mine arm.
But when he saw my best alarum'd spirits,
Bold in the quarrel's right, roused to the encounter,
Or whether gasted by the noise I made,
Full suddenly he fled.

GLOUCESTER   Let him fly far.
Not in this land shall he remain uncaught;
And found—dispatch. The noble Duke my master,
My worthy arch and patron, comes to-night.
By his authority I will proclaim it,
That he which finds him shall deserve our thanks,
Bringing the murderous coward to the stake;
He that conceals him, death.

EDMUND   When I dissuaded him from his intent,
And found him pight to do it, with curst speech
I threaten'd to discover him; he replied,
"Thou unpossessing bastard! dost thou think,
If I would stand against thee, would the reposal
Of any trust, virtue, or worth in thee
Make thy words faith'd? No. What I should deny—
As this I would; ay, though thou didst produce
My very character—I'd turn it all
To thy suggestion, plot, and damned practice.
And thou must make a dullard of the world,
If they not thought the profits of my death
Were very pregnant and potential spurs
To make thee seek it."

GLOUCESTER   Strong and fasten'd villain!
Would he deny his letter? I never got him.

Tucket within.

Hark, the Duke's trumpets! I know not why he comes.
All ports I'll bar; the villain shall not 'scape;
The Duke must grant me that. Besides, his picture
I will send far and near, that all the kingdom
May have due note of him; and of my land,
Loyal and natural boy, I'll work the means
To make thee capable.

ACT II   Scene 1

Enter Cornwall, Regan, and Attendants.

CORNWALL   How now, my noble friend! since I came hither,
Which I can call but now, I have heard strange news.

REGAN   If it be true, all vengeance comes too short
Which can pursue the offender. How dost, my lord?

GLOUCESTER   O, madam, my old heart is crack'd, is crack'd!

REGAN   What, did my father's godson seek your life?
He whom my father named? your Edgar?

GLOUCESTER   O, lady, lady, shame would have it hid!

REGAN   Was he not companion with the riotous knights
That tend upon my father?

GLOUCESTER   I know not, madam. 'Tis too bad, too bad.

EDMUND   Yes, madam, he was of that consort.

REGAN   No marvel, then, though he were ill affected.
'Tis they have put him on the old man's death,
To have the expense and waste of his revenues.
I have this present evening from my sister
Been well inform'd of them; and with such cautions,
That if they come to sojourn at my house,
I'll not be there.

CORNWALL   Nor I, assure thee, Regan.
Edmund, I hear that you have shown your father
A child-like office.

EDMUND   'Twas my duty, sir.

GLOUCESTER   He did bewray his practice; and received
This hurt you see, striving to apprehend him.

CORNWALL   Is he pursued?

GLOUCESTER   Ay, my good lord.

CORNWALL   If he be taken, he shall never more
Be fear'd of doing harm. Make your own purpose,
How in my strength you please. For you, Edmund,
Whose virtue and obedience doth this instant
So much commend itself, you shall be ours.

433

Natures of such deep trust we shall much need;
You we first seize on.

EDMUND   I shall serve you, sir,
  Truly, however else.

GLOUCESTER   For him I thank your Grace.

CORNWALL   You know not why we came to visit you—

REGAN   Thus out of season, threading dark-eyed night.
  Occasions, noble Gloucester, of some poise,
  Wherein we must have use of your advice.
  Our father he hath writ, so hath our sister,
  Of differences, which I least thought it fit
  To answer from our home; the several messengers
  From hence attend dispatch. Our good old friend,
  Lay comforts to your bosom; and bestow
  Your needful counsel to our business,
  Which craves the instant use.

GLOUCESTER   I serve you, madam.
  Your Graces are right welcome.   *Exeunt.*

SCENE 2   *Before Gloucester's castle.*

Enter Kent and Oswald, severally.

OSWALD   Good dawning to thee, friend. Art of this house?

KENT   Ay.

OSWALD   Where may we set our horses?

KENT   I' the mire.

OSWALD   Prithee, if thou lovest me, tell me.

KENT   I love thee not.

OSWALD   Why, then, I care not for thee.

KENT   If I had thee in Lipsbury pinfold, I would make thee care for me.

OSWALD   Why dost thou use me thus? I know thee not.

KENT   Fellow, I know thee.

OSWALD   What dost thou know me for?

KENT   A knave; a rascal; an eater of broken meats; a base, proud, shallow, beggarly, three-suited, hundred-pound, filthy, worsted-stocking knave; a lily-livered, action-taking knave, a whoreson, glass-gazing, superserviceable, finical rogue; one-trunk-inheriting slave; one that wouldst be a bawd, in way of good service, and art nothing but the composition of a knave, beggar, coward, pandar, and the son and heir of a mongrel bitch; one whom I will beat into clamorous whining, if thou deniest the least syllable of thy addition.

OSWALD   Why, what a monstrous fellow art thou, thus to rail on one that is neither known of thee nor knows thee!

KENT   What a brazen-faced varlet art thou, to deny thou knowest me! Is it two days ago since I tripped up thy heels, and beat thee before the King? Draw, you rogue; for, though it be night, yet the moon shines; I'll make a sop o' the moonshine of you. Draw, you whoreson cullionly barber-monger, draw.

Drawing his sword.

OSWALD   Away! I have nothing to do with thee.

KENT   Draw, you rascal. You come with letters against the King; and take vanity the puppet's part against the royalty of her father. Draw, you rogue, or I'll so carbonado your shanks. Draw, you rascal; come your ways.

OSWALD   Help, ho! murder! help!

KENT   Strike, you slave; stand, rogue, stand; you neat slave, strike.

Beating him.

OSWALD   Help, ho! murder! murder!

Enter Edmund, with his rapier drawn, Cornwall, Regan, Gloucester, and Servants.

EDMUND   How now! What's the matter?

KENT   With you, goodman boy, an you please.
   Come, I'll flesh ye; come on, young master.

GLOUCESTER   Weapons! arms! What's the matter here?

CORNWALL   Keep peace, upon your lives;
   He dies that strikes again. What is the matter?

REGAN   The messengers from our sister and the King.

435

CORNWALL   What is your difference? Speak.

OSWALD   I am scarce in breath, my lord.

KENT   No marvel, you have so bestirred your valour. You cowardly rascal, nature disclaims in thee. A tailor made thee.

CORNWALL   Thou art a strange fellow. A tailor make a man?

KENT   Ay, a tailor, sir. A stone-cutter or a painter could not have made him so ill, though he had been but two hours at the trade.

CORNWALL   Speak yet, how grew your quarrel?

OSWALD   This ancient ruffian, sir, whose life I have spared at suit of his gray beard—

KENT   Thou whoreson zed! thou unnecessary letter! My lord, if you will give me leave, I will tread this unbolted villain into mortar, and daub the walls of a jakes with him. Spare my gray beard, you wagtail?

CORNWALL   Peace, sirrah!
You beastly knave, know you no reverence?

KENT   Yes, sir; but anger hath a privilege.

CORNWALL   Why art thou angry?

KENT   That such a slave as this should wear a sword,
Who wears no honesty. Such smiling rogues as these,
Like rats, oft bite the holy cords a-twain
Which are too intrinse t' unloose; smooth every passion
That in the natures of their lords rebel;
Bring oil to fire, snow to their colder moods;
Renege, affirm, and turn their halcyon beaks
With every gale and vary of their masters,
Knowing nought, like dogs, but following.
A plague upon your epileptic visage!
Smile you my speeches, as I were a fool?
Goose, if I had you upon Sarum plain,
I'd drive ye cackling home to Camelot.

CORNWALL   What, art thou mad, old fellow?

GLOUCESTER   How fell you out? say that.

KENT   No contraries hold more antipathy
Than I and such a knave.

436

CORNWALL   Why dost thou call him knave? What's his offence?

KENT   His countenance likes me not.

CORNWALL   No more, perchance, does mine, nor his, nor hers.

KENT   Sir, 'tis my occupation to be plain.
  I have seen better faces in my time
  Than stands on any shoulder that I see
  Before me at this instant.

CORNWALL   This is some fellow,
  Who, having been praised for bluntness, doth affect
  A saucy roughness, and constrains the garb
  Quite from his nature. He cannot flatter, he,
  An honest mind and plain, he must speak truth!
  An they will take it, so; if not, he's plain.
  These kind of knaves I know, which in this plainness
  Harbour more craft and more corrupter ends
  Than twenty silly ducking observants
  That stretch their duties nicely.

KENT   Sir, in good sooth, in sincere verity,
  Under the allowance of your great aspect,
  Whose influence, like the wreath of radiant fire
  On flickering Phoebus' front—

CORNWALL   What mean'st by this?

KENT   To go out of my dialect, which you discommend so much. I
  know, sir, I am no flatterer. He that beguiled you in a plain accent was a
  plain knave; which for my part I will not be, though I should win your
  displeasure to entreat me to't.

CORNWALL   What was the offence you gave him?

OSWALD   I never gave him any.
  It pleased the King his master very late
  To strike at me, upon his misconstruction;
  When he, conjunct, and flattering his displeasure,
  Tripp'd me behind; being down, insulted, rail'd,
  And put upon him such a deal of man,
  That worthied him, got praises of the King
  For him attempting who was self-subdued;
  And, in the fleshment of this dread exploit,
  Drew on me here again.

437

KENT   None of these rogues and cowards
   But Ajax is their fool.

CORNWALL   Fetch forth the stocks!
   You stubborn ancient knave, you reverend braggart,
   We'll teach you—

KENT   Sir, I am too old to learn.
   Call not your stocks for me. I serve the King;
   On whose employment I was sent to you:
   You shall do small respect, show too bold malice
   Against the grace and person of my master,
   Stocking his messenger.

CORNWALL   Fetch forth the stocks! As I have life and honour,
   There shall he sit till noon.

REGAN   Till noon! till night, my lord; and all night too.

KENT   Why, madam, if I were your father's dog,
   You should not use me so.

REGAN   Sir, being his knave, I will.

CORNWALL   This is a fellow of the self-same colour
   Our sister speaks of. Come, bring away the stocks!

Stocks brought out.

GLOUCESTER   Let me beseech your Grace not to do so:
   His fault is much, and the good King his master
   Will check him for't. Your purposed low correction
   Is such as basest and contemned'st wretches
   For pilferings and most common trespasses
   Are punish'd with. The King must take it ill
   That he's so slightly valued in his messenger,
   Should have him thus restrain'd.

CORNWALL   I'll answer that.

REGAN   My sister may receive it much more worse,
   To have her gentleman abused, assaulted,
   For following her affairs. Put in his legs.

Kent is put in the stocks.

   Come, my good lord, away.   *Exeunt all but Gloucester and Kent.*

GLOUCESTER   I am sorry for thee, friend; 'tis the Duke's pleasure,
  Whose disposition, all the world well knows,
  Will not be rubb'd nor stopp'd. I'll entreat for thee.

KENT   Pray, do not, sir. I have watched and travell'd hard;
  Some time I shall sleep out, the rest I'll whistle.
  A good man's fortune may grow out at heels.
  Give you good morrow!

GLOUCESTER   The Duke's to blame in this; 'twill be ill taken.   *Exit.*

KENT   Good King, that must approve the common saw,
  Thou out of heaven's benediction comest
  To the warm sun!
  Approach, thou beacon to this under globe,
  That by thy comfortable beams I may
  Peruse this letter! Nothing almost sees miracles
  But misery. I know 'tis from Cordelia,
  Who hath most fortunately been inform'd
  Of my obscured course; and [*Reads.*] "shall find time
  From this enormous state, seeking to give
  Losses their remedies." All weary and o'er-watch'd,
  Take vantage, heavy eyes, not to behold
  This shameful lodging.
  Fortune, good night. Smile once more; turn thy wheel!

Sleeps.

SCENE 3   *A wood.*

Enter Edgar.

EDGAR   I heard myself proclaim'd;
  And by the happy hollow of a tree
  Escaped the hunt. No port is free; no place
  That guard and most unusual vigilance
  Does not attend my taking. Whiles I may 'scape,
  I will preserve myself. And am bethought
  To take the basest and most poorest shape
  That ever penury, in contempt of man,
  Brought near to beast. My face I'll grime with filth;
  Blanket my loins; elf all my hair in knots;
  And with presented nakedness out-face
  The winds and persecutions of the sky.

439

The country gives me proof and precedent
Of Bedlam beggars, who, with roaring voices,
Strike in their numb'd and mortified bare arms
Pins, wooden pricks, nails, sprigs of rosemary;
And with this horrible object, from low farms,
Poor pelting villages, sheep-cotes, and mills,
Sometime with lunatic bans, sometime with prayers,
Enforce their charity. Poor Turlygod! poor Tom!
That's something yet. Edgar I nothing am. *Exit.*

SCENE 4 *Before Gloucester's castle. Kent in the stocks.*

Enter Lear, Fool, and Gentleman.

LEAR 'Tis strange that they should so depart from home,
And not send back my messenger.

GENTLEMAN   As I learn'd,
The night before there was no purpose in them
Of this remove.

KENT   Hail to thee, noble master!

LEAR Ha!
Makest thou this shame thy pastime?

KENT   No, my lord.

FOOL Ha, ha! he wears cruel garters. Horses are tied by the heads, dogs
and bears by the neck, monkeys by the loins, and men by the legs.
When a man's over-lusty at legs, then he wears wooden nether-stocks.

LEAR What's he that hath so much thy place mistook
To set thee here?

KENT   It is both he and she;
Your son and daughter.

LEAR No.

KENT Yes.

LEAR No, I say.

KENT I say, yea.

LEAR No, no, they would not.

440

KENT   Yes, they have.

LEAR   By Jupiter, I swear, no.

KENT   By Juno, I swear, ay.

LEAR   They durst not do't;
  They could not, would not do't; 'tis worse than murder,
  To do upon respect such violent outrage.
  Resolve me, with all modest haste, which way
  Thou mightst deserve, or they impose, this usage,
  Coming from us.

KENT   My lord, when at their home
  I did commend your Highness' letters to them,
  Ere I was risen from the place that show'd
  My duty kneeling, came there a reeking post,
  Stew'd in his haste, half breathless, panting forth
  From Goneril his mistress salutations;
  Deliver'd letters, spite of intermission,
  Which presently they read. On whose contents,
  They summon'd up their meiny, straight took horse;
  Commanded me to follow and attend
  The leisure of their answer; gave me cold looks;
  And meeting here the other messenger,
  Whose welcome, I perceived, had poison'd mine—
  Being the very fellow that of late
  Display'd so saucily against your Highness—
  Having more man than wit about me, drew.
  He raised the house with loud and coward cries.
  Your son and daughter found this trespass worth
  The shame which here it suffers.

FOOL   Winter's not gone yet, if the wild-geese fly that way.

        "Fathers that wear rags
          Do make their children blind;
        But fathers that bear bags
          Shall see their children kind.
        Fortune, that arrant whore,
          Ne'er turns the key to the poor."

But, for all this, thou shalt have as many dolours
For thy daughters as thou canst tell in a year.

LEAR   O, how this mother swells up toward my heart!

441

Hysterica passio, down, thou climbing sorrow,
Thy element's below! Where is this daughter?

KENT   With the Earl, sir, here within.

LEAR   Follow me not;
   Stay here.   *Exit.*

GENTLEMAN   Made you no more offence but what you speak of?

KENT   None.
   How chance the King comes with so small a train?

FOOL   An thou hadst been set i' the stocks for that question, thou hadst
   well deserved it.

KENT   Why, fool?

FOOL   We'll set thee to school to an ant, to teach thee there's no labouring i' the winter. All that follow their noses are led by their eyes but
   blind men; and there's not a nose among twenty but can smell him
   that's stinking. Let go thy hold when a great wheel runs down a hill,
   lest it break thy neck with following it; but the great one that goes up
   the hill, let him draw thee after. When a wise man gives thee better
   counsel, give me mine again. I would have none but knaves follow it,
   since a fool gives it.

> "That sir which serves and seeks for gain,
>   And follows but for form,
> Will pack when it begins to rain,
>   And leave thee in the storm.
> But I will tarry; the fool will stay,
>   And let the wise man fly.
> The knave turns fool that runs away;
>   The fool no knave, perdy."

KENT   Where learned you this, fool?

FOOL   Not i' the stocks, fool.

Re-enter Lear, with Gloucester.

LEAR   Deny to speak with me? They are sick? they are weary?
   They have travell'd all the night? Mere fetches;
   The images of revolt and flying off.
   Fetch me a better answer.

GLOUCESTER   My dear lord,

You know the fiery quality of the Duke;
How unremovable and fix'd he is
In his own course.

LEAR   Vengeance! plague! death! confusion!
Fiery? what quality? Why, Gloucester, Gloucester,
I'd speak with the Duke of Cornwall and his wife.

GLOUCESTER   Well, my good lord, I have inform'd them so.

LEAR   Inform'd them! Dost thou understand me, man?

GLOUCESTER   Ay, my good lord.

LEAR   The King would speak with Cornwall; the dear father
Would with his daughter speak, commands her service.
Are they "inform'd" of this? My breath and blood!
"Fiery"? the fiery Duke? Tell the hot Duke that—
No, but not yet; may be he is not well.
Infirmity doth still neglect all office
Whereto our health is bound; we are not ourselves
When nature, being oppress'd, commands the mind
To suffer with the body. I'll forbear;
And am fall'n out with my more headier will,
To take the indisposed and sickly fit
For the sound man. Death on my state! wherefore

Looking on Kent.

Should he sit here? This act persuades me
That this remotion of the Duke and her
Is practice only. Give me my servant forth.
Go tell the Duke and's wife I'd speak with them,
Now, presently. Bid them come forth and hear me,
Or at their chamber-door I'll beat the drum
Till it cry sleep to death.

GLOUCESTER   I would have all well betwixt you.   *Exit.*

LEAR   O me, my heart, my rising heart! but, down!

FOOL   Cry to it, nuncle, as the cockney did to the eels when she put 'em
i' the paste alive; she knapped 'em o' the coxcombs with a stick, and
cried, "Down, wantons, down!" 'Twas her brother that, in pure kindness to his horse, buttered his hay.

Enter Cornwall, Regan, Gloucester, and Servants.

443

LEAR   Good morrow to you both.

CORNWALL   Hail to your Grace!

Kent is set at liberty.

REGAN   I am glad to see your Highness.

LEAR   Regan, I think you are; I know what reason
I have to think so. If thou shouldst not be glad,
I would divorce me from thy mother's tomb,
Sepulchring an adultress. [*To Kent.*] O, are you free?
Some other time for that. Beloved Regan,
Thy sister's naught. O Regan, she hath tied
Sharp-tooth'd unkindness, like a vulture, here.

Points to his heart.

I can scarce speak to thee; thou'lt not believe
With how depraved a quality— O Regan!

REGAN   I pray you, sir, take patience. I have hope
You less know how to value her desert
Than she to scant her duty.

LEAR   Say, how is that?

REGAN   I cannot think my sister in the least
Would fail her obligation. If, sir, perchance
She have restrain'd the riots of your followers,
'Tis on such ground, and to such wholesome end,
As clears her from all blame.

LEAR   My curses on her!

REGAN   O, sir, you are old;
Nature in you stands on the very verge
Of her confine. You should be ruled and led
By some discretion that discerns your state
Better than you yourself. Therefore, I pray you
That to our sister you do make return;
Say you have wrong'd her, sir.

LEAR   Ask her forgiveness?
Do you but mark how this becomes the house:

Kneeling.

"Dear daughter, I confess that I am old;

444

Age is unnecessary. On my knees I beg
That you'll vouchsafe me raiment, bed, and food.''

REGAN   Good sir, no more; these are unsightly tricks.
Return you to my sister.

LEAR   [*Rising.*]   Never, Regan.
She hath abated me of half my train;
Look'd black upon me; struck me with her tongue,
Most serpent-like, upon the very heart.
All the stored vengeances of heaven fall
On her ingrateful top! Strike her young bones,
You taking airs, with lameness!

CORNWALL   Fie, sir, fie!

LEAR   You nimble lightnings, dart your blinding flames
Into her scornful eyes! Infect her beauty,
You fen-suck'd fogs, drawn by the powerful sun,
To fall and blast her pride!

REGAN   O the blest gods! so will you wish on me,
When the rash mood is on.

LEAR   No, Regan, thou shalt never have my curse.
Thy tender-hefted nature shall not give
Thee o'er to harshness. Her eyes are fierce; but thine
Do comfort and not burn. 'Tis not in thee
To grudge my pleasures, to cut off my train,
To bandy hasty words, to scant my sizes,
And in conclusion to oppose the bolt
Against my coming in. Thou better know'st
The offices of nature, bond of childhood,
Effects of courtesy, dues of gratitude;
Thy half o' the kingdom hast thou not forgot,
Wherein I thee endow'd.

REGAN   Good sir, to the purpose.

LEAR   Who put my man i' the stocks?

Tucket within.

CORNWALL   What trumpet's that?

445

REGAN   I know't, my sister's. This approves her letter,
 That she would soon be here.

Enter Oswald.

                                   Is your lady come?

LEAR   This is a slave, whose easy-borrow'd pride
 Dwells in the fickle grace of her he follows.
 Out, varlet, from my sight!

CORNWALL   What means your Grace?

LEAR   Who stock'd my servant? Regan, I have good hope
 Thou didst not know on't. Who comes here? O heavens.

Enter Goneril.

 If you do love old men, if your sweet sway
 Allow obedience, if yourselves are old,
 Make it your cause; send down, and take my part!
 [*To Goneril.*] Art not ashamed to look upon this beard?
 O Regan, wilt thou take her by the hand?

GONERIL   Why not by the hand, sir? How have I offended?
 All's not offence that indiscretion finds
 And dotage terms so.

LEAR   O sides, you are too tough;
 Will you yet hold? How came my man i' the stocks?

CORNWALL   I set him there, sir; but his own disorders
 Deserved much less advancement.

LEAR   You! did you?

REGAN   I pray you, father, being weak, seem so.
 If, till the expiration of your month,
 You will return and sojourn with my sister,
 Dismissing half your train, come then to me.
 I am now from home, and out of that provision
 Which shall be needful for your entertainment.

LEAR   Return to her, and fifty men dismiss'd?
 No, rather I abjure all roofs, and choose
 To wage against the enmity o' the air;
 To be a comrade with the wolf and owl—
 Necessity's sharp pinch! Return with her?

Why, the hot-blooded France, that dowerless took
Our youngest born, I could as well be brought
To knee his throne, and, squire-like, pension beg
To keep base life afoot. Return with her?
Persuade me rather to be slave and sumpter
To this detested groom.

Pointing at Oswald.

GONERIL   At your choice, sir.

LEAR   I prithee, daughter, do not make me mad.
I will not trouble thee, my child; farewell.
We'll no more meet, no more see one another.
But yet thou art my flesh, my blood, my daughter;
Or rather a disease that's in my flesh,
Which I must needs call mine; thou art a boil,
A plague-sore, an embossed carbuncle,
In my corrupted blood. But I'll not chide thee;
Let shame come when it will, I do not call it.
I do not bid the thunder-bearer shoot,
Nor tell tales of thee to high-judging Jove.
Mend when thou canst; be better at thy leisure.
I can be patient; I can stay with Regan,
I and my hundred knights.

REGAN   Not altogether so.
I look'd not for you yet, nor am provided
For your fit welcome. Give ear, sir, to my sister;
For those that mingle reason with your passion
Must be content to think you old, and so—
But she knows what she does.

LEAR   Is this well spoken?

REGAN   I dare avouch it, sir. What, fifty followers?
Is it not well? What should you need of more?
Yea, or so many, sith that both charge and danger
Speak 'gainst so great a number? How, in one house,
Should many people, under two commands,
Hold amity? 'Tis hard; almost impossible.

GONERIL   Why might not you, my lord, receive attendance
From those that she calls servants or from mine?

REGAN   Why not, my lord? If then they chanced to slack you,

447

We could control them. If you will come to me—
For now I spy a danger—I entreat you
To bring but five and twenty. To no more
Will I give place or notice.

LEAR   I gave you all—

REGAN   And in good time you gave it.

LEAR   Made you my guardians, my depositaries;
  But kept a reservation to be follow'd
  With such a number. What, must I come to you
  With five and twenty, Regan? said you so?

REGAN   And speak't again, my lord; no more with me.

LEAR   Those wicked creatures yet do look well-favour'd,
  When others are more wicked; not being the worst
  Stands in some rank of praise. [To Goneril.] I'll go with thee.
  Thy fifty yet doth double five and twenty,
  And thou art twice her love.

GONERIL   Hear me, my lord.
  What need you five and twenty, ten, or five,
  To follow in a house where twice so many
  Have a command to tend you?

REGAN   What need one?

LEAR   O, reason not the need. Our basest beggars
  Are in the poorest thing superfluous.
  Allow not nature more than nature needs,
  Man's life's as cheap as beast's. Thou art a lady;
  If only to go warm were gorgeous,
  Why, nature needs not what thou gorgeous wear'st,
  Which scarcely keeps thee warm. But, for true need—
  You heavens, give me that patience, patience I need!
  You see me here, you gods, a poor old man,
  As full of grief as age; wretched in both!
  If it be you that stirs these daughters' hearts
  Against their father, fool me not so much
  To bear it tamely; touch me with noble anger,
  And let not women's weapons, water-drops,
  Stain my man's cheeks! No, you unnatural hags,
  I will have such revenges on you both,
  That all the world shall—I will do such things—

448

What they are, yet I know not; but they shall be
The terrors of the earth. You think I'll weep;
No, I'll not weep.
I have full cause of weeping; but this heart
Shall break into a hundred thousand flaws,
Or ere I'll weep. O fool, I shall go mad!

                    Exeunt Lear, Gloucester, Kent, and Fool.

Storm and tempest.

CORNWALL   Let us withdraw; 'twill be a storm.

REGAN   This house is little. The old man and his people
  Cannot be well bestow'd.

GONERIL   'Tis his own blame; hath put himself from rest,
  And must needs taste his folly.

REGAN   For his particular, I'll receive him gladly,
  But not one follower.

GONERIL   So am I purposed.
  Where is my Lord of Gloucester?

CORNWALL   Follow'd the old man forth. He is return'd.

Re-enter Gloucester.

GLOUCESTER   The King is in high rage.

CORNWALL   Whither is he going?

GLOUCESTER   He calls to horse; but will I know not whither.

CORNWALL   'Tis best to give him way; he leads himself.

GONERIL   My lord, entreat him by no means to stay.

GLOUCESTER   Alack, the night comes on, and the bleak winds
  Do sorely ruffle; for many miles about
  There's scarce a bush.

REGAN   O, sir, to wilful men,
  The injuries that they themselves procure
  Must be their schoolmasters. Shut up your doors.
  He is attended with a desperate train;
  And what they may incense him to, being apt
  To have his ear abused, wisdom bids fear.

CORNWALL   Shut up your doors, my lord; 'tis a wild night;
  My Regan counsels well. Come out o' the storm.   *Exeunt.*

ACT III

❀ SCENE 1 *A heath.*

Storm still. Enter Kent and a Gentleman, meeting.

KENT   Who's there, besides foul weather?

GENTLEMAN   One minded like the weather, most unquietly.

KENT   I know you. Where's the King?

GENTLEMAN   Contending with the fretful elements;
  Bids the wind blow the earth into the sea,
  Or swell the curled waters 'bove the main,
  That things might change or cease; tears his white hair,
  Which the impetuous blasts, with eyeless rage,
  Catch in their fury, and make nothing of;
  Strives in his little world of man to out-scorn
  The to-and-fro-conflicting wind and rain.
  This night, wherein the cub-drawn bear would couch,
  The lion and the belly-pinched wolf
  Keep their fur dry, unbonneted he runs,
  And bids what will take all.

KENT   But who is with him?

GENTLEMAN   None but the fool; who labours to outjest
  His heart-struck injuries.

KENT   Sir, I do know you;
  And dare, upon the warrant of my note,
  Commend a dear thing to you. There is division,
  Although as yet the face of it be cover'd

450

With mutual cunning, 'twixt Albany and Cornwall;
Who have—as who have not, that their great stars
Throned and set high?—servants, who seem no less,
Which are to France the spies and speculations
Intelligent of our state; what hath been seen,
Either in snuffs and packings of the Dukes,
Or the hard rein which both of them have borne
Against the old kind King; or something deeper,
Whereof perchance these are but furnishings;
But, true it is, from France there comes a power
Into this scatter'd kingdom; who already,
Wise in our negligence, have secret feet
In some of our best ports, and are at point
To show their open banner. Now to you.
If on my credit you dare build so far
To make your speed to Dover, you shall find
Some that will thank you, making just report
Of how unnatural and bemadding sorrow
The King hath cause to plain.
I am a gentleman of blood and breeding;
And, from some knowledge and assurance, offer
This office to you.

GENTLEMAN   I will talk further with you.

KENT   No, do not.
For confirmation that I am much more
Than my out-wall, open this purse, and take
What it contains. If you shall see Cordelia—
As fear not but you shall—show her this ring;
And she will tell you who your fellow is
That yet you do not know. Fie on this storm!
I will go seek the King.

GENTLEMAN   Give me your hand. Have you no more to say?

KENT   Few words, but, to effect, more than all yet;
That, when we have found the King—in which your pain
That way, I'll this—he that first lights on him
Holla the other.   *Exeunt severally.*

451

SCENE 2 *Another part of the heath. Storm still.*

Enter Lear and Fool.

LEAR Blow, winds, and crack your cheeks! rage! blow!
You cataracts and hurricanoes, spout
Till you have drench'd our steeples, drown'd the cocks!
You sulphurous and thought-executing fires,
Vaunt-couriers to oak-cleaving thunderbolts,
Singe my white head! And thou, all-shaking thunder,
Smite flat the thick rotundity o' the world!
Crack nature's moulds, all germens spill at once,
That make ingrateful man!

FOOL O nuncle, court holy-water in a dry house is better than this rain-
water out o' door. Good nuncle, in, and ask thy daughters' blessing.
Here's a night pities neither wise man nor fool.

LEAR Rumble thy bellyful! Spit, fire! spout, rain!
Nor rain, wind, thunder, fire, are my daughters.
I tax not you, you elements, with unkindness;
I never gave you kingdom, call'd you children,
You owe me no subscription. Then let fall
Your horrible pleasure; here I stand, your slave,
A poor, infirm, weak, and despised old man:
But yet I call you servile ministers,
That have with two pernicious daughters join'd
Your high engender'd battles 'gainst a head
So old and white as this. O! O! 'tis foul!

FOOL He that has a house to put's head in has a good head-piece.

> "The cod-piece that will house
>   Before the head has any,
> The head and he shall louse;
>   So beggars marry many.
> The man that makes his toe
>   What he his heart should make
> Shall of a corn cry woe,
>   And turn his sleep to wake."

For there was never yet fair woman but she made mouths in a glass.

LEAR No, I will be the pattern of all patience; I will say nothing.

Enter Kent.

KENT   Who's there?

FOOL   Marry, here's grace and a cod-piece; that's a wise man and a fool.

KENT   Alas, sir, are you here? things that love night
Love not such nights as these; the wrathful skies
Gallow the very wanderers of the dark,
And make them keep their caves. Since I was man,
Such sheets of fire, such bursts of horrid thunder,
Such groans of roaring wind and rain, I never
Remember to have heard. Man's nature cannot carry
The affliction nor the fear.

LEAR   Let the great gods,
That keep this dreadful pother o'er our heads,
Find out their enemies now. Tremble, thou wretch,
That hast within thee undivulged crimes,
Unwhipp'd of justice. Hide thee, thou bloody hand;
Thou perjured, and thou simular man of virtue
That are incestuous. Caitiff, to pieces shake,
That under covert and convenient seeming
Hast practised on man's life. Close pent-up guilts,
Rive your concealing continents, and cry
These dreadful summoners grace. I am a man
More sinn'd against than sinning.

KENT   Alack, bare-headed!
Gracious my lord, hard by here is a hovel;
Some friendship will it lend you 'gainst the tempest.
Repose you there; while I to this hard house—
More harder than the stones whereof 'tis raised;
Which even but now, demanding after you,
Denied me to come in—return, and force
Their scanted courtesy.

LEAR   My wits begin to turn.
Come on, my boy. How dost, my boy? art cold?
I am cold myself. Where is this straw, my fellow?
The art of our necessities is strange,
That can make vile things precious. Come, your hovel.
Poor fool and knave, I have one part in my heart
That's sorry yet for thee.

FOOL   [Sings.]
            "He that has and a little tiny wit—

453

> With hey, ho, the wind and the rain—
> Must make content with his fortunes fit,
> For the rain it raineth every day."

LEAR   True, my good boy. Come, bring us to this hovel.

Exeunt Lear and Kent.

FOOL   This is a brave night to cool a courtesan. I'll speak a prophecy ere I
go:

> "When priests are more in word than matter;
> When brewers mar their malt with water;
> When nobles are their tailors' tutors;
> No heretics burn'd, but wenches' suitors;
> When every case in law is right;
> No squire in debt, nor no poor knight;
> When slanders do not live in tongues;
> Nor cutpurses come not to throngs;
> When usurers tell their gold i' the field;
> And bawds and whores do churches build;
> Then shall the realm of Albion
> Come to great confusion.
> Then comes the time, who lives to see't,
> That going shall be used with feet."

This prophecy Merlin shall make; for I live before his time.   *Exit.*

 SCENE 3   *Gloucester's castle.*

Enter Gloucester and Edmund.

GLOUCESTER   Alack, alack, Edmund, I like not this unnatural dealing.
When I desired their leave that I might pity him, they took from me
the use of mine own house; charged me, on pain of their perpetual displeasure, neither to speak of him, entreat for him, nor any way sustain
him.

EDMUND   Most savage and unnatural!

GLOUCESTER   Go to; say you nothing. There's a division betwixt the
Dukes; and a worse matter than that. I have received a letter this night;
'tis dangerous to be spoken; I have locked the letter in my closet. These
injuries the King now bears will be revenged home; there's part of a
power already footed. We must incline to the King. I will seek him,

and privily relieve him. Go you and maintain talk with the Duke, that my charity be not of him perceived. If he ask for me, I am ill and gone to bed. Though I die for it, as no less is threatened me, the King my old master must be relieved. There is some strange thing toward, Edmund; pray you, be careful. *Exit.*

EDMUND   This courtesy, forbid thee, shall the Duke
Instantly know; and of that letter too.
This seems a fair deserving, and must draw me
That which my father loses; no less than all.
The younger rises when the old doth fall.   *Exit.*

 SCENE 4   *The heath. Before a hovel.*

Enter Lear, Kent, and Fool.

KENT   Here is the place, my lord; good my lord, enter.
The tyranny of the open night's too rough
For nature to endure.

Storm still.

LEAR   Let me alone.

KENT   Good my lord, enter here.

LEAR   Wilt break my heart?

KENT   I had rather break mine own. Good my lord, enter.

LEAR   Thou think'st 'tis much that this contentious storm
Invades us to the skin. So 'tis to thee;
But where the greater malady is fix'd,
The lesser is scarce felt. Thou'dst shun a bear;
But if thy flight lay toward the raging sea,
Thou'dst meet the bear i' the mouth. When the mind's free,
The body's delicate. The tempest in my mind
Doth from my senses take all feeling else
Save what beats there. Filial ingratitude!
Is it not as this mouth should tear this hand
For lifting food to't? But I will punish home.
No, I will weep no more. In such a night
To shut me out! Pour on; I will endure.
In such a night as this! O Regan, Goneril!

455

Your old kind father, whose frank heart gave all—
O, that way madness lies; let me shun that;
No more of that.

KENT   Good my lord, enter here.

LEAR   Prithee, go in thyself; seek thine own ease.
This tempest will not give me leave to ponder
On things would hurt me more. But I'll go in.
[*To the Fool.*] In, boy; go first. You houseless poverty—
Nay, get thee in. I'll pray, and then I'll sleep.

The Fool goes in.

Poor naked wretches, wheresoe'er you are,
That bide the pelting of this pitiless storm,
How shall your houseless heads and unfed sides,
Your loop'd and window'd raggedness, defend you
From reasons such as these? O, I have ta'en
Too little care of this! Take physic, pomp;
Expose thyself to feel what wretches feel,
That thou mayst shake the superflux to them,
And show the heavens more just.

EDGAR   [*Within.*] Fathom and half, fathom and half! Poor Tom!

The Fool runs out from the hovel.

FOOL   Come not in here, nuncle, here's a spirit. Help me, help me!

KENT   Give me thy hand. Who's there?

FOOL   A spirit, a spirit. He says his name's poor Tom.

KENT   What art thou that dost grumble there i' the straw? Come forth.

Enter Edgar disguised as a madman.

EDGAR   Away! the foul fiend follows me!
Through the sharp hawthorn blows the cold wind.
Hum! go to thy cold bed and warm thee.

LEAR   Hast thou given all to thy two daughters? And art thou come to this?

EDGAR   Who gives anything to poor Tom? whom the foul fiend hath led through fire and through flame, through ford and whirlpool, o'er bog and quagmire; that hath laid knives under his pillow, and halters in his

456

pew; set ratsbane by his porridge; made him proud of heart, to ride on a bay trotting-horse over four-inched bridges, to course his own shadow for a traitor. Bless thy five wits! Tom's a-cold—O, do de, do de, do de. Bless thee from whirlwinds, star-blasting and taking! Do poor Tom some charity, whom the foul fiend vexes. There could I have him now—and there—and there again, and there.

Storm still.

LEAR   What, have his daughters brought him to this pass?
Couldst thou save nothing? Didst thou give them all?

FOOL   Nay, he reserved a blanket, else we had been all shamed.

LEAR   Now, all the plagues that in the pendulous air
Hang fated o'er men's faults light on thy daughters!

KENT   He hath no daughters, sir.

LEAR   Death, traitor! nothing could have subdued nature
To such a lowness but his unkind daughters.
Is it the fashion, that discarded fathers
Should have thus little mercy on their flesh?
Judicious punishment! 'twas this flesh begot
Those pelican daughters.

EDGAR   "Pillicock sat on Pillicock-hill.
                      Halloo, halloo, loo, loo!"

FOOL   This cold night will turn us all to fools and madmen.

EDGAR   Take heed o' the foul fiend. Obey thy parents; keep thy word justly; swear not; commit not with man's sworn spouse; set not thy sweet heart on proud array. Tom's a-cold.

LEAR   What hast thou been?

EDGAR   A serving-man, proud in heart and mind; that curled my hair; wore gloves in my cap; served the lust of my mistress' heart, and did the act of darkness with her; swore as many oaths as I spake words, and broke them in the sweet face of heaven: one that slept in the contriving of lust, and waked to do it. Wine loved I deeply, dice dearly; and in woman out-paramoured the Turk: false of heart, light of ear, bloody of hand; hog in sloth, fox in stealth, wolf in greediness, dog in madness, lion in prey. Let the creaking of shoes nor the rustling of silks betray thy poor heart to woman. Keep thy foot out of brothels, thy hand out of plackets, thy pen from lenders' books, and defy the foul

457

fiend. Still through the hawthorn blows the cold wind; says suum, mun, ha, no, nonny. Dolphin my boy, my boy, sessa! let him trot by.

Storm still.

LEAR   Why, thou wert better in thy grave than to answer with thy uncovered body this extremity of the skies. Is man no more than this? Consider him well. Thou owest the worm no silk, the beast no hide, the sheep no wool, the cat no perfume. Ha! here's three on's are sophisticated! Thou art the thing itself. Unaccommodated man is no more but such a poor, bare, forked animal as thou art. Off, off, you lendings! come, unbutton here.

Tearing off his clothes.

FOOL   Prithee, nuncle, be contented; 'tis a naughty night to swim in. Now a little fire in a wild field were like an old lecher's heart; a small spark, all the rest on's body cold. Look, here comes a walking fire.

Enter Gloucester, with a torch.

EDGAR   This is the foul fiend Flibbertigibbet. He begins at curfew, and walks till the first cock; he gives the web and the pin, squints the eye, and makes the hare-lip; mildews the white wheat, and hurts the poor creature of earth.

> "Swithold footed thrice the old;
>   He met the night-mare, and her nine-fold;
>   Bid her alight,
>   And her troth plight,
>   And, aroint thee, witch, aroint thee!"

KENT   How fares your Grace?

LEAR   What's he?

KENT   Who's there? What is't you seek?

GLOUCESTER   What are you there? Your names?

EDGAR   Poor Tom; that eats the swimming frog, the toad, the tadpole, the wall-newt, and the water; that in the fury of his heart, when the foul fiend rages, eats cow-dung for sallets; swallows the old rat and the ditch-dog; drinks the green mantle of the standing pool; who is whipped from tithing to tithing, and stock-punished, and imprisoned; who hath had three suits to his back, six shirts to his body, horse to ride, and weapon to wear:

"But mice and rats, and such small deer,
   Have been Tom's food for seven long year."

Beware my follower. Peace, Smulkin; peace, thou fiend!

GLOUCESTER   What, hath your Grace no better company?

EDGAR   The prince of darkness is a gentleman. Modo he's call'd, and
Mahu.

GLOUCESTER   Our flesh and blood is grown so vile, my lord,
   That it doth hate what gets it.

EDGAR   Poor Tom's a-cold.

GLOUCESTER   Go in with me; my duty cannot suffer
   To obey in all your daughters' hard commands.
   Though their injunction be to bar my doors,
   And let this tyrannous night take hold upon you,
   Yet have I ventured to come seek you out,
   And bring you where both fire and food is ready.

LEAR   First let me talk with this philosopher.
   What is the cause of thunder?

KENT   Good my lord, take his offer; go into the house.

LEAR   I'll talk a word with this same learned Theban.
   What is your study?

EDGAR   How to prevent the fiend, and to kill vermin.

LEAR   Let me ask you one word in private.

KENT   Importune him once more to go, my lord;
   His wits begin to unsettle.

GLOUCESTER   Canst thou blame him?

Storm still.

His daughters seek his death. Ah, that good Kent!
He said it would be thus, poor banish'd man!
Thou say'st the King grows mad; I'll tell thee, friend,
I am almost mad myself. I had a son,
Now outlaw'd from my blood; he sought my life,
But lately, very late. I loved him, friend;
No father his son dearer. Truth to tell thee,

459

The grief hath crazed my wits. What a night's this!
I do beseech your Grace—

LEAR   O, cry you mercy, sir.
Noble philosopher, your company.

EDGAR   Tom's a-cold.

GLOUCESTER   In, fellow, there, into the hovel. Keep thee warm.

LEAR   Come, let's in all.

KENT   This way, my lord.

LEAR   With him;
I will keep still with my philosopher.

KENT   Good my lord, soothe him; let him take the fellow.

GLOUCESTER   Take him you on.

KENT   Sirrah, come on; go along with us.

LEAR   Come, good Athenian.

GLOUCESTER   No words, no words; hush.

EDGAR   "Child Rowland to the dark tower came,
               His word was still, 'Fie, foh, and fum,
               I smell the blood of a British man.'"   *Exeunt.*

SCENE 5   *Gloucester's castle.*

Enter Cornwall and Edmund.

CORNWALL   I will have my revenge ere I depart his house.

EDMUND   How, my lord, I may be censured that nature thus gives way
to loyalty, something fears me to think of.

CORNWALL   I now perceive, it was not altogether your brother's evil disposition made him seek his death; but a provoking merit, set a-work
by a reprovable badness in himself.

EDMUND   How malicious is my fortune that I must repent to be just! this
is the letter he spoke of, which approves him an intelligent party to the
advantages of France. O heavens! that this treason were not, or not I
the detector!

CORNWALL   Go with me to the Duchess.

460

EDMUND   If the matter of this paper be certain, you have mighty business in hand.

CORNWALL   True or false, it hath made thee Earl of Gloucester. Seek out where thy father is, that he may be ready for our apprehension.

EDMUND   [*Aside.*] If I find him comforting the King, it will stuff his suspicion more fully. I will persevere in my course of loyalty, though the conflict be sore between that and my blood.

CORNWALL   I will lay trust upon thee; and thou shalt find a dearer father in my love.   *Exeunt.*

SCENE 6   *A chamber in a farmhouse adjoining the castle.*

Enter Gloucester, Lear, Kent, Fool, and Edgar.

GLOUCESTER   Here is better than the open air; take it thankfully. I will piece out the comfort with what addition I can. I will not be long from you.

KENT   All the power of his wits have given way to his impatience. The gods reward your kindness!   *Exit Gloucester.*

EDGAR   Frateretto calls me; and tells me Nero is an angler in the lake of darkness. Pray, innocent, and beware the foul fiend.

FOOL   Prithee, nuncle, tell me whether a madman be a gentleman or a yeoman?

LEAR   A king, a king!

FOOL   No, he's a yeoman that has a gentleman to his son; for he's a mad yeoman that sees his son a gentleman before him.

LEAR   To have a thousand with red burning spits
Come hissing in upon 'em—

EDGAR   The foul fiend bites my back.

FOOL   He's mad that trusts in the tameness of a wolf, a horse's health, a boy's love, or a whore's oath.

LEAR   It shall be done; I will arraign them straight.
[*To Edgar.*] Come, sit thou here, most learned justicer;
[*To the Fool.*] Thou, sapient sir, sit here. Now, you she foxes!

461

EDGAR   Look, where he stands and glares!
Wantest thou eyes at trial, madam? [*Sings.*]

"Come o'er the bourn, Bessy, to me."

FOOL   [*Sings.*]
"Her boat hath a leak,
    And she must not speak
Why she dares not come over to thee."

EDGAR   The foul fiend haunts poor Tom in the voice of a nightingale.
Hopdance cries in Tom's belly for two white herring. Croak not, black
angel; I have no food for thee.

KENT   How do you, sir? Stand you not so amazed.
Will you lie down and rest upon the cushions?

LEAR   I'll see their trial first. Bring in the evidence.
[*To Edgar.*] Thou robed man of justice, take thy place;
[*To the Fool.*] And thou, his yoke-fellow of equity,
Bench by his side. [*To Kent.*] You are o' the commission,
Sit you too.

EDGAR   Let us deal justly. [*Sings.*]

"Sleepest or wakest thou, jolly shepherd?
    Thy sheep be in the corn;
And for one blast of thy minikin mouth,
    Thy sheep shall take no harm."

Pur! the cat is gray.

LEAR   Arraign her first; 'tis Goneril. I here take my oath before this honourable assembly, she kicked the poor King her father.

FOOL   Come hither, mistress. Is your name Goneril?

LEAR   She cannot deny it.

FOOL   Cry you mercy, I took you for a joint-stool.

LEAR   And here's another, whose warp'd looks proclaim
What store her heart is made on. Stop her there!
Arms, arms, sword, fire! Corruption in the place!
False justicer, why hast thou let her 'scape?

EDGAR   Bless thy five wits!

KENT   O pity! Sir, where is the patience now
  That you so oft have boasted to retain?

EDGAR   [*Aside.*] My tears begin to take his part so much,
  They'll mar my counterfeiting.

LEAR   The little dogs and all,
  Tray, Blanch, and Sweetheart, see, they bark at me.

EDGAR   Tom will throw his head at them. Avaunt, you curs!

        "Be thy mouth or black or white,
         Tooth that poisons if it bite;
         Mastiff, greyhound, mongrel grim,
         Hound or spaniel, brach or lym,
         Or bobtail tike or trundle-tail,
         Tom will make them weep and wail;
         For, with throwing thus my head,
         Dogs leap the hatch, and all are fled."

Do de, de, de. Sessa! come, march to wakes and fairs and market-
towns. Poor Tom, thy horn is dry.

LEAR   Then let them anatomize Regan; see what breeds about her heart.
Is there any cause in nature that makes these hard hearts? [*To Edgar.*]
You, sir, I entertain for one of my hundred; only I do not like the fashion of your garments. You will say they are Persian attire; but let them
be changed.

KENT   Now, good my lord, lie here and rest awhile.

LEAR   Make no noise, make no noise; draw the curtains; so, so, so. We'll
go to supper i' the morning. So, so, so.

FOOL   And I'll go to bed at noon.

Re-enter Gloucester.

GLOUCESTER   Come hither, friend; where is the King my master?

KENT   Here, sir; but trouble him not, his wits are gone.

GLOUCESTER   Good friend, I prithee, take him in thy arms;
  I have o'erheard a plot of death upon him.
  There is a litter ready; lay him in't,
  And drive towards Dover, friend, where thou shalt meet
  Both welcome and protection. Take up thy master.
  If thou shouldst dally half an hour, his life,

With thine and all that offer to defend him,
Stand in assured loss. Take up, take up;
And follow me, that will to some provision
Give thee quick conduct.

KENT   Oppressed nature sleeps.
  This rest might yet have balm'd thy broken sinews,
  Which, if convenience will not allow,
  Stand in hard cure. [*To the Fool.*] Come, help to bear thy master:
  Thou must not stay behind.

GLOUCESTER   Come, come, away.
                                                                    Exeunt all but Edgar.

EDGAR   When we our betters see bearing our woes,
  We scarcely think our miseries our foes.
  Who alone suffers, suffers most i' the mind.
  Leaving free things and happy shows behind;
  But then the mind much sufferance doth o'erskip,
  When grief hath mates, and bearing fellowship.
  How light and portable my pain seems now,
  When that which makes me bend makes the King bow,
  He childed as I father'd! Tom, away!
  Mark the high noises; and thyself bewray,
  When false opinion, whose wrong thought defiles thee,
  In thy just proof, repeals and reconciles thee.
  What will hap more to-night, safe 'scape the King!
  Lurk, lurk.   *Exit.*

SCENE 7   *Gloucester's castle.*

Enter Cornwall, Regan, Goneril, Edmund, and Servants.

CORNWALL   Post speedily to my lord your husband; show him this letter.
  The army of France is landed. Seek out the villain Gloucester.
                                                        Exeunt some of the Servants.

REGAN   Hang him instantly.

GONERIL   Pluck out his eyes.

CORNWALL   Leave him to my displeasure. Edmund, keep you our sister
  company. The revenges we are bound to take upon your traitorous father are not fit for your beholding. Advise the Duke, where you are
  going, to a most festinate preparation; we are bound to the like. Our

posts shall be swift and intelligent betwixt us. Farewell, dear sister; farewell, my Lord of Gloucester.

Enter Oswald.

How now! where's the King?

OSWALD   My Lord of Gloucester hath convey'd him hence.
Some five or six and thirty of his knights,
Hot questrists after him, met him at gate;
Who, with some other of the lord's dependants,
Are gone with him towards Dover; where they boast
To have well-armed friends.

CORNWALL   Get horses for your mistress.

GONERIL   Farewell, sweet lord, and sister.

CORNWALL   Edmund, farewell.   *Exeunt Goneril, Edmund, and Oswald.*
                              Go seek the traitor Gloucester,
Pinion him like a thief, bring him before us.   *Exeunt other Servants.*
Though well we may not pass upon his life
Without the form of justice, yet our power
Shall do a courtesy to our wrath, which men
May blame, but not control. Who's there? the traitor?

Enter Gloucester, brought in by two or three Servants.

REGAN   Ingrateful fox! 'tis he.

CORNWALL   Bind fast his corky arms.

GLOUCESTER   What mean your Graces? Good my friends, consider
You are my guests. Do me no foul play, friends.

CORNWALL   Bind him, I say.

Servants bind him.

REGAN   Hard, hard. O filthy traitor!

GLOUCESTER   Unmerciful lady as you are, I'm none.

CORNWALL   To this chair bind him. Villain, thou shalt find —

Regan plucks his beard.

GLOUCESTER   By the kind gods, 'tis most ignobly done
To pluck me by the beard.

REGAN   So white, and such a traitor!

GLOUCESTER   Naughty lady,
  These hairs, which thou dost ravish from my chin,
  Will quicken, and accuse thee. I am your host.
  With robbers' hands my hospitable favours
  You should not ruffle thus. What will you do?

CORNWALL   Come, sir, what letters had you late from France?

REGAN   Be simple answerer, for we know the truth.

CORNWALL   And what confederacy have you with the traitors
  Late footed in the kingdom?

REGAN   To whose hands have you sent the lunatic King?
  Speak.

GLOUCESTER   I have a letter guessingly set down,
  Which came from one that's of a neutral heart,
  And not from one opposed.

CORNWALL   Cunning.

REGAN   And false.

CORNWALL   Where hast thou sent the King?

GLOUCESTER   To Dover.

REGAN   Wherefore to Dover? Wast thou not charged at peril—

CORNWALL   Wherefore to Dover? Let him first answer that.

GLOUCESTER   I am tied to the stake, and I must stand the course.

REGAN   Wherefore to Dover, sir?

GLOUCESTER   Because I would not see thy cruel nails
  Pluck out his poor old eyes; nor thy fierce sister
  In his anointed flesh stick boarish fangs.
  The sea, with such a storm as his bare head
  In hell-black night endured, would have bouy'd up,
  And quench'd the stelled fires;
  Yet, poor old heart, he holp the heavens to rain.
  If wolves had at thy gate howl'd that stern time,
  Thou shouldst have said, "Good porter, turn the key,"
  All cruels else subscribed; but I shall see
  The winged vengeance overtake such children.

CORNWALL   See't shalt thou never. Fellows, hold the chair.
　　Upon these eyes of thine I'll set my foot.

GLOUCESTER   He that will think to live till he be old,
　　Give me some help! O cruel! O you gods!

REGAN   One side will mock another; the other too.

CORNWALL   If you see vengeance—

FIRST SERVANT　　　　　　　　Hold your hand, my lord.
　　I have served you ever since I was a child;
　　But better service have I never done you
　　Than now to bid you hold.

REGAN　　　　　　　　　　How now, you dog!

FIRST SERVANT   If you did wear a beard upon your chin,
　　I'd shake it on this quarrel. What do you mean?

CORNWALL   My villain!

They draw and fight.

FIRST SERVANT   Nay, then, come on, and take the chance of anger.

REGAN   Give me thy sword. A peasant stand up thus!

Takes a sword, and runs at him behind.

FIRST SERVANT   O, I am slain! My lord, you have one eye left
　　To see some mischief on him. O!　　　　　　　*Dies.*

CORNWALL   Lest it see more, prevent it. Out, vile jelly!
　　Where is thy lustre now?

GLOUCESTER   All dark and comfortless. Where's my son Edmund?
　　Edmund, enkindle all the sparks of nature,
　　To quit this horrid act.

REGAN　　　　　　　　　Out, treacherous villain!
　　Thou call'st on him that hates thee. It was he
　　That made the overture of thy treasons to us;
　　Who is too good to pity thee.

GLOUCESTER   O my follies! then Edgar was abused.
　　Kind gods, forgive me that, and prosper him!

467

REGAN   Go thrust him out at gates, and let him smell
   His way to Dover.   *Exit one Servant with Gloucester.*
                        How is't, my lord? how look you?

CORNWALL   I have received a hurt. Follow me, lady.
   Turn out that eyeless villain; throw this slave
   Upon the dunghill. Regan, I bleed apace.
   Untimely comes this hurt; give me your arm.
                                    Exit Cornwall, led by Regan.

SECOND SERVANT   I'll never care what wickedness I do,
   If this man come to good.

THIRD SERVANT   If she live long,
   And in the end meet the old course of death,
   Women will all turn monsters.

SECOND SERVANT   Let's follow the old Earl, and get the Bedlam
   To lead him where he would. His roguish madness
   Allows itself to anything.

THIRD SERVANT   Go thou. I'll fetch some flax and whites of eggs
   To apply to his bleeding face. Now, Heaven help him!
                                        Exeunt severally.

ACT IV

❧ SCENE 1 *The heath.*

Enter Edgar.

EDGAR Yet better thus, and known to be contemn'd,
Than still contemn'd and flatter'd. To be worst,
The lowest and most dejected thing of fortune,
Stands still in esperance, lives not in fear.
The lamentable change is from the best;
The worst returns to laughter. Welcome, then,
Thou unsubstantial air that I embrace!
The wretch that thou hast blown unto the worst
Owes nothing to thy blasts. But who comes here?

Enter Gloucester, led by an Old Man.

My father, poorly led? World, world, O world!
But that thy strange mutations make us hate thee,
Life would not yield to age.

OLD MAN O, my good lord, I have been your tenant, and your father's
tenant, these fourscore years.

GLOUCESTER Away, get thee away; good friend, be gone.
Thy comforts can do me no good at all;
Thee they may hurt.

OLD MAN Alack, sir, you cannot see your way.

GLOUCESTER I have no way, and therefore want no eyes;
I stumbled when I saw. Full oft 'tis seen,
Our means secure us, and our mere defects

Prove our commodities. O dear son Edgar,
The food of thy abused father's wrath!
Might I but live to see thee in my touch,
I'd say I had eyes again!

OLD MAN   How now! Who's there?

EDGAR   [*Aside.*] O gods! Who is't can say, "I am at the worst"?
I am worse than e'er I was.

OLD MAN   'Tis poor mad Tom.

EDGAR   [*Aside.*] And worse I may be yet; the worst is not
So long as we can say, "This is the worst."

OLD MAN   Fellow, where goest?

GLOUCESTER   Is it a beggar-man?

OLD MAN   Madman and beggar too.

GLOUCESTER   He has some reason, else he could not beg.
I' the last night's storm I such a fellow saw;
Which made me think a man a worm. My son
Came then into my mind; and yet my mind
Was then scarce friends with him. I have heard more since.
As flies to wanton boys, are we to the gods,
They kill us for their sport.

EDGAR   [*Aside.*]   How should this be?
Bad is the trade that must play fool to sorrow,
Angering itself and others. Bless thee, master!

GLOUCESTER   Is that the naked fellow?

OLD MAN   Ay, my lord.

GLOUCESTER   Then, prithee, get thee gone. If, for my sake,
Thou wilt o'ertake us, hence a mile or twain,
I' the way toward Dover, do it for ancient love;
And bring some covering for this naked soul,
Who I'll entreat to lead me.

OLD MAN   Alack, sir, he is mad.

GLOUCESTER   'Tis the times' plague, when madmen lead the blind.
Do as I bid thee, or rather do thy pleasure;
Above the rest, be gone.

470

OLD MAN   I'll bring him the best 'parel that I have,
Come on't what will.   *Exit.*

GLOUCESTER   Sirrah, naked fellow—

EDGAR   Poor Tom's a-cold. [*Aside.*] I cannot daub it further.

GLOUCESTER   Come hither, fellow.

EDGAR   [*Aside.*] And yet I must. Bless thy sweet eyes, they bleed.

GLOUCESTER   Know'st thou the way to Dover?

EDGAR   Both stile and gate, horse-way and foot-path. Poor Tom hath
been scared out of his good wits. Bless thee, good man's son, from the
foul fiend! five fiends have been in poor Tom at once; of lust, as Obidi-
cut; Hobbididance, prince of dumbness; Mahu, of stealing; Modo, of
murder; Flibbertigibbet, of mopping and mowing, who since possesses chambermaids and waiting-women. So, bless thee, master!

GLOUCESTER   Here, take this purse, thou whom the heavens' plagues
Have humbled to all strokes. That I am wretched
Makes thee the happier. Heavens, deal so still!
Let the superfluous and lust-dieted man,
That slaves your ordinance, that will not see
Because he doth not feel, feel your power quickly;
So distribution should undo excess,
And each man have enough. Dost thou know Dover?

EDGAR   Ay, master.

GLOUCESTER   There is a cliff, whose high and bending head
Looks fearfully in the confined deep.
Bring me but to the very brim of it,
And I'll repair the misery thou dost bear
With something rich about me. From that place
I shall no leading need.

EDGAR   Give me thy arm:
Poor Tom shall lead thee.   *Exeunt.*

❧ SCENE 2   *Before the Duke of Albany's palace.*

Enter Goneril and Edmund.

GONERIL   Welcome, my lord. I marvel our mild husband
Not met us on the way.

471

Enter Oswald.

Now, where's your master?

OSWALD Madam, within; but never man so changed.
I told him of the army that was landed;
He smiled at it. I told him you were coming;
His answer was, "The worse"; of Gloucester's treachery,
And of the loyal service of his son,
When I inform'd him, then he call'd me sot,
And told me I had turn'd the wrong side out.
What most he should dislike seems pleasant to him;
What like, offensive.

GONERIL [*To Edmund.*] Then shall you go no further.
It is the cowish terror of his spirit,
That dares not undertake. He'll not feel wrongs
Which tie him to an answer. Our wishes on the way
May prove effects. Back, Edmund, to my brother;
Hasten his musters and conduct his powers.
I must change arms at home, and give the distaff
Into my husband's hands. This trusty servant
Shall pass between us. Ere long you are like to hear,
If you dare venture in your own behalf,
A mistress's command. Wear this; spare speech;

Giving a favour.

Decline your head. This kiss, if it durst speak,
Would stretch thy spirits up into the air.
Conceive, and fare thee well.

EDMUND Yours in the ranks of death.

GONERIL   My most dear Gloucester!
                                             Exit Edmund.

O, the difference of man and man!
To thee a woman's services are due;
My fool usurps my body.

OSWALD   Madam, here comes my lord.   *Exit.*

Enter Albany.

GONERIL I have been worth the whistle.

472

ALBANY   O Goneril!
You are not worth the dust which the rude wind
Blows in your face. I fear your disposition.
That nature, which contemns it origin,
Cannot be border'd certain in itself;
She that herself will sliver and disbranch
From her material sap, perforce must wither
And come to deadly use.

GONERIL   No more; the text is foolish.

ALBANY   Wisdom and goodness to the vile seem vile;
Filths savour but themselves. What have you done?
Tigers, not daughters, what have you perform'd?
A father, and a gracious aged man,
Whose reverence even the head-lugg'd bear would lick,
Most barbarous, most degenerate! have you madded.
Could my good brother suffer you to do it?
A man, a prince, by him so benefited!
If that the heavens do not their visible spirits
Send quickly down to tame these vile offences,
It will come,
Humanity must perforce prey on itself,
Like monsters of the deep.

GONERIL   Milk-liver'd man!
That bear'st a cheek for blows, a head for wrongs;
Who hast not in thy brows an eye discerning
Thine honour from thy suffering; that not know'st
Fools do those villains pity who are punish'd
Ere they have done their mischief. Where's thy drum?
France spreads his banners in our noiseless land,
With plumed helm thy state begins to threat;
Whiles thou, a moral fool, sit'st still, and criest,
"Alack, why does he so?"

ALBANY   See thyself, devil!
Proper deformity seems not in the fiend
So horrid as in woman.

GONERIL   O vain fool!

ALBANY   Thou changed and self-cover'd thing, for shame,
Be-monster not thy feature. Were't my fitness

473

To let these hands obey my blood,
They are apt enough to dislocate and tear
Thy flesh and bones. Howe'er thou art a fiend,
A woman's shape doth shield thee.

GONERIL   Marry, your manhood now —

Enter a Messenger.

ALBANY   What news?

MESSENGER   O, my good lord, the Duke of Cornwall's dead;
Slain by his servant, going to put out
The other eye of Gloucester.

ALBANY   Gloucester's eyes!

MESSENGER   A servant that he bred, thrill'd with remorse,
Opposed against the act, bending his sword
To his great master; who, thereat enraged,
Flew on him, and amongst them fell'd him dead;
But not without that harmful stroke, which since
Hath pluck'd him after.

ALBANY   This shows you are above,
You justicers, that these our nether crimes
So speedily can venge! But, O poor Gloucester!
Lost he his other eye?

MESSENGER   Both, both, my lord.
This letter, madam, craves a speedy answer;
'Tis from your sister.

GONERIL   [*Aside.*] One way I like this well;
But being widow, and my Gloucester with her,
May all the building in my fancy pluck
Upon my hateful life; another way,
The news is not so tart. I'll read, and answer.   *Exit.*

ALBANY   Where was his son when they did take his eyes?

MESSENGER   Come with my lady hither.

ALBANY   He is not here.

MESSENGER   No, my good lord; I met him back again.

ALBANY   Knows he the wickedness?

474

MESSENGER   Ay, my good lord; 'twas he inform'd against him;
And quit the house on purpose, that their punishment
Might have the freer course.

ALBANY   Gloucester, I live
To thank thee for the love thou show'dst the King,
And to revenge thine eyes. Come hither, friend.
Tell me what more thou know'st.   *Exeunt.*

❧ SCENE 3   *The French camp near Dover.*

Enter Kent and a Gentleman.

KENT   Why the King of France is so suddenly gone back know you the
reason?

GENTLEMAN   Something he left imperfect in the state, which since his
coming forth is thought of; which imports to the kingdom so much
fear and danger, that his personal return was most required and necessary.

KENT   Who hath he left behind him general?

GENTLEMAN   The Marshal of France, Monsieur La Far.

KENT   Did your letters pierce the Queen to any demonstration of grief?

GENTLEMAN   Ay, sir; she took them, read them in my presence;
And now and then an ample tear trill'd down
Her delicate cheek. It seem'd she was a queen
Over her passion; who, most rebel-like,
Sought to be king o'er her.

KENT   O, then it moved her.

GENTLEMAN   Not to a rage: patience and sorrow strove
Who should express her goodliest. You have seen
Sunshine and rain at once: her smiles and tears
Were like a better way; those happy smilets,
That play'd on her ripe lip, seem'd not to know
What guests were in her eyes; which parted thence,
As pearls from diamonds dropp'd. In brief,
Sorrow would be a rarity most beloved,
If all could so become it.

KENT   Made she no verbal question?

475

GENTLEMAN   'Faith, once or twice she heaved the name of "father"
   Pantingly forth, as if it press'd her heart;
   Cried "Sisters! sisters! Shame of ladies! sisters!
   Kent! father! sisters! What, i' the storm? i' the night?
   Let pity not be believed!" There she shook
   The holy water from her heavenly eyes,
   And clamour moisten'd; then away she started
   To deal with grief alone.

KENT   It is the stars,
   The stars above us, govern our conditions;
   Else one self mate and mate could not beget
   Such different issues. You spoke not with her since?

GENTLEMAN   No.

KENT   Was this before the King returned?

GENTLEMAN   No, since.

KENT   Well, sir, the poor distressed Lear's i' the town;
   Who sometime, in his better tune, remembers
   What we are come about, and by no means
   Will yield to see his daughter.

GENTLEMAN   Why, good sir?

KENT   A sovereign shame so elbows him. His own unkindness,
   That stripp'd her from his benediction, turn'd her
   To foreign casualties, gave her dear rights
   To his dog-hearted daughters, these things sting
   His mind so venomously, that burning shame
   Detains him from Cordelia.

GENTLEMAN   Alack, poor gentleman!

KENT   Of Albany's and Cornwall's powers you heard not?

GENTLEMAN   'Tis so, they are afoot.

KENT   Well, sir, I'll bring you to our master Lear,
   And leave you to attend him. Some dear cause
   Will in concealment wrap me up awhile;
   When I am known aright, you shall not grieve
   Lending me this acquaintance. I pray you, go
   Along with me.   *Exeunt.*

❧ SCENE 4   *The same. A tent.*

Enter, with drum and colours, Cordelia, Doctor, and Soldiers.

CORDELIA   Alack, 'tis he. Why, he was met even now
  As mad as the vex'd sea; singing aloud;
  Crown'd with rank fumiter and furrow-weeds,
  With bur-docks, hemlock, nettles, cuckoo-flowers,
  Darnel, and all the idle weeds that grow
  In our sustaining corn. A century send forth;
  Search every acre in the high-grown field,
  And bring him to our eye.   *Exit an Officer.*
                   What can man's wisdom
  In the restoring his bereaved sense?
  He that helps him take all my outward worth.

DOCTOR   There is means, madam.
  Our foster-nurse of nature is repose,
  The which he lacks; that to provoke in him,
  Are many simples operative, whose power
  Will close the eye of anguish.

CORDELIA   All blest secrets,
  All you unpublish'd virtues of the earth,
  Spring with my tears! be aidant and remediate
  In the good man's distress! Seek, seek for him;
  Lest his ungovern'd rage dissolve the life
  That wants the means to lead it.

Enter a Messenger.

MESSENGER   News, madam;
  The British powers are marching hitherward.

CORDELIA   'Tis known before; our preparation stands
  In expectation of them. O dear father,
  It is thy business that I go about;
  Therefore great France
  My mourning and important tears hath pitied.
  No blown ambition doth our arms incite,
  But love, dear love, and our aged father's right.
  Soon may I hear and see him!   *Exeunt.*

❧ SCENE 5 *Gloucester's castle.*

Enter Regan and Oswald.

REGAN   But are my brother's powers set forth?

OSWALD   Ay, madam.

REGAN   Himself in person there?

OSWALD   Madam, with much ado.
Your sister is the better soldier.

REGAN   Lord Edmund spake not with your lord at home?

OSWALD   No, madam.

REGAN   What might import my sister's letter to him?

OSWALD   I know not, lady.

REGAN   'Faith, he is posted hence on serious matter.
It was great ignorance, Gloucester's eyes being out,
To let him live; where he arrives he moves
All hearts against us. Edmund, I think, is gone,
In pity of his misery, to dispatch
His nighted life, moreover, to descry
The strength o' the enemy.

OSWALD   I must needs after him, madam, with my letter.

REGAN   Our troops set forth to-morrow. Stay with us;
The ways are dangerous.

OSWALD   I may not, madam.
My lady charged my duty in this business.

REGAN   Why should she write to Edmund? Might not you
Transport her purposes by word? Belike,
Something—I know not what. I'll love thee much,
Let me unseal the letter.

OSWALD   Madam, I had rather—

REGAN   I know your lady does not love her husband;
I am sure of that. And at her late being here
She gave strange oeillades and most speaking looks
To noble Edmund. I know you are of her bosom.

OSWALD   I, madam?

REGAN   I speak in understanding; you are, I know't.
 Therefore I do advise you, take this note.
 My lord is dead; Edmund and I have talk'd;
 And more convenient is he for my hand
 Than for your lady's. You may gather more.
 If you do find him, pray you, give him this;
 And when your mistress hears thus much from you,
 I pray, desire her call her wisdom to her.
 So, fare you well.
 If you do chance to hear of that blind traitor,
 Preferment falls on him that cuts him off.

OSWALD   Would I could meet him, madam! I should show
 What party I do follow.

REGAN   Fare thee well.   *Exeunt.*

❧ SCENE 6   *Fields near Dover.*

Enter Gloucester, and Edgar dressed like a peasant.

GLOUCESTER   When shall we come to the top of that same hill?

EDGAR   You do climb up it now. Look, how we labour.

GLOUCESTER   Methinks the ground is even.

EDGAR   Horrible steep.
 Hark, do you hear the sea?

GLOUCESTER   No, truly.

EDGAR   Why, then, your other senses grow imperfect
 By your eyes' anguish.

GLOUCESTER   So may it be, indeed.
 Methinks thy voice is alter'd; and thou speak'st
 In better phrase and matter than thou didst.

EDGAR   You're much deceived. In nothing am I changed
 But in my garments.

GLOUCESTER   Methinks you're better spoken.

EDGAR   Come on, sir; here's the place. Stand still. How fearful
 And dizzy 'tis, to cast one's eyes so low!
 The crows and choughs that wing the midway air

479

Show scarce so gross as beetles. Half way down
Hangs one that gathers samphire, dreadful trade!
Methinks he seems no bigger than his head.
The fishermen, that walk upon the beach,
Appear like mice; and yond tall anchoring bark,
Diminish'd to her cock; her cock, a buoy
Almost too small for sight. The murmuring surge,
That on the unnumber'd idle pebbles chafes,
Cannot be heard so high. I'll look no more;
Lest my brain turn, and the deficient sight
Topple down headlong.

GLOUCESTER   Set me where you stand.

EDGAR   Give me your hand. You are now within a foot
Of the extreme verge. For all beneath the moon
Would I not leap upright.

GLOUCESTER   Let go my hand.
Here, friend, 's another purse; in it a jewel
Well worth a poor man's taking. Fairies and gods
Prosper it with thee! Go thou farther off;
Bid me farewell, and let me hear thee going.

EDGAR   Now fare you well, good sir.

GLOUCESTER   With all my heart.

EDGAR   Why I do trifle thus with his despair
Is done to cure it.

GLOUCESTER   [*Kneeling.*] O you mighty gods!
This world I do renounce, and, in your sights,
Shake patiently my great affliction off.
If I could bear it longer, and not fall
To quarrel with your great opposeless wills,
My snuff and loathed part of nature should
Burn itself out. If Edgar live, O, bless him!
Now, fellow, fare thee well.

He falls forward.

EDGAR   Gone, sir; farewell.
And yet I know not how conceit may rob
The treasury of life, when life itself
Yields to the theft. Had he been where he thought,

By this, had thought been past. Alive or dead?
Ho, you sir! friend! Hear you, sir! speak!
Thus might he pass indeed. Yet he revives.
What are you, sir?

GLOUCESTER   Away, and let me die.

EDGAR   Hadst thou been aught but gossamer, feathers, air,
So many fathom down precipitating,
Thou'dst shiver'd like an egg. But thou dost breathe;
Hast heavy substance; bleed'st not; speak'st; art sound.
Ten masts at each make not the altitude
Which thou hast perpendicularly fell.
Thy life's a miracle. Speak yet again.

GLOUCESTER   But have I fall'n, or no?

EDGAR   From the dread summit of this chalky bourn.
Look up a-height; the shrill-gorged lark so far
Cannot be seen or heard. Do but look up.

GLOUCESTER   Alack, I have no eyes.
Is wretchedness deprived that benefit,
To end itself by death? 'Twas yet some comfort,
When misery could beguile the tyrant's rage,
And frustrate his proud will.

EDGAR   Give me your arm.
Up: so. How is't? Feel you your legs? You stand.

GLOUCESTER   Too well, too well.

EDGAR   This is above all strangeness.
Upon the crown o' the cliff, what thing was that
Which parted from you?

GLOUCESTER   A poor unfortunate beggar.

EDGAR   As I stood here below, methought his eyes
Were two full moons; he had a thousand noses,
Horns whelk'd and waved like the enridged sea.
It was some fiend; therefore, thou happy father,
Think that the clearest gods, who make them honours
Of men's impossibilities, have preserved thee.

GLOUCESTER   I do remember now. Henceforth I'll bear
Affliction till it do cry out itself

481

"Enough, enough," and die. That thing you speak of,
I took it for a man; often 'twould say
"The fiend, the fiend." He led me to that place.

EDGAR   Bear free and patient thoughts.

Enter Lear, fantastically dressed with wild flowers.

But who comes here?
The safer sense will ne'er accommodate
His master thus.

LEAR   No, they cannot touch me for coining;
I am the King himself.

EDGAR   O thou side-piercing sight!

LEAR   Nature's above art in that respect. There's your press-money.
That fellow handles his bow like a crow-keeper. Draw me a clothier's
yard. Look, look, a mouse! Peace, peace; this piece of toasted cheese
will do't. There's my gauntlet; I'll prove it on a giant. Bring up the
brown bills. O, well flown, bird! i' the clout, i' the clout. Hewgh! Give
the word.

EDGAR   Sweet marjoram.

LEAR   Pass.

GLOUCESTER   I know that voice.

LEAR   Ha! Goneril, with a white beard! They flattered me like a dog; and
told me I had white hairs in my beard ere the black ones were there. To
say "ay" and "no" to everything that I said! "Ay" and "no" too was
no good divinity. When the rain came to wet me once, and the wind to
make me chatter; when the thunder would not peace at my bidding;
there I found 'em, there I smelt 'em out. Go to, they are not men o'
their words. They told me I was every thing; 'tis a lie, I am not ague-
proof.

GLOUCESTER   The trick of that voice I do well remember.
Is't not the King?

LEAR   Ay, every inch a king!
When I do stare, see how the subject quakes.
I pardon that man's life. What was thy cause?
Adultery?
Thou shalt not die. Die for adultery! No:
The wren goes to it, and the small gilded fly

Does lecher in my sight.
Let copulation thrive; for Gloucester's bastard son
Was kinder to his father than my daughters
Got 'tween the lawful sheets.
To it, luxury, pell-mell; for I lack soldiers.
Behold yond simpering dame,
Whose face between her forks presages snow;
That minces virtue, and does shake the head
To hear of pleasure's name;
The fitchew, nor the soiled horse, goes to it
With a more riotous appetite.
Down from the waist they are Centaurs,
Though women all above;
But to the girdle do the gods inherit,
Beneath is all the fiends';
There's hell, there's darkness, there's the sulphurous pit,
Burning, scalding, stench, consumption; fie, fie, fie! pah, pah! Give me
an ounce of civet, good apothecary, to sweeten my imagination.
There's money for thee.

GLOUCESTER   O, let me kiss that hand!

LEAR   Let me wipe it first; it smells of mortality.

GLOUCESTER   O ruin'd piece of nature! This great world
Shall so wear out to nought. Dost thou know me?

LEAR   I remember thine eyes well enough. Dost thou squiny at me? No,
do thy worst, blind Cupid; I'll not love. Read thou this challenge;
mark but the penning of it.

GLOUCESTER   Were all the letters suns, I could not see one.

EDGAR   I would not take this from report; it is,
And my heart breaks at it.

LEAR   Read.

GLOUCESTER   What, with the case of eyes?

LEAR   O, ho, are you there with me? No eyes in your head, nor no
money in your purse? Your eyes are in a heavy case, your purse in a
light. Yet you see how this world goes.

GLOUCESTER   I see it feelingly.

LEAR   What, art mad? A man may see how this world goes with no eyes.

Look with thine ears: see how yond justice rails upon yond simple thief. Hark, in thine ear: change places; and, handy-dandy, which is the justice, which is the thief? Thou hast seen a farmer's dog bark at a beggar?

GLOUCESTER   Ay, sir.

LEAR   And the creature run from the cur?
There thou mightst behold the great image of authority: a dog's obeyed in office.
Thou rascal beadle, hold thy bloody hand!
Why dost thou lash that whore? Strip thine own back;
Thou hotly lust'st to use her in that kind
For which thou whipp'st her. The usurer hangs the cozener.
Through tatter'd clothes small vices do appear;
Robes and furr'd gowns hide all. Plate sin with gold,
And the strong lance of justice hurtless breaks;
Arm it in rags, a pigmy's straw does pierce it.
None does offend, none, I say, none; I'll able 'em.
Take that of me, my friend, who have the power
To seal the accuser's lips. Get thee glass eyes;
And, like a scurvy politician, seem
To see the things thou dost not. Now, now, now, now.
Pull off my boots: harder, harder; so.

EDGAR   O, matter and impertinency mix'd!
Reason in madness!

LEAR   If thou wilt weep my fortunes, take my eyes.
I know thee well enough; thy name is Gloucester.
Thou must be patient; we came crying hither.
Thou know'st, the first time that we smell the air,
We wawl and cry. I will preach to thee; mark.

GLOUCESTER   Alack, alack the day!

LEAR   When we are born, we cry that we are come
To this great stage of fools. This' a good block;
It were a delicate stratagem, to shoe
A troop of horse with felt. I'll put't in proof;
And when I have stol'n upon these sons-in-law,
Then, kill, kill, kill, kill, kill, kill!

Enter a Gentleman, with Attendants.

484

GENTLEMAN   O, here he is. Lay hand upon him. Sir,
  Your most dear daughter—

LEAR   No rescue? What, a prisoner? I am even
  The natural fool of fortune. Use me well;
  You shall have ransom. Let me have surgeons;
  I am cut to the brains.

GENTLEMAN   You shall have anything.

LEAR   No seconds? All myself?
  Why, this would make a man a man of salt,
  To use his eyes for garden water-pots,
  Ay, and laying autumn's dust.

GENTLEMAN   Good sir—

LEAR   I will die bravely, like a smug bridegroom. What!
  I will be jovial. Come, come; I am a king,
  My masters, know you that.

GENTLEMAN   You are a royal one, and we obey you.

LEAR   Then there's life in't. Nay, if you get it, you shall get it with running. Sa, sa, sa, sa.   *Exit running; Attendants follow.*

GENTLEMAN   A sight most pitiful in the meanest wretch,
  Past speaking of in a king! Thou hast one daughter,
  Who redeems nature from the general curse
  Which twain have brought her to.

EDGAR   Hail, gentle sir.

GENTLEMAN   Sir, speed you. What's your will?

EDGAR   Do you hear aught, sir, of a battle toward?

GENTLEMAN   Most sure and vulgar. Every one hears that,
  Which can distinguish sound.

EDGAR   But, by your favour,
  How near's the other army?

GENTLEMAN   Near and on speedy foot; the main descry
  Stands on the hourly thought.

EDGAR   I thank you, sir. That's all.

GENTLEMAN   Though that the Queen on special cause is here,
  Her army is moved on.

485

EDGAR   I thank you, sir.   *Exit Gentleman.*

GLOUCESTER   You ever-gentle gods, take my breath from me;
  Let not my worser spirit tempt me again
  To die before you please!

EDGAR   Well pray you, father.

GLOUCESTER   Now, good sir, what are you?

EDGAR   A most poor man, made tame to fortune's blows;
  Who, by the art of known and feeling sorrows,
  Am pregnant to good pity. Give me your hand,
  I'll lead you to some biding.

GLOUCESTER   Hearty thanks.
  The bounty and the benison of Heaven
  To boot, and boot!

Enter Oswald.

OSWALD   A proclaim'd prize! Most happy!
  That eyeless head of thine was first framed flesh
  To raise my fortunes. Thou old unhappy traitor,
  Briefly thyself remember; the sword is out
  That must destroy thee.

GLOUCESTER   Now let thy friendly hand
  Put strength enough to't.

Edgar interposes.

OSWALD   Wherefore, bold peasant,
  Darest thou support a publish'd traitor? Hence;
  Lest that the infection of his fortune take
  Like hold on thee. Let go his arm.

EDGAR   Chill not let go, zir, without vurther 'casion.

OSWALD   Let go, slave, or thou diest!

EDGAR   Good gentleman, go your gait, and let poor volk pass. An chud
  ha' bin zwaggered out of my life, 'twould not ha' bin zo long as 'tis by
  a vortnight. Nay, come not near th' old man; keep out, che vor ye, or
  ise try whether your costard or my ballow be the harder. Chill be plain
  with you.

OSWALD   Out, dunghill!

486

EDGAR   Chill pick your teeth, zir. Come; no matter vor your foins.

They fight, and Edgar knocks him down.

OSWALD   Slave, thou hast slain me. Villain, take my purse.
  If ever thou wilt thrive, bury my body;
  And give the letters which thou find'st about me
  To Edmund Earl of Gloucester; seek him out
  Upon the British party. O, untimely death!   *Dies.*

EDGAR   I know thee well. A serviceable villain;
  As duteous to the vices of thy mistress
  As badness would desire.

GLOUCESTER   What, is he dead?

EDGAR   Sit you down, father; rest you.
  Let's see these pockets. The letters that he speaks of
  May be my friends. He's dead; I am only sorry
  He had no other death's-man. Let us see;
  Leave, gentle wax; and, manners, blame us not.
  To know our enemies' minds, we'd rip their hearts;
  Their papers, is more lawful. [*Reads.*]

"Let our reciprocal vows be remembered. You have many opportuni-
ties to cut him off. If your will want not, time and place will be fruit-
fully offered. There is nothing done, if he return the conqueror. Then
am I the prisoner, and his bed my gaol; from the loathed warmth
whereof deliver me, and supply the place for your labour.
      Your—wife, so I would say—affectionate servant, Goneril."

O undistinguish'd space of woman's will!
A plot upon her virtuous husband's life;
And the exchange my brother! Here, in the sands,
Thee I'll rake up, the post unsanctified
Of murderous lechers. And in the mature time
With this ungracious paper strike the sight
Of the death-practised Duke; for him 'tis well
That of thy death and business I can tell.

GLOUCESTER   The King is mad. How stiff is my vile sense,
  That I stand up, and have ingenious feeling
  Of my huge sorrows! Better I were distract.
  So should my thoughts be sever'd from my griefs,
  And woes by wrong imaginations lose
  The knowledge of themselves.

487

EDGAR   Give me your hand:

Drum afar off.

   Far off, methinks, I hear the beaten drum.
   Come, father, I'll bestow you with a friend.   *Exeunt.*

❀ SCENE 7   *A tent in the French camp. Lear on a bed*
            asleep, soft music playing; Gentleman, and
            others attending.

Enter Cordelia, Kent, and Doctor.

CORDELIA   O thou good Kent, how shall I live and work,
   To match thy goodness? My life will be too short,
   And every measure fail me.

KENT   To be acknowledged, madam, is o'erpaid.
   All my reports go with the modest truth;
   Nor more nor clipp'd, but so.

CORDELIA   Be better suited;
   These weeds are memories of those worser hours.
   I prithee, put them off.

KENT   Pardon me, dear madam;
   Yet to be known shortens my made intent.
   My boon I make it, that you know me not
   Till time and I think meet.

CORDELIA   Then be't so, my good lord. [*To the Doctor.*] How does the
   King?

DOCTOR   Madam, sleeps still.

CORDELIA   O you kind gods,
   Cure this great breach in his abused nature!
   The untuned and jarring senses, O, wind up
   Of this child-changed father!

DOCTOR   So please your Majesty
   That we may wake the King? He hath slept long.

CORDELIA   Be govern'd by your knowledge, and proceed
   I' the sway of your own will. Is he array'd?

488

GENTLEMAN   Ay, madam; in the heaviness of his sleep
We put fresh garments on him.

DOCTOR   Be by, good madam, when we do awake him;
I doubt not of his temperance.

CORDELIA   Very well.

DOCTOR   Please you, draw near. Louder the music there!

CORDELIA   O my dear father! Restoration hang
Thy medicine on my lips; and let this kiss
Repair those violent harms that my two sisters
Have in thy reverence made!

KENT   Kind and dear Princess!

CORDELIA   Had you not been their father, these white flakes
Had challenged pity of them. Was this a face
To be opposed against the warring winds?
To stand against the deep dread-bolted thunder?
In the most terrible and nimble stroke
Of quick, cross lightning? to watch—poor perdu!—
With this thin helm? Mine enemy's dog,
Though he had bit me, should have stood that night
Against my fire; and wast thou fain, poor father,
To hovel thee with swine and rogues forlorn
In short and musty straw? Alack, alack!
'Tis wonder that thy life and wits at once
Had not concluded all. He wakes; speak to him.

DOCTOR   Madam, do you; 'tis fittest.

CORDELIA   How does my royal lord? How fares your Majesty?

LEAR   You do me wrong to take me out o' the grave.
Thou art a soul in bliss; but I am bound
Upon a wheel of fire, that mine own tears
Do scald like molten lead.

CORDELIA   Sir, do you know me?

LEAR   You are a spirit, I know. When did you die?

CORDELIA   Still, still, far wide!

DOCTOR   He's scarce awake. Let him alone awhile.

489

LEAR   Where have I been? Where am I? Fair daylight?
  I am mightily abused. I should e'en die with pity,
  To see another thus. I know not what to say.
  I will not swear these are my hands. Let's see;
  I feel this pin prick. Would I were assured
  Of my condition!

CORDELIA   O, look upon me, sir,
  And hold your hands in benediction o'er me.
  No, sir, you must not kneel.

LEAR   Pray, do not mock me.
  I am a very foolish fond old man,
  Fourscore and upward, not an hour more nor less;
  And, to deal plainly,
  I fear I am not in my perfect mind.
  Methinks I should know you, and know this man;
  Yet I am doubtful; for I am mainly ignorant
  What place this is; and all the skill I have
  Remembers not these garments; nor I know not
  Where I did lodge last night. Do not laugh at me;
  For, as I am a man, I think this lady
  To be my child Cordelia.

CORDELIA   And so I am, I am.

LEAR   Be your tears wet? yes, 'faith. I pray, weep not.
  If you have poison for me, I will drink it.
  I know you do not love me; for your sisters
  Have, as I do remember, done me wrong.
  You have some cause, they have not.

CORDELIA   No cause, no cause.

LEAR   Am I in France?

KENT   In your own kingdom, sir.

LEAR   Do not abuse me.

DOCTOR   Be comforted, good madam. The great rage,
  You see, is kill'd in him; and yet it is danger
  To make him even o'er the time he has lost.
  Desire him to go in; trouble him no more
  Till further settling.

CORDELIA   Will't please your Highness walk?

LEAR   You must bear with me.
  Pray you now, forget and forgive. I am old and foolish.

Exeunt all but Kent and Gentleman.

GENTLEMAN   Holds it true, sir, that the Duke of Cornwall was so slain?

KENT   Most certain, sir.

GENTLEMAN   Who is conductor of his people?

KENT   As 'tis said, the bastard son of Gloucester.

GENTLEMAN   They say Edgar, his banished son, is with the Earl of Kent
  in Germany.

KENT   Report is changeable. 'Tis time to look about; the powers of the
  kingdom approach apace.

GENTLEMAN   The arbitrement is like to be bloody. Fare you well, sir.

Exit.

KENT   My point and period will be thoroughly wrought,
  Or well or ill, as this day's battle's fought.   *Exit.*

ACT V

The British camp, near Dover.

Enter, with drum and colours, Edmund, Regan, Gentlemen, and Soldiers.

EDMUND Know of the Duke if his last purpose hold,
  Or whether since he is advised by aught
  To change the course. He's full of alteration
  And self-reproving; bring his constant pleasure.   *Exit an Officer.*

REGAN Our sister's man is certainly miscarried.

EDMUND 'Tis to be doubted, madam.

REGAN   Now, sweet lord,
  You know the goodness I intend upon you.
  Tell me—but truly—but then speak the truth,
  Do you not love my sister?

EDMUND   In honour'd love.

REGAN But have you never found my brother's way
  To the forfended place?

EDMUND   That thought abuses you.

REGAN I am doubtful that you have been conjunct
  And bosom'd with her, as far as we call hers.

EDMUND No, by mine honour, madam.

REGAN I never shall endure her. Dear my lord,
  Be not familiar with her.

492

EDMUND   Fear me not.
  She and the Duke her husband!

Enter, with drum and colours, Albany, Goneril, and Soldiers.

GONERIL   [*Aside.*] I had rather lose the battle than that sister
  Should loosen him and me.

ALBANY   Our very loving sister, well be-met.
  Sir, this I hear; the King is come to his daughter,
  With others whom the rigour of our state
  Forced to cry out. Where I could not be honest,
  I never yet was valiant; for this business,
  It toucheth us, as France invades our land,
  Not bolds the King, with others, whom, I fear,
  Most just and heavy causes make oppose.

EDMUND   Sir, you speak nobly.

REGAN   Why is this reason'd?

GONERIL   Combine together 'gainst the enemy;
  For these domestic and particular broils
  Are not the question here.

ALBANY   Let's then determine
  With the ancient of war on our proceedings.

EDMUND   I shall attend you presently at your tent.

REGAN   Sister, you'll go with us?

GONERIL   No.

REGAN   'Tis most convenient; pray you, go with us.

GONERIL   [*Aside.*] O, ho, I know the riddle. I will go.

As they are going out, enter Edgar disguised.

EDGAR   If e'er your Grace had speech with man so poor,
  Hear me one word.

ALBANY   I'll overtake you. Speak.
                    Exeunt all but Albany and Edgar.

EDGAR   Before you fight the battle, ope this letter.
  If you have victory, let the trumpet sound
  For him that brought it. Wretched though I seem,
  I can produce a champion that will prove

493

What is avouched there. If you miscarry,
Your business of the world hath so an end,
And machination ceases. Fortune love you!

ALBANY   Stay till I have read the letter.

EDGAR   I was forbid it.
When time shall serve, let but the herald cry,
And I'll appear again.

ALBANY   Why, fare thee well. I will o'erlook thy paper.   *Exit Edgar.*

Re-enter Edmund.

EDMUND   The enemy's in view; draw up your powers.
Here is the guess of their true strength and forces
By diligent discovery; but your haste
Is now urged on you.

ALBANY   We will greet the time.   *Exit.*

EDMUND   To both these sisters have I sworn my love;
Each jealous of the other, as the stung
Are of the adder. Which of them shall I take?
Both? one? or neither? Neither can be enjoy'd,
If both remain alive. To take the widow
Exasperates, makes mad her sister Goneril;
And hardly shall I carry out my side,
Her husband being alive. Now then we'll use
His countenance for the battle; which being done,
Let her who would be rid of him devise
His speedy taking off. As for the mercy
Which he intends to Lear and to Cordelia,
The battle done, and they within our power,
Shall never see his pardon; for my state
Stands on me to defend, not to debate.   *Exit.*

SCENE 2   *A field between the two camps.*

Alarum within. Enter, with drum and colours, Lear, Cordelia, and Soldiers, over the stage; and exeunt. Enter Edgar and Gloucester.

EDGAR   Here, father, take the shadow of this tree
For your good host; pray that the right may thrive.

If ever I return to you again,
I'll bring you comfort.

GLOUCESTER   Grace go with you, sir!
                              Exit Edgar. Alarum and retreat within.

Re-enter Edgar.

EDGAR   Away, old man; give me thy hand; away!
  King Lear hath lost, he and his daughter ta'en.
  Give me thy hand; come on.

GLOUCESTER   No farther, sir; a man may rot even here.

EDGAR   What, in ill thoughts again? Men must endure
  Their going hence, even as their coming hither;
  Ripeness is all. Come on.

GLOUCESTER   And that's true too.   *Exeunt.*

SCENE 3   *The British camp near Dover.*

*Enter, in conquest, with drum and colours, Edmund; Lear and Cordelia, prison-
ers; Captain, Soldiers, &c.*

EDMUND   Some officers take them away. Good guard,
  Until their greater pleasures first be known
  That are to censure them.

CORDELIA   We are not the first
  Who, with best meaning, have incurr'd the worst.
  For thee, oppressed King, am I cast down;
  Myself could else out-frown false Fortune's frown.
  Shall we not see these daughters and these sisters?

LEAR   No, no, no, no! Come, let's away to prison.
  We two alone will sing like birds i' the cage;
  When thou dost ask me blessing, I'll kneel down,
  And ask of thee forgiveness; so we'll live,
  And pray, and sing, and tell old tales, and laugh
  At gilded butterflies, and hear poor rogues
  Talk of court news; and we'll talk with them too,
  Who loses and who wins; who's in, who's out;
  And take upon's the mystery of things,
  As if we were God's spies; and we'll wear out,

In a wall'd prison, packs and sects of great ones,
That ebb and flow by the moon.

EDMUND   Take them away.

LEAR   Upon such sacrifices, my Cordelia,
The gods themselves throw incense. Have I caught thee?
He that parts us shall bring a brand from heaven,
And fire us hence like foxes. Wipe thine eyes;
The good-years shall devour them, flesh and fell,
Ere they shall make us weep. We'll see 'em starve first.
Come.   *Exeunt Lear and Cordelia, guarded.*

EDMUND   Come hither, captain; hark.
Take thou this note. [*Gives a paper.*] Go follow them to prison.
One step I have advanced thee; if thou dost
As this instructs thee, thou dost make thy way
To noble fortunes. Know thou this, that men
Are as the time is; to be tender-minded
Does not become a sword. Thy great employment
Will not bear question; either say thou'lt do't,
Or thrive by other means.

CAPTAIN   I'll do't, my lord.

EDMUND   About it; and write happy when thou hast done.
Mark, I say, instantly; and carry it so
As I have set it down.

CAPTAIN   I cannot draw a cart, nor eat dried oats;
If it be man's work, I'll do't.   *Exit.*

Flourish. Enter Albany, Goneril, Regan, another Captain, and Soldiers.

ALBANY   Sir, you have shown to-day your valiant strain,
And fortune led you well. You have the captives
That were the opposites of this day's strife;
We do require them of you, so to use them
As we shall find their merits and our safety
May equally determine.

EDMUND   Sir, I thought it fit
To send the old and miserable King
To some retention and appointed guard;
Whose age has charms in it, whose title more,
To pluck the common bosom on his side,

496

And turn our impress'd lances in our eyes
Which do command them. With him I sent the Queen;
My reason all the same; and they are ready
To-morrow, or at further space, to appear
Where you shall hold your session. At this time
We sweat and bleed; the friend hath lost his friend;
And the best quarrels, in the heat, are cursed
By those that feel their sharpness.
The question of Cordelia and her father
Requires a fitter place.

ALBANY   Sir, by your patience,
I hold you but a subject of this war,
Not as a brother.

REGAN   That's as we list to grace him.
Methinks our pleasure might have been demanded,
Ere you had spoke so far. He led our powers;
Bore the commission of my place and person;
The which immediacy may well stand up,
And call itself your brother.

GONERIL   Not so hot:
In his own grace he doth exalt himself,
More than in your addition.

REGAN   In my rights,
By me invested, he compeers the best.

GONERIL   That were the most, if he should husband you.

REGAN   Jesters do oft prove prophets.

GONERIL   Holla, holla!
That eye that told you so look'd but a-squint.

REGAN   Lady, I am not well; else I should answer
From a full-flowing stomach. General,
Take thou my soldiers, prisoners, patrimony;
Dispose of them, of me; the walls are thine.
Witness the world, that I create thee here
My lord and master.

GONERIL   Mean you to enjoy him?

ALBANY   The let-alone lies not in your good will.

EDMUND   Nor in thine, lord.

ALBANY   Half-blooded fellow, yes.

REGAN   [*To Edmund*.] Let the drum strike, and prove my title thine.

ALBANY   Stay yet; hear reason. Edmund, I arrest thee
On capital treason; and, in thine attaint,
This gilded serpent. [*Points to Goneril*.] For your claim, fair sister,
I bar it in the interest of my wife;
'Tis she is sub-contracted to this lord,
And I, her husband, contradict your bans.
If you will marry, make your loves to me,
My lady is bespoke.

GONERIL   An interlude!

ALBANY   Thou art arm'd, Gloucester. Let the trumpet sound.
If none appear to prove upon thy head
Thy heinous, manifest, and many treasons,
There is my pledge. [*Throws down a glove*.] I'll prove it on thy heart,
Ere I taste bread, thou art in nothing less
Than I have here proclaim'd thee.

REGAN   Sick, O, sick!

GONERIL   [*Aside*.] If not, I'll ne'er trust medicine.

EDMUND   There's my exchange. [*Throws down a glove*.] What in the
world he is
That names me traitor, villain-like he lies.
Call by thy trumpet; he that dares approach,
On him, on you, who not? I will maintain
My truth and honour firmly.

ALBANY   A herald, ho!

EDMUND   A herald, ho, a herald!

ALBANY   Trust to thy single virtue; for thy soldiers,
All levied in my name, have in my name
Took their discharge.

REGAN   My sickness grows upon me.

ALBANY   She is not well; convey her to my tent.   *Exit Regan, led.*

Enter a Herald.

Come hither, herald. Let the trumpet sound,
And read out this.

CAPTAIN Sound, trumpet!

A trumpet sounds.

HERALD [*Reads.*]
"If any man of quality or degree within the lists of the army will maintain upon Edmund, supposed Earl of Gloucester, that he is a manifold
traitor, let him appear by the third sound of the trumpet. He is bold in
his defence."

EDMUND Sound!

First trumpet.

HERALD Again!

Second trumpet.

HERALD Again!

*Third trumpet. Trumpet answers within. Enter Edgar, at the third sound,
armed, with a trumpet before him.*

ALBANY Ask him his purposes, why he appears
Upon this call o' the trumpet.

HERALD   What are you?
Your name, your quality? and why you answer
This present summons?

EDGAR   Know, my name is lost;
By treason's tooth bare-gnawn and canker-bit.
Yet am I noble as the adversary
I come to cope.

ALBANY   Which is that adversary?

EDGAR What's he that speaks for Edmund Earl of Gloucester?

EDMUND Himself. What say'st thou to him?

EDGAR   Draw thy sword,
That, if my speech offend a noble heart,
Thy arm may do thee justice; here is mine.
Behold, it is the privilege of mine honours,
My oath, and my profession. I protest,
Maugre thy strength, youth, place, and eminence,

499

Despite thy victor sword and fire-new fortune,
Thy valour and thy heart, thou art a traitor;
False to thy gods, thy brother, and thy father;
Conspirant 'gainst this high-illustrious prince;
And, from the extremest upward of thy head
To the descent and dust below thy foot,
A most toad-spotted traitor. Say thou "No,"
This sword, this arm, and my best spirits are bent
To prove upon thy heart, whereto I speak,
Thou liest.

EDMUND   In wisdom I should ask thy name;
But, since thy outside looks so fair and warlike,
And that thy tongue some say of breeding breathes,
What safe and nicely I might well delay
By rule of knighthood, I disdain and spurn.
Back do I toss these treasons to thy head;
With the hell-hated lie o'erwhelm thy heart;
Which, for they yet glance by and scarcely bruise,
This sword of mine shall give them instant way,
Where they shall rest for ever. Trumpets, speak!

Alarums. They fight. Edmund falls.

ALBANY   Save him, save him!

GONERIL   This is practice, Gloucester.
By the law of arms thou wast not bound to answer
An unknown opposite; thou art not vanquish'd,
But cozen'd and beguiled.

ALBANY   Shut your mouth, dame,
Or with this paper shall I stop it. Hold, sir.
Thou worse than any name, read thine own evil.
No tearing, lady; I perceive you know it.

Gives the letter to Edmund.

GONERIL   Say, if I do, the laws are mine, not thine.
Who can arraign me for't?

ALBANY   Most monstrous! oh!
Know'st thou this paper?

GONERIL   Ask me not what I know.   *Exit.*

ALBANY   Go after her. She's desperate; govern her.

EDMUND   What you have charged me with, that have I done;
And more, much more; the time will bring it out.
'Tis past, and so am I. But what art thou
That hast this fortune on me? If thou'rt noble,
I do forgive thee.

EDGAR   Let's exchange charity.
I am no less in blood than thou art, Edmund;
If more, the more thou hast wrong'd me.
My name is Edgar, and thy father's son.
The gods are just, and of our pleasant vices
Make instruments to plague us.
The dark and vicious place where thee he got
Cost him his eyes.

EDMUND   Thou hast spoken right, 'tis true;
The wheel is come full circle; I am here.

ALBANY   Methought thy very gait did prophesy
A royal nobleness. I must embrace thee.
Let sorrow split my heart, if ever I
Did hate thee or thy father!

EDGAR   Worthy Prince, I know't.

ALBANY   Where have you hid yourself?
How have you known the miseries of your father?

EDGAR   By nursing them, my lord. List a brief tale;
And when 'tis told, O, that my heart would burst!
The bloody proclamation to escape,
That follow'd me so near—O, our lives' sweetness!
That we the pain of death would hourly die
Rather than die at once!—taught me to shift
Into a madman's rags; to assume a semblance
That very dogs disdain'd; and in this habit
Met I my father with his bleeding rings,
Their precious stones new lost; became his guide,
Led him, begg'd for him, saved him from despair;
Never—O fault!—reveal'd myself unto him,
Until some half-hour past, when I was arm'd.
Not sure, though hoping, of this good success,
I ask'd his blessing, and from first to last
Told him my pilgrimage. But his flaw'd heart,
Alack, too weak the conflict to support!

501

'Twixt two extremes of passion, joy and grief,
Burst smilingly.

EDMUND   This speech of yours hath moved me,
And shall perchance do good. But speak you on;
You look as you had something more to say.

ALBANY   If there be more, more woeful, hold it in;
For I am almost ready to dissolve,
Hearing of this.

EDGAR   This would have seem'd a period
To such as love not sorrow; but another,
To amplify too much, would make much more,
And top extremity.
Whilst I was big in clamour came there in a man,
Who, having seen me in my worst estate,
Shunn'd my abhorr'd society; but then, finding
Who 'twas that so endured, with his strong arms
He fasten'd on my neck, and bellow'd out
As he'd burst heaven; threw him on my father;
Told the most piteous tale of Lear and him
That ever ear received; which in recounting
His grief grew puissant, and the strings of life
Began to crack. Twice then the trumpets sounded,
And there I left him tranced.

ALBANY   But who was this?

EDGAR   Kent, sir, the banish'd Kent; who in disguise
Follow'd his enemy King, and did him service
Improper for a slave.

Enter a Gentleman, with a bloody knife.

GENTLEMAN   Help, help, O, help!

EDGAR   What kind of help?

ALBANY   Speak, man.

EDGAR   What means that bloody knife?

GENTLEMAN   'Tis hot, it smokes;
It came even from the heart of—O, she's dead!

ALBANY   Who dead? speak, man.

502

GENTLEMAN   Your lady, sir, your lady. And her sister
By her is poisoned; she hath confess'd it.

EDMUND   I was contracted to them both. All three
Now marry in an instant.

EDGAR   Here comes Kent.

ALBANY   Produce their bodies, be they alive or dead.
This judgement of the heavens, that makes us tremble,
Touches us not with pity.   *Exit Gentleman.*

Enter Kent.

                              O, is this he?
The time will not allow the compliment
Which very manners urges.

KENT   I am come
To bid my King and master aye good night.
Is he not here?

ALBANY   Great thing of us forgot!
Speak, Edmund, where's the King? and where's Cordelia?
See'st thou this object, Kent?

The bodies of Goneril and Regan are brought in.

KENT   Alack, why thus?

EDMUND   Yet Edmund was beloved.
The one the other poison'd for my sake,
And after slew herself.

ALBANY   Even so. Cover their faces.

EDMUND   I pant for life. Some good I mean to do,
Despite of mine own nature. Quickly send,
Be brief in it, to the castle; for my writ
Is on the life of Lear and on Cordelia.
Nay, send in time.

ALBANY   Run, run, O, run!

EDGAR   To who, my lord? Who hath the office? Send
Thy token of reprieve.

503

EDMUND Well thought on. Take my sword,
Give it the captain.

ALBANY   Haste thee, for thy life.   *Exit Edgar.*

EDMUND He hath commission from thy wife and me
To hang Cordelia in the prison, and
To lay the blame upon her own despair,
That she fordid herself.

ALBANY The gods defend her! Bear him hence awhile.
                                    Edmund is borne off.

Re-enter Lear, with Cordelia dead in his arms; Edgar, Captain, and others following.

LEAR Howl, howl, howl, howl! O, you are men of stones!
Had I your tongues and eyes, I'd use them so
That heaven's vault should crack. She's gone for ever!
I know when one is dead, and when one lives;
She's dead as earth. Lend me a looking-glass;
If that her breath will mist or stain the stone,
Why, then she lives.

KENT   Is this the promised end?

EDGAR Or image of that horror?

ALBANY   Fall, and cease!

LEAR This feather stirs; she lives! if it be so,
It is a chance which does redeem all sorrows
That ever I have felt.

KENT [*Kneeling.*] O my good master!

LEAR Prithee, away.

EDGAR   'Tis noble Kent, your friend.

LEAR A plague upon you, murderers, traitors all!
I might have saved her; now she's gone for ever!
Cordelia, Cordelia! stay a little. Ha!
What is't thou say'st. Her voice was ever soft,
Gentle, and low, an excellent thing in woman.
I kill'd the slave that was a-hanging thee.

CAPTAIN 'Tis true, my lords, he did.

504

LEAR   Did I not, fellow?
I have seen the day, with my good biting falchion
I would have made them skip. I am old now,
And these same crosses spoil me. Who are you?
Mine eyes are not o' the best. I'll tell you straight.

KENT   If fortune brag of two she loved and hated,
One of them we behold.

LEAR   This is a dull sight. Are you not Kent?

KENT   The same.
Your servant Kent. Where is your servant Caius?

LEAR   He's a good fellow, I can tell you that;
He'll strike, and quickly too. He's dead and rotten.

KENT   No, my good lord; I am the very man—

LEAR   I'll see that straight.

KENT   That, from your first of difference and decay,
Have follow'd your sad steps.

LEAR   You are welcome hither.

KENT   Nor no man else. All's cheerless, dark, and deadly.
Your eldest daughters have fordone themselves,
And desperately are dead.

LEAR   Ay, so I think.

ALBANY   He knows not what he says; and vain it is
That we present us to him.

EDGAR   Very bootless.

Enter a Captain.

CAPTAIN   Edmund is dead, my lord.

ALBANY   That's but a trifle here.
You lords and noble friends, know our intent.
What comfort to this great decay may come
Shall be applied. For us, we will resign,
During the life of this old majesty,
To him our absolute power; [*To Edgar and Kent.*] you, to your rights;
With boot, and such addition as your honours
Have more than merited. All friends shall taste

505

The wages of their virtue, and all foes
The cup of their deservings. O, see, see!

LEAR   And my poor fool is hang'd! No, no, no life!
Why should a dog, a horse, a rat, have life,
And thou no breath at all? Thou'lt come no more,
Never, never, never, never, never!
Pray you undo this button. Thank you, sir.
Do you see this? Look on her, look, her lips,
Look there, look there!   *Dies.*

EDGAR   He faints! My lord, my lord!

KENT   Break, heart; I prithee, break!

EDGAR   Look up, my lord.

KENT   Vex not his ghost. O, let him pass! he hates him much
That would upon the rack of this tough world
Stretch him out longer.

EDGAR   He is gone, indeed.

KENT   The wonder is he hath endured so long.
He but usurp'd his life.

ALBANY   Bear them from hence. Our present business
Is general woe. [*To Kent and Edgar.*] Friends of my soul, you twain
Rule in this realm, and the gored state sustain.

KENT   I have a journey, sir, shortly to go;
My master calls me, I must not say no.

ALBANY   The weight of this sad time we must obey;
Speak what we feel, not what we ought to say.
The oldest hath borne most; we that are young
Shall never see so much, nor live so long.   *Exeunt, with a dead march.*

MACBETH

THE ACTORS

DUNCAN, *King of Scotland*

MALCOLM
DONALBAIN } *his sons*

MACBETH
BANQUO } *generals of the King's army*

MACDUFF
LENNOX
ROSS
MENTEITH } *noblemen of Scotland*
ANGUS
CAITHNESS

FLEANCE, *son to Banquo*

SIWARD, *Earl of Northumberland, general of the English forces*

YOUNG SIWARD, *his son*

SEYTON, *an officer attending on Macbeth*

BOY, *son to Macduff*

AN ENGLISH DOCTOR

A SCOTCH DOCTOR

A LORD

A PORTER

AN OLD MAN

A SERGEANT

TWO MESSENGERS

AN ATTENDANT *on Macbeth*

A SERVANT *to Lady Macbeth*

THREE MURDERERS

LADY MACBETH

LADY MACDUFF

A GENTLEWOMAN, *attending on Lady Macbeth*

HECATE

THREE WITCHES

THREE APPARITIONS

Non-Speaking: Lords, Ladies, Officers, Soldiers, Ghosts, and Attendants

SCENE: *Scotland and England*

ACT I

❧ SCENE 1 *A desert place.*

Thunder and lightning. Enter Three Witches.

FIRST WITCH   When shall we three meet again
  In thunder, lightning, or in rain?

SECOND WITCH   When the hurlyburly's done,
  When the battle's lost and won.

THIRD WITCH   That will be ere the set of sun.

FIRST WITCH   Where the place?

SECOND WITCH   Upon the heath.

THIRD WITCH   There to meet with Macbeth.

FIRST WITCH   I come, Graymalkin!

SECOND WITCH   Paddock calls.

THIRD WITCH   Anon.

ALL   Fair is foul, and foul is fair;
  Hover through the fog and filthy air.   *Exeunt.*

❧ SCENE 2 *A camp near Forres.*

*Alarum within. Enter Duncan, Malcolm, Donalbain, Lennox, with Attend-
ants, meeting a bleeding Sergeant.*

DUNCAN   What bloody man is that? He can report,
  As seemeth by his plight, of the revolt
  The newest state.

511

MALCOLM   This is the sergeant
Who like a good and hardy soldier fought
'Gainst my captivity. Hail, brave friend!
Say to the King the knowledge of the broil
As thou didst leave it.

SERGEANT   Doubtful it stood;
As two spent swimmers that do cling together
And choke their art. The merciless Macdonwald—
Worthy to be a rebel, for to that
The multiplying villanies of nature
Do swarm upon him—from the western isles
Of kerns and gallowglasses is supplied;
And Fortune, on his damned quarrel smiling,
Show'd like a rebel's whore. But all's too weak;
For brave Macbeth—well he deserves that name—
Disdaining Fortune, with his brandish'd steel,
Which smoked with bloody execution,
Like valour's minion carved out his passage
Till he faced the slave;
Which ne'er shook hands, nor bade farewell to him,
Till he unseam'd him from the nave to the chaps,
And fix'd his head upon our battlements.

DUNCAN   O valiant cousin! worthy gentleman!

SERGEANT   As whence the sun 'gins his reflection
Shipwrecking storms and direful thunders break,
So from that spring whence comfort seem'd to come
Discomfort swells. Mark, King of Scotland, mark!
No sooner justice had, with valour arm'd,
Compell'd these skipping kerns to trust their heels,
But the Norweyan lord surveying vantage,
With furbish'd arms and new supplies of men
Began a fresh assault.

DUNCAN   Dismay'd not this
Our captains, Macbeth and Banquo?

SERGEANT   Yes;
As sparrows eagles, or the hare the lion.
If I say sooth, I must report they were
As cannons overcharged with double cracks, so they

Doubly redoubled strokes upon the foe.
Except they meant to bathe in reeking wounds,
Or memorize another Golgotha,
I cannot tell.
But I am faint, my gashes cry for help.

DUNCAN   So well thy words become thee as thy wounds;
They smack of honour both. Go get him surgeons.

Exit Sergeant, attended.

Who comes here?

Enter Ross.

MALCOLM   The worthy thane of Ross.

LENNOX   What a haste looks through his eyes!
So should he look
That seems to speak things strange.

ROSS   God save the King!

DUNCAN   Whence camest thou, worthy thane?

ROSS   From Fife, great King;
Where the Norweyan banners flout the sky
And fan our people cold. Norway himself,
With terrible numbers,
Assisted by that most disloyal traitor
The thane of Cawdor, began a dismal conflict;
Till that Bellona's bridegroom, lapp'd in proof,
Confronted him with self-comparisons,
Point against point rebellious, arm 'gainst arm,
Curbing his lavish spirit; and, to conclude,
The victory fell on us.

DUNCAN   Great happiness!

ROSS   That now
Sweno, the Norways' king, craves composition;
Nor would we deign him burial of his men
Till he disbursed at Saint Colme's inch
Ten thousand dollars to our general use.

DUNCAN   No more that thane of Cawdor shall deceive
Our bosom interest. Go pronounce his present death,
And with his former title greet Macbeth.

513

ross   I'll see it done.

duncan   What he hath lost, noble Macbeth hath won.   *Exeunt.*

🎔 SCENE 3   *A heath near Forres.*

Thunder. Enter the Three Witches.

first witch   Where hast thou been, sister?

second witch   Killing swine.

third witch   Sister, where thou?

first witch   A sailor's wife had chestnuts in her lap,
   And munch'd, and munch'd, and munch'd. "Give me," quoth I.
   "Aroint thee, witch!" the rump-fed ronyon cries.
   Her husband's to Aleppo gone, master o' the Tiger;
   But in a sieve I'll thither sail,
   And, like a rat without a tail,
   I'll do, I'll do, and I'll do.

second witch   I'll give thee a wind.

first witch   Th'art kind.

third witch   And I another.

first witch   I myself have all the other,
   And the very ports they blow,
   All the quarters that they know
   I' the shipman's card.
   I will drain him dry as hay.
   Sleep shall neither night nor day
   Hang upon his pent-house lid;
   He shall live a man forbid.
   Weary se'nnights nine times nine
   Shall he dwindle, peak and pine.
   Though his bark cannot be lost,
   Yet it shall be tempest-tost.
   Look what I have.

second witch   Show me, show me.

first witch   Here I have a pilot's thumb,
   Wreck'd as homeward he did come.

Drum within.

THIRD WITCH   A drum, a drum!
  Macbeth doth come.

ALL   The weird sisters, hand in hand,
  Posters of the sea and land,
  Thus do go about, about;
  Thrice to thine and thrice to mine
  And thrice again, to make up nine.
  Peace! the charm's wound up.

Enter Macbeth and Banquo.

MACBETH   So foul and fair a day I have not seen.

BANQUO   How far is't call'd to Forres? What are these
  So wither'd and so wild in their attire,
  That look not like the inhabitants o' the earth,
  And yet are on't? Live you? or are you aught
  That man may question? You seem to understand me,
  By each at once her choppy finger laying
  Upon her skinny lips. You should be women,
  And yet your beards forbid me to interpret
  That you are so.

MACBETH   Speak, if you can. What are you?

FIRST WITCH   All hail, Macbeth! hail to thee, thane of Glamis!

SECOND WITCH   All hail, Macbeth! hail to thee, thane of Cawdor!

THIRD WITCH   All hail, Macbeth, that shalt be King hereafter!

BANQUO   Good sir, why do you start, and seem to fear
  Things that do sound so fair? I' the name of truth,
  Are ye fantastical, or that indeed
  Which outwardly ye show? My noble partner
  You greet with present grace and great prediction
  Of noble having and of royal hope,
  That he seems rapt withal. To me you speak not.
  If you can look into the seeds of time,
  And say which grain will grow and which will not,
  Speak then to me, who neither beg nor fear
  Your favours nor your hate.

FIRST WITCH   Hail!

515

SECOND WITCH   Hail!

THIRD WITCH   Hail!

FIRST WITCH   Lesser than Macbeth, and greater.

SECOND WITCH   Not so happy, yet much happier.

THIRD WITCH   Thou shalt get kings, though thou be none.
   So all hail, Macbeth and Banquo!

FIRST WITCH   Banquo and Macbeth, all hail!

MACBETH   Stay, you imperfect speakers, tell me more.
   By Sinel's death I know I am thane of Glamis;
   But how of Cawdor? the thane of Cawdor lives,
   A prosperous gentleman; and to be King
   Stands not within the prospect of belief,
   No more than to be Cawdor. Say from whence
   You owe this strange intelligence? or why
   Upon this blasted heath you stop our way
   With such prophetic greeting? Speak, I charge you.   *Witches vanish.*

BANQUO   The earth hath bubbles, as the water has,
   And these are of them. Whither are they vanish'd?

MACBETH   Into the air; and what seem'd corporal melted
   As breath into the wind. Would they had stay'd!

BANQUO   Were such things here as we do speak about?
   Or have we eaten on the insane root
   That takes the reason prisoner?

MACBETH   Your children shall be kings.

BANQUO   You shall be King.

MACBETH   And thane of Cawdor too; went it not so?

BANQUO   To the selfsame tune and words. Who's here?

Enter Ross and Angus.

ROSS   The King hath happily received, Macbeth,
   The news of thy success; and when he reads
   Thy personal venture in the rebels' fight,
   His wonders and his praises do contend
   Which should be thine or his. Silenced with that,
   In viewing o'er the rest o' the selfsame day,

He finds thee in the stout Norweyan ranks,
Nothing afeard of what thyself didst make,
Strange images of death. As thick as hail
Came post with post; and every one did bear
Thy praises in his kingdom's great defence,
And pour'd them down before him.

ANGUS   We are sent
  To give thee from our royal master thanks;
  Only to herald thee into his sight,
  Not pay thee.

ROSS   And, for an earnest of a greater honour,
  He bade me, from him, call thee thane of Cawdor;
  In which addition, hail, most worthy thane!
  For it is thine.

BANQUO   What, can the devil speak true?

MACBETH   The thane of Cawdor lives. Why do you dress me
  In borrow'd robes?

ANGUS   Who was the thane lives yet;
  But under heavy judgement bears that life
  Which he deserves to lose. Whether he was combined
  With those of Norway, or did line the rebel
  With hidden help and vantage, or that with both
  He labour'd in his country's wreck, I know not;
  But treasons capital, confess'd, and proved,
  Have overthrown him.

MACBETH   [*Aside.*] Glamis, and thane of Cawdor!
  The greatest is behind. [*To Ross and Angus.*] Thanks for your pains.
  [*To Banquo.*] Do you not hope your children shall be kings,
  When those that gave the thane of Cawdor to me
  Promised no less to them?

BANQUO   That trusted home
  Might yet enkindle you unto the crown,
  Besides the thane of Cawdor. But 'tis strange;
  And oftentimes, to win us to our harm,
  The instruments of darkness tell us truths,
  Win us with honest trifles, to betray's
  In deepest consequence.
  Cousins, a word, I pray you.

MACBETH   [*Aside.*]   Two truths are told,
  As happy prologues to the swelling act
  Of the imperial theme. I thank you, gentlemen.
  [*Aside.*] This supernatural soliciting
  Cannot be ill, cannot be good. If ill,
  Why hath it given me earnest of success,
  Commencing in a truth? I am thane of Cawdor.
  If good, why do I yield to that suggestion
  Whose horrid image doth unfix my hair
  And make my seated heart knock at my ribs,
  Against the use of nature? Present fears
  Are less than horrible imaginings.
  My thought, whose murder yet is but fantastical,
  Shakes so my single state of man that function
  Is smother'd in surmise, and nothing is
  But what is not.

BANQUO   Look, how our partner's rapt.

MACBETH   [*Aside.*] If chance will have me King, why, chance may crown
  me
  Without my stir.

BANQUO   New honours come upon him,
  Like our strange garments, cleave not to their mould
  But with the aid of use.

MACBETH   [*Aside.*]   Come what come may,
  Time and the hour runs through the roughest day.

BANQUO   Worthy Macbeth, we stay upon your leisure.

MACBETH   Give me your favour. My dull brain was wrought
  With things forgotten. Kind gentlemen, your pains
  Are register'd where every day I turn
  The leaf to read them. Let us toward the King.
  [*To Banquo.*] Think upon what hath chanced, and, at more time,
  The interim having weigh'd it, let us speak
  Our free hearts each to other.

BANQUO   Very gladly.

MACBETH   Till then, enough. Come, friends.   *Exeunt.*

SCENE 4 *Forres. The palace.*

Flourish. Enter Duncan, Malcolm, Donalbain, Lennox, and Attendants.

DUNCAN   Is execution done on Cawdor? Are not
   Those in commission yet return'd?

MALCOLM   My liege,
   They are not yet come back. But I have spoke
   With one that saw him die; who did report
   That very frankly he confess'd his treasons,
   Implor'd your Highness' pardon, and set forth
   A deep repentance. Nothing in his life
   Became him like the leaving it; he died
   As one that had been studied in his death
   To throw away the dearest thing he owed,
   As 'twere a careless trifle.

DUNCAN   There's no art
   To find the mind's construction in the face.
   He was a gentleman on whom I built
   An absolute trust.

Enter Macbeth, Banquo, Ross, and Angus.

                 O worthiest cousin!
   The sin of my ingratitude even now
   Was heavy on me. Thou art so far before
   That swiftest wing of recompense is slow
   To overtake thee. Would thou hadst less deserved,
   That the proportion both of thanks and payment
   Might have been mine! only I have left to say,
   More is thy due than more than all can pay.

MACBETH   The service and the loyalty I owe,
   In doing it, pays itself. Your Highness' part
   Is to receive our duties; and our duties
   Are to your throne and state, children and servants,
   Which do but what they should, by doing everything
   Safe toward your love and honour.

DUNCAN   Welcome hither.
   I have begun to plant thee, and will labour
   To make thee full of growing. Noble Banquo,
   That hast no less deserved, nor must be known

No less to have done so, let me infold thee
And hold thee to my heart.

BANQUO   There if I grow,
  The harvest is your own.

DUNCAN   My plenteous joys,
  Wanton in fulness, seek to hide themselves
  In drops of sorrow. Sons, kinsmen, thanes,
  And you whose places are the nearest, know
  We will establish our estate upon
  Our eldest, Malcolm, whom we name hereafter
  The Prince of Cumberland; which honour must
  Not unaccompanied invest him only,
  But signs of nobleness, like stars, shall shine
  On all deservers. From hence to Inverness,
  And bind us further to you.

MACBETH   The rest is labour, which is not used for you.
  I'll be myself the harbinger and make joyful
  The hearing of my wife with your approach;
  So humbly take my leave.

DUNCAN   My worthy Cawdor!

MACBETH   [*Aside.*] The Prince of Cumberland! that is a step
  On which I must fall down, or else o'erleap,
  For in my way it lies. Stars, hide your fires;
  Let not light see my black and deep desires;
  The eye wink at the hand; yet let that be
  Which the eye fears, when it is done, to see.   *Exit.*

DUNCAN   True, worthy Banquo; he is full so valiant,
  And in his commendations I am fed;
  It is a banquet to me. Let's after him,
  Whose care is gone before to bid us welcome.
  It is a peerless kinsman.   *Flourish. Exeunt.*

SCENE 5 *Inverness. Macbeth's castle.*

Enter Lady Macbeth, alone, with a letter.

LADY MACBETH   [*Reads.*]
  "They met me in the day of success; and I have learned by the perfect-
  est report, they have more in them than mortal knowledge. When I

520

burned in desire to question them further, they made themselves air, into which they vanished. Whiles I stood rapt in the wonder of it, came missives from the King, who all-hailed me 'Thane of Cawdor'; by which title, before, these weird sisters saluted me, and referred me to the coming on of time with 'Hail, King that shalt be!' This have I thought good to deliver thee, my dearest partner of greatness, that thou mightst not lose the dues of rejoicing by being ignorant of what greatness is promised thee. Lay it to thy heart, and farewell."

Glamis thou art, and Cawdor; and shalt be
What thou art promised. Yet do I fear thy nature;
It is too full o' the milk of human kindness
To catch the nearest way. Thou wouldst be great;
Art not without ambition, but without
The illness should attend it. What thou wouldst highly,
That wouldst thou holily; wouldst not play false,
And yet wouldst wrongly win. Thou'dst have, great Glamis,
That which cries "Thus thou must do, if thou have it;
And that which rather thou dost fear to do
Than wishest should be undone." Hie thee hither,
That I may pour my spirits in thine ear;
And chastise with the valour of my tongue
All that impedes thee from the golden round,
Which fate and metaphysical aid doth seem
To have thee crown'd withal.

Enter a Messenger.

What is your tidings?

MESSENGER   The King comes here to-night.

LADY MACBETH   Th'art mad to say it!
Is not thy master with him? who, were't so,
Would have inform'd for preparation.

MESSENGER   So please you, it is true; our thane is coming.
One of my fellows had the speed of him,
Who, almost dead for breath, had scarcely more
Than would make up his message.

LADY MACBETH   Give him tending;
He brings great news.   *Exit Messenger.*
                    The raven himself is hoarse
That croaks the fatal entrance of Duncan

521

Under my battlements. Come, you spirits
That tend on mortal thoughts, unsex me here,
And fill me from the crown to the toe top-full
Of direst cruelty! make thick my blood;
Stop up the access and passage to remorse.
That no compunctious visitings of nature
Shake my fell purpose, nor keep peace between
The effect and it! Come to my woman's breasts,
And take my milk for gall, you murdering ministers,
Wherever in your sightless substances
You wait on nature's mischief! Come, thick night,
And pall thee in the dunnest smoke of hell,
That my keen knife see not the wound it makes,
Nor heaven peep through the blanket of the dark,
To cry, "Hold, hold!"

Enter Macbeth.

                    Great Glamis! worthy Cawdor!
Greater than both, by the all-hail hereafter!
Thy letters have transported me beyond
This ignorant present, and I feel now
The future in the instant.

MACBETH   My dearest love,
Duncan comes here to-night.

LADY MACBETH   And when goes hence?

MACBETH   To-morrow, as he purposes.

LADY MACBETH   O, never
Shall sun that morrow see!
Your face, my thane, is as a book where men
May read strange matters. To beguile the time,
Look like the time; bear welcome in your eye,
Your hand, your tongue; look like the innocent flower,
But be the serpent under't. He that's coming
Must be provided for; and you shall put
This night's great business into my dispatch;
Which shall to all our nights and days to come
Give solely sovereign sway and masterdom.

MACBETH   We will speak further.

522

LADY MACBETH   Only look up clear;
   To alter favour ever is to fear.
   Leave all the rest to me.   *Exeunt.*

SCENE 6   *Before Macbeth's castle.*

Hautboys and torches. Enter Duncan, Malcolm, Donalbain, Banquo, Lennox,
Macduff, Ross, Angus, and Attendants.

DUNCAN   This castle hath a pleasant seat; the air
   Nimbly and sweetly recommends itself
   Unto our gentle senses.

BANQUO   This guest of summer,
   The temple-haunting martlet, does approve,
   By his loved mansionry, that the heaven's breath
   Smells wooingly here; no jutty, frieze,
   Buttress, nor coign of vantage, but this bird
   Hath made his pendent bed and procreant cradle.
   Where they most breed and haunt, I have observed,
   The air is delicate.

Enter Lady Macbeth.

DUNCAN   See, see, our honour'd hostess!
   The love that follows us sometime is our trouble,
   Which still we thank as love. Herein I teach you
   How you shall bid God 'ild us for your pains,
   And thank us for your trouble.

LADY MACBETH   All our service
   In every point twice done and then done double
   Were poor and single business to contend
   Against those honours deep and broad wherewith
   Your Majesty loads our house. For those of old,
   And the late dignities heap'd up to them,
   We rest your hermits.

DUNCAN   Where's the thane of Cawdor?
   We coursed him at the heels, and had a purpose
   To be his purveyor; but he rides well
   And his great love, sharp as his spur, hath holp him
   To his home before us. Fair and noble hostess,
   We are your guest to-night.

523

LADY MACBETH   Your servants ever
  Have theirs, themselves, and what is theirs, in compt,
  To make their audit at your Highness' pleasure,
  Still to return your own.

DUNCAN   Give me your hand;
  Conduct me to mine host. We love him highly,
  And shall continue our graces towards him.
  By your leave, hostess.   *Exeunt.*

SCENE 7 *Macbeth's castle.*

Hautboys and torches. Enter a Sewer, and divers Servants with dishes and service, and pass over the stage. Then enter Macbeth.

MACBETH   If it were done when 'tis done, then 'twere well
  It were done quickly. If the assassination
  Could trammel up the consequence, and catch
  With his surcease success; that but this blow
  Might be the be-all and the end-all here,
  But here, upon this bank and shoal of time,
  We'd jump the life to come. But in these cases
  We still have judgement here; that we but teach
  Bloody instructions, which, being taught, return
  To plague the inventor. This even-handed justice
  Commends the ingredients of our poison'd chalice
  To our own lips. He's here in double trust;
  First, as I am his kinsman and his subject,
  Strong both against the deed; then, as his host,
  Who should against his murderer shut the door,
  Not bear the knife myself. Besides, this Duncan
  Hath borne his faculties so meek, hath been
  So clear in his great office, that his virtues
  Will plead like angels, trumpet-tongued, against
  The deep damnation of his taking-off;
  And pity, like a naked new-born babe,
  Striding the blast, or heaven's cherubim, horsed
  Upon the sightless couriers of the air,
  Shall blow the horrid deed in every eye,
  That tears shall drown the wind. I have no spur
  To prick the sides of my intent, but only

Vaulting ambition, which o'erleaps itself
And falls on the other.

Enter Lady Macbeth.

How now! what news?

LADY MACBETH   He has almost supp'd. Why have you left the chamber?

MACBETH   Hath he ask'd for me?

LADY MACBETH   Know you not he has?

MACBETH   We will proceed no further in this business.
   He hath honour'd me of late; and I have bought
   Golden opinions from all sorts of people,
   Which would be worn now in their newest gloss,
   Not cast aside so soon.

LADY MACBETH   Was the hope drunk
   Wherein you dress'd yourself? Hath it slept since?
   And wakes it now, to look so green and pale
   At what it did so freely? From this time
   Such I account thy love. Art thou afeard
   To be the same in thine own act and valour
   As thou art in desire? Wouldst thou have that
   Which thou esteem'st the ornament of life,
   And live a coward in thine own esteem,
   Letting "I dare not" wait upon "I would,"
   Like the poor cat i' the adage?

MACBETH   Prithee, peace.
   I dare do all that may become a man;
   Who dares do more is none.

LADY MACBETH   What beast was't, then,
   That made you break this enterprise to me?
   When you durst do it, then you were a man;
   And, to be more than what you were, you would
   Be so much more the man. Nor time nor place
   Did then adhere, and yet you would make both.
   They have made themselves, and that their fitness now
   Does unmake you. I have given suck, and know
   How tender 'tis to love the babe that milks me;
   I would, while it was smiling in my face,

525

Have pluck'd my nipple from his boneless gums
And dash'd the brains out, had I so sworn as you
Have done to this.

MACBETH   If we should fail?

LADY MACBETH   We fail!
But screw your courage to the sticking-place,
And we'll not fail. When Duncan is asleep—
Whereto the rather shall his day's hard journey
Soundly invite him—his two chamberlains
Will I with wine and wassail so convince
That memory, the warder of the brain,
Shall be a fume, and the receipt of reason
A limbeck only. When in swinish sleep
Their drenched natures lie as in a death,
What cannot you and I perform upon
The unguarded Duncan? what not put upon
His spongy officers, who shall bear the guilt
Of our great quell?

MACBETH   Bring forth men-children only;
For thy undaunted mettle should compose
Nothing but males. Will it not be received,
When we have mark'd with blood those sleepy two
Of his own chamber and used their very daggers,
That they have done't?

LADY MACBETH   Who dares receive it other,
As we shall make our griefs and clamour roar
Upon his death?

MACBETH   I am settled, and bend up
Each corporal agent to this terrible feat.
Away, and mock the time with fairest show;
False face must hide what the false heart doth know.   *Exeunt.*

ACT II

SCENE 1 *Court of Macbeth's castle.*

Enter Banquo, and Fleance bearing a torch before him.

BANQUO How goes the night, boy?

FLEANCE The moon is down; I have not heard the clock.

BANQUO And she goes down at twelve.

FLEANCE   I take't, 'tis later, sir.

BANQUO Hold, take my sword. There's husbandry in heaven;
Their candles are all out. Take thee that too.
A heavy summons lies like lead upon me,
And yet I would not sleep. Merciful powers,
Restrain in me the cursed thoughts that nature
Gives way to in repose!

Enter Macbeth, and a Servant with a torch.

                                        Give me my sword.
Who's there?

MACBETH A friend.

BANQUO What, sir, not yet at rest? The King's a-bed.
He hath been in unusual pleasure, and
Sent forth great largess to your offices.
This diamond he greets your wife withal,
By the name of most kind hostess; and shut up
In measureless content.

MACBETH   Being unprepared,

Our will became the servant to defect;
Which else should free have wrought.

BANQUO   All's well.
I dreamt last night of the three weird sisters.
To you they have show'd some truth.

MACBETH   I think not of them:
Yet, when we can entreat an hour to serve,
We would spend it in some words upon that business,
If you would grant the time.

BANQUO   At your kind'st leisure.

MACBETH   If you shall cleave to my consent, when 'tis,
It shall make honour for you.

BANQUO   So I lose none
In seeking to augment it, but still keep
My bosom franchised and allegiance clear,
I shall be counsell'd.

MACBETH   Good repose the while!

BANQUO   Thanks, sir; the like to you!   *Exeunt Banquo and Fleance.*

MACBETH   Go bid thy mistress, when my drink is ready,
She strike upon the bell. Get thee to bed.   *Exit Servant.*
Is this a dagger which I see before me,
The handle toward my hand? Come, let me clutch thee.
I have thee not, and yet I see thee still.
Art thou not, fatal vision, sensible
To feeling as to sight? or art thou but
A dagger of the mind, a false creation,
Proceeding from the heat-oppressed brain?
I see thee yet, in form as palpable
As this which now I draw.
Thou marshall'st me the way that I was going;
And such an instrument I was to use.
Mine eyes are made the fools o' the other senses,
Or else worth all the rest; I see thee still,
And on thy blade and dudgeon gouts of blood,
Which was not so before. There's no such thing.
It is the bloody business which informs
Thus to mine eyes. Now o'er the one half-world
Nature seems dead, and wicked dreams abuse

528

The curtain'd sleep; witchcraft celebrates
Pale Hecate's offerings, and wither'd murder,
Alarum'd by his sentinel, the wolf,
Whose howl's his watch, thus with his stealthy pace,
With Tarquin's ravishing strides, towards his design
Moves like a ghost. Thou sure and firm-set earth,
Hear not my steps, which way they walk, for fear
Thy very stones prate of my whereabout,
And take the present horror from the time,
Which now suits with it. Whiles I threat, he lives:
Words to the heat of deeds too cold breath gives.

A bell rings.

I go, and it is done; the bell invites me.
Hear it not, Duncan; for it is a knell
That summons thee to heaven or to hell.   *Exit.*

❧ SCENE 2   *The same.*

Enter Lady Macbeth.

LADY MACBETH   That which hath made them drunk hath made me bold;
What hath quench'd them hath given me fire. Hark! Peace!
It was the owl that shriek'd, the fatal bellman,
Which gives the stern'st good-night. He is about it.
The doors are open, and the surfeited grooms
Do mock their charge with snores. I have drugg'd their possets,
That death and nature do contend about them,
Whether they live or die.

MACBETH   [*Within.*] Who's there? what, ho!

LADY MACBETH   Alack, I am afraid they have awaked,
And 'tis not done. The attempt and not the deed
Confounds us. Hark! I laid their daggers ready;
He could not miss 'em. Had he not resembled
My father as he slept, I had done't.

Enter Macbeth.

My husband!

MACBETH   I have done the deed. Didst thou not hear a noise?

529

LADY MACBETH   I heard the owl scream and the crickets cry.
Did not you speak?

MACBETH   When?

LADY MACBETH   Now.

MACBETH   As I descended?

LADY MACBETH   Ay.

MACBETH   Hark!
Who lies i' the second chamber?

LADY MACBETH   Donalbain.

MACBETH   This is a sorry sight.

Looking on his hands.

LADY MACBETH   A foolish thought, to say a sorry sight.

MACBETH   There's one did laugh in's sleep, and one cried "Murder!"
That they did wake each other. I stood and heard them;
But they did say their prayers, and address'd them
Again to sleep.

LADY MACBETH   There are two lodged together.

MACBETH   One cried "God bless us!" and "Amen" the other;
As they had seen me with these hangman's hands.
Listening their fear, I could not say "Amen,"
When they did say "God bless us!"

LADY MACBETH   Consider it not so deeply.

MACBETH   But wherefore could not I pronounce "Amen"?
I had most need of blessing, and "Amen"
Stuck in my throat.

LADY MACBETH   These deeds must not be thought
After these ways; so, it will make us mad.

MACBETH   Methought I heard a voice cry, "Sleep no more!
Macbeth does murder sleep," the innocent sleep,
Sleep that knits up the ravell'd sleave of care,
The death of each day's life, sore labour's bath,
Balm of hurt minds, great nature's second course,
Chief nourisher in life's feast—

LADY MACBETH   What do you mean?

MACBETH   Still it cried, "Sleep no more!" to all the house;
  "Glamis hath murder'd sleep, and therefore Cawdor
  Shall sleep no more; Macbeth shall sleep no more."

LADY MACBETH   Who was it that thus cried? Why, worthy thane,
  You do unbend your noble strength, to think
  So brainsickly of things. Go get some water,
  And wash this filthy witness from your hand.
  Why did you bring these daggers from the place?
  They must lie there. Go carry them; and smear
  The sleepy grooms with blood.

MACBETH   I'll go no more.
  I am afraid to think what I have done;
  Look on't again I dare not.

LADY MACBETH   Infirm of purpose!
  Give me the daggers. The sleeping and the dead
  Are but as pictures; 'tis the eye of childhood
  That fears a painted devil. If he do bleed,
  I'll gild the faces of the grooms withal;
  For it must seem their guilt.   *Exit.*

Knock within.

MACBETH   Whence is that knocking?
  How is't with me, when every noise appals me?
  What hands are here? Ha! they pluck out mine eyes.
  Will all great Neptune's ocean wash this blood
  Clean from my hand? No, this my hand will rather
  The multitudinous seas incarnadine,
  Making the green one red.

Re-enter Lady Macbeth.

LADY MACBETH   My hands are of your colour; but I shame
  To wear a heart so white. [*Knock.*] I hear a knocking
  At the south entry. Retire we to our chamber.
  A little water clears us of this deed;
  How easy is it, then! Your constancy
  Hath left you unattended. [*Knock.*] Hark! more knocking.
  Get on your nightgown, lest occasion call us,
  And show us to be watchers. Be not lost
  So poorly in your thoughts.

MACBETH   To know my deed, 'twere best not know myself. [*Knock.*]
Wake Duncan with thy knocking! I would thou couldst!   *Exeunt.*

✻ SCENE 3   *The same.*

Knocking within. Enter a Porter.

PORTER   Here's a knocking indeed! If a man were porter of hell-gate, he
should have old turning the key. [*Knock.*] Knock, knock, knock! Who's
there, i' the name of Beelzebub? Here's a farmer, that hanged himself
on the expectation of plenty. Come in time; have napkins enow about
you; here you'll sweat for't. [*Knock.*] Knock, knock! Who's there, in
the other devil's name? Faith, here's an equivocator, that could swear
in both the scales against either scale; who committed treason enough
for God's sake, yet could not equivocate to heaven. O, come in, equivocator. [*Knock.*] Knock, knock, knock! Who's there? Faith, here's an
English tailor come hither for stealing out of a French hose. Come in,
tailor; here you may roast your goose. [*Knock.*] Knock, knock; never at
quiet! What are you? But this place is too cold for hell. I'll devil-porter
it no further. I had thought to have let in some of all professions that go
the primrose way to the everlasting bonfire. [*Knock.*] Anon, anon! I
pray you, remember the porter.

Opens the gate. Enter Macduff and Lennox.

MACDUFF   Was it so late, friend, ere you went to bed,
That you do lie so late?

PORTER   'Faith, sir, we were carousing till the second cock. And drink,
sir, is a great provoker of three things.

MACDUFF   What three things does drink especially provoke?

PORTER   Marry, sir, nose-painting, sleep, and urine. Lechery, sir, it provokes, and unprovokes; it provokes the desire but it takes away the
performance; therefore, much drink may be said to be an equivocator
with lechery: it makes him, and it mars him; it sets him on, and it takes
him off; it persuades him, and disheartens him; makes him stand to,
and not stand to; in conclusion, equivocates him in sleep, and, giving
him the lie, leaves him.

MACDUFF   I believe drink gave thee the lie last night.

PORTER   That it did, sir, i' the very throat on me. But I requited him for

his lie; and, I think, being too strong for him, though he took up my legs sometime, yet I made a shift to cast him.

MACDUFF   Is thy master stirring?

Enter Macbeth.

Our knocking has awakened him; here he comes.

LENNOX   Good morrow, noble sir.

MACBETH   Good morrow, both.

MACDUFF   Is the King stirring, worthy thane?

MACBETH   Not yet.

MACDUFF   He did command me to call timely on him.
I have almost slipp'd the hour.

MACBETH   I'll bring you to him.

MACDUFF   I know this is a joyful trouble to you;
But yet 'tis one.

MACBETH   The labour we delight in physics pain.
This is the door.

MACDUFF   I'll make so bold to call,
For 'tis my limited service.   *Exit.*

LENNOX   Goes the King hence to-day?

MACBETH   He does; he did appoint so.

LENNOX   The night has been unruly. Where we lay,
Our chimneys were blown down; and, as they say,
Lamentings heard i' the air; strange screams of death,
And prophesying with accents terrible
Of dire combustion and confused events
New hatch'd to the woeful time. The obscure bird
Clamour'd the livelong night; some say, the earth
Was feverous and did shake.

MACBETH   'Twas a rough night.

LENNOX   My young remembrance cannot parallel
A fellow to it.

Re-enter Macduff.

533

MACDUFF   O horror, horror, horror! Tongue nor heart
Cannot conceive nor name thee.

MACBETH AND LENNOX   What's the matter?

MACDUFF   Confusion now hath made his masterpiece!
Most sacrilegious murder hath broke ope
The Lord's anointed temple, and stole thence
The life o' the building!

MACBETH   What is't you say? the life?

LENNOX   Mean you his Majesty?

MACDUFF   Approach the chamber, and destroy your sight
With a new Gorgon. Do not bid me speak;
See, and then speak yourselves.   *Exeunt Macbeth and Lennox.*
                              Awake, awake!
Ring the alarum-bell. Murder and treason!
Banquo and Donalbain! Malcolm! awake!
Shake off this downy sleep, death's counterfeit,
And look on death itself! Up, up, and see
The great doom's image! Malcolm! Banquo!
As from your graves rise up, and walk like sprites,
To countenance this horror! Ring the bell.

Bell rings. Enter Lady Macbeth.

LADY MACBETH   What's the business,
That such a hideous trumpet calls to parley
The sleepers of the house? Speak, speak!

MACDUFF   O gentle lady,
'Tis not for you to hear what I can speak.
The repetition, in a woman's ear,
Would murder as it fell.

Enter Banquo.

                    O Banquo, Banquo,
Our royal master's murder'd!

LADY MACBETH   Woe, alas!
What, in our house?

BANQUO   Too cruel anywhere.
Dear Duff, I prithee, contradict thyself,
And say it is not so.

534

ACT II   Scene 3

Re-enter Macbeth and Lennox, with Ross.

MACBETH   Had I but died an hour before this chance,
I had lived a blessed time; for, from this instant,
There's nothing serious in mortality;
All is but toys. Renown and grace is dead;
The wine of life is drawn, and the mere lees
Is left this vault to brag of.

Enter Malcolm and Donalbain.

DONALBAIN   What is amiss?

MACBETH   You are, and do not know't.
The spring, the head, the fountain of your blood
Is stopp'd; the very source of it is stopp'd.

MACDUFF   Your royal father's murder'd.

MALCOLM   O, by whom?

LENNOX   Those of his chamber, as it seem'd, had done't.
Their hands and faces were all badged with blood;
So were their daggers, which unwiped we found
Upon their pillows.
They stared, and were distracted; no man's life
Was to be trusted with them.

MACBETH   O, yet I do repent me of my fury,
That I did kill them.

MACDUFF   Wherefore did you so?

MACBETH   Who can be wise, amazed, temperate, and furious,
Loyal and neutral, in a moment? No man.
The expedition of my violent love
Outrun the pauser, reason. Here lay Duncan,
His silver skin laced with his golden blood;
And his gash'd stabs look'd like a breach in nature
For ruin's wasteful entrance; there, the murderers,
Steep'd in the colours of their trade, their daggers
Unmannerly breech'd with gore. Who could refrain,
That had a heart to love, and in that heart
Courage to make's love known?

LADY MACBETH   Help me hence, ho!

MACDUFF   Look to the lady.

MALCOLM   [*Aside to Donalbain.*] Why do we hold our tongues,
   That most may claim this argument for ours?

DONALBAIN   [*Aside to Malcolm.*] What should be spoken here, where our fate,
   Hid in an auger-hole, may rush, and seize us?
   Let's away;
   Our tears are not yet brew'd.

MALCOLM   [*Aside to Donalbain.*] Nor our strong sorrow
   Upon the foot of motion.

BANQUO   Look to the lady;
                           Lady Macbeth is carried out.

   And when we have our naked frailties hid,
   That suffer in exposure, let us meet
   And question this most bloody piece of work,
   To know it further. Fears and scruples shake us.
   In the great hand of God I stand; and thence
   Against the undivulged pretence I fight
   Of treasonous malice.

MACDUFF   And so do I.

ALL   So all.

MACBETH   Let's briefly put on manly readiness,
   And meet i' the hall together.

ALL   Well contented.

                           Exeunt all but Malcolm and Donalbain.

MALCOLM   What will you do? Let's not consort with them;
   To show an unfelt sorrow is an office
   Which the false man does easy. I'll to England.

DONALBAIN   To Ireland, I; our separated fortune
   Shall keep us both the safer. Where we are,
   There's daggers in men's smiles; the near in blood,
   The nearer bloody.

MALCOLM   This murderous shaft that's shot
   Hath not yet lighted, and our safest way
   Is to avoid the aim. Therefore, to horse;
   And let us not be dainty of leave-taking,

But shift away. There's warrant in that theft
Which steals itself, when there's no mercy left.   *Exeunt.*

 SCENE 4   *Outside Macbeth's castle.*

Enter Ross and an Old Man.

OLD MAN   Threescore and ten I can remember well;
  Within the volume of which time I have seen
  Hours dreadful and things strange; but this sore night
  Hath trifled former knowings.

ROSS   Ah, good father,
  Thou seest, the heavens, as troubled with man's act,
  Threaten his bloody stage. By the clock, 'tis day,
  And yet dark night strangles the travelling lamp.
  Is't night's predominance, or the day's shame,
  That darkness does the face of earth entomb,
  When living light should kiss it?

OLD MAN   'Tis unnatural,
  Even like the deed that's done. On Tuesday last,
  A falcon, towering in her pride of place,
  Was by a mousing owl hawk'd at and kill'd.

ROSS   And Duncan's horses—a thing most strange and certain—
  Beauteous and swift, the minions of their race,
  Turn'd wild in nature, broke their stalls, flung out,
  Contending 'gainst obedience, as they would make
  War with mankind.

OLD MAN   'Tis said they eat each other.

ROSS   They did so, to the amazement of mine eyes
  That look'd upon't. Here comes the good Macduff.

Enter Macduff.

  How goes the world, sir, now?

MACDUFF   Why, see you not?

ROSS   Is't known who did this more than bloody deed?

MACDUFF   Those that Macbeth hath slain.

537

ROSS   Alas, the day!
  What good could they pretend?

MACDUFF   They were suborn'd.
  Malcolm and Donalbain, the King's two sons,
  Are stol'n away and fled; which puts upon them
  Suspicion of the deed.

ROSS   'Gainst nature still!
  Thriftless ambition, that wilt ravin up
  Thine own life's means! Then 'tis most like
  The sovereignty will fall upon Macbeth.

MACDUFF He is already named, and gone to Scone
  To be invested.

ROSS   Where is Duncan's body?

MACDUFF Carried to Colmekill,
  The sacred storehouse of his predecessors,
  And guardian of their bones.

ROSS   Will you to Scone?

MACDUFF No, cousin, I'll to Fife.

ROSS   Well, I will thither.

MACDUFF Well, may you see things well done there, adieu!
  Lest our old robes sit easier than our new!

ROSS Farewell, father.

OLD MAN God's benison go with you; and with those
  That would make good of bad, and friends of foes!   *Exeunt.*

ACT III

SCENE 1 *Forres. The palace.*

Enter Banquo.

BANQUO   Thou hast it now: King, Cawdor, Glamis, all,
As the weird women promised, and, I fear,
Thou play'dst most foully for't; yet it was said
It should not stand in thy posterity,
But that myself should be the root and father
Of many kings. If there come truth from them—
As upon thee, Macbeth, their speeches shine—
Why, by the verities on thee made good,
May they not be my oracles as well,
And set me up in hope? But hush! no more.

*Sennet sounded. Enter Macbeth, as King, Lady Macbeth, as Queen, Lennox,
Ross, Lords, Ladies, and Attendants.*

MACBETH   Here's our chief guest.

LADY MACBETH   If he had been forgotten,
It had been as a gap in our great feast,
And all-thing unbecoming.

MACBETH   To-night we hold a solemn supper, sir,
And I'll request your presence.

BANQUO   Let your Highness
Command upon me; to the which my duties
Are with a most indissoluble tie
For ever knit.

539

MACBETH   Ride you this afternoon?

BANQUO   Ay, my good lord.

MACBETH   We should have else desired your good advice,
Which still hath been both grave and prosperous,
In this day's council; but we'll take to-morrow.
Is't far you ride?

BANQUO   As far, my lord, as will fill up the time
'Twixt this and supper. Go not my horse the better,
I must become a borrower of the night
For a dark hour or twain.

MACBETH   Fail not our feast.

BANQUO   My lord, I will not.

MACBETH   We hear, our bloody cousins are bestow'd
In England and in Ireland, not confessing
Their cruel parricide, filling their hearers
With strange invention. But of that to-morrow,
When therewithal we shall have cause of state
Craving us jointly. Hie you to horse; adieu.
Till you return at night. Goes Fleance with you?

BANQUO   Ay, my good lord. Our time does call upon's.

MACBETH   I wish your horses swift and sure of foot;
And so I do commend you to their backs.
Farewell.   *Exit Banquo.*
Let every man be master of his time
Till seven at night. To make society
The sweeter welcome, we will keep ourself
Till supper-time alone; while then, God be with you!
                    Exeunt all but Macbeth, and an Attendant.
Sirrah, a word with you. Attend those men
Our pleasure?

ATTENDANT   They are, my lord, without the palace gate.

MACBETH   Bring them before us.   *Exit Attendant.*
                    To be thus is nothing;
But to be safely thus. Our fears in Banquo
Stick deep; and in his royalty of nature
Reigns that which would be fear'd. 'Tis much he dares;
And, to that dauntless temper of his mind,

He hath a wisdom that doth guide his valour
To act in safety. There is none but he
Whose being I do fear; and, under him,
My Genius is rebuked, as, it is said,
Mark Antony's was by Caesar. He chid the sisters
When first they put the name of King upon me,
And bade them speak to him; then prophet-like
They hail'd him father to a line of kings;
Upon my head they placed a fruitless crown,
And put a barren sceptre in my gripe,
Thence to be wrench'd with an unlineal hand,
No son of mine succeeding. If't be so,
For Banquo's issue have I filed my mind;
For them the gracious Duncan have I murder'd;
Put rancours in the vessel of my peace
Only for them; and mine eternal jewel
Given to the common enemy of man,
To make them kings, the seed of Banquo kings!
Rather than so, come fate into the list,
And champion me to the utterance! Who's there?

Re-enter Attendant, with Two Murderers.

Now go to the door, and stay there till we call.   *Exit Attendant.*
Was it not yesterday we spoke together?

FIRST MURDERER   It was, so please your Highness.

MACBETH   Well then, now
Have you consider'd of my speeches? Know
That it was he in the times past which held you
So under fortune, which you thought had been
Our innocent self. This I made good to you
In our last conference, pass'd in probation with you,
How you were borne in hand, how cross'd, the instruments,
Who wrought with them, and all things else that might
To half a soul and to a notion crazed
Say "Thus did Banquo."

FIRST MURDERER   You made it known to us.

MACBETH   I did so, and went further, which is now
Our point of second meeting. Do you find
Your patience so predominant in your nature
That you can let this go? Are you so gospell'd

541

To pray for this good man and for his issue,
Whose heavy hand hath bow'd you to the grave
And beggar'd yours for ever?

FIRST MURDERER We are men, my liege.

MACBETH Ay, in the catalogue ye go for men;
As hounds and greyhounds, mongrels, spaniels, curs,
Shoughs, water-rugs and demi-wolves are clept
All by the name of dogs; the valued file
Distinguishes the swift, the slow, the subtle,
The housekeeper, the hunter, every one
According to the gift which bounteous nature
Hath in him closed, whereby he does receive
Particular addition, from the bill
That writes them all alike; and so of men.
Now, if you have a station in the file,
Not i' the worst rank of manhood, say't;
And I will put that business in your bosoms,
Whose execution takes your enemy off,
Grapples you to the heart and love of us,
Who wear our health but sickly in his life,
Which in his death were perfect.

SECOND MURDERER I am one, my liege,
Whom the vile blows and buffets of the world
Have so incensed that I am reckless what
I do to spite the world.

FIRST MURDERER And I another
So weary with disasters, tugg'd with fortune,
That I would set my life on any chance,
To mend it, or be rid on't.

MACBETH Both of you
Know Banquo was your enemy.

BOTH MURDERERS True, my lord.

MACBETH So is he mine; and in such bloody distance,
That every minute of his being thrusts
Against my near'st of life; and though I could
With barefaced power sweep him from my sight
And bid my will avouch it, yet I must not,
For certain friends that are both his and mine,

542

Whose loves I may not drop, but wail his fall
Who I myself struck down; and thence it is,
That I to your assistance do make love,
Masking the business from the common eye
For sundry weighty reasons.

SECOND MURDERER   We shall, my lord,
Perform what you command us.

FIRST MURDERER   Though our lives—

MACBETH   Your spirits shine through you. Within this hour at most
I will advise you where to plant yourselves;
Acquaint you with the perfect spy o' the time,
The moment on't; for't must be done to-night,
And something from the palace; always thought
That I require a clearness: and with him—
To leave no rubs nor botches in the work—
Fleance his son, that keeps him company,
Whose absence is no less material to me
Than is his father's, must embrace the fate
Of that dark hour. Resolve yourselves apart;
I'll come to you anon.

BOTH MURDERERS   We are resolved, my lord.

MACBETH   I'll call upon you straight; abide within.   *Exeunt Murderers.*
It is concluded. Banquo, thy soul's flight,
If it find heaven, must find it out to-night.   *Exit.*

SCENE 2   *The palace.*

Enter Lady Macbeth and a Servant.

LADY MACBETH   Is Banquo gone from court?

SERVANT   Ay, madam, but returns again to-night.

LADY MACBETH   Say to the King, I would attend his leisure
For a few words.

SERVANT   Madam, I will.   *Exit.*

LADY MACBETH   Nought's had, all's spent,
Where our desire is got without content.

543

'Tis safer to be that which we destroy
Than by destruction dwell in doubtful joy.

Enter Macbeth.

How now, my lord! why do you keep alone,
Of sorriest fancies your companions making,
Using those thoughts which should indeed have died
With them they think on? Things without all remedy
Should be without regard; what's done is done.

MACBETH   We have scotch'd the snake, not kill'd it;
She'll close and be herself, whilst our poor malice
Remains in danger of her former tooth,
But let the frame of things disjoint, both the worlds suffer,
Ere we will eat our meal in fear and sleep
In the affliction of these terrible dreams
That shake us nightly. Better be with the dead,
Whom we, to gain our peace, have sent to peace,
Than on the torture of the mind to lie
In restless ecstasy. Duncan is in his grave;
After life's fitful fever he sleeps well;
Treason has done his worst; nor steel, nor poison,
Malice domestic, foreign levy, nothing,
Can touch him further.

LADY MACBETH   Come on;
Gentle my lord, sleek o'er your rugged looks;
Be bright and jovial among your guests to-night.

MACBETH   So shall I, love; and so, I pray, be you.
Let your remembrance apply to Banquo;
Present him eminence, both with eye and tongue.
Unsafe the while, that we
Must lave our honours in these flattering streams,
And make our faces vizards to our hearts,
Disguising what they are.

LADY MACBETH   You must leave this.

MACBETH   O, full of scorpions is my mind, dear wife!
Thou know'st that Banquo, and his Fleance, lives.

LADY MACBETH   But in them nature's copy's not eterne.

MACBETH   There's comfort yet; they are assailable;

Then be thou jocund; ere the bat hath flown
His cloister'd flight, ere to black Hecate's summons
The shard-borne beetle with his drowsy hums
Hath rung night's yawning peal, there shall be done
A deed of dreadful note.

LADY MACBETH   What's to be done?

MACBETH   Be innocent of the knowledge, dearest chuck,
  Till thou applaud the deed. Come, seeling night,
  Scarf up the tender eye of pitiful day;
  And with thy bloody and invisible hand
  Cancel and tear to pieces that great bond
  Which keeps me pale! Light thickens; and the crow
  Makes wing to the rooky wood;
  Good things of day begin to droop and drowse;
  Whiles night's black agents to their preys do rouse.
  Thou marvell'st at my words, but hold thee still;
  Things bad begun make strong themselves by ill.
  So, prithee, go with me.   *Exeunt.*

☙ SCENE 3   *A park near the palace.*

Enter Three Murderers.

FIRST MURDERER   But who did bid thee join with us?

THIRD MURDERER   Macbeth.

SECOND MURDERER   He needs not our mistrust, since he delivers
  Our offices and what we have to do
  To the direction just.

FIRST MURDERER   Then stand with us.
  The west yet glimmers with some streaks of day;
  Now spurs the lated traveller apace
  To gain the timely inn; and near approaches
  The subject of our watch.

THIRD MURDERER   Hark! I hear horses.

BANQUO   [*Within.*] Give us a light there, ho!

SECOND MURDERER   Then 'tis he; the rest
  That are within the note of expectation
  Already are i' the court.

545

FIRST MURDERER   His horses go about.

THIRD MURDERER   Almost a mile; but he does usually,
So all men do, from hence to the palace gate
Make it their walk.

SECOND MURDERER   A light, a light!

Enter Banquo, and Fleance with a torch.

THIRD MURDERER   'Tis he.

FIRST MURDERER   Stand to't.

BANQUO   It will be rain to-night.

FIRST MURDERER   Let it come down.

They set upon Banquo.

BANQUO   O, treachery! Fly, good Fleance, fly, fly, fly!
Thou mayst revenge. O slave!   *Dies. Fleance escapes.*

THIRD MURDERER   Who did strike out the light?

FIRST MURDERER   Was't not the way?

THIRD MURDERER   There's but one down; the son is fled.

SECOND MURDERER   We have lost
Best half of our affair.

FIRST MURDERER   Well, let's away, and say how much is done.   *Exeunt.*

❀ SCENE 4   *The same. Hall in the palace.*

A banquet prepared. Enter Macbeth, Lady Macbeth, Ross, Lennox, Lords, and Attendants.

MACBETH   You know your own degrees; sit down. At first
And last the hearty welcome.

LORDS   Thanks to your Majesty.

MACBETH   Ourself will mingle with society,
And play the humble host.
Our hostess keeps her state, but in best time
We will require her welcome.

LADY MACBETH   Pronounce it for me, sir, to all our friends;
  For my heart speaks they are welcome.

First Murderer appears at the door.

MACBETH   See, they encounter thee with their hearts' thanks.
  Both sides are even; here I'll sit i' the midst.
  Be large in mirth; anon we'll drink a measure
  The table round. [*Approaching the door.*] There's blood upon thy face.

FIRST MURDERER   'Tis Banquo's then.

MACBETH   'Tis better thee without than he within.
  Is he dispatch'd?

FIRST MURDERER   My lord, his throat is cut; that I did for him.

MACBETH   Thou art the best o' the cut-throats; yet he's good
  That did the like for Fleance. If thou didst it,
  Thou art the nonpareil.

FIRST MURDERER   Most royal sir,
  Fleance is 'scaped.

MACBETH   Then comes my fit again. I had else been perfect,
  Whole as the marble, founded as the rock,
  As broad and general as the casing air;
  But now I am cabin'd, cribb'd, confined, bound in
  To saucy doubts and fears. But Banquo's safe?

FIRST MURDERER   Ay, my good lord; safe in a ditch he bides,
  With twenty trenched gashes on his head;
  The least a death to nature.

MACBETH   Thanks for that.
  There the grown serpent lies; the worm that's fled
  Hath nature that in time will venom breed,
  No teeth for the present. Get thee gone; to-morrow
  We'll hear, ourselves, again.   *Exit Murderer.*

LADY MACBETH   My royal lord,
  You do not give the cheer. The feast is sold
  That is not often vouch'd, while 'tis a-making,
  'Tis given with welcome. To feed were best at home;
  From thence the sauce to meat is ceremony;
  Meeting were bare without it.

547

MACBETH   Sweet remembrancer!
  Now, good digestion wait on appetite,
  And health on both!

LENNOX   May't please your Highness sit.

The Ghost of Banquo enters, and sits in Macbeth's place.

MACBETH   Here had we now our country's honour roof'd,
  Were the graced person of our Banquo present;
  Who may I rather challenge for unkindness
  Than pity for mischance!

ROSS   His absence, sir,
  Lays blame upon his promise. Please't your Highness
  To grace us with your royal company.

MACBETH   The table's full.

LENNOX   Here is a place reserved, sir.

MACBETH   Where?

LENNOX   Here, my good lord. What is't that moves your Highness?

MACBETH   Which of you have done this?

LORDS   What, my good lord?

MACBETH   Thou canst not say I did it. Never shake
  Thy gory locks at me.

ROSS   Gentlemen, rise: his Highness is not well.

LADY MACBETH   Sit, worthy friends; my lord is often thus,
  And hath been from his youth. Pray you, keep seat;
  The fit is momentary; upon a thought
  He will again be well. If much you note him,
  You shall offend him and extend his passion.
  Feed, and regard him not. Are you a man?

MACBETH   Ay, and a bold one, that dare look on that
  Which might appal the devil.

LADY MACBETH   O proper stuff!
  This is the very painting of your fear;
  This is the air-drawn dagger which, you said,
  Led you to Duncan. O, these flaws and starts,
  Impostors to true fear, would well become

548

A woman's story at a winter's fire,
Authorized by her grandam. Shame itself!
Why do you make such faces? When all's done,
You look but on a stool.

MACBETH   Prithee, see there! behold! look! lo! how say you?
Why, what care I? If thou canst nod, speak too.
If charnel-houses and our graves must send
Those that we bury back, our monuments
Shall be the maws of kites.   *Ghost vanishes.*

LADY MACBETH   What, quite unmann'd in folly?

MACBETH   If I stand here, I saw him.

LADY MACBETH   Fie, for shame!

MACBETH   Blood hath been shed ere now, i' the olden time,
Ere humane statute purged the gentle weal;
Ay, and since too, murders have been perform'd
Too terrible for the ear. The time has been
That, when the brains were out, the man would die,
And there an end; but now they rise again,
With twenty mortal murders on their crowns,
And push us from our stools. This is more strange
Than such a murder is.

LADY MACBETH   My worthy lord,
Your noble friends do lack you.

MACBETH   I do forget.
Do not muse at me, my most worthy friends;
I have a strange infirmity, which is nothing
To those that know me. Come, love and health to all;
Then I'll sit down. Give me some wine; fill full.
I drink to the general joy o' the whole table,
And to our dear friend Banquo, whom we miss;
Would he were here! to all, and him, we thirst,
And all to all.

LORDS   Our duties, and the pledge.

Re-enter Ghost.

MACBETH   Avaunt! and quit my sight! let the earth hide thee!
Thy bones are marrowless, thy blood is cold;

Thou hast no speculation in those eyes
Which thou dost glare with!

LADY MACBETH   Think of this, good peers,
But as a thing of custom; 'tis no other.
Only it spoils the pleasure of the time.

MACBETH   What man dare, I dare.
Approach thou like the rugged Russian bear,
The arm'd rhinoceros, or the Hyrcan tiger;
Take any shape but that, and my firm nerves
Shall never tremble. Or be alive again,
And dare me to the desert with thy sword;
If trembling I inhabit then, protest me
The baby of a girl. Hence, horrible shadow!
Unreal mockery, hence!   *Ghost vanishes.*
                    Why, so; being gone,
I am a man again. Pray you, sit still.

LADY MACBETH   You have displaced the mirth, broke the good meeting,
With most admired disorder.

MACBETH   Can such things be,
And overcome us like a summer's cloud,
Without our special wonder? You make me strange
Even to the disposition that I owe,
When now I think you can behold such sights,
And keep the natural ruby of your cheeks,
When mine is blanch'd with fear.

ROSS   What sights, my lord?

LADY MACBETH   I pray you, speak not; he grows worse and worse;
Question enrages him. At once, good night.
Stand not upon the order of your going,
But go at once.

LENNOX   Good night; and better health
Attend his Majesty!

LADY MACBETH   A kind good night to all!
                    Exeunt all but Macbeth and Lady Macbeth.

MACBETH   It will have blood; they say, blood will have blood.
Stones have been known to move and trees to speak;
Augurs and understood relations have

550

By magot-pies and choughs and rooks brought forth
The secret'st man of blood. What is the night?

LADY MACBETH   Almost at odds with morning, which is which.

MACBETH   How say'st thou, that Macduff denies his person
At our great bidding?

LADY MACBETH   Did you send to him, sir?

MACBETH   I hear it by the way; but I will send.
There's not a one of them but in his house
I keep a servant fee'd. I will to-morrow,
And betimes I will, to the weird sisters.
More shall they speak; for now I am bent to know,
By the worst means, the worst. For mine own good,
All causes shall give way. I am in blood
Stepp'd in so far that, should I wade no more,
Returning were as tedious as go o'er.
Strange things I have in head, that will to hand;
Which must be acted ere they may be scann'd.

LADY MACBETH   You lack the season of all natures, sleep.

MACBETH   Come, we'll to sleep. My strange and self-abuse
Is the initiate fear that wants hard use.
We are yet but young in deed.   *Exeunt.*

SCENE 5 *A heath.*

Thunder. Enter the Three Witches, meeting Hecate.

FIRST WITCH   Why, how now, Hecate! you look angerly.

HECATE   Have I not reason, beldams as you are,
Saucy and overbold? How did you dare
To trade and traffic with Macbeth
In riddles and affairs of death;
And I, the mistress of your charms,
The close contriver of all harms,
Was never call'd to bear my part,
Or show the glory of our art?
And, which is worse, all you have done
Hath been but for a wayward son,
Spiteful and wrathful, who, as others do,

551

Loves for his own ends, not for you.
But make amends now; get you gone,
And at the pit of Acheron
Meet me i' the morning; thither he
Will come to know his destiny.
Your vessels and your spells provide,
Your charms and everything beside.
I am for the air; this night I'll spend
Unto a dismal and a fatal end;
Great business must be wrought ere noon.
Upon the corner of the moon
There hangs a vaporous drop profound;
I'll catch it ere it come to ground;
And that distill'd by magic sleights
Shall raise such artificial sprites
As by the strength of their illusion
Shall draw him on to his confusion.
He shall spurn fate, scorn death, and bear
His hopes 'bove wisdom, grace and fear;
And you all know, security
Is mortals' chiefest enemy.

Music and a song within: "Come away, come away," &c.

Hark! I am call'd; my little spirit, see,
Sits in a foggy cloud, and stays for me.   *Exit.*

FIRST WITCH   Come, let's make haste; she'll soon be back again.
                                                        Exeunt.

 SCENE 6   *Forres. The palace.*

Enter Lennox and another Lord.

LENNOX   My former speeches have but hit your thoughts,
Which can interpret further; only, I say,
Things have been strangely borne. The gracious Duncan
Was pitied of Macbeth; marry, he was dead.
And the right-valiant Banquo walk'd too late;
Whom, you may say, if 't please you, Fleance kill'd,
For Fleance fled. Men must not walk too late.

552

Who cannot want the thought how monstrous
It was for Malcolm and for Donalbain
To kill their gracious father? damned fact!
How it did grieve Macbeth! did he not straight
In pious rage the two delinquents tear,
That were the slaves of drink and thralls of sleep?
Was not that nobly done? Ay, and wisely too;
For 'twould have anger'd any heart alive
To hear the men deny't. So that, I say,
He has borne all things well; and I do think
That had he Duncan's sons under his key —
As, an't please heaven, he shall not — they should find
What 'twere to kill a father; so should Fleance.
But, peace! for from broad words and 'cause he fail'd
His presence at the tyrant's feast, I hear
Macduff lives in disgrace. Sir, can you tell
Where he bestows himself?

LORD   The son of Duncan,
   From whom this tyrant holds the due of birth,
   Lives in the English court, and is received
   Of the most pious Edward with such grace
   That the malevolence of Fortune nothing
   Takes from his high respect. Thither Macduff
   Is gone to pray the holy King, upon his aid
   To wake Northumberland and warlike Siward;
   That, by the help of these — with Him above
   To ratify the work — we may again
   Give to our tables meat, sleep to our nights,
   Free from our feasts and banquets bloody knives,
   Do faithful homage, and receive free honours;
   All which we pine for now. And this report
   Hath so exasperate the King that he
   Prepares for some attempt of war.

LENNOX   Sent he to Macduff?

LORD   He did; and with an absolute "Sir, not I,"
   The cloudy messenger turns me his back,
   And hums, as who should say, "You'll rue the time
   That clogs me with this answer."

553

LENNOX   And that well might
  Advise him to a caution, to hold what distance
  His wisdom can provide. Some holy angel
  Fly to the court of England and unfold
  His message ere he come, that a swift blessing
  May soon return to this our suffering country
  Under a hand accursed!

LORD   I'll send my prayers with him.   *Exeunt.*

ACT IV

 SCENE 1 *A cavern. In the middle, a boiling cauldron.*

Thunder. Enter the Three Witches.

FIRST WITCH   Thrice the brinded cat hath mew'd.

SECOND WITCH   Thrice and once the hedge-pig whined.

THIRD WITCH   Harpier cries; 'tis time, 'tis time.

FIRST WITCH   Round about the cauldron go;
  In the poison'd entrails throw.
  Toad, that under cold stone
  Days and nights has thirty-one
  Swelter'd venom sleeping got,
  Boil thou first i' the charmed pot.

ALL   Double, double, toil and trouble;
  Fire burn and cauldron bubble.

SECOND WITCH   Fillet of a fenny snake,
  In the cauldron boil and bake;
  Eye of newt and toe of frog,
  Wool of bat and tongue of dog,
  Adder's fork and blind-worm's sting,
  Lizard's leg and howlet's wing,
  For a charm of powerful trouble,
  Like a hell-broth boil and bubble.

ALL   Double, double, toil and trouble;
  Fire burn and cauldron bubble.

THIRD WITCH   Scale of dragon, tooth of wolf,

555

Witches' mummy, maw and gulf
Of the ravin'd salt-sea shark,
Root of hemlock digg'd i' the dark,
Liver of blaspheming Jew,
Gall of goat, and slips of yew
Sliver'd in the moon's eclipse,
Nose of Turk and Tartar's lips,
Finger of birth-strangled babe
Ditch-deliver'd by a drab,
Make the gruel thick and slab.
Add thereto a tiger's chaudron,
For the ingredients of our cauldron.

ALL   Double, double, toil and trouble;
Fire burn and cauldron bubble.

SECOND WITCH   Cool it with a baboon's blood,
Then the charm is firm and good.

Enter Hecate to the other Three Witches.

HECATE   O, well done! I commend your pains;
And every one shall share i' the gains.
And now about the cauldron sing,
Like elves and fairies in a ring,
Enchanting all that you put in.
            Music and a song: "Black spirits," &c. Hecate retires.

SECOND WITCH   By the pricking of my thumbs,
Something wicked this way comes.
                    Open, locks,
                    Whoever knocks!

Enter Macbeth.

MACBETH   How now, you secret, black, and midnight hags!
What is't you do?

ALL   A deed without a name.

MACBETH   I conjure you by that which you profess,
Howe'er you come to know it, answer me:
Though you untie the winds and let them fight
Against the churches; though the yesty waves
Confound and swallow navigation up;
Though bladed corn be lodged and trees blown down;

556

Though castles topple on their warders' heads;
Though palaces and pyramids do slope
Their heads to their foundations; though the treasure
Of nature's germens tumble all together,
Even till destruction sicken; answer me
To what I ask you.

FIRST WITCH   Speak.

SECOND WITCH   Demand.

THIRD WITCH   We'll answer.

FIRST WITCH   Say, if thou'dst rather hear it from our mouths,
Or from our masters?

MACBETH   Call 'em; let me see 'em.

FIRST WITCH   Pour in sow's blood, that hath eaten
Her nine farrow; grease that's sweaten
From the murderer's gibbet throw
Into the flame.

ALL   Come, high or low;
Thyself and office deftly show!

Thunder. First Apparition, an Armed Head.

MACBETH   Tell me, thou unknown power—

FIRST WITCH   He knows thy thought.
Hear his speech, but say thou nought.

FIRST APPARITION   Macbeth! Macbeth! Macbeth! beware Macduff;
Beware the thane of Fife. Dismiss me. Enough.   *Descends.*

MACBETH   Whate'er thou art, for thy good caution, thanks;
Thou hast harp'd my fear aright. But one word more—

FIRST WITCH   He will not be commanded. Here's another,
More potent than the first.

Thunder. Second Apparition, a Bloody Child.

SECOND APPARITION   Macbeth! Macbeth! Macbeth!

MACBETH   Had I three ears, I'd hear thee.

SECOND APPARITION   Be bloody, bold, and resolute; laugh to scorn

557

The power of man, for none of woman born
Shall harm Macbeth.   *Descends.*

MACBETH   Then live, Macduff; what need I fear of thee?
But yet I'll make assurance double sure,
And take a bond of fate. Thou shalt not live;
That I may tell pale-hearted fear it lies,
And sleep in spite of thunder.

Thunder. Third Apparition, a Child Crowned, with a tree in his hand.

What is this
That rises like the issue of a king,
And wears upon his baby-brow the round
And top of sovereignty?

ALL   Listen, but speak not to't.

THIRD APPARITION   Be lion-mettled, proud; and take no care
Who chafes, who frets, or where conspirers are.
Macbeth shall never vanquish'd be until
Great Birnam wood to high Dunsinane hill
Shall come against him.   *Descends.*

MACBETH   That will never be.
Who can impress the forest, bid the tree
Unfix his earth-bound root? Sweet bodements! good!
Rebellion's head, rise never till the wood
Of Birnam rise, and our high-placed Macbeth
Shall live the lease of nature, pay his breath
To time and mortal custom. Yet my heart
Throbs to know one thing. Tell me, if your art
Can tell so much: shall Banquo's issue ever
Reign in this kingdom?

ALL   Seek to know no more.

MACBETH   I will be satisfied; deny me this,
And an eternal curse fall on you! Let me know.
Why sinks that cauldron? and what noise is this?

Hautboys.

FIRST WITCH   Show!

SECOND WITCH   Show!

THIRD WITCH   Show!

ALL   Show his eyes, and grieve his heart;
  Come like shadows, so depart!

*A show of Eight Kings, the last with a glass in his hand; Banquo's Ghost
following.*

MACBETH   Thou art too like the spirit of Banquo; down!
  Thy crown does sear mine eye-balls. And thy hair,
  Thou other gold-bound brow, is like the first.
  A third is like the former. Filthy hags!
  Why do you show me this? A fourth! Start, eyes!
  What, will the line stretch out to the crack of doom?
  Another yet! A seventh! I'll see no more.
  And yet the eighth appears, who bears a glass
  Which shows me many more; and some I see
  That two-fold balls and treble sceptres carry.
  Horrible sight! Now, I see, 'tis true;
  For the blood-bolter'd Banquo smiles upon me,
  And points at them for his.   *Apparitions vanish.*
                        What, is this so?

FIRST WITCH   Ay, sir, all this is so. But why
  Stands Macbeth thus amazedly?
  Come, sisters, cheer we up his sprites,
  And show the best of our delights.
  I'll charm the air to give a sound,
  While you perform your antic round;
  That this great king may kindly say,
  Our duties did his welcome pay.
            Music. The Witches dance, and then vanish, with Hecate.

MACBETH   Where are they? Gone? Let this pernicious hour
  Stand aye accursed in the calendar!
  Come in, without there!

Enter Lennox.

LENNOX   What's your Grace's will?

MACBETH   Saw you the weird sisters?

LENNOX   No, my lord.

MACBETH   Came they not by you?

LENNOX   No, indeed, my lord.

MACBETH   Infected be the air whereon they ride;
  And damn'd all those that trust them! I did hear
  The galloping of horse; who was't came by?

LENNOX   'Tis two or three, my lord, that bring you word
  Macduff is fled to England.

MACBETH   Fled to England!

LENNOX   Ay, my good lord.

MACBETH   Time, thou anticipatest my dread exploits;
  The flighty purpose never is o'ertook
  Unless the deed go with it. From this moment
  The very firstlings of my heart shall be
  The firstlings of my hand. And even now,
  To crown my thoughts with acts, be it thought and done.
  The castle of Macduff I will surprise;
  Seize upon Fife; give to the edge o' the sword
  His wife, his babes, and all unfortunate souls
  That trace him in his line. No boasting like a fool;
  This deed I'll do before this purpose cool.
  But no more sights! Where are these gentlemen?
  Come, bring me where they are.   *Exeunt.*

SCENE 2   *Fife. Macduff's castle.*

Enter Lady Macduff, her Son, and Ross.

LADY MACDUFF   What had he done, to make him fly the land?

ROSS   You must have patience, madam.

LADY MACDUFF   He had none;
  His flight was madness. When our actions do not,
  Our fears do make us traitors.

ROSS   You know not
  Whether it was his wisdom or his fear.

LADY MACDUFF   Wisdom! to leave his wife, to leave his babes,
  His mansion, and his titles in a place
  From whence himself does fly? He loves us not;
  He wants the natural touch; for the poor wren,
  The most diminutive of birds, will fight,
  Her young ones in her nest, against the owl.

All is the fear and nothing is the love;
As little is the wisdom, where the flight
So runs against all reason.

ROSS   My dearest coz,
 I pray you, school yourself; but for your husband,
 He is noble, wise, judicious, and best knows
 The fits o' the season. I dare not speak much further;
 But cruel are the times, when we are traitors
 And do not know ourselves, when we hold rumour
 From what we fear, yet know not what we fear,
 But float upon a wild and violent sea
 Each way and move. I take my leave of you;
 Shall not be long but I'll be here again.
 Things at the worst will cease, or else climb upward
 To what they were before. My pretty cousin,
 Blessing upon you!

LADY MACDUFF   Father'd he is, and yet he's fatherless.

ROSS   I am so much a fool, should I stay longer,
 It would be my disgrace and your discomfort.
 I take my leave at once.   *Exit.*

LADY MACDUFF   Sirrah, your father's dead;
 And what will you do now? How will you live?

SON   As birds do, mother.

LADY MACDUFF   What, with worms and flies?

SON   With what I get, I mean; and so do they.

LADY MACDUFF   Poor bird! thou'dst never fear the net nor lime,
 The pitfall nor the gin.

SON   Why should I, mother? Poor birds they are not set for.
 My father is not dead, for all your saying.

LADY MACDUFF   Yes, he is dead. How wilt thou do for a father?

SON   Nay, how will you do for a husband?

LADY MACDUFF   Why, I can buy me twenty at any market.

SON   Then you'll buy 'em to sell again.

LADY MACDUFF   Thou speak'st with all thy wit; and yet, i' faith,
 With wit enough for thee.

SON Was my father a traitor, mother?

LADY MACDUFF Ay, that he was.

SON What is a traitor?

LADY MACDUFF Why, one that swears and lies.

SON And be all traitors that do so?

LADY MACDUFF Every one that does so is a traitor, and must be hanged.

SON And must they all be hanged that swear and lie?

LADY MACDUFF Every one.

SON Who must hang them?

LADY MACDUFF Why, the honest men.

SON Then the liars and swearers are fools, for there are liars and
    swearers enow to beat the honest men and hang up them.

LADY MACDUFF Now, God help thee, poor monkey!
    But how wilt thou do for a father?

SON If he were dead, you'd weep for him; if you would not, it were a
    good sign that I should quickly have a new father.

LADY MACDUFF Poor prattler, how thou talk'st!

Enter a Messenger.

MESSENGER Bless you, fair dame! I am not to you known,
    Though in your state of honour I am perfect.
    I doubt some danger does approach you nearly.
    If you will take a homely man's advice,
    Be not found here; hence, with your little ones.
    To fright you thus, methinks, I am too savage;
    To do worse to you were fell cruelty,
    Which is too nigh your person. Heaven preserve you!
    I dare abide no longer.   *Exit.*

LADY MACDUFF   Whither should I fly?
    I have done no harm. But I remember now
    I am in this earthly world; where to do harm
    Is often laudable, to do good sometime
    Accounted dangerous folly. Why then, alas,
    Do I put up that womanly defence,
    To say I have done no harm?

Enter Murderers.

                              What are these faces?

FIRST MURDERER   Where is your husband?

LADY MACDUFF   I hope, in no place so unsanctified
  Where such as thou mayst find him.

FIRST MURDERER   He's a traitor.

SON   Thou liest, thou shag-hair'd villain!

FIRST MURDERER   What, you egg!

Stabbing him.

    Young fry of treachery!

SON   He has kill'd me, mother.
  Run away, I pray you!
                    Dies. Exit Lady Macduff, crying "Murder!" Exeunt Murderers,
                                            following her.

 SCENE 3   *England. Before the King's palace.*

Enter Malcolm and Macduff.

MALCOLM   Let us seek out some desolate shade, and there
  Weep our sad bosoms empty.

MACDUFF   Let us rather
  Hold fast the mortal sword, and like good men
  Bestride our down-fall'n birthdom. Each new morn
  New widows howl, new orphans cry, new sorrows
  Strike heaven on the face, that it resounds
  As if it felt with Scotland and yell'd out
  Like syllable of dolour.

MALCOLM   What I believe I'll wail,
  What know believe, and what I can redress,
  As I shall find the time to friend, I will.
  What you have spoke, it may be so perchance.
  This tyrant, whose sole name blisters our tongues,
  Was once thought honest; you have loved him well.
  He hath not touch'd you yet. I am young; but something
  You may deserve of him through me, and wisdom

563

MACBETH

To offer up a weak poor innocent lamb
To appease an angry god.

MACDUFF   I am not treacherous.

MALCOLM   But Macbeth is.
A good and virtuous nature may recoil
In an imperial charge. But I shall crave your pardon;
That which you are my thoughts cannot transpose.
Angels are bright still, though the brightest fell.
Though all things foul would wear the brows of grace,
Yet grace must still look so.

MACDUFF   I have lost my hopes.

MALCOLM   Perchance even there where I did find my doubts.
Why in that rawness left you wife and child,
Those precious motives, those strong knots of love,
Without leave-taking? I pray you,
Let not my jealousies be your dishonours,
But mine own safeties. You may be rightly just,
Whatever I shall think.

MACDUFF   Bleed, bleed, poor country!
Great tyranny! lay thou thy basis sure,
For goodness dare not check thee. Wear thou thy wrongs;
The title is affeer'd! Fare thee well, lord.
I would not be the villain that thou think'st
For the whole space that's in the tyrant's grasp,
And the rich East to boot.

MALCOLM   Be not offended.
I speak not as in absolute fear of you.
I think our country sinks beneath the yoke;
It weeps, it bleeds; and each new day a gash
Is added to her wounds. I think withal
There would be hands uplifted in my right;
And here from gracious England have I offer
Of goodly thousands. But, for all this,
When I shall tread upon the tyrant's head,
Or wear it on my sword, yet my poor country
Shall have more vices than it had before,
More suffer and more sundry ways than ever,
By him that shall succeed.

MACDUFF   What should he be?

MALCOLM   It is myself I mean; in whom I know
All the particulars of vice so grafted
That, when they shall be open'd, black Macbeth
Will seem as pure as snow, and the poor state
Esteem him as a lamb, being compared
With my confineless harms.

MACDUFF   Not in the legions
Of horrid hell can come a devil more damn'd
In evils to top Macbeth.

MALCOLM   I grant him bloody,
Luxurious, avaricious, false, deceitful,
Sudden, malicious, smacking of every sin
That has a name; but there's no bottom, none,
In my voluptuousness. Your wives, your daughters,
Your matrons, and your maids, could not fill up
The cistern of my lust, and my desire
All continent impediments would o'erbear
That did oppose my will. Better Macbeth
Than such a one to reign.

MACDUFF   Boundless intemperance
In nature is a tyranny; it hath been
The untimely emptying of the happy throne
And fall of many kings. But fear not yet
To take upon you what is yours; you may
Convey your pleasures in a spacious plenty,
And yet seem cold, the time you may so hoodwink.
We have willing dames enough; there cannot be
That vulture in you, to devour so many
As will to greatness dedicate themselves,
Finding it so inclined.

MALCOLM   With this there grows
In my most ill-composed affection such
A stanchless avarice that, were I king,
I should cut off the nobles for their lands,
Desire his jewels and this other's house;
And my more-having would be as a sauce
To make me hunger more; that I should forge

565

Quarrels unjust against the good and loyal,
Destroying them for wealth.

MACDUFF   This avarice
Sticks deeper, grows with more pernicious root
Than summer-seeming lust, and it hath been
The sword of our slain kings. Yet do not fear;
Scotland hath foisons to fill up your will,
Of your mere own. All these are portable,
With other graces weigh'd.

MALCOLM   But I have none. The king-becoming graces,
As justice, verity, temperance, stableness,
Bounty, perseverance, mercy, lowliness,
Devotion, patience, courage, fortitude,
I have no relish of them, but abound
In the division of each several crime,
Acting it many ways. Nay, had I power, I should
Pour the sweet milk of concord into hell,
Uproar the universal peace, confound
All unity on earth.

MACDUFF   O Scotland, Scotland!

MALCOLM   If such a one be fit to govern, speak.
I am as I have spoken.

MACDUFF   Fit to govern!
No, not to live. O nation miserable,
With an untitled tyrant bloody-scepter'd,
When shalt thou see thy wholesome days again,
Since then the truest issue of thy throne
By his own interdiction stands accursed,
And does blaspheme his breed? Thy royal father
Was a most sainted king; the queen that bore thee,
Oftener upon her knees than on her feet,
Died every day she lived. Fare thee well!
These evils thou repeat'st upon thyself
Have banish'd me from Scotland. O my breast,
Thy hope ends here!

MALCOLM   Macduff, this noble passion,
Child of integrity, hath from my soul
Wiped the black scruples, reconciled my thoughts
To thy good truth and honour. Devilish Macbeth

566

By many of these trains hath sought to win me
Into his power, and modest wisdom plucks me
From over-credulous haste. But God above
Deal between thee and me! for even now
I put myself to thy direction, and
Unspeak mine own detraction, here abjure
The taints and blames I laid upon myself,
For strangers to my nature. I am yet
Unknown to woman, never was forsworn,
Scarcely have coveted what was mine own,
At no time broke my faith, would not betray
The devil to his fellow, and delight
No less in truth than life. My first false speaking
Was this upon myself; what I am truly,
Is thine and my poor country's to command.
Whither indeed, before thy here-approach,
Old Siward, with ten thousand warlike men,
Already at a point, was setting forth.
Now we'll together; and the chance of goodness
Be like our warranted quarrel! Why are you silent?

MACDUFF   Such welcome and unwelcome things at once
'Tis hard to reconcile.

Enter a Doctor.

MALCOLM   Well; more anon. Comes the King forth, I pray you?

DOCTOR   Ay, sir; there are a crew of wretched souls
That stay his cure. Their malady convinces
The great assay of art; but at his touch—
Such sanctity hath heaven given his hand—
They presently amend.

MALCOLM   I thank you, doctor.   *Exit Doctor.*

MACDUFF   What's the disease he means?

MALCOLM   'Tis call'd the evil:
A most miraculous work in this good king;
Which often, since my here-remain in England,
I have seen him do. How he solicits Heaven,
Himself best knows; but strangely-visited people,
All swoln and ulcerous, pitiful to the eye,
The mere despair of surgery, he cures,

567

Hanging a golden stamp about their necks,
Put on with holy prayers. And 'tis spoken,
To the succeeding royalty he leaves
The healing benediction. With this strange virtue,
He hath a heavenly gift of prophecy,
And sundry blessings hang about his throne
That speak him full of grace.

Enter Ross.

MACDUFF   See, who comes here?

MALCOLM   My countryman; but yet I know him not.

MACDUFF   My ever-gentle cousin, welcome hither.

MALCOLM   I know him now. Good God, betimes remove
The means that makes us strangers!

ROSS   Sir, amen.

MACDUFF   Stands Scotland where it did?

ROSS   Alas, poor country!
Almost afraid to know itself. It cannot
Be call'd our mother, but our grave; where nothing,
But who knows nothing, is once seen to smile;
Where sighs and groans and shrieks that rend the air
Are made, not mark'd; where violent sorrow seems
A modern ecstasy. The dead man's knell
Is there scarce ask'd for who; and good men's lives
Expire before the flowers in their caps,
Dying or ere they sicken.

MACDUFF   O, relation
Too nice, and yet too true!

MALCOLM   What's the newest grief?

ROSS   That of an hour's age doth hiss the speaker;
Each minute teems a new one.

MACDUFF   How does my wife?

ROSS   Why, well.

MACDUFF   And all my children?

568

ROSS   Well too.

MACDUFF   The tyrant has not batter'd at their peace?

ROSS   No; they were well at peace when I did leave 'em.

MACDUFF   Be not a niggard of your speech; how goes't?

ROSS   When I came hither to transport the tidings,
Which I have heavily borne, there ran a rumour
Of many worthy fellows that were out;
Which was to my belief witness'd the rather,
For that I saw the tyrant's power a-foot.
Now is the time of help; your eye in Scotland
Would create soldiers, make our women fight,
To doff their dire distresses.

MALCOLM   Be't their comfort
We are coming thither. Gracious England hath
Lent us good Siward and ten thousand men;
An older and a better soldier none
That Christendom gives out.

ROSS   Would I could answer
This comfort with the like! But I have words
That would be howl'd out in the desert air,
Where hearing should not latch them.

MACDUFF   What concern they?
The general cause? or is it a fee-grief
Due to some single breast?

ROSS   No mind that's honest
But in it shares some woe; though the main part
Pertains to you alone.

MACDUFF   If it be mine,
Keep it not from me, quickly let me have it.

ROSS   Let not your ears despise my tongue for ever,
Which shall possess them with the heaviest sound
That ever yet they heard.

MACDUFF   Hum! I guess at it.

ROSS   Your castle is surprised; your wife and babes
Savagely slaughter'd. To relate the manner

569

Were, on the quarry of these murder'd deer,
To add the death of you.

MALCOLM   Merciful heaven!
What, man! ne'er pull your hat upon your brows;
Give sorrow words. The grief that does not speak
Whispers the o'er-fraught heart and bids it break.

MACDUFF   My children too?

ROSS   Wife, children, servants, all
That could be found.

MACDUFF   And I must be from thence!
My wife kill'd too?

ROSS   I have said.

MALCOLM   Be comforted.
Let's make us medicines of our great revenge
To cure this deadly grief.

MACDUFF   He has no children. All my pretty ones?
Did you say all? O hell-kite! All?
What, all my pretty chickens and their dam
At one fell swoop?

MALCOLM   Dispute it like a man.

MACDUFF   I shall do so;
But I must also feel it as a man.
I cannot but remember such things were,
That were most precious to me. Did heaven look on,
And would not take their part? Sinful Macduff,
They were all struck for thee! naught that I am,
Not for their own demerits, but for mine,
Fell slaughter on their souls. Heaven rest them now!

MALCOLM   Be this the whetstone of your sword; let grief
Convert to anger; blunt not the heart, enrage it.

MACDUFF   O, I could play the woman with mine eyes
And braggart with my tongue! But, gentle heavens,
Cut short all intermission; front to front
Bring thou this fiend of Scotland and myself;
Within my sword's length set him; if he 'scape,
Heaven forgive him too!

570

MALCOLM   This tune goes manly.
  Come, go we to the King; our power is ready;
  Our lack is nothing but our leave. Macbeth
  Is ripe for shaking, and the powers above
  Put on their instruments. Receive what cheer you may;
  The night is long that never finds the day.   *Exeunt.*

ACT V

 SCENE 1 *Dunsinane. Ante-room in the castle.*

Enter a Doctor of Physic and a Waiting-Gentlewoman.

DOCTOR   I have two nights watched with you, but can perceive no truth in your report. When was it she last walked?

WAITING–GENTLEWOMAN   Since his Majesty went into the field, I have seen her rise from her bed, throw her nightgown upon her, unlock her closet, take forth paper, fold it, write upon't, read it, afterwards seal it, and again return to bed; yet all this while in a most fast sleep.

DOCTOR   A great perturbation in nature, to receive at once the benefit of sleep, and do the effects of watching! In this slumbery agitation, besides her walking and other actual performances, what, at any time, have you heard her say?

WAITING–GENTLEWOMAN   That, sir, which I will not report after her.

DOCTOR   You may to me; and 'tis most meet you should.

WAITING–GENTLEWOMAN   Neither to you nor any one; having no witness to confirm my speech.

Enter Lady Macbeth, with a taper.

Lo you, here she comes! This is her very guise; and, upon my life, fast asleep. Observe her; stand close.

DOCTOR   How came she by that light?

WAITING–GENTLEWOMAN   Why, it stood by her. She has light by her continually; 'tis her command.

572

ACT V   Scene 1

DOCTOR   You see, her eyes are open.

WAITING-GENTLEWOMAN   Ay, but their sense is shut.

DOCTOR   What is it she does now? Look, how she rubs her hands.

WAITING-GENTLEWOMAN   It is an accustomed action with her, to seem
thus washing her hands. I have known her continue in this a quarter of
an hour.

LADY MACBETH   Yet here's a spot.

DOCTOR   Hark! she speaks. I will set down what comes from her, to satisfy my remembrance the more strongly.

LADY MACBETH   Out, damned spot! out, I say! One; two. Why, then 'tis
time to do't. Hell is murky! Fie, my lord, fie! a soldier, and afeard?
What need we fear who knows it, when none can call our power to
account? Yet who would have thought the old man to have had so
much blood in him.

DOCTOR   Do you mark that?

LADY MACBETH   The thane of Fife had a wife. Where is she now? What,
will these hands ne'er be clean? No more o' that, my lord, no more o'
that! You mar all with this starting.

DOCTOR   Go to, go to; you have known what you should not.

WAITING-GENTLEWOMAN   She has spoke what she should not, I am sure
of that. Heaven knows what she has known.

LADY MACBETH   Here's the smell of the blood still. All the perfumes of
Arabia will not sweeten this little hand. Oh, oh, oh!

DOCTOR   What a sigh is there! The heart is sorely charged.

WAITING-GENTLEWOMAN   I would not have such a heart in my bosom for
the dignity of the whole body.

DOCTOR   Well, well, well—

WAITING-GENTLEWOMAN   Pray God it be, sir.

DOCTOR   This disease is beyond my practice. Yet I have known those
which have walked in their sleep who have died holily in their beds.

LADY MACBETH   Wash your hands, put on your nightgown; look not so
pale. I tell you yet again, Banquo's buried; he cannot come out on's
grave.

573

DOCTOR   Even so?

LADY MACBETH   To bed, to bed! there's knocking at the gate. Come, come, come, come, give me your hand. What's done cannot be un-done. To bed, to bed, to bed!   *Exit.*

DOCTOR   Will she go now to bed?

WAITING-GENTLEWOMAN   Directly.

DOCTOR   Foul whisperings are abroad. Unnatural deeds
   Do breed unnatural troubles. Infected minds
   To their deaf pillows will discharge their secrets.
   More needs she the divine than the physician.
   God, God forgive us all! Look after her;
   Remove from her the means of all annoyance,
   And still keep eyes upon her. So, good night.
   My mind she has mated, and amazed my sight.
   I think, but dare not speak.

WAITING-GENTLEWOMAN   Good night, good doctor.   *Exeunt.*

SCENE 2   *The country near Dunsinane.*

Drum and colours. Enter Menteith, Caithness, Angus, Lennox, and Soldiers.

MENTEITH   The English power is near, led on by Malcolm,
   His uncle Siward, and the good Macduff.
   Revenges burn in them; for their dear causes
   Would to the bleeding and the grim alarm
   Excite the mortified man.

ANGUS   Near Birnam wood
   Shall we well meet them; that way are they coming.

CAITHNESS   Who knows if Donalbain be with his brother?

LENNOX   For certain, sir, he is not; I have a file
   Of all the gentry. There is Siward's son,
   And many unrough youths that even now
   Protest their first of manhood.

MENTEITH   What does the tyrant?

CAITHNESS   Great Dunsinane he strongly fortifies.
   Some say he's mad; others that lesser hate him
   Do call it valiant fury; but, for certain,

He cannot buckle his distemper'd cause
Within the belt of rule.

ANGUS   Now does he feel
His secret murders sticking on his hands;
Now minutely revolts upbraid his faith-breach;
Those he commands move only in command,
Nothing in love; now does he feel his title
Hang loose about him, like a giant's robe
Upon a dwarfish thief.

MENTEITH   Who then shall blame
His pester'd senses to recoil and start,
When all that is within him does condemn
Itself for being there?

CAITHNESS   Well, march we on,
To give obedience where 'tis truly owed.
Meet we the medicine of the sickly weal,
And with him pour we in our country's purge
Each drop of us.

LENNOX   Or so much as it needs,
To dew the sovereign flower and drown the weeds.
Make we our march towards Birnam.   *Exeunt, marching.*

 SCENE 3   *Dunsinane. A room in the castle.*

Enter Macbeth, Doctor, and Attendants.

MACBETH   Bring me no more reports; let them fly all.
Till Birnam wood remove to Dunsinane,
I cannot taint with fear. What's the boy Malcolm?
Was he not born of woman? The spirits that know
All mortal consequences have pronounced me thus:
"Fear not, Macbeth; no man that's born of woman
Shall e'er have power upon thee." Then fly, false thanes,
And mingle with the English epicures.
The mind I sway by and the heart I bear
Shall never sag with doubt nor shake with fear.

Enter a Servant.

The devil damn thee black, thou cream-faced loon!
Where got'st thou that goose look?

575

SERVANT   There is ten thousand—

MACBETH   Geese, villain?

SERVANT   Soldiers, sir.

MACBETH   Go prick thy face, and over-red thy fear,
  Thou lily-liver'd boy. What soldiers, patch?
  Death of thy soul! those linen cheeks of thine
  Are counsellors to fear. What soldiers, whey-face?

SERVANT   The English force, so please you.

MACBETH   Take thy face hence.   *Exit Servant.*
                      Seyton! I am sick at heart,
  When I behold— Seyton, I say! This push
  Will cheer me ever, or disseat me now.
  I have lived long enough; my way of life
  Is fall'n into the sear, the yellow leaf;
  And that which should accompany old age,
  As honour, love, obedience, troops of friends,
  I must not look to have; but, in their stead,
  Curses, not loud but deep, mouth-honour, breath,
  Which the poor heart would fain deny, and dare not.
  Seyton!

Enter Seyton.

SEYTON   What is your gracious pleasure?

MACBETH   What news more?

SEYTON   All is confirm'd, my lord, which was reported.

MACBETH   I'll fight till from my bones my flesh be hack'd.
  Give me my armour.

SEYTON   'Tis not needed yet.

MACBETH   I'll put it on.
  Send out more horses; skirr the country round;
  Hang those that talk of fear. Give me mine armour.
  How does your patient, doctor?

DOCTOR   Not so sick, my lord,
  As she is troubled with thick-coming fancies,
  That keep her from her rest.

MACBETH   Cure her of that.

Canst thou not minister to a mind diseased,
Pluck from the memory a rooted sorrow,
Raze out the written troubles of the brain,
And with some sweet oblivious antidote
Cleanse the stuff'd bosom of that perilous stuff
Which weighs upon the heart?

DOCTOR   Therein the patient
Must minister to himself.

MACBETH   Throw physic to the dogs; I'll none of it.
Come, put mine armour on; give me my staff.
Seyton, send out. Doctor, the thanes fly from me.
Come, sir, dispatch. If thou couldst, doctor, cast
The water of my land, find her disease,
And purge it to a sound and pristine health,
I would applaud thee to the very echo,
That should applaud again. Pull't off, I say.
What rhubarb, senna, or what purgative drug,
Would scour these English hence? Hear'st thou of them?

DOCTOR   Ay, my good lord; your royal preparation
Makes us hear something.

MACBETH   Bring it after me.
I will not be afraid of death and bane,
Till Birnam forest come to Dunsinane.

DOCTOR   [*Aside.*] Were I from Dunsinane away and clear,
Profit again should hardly draw me here.   *Exeunt.*

SCENE 4   *Country near Birnam wood.*

*Drum and colours. Enter Malcolm, Old Siward and his son, Macduff, Menteith,
Caithness, Angus, Lennox, Ross, and Soldiers, marching.*

MALCOLM   Cousins, I hope the days are near at hand
That chambers will be safe.

MENTEITH   We doubt it nothing.

SIWARD   What wood is this before us?

MENTEITH   The wood of Birnam.

MALCOLM   Let every soldier hew him down a bough

577

And bear't before him; thereby shall we shadow
The numbers of our host and make discovery
Err in report of us.

SOLDIERS   It shall be done.

SIWARD   We learn no other but the confident tyrant
Keeps still in Dunsinane, and will endure
Our setting down before't.

MALCOLM   'Tis his main hope;
For where there is advantage to be given,
Both more and less have given him the revolt,
And none serve with him but constrained things
Whose hearts are absent too.

MACDUFF   Let our just censures
Attend the true event, and put we on
Industrious soldiership.

SIWARD   The time approaches
That will with due decision make us know
What we shall say we have and what we owe.
Thoughts speculative their unsure hopes relate,
But certain issue strokes must arbitrate;
Towards which advance the war.   *Exeunt, marching.*

SCENE 5 *Dunsinane. Within the castle.*

Enter Macbeth, Seyton, and Soldiers, with drum and colours.

MACBETH   Hang out our banners on the outward walls;
The cry is still "They come." Our castle's strength
Will laugh a siege to scorn; here let them lie
Till famine and the ague eat them up.
Were they not forced with those that should be ours,
We might have met them dareful, beard to beard,
And beat them backward home.

A cry of women within.

                              What is that noise?

SEYTON   It is the cry of women, my good lord.   *Exit.*

MACBETH   I have almost forgot the taste of fears.

578

The time has been, my senses would have cool'd
To hear a night-shriek; and my fell of hair
Would at a dismal treatise rouse and stir
As life were in't. I have supp'd full with horrors;
Direness, familiar to my slaughterous thoughts,
Cannot once start me.

Re-enter Seyton.

                              Wherefore was that cry?

SEYTON   The Queen, my lord, is dead.

MACBETH   She should have died hereafter;
There would have been a time for such a word.
To-morrow, and to-morrow, and to-morrow,
Creeps in this petty pace from day to day
To the last syllable of recorded time,
And all our yesterdays have lighted fools
The way to dusty death. Out, out, brief candle!
Life's but a walking shadow, a poor player
That struts and frets his hour upon the stage
And then is heard no more. It is a tale
Told by an idiot, full of sound and fury,
Signifying nothing.

Enter a Messenger.

Thou comest to use thy tongue; thy story quickly.

MESSENGER   Gracious my lord,
I should report that which I say I saw,
But know not how to do it.

MACBETH   Well, say, sir.

MESSENGER   As I did stand my watch upon the hill,
I look'd toward Birnam, and anon, methought,
The wood began to move.

MACBETH   Liar and slave!

MESSENGER   Let me endure your wrath, if't be not so.
Within this three mile may you see it coming;
I say, a moving grove.

MACBETH   If thou speak'st false,
Upon the next tree shalt thou hang alive,

Till famine cling thee. If thy speech be sooth,
I care not if thou dost for me as much.
I pull in resolution, and begin
To doubt the equivocation of the fiend
That lies like truth: "Fear not, till Birnam wood
Do come to Dunsinane"; and now a wood
Comes toward Dunsinane. Arm, arm, and out!
If this which he avouches does appear,
There is nor flying hence nor tarrying here.
I 'gin to be aweary of the sun,
And wish the estate o' the world were now undone.
Ring the alarum-bell! Blow, wind! come, wrack!
At least we'll die with harness on our back.   *Exeunt.*

SCENE 6   *Dunsinane. Before the castle.*

Drum and colours. Enter Malcolm, Old Siward, Macduff, and their Army, with boughs.

MALCOLM   Now near enough. Your leavy screens throw down,
And show like those you are. You, worthy uncle,
Shall, with my cousin, your right-noble son,
Lead our first battle. Worthy Macduff and we
Shall take upon's what else remains to do,
According to our order.

SIWARD   Fare you well.
Do we but find the tyrant's power to-night,
Let us be beaten, if we cannot fight.

MACDUFF   Make all our trumpets speak; give them all breath
Those clamorous harbingers of blood and death.   *Exeunt.*

SCENE 7   *Another part of the field.*

Alarums. Enter Macbeth.

MACBETH   They have tied me to a stake; I cannot fly,
But, bear-like, I must fight the course. What's he
That was not born of woman? Such a one
Am I to fear, or none.

Enter Young Siward.

580

YOUNG SIWARD   What is thy name?

MACBETH   Thou'lt be afraid to hear it.

YOUNG SIWARD   No; though thou call'st thyself a hotter name
  Than any is in hell.

MACBETH   My name's Macbeth.

YOUNG SIWARD   The devil himself could not pronounce a title
  More hateful to mine ear.

MACBETH   No, nor more fearful.

YOUNG SIWARD   Thou liest, abhorred tyrant; with my sword
  I'll prove the lie thou speak'st.

They fight and Young Siward is slain.

MACBETH   Thou wast born of woman.
  But swords I smile at, weapons laugh to scorn,
  Brandish'd by man that's of a woman born.   *Exit.*

Alarums. Enter Macduff.

MACDUFF   That way the noise is. Tyrant, show thy face!
  If thou be'st slain and with no stroke of mine,
  My wife and children's ghosts will haunt me still.
  I cannot strike at wretched kerns, whose arms
  Are hired to bear their staves. Either thou, Macbeth,
  Or else my sword with an unbatter'd edge
  I sheathe again undeeded. There thou shouldst be;
  By this great clatter, one of greatest note
  Seems bruited. Let me find him, fortune!
  And more I beg not.   *Exit. Alarums.*

Enter Malcolm and Old Siward.

SIWARD   This way, my lord; the castle's gently render'd.
  The tyrant's people on both sides do fight;
  The noble thanes do bravely in the war;
  The day almost itself professes yours,
  And little is to do.

MALCOLM   We have met with foes
  That strike beside us.

SIWARD   Enter, sir, the castle.   *Exeunt. Alarums.*

581

SCENE 8 *Another part of the field.*

Enter Macbeth.

MACBETH Why should I play the Roman fool, and die
On mine own sword? whiles I see lives, the gashes
Do better upon them.

Enter Macduff.

MACDUFF   Turn, hell-hound, turn!

MACBETH Of all men else I have avoided thee.
But get thee back; my soul is too much charged
With blood of thine already.

MACDUFF   I have no words;
My voice is in my sword. Thou bloodier villain
Than terms can give thee out!

They fight.

MACBETH   Thou losest labour.
As easy mayst thou the intrenchant air
With thy keen sword impress as make me bleed.
Let fall thy blade on vulnerable crests;
I bear a charmed life, which must not yield
To one of woman born.

MACDUFF   Despair thy charm;
And let the angel whom thou still hast served
Tell thee, Macduff was from his mother's womb
Untimely ripp'd.

MACBETH Accursed be that tongue that tells me so,
For it hath cow'd my better part of man!
And be these juggling fiends no more believed
That palter with us in a double sense;
That keep the word of promise to our ear,
And break it to our hope. I'll not fight with thee.

MACDUFF Then yield thee, coward,
And live to be the show and gaze o' the time!
We'll have thee, as our rarer monsters are,
Painted upon a pole, and underwrit,
"Here may you see the tyrant."

582

MACBETH   I will not yield,
  To kiss the ground before young Malcolm's feet
  And to be baited with the rabble's curse.
  Though Birnam wood be come to Dunsinane,
  And thou opposed, being of no woman born,
  Yet I will try the last. Before my body
  I throw my warlike shield. Lay on, Macduff,
  And damn'd be him that first cries, "Hold, enough!"

Exeunt, fighting. Alarums.

*Retreat. Flourish. Enter, with drum and colours, Malcolm, Old Siward, Ross,
the other Thanes, and Soldiers.*

MALCOLM   I would the friends we miss were safe arrived.

SIWARD   Some must go off; and yet, by these I see,
  So great a day as this is cheaply bought.

MALCOLM   Macduff is missing, and your noble son.

ROSS   Your son, my lord, has paid a soldier's debt.
  He only lived but till he was a man;
  The which no sooner had his prowess confirm'd
  In the unshrinking station where he fought,
  But like a man he died.

SIWARD   Then he is dead?

ROSS   Ay, and brought off the field. Your cause of sorrow
  Must not be measured by his worth, for then
  It hath no end.

SIWARD   Had he his hurts before?

ROSS   Ay, on the front.

SIWARD   Why then, God's soldier be he!
  Had I as many sons as I have hairs,
  I would not wish them to a fairer death.
  And so, his knell is knoll'd.

MALCOLM   He's worth more sorrow,
  And that I'll spend for him.

SIWARD   He's worth no more.
  They say he parted well, and paid his score;
  And so, God be with him! Here comes newer comfort.

Re-enter Macduff, with Macbeth's head.

MACDUFF   Hail, King! for so thou art. Behold, where stands
The usurper's cursed head. The time is free.
I see thee compass'd with thy kingdom's pearl,
That speak my salutation in their minds;
Whose voices I desire aloud with mine:
Hail, King of Scotland!

ALL   Hail, King of Scotland!

Flourish.

MALCOLM   We shall not spend a large expense of time
Before we reckon with your several loves,
And make us even with you. My thanes and kinsmen,
Henceforth be earls, the first that ever Scotland
In such an honour named. What's more to do,
Which would be planted newly with the time,
As calling home our exiled friends abroad
That fled the snares of watchful tyranny;
Producing forth the cruel ministers
Of this dead butcher and his fiend-like queen,
Who, as 'tis thought, by self and violent hands
Took off her life; this, and what needful else
That calls upon us, by the grace of Grace,
We will perform in measure, time and place.
So, thanks to all at once and to each one,
Whom we invite to see us crown'd at Scone.   *Flourish. Exeunt.*

THE TEMPEST

THE ACTORS

ALONSO, *King of Naples*

SEBASTIAN, *his brother*

PROSPERO, *the right Duke of Milan*

ANTONIO, *his brother, the usurping Duke of Milan*

FERDINAND, *son to the King of Naples*

GONZALO, *an honest old counsellor*

ADRIAN
FRANCISCO } *Lords*

CALIBAN, *a savage and deformed slave*

TRINCULO, *a jester*

STEPHANO, *a drunken butler*

MASTER *of a ship*

BOATSWAIN

MARINERS

MIRANDA, *daughter to Prospero*

ARIEL, *an airy Spirit*

IRIS
CERES } *Spirits*
JUNO

Non-Speaking: Nymphs and Reapers, presented by Spirits; and other Spirits attending on Prospero

SCENE: *A ship at sea, and an island*

ACT I

On a ship at sea. A tempestuous noise of thunder and lightning heard.

Enter a Ship-Master and a Boatswain.

MASTER Boatswain!

BOATSWAIN Here, master. What cheer?

MASTER Good, speak to the mariners. Fall to't, yarely, or we run ourselves aground. Bestir, bestir.   *Exit.*

Enter Mariners.

BOATSWAIN Heigh, my hearts! Cheerly, cheerly, my hearts! Yare, yare! Take in the topsail. Tend to the master's whistle. Blow, till thou burst thy wind, if room enough!

Enter Alonso, Sebastian, Antonio, Ferdinand, Gonzalo, and others.

ALONSO Good boatswain, have care. Where's the master? Play the men.

BOATSWAIN I pray now, keep below.

ANTONIO Where is the master, boatswain?

BOATSWAIN Do you not hear him? You mar our labour. Keep your cabins; you do assist the storm.

GONZALO Nay, good, be patient.

BOATSWAIN When the sea is. Hence! What cares these roarers for the name of king? To cabin. Silence! Trouble us not.

GONZALO Good, yet remember whom thou hast aboard.

589

BOATSWAIN   None that I more love than myself. You are a counsellor; if you can command these elements to silence, and work the peace of the present, we will not hand a rope more; use your authority. If you cannot, give thanks you have lived so long, and make yourself ready in your cabin for the mischance of the hour, if it so hap. Cheerly, good hearts! Out of our way, I say.   *Exit.*

GONZALO   I have great comfort from this fellow. Methinks he hath no drowning mark upon him; his complexion is perfect gallows. Stand fast, good Fate, to his hanging. Make the rope of his destiny our cable, for our own doth little advantage. If he be not born to be hanged, our case is miserable.   *Exeunt.*

Re-enter Boatswain.

BOATSWAIN   Down with the topmast! yare! lower, lower! Bring her to try with main-course. [*A cry within.*] A plague upon this howling! they are louder than the weather or our office.

Re-enter Sebastian, Antonio, and Gonzalo.

Yet again! what do you here? Shall we give o'er and drown? Have you a mind to sink?

SEBASTIAN   A pox o' your throat, you bawling, blasphemous, incharitable dog!

BOATSWAIN   Work you then.

ANTONIO   Hang, cur! hang, you whoreson, insolent noisemaker! We are less afraid to be drowned than thou art.

GONZALO   I'll warrant him for drowning; though the ship were no stronger than a nutshell and as leaky as an unstanched wench.

BOATSWAIN   Lay her a-hold, a-hold! set her two courses off to sea again; lay her off.

Enter Mariners wet.

MARINERS   All lost! to prayers, to prayers! all lost!

BOATSWAIN   What, must our mouths be cold?

GONZALO   The King and Prince at prayers! let's assist them, For our case is as theirs.

SEBASTIAN   I'm out of patience.

ANTONIO   We are merely cheated of our lives by drunkards.

590

This wide-chapp'd rascal—would thou mightst lie drowning
The washing of ten tides!

GONZALO   He'll be hang'd yet,
   Though every drop of water swear against it
   And gape at widest to glut him.

*A confused noise within: "Mercy on us! We split, we split! Farewell, my wife
and children! Farewell, brother! We split, we split, we split!" Exit Boatswain.*

ANTONIO   Let's all sink with the King.

SEBASTIAN   Let's take leave of him.   *Exeunt Antonio and Sebastian.*

GONZALO   Now would I give a thousand furlongs of sea for an acre of
   barren ground, long heath, brown furze, anything. The wills above be
   done! but I would fain die a dry death.   *Exeunt.*

SCENE 2   *The island. Before Prospero's cell.*

Enter Prospero and Miranda.

MIRANDA   If by your art, my dearest father, you have
   Put the wild waters in this roar, allay them.
   The sky, it seems, would pour down stinking pitch,
   But that the sea, mounting to the welkin's cheek,
   Dashes the fire out. O, I have suffer'd
   With those that I saw suffer. A brave vessel,
   Who had, no doubt, some noble creature in her,
   Dash'd all to pieces. O, the cry did knock
   Against my very heart. Poor souls, they perish'd.
   Had I been any god of power, I would
   Have sunk the sea within the earth or ere
   It should the good ship so have swallow'd and
   The fraughting souls within her.

PROSPERO   Be collected;
   No more amazement. Tell your piteous heart
   There's no harm done.

MIRANDA   O, woe the day!

PROSPERO   No harm.
   I have done nothing but in care of thee,
   Of thee, my dear one, thee, my daughter, who
   Art ignorant of what thou art, nought knowing

591

Of whence I am, nor that I am more better
Than Prospero, master of a full poor cell,
And thy no greater father.

MIRANDA   More to know
  Did never meddle with my thoughts.

PROSPERO   'Tis time
  I should inform thee farther. Lend thy hand,
  And pluck my magic garment from me. So,

Lays down his mantle.

  Lie there, my art. Wipe thou thine eyes; have comfort.
  The direful spectacle of the wreck, which touch'd
  The very virtue of compassion in thee,
  I have with such provision in mine art
  So safely ordered that there is no soul—
  No, not so much perdition as an hair
  Betid to any creature in the vessel
  Which thou heard'st cry, which thou saw'st sink. Sit down;
  For thou must now know farther.

MIRANDA   You have often
  Begun to tell me what I am, but stopp'd
  And left me to a bootless inquisition,
  Concluding, "Stay; not yet."

PROSPERO   The hour's now come;
  The very minute bids thee ope thine ear;
  Obey and be attentive. Canst thou remember
  A time before we came unto this cell?
  I do not think thou canst, for then thou wast not
  Out three years old.

MIRANDA   Certainly, sir, I can.

PROSPERO   By what? by any other house or person?
  Of anything the image tell me that
  Hath kept with thy remembrance.

MIRANDA   'Tis far off
  And rather like a dream than an assurance
  That my remembrance warrants. Had I not
  Four or five women once that tended me?

PROSPERO   Thou hadst, and more, Miranda. But how is it

That this lives in thy mind? What seest thou else
In the dark backward and abysm of time?
If thou remember'st aught ere thou camest here,
How thou camest here thou mayst.

MIRANDA   But that I do not.

PROSPERO   Twelve year since, Miranda, twelve year since,
   Thy father was the Duke of Milan and
   A prince of power.

MIRANDA   Sir, are not you my father?

PROSPERO   Thy mother was a piece of virtue, and
   She said thou wast my daughter; and thy father
   Was Duke of Milan; and thou his only heir
   And princess no worse issued.

MIRANDA   O the heavens!
   What foul play had we, that we came from thence?
   Or blessed was't we did?

PROSPERO   Both, both, my girl.
   By foul play, as thou say'st, were we heaved thence,
   But blessedly holp hither.

MIRANDA   O, my heart bleeds
   To think o' the teen that I have turn'd you to,
   Which is from my remembrance! Please you, farther.

PROSPERO   My brother and thy uncle, call'd Antonio—
   I pray thee, mark me—that a brother should
   Be so perfidious!—he whom next thyself
   Of all the world I loved and to him put
   The manage of my state; as at that time
   Through all the signories it was the first
   And Prospero the prime duke, being so reputed
   In dignity, and for the liberal arts
   Without a parallel; those being all my study,
   The government I cast upon my brother
   And to my state grew stranger, being transported
   And rapt in secret studies. Thy false uncle—
   Dost thou attend me?

MIRANDA   Sir, most heedfully.

PROSPERO   Being once perfected how to grant suits,

593

How to deny them, who to advance and who
To trash for over-topping, new created
The creatures that were mine, I say, or changed 'em,
Or else new form'd 'em; having both the key
Of officer and office, set all hearts i' the state
To what tune pleased his ear; that now he was
The ivy which had hid my princely trunk,
And suck'd my verdure out on't. Thou attend'st not.

MIRANDA   O, good sir, I do.

PROSPERO   I pray thee, mark me.
   I, thus neglecting worldly ends, all dedicated
   To closeness and the bettering of my mind
   With that which, but by being so retired,
   O'er-prized all popular rate, in my false brother
   Awaked an evil nature; and my trust,
   Like a good parent, did beget of him
   A falsehood in its contrary as great
   As my trust was; which had indeed no limit,
   A confidence sans bound. He being thus lorded,
   Not only with what my revenue yielded,
   But what my power might else exact, like one
   Who having into truth, by telling of it,
   Made such a sinner of his memory,
   To credit his own lie, he did believe
   He was indeed the Duke. Out o' the substitution,
   And executing the outward face of royalty,
   With all prerogative, hence his ambition growing—
   Dost thou hear?

   MIRANDA   Your tale, sir, would cure deafness.

PROSPERO   To have no screen between this part he play'd
   And him he play'd it for, he needs will be
   Absolute Milan. Me, poor man, my library
   Was dukedom large enough. Of temporal royalties
   He thinks me now incapable; confederates—
   So dry he was for sway—wi' the King of Naples
   To give him annual tribute, do him homage,
   Subject his coronet to his crown and bend
   The dukedom yet unbow'd—alas, poor Milan!—
   To most ignoble stooping.

594

MIRANDA   O the heavens!

PROSPERO Mark his condition and the event; then tell me
    If this might be a brother.

MIRANDA   I should sin
    To think but nobly of my grandmother.
    Good wombs have borne bad sons.

PROSPERO   Now the condition.
    This King of Naples, being an enemy
    To me inveterate, hearkens my brother's suit;
    Which was, that he, in lieu o' the premises
    Of homage and I know not how much tribute,
    Should presently extirpate me and mine
    Out of the dukedom and confer fair Milan
    With all the honours on my brother; whereon,
    A treacherous army levied, one midnight
    Fated to the purpose did Antonio open
    The gates of Milan, and, i' the dead of darkness,
    The ministers for the purpose hurried thence
    Me and thy crying self.

MIRANDA   Alack, for pity!
    I, not remembering how I cried out then,
    Will cry it o'er again. It is a hint
    That wrings mine eyes to't.

PROSPERO   Hear a little further
    And then I'll bring thee to the present business
    Which now's upon's; without the which this story
    Were most impertinent.

MIRANDA   Wherefore did they not
    That hour destroy us?

PROSPERO   Well demanded, wench;
    My tale provokes that question. Dear, they durst not,
    So dear the love my people bore me, nor set
    A mark so bloody on the business, but
    With colours fairer painted their foul ends.
    In few, they hurried us aboard a bark,
    Bore us some leagues to sea; where they prepared
    A rotten carcass of a boat, not rigg'd,
    Nor tackle, sail, nor mast; the very rats

595

Instinctively have quit it. There they hoist us,
To cry to the sea that roar'd to us, to sigh
To the winds whose pity, sighing back again,
Did us but loving wrong.

MIRANDA   Alack, what trouble
Was I then to you!

PROSPERO   O, a cherubin
Thou wast that did preserve me. Thou didst smile,
Infused with a fortitude from heaven,
When I have deck'd the sea with drops full salt,
Under my burthen groan'd; which raised in me
An undergoing stomach, to bear up
Against what should ensue.

MIRANDA   How came we ashore?

PROSPERO   By Providence divine.
Some food we had and some fresh water that
A noble Neapolitan, Gonzalo,
Out of his charity, who being then appointed
Master of this design, did give us, with
Rich garments, linens, stuffs and necessaries,
Which since have steaded much; so, of his gentleness,
Knowing I loved my books, he furnish'd me
From mine own library with volumes that
I prize above my dukedom.

MIRANDA   Would I might
But ever see that man!

PROSPERO   Now I arise.

Puts on his mantle.

Sit still, and hear the last of our sea-sorrow.
Here in this island we arrived; and here
Have I, thy schoolmaster, made thee more profit
Than other princesses can that have more time
For vainer hours and tutors not so careful.

MIRANDA   Heavens thank you for't! And now, I pray you, sir,
For still 'tis beating in my mind, your reason
For raising this sea-storm?

PROSPERO   Know thus far forth.

By accident most strange, bountiful Fortune,
Now my dear lady, hath mine enemies
Brought to this shore; and by my prescience
I find my zenith doth depend upon
A most auspicious star, whose influence
If now I court not but omit, my fortunes
Will ever after droop. Here cease more questions.
Thou art inclined to sleep; 'tis a good dulness,
And give it way; I know thou canst not choose.

Miranda sleeps.

Come away, servant, come. I am ready now.
Approach, my Ariel, come.

Enter Ariel.

ARIEL   All hail, great master! grave sir, hail! I come
To answer thy best pleasure, be't to fly,
To swim, to dive into the fire, to ride
On the curl'd clouds, to thy strong bidding task
Ariel and all his quality.

PROSPERO   Hast thou, spirit,
Perform'd to point the tempest that I bade thee?

ARIEL   To every article.
I boarded the King's ship; now on the beak,
Now in the waist, the deck, in every cabin,
I flamed amazement. Sometime I'd divide,
And burn in many places; on the topmast,
The yards and bowsprit, would I flame distinctly,
Then meet and join. Jove's lightnings, the precursors
O' the dreadful thunder-claps, more momentary
And sight-outrunning were not; the fire and cracks
Of sulphurous roaring the most mighty Neptune
Seem to besiege and make his bold waves tremble,
Yea, his dread trident shake.

PROSPERO   My brave spirit!
Who was so firm, so constant, that this coil
Would not infect his reason?

ARIEL   Not a soul
But felt a fever of the mad and play'd
Some tricks of desperation. All but mariners

597

Plunged in the foaming brine and quit the vessel,
Then all afire with me. The King's son, Ferdinand,
With hair up-staring—then like reeds, not hair—
Was the first man that leap'd; cried, "Hell is empty,
And all the devils are here."

PROSPERO   Why, that's my spirit!
But was not this nigh shore?

ARIEL   Close by, my master.

PROSPERO   But are they, Ariel, safe?

ARIEL   Not a hair perish'd;
On their sustaining garments not a blemish,
But fresher than before; and, as thou badest me,
In troops I have dispersed them 'bout the isle.
The King's son have I landed by himself;
Whom I left cooling of the air with sighs
In an odd angle of the isle and sitting,
His arms in this sad knot.

PROSPERO   Of the King's ship
The mariners say how thou hast disposed
And all the rest o' the fleet.

ARIEL   Safely in harbour
Is the King's ship; in the deep nook, where once
Thou call'dst me up at midnight to fetch dew
From the still-vex'd Bermoothes, there she's hid.
The mariners all under hatches stow'd;
Who, with a charm join'd to their suffer'd labour,
I have left asleep; and for the rest o' the fleet
Which I dispersed, they all have met again
And are upon the Mediterranean float,
Bound sadly home for Naples,
Supposing that they saw the King's ship wreck'd
And his great person perish.

PROSPERO   Ariel, thy charge
Exactly is perform'd; but there's more work.
What is the time o' the day?

ARIEL   Past the mid season.

598

PROSPERO   At least two glasses. The time 'twixt six and now
  Must by us both be spent most preciously.

ARIEL   Is there more toil? Since thou dost give me pains,
  Let me remember thee what thou hast promised,
  Which is not yet perform'd me.

PROSPERO   How now? moody?
  What is't thou canst demand?

ARIEL   My liberty.

PROSPERO   Before the time be out? no more!

ARIEL   I prithee,
  Remember I have done thee worthy service;
  Told thee no lies, made thee no mistakings, served
  Without or grudge or grumblings. Thou didst promise
  To bate me a full year.

PROSPERO   Dost thou forget
  From what a torment I did free thee?

ARIEL   No.

PROSPERO   Thou dost, and think'st it much to tread the ooze
  Of the salt deep,
  To run upon the sharp wind of the north,
  To do me business in the veins o' the earth
  When it is baked with frost.

ARIEL   I do not, sir.

PROSPERO   Thou liest, malignant thing! Hast thou forgot
  The foul witch Sycorax, who with age and envy
  Was grown into a hoop? Hast thou forgot her?

ARIEL   No, sir.

PROSPERO   Thou hast. Where was she born? speak; tell me.

ARIEL   Sir, in Argier.

PROSPERO   O, was she so? I must
  Once in a month recount what thou hast been,
  Which thou forget'st. This damn'd witch Sycorax,
  For mischiefs manifold and sorceries terrible
  To enter human hearing, from Argier,

Thou know'st, was banish'd; for one thing she did
They would not take her life. Is not this true?

ARIEL   Ay, sir.

PROSPERO   This blue-eyed hag was hither brought with child
And here was left by the sailors. Thou, my slave,
As thou report'st thyself, wast then her servant;
And, for thou wast a spirit too delicate
To act her earthy and abhorr'd commands,
Refusing her grand hests, she did confine thee,
By help of her more potent ministers
And in her most unmitigable rage,
Into a cloven pine; within which rift
Imprison'd thou didst painfully remain
A dozen years; within which space she died
And left thee there; where thou didst vent thy groans
As fast as mill-wheels strike. Then was this island—
Save for the son that she did litter here,
A freckled whelp hag-born—not honour'd with
A human shape.

ARIEL   Yes, Caliban her son.

PROSPERO   Dull thing, I say so; he, that Caliban
Whom now I keep in service. Thou best know'st
What torment I did find thee in; thy groans
Did make wolves howl and penetrate the breasts
Of ever angry bears. It was a torment
To lay upon the damn'd, which Sycorax
Could not again undo. It was mine art,
When I arrived and heard thee, that made gape
The pine and let thee out.

ARIEL   I thank thee, master.

PROSPERO   If thou more murmur'st, I will rend an oak
And peg thee in his knotty entrails till
Thou hast howl'd away twelve winters.

ARIEL   Pardon, master;
I will be correspondent to command
And do my spiriting gently.

PROSPERO   Do so, and after two days
I will discharge thee.

600

ARIEL   That's my noble master!
  What shall I do? Say what; what shall I do?

PROSPERO   Go make thyself like a nymph o' the sea; be subject
  To no sight but thine and mine, invisible
  To every eyeball else. Go take this shape
  And hither come in't. Go, hence with diligence!   *Exit Ariel.*
  Awake, dear heart, awake! thou hast slept well;
  Awake!

MIRANDA   The strangeness of your story put
  Heaviness in me.

PROSPERO   Shake it off. Come on;
  We'll visit Caliban my slave, who never
  Yields us kind answer.

MIRANDA   'Tis a villain, sir,
  I do not love to look on.

PROSPERO   But, as 'tis,
  We cannot miss him: he does make our fire,
  Fetch in our wood, and serves in offices
  That profit us. What, ho! slave! Caliban!
  Thou earth, thou! speak.

CALIBAN   [*Within.*]   There's wood enough within.

PROSPERO   Come forth, I say! there's other business for thee.
  Come, thou tortoise! when?

Re-enter Ariel like a water-nymph.

  Fine apparition! My quaint Ariel,
  Hark in thine ear.

ARIEL   My lord, it shall be done.   *Exit.*

PROSPERO   Thou poisonous slave, got by the devil himself
  Upon thy wicked dam, come forth!

Enter Caliban.

CALIBAN   As wicked dew as e'er my mother brush'd
  With raven's feather from unwholesome fen
  Drop on you both! a south-west blow on ye
  And blister you all o'er!

PROSPERO   For this, be sure, to-night thou shalt have cramps,

601

Side-stitches that shall pen thy breath up; urchins
Shall, for that vast of night that they may work,
All exercise on thee; thou shalt be pinch'd
As thick as honeycomb, each pinch more stinging
Than bees that made 'em.

CALIBAN   I must eat my dinner.
This island's mine, by Sycorax my mother,
Which thou takest from me. When thou camest first,
Thou strokedst me and madest much of me, wouldst give me
Water with berries in't, and teach me how
To name the bigger light, and how the less,
That burn by day and night; and then I loved thee
And show'd thee all the qualities o' the isle,
The fresh springs, brine-pits, barren place and fertile.
Cursed be I that did so! All the charms
Of Sycorax, toads, beetles, bats, light on you!
For I am all the subjects that you have,
Which first was mine own king; and here you sty me
In this hard rock, whiles you do keep from me
The rest o' the island.

PROSPERO   Thou most lying slave,
Whom stripes may move, not kindness! I have used thee,
Filth as thou art, with human care, and lodged thee
In mine own cell, till thou didst seek to violate
The honour of my child.

CALIBAN   O ho, O ho! Would't had been done!
Thou didst prevent me; I had peopled else
This isle with Calibans.

PROSPERO   Abhorred slave,
Which any print of goodness wilt not take,
Being capable of all ill! I pitied thee,
Took pains to make thee speak, taught thee each hour
One thing or other. When thou didst not, savage,
Know thine own meaning, but wouldst gabble like
A thing most brutish, I endow'd thy purposes
With words that made them known. But thy vile race,
Though thou didst learn, had that in't which good natures
Could not abide to be with; therefore wast thou
Deservedly confined into this rock,
Who hadst deserved more than a prison.

602

CALIBAN   You taught me language; and my profit on't
Is, I know how to curse. The red plague rid you
For learning me your language!

PROSPERO   Hag-seed, hence!
Fetch us in fuel; and be quick, thou'rt best,
To answer other business. Shrug'st thou, malice?
If thou neglect'st or dost unwillingly
What I command, I'll rack thee with old cramps,
Fill all thy bones with aches, make thee roar
That beasts shall tremble at thy din.

CALIBAN   No, pray thee.
[*Aside.*] I must obey. His art is of such power,
It would control my dam's god, Setebos,
And make a vassal of him.

PROSPERO   So, slave; hence!   *Exit Caliban.*

Re-enter Ariel, invisible, playing and singing; Ferdinand following.

Ariel's Song

"Come unto these yellow sands,
        And then take hands,
Courtsied when you have and kiss'd
        The wild waves whist,
Foot it featly here and there;
And, sweet sprites, the burthen bear.
        Hark, hark!"

Burthen dispersedly, within, "Bow-wow."

"The watch-dogs bark!"

Burthen, dispersedly, within, "Bow-wow."

"Hark, hark! I hear
The strain of strutting chanticleer."

Cry, within, "Cock-a-diddle-dow."

FERDINAND   Where should this music be? i' the air or the earth?
It sounds no more; and, sure, it waits upon
Some god o' the island. Sitting on a bank,
Weeping again the King my father's wreck,
This music crept by me upon the waters,
Allaying both their fury and my passion

603

With its sweet air. Thence I have follow'd it,
Or it hath drawn me rather. But 'tis gone.
No, it begins again.

Ariel's Song

"Full fathom five thy father lies;
    Of his bones are coral made;
Those are pearls that were his eyes:
    Nothing of him that doth fade
But doth suffer a sea-change
Into something rich and strange.
Sea-nymphs hourly ring his knell."

Burthen, within, "Ding-dong."

"Hark! now I hear them—ding-dong, bell."

FERDINAND   The ditty does remember my drown'd father.
This is no mortal business, nor no sound
That the earth owes. I hear it now above me.

PROSPERO   The fringed curtains of thine eye advance
And say what thou seest yond.

MIRANDA   What is't? a spirit?
Lord, how it looks about! Believe me, sir,
It carries a brave form. But 'tis a spirit.

PROSPERO   No, wench; it eats and sleeps and hath such senses
As we have, such. This gallant which thou seest
Was in the wreck; and, but he's something stain'd
With grief that's beauty's canker, thou mightst call him
A goodly person. He hath lost his fellows
And strays about to find 'em.

MIRANDA   I might call him
A thing divine, for nothing natural
I ever saw so noble.

PROSPERO [*Aside.*]   It goes on, I see,
As my soul prompts it. Spirit, fine spirit! I'll free thee
Within two days for this.

FERDINAND   Most sure, the goddess
On whom these airs attend! Vouchsafe my prayer
May know if you remain upon this island;
And that you will some good instruction give

How I may bear me here. My prime request,
Which I do last pronounce, is, O you wonder!
If you be maid or no?

MIRANDA   No wonder, sir;
   But certainly a maid.

FERDINAND   My language! heavens!
   I am the best of them that speak this speech,
   Were I but where 'tis spoken.

PROSPERO   How? the best?
   What wert thou, if the King of Naples heard thee?

FERDINAND   A single thing, as I am now, that wonders
   To hear thee speak of Naples. He does hear me:
   And that he does I weep. Myself am Naples,
   Who with mine eyes, never since at ebb, beheld
   The King my father wreck'd.

MIRANDA   Alack, for mercy!

FERDINAND   Yes, faith, and all his lords; the Duke of Milan
   And his brave son being twain.

PROSPERO   [*Aside*.]   The Duke of Milan
   And his more braver daughter could control thee,
   If now 'twere fit to do't. At the first sight
   They have changed eyes. Delicate Ariel,
   I'll set thee free for this. [*To Ferdinand*.] A word, good sir;
   I fear you have done yourself some wrong; a word.

MIRANDA   Why speaks my father so ungently? This
   Is the third man that e'er I saw, the first
   That e'er I sigh'd for. Pity move my father
   To be inclined my way!

FERDINAND   O, if a virgin,
   And your affection not gone forth, I'll make you
   The Queen of Naples.

PROSPERO   Soft, sir! one word more.
   [*Aside*.] They are both in either's powers; but this swift business
   I must uneasy make, lest too light winning
   Make the prize light. [*To Ferdinand*.] One word more; I charge thee
   That thou attend me. Thou dost here usurp
   The name thou owest not; and hast put thyself

Upon this island as a spy, to win it
From me, the lord on't.

FERDINAND   No, as I am a man.

MIRANDA   There's nothing ill can dwell in such a temple.
If the ill spirit have so fair a house,
Good things will strive to dwell with't.

PROSPERO   Follow me.
Speak not you for him; he's a traitor. Come;
I'll manacle thy neck and feet together;
Sea-water shalt thou drink; thy food shall be
The fresh-brook muscles, wither'd roots, and husks
Wherein the acorn cradled. Follow.

FERDINAND   No;
I will resist such entertainment till
Mine enemy has more power.

He draws, and is charmed from moving.

MIRANDA   O dear father,
Make not too rash a trial of him, for
He's gentle and not fearful.

PROSPERO   What? I say,
My foot my tutor? Put thy sword up, traitor;
Who makest a show but darest not strike, thy conscience
Is so possess'd with guilt. Come from thy ward,
For I can here disarm thee with this stick
And make thy weapon drop.

MIRANDA   Beseech you, father.

PROSPERO   Hence! hang not on my garments.

MIRANDA   Sir, have pity;
I'll be his surety.

PROSPERO   Silence! one word more
Shall make me chide thee, if not hate thee. What!
An advocate for an impostor! Hush!
Thou think'st there is no more such shapes as he,
Having seen but him and Caliban. Foolish wench!
To the most of men this is a Caliban
And they to him are angels.

606

MIRANDA   My affections
Are then most humble; I have no ambition
To see a goodlier man.

PROSPERO   Come on; obey.
Thy nerves are in their infancy again
And have no vigour in them.

FERDINAND   So they are;
My spirits, as in a dream, are all bound up.
My father's loss, the weakness which I feel,
The wreck of all my friends, nor this man's threats,
To whom I am subdued, are but light to me,
Might I but through my prison once a day
Behold this maid. All corners else o' the earth
Let liberty make use of; space enough
Have I in such a prison.

PROSPERO   [*Aside.*]   It works. [*To Ferdinand.*] Come on.
Thou hast done well, fine Ariel! [*To Ferdinand.*] Follow me.
[*To Ariel.*] Hark what thou else shalt do me.

MIRANDA   Be of comfort;
My father's of a better nature, sir,
Than he appears by speech. This is unwonted
Which now came from him.

PROSPERO   Thou shalt be as free
As mountain winds. But then exactly do
All points of my command.

ARIEL   To the syllable.

PROSPERO   Come, follow. Speak not for him.   *Exeunt.*

ACT II

SCENE 1 *Another part of the island.*

Enter Alonso, Sebastian, Antonio, Gonzalo, Adrian, Francisco, and others.

GONZALO Beseech you, sir, be merry; you have cause,
So have we all, of joy; for our escape
Is much beyond our loss. Our hint of woe
Is common; every day some sailor's wife,
The masters of some merchant, and the merchant
Have just our theme of woe; but for the miracle,
I mean our preservation, few in millions
Can speak like us. Then wisely, good sir, weigh
Our sorrow with our comfort.

ALONSO   Prithee, peace.

SEBASTIAN He receives comfort like cold porridge.

ANTONIO The visitor will not give him o'er so.

SEBASTIAN Look, he's winding up the watch of his wit; by and by it will
strike.

GONZALO Sir—

SEBASTIAN One. Tell.

GONZALO When every grief is entertain'd that's offer'd,
Comes to the entertainer—

SEBASTIAN A dollar.

GONZALO Dolour comes to him, indeed; you have spoken truer than
you purposed.

608

SEBASTIAN You have taken it wiselier than I meant you should.

GONZALO Therefore, my lord—

ANTONIO Fie, what a spendthrift is he of his tongue!

ALONSO I prithee, spare.

GONZALO Well, I have done. But yet—

SEBASTIAN He will be talking.

ANTONIO Which, of he or Adrian, for a good wager, first begins to crow?

SEBASTIAN The old cock.

ANTONIO The cockerel.

SEBASTIAN Done. The wager?

ANTONIO A laughter.

SEBASTIAN A match!

ADRIAN Though this island seem to be desert—

SEBASTIAN Ha, ha, ha! So, you're paid.

ADRIAN Uninhabitable and almost inaccessible—

SEBASTIAN Yet—

ADRIAN Yet—

ANTONIO He could not miss't.

ADRIAN It must needs be of subtle, tender, and delicate temperance.

ANTONIO Temperance was a delicate wench.

SEBASTIAN Ay, and a subtle; as he most learnedly delivered.

ADRIAN The air breathes upon us here most sweetly.

SEBASTIAN As if it had lungs and rotten ones.

ANTONIO Or as 'twere perfumed by a fen.

GONZALO Here is everything advantageous to life.

ANTONIO True; save means to live.

SEBASTIAN Of that there's none, or little.

GONZALO   How lush and lusty the grass looks! how green!

ANTONIO   The ground indeed is tawny.

SEBASTIAN   With an eye of green in't.

ANTONIO   He misses not much.

SEBASTIAN   No; he doth but mistake the truth totally.

GONZALO   But the rarity of it is—which is indeed almost beyond credit—

SEBASTIAN   As many vouched rarities are.

GONZALO   That our garments, being, as they were, drenched in the sea, hold notwithstanding their freshness and glosses, being rather new-dyed than stained with salt water.

ANTONIO   If but one of his pockets could speak, would it not say he lies?

SEBASTIAN   Ay, or very falsely pocket up his report.

GONZALO   Methinks our garments are now as fresh as when we put them on first in Afric, at the marriage of the King's fair daughter Claribel to the King of Tunis.

SEBASTIAN   'Twas a sweet marriage, and we prosper well in our return.

ADRIAN   Tunis was never graced before with such a paragon to their queen.

GONZALO   Not since widow Dido's time.

ANTONIO   Widow! a pox o' that! How came that widow in? widow Dido!

SEBASTIAN   What if he had said "widower Aeneas" too? Good Lord, how you take it!

ADRIAN   "Widow Dido" said you? you make me study of that. She was of Carthage, not of Tunis.

GONZALO   This Tunis, sir, was Carthage.

ADRIAN   Carthage?

GONZALO   I assure you, Carthage.

SEBASTIAN   His word is more than the miraculous harp; he hath raised the wall and houses too.

ANTONIO   What impossible matter will he make easy next?

SEBASTIAN   I think he will carry this island home in his pocket and give it his son for an apple.

ANTONIO   And, sowing the kernels of it in the sea, bring forth more islands.

GONZALO   Ay.

ANTONIO   Why, in good time.

GONZALO   Sir, we were talking that our garments seem now as fresh as when we were at Tunis at the marriage of your daughter, who is now Queen.

ANTONIO   And the rarest that e'er came there.

SEBASTIAN   Bate, I beseech you, widow Dido.

ANTONIO   O, widow Dido! ay, widow Dido.

GONZALO   Is not, sir, my doublet as fresh as the first day I wore it? I mean, in a sort.

ANTONIO   That sort was well fished for.

GONZALO   When I wore it at your daughter's marriage?

ALONSO   You cram these words into mine ears against
The stomach of my sense. Would I had never
Married my daughter there! for, coming thence,
My son is lost and, in my rate, she too,
Who is so far from Italy removed
I ne'er again shall see her. O thou mine heir
Of Naples and of Milan, what strange fish
Hath made his meal on thee?

FRANCISCO   Sir, he may live.
I saw him beat the surges under him
And ride upon their backs; he trod the water,
Whose enmity he flung aside, and breasted
The surge most swoln that met him; his bold head
'Bove the contentious waves he kept, and oar'd
Himself with his good arms in lusty stroke
To the shore, that o'er his wave-worn basis bow'd,
As stooping to relieve him. I not doubt
He came alive to land.

611

ALONSO   No, no, he's gone.

SEBASTIAN   Sir, you may thank yourself for this great loss,
That would not bless our Europe with your daughter,
But rather lose her to an African;
Where she at least is banish'd from your eye,
Who hath cause to wet the grief on't.

ALONSO   Prithee, peace.

SEBASTIAN   You were kneel'd to and importuned otherwise
By all of us, and the fair soul herself
Weigh'd between loathness and obedience, at
Which end o' the beam should bow. We have lost your son,
I fear, for ever. Milan and Naples have
Moe widows in them of this business' making
Than we bring men to comfort them.
The fault's your own.

ALONSO   So is the dear'st o' the loss.

GONZALO   My lord Sebastian,
The truth you speak doth lack some gentleness
And time to speak it in. You rub the sore,
When you should bring the plaster.

SEBASTIAN   Very well.

ANTONIO   And most chirurgeonly.

GONZALO   It is foul weather in us all, good sir,
When you are cloudy.

SEBASTIAN   Foul weather?

ANTONIO   Very foul.

GONZALO   Had I plantation of this isle, my lord—

ANTONIO   He'd sow't with nettle-seed.

SEBASTIAN   Or docks, or mallows.

GONZALO   And were the king on't, what would I do?

SEBASTIAN   'Scape being drunk for want of wine.

GONZALO   I' the commonwealth I would by contraries
Execute all things; for no kind of traffic
Would I admit; no name of magistrate;

Letters should not be known; riches, poverty,
And use of service, none; contract, succession,
Bourn, bound of land, tilth, vineyard, none;
No use of metal, corn, or wine, or oil;
No occupation; all men idle, all;
And women too, but innocent and pure;
No sovereignty —

SEBASTIAN   Yet he would be king on't.

ANTONIO   The latter end of his commonwealth forgets the beginning.

GONZALO   All things in common nature should produce
Without sweat or endeavour. Treason, felony,
Sword, pike, knife, gun, or need of any engine,
Would I not have; but nature should bring forth,
Of it own kind, all foison, all abundance,
To feed my innocent people.

SEBASTIAN   No marrying 'mong his subjects?

ANTONIO   None, man; all idle. Whores and knaves.

GONZALO   I would with such perfection govern, sir,
To excel the golden age.

SEBASTIAN   God save his Majesty!

ANTONIO   Long live Gonzalo!

GONZALO   And — do you mark me, sir?

ALONSO   Prithee, no more. Thou dost talk nothing to me.

GONZALO   I do well believe your Highness; and did it to minister occasion to these gentlemen, who are of such sensible and nimble lungs
that they always use to laugh at nothing.

ANTONIO   'Twas you we laughed at.

GONZALO   Who in this kind of merry fooling am nothing to you. So you
may continue and laugh at nothing still.

ANTONIO   What a blow was there given!

SEBASTIAN   An it had not fallen flatlong.

GONZALO   You are gentlemen of brave mettle; you would lift the moon
out of her sphere, if she would continue in it five weeks without
changing.

613

Enter Ariel, invisible, playing solemn music.

SEBASTIAN   We would so, and then go a bat-fowling.

ANTONIO   Nay, good my lord, be not angry.

GONZALO   No, I warrant you; I will not adventure my discretion so
weakly. Will you laugh me asleep, for I am very heavy?

ANTONIO   Go sleep, and hear us.

All sleep except Alonso, Sebastian, and Antonio.

ALONSO   What, all so soon asleep! I wish mine eyes
Would, with themselves, shut up my thoughts. I find
They are inclined to do so.

SEBASTIAN   Please you, sir,
Do not omit the heavy offer of it.
It seldom visits sorrow; when it doth,
It is a comforter.

ANTONIO   We two, my lord,
Will guard your person while you take your rest,
And watch your safety.

ALONSO   Thank you. Wondrous heavy.
                                   Alonso sleeps. Exit Ariel.

SEBASTIAN   What a strange drowsiness possesses them!

ANTONIO   It is the quality o' the climate.

SEBASTIAN   Why
Doth it not then our eyelids sink? I find not
Myself disposed to sleep.

ANTONIO   Nor I; my spirits are nimble.
They fell together all, as by consent;
They dropp'd, as by a thunder-stroke. What might,
Worthy Sebastian? O, what might? No more;
And yet methinks I see it in thy face,
What thou shouldst be. The occasion speaks thee, and
My strong imagination sees a crown
Dropping upon thy head.

SEBASTIAN   What, art thou waking?

ANTONIO   Do you not hear me speak?

SEBASTIAN   I do; and surely
  It is a sleepy language and thou speak'st
  Out of thy sleep. What is it thou didst say?
  This is a strange repose, to be asleep
  With eyes wide open; standing, speaking, moving,
  And yet so fast asleep.

ANTONIO   Noble Sebastian,
  Thou let'st thy fortune sleep—die, rather; wink'st
  Whiles thou art waking.

SEBASTIAN   Thou dost snore distinctly;
  There's meaning in thy snores.

ANTONIO   I am more serious than my custom. You
  Must be so too, if heed me; which to do
  Trebles thee o'er.

SEBASTIAN   Well, I am standing water.

ANTONIO   I'll teach you how to flow.

SEBASTIAN   Do so. To ebb
  Hereditary sloth instructs me.

ANTONIO   O,
  If you but knew how you the purpose cherish
  Whiles thus you mock it! how, in stripping it,
  You more invest it! Ebbing men, indeed,
  Most often do so near the bottom run
  By their own fear or sloth.

SEBASTIAN   Prithee, say on.
  The setting of thine eye and cheek proclaim
  A matter from thee, and a birth indeed
  Which throes thee much to yield.

ANTONIO   Thus, sir:
  Although this lord of weak remembrance, this,
  Who shall be of as little memory
  When he is earth'd, hath here almost persuaded—
  For he's a spirit of persuasion, only
  Professes to persuade—the King his son's alive,
  'Tis as impossible that he's undrown'd
  As he that sleeps here swims.

615

SEBASTIAN   I have no hope
  That he's undrown'd.

ANTONIO   O, out of that "no hope"
  What great hope have you! no hope that way is
  Another way so high a hope that even
  Ambition cannot pierce a wink beyond,
  But doubt discovery there. Will you grant with me
  That Ferdinand is drown'd?

SEBASTIAN   He's gone.

ANTONIO   Then, tell me,
  Who's the next heir of Naples?

SEBASTIAN   Claribel.

ANTONIO   She that is Queen of Tunis; she that dwells
  Ten leagues beyond man's life; she that from Naples
  Can have no note, unless the sun were post—
  The man i' the moon's too slow—till new-born chins
  Be rough and razorable; she that—from whom?
  We all were sea-swallow'd, though some cast again,
  And by that destiny to perform an act
  Whereof what's past is prologue, what to come
  In yours and my discharge.

SEBASTIAN   What stuff is this! how say you?
  'Tis true, my brother's daughter's Queen of Tunis;
  So is she heir of Naples; 'twixt which regions
  There is some space.

ANTONIO   A space whose every cubit
  Seems to cry out, "How shall that Claribel
  Measure us back to Naples? Keep in Tunis,
  And let Sebastian wake." Say, this were death
  That now hath seized them; why, they were no worse
  Than now they are. There be that can rule Naples
  As well as he that sleeps; lords that can prate
  As amply and unnecessarily
  As this Gonzalo; I myself could make
  A chough of as deep chat. O, that you bore
  The mind that I do! what a sleep were this   .
  For your advancement! Do you understand me?

SEBASTIAN   Methinks I do.

616

ANTONIO   And how does your content
  Tender your own good fortune?

SEBASTIAN   I remember
  You did supplant your brother Prospero.

ANTONIO   True;
  And look how well my garments sit upon me;
  Much feater than before. My brother's servants
  Were then my fellows; now they are my men.

SEBASTIAN   But, for your conscience?

ANTONIO   Ay, sir; where lies that? if 'twere a kibe,
  'Twould put me to my slipper: but I feel not
  This deity in my bosom. Twenty consciences,
  That stand 'twixt me and Milan, candied be they
  And melt ere they molest! Here lies your brother,
  No better than the earth he lies upon,
  If he were that which now he's like, that's dead;
  Whom I, with this obedient steel, three inches of it,
  Can lay to bed for ever; whiles you, doing thus,
  To the perpetual wink for aye might put
  This ancient morsel, this Sir Prudence, who
  Should not upbraid our course. For all the rest,
  They'll take suggestion as a cat laps milk;
  They'll tell the clock to any business that
  We say befits the hour.

SEBASTIAN   Thy case, dear friend,
  Shall be my precedent; as thou got'st Milan,
  I'll come by Naples. Draw thy sword. One stroke
  Shall free thee from the tribute which thou payest;
  And I the King shall love thee.

ANTONIO   Draw together;
  And when I rear my hand, do you the like,
  To fall it on Gonzalo.

SEBASTIAN   O, but one word.

They talk apart. Re-enter Ariel, invisible.

ARIEL   My master through his art foresees the danger
  That you, his friend, are in; and sends me forth—
  For else his project dies—to keep them living. [*Sings in Gonzalo's ear.*]

"While you here do snoring lie,
Open-eyed conspiracy
His time doth take.
If of life you keep a care,
Shake off slumber, and beware;
Awake, awake!"

ANTONIO   Then let us both be sudden.

GONZALO   Now, good angels
Preserve the King.

They wake.

ALONSO   Why, how now? ho, awake! Why are you drawn?
Wherefore this ghastly looking?

GONZALO   What's the matter?

SEBASTIAN   Whiles we stood here securing your repose,
Even now, we heard a hollow burst of bellowing
Like bulls, or rather lions. Did't not wake you?
It struck mine ear most terribly.

ALONSO   I heard nothing.

ANTONIO   O, 'twas a din to fright a monster's ear,
To make an earthquake! sure, it was the roar
Of a whole herd of lions.

ALONSO   Heard you this, Gonzalo?

GONZALO   Upon mine honour, sir, I heard a humming,
And that a strange one too, which did awake me.
I shaked you, sir, and cried. As mine eyes open'd,
I saw their weapons drawn. There was a noise,
That's verily. 'Tis best we stand upon our guard,
Or that we quit this place. Let's draw our weapons.

ALONSO   Lead off this ground; and let's make further search
For my poor son.

GONZALO   Heavens keep him from these beasts!
For he is, sure, i' the island.

ALONSO   Lead away.

ARIEL   Prospero my lord shall know what I have done.
So, King, go safely to seek thy son.   *Exeunt.*

618

❦ SCENE 2 *Another part of the island.*

Enter Caliban with a burthen of wood. A noise of thunder heard.

CALIBAN All the infections that the sun sucks up
From bogs, fens, flats, on Prosper fall and make him
By inch-meal a disease! His spirits hear me
And yet I needs must curse. But they'll nor pinch,
Fright me with urchin-shows, pitch me i' the mire,
Nor lead me, like a firebrand, in the dark
Out of my way, unless he bid 'em; but
For every trifle are they set upon me;
Sometime like apes that mow and chatter at me
And after bite me, then like hedgehogs which
Lie tumbling in my barefoot way and mount
Their pricks at my footfall; sometime am I
All wound with adders who with cloven tongues
Do hiss me into madness.

Enter Trinculo.

Lo, now, lo!
Here comes a spirit of his, and to torment me
For bringing wood in slowly. I'll fall flat;
Perchance he will not mind me.

TRINCULO Here's neither bush nor shrub, to bear off any weather at all,
and another storm brewing; I hear it sing i' the wind. Yond same black
cloud, yond huge one, looks like a foul bombard that would shed his
liquor. If it should thunder as it did before, I know not where to hide
my head; yond same cloud cannot choose but fall by pailfuls. What
have we here? a man or a fish? Dead or alive? A fish; he smells like a
fish; a very ancient and fish-like smell; a kind of not-of-the newest
Poor-John. A strange fish! Were I in England now, as once I was, and
had but this fish painted, not a holiday fool there but would give a
piece of silver. There would this monster make a man; any strange
beast there makes a man; when they will not give a doit to relieve a
lame beggar, they will lay out ten to see a dead Indian. Legged like a
man! and his fins like arms! Warm o' my troth! I do now let loose my
opinion; hold it no longer. This is no fish, but an islander, that hath
lately suffered by a thunderbolt. [*Thunder.*] Alas, the storm is come
again! my best way is to creep under his gaberdine; there is no other
shelter hereabout. Misery acquaints a man with strange bedfellows. I
will here shroud till the dregs of the storm be past.

619

Enter Stephano, singing, a bottle in his hand.

STEPHANO   "I shall no more to sea, to sea,
                                    Here shall I die ashore—"

This is a very scurvy tune to sing at a man's funeral.
Well, here's my comfort. [*Drinks.*]

[*Sings.*]
                    "The master, the swabber, the boatswain and I,
                            The gunner and his mate
                    Loved Mall, Meg, and Marian, and Margery,
                            But none of us cared for Kate;
                            For she had a tongue with a tang,
                            Would cry to a sailor, 'Go hang!'
                    She loved not the savour of tar nor of pitch,
                    Yet a tailor might scratch her where'er she did itch;
                            Then to sea, boys, and let her go hang!"

This is a scurvy tune too; but here's my comfort. [*Drinks.*]

CALIBAN   Do not torment me! Oh!

STEPHANO   What's the matter? Have we devils here? Do you put tricks
upon's with savages and men of Ind, ha? I have not 'scaped drowning
to be afeard now of your four legs; for it hath been said, "As proper a
man as ever went on four legs cannot make him give ground"; and it
shall be said so again while Stephano breathes at nostrils.

CALIBAN   The spirit torments me; Oh!

STEPHANO   This is some monster of the isle with four legs, who hath
got, as I take it, an ague. Where the devil should he learn our language?
I will give him some relief, if it be but for that. If I can recover him and
keep him tame and get to Naples with him, he's a present for any emperor that ever trod on neat's-leather.

CALIBAN   Do not torment me, prithee; I'll bring my wood home faster.

STEPHANO   He's in his fit now and does not talk after the wisest. He shall
taste of my bottle. If he have never drunk wine afore, it will go near to
remove his fit. If I can recover him and keep him tame, I will not take
too much for him; he shall pay for him that hath him, and that
soundly.

CALIBAN   Thou dost me yet but little hurt; thou wilt anon, I know it by
thy trembling. Now, Prosper works upon thee.

620

STEPHANO   Come on your ways; open your mouth; here is that which will give language to you, cat. Open your mouth; this will shake your shaking, I can tell you, and that soundly. You cannot tell who's your friend. Open your chaps again.

TRINCULO   I should know that voice. It should be—but he is drowned; and these are devils. O defend me!

STEPHANO   Four legs and two voices; a most delicate monster! His forward voice now is to speak well of his friend; his backward voice is to utter foul speeches and to detract. If all the wine in my bottle will recover him, I will help his ague. Come. Amen! I will pour some in thy other mouth.

TRINCULO   Stephano!

STEPHANO   Doth thy other mouth call me? Mercy, mercy! This is a devil, and no monster. I will leave him; I have no long spoon.

TRINCULO   Stephano! If thou beest Stephano, touch me and speak to me; for I am Trinculo—be not afeard—thy good friend Trinculo.

STEPHANO   If thou beest Trinculo, come forth. I'll pull thee by the lesser legs. If any be Trinculo's legs, these are they. Thou art very Trinculo indeed! How camest thou to be the siege of this moon-calf? Can he vent Trinculos?

TRINCULO   I took him to be killed with a thunder-stroke. But art thou not drowned, Stephano? I hope now thou art not drowned. Is the storm overblown? I hid me under the dead moon-calf's gaberdine for fear of the storm. And art thou living, Stephano? O Stephano, two Neapolitans 'scaped!

STEPHANO   Prithee, do not turn me about; my stomach is not constant.

CALIBAN   [*Aside.*] These be fine things, an if they be not sprites.
That's a brave god and bears celestial liquor.
I will kneel to him.

STEPHANO   How didst thou 'scape? How camest thou hither? Swear by this bottle how thou camest hither. I escaped upon a butt of sack which the sailors heaved o'erboard, by this bottle, which I made of the bark of a tree with mine own hands since I was cast ashore.

CALIBAN   I'll swear upon that bottle to be thy true subject; for the liquor is not earthly.

STEPHANO   Here; swear then how thou escapedst.

621

TRINCULO   Swum ashore, man, like a duck. I can swim like a duck, I'll be sworn.

STEPHANO   Here, kiss the book. [*Passing the bottle.*] Though thou canst swim like a duck, thou art made like a goose.

TRINCULO   O Stephano, hast any more of this?

STEPHANO   The whole butt, man. My cellar is in a rock by the sea-side where my wine is hid. How now, moon-calf! how does thine ague?

CALIBAN   Hast thou not dropp'd from heaven?

STEPHANO   Out o' the moon, I do assure thee. I was the man i' the moon when time was.

CALIBAN   I have seen thee in her and I do adore thee.
My mistress show'd me thee and thy dog and thy bush.

STEPHANO   Come, swear to that; kiss the book. I will furnish it anon with new contents. Swear. [*Caliban drinks.*]

TRINCULO   By this good light, this is a very shallow monster! I afeard of him! A very weak monster! The man i' the moon! A most poor credulous monster! Well drawn, monster, in good sooth!

CALIBAN   I'll show thee every fertile inch o' th' island; And I will kiss thy foot. I prithee, be my god.

TRINCULO   By this light, a most perfidious and drunken monster! When's god's asleep, he'll rob his bottle.

CALIBAN   I'll kiss thy foot; I'll swear myself thy subject.

STEPHANO   Come on then; down, and swear.

TRINCULO   I shall laugh myself to death at this puppy-headed monster. A most scurvy monster! I could find in my heart to beat him—

STEPHANO   Come, kiss.

TRINCULO   But that the poor monster's in drink. An abominable monster!

CALIBAN   I'll show thee the best springs; I'll pluck thee berries;
I'll fish for thee and get thee wood enough.
A plague upon the tyrant that I serve!
I'll bear him no more sticks, but follow thee,
Thou wondrous man.

622

TRINCULO   A most ridiculous monster, to make a wonder of a poor drunkard!

CALIBAN   I prithee, let me bring thee where crabs grow;
And I with my long nails will dig thee pig-nuts;
Show thee a jay's nest and instruct thee how
To snare the nimble marmoset; I'll bring thee
To clustering filberts and sometimes I'll get thee
Young scamels from the rock. Wilt thou go with me?

STEPHANO   I prithee now, lead the way without any more talking. Trinculo, the King and all our company else being drowned, we will inherit here. Here; bear my bottle. Fellow Trinculo, we'll fill him by and by again.

CALIBAN   [*Sings drunkenly.*]
        "Farewell, master; farewell, farewell!"

TRINCULO   A howling monster; a drunken monster!

CALIBAN   [*Sings.*]
            "No more dams I'll make for fish;
                Nor fetch in firing
                At requiring;
            Nor scrape trencher, nor wash dish.
                'Ban, 'Ban, Cacaliban
            Has a new master, get a new man."

Freedom, hey-day! hey-day, freedom! freedom, hey-day, freedom!

STEPHANO   O brave monster! Lead the way.   *Exeunt.*

623

ACT III

 SCENE 1 *Before Prospero's cell.*

Enter Ferdinand, bearing a log.

FERDINAND   There be some sports are painful, and their labour
Delight in them sets off; some kinds of baseness
Are nobly undergone and most poor matters
Point to rich ends. This my mean task
Would be as heavy to me as odious, but
The mistress which I serve quickens what's dead
And makes my labours pleasures. O, she is
Ten times more gentle than her father's crabbed,
And he's composed of harshness. I must remove
Some thousands of these logs and pile them up,
Upon a sore injunction. My sweet mistress
Weeps when she sees me work, and says, such baseness
Had never like executor. I forget;
But these sweet thoughts do even refresh my labours
Most busiest when I do it.

Enter Miranda; and Prospero at a distance, unseen.

MIRANDA   Alas, now, pray you,
Work not so hard. I would the lightning had
Burnt up those logs that you are enjoin'd to pile!
Pray, set it down and rest you. When this burns,
'Twill weep for having wearied you. My father
Is hard at study; pray now, rest yourself;
He's safe for these three hours.

FERDINAND   O most dear mistress,

624

The sun will set before I shall discharge
What I must strive to do.

MIRANDA   If you'll sit down,
    I'll bear your logs the while. Pray, give me that;
    I'll carry it to the pile.

FERDINAND   No, precious creature;
    I had rather crack my sinews, break my back,
    Than you should such dishonour undergo,
    While I sit lazy by.

MIRANDA   It would become me
    As well as it does you; and I should do it
    With much more ease; for my good will is to it,
    And yours it is against.

PROSPERO   Poor worm, thou art infected!
    This visitation shows it.

MIRANDA   You look wearily.

FERDINAND   No, noble mistress; 'tis fresh morning with me
    When you are by at night. I do beseech you—
    Chiefly that I might set it in my prayers—
    What is your name?

MIRANDA   Miranda. O my father,
    I have broke your hest to say so!

FERDINAND   Admired Miranda!
    Indeed the top of admiration! worth
    What's dearest to the world! Full many a lady
    I have eyed with best regard and many a time
    The harmony of their tongues hath into bondage
    Brought my too diligent ear; for several virtues
    Have I liked several women; never any
    With so full soul, but some defect in her
    Did quarrel with the noblest grace she owed
    And put it to the foil; but you, O you,
    So perfect and so peerless, are created
    Of every creature's best!

MIRANDA   I do not know
    One of my sex; no woman's face remember,
    Save, from my glass, mine own; nor have I seen

625

More that I may call men than you, good friend,
And my dear father. How features are abroad,
I am skilless of; but, by my modesty,
The jewel in my dower, I would not wish
Any companion in the world but you,
Nor can imagination form a shape,
Besides yourself, to like of. But I prattle
Something too wildly and my father's precepts
I therein do forget.

FERDINAND   I am in my condition
A prince, Miranda; I do think, a king;
I would, not so!—and would no more endure
This wooden slavery than to suffer
The flesh-fly blow my mouth. Hear my soul speak.
The very instant that I saw you, did
My heart fly to your service; there resides,
To make me slave to it; and for your sake
Am I this patient log-man.

MIRANDA   Do you love me?

FERDINAND   O heaven, O earth, bear witness to this sound
And crown what I profess with kind event
If I speak true! if hollowly, invert
What best is boded me to mischief! I
Beyond all limit of what else i' the world
Do love, prize, honour you.

MIRANDA   I am a fool
To weep at what I am glad of.

PROSPERO   Fair encounter
Of two most rare affections! Heavens rain grace
On that which breeds between 'em!

FERDINAND   Wherefore weep you?

MIRANDA   At mine unworthiness that dare not offer
What I desire to give, and much less take
What I shall die to want. But this is trifling;
And all the more it seeks to hide itself,
The bigger bulk it shows. Hence, bashful cunning!
And prompt me, plain and holy innocence!
I am your wife, if you will marry me;

626

If not, I'll die your maid. To be your fellow
You may deny me; but I'll be your servant,
Whether you will or no.

FERDINAND   My mistress, dearest;
And I thus humble ever.

MIRANDA   My husband, then?

FERDINAND   Ay, with a heart as willing
As bondage e'er of freedom. Here's my hand.

MIRANDA   And mine, with my heart in't. And now farewell
Till half an hour hence.

FERDINAND   A thousand thousand!

                            Exeunt Ferdinand and Miranda severally.

PROSPERO   So glad of this as they I cannot be,
Who are surprised withal; but my rejoicing
At nothing can be more. I'll to my book,
For yet ere supper-time must I perform
Much business appertaining.   *Exit.*

 SCENE 2   *Another part of the island.*

Enter Caliban, Stephano, and Trinculo.

STEPHANO   Tell not me; when the butt is out, we will drink water; not a
drop before; therefore bear up, and board 'em. Servant-monster, drink
to me.

TRINCULO   Servant-monster! the folly of this island! They say there's but
five upon this isle; we are three of them; if th' other two be brained like
us, the state totters.

STEPHANO   Drink, servant-monster, when I bid thee. Thy eyes are almost set in thy head.

TRINCULO   Where should they be set else? He were a brave monster indeed, if they were set in his tail.

STEPHANO   My man-monster hath drown'd his tongue in sack. For my
part, the sea cannot drown me; I swam, ere I could recover the shore,
five and thirty leagues off and on. By this light, thou shalt be my lieutenant, monster, or my standard.

627

TRINCULO   Your lieutenant, if you list; he's no standard.

STEPHANO   We'll not run, Monsieur Monster.

TRINCULO   Nor go neither; but you'll lie like dogs and yet say nothing neither.

STEPHANO   Moon-calf, speak once in thy life, if thou beest a good moon-calf.

CALIBAN   How does thy honour? Let me lick thy shoe.
I'll not serve him; he is not valiant.

TRINCULO   Thou liest, most ignorant monster. I am in case to justle a constable. Why, thou deboshed fish, thou, was there ever man a coward that hath drunk so much sack as I to-day? Wilt thou tell a monstrous lie, being but half a fish and half a monster?

CALIBAN   Lo, how he mocks me! wilt thou let him, my lord?

TRINCULO   "Lord" quoth he! That a monster should be such a natural!

CALIBAN   Lo, lo, again! bite him to death, I prithee.

STEPHANO   Trinculo, keep a good tongue in your head. If you prove a mutineer—the next tree! The poor monster's my subject, and he shall not suffer indignity.

CALIBAN   I thank my noble lord. Wilt thou be pleased to hearken once again to the suit I made to thee?

STEPHANO   Marry, will I; kneel and repeat it; I will stand, and so shall Trinculo.

Enter Ariel, invisible.

CALIBAN   As I told thee before, I am subject to a tyrant,
A sorcerer, that by his cunning hath
Cheated me of the island.

ARIEL   Thou liest.

CALIBAN   Thou liest, thou jesting monkey, thou.
I would my valiant master would destroy thee!
I do not lie.

STEPHANO   Trinculo, if you trouble him any more in's tale, by this hand, I will supplant some of your teeth.

TRINCULO   Why, I said nothing.

STEPHANO   Mum, then, and no more. Proceed.

CALIBAN   I say, by sorcery he got this isle;
From me he got it. If thy greatness will
Revenge it on him—for I know thou darest,
But this thing dare not—

STEPHANO   That's most certain.

CALIBAN   Thou shalt be lord of it and I'll serve thee.

STEPHANO   How now shall this be compassed? Canst thou bring me to
the party?

CALIBAN   Yea, yea, my lord. I'll yield him thee asleep,
Where thou mayst knock a nail into his head.

ARIEL   Thou liest; thou canst not.

CALIBAN   What a pied ninny's this! Thou scurvy patch!
I do beseech thy greatness, give him blows
And take his bottle from him. When that's gone
He shall drink nought but brine; for I'll not show him
Where the quick freshes are.

STEPHANO   Trinculo, run into no further danger. Interrupt the monster
one word further, and, by this hand, I'll turn my mercy out o' doors
and make a stock-fish of thee.

TRINCULO   Why, what did I? I did nothing. I'll go farther off.

STEPHANO   Didst thou not say he lied?

ARIEL   Thou liest.

STEPHANO   Do I so? take thou that. [*Beats Trinculo.*] As you like this, give
me the lie another time.

TRINCULO   I did not give the lie. Out o' your wits and hearing too? A
pox o' your bottle! this can sack and drinking do. A murrain on your
monster, and the devil take your fingers!

CALIBAN   Ha, ha, ha!

STEPHANO   Now, forward with your tale. Prithee, stand farther off.

CALIBAN   Beat him enough. After a little time
I'll beat him too.

STEPHANO   Stand farther. Come, proceed.

CALIBAN   Why, as I told thee, 'tis a custom with him, i' th' afternoon to
  sleep. There thou mayst brain him,
  Having first seized his books, or with a log
  Batter his skull, or paunch him with a stake,
  Or cut his wezand with thy knife. Remember
  First to possess his books; for without them
  He's but a sot, as I am, nor hath not
  One spirit to command. They all do hate him
  As rootedly as I. Burn but his books.
  He has brave utensils—for so he calls them—
  Which, when he has a house, he'll deck withal.
  And that most deeply to consider is
  The beauty of his daughter; he himself
  Calls her a nonpareil. I never saw a woman,
  But only Sycorax my dam and she;
  But she as far surpasseth Sycorax
  As great'st does least.

STEPHANO   Is it so brave a lass?

CALIBAN   Ay, lord; she will become thy bed, I warrant.
  And bring thee forth brave brood.

STEPHANO   Monster, I will kill this man. His daughter and I will be king
  and queen—save our graces!—and Trinculo and thyself shall be vice-
  roys. Dost thou like the plot, Trinculo?

TRINCULO   Excellent.

STEPHANO   Give me thy hand. I am sorry I beat thee; but, while thou
  livest, keep a good tongue in thy head.

CALIBAN   Within this half hour will he be asleep.
  Wilt thou destroy him then?

STEPHANO   Ay, on mine honour.

ARIEL   This will I tell my master.

CALIBAN   Thou makest me merry; I am full of pleasure.
  Let us be jocund. Will you troll the catch
  You taught me but while-ere?

STEPHANO   At thy request, monster, I will do reason, any reason. Come
  on, Trinculo, let us sing. [*Sings.*]

"Flout 'em and scout 'em
And scout 'em and flout 'em;
Thought is free."

CALIBAN   That's not the tune.

Ariel plays the tune on a tabor and pipe.

STEPHANO   What is this same?

TRINCULO   This is the tune of our catch, played by the picture of Nobody.

STEPHANO   If thou beest a man, show thyself in thy likeness. If thou
beest a devil, take't as thou list.

TRINCULO   O, forgive me my sins!

STEPHANO   He that dies pays all debts. I defy thee.
Mercy upon us!

CALIBAN   Art thou afeard?

STEPHANO   No, monster, not I.

CALIBAN   Be not afeard; the isle is full of noises,
Sounds and sweet airs, that give delight and hurt not.
Sometimes a thousand twangling instruments
Will hum about mine ears, and sometimes voices
That, if I then had waked after long sleep,
Will make me sleep again; and then, in dreaming,
The clouds methought would open and show riches
Ready to drop upon me, that, when I waked,
I cried to dream again.

STEPHANO   This will prove a brave kingdom to me, where I shall have
my music for nothing.

CALIBAN   When Prospero is destroyed.

STEPHANO   That shall be by and by. I remember the story.

TRINCULO   The sound is going away; let's follow it, and after do our
work.

STEPHANO   Lead, monster; we'll follow. I would I could see this taborer;
he lays it on.

TRINCULO   Wilt come? I'll follow, Stephano.   *Exeunt.*

❧ SCENE 3 *Another part of the island.*

Enter Alonso, Sebastian, Antonio, Gonzalo, Adrian, Francisco, and others.

GONZALO By'r lakin, I can go no further, sir;
  My old bones ache. Here's a maze trod indeed
  Through forth-rights and meanders! By your patience,
  I needs must rest me.

ALONSO   Old lord, I cannot blame thee,
  Who am myself attach'd with weariness,
  To the dulling of my spirits. Sit down, and rest.
  Even here I will put off my hope and keep it
  No longer for my flatterer. He is drown'd
  Whom thus we stray to find, and the sea mocks
  Our frustrate search on land. Well, let him go.

ANTONIO [*Aside to Sebastian.*] I am right glad that he's so out of hope.
  Do not, for one repulse, forego the purpose
  That you resolved to effect.

SEBASTIAN [*Aside to Antonio.*] The next advantage
  Will we take throughly.

ANTONIO [*Aside to Sebastian.*] Let it be to-night;
  For, now they are oppress'd with travel, they
  Will not, nor cannot, use such vigilance
  As when they are fresh.

SEBASTIAN [*Aside to Antonio.*] I say, to-night. No more.

Solemn and strange music.

ALONSO What harmony is this? My good friends, hark!

GONZALO Marvellous sweet music!

Enter Prospero above, invisible. Enter several strange Shapes, bringing in a ban-quet; they dance about it with gentle actions of salutation; and, inviting the King, &c. to eat, they depart.

ALONSO Give us kind keepers, heavens! What were these?

SEBASTIAN A living drollery. Now I will believe
  That there are unicorns, that in Arabia
  There is one tree, the phoenix' throne, one phoenix
  At this hour reigning there.

632

ANTONIO   I'll believe both;
  And what does else want credit, come to me,
  And I'll be sworn 'tis true. Travellers ne'er did lie,
  Though fools at home condemn 'em.

GONZALO   If in Naples
  I should report this now, would they believe me?
  If I should say, I saw such islanders —
  For, certes, these are people of the island —
  Who, though they are of monstrous shape, yet, note,
  Their manners are more gentle-kind than of
  Our human generation you shall find
  Many, nay, almost any.

PROSPERO   [*Aside.*]   Honest lord,
  Thou hast said well; for some of you there present
  Are worse than devils.

ALONSO   I cannot too much muse
  Such shapes, such gesture and such sound, expressing,
  Although they want the use of tongue, a kind
  Of excellent dumb discourse.

PROSPERO   [*Aside.*]   Praise in departing.

FRANCISCO   They vanish'd strangely.

SEBASTIAN   No matter, since
  They have left their viands behind; for we have stomachs.
  Will't please you taste of what is here?

ALONSO   Not I.

GONZALO   Faith, sir, you need not fear. When we were boys,
  Who would believe that there were mountaineers
  Dew-lapp'd like bulls, whose throats had hanging at 'em
  Wallets of flesh? or that there were such men
  Whose heads stood in their breasts? which now we find
  Each putter-out of five for one will bring us
  Good warrant of.

ALONSO   I will stand to and feed,
  Although my last. No matter, since I feel
  The best is past. Brother, my lord the Duke,
  Stand to and do as we.

633

Thunder and lightning. Enter Ariel, like a harpy; claps his wings upon the table; and, with a quaint device, the banquet vanishes.

ARIEL   You are three men of sin, whom Destiny,
That hath to instrument this lower world
And what is in't, the never-surfeited sea
Hath caused to belch up you; and on this island
Where man doth not inhabit; you 'mongst men
Being most unfit to live. I have made you mad;
And even with such-like valour men hang and drown
Their proper selves.

Alonso, Sebastian, &c. draw their swords.

                    You fools! I and my fellows
Are ministers of Fate. The elements,
Of whom your swords are temper'd, may as well
Wound the loud winds, or with bemock'd-at-stabs
Kill the still-closing waters, as diminish
One dowle that's in my plume. My fellow-ministers
Are like invulnerable. If you could hurt,
Your swords are now too massy for your strengths
And will not be uplifted. But remember—
For that's my business to you—that you three
From Milan did supplant good Prospero;
Exposed unto the sea, which hath requit it,
Him and his innocent child; for which foul deed
The powers, delaying, not forgetting, have
Incensed the seas and shores, yea, all the creatures,
Against your peace. Thee of thy son, Alonso,
They have bereft; and do pronounce by me
Lingering perdition, worse than any death
Can be at once, shall step by step attend
You and your ways; whose wraths to guard you from—
Which here, in this most desolate isle, else falls
Upon your heads—is nothing but heart-sorrow
And a clear life ensuing.   *He vanishes in thunder.*

Then, to soft music, enter the Shapes again, and dance, with mocks and mows, and carrying out the table.

PROSPERO   Bravely the figure of this harpy hast thou
Perform'd, my Ariel; a grace it had, devouring.
Of my instruction hast thou nothing bated

634

In what thou hadst to say. So, with good life
And observation strange, my meaner ministers
Their several kinds have done. My high charms work
And these mine enemies are all knit up
In their distractions; they now are in my power;
And in these fits I leave them, while I visit
Young Ferdinand, whom they suppose is drown'd,
And his and mine loved darling.   *Exit above.*

GONZALO   I' the name of something holy, sir, why stand you
In this strange stare?

ALONSO   O, it is monstrous, monstrous!
Methought the billows spoke and told me of it;
The winds did sing it to me, and the thunder,
That deep and dreadful organ-pipe, pronounced
The name of Prosper; it did bass my trespass.
Therefore my son i' the ooze is bedded, and
I'll seek him deeper than e'er plummet sounded
And with him there lie mudded.   *Exit.*

SEBASTIAN   But one fiend at a time,
I'll fight their legions o'er.

ANTONIO   I'll be thy second.
                    Exeunt Sebastian and Antonio.

GONZALO   All three of them are desperate. Their great guilt,
Like poison given to work a great time after,
Now 'gins to bite the spirits. I do beseech you
That are of suppler joints, follow them swiftly
And hinder them from what this ecstasy
May now provoke them to.

ADRIAN   Follow, I pray you.   *Exeunt.*

635

ACT IV

SCENE 1 *Before Prospero's cell.*

Enter Prospero, Ferdinand, and Miranda.

PROSPERO   If I have too austerely punish'd you,
  Your compensation makes amends, for I
  Have given you here a third of mine own life,
  Or that for which I live; who once again
  I tender to thy hand. All thy vexations
  Were but my trials of thy love, and thou
  Hast strangely stood the test. Here, afore Heaven,
  I ratify this my rich gift. O Ferdinand,
  Do not smile at me that I boast her off,
  For thou shalt find she will outstrip all praise
  And make it halt behind her.

FERDINAND   I do believe it
  Against an oracle.

PROSPERO   Then, as my gift and thine own acquisition
  Worthily purchased, take my daughter; but
  If thou dost break her virgin-knot before
  All sanctimonious ceremonies may
  With full and holy rite be minister'd,
  No sweet aspersion shall the heavens let fall
  To make this contract grow; but barren hate,
  Sour-eyed disdain, and discord shall bestrew
  The union of your bed with weeds so loathly
  That you shall hate it both. Therefore take heed,
  As Hymen's lamps shall light you.

636

FERDINAND   As I hope
  For quiet days, fair issue, and long life,
  With such love as 'tis now, the murkiest den,
  The most opportune place, the strong'st suggestion
  Our worser genius can, shall never melt
  Mine honour into lust, to take away
  The edge of that day's celebration
  When I shall think, or Phoebus' steeds are founder'd,
  Or Night kept chain'd below.

PROSPERO   Fairly spoke.
  Sit then and talk with her; she is thine own.
  What, Ariel! my industrious servant, Ariel!

Enter Ariel.

ARIEL   What would my potent master? here I am.

PROSPERO   Thou and thy meaner fellows your last service
  Did worthily perform; and I must use you
  In such another trick. Go bring the rabble,
  O'er whom I give thee power, here to this place;
  Incite them to quick motion; for I must
  Bestow upon the eyes of this young couple
  Some vanity of mine art. It is my promise,
  And they expect it from me.

ARIEL   Presently?

PROSPERO   Ay, with a twink.

ARIEL   Before you can say "come" and "go,"
  And breathe twice and cry "so, so,"
  Each one, tripping on his toe,
  Will be here with mop and mow.
  Do you love me, master? No?

PROSPERO   Dearly, my delicate Ariel. Do not approach
  Till thou dost hear me call.

ARIEL   Well, I conceive.   *Exit.*

PROSPERO   Look thou be true; do not give dalliance
  Too much the rein. The strongest oaths are straw
  To the fire i' the blood. Be more abstemious,
  Or else, good night your vow!

FERDINAND   I warrant you, sir;
   The white cold virgin snow upon my heart
   Abates the ardour of my liver.

PROSPERO   Well.
   Now come, my Ariel! bring a corollary,
   Rather than want a spirit. Appear, and pertly!
   No tongue! all eyes! be silent.

Soft music. Enter Iris.

IRIS   "Ceres, most bounteous lady, thy rich leas
   Of wheat, rye, barley, vetches, oats, and pease;
   Thy turfy mountains, where live nibbling sheep,
   And flat meads thatch'd with stover, them to keep;
   Thy banks with pioned and twilled brims,
   Which spongy April at thy hest betrims,
   To make cold nymphs chaste crowns; and thy broom-groves,
   Whose shadow the dismissed bachelor loves,
   Being lass-lorn; thy pole-clipt vineyard;
   And thy sea-marge, sterile and rock-hard,
   Where thou thyself dost air—the queen o' the sky,
   Whose watery arch and messenger am I,
   Bids thee leave these, and with her sovereign grace,
   Here on this grass-plot, in this very place,
   To come and sport; here peacocks fly amain.
   Approach, rich Ceres, her to entertain."

Enter Ceres.

CERES   "Hail, many-colour'd messenger, that ne'er
   Dost disobey the wife of Jupiter;
   Who with thy saffron wings upon my flowers
   Diffusest honey-drops, refreshing showers,
   And with each end of thy blue bow dost crown
   My bosky acres and my unshrubb'd down,
   Rich scarf to my proud earth; why hath thy queen
   Summon'd me hither, to this short-grass'd green?"

IRIS   "A contract of true love to celebrate;
   And some donation freely to estate
   On the blest lovers."

CERES   "Tell me, heavenly bow,
   If Venus or her son, as thou dost know,

Do now attend the Queen? Since they did plot
The means that dusky Dis my daughter got,
Her and her blind boy's scandal'd company
I have forsworn."

IRIS   "Of her society
Be not afraid. I met her deity
Cutting the clouds towards Paphos and her son
Dove-drawn with her. Here thought they to have done
Some wanton charm upon this man and maid,
Whose vows are, that no bed-right shall be paid
Till Hymen's torch be lighted; but in vain;
Mar's hot minion is return'd again;
Her waspish-headed son has broke his arrows,
Swears he will shoot no more but play with sparrows
And be a boy right out."

CERES   "High'st queen of state,
Great Juno, comes; I know her by her gait."

Enter Juno.

JUNO   "How does my bounteous sister? Go with me
To bless this twain, that they may prosperous be
And honour'd in their issue."

They sing.

JUNO   "Honour, riches, marriage-blessing,
                  Long continuance, and increasing,
                  Hourly joys be still upon you!
                  Juno sings her blessings on you."

CERES   "Earth's increase, foison plenty,
                  Barns and garners never empty,
                  Vines with clustering bunches growing,
                  Plants with goodly burthen bowing;
                  Spring come to you at the farthest
                  In the very end of harvest!
                  Scarcity and want shall shun you;
                  Ceres' blessing so is on you."

FERDINAND   This is a most majestic vision, and
Harmonious charmingly. May I be bold
To think these spirits?

639

PROSPERO   Spirits, which by mine art
  I have from their confines call'd to enact
  My present fancies.

FERDINAND   Let me live here ever;
  So rare a wonder'd father and a wife
  Makes this place Paradise.

Juno and Ceres whisper, and send Iris on employment.

PROSPERO   Sweet, now, silence!
  Juno and Ceres whisper seriously;
  There's something else to do. Hush, and be mute,
  Or else our spell is marr'd.

IRIS "You nymphs, call'd Naiads, of the windring brooks,
  With your sedged crowns and ever-harmless looks,
  Leave your crisp channels and on this green land
  Answer your summons; Juno does command.
  Come, temperate nymphs, and help to celebrate
  A contract of true love; be not too late."

Enter certain Nymphs.

  "You sunburnt sicklemen, of August weary,
  Come hither from the furrow and be merry;
  Make holiday; your rye-straw hats put on
  And these fresh nymphs encounter every one
  In country footing."

*Enter certain Reapers, properly habited; they join with the Nymphs in a graceful
dance; towards the end whereof Prospero starts suddenly, and speaks; after which,
to a strange, hollow, and confused noise, they heavily vanish.*

PROSPERO [*Aside.*] I had forgot that foul conspiracy
  Of the beast Caliban and his confederates
  Against my life; the minute of their plot
  Is almost come. [*To the Spirits.*] Well done! avoid; no more!

FERDINAND   This is strange. Your father's in some passion
  That works him strongly.

MIRANDA   Never till this day
  Saw I him touch'd with anger so distemper'd.

PROSPERO   You do look, my son, in a moved sort,
  As if you were dismay'd; be cheerful, sir.

Our revels now are ended. These our actors,
As I foretold you, were all spirits and
Are melted into air, into thin air,
And, like the baseless fabric of this vision,
The cloud-capp'd towers, the gorgeous palaces,
The solemn temples, the great globe itself,
Yea, all which it inherit, shall dissolve
And, like this insubstantial pageant faded,
Leave not a rack behind. We are such stuff
As dreams are made on, and our little life
Is rounded with a sleep. Sir, I am vex'd;
Bear with my weakness; my old brain is troubled.
Be not disturb'd with my infirmity.
If you be pleased, retire into my cell
And there repose. A turn or two I'll walk,
To still my beating mind.

FERDINAND AND MIRANDA   We wish your peace.   *Exeunt.*

PROSPERO   Come with a thought. I thank thee, Ariel; come.

Enter Ariel.

ARIEL   Thy thoughts I cleave to. What's thy pleasure?

PROSPERO   Spirit,
We must prepare to meet with Caliban.

ARIEL   Ay, my commander. When I presented Ceres,
I thought to have told thee of it, but I fear'd
Lest I might anger thee.

PROSPERO   Say again, where didst thou leave these varlets?

ARIEL   I told you, sir, they were red-hot with drinking;
So full of valour that they smote the air
For breathing in their faces; beat the ground
For kissing of their feet; yet always bending
Towards their project. Then I beat my tabor;
At which, like unback'd colts, they prick'd their ears,
Advanced their eyelids, lifted up their noses
As they smelt music. So I charm'd their ears
That calf-like they my lowing follow'd through
Tooth'd briers, sharp furzes, pricking goss, and thorns,
Which enter'd their frail shins. At last I left them
I' the filthy-mantled pool beyond your cell,

641

There dancing up to the chins, that the foul lake
O'erstunk their feet.

PROSPERO   This was well done, my bird.
Thy shape invisible retain thou still.
The trumpery in my house, go bring it hither,
For stale to catch these thieves.

ARIEL   I go, I go.   *Exit.*

PROSPERO   A devil, a born devil, on whose nature
Nurture can never stick, on whom my pains,
Humanely taken, all, all lost, quite lost;
And as with age his body uglier grows,
So his mind cankers. I will plague them all,
Even to roaring.

Re-enter Ariel, loaden with glistering apparel, &c.

         Come, hang them on this line.

Prospero and Ariel remain, invisible. Enter Caliban, Stephano, and Trinculo, all wet.

CALIBAN   Pray you, tread softly, that the blind mole may not
Hear a foot fall. We now are near his cell.

STEPHANO   Monster, your fairy, which you say is a harmless fairy, has done little better than played the Jack with us.

TRINCULO   Monster, I do smell all horse-piss; at which my nose is in great indignation.

STEPHANO   So is mine. Do you hear, monster? If I should take a displeasure against you, look you—

TRINCULO   Thou wert but a lost monster.

CALIBAN   Good my lord, give me thy favour still.
Be patient, for the prize I'll bring thee to
Shall hoodwink this mischance; therefore speak softly.
All's hush'd as midnight yet.

TRINCULO   Ay, but to lose our bottles in the pool—

STEPHANO   There is not only disgrace and dishonour in that, monster, but an infinite loss.

TRINCULO   That's more to me than my wetting; yet this is your harmless
fairy, monster.

STEPHANO   I will fetch off my bottle, though I be o'er ears for my labour.

CALIBAN   Prithee, my king, be quiet. See'st thou here,
This is the mouth o' the cell. No noise, and enter.
Do that good mischief which may make this island
Thine own for ever, and I, thy Caliban,
For aye thy foot-licker.

STEPHANO   Give me thy hand. I do begin to have bloody thoughts.

TRINCULO   O King Stephano! O peer! O worthy Stephano! look what a
wardrobe here is for thee!

CALIBAN   Let it alone, thou fool; it is but trash.

TRINCULO   O, ho, monster! we know what belongs to a frippery. O
King Stephano!

STEPHANO   Put off that gown, Trinculo; by this hand, I'll have that
gown.

TRINCULO   Thy grace shall have it.

CALIBAN   The dropsy drown this fool! what do you mean
To dote thus on such luggage? Let's alone
And do the murder first. If he awake,
From toe to crown he'll fill our skins with pinches,
Make us strange stuff.

STEPHANO   Be quiet, monster. Mistress line, is not this my jerkin? Now
is the jerkin under the line. Now, jerkin, you are like to lose your hair
and prove a bald jerkin.

TRINCULO   Do, do; we steal by line and level, an't like your Grace.

STEPHANO   I thank thee for that jest; here's a garment for't. Wit shall not
go unrewarded while I am king of this country. "Steal by line and
level" is an excellent pass of pate; there's another garment for't.

TRINCULO   Monster, come, put some lime upon your fingers, and away
with the rest.

CALIBAN   I will have none on't. We shall lose our time,
And all be turn'd to barnacles, or to apes
With foreheads villainous low.

643

THE TEMPEST

STEPHANO Monster, lay-to your fingers. Help to bear this away where my hogshead of wine is, or I'll turn you out of my kingdom. Go to, carry this.

TRINCULO And this.

STEPHANO Ay, and this.

A noise of hunters heard. Enter divers Spirits, in shapes of dogs and hounds, and hunt them about, Prospero and Ariel setting them on.

PROSPERO Hey, Mountain, hey!

ARIEL Silver! there it goes, Silver!

PROSPERO Fury, Fury! there, Tyrant, there! hark! hark!
                    Caliban, Stephano, and Trinculo are driven out.

Go charge my goblins that they grind their joints
With dry convulsions, shorten up their sinews
With aged cramps, and more pinch-spotted make them
Than pard or cat o' mountain.

ARIEL   Hark, they roar!

PROSPERO Let them be hunted soundly. At this hour
Lie at my mercy all mine enemies.
Shortly shall all my labours end, and thou
Shalt have the air at freedom. For a little
Follow, and do me service.   *Exeunt.*

ACT V

Before Prospero's cell.

Enter Prospero in his magic robes, and Ariel.

PROSPERO Now does my project gather to a head.
  My charms crack not; my spirits obey; and time
  Goes upright with his carriage. How's the day?

ARIEL On the sixth hour; at which time, my lord,
  You said our work should cease.

PROSPERO   I did say so,
  When first I raised the tempest. Say, my spirit,
  How fares the King and's followers?

ARIEL   Confined together
  In the same fashion as you gave in charge,
  Just as you left them; all prisoners, sir,
  In the line-grove which weather-fends your cell;
  They cannot budge till your release. The King,
  His brother, and yours, abide all three distracted
  And the remainder mourning over them,
  Brimful of sorrow and dismay; but chiefly
  Him that you term'd, sir, "The good old lord, Gonzalo";
  His tears run down his beard, like winter's drops
  From eaves of reeds. Your charm so strongly works 'em
  That if you now beheld them, your affections
  Would become tender.

PROSPERO   Dost thou think so, spirit?

645

ARIEL   Mine would, sir, were I human.

PROSPERO   And mine shall.
Hast thou, which art but air, a touch, a feeling
Of their afflictions, and shall not myself,
One of their kind, that relish all as sharply,
Passion as they, be kindlier moved than thou art?
Though with their high wrongs I am struck to the quick,
Yet with my nobler reason 'gainst my fury
Do I take part. The rarer action is
In virtue than in vengeance. They being penitent,
The sole drift of my purpose doth extend
Not a frown further. Go release them, Ariel.
My charms I'll break, their sense I'll restore,
And they shall be themselves.

ARIEL   I'll fetch them, sir.   *Exit.*

PROSPERO   Ye elves of hills, brooks, standing lakes, and groves,
And ye that on the sands with printless foot
Do chase the ebbing Neptune and do fly him
When he comes back; you demi-puppets that
By moonshine do the green sour ringlets make,
Whereof the ewe not bites, and you whose pastime
Is to make midnight mushrooms, that rejoice
To hear the solemn curfew; by whose aid,
Weak masters though ye be, I have bedimm'd
The noontide sun, call'd forth the mutinous winds,
And 'twixt the green sea and the azured vault
Set roaring war; to the dread rattling thunder
Have I given fire and rifted Jove's stout oak
With his own bolt; the strong-based promontory
Have I made shake and by the spurs pluck'd up
The pine and cedar; graves at my command
Have waked their sleepers, oped, and let 'em forth
By my so potent art. But this rough magic
I here abjure, and, when I have required
Some heavenly music, which even now I do,
To work mine end upon their senses that
This airy charm is for, I'll break my staff,
Bury it certain fathoms in the earth,
And deeper than did ever plummet sound
I'll drown my book.

ACT V   Scene 1

Solemn music. Re-enter Ariel before; then Alonso, with a frantic gesture, attended by Gonzalo; Sebastian and Antonio in like manner, attended by Adrian and Francisco. They all enter the circle which Prospero had made, and there stand charmed; which Prospero observing, speaks.

A solemn air and the best comforter
To an unsettled fancy cure thy brains,
Now useless, boil'd within thy skull! There stand,
For you are spell-stopp'd.
Holy Gonzalo, honourable man,
Mine eyes, even sociable to the show of thine,
Fall fellowly drops. The charm dissolves apace,
And as the morning steals upon the night,
Melting the darkness, so their rising senses
Begin to chase the ignorant fumes that mantle
Their clearer reason. O good Gonzalo,
My true preserver, and a loyal sir
To him thou follow'st! I will pay thy graces
Home both in word and deed. Most cruelly
Didst thou, Alonso, use me and my daughter;
Thy brother was a furtherer in the act.
Thou art pinch'd for't now, Sebastian. Flesh and blood,
You, brother mine, that entertain'd ambition,
Expell'd remorse and nature; who, with Sebastian,
Whose inward pinches therefore are most strong,
Would here have kill'd your king, I do forgive thee,
Unnatural though thou art. Their understanding
Begins to swell, and the approaching tide
Will shortly fill the reasonable shore
That now lies foul and muddy. Not one of them
That yet looks on me, or would know me. Ariel,
Fetch me the hat and rapier in my cell.
I will discase me, and myself present
As I was sometime Milan. Quickly, spirit;
Thou shalt ere long be free.

Ariel sings and helps to attire him.

"Where the bee sucks, there suck I.
In a cowslip's bell I lie;
There I couch when owls do cry.
On the bat's back I do fly
After summer merrily.

647

> Merrily, merrily shall I live now
> Under the blossom that hangs on the bough.''

PROSPERO   Why, that's my dainty Ariel! I shall miss thee;
But yet thou shalt have freedom. So, so, so.
To the King's ship, invisible as thou art;
There shalt thou find the mariners asleep
Under the hatches; the master and the boatswain
Being awake, enforce them to this place,
And presently, I prithee.

ARIEL   I drink the air before me, and return
Or ere your pulse twice beat.   *Exit.*

GONZALO   All torment, trouble, wonder, and amazement
Inhabits here. Some heavenly power guide us
Out of this fearful country!

PROSPERO   Behold, sir King,
The wronged Duke of Milan, Prospero.
For more assurance that a living prince
Does now speak to thee, I embrace thy body;
And to thee and thy company I bid
A hearty welcome.

ALONSO   Whether thou be'st he or no,
Or some enchanted trifle to abuse me,
As late I have been, I not know. Thy pulse
Beats as of flesh and blood; and, since I saw thee,
The affliction of my mind amends, with which,
I fear, a madness held me. This must crave,
An if this be at all, a most strange story.
Thy dukedom I resign and do entreat
Thou pardon me my wrongs. But how should Prospero
Be living and be here?

PROSPERO   First, noble friend,
Let me embrace thine age, whose honour cannot
Be measured or confined.

GONZALO   Whether this be
Or be not, I'll not swear.

PROSPERO   You do yet taste
Some subtilties o' the isle, that will not let you
Believe things certain. Welcome, my friends all!

648

[*Aside to Sebastian and Antonio.*] But you, my brace of lords, were I so minded,
I here could pluck his Highness' frown upon you
And justify you traitors. At this time
I will tell no tales.

SEBASTIAN   [*Aside.*] The devil speaks in him.

PROSPERO   No.
For you, most wicked sir, whom to call brother
Would even infect my mouth, I do forgive
Thy rankest fault; all of them; and require
My dukedom of thee, which perforce, I know,
Thou must restore.

ALONSO   If thou be'st Prospero,
Give us particulars of thy preservation;
How thou hast met us here, who three hours since
Were wreck'd upon this shore; where I have lost—
How sharp the point of this remembrance is!
My dear son Ferdinand.

PROSPERO   I am woe for't, sir.

ALONSO   Irreparable is the loss, and Patience
Says it is past her cure.

PROSPERO   I rather think
You have not sought her help, of whose soft grace
For the like loss I have her sovereign aid
And rest myself content.

ALONSO   You the like loss!

PROSPERO   As great to me as late; and, supportable
To make the dear loss, have I means much weaker
Than you may call to comfort you, for I
Have lost my daughter.

ALONSO   A daughter?
O heavens, that they were living both in Naples,
The King and Queen there! that they were, I wish
Myself were mudded in that oozy bed
Where my son lies. When did you lose your daughter?

PROSPERO   In this last tempest. I perceive, these lords
At this encounter do so much admire

That they devour their reason and scarce think
Their eyes do offices of truth, their words
Are natural breath; but, howsoe'er you have
Been justled from your senses, know for certain
That I am Prospero and that very duke
Which was thrust forth of Milan, who most strangely
Upon this shore, where you were wreck'd, was landed,
To be the lord on't. No more yet of this;
For 'tis a chronicle of day by day,
Not a relation for a breakfast nor
Befitting this first meeting. Welcome, sir;
This cell's my court. Here have I few attendants
And subjects none abroad. Pray you, look in.
My dukedom since you have given me again,
I will requite you with as good a thing;
At least bring forth a wonder, to content ye
As much as me my dukedom.

Here Prospero discovers Ferdinand and Miranda playing at chess.

MIRANDA   Sweet lord, you play me false.

FERDINAND   No, my dear'st love,
   I would not for the world.

MIRANDA   Yes, for a score of kingdoms you should wrangle,
   And I would call it fair play.

ALONSO   If this prove
   A vision of the island, one dear son
   Shall I twice lose.

SEBASTIAN   A most high miracle!

FERDINAND   Though the seas threaten, they are merciful;
   I have cursed them without cause. [*Kneels.*]

ALONSO   Now all the blessings
   Of a glad father compass thee about!
   Arise, and say how thou camest here.

MIRANDA   O, wonder!
   How many goodly creatures are there here!
   How beauteous mankind is! O brave new world,
   That has such people in't!

PROSPERO   'Tis new to thee.

ACT V   Scene 1

ALONSO   What is this maid with whom thou wast at play?
Your eld'st acquaintance cannot be three hours.
Is she the goddess that hath sever'd us,
And brought us thus together?

FERDINAND   Sir, she is mortal;
But by immortal Providence she's mine.
I chose her when I could not ask my father
For his advice, nor thought I had one. She
Is daughter to this famous Duke of Milan,
Of whom so often I have heard renown,
But never saw before; of whom I have
Received a second life; and second father
This lady makes him to me.

ALONSO   I am hers.
But, O, how oddly will it sound that I
Must ask my child forgiveness!

PROSPERO   There, sir, stop.
Let us not burthen our remembrance with
A heaviness that's gone.

GONZALO   I have inly wept,
Or should have spoke ere this. Look down, you gods,
And on this couple drop a blessed crown!
For it is you that have chalk'd forth the way
Which brought us hither.

ALONSO   I say, Amen, Gonzalo!

GONZALO   Was Milan thrust from Milan, that his issue
Should become kings of Naples? O, rejoice
Beyond a common joy, and set it down
With gold on lasting pillars. In one voyage
Did Claribel her husband find at Tunis
And Ferdinand, her brother, found a wife
Where he himself was lost, Prospero his dukedom
In a poor isle, and all of us ourselves
When no man was his own.

ALONSO   [*To Ferdinand and Miranda.*] Give me your hands.
Let grief and sorrow still embrace his heart
That doth not wish you joy!

651

GONZALO   Be it so! Amen!

Re-enter Ariel, with the Master and Boatswain amazedly following.

O, look, sir, look, sir! here is more of us.
I prophesied, if a gallows were on land,
This fellow could not drown. Now, blasphemy,
That swear'st grace o'erboard, not an oath on shore?
Hast thou no mouth by land? What is the news?

BOATSWAIN   The best news is that we have safely found
Our King and company; the next, our ship—
Which, but three glasses since, we gave out split—
Is tight and yare and bravely rigg'd as when
We first put out to sea.

ARIEL   [*Aside to Prospero.*] Sir, all this service
Have I done since I went.

PROSPERO   [*Aside to Ariel.*] My tricksy spirit!

ALONSO   These are not natural events; they strengthen
From strange to stranger. Say, how came you hither?

BOATSWAIN   If I did think, sir, I were well awake,
I'd strive to tell you. We were dead of sleep,
And—how we know not—all clapp'd under hatches;
Where but even now with strange and several noises
Of roaring, shrieking, howling, jingling chains,
And moe diversity of sounds, all horrible,
We were awaked; straightway, at liberty;
Where we, in all her trim, freshly beheld
Our royal, good, and gallant ship, our master
Capering to eye her. On a trice, so please you,
Even in a dream, were we divided from them
And were brought moping hither.

ARIEL   [*Aside to Prospero.*]   Was't well done?

PROSPERO   [*Aside to Ariel.*] Bravely, my diligence. Thou shalt be free.

ALONSO   This is as strange a maze as e'er men trod;
And there is in this business more than nature
Was ever conduct of. Some oracle
Must rectify our knowledge.

PROSPERO   Sir, my liege,

Do not infest your mind with beating on
The strangeness of this business; at pick'd leisure
Which shall be shortly, single I'll resolve you,
Which to you shall seem probable, of every
These happen'd accidents; till when, be cheerful
And think of each thing well. [*Aside to Ariel.*] Come hither, spirit.
Set Caliban and his companions free;
Untie the spell.   *Exit Ariel.*
                    How fares my gracious sir?
There are yet missing of your company
Some few odd lads that you remember not.

Re-enter Ariel, driving in Caliban, Stephano, and Trinculo, in their stolen apparel.

STEPHANO   Every man shift for all the rest, and let no man take care for
himself; for all is but fortune. Coragio, bully-monster, coragio!

TRINCULO   If these be true spies which I wear in my head, here's a
goodly sight.

CALIBAN   O Setebos, these be brave spirits indeed!
How fine my master is! I am afraid
He will chastise me.

SEBASTIAN   Ha, ha!
What things are these, my lord Antonio?
Will money buy 'em?

ANTONIO   Very like; one of them
Is a plain fish, and, no doubt, marketable.

PROSPERO   Mark but the badges of these men, my lords,
Then say if they be true. This mis-shapen knave,
His mother was a witch, and one so strong
That could control the moon, make flows and ebbs,
And deal in her command without her power.
These three have robb'd me; and this demi-devil—
For he's a bastard one—had plotted with them
To take my life. Two of these fellows you
Must know and own; this thing of darkness I
Acknowledge mine.

CALIBAN   I shall be pinch'd to death.

ALONSO   Is not this Stephano, my drunken butler?

653

SEBASTIAN   He is drunk now. Where had he wine?

ALONSO   And Trinculo is reeling ripe. Where should they
Find this grand liquor that hath gilded 'em?
How camest thou in this pickle?

TRINCULO   I have been in such a pickle since I saw you last that, I fear
me, will never out of my bones. I shall not fear fly-blowing.

SEBASTIAN   Why, how now, Stephano!

STEPHANO   O, touch me not; I am not Stephano, but a cramp.

PROSPERO   You'd be king o' the isle, sirrah?

STEPHANO   I should have been a sore one then.

ALONSO   [Pointing to Caliban.] This is a strange thing as e'er I look'd on.

PROSPERO   He is as disproportion'd in his manners
As in his shape. Go, sirrah, to my cell;
Take with you your companions; as you look
To have my pardon, trim it handsomely.

CALIBAN   Ay, that I will; and I'll be wise hereafter
And seek for grace. What a thrice-double ass
Was I, to take this drunkard for a god
And worship this dull fool!

PROSPERO   Go to; away!

ALONSO   Hence, and bestow your luggage where you found it.

SEBASTIAN   Or stole it, rather.   *Exeunt Caliban, Stephano, and Trinculo.*

PROSPERO   Sir, I invite your Highness and your train
To my poor cell, where you shall take your rest
For this one night; which, part of it, I'll waste
With such discourse as, I not doubt, shall make it
Go quick away; the story of my life
And the particular accidents gone by
Since I came to this isle. And in the morn
I'll bring you to your ship and so to Naples,
Where I have hope to see the nuptial
Of these our dear-beloved solemnized;
And thence retire me to my Milan, where
Every third thought shall be my grave.

ALONSO   I long
  To hear the story of your life, which must
  Take the ear strangely.

PROSPERO   I'll deliver all;
  And promise you calm seas, auspicious gales,
  And sail so expeditious that shall catch
  Your royal fleet far off. [*Aside to Ariel.*] My Ariel, chick,
  That is thy charge. Then to the elements
  Be free, and fare thou well! Please you, draw near.   *Exeunt.*

❀ EPILOGUE

PROSPERO   Now my charms are all o'erthrown,
               And what strength I have's mine own,
               Which is most faint. Now, 'tis true,
               I must be here confined by you,
               Or sent to Naples. Let me not,
               Since I have my dukedom got
               And pardon'd the deceiver, dwell
               In this bare island by your spell;
               But release me from my bands
               With the help of your good hands.
               Gentle breath of yours my sails
               Must fill, or else my project fails,
               Which was to please. Now I want
               Spirits to enforce, art to enchant,
               And my ending is despair,
               Unless I be relieved by prayer,
               Which pierces so that it assaults
               Mercy itself and frees all faults.
               As you from crimes would pardon'd be,
               Let your indulgence set me free.

D1131509